The Dynamics and Treatment of Alcoholism: Essential Papers

The Dynamics and Treatment of Alcoholism: Essential Papers

Edited by
Jerome D. Levin, Ph.D. and
Ronna H. Weiss, Ph.D.

JASON ARONSON INC.
Northvale, New Jersey
London

This book was set in 10 point Baskerville by Lind Graphics of Upper Saddle River, New Jersey, and printed and bound by Haddon Craftsmen of Scranton, Pennsylvania.

Library of Congress Cataloging-in-Publication Data

Dynamics and treament of alcoholism : essential papers / [edited] by
    Jerome D. Levin and Ronna H. Weiss.
        p. cm.
    Includes bibliographical references and index.
    ISBN 1-56821-072-8
    1. Alcoholism—Psychological aspects.   2. Alcoholism—Treatment.
3. Psychotherapy.   I. Levin, Jerome D. (Jerome David)   II. Weiss,
Ronna Helene.
RC565.D93   1994
616.86'1—dc20   93-8825

Manufactured in the United States of America. Jason Aronson Inc. offers books and cassettes. For information and catalog write to Jason Aronson Inc., 230 Livingston Street, Northvale, New Jersey 07647.

CONTENTS

INTRODUCTION
Part I

INTRODUCTION

Psychoanalysis and addiction have a long, tangled, ambivalent relationship characterized by denial, minimalization, projection, and devaluation. Somehow addiction, including addiction to alcohol, has seemed less than analytic and not of the essence of the psychopathology treated by analysis. Nevertheless, analysis that addresses the human condition has not been able to ignore such a central phenomenon in human experience. Indeed, analysis has, almost in spite of itself, made highly significant contributions to our understanding of addiction from its very beginnings and has done this in the face of denial by psychodynamicists, both famous and obscure, of their own addictions.

Anna O., the Ur-patient of psychoanalysis, was addicted to both chloral hydrate and morphine, as were several other patients whose cases Freud and Breuer described in *Studies on Hysteria*. Freud himself was seriously involved with cocaine from his mid-twenties well into his forties. His masterpiece *Interpretation of Dreams* is, importantly, "about" his cocaine use with his associations to dream after dream, revealing his feelings about his relationship to the drug. If Freud was able to "benefit" from his cocaine use, the same cannot be said of his addiction to tobacco. It killed him. As Freud suffered one mutilating operation after another to remove the leukoplakias brought on by his heavy cigar smoking, Max Schur, his personal physician, would beg him to stop smoking. Sounding like an addict defending his addiction, he refused, saying that he couldn't be creative without his cigars.

Ruth Mack Brunswick, the Wolf Man's second analyst and a favorite of Freud, was addicted to both alcohol and drugs. She died as the consequence of a fall during a blackout. Otto Rank, whom Freud rescued from the slums of Vienna, educated, and virtually adopted, was the son of a hopeless alcoholic. Loë Kann, Ernest Jones's "wife" and Freud's analysand, was addicted to morphine. Her analysis failed to cure her addiction. Ronald Fairbairn was married to an alcoholic and was himself a very heavy drinker. One could go on, but it is abundantly clear that the psychodynamic fascination with addiction to alcohol and other substances is far more than theoretical. It is existential and personal. Although *Dynamics and Treatment of Alcoholism* is a clinical and, to a lesser extent, a theoretical work, its editors are acutely aware that the insights of our various authors are personal and deeply felt, however brilliant their intellectual formulations.

Dynamics and Treatment of Alcoholism is a historical survey of the evolution of psychodynamic theory as exemplified by the evolving psychodynamic understanding of alcoholism, ranging from the drive formulations of Freud and the early analysts to current ego, object relational, and self-conceptualizations. It is a collection of classical papers written across two centuries, all of which are relevant for the present-day clinician, deepening empathy and understanding, guiding observation, and suggesting treatment approaches to the men and women who suffer so egregiously from their addictions to alcohol. Thus, both the historically minded and the clinically oriented will find much of value in this unique compilation of the seminal psychoanalytic papers on addiction. They were selected for their insight, readability, historical relevance, and clinical utility. Collectively, they offer a polyvariate understanding of one of the most overdetermined of psychopathologies. Although this book concentrates on the psychodynamic correlatives of alcoholism, the reader should keep in mind that alcoholism is a biopsychosocial disorder with pharmacological, genetically mediated neurochemical, sociological, and cultural, as well as psychodynamic, determinants.

Because the dynamics of various addictions are basically similar, we include papers—such as Freud's on Dostoevsky, which deals with compulsive gambling—that have best presented a psychodynamic component of addictive behavior. The reader can easily substitute alcoholism for the author's model of addiction. There is a voluminous polemical literature on the status of the disease model of alcoholism. It is our view that alcoholism is usefully regarded as *both* a symptom and a disease in its own right, just as electromagnetic energy is sometimes best understood as a wave phenomenon and sometimes as a particle phenomenon. Alcoholism is best regarded as a disease when helping the patient deal with guilt and come to understand the necessity of sobriety if medical and psychological progress is to be achieved. Alcoholism is best regarded as a symptom when the therapist is focusing on the remediation of deficits and the resolution of conflict. By borrowing the principle of complementarity from physics, we are suggesting a possible resolution of this vexed issue, so intensely struggled with by a number of our authors, particularly by those in the historical section.

HISTORICAL PAPERS

Benjamin Rush, the Surgeon General of the American Revolutionary Army and America's first professor of medicine, came to believe that pathological drinking was a disease. Although he was not a prohibitionist, Rush powerfully influenced the Prohibitionist movement. Written in 1785, his article is included for its intrinsic as well as its historical interest. In 1805, British naval physician Thomas Trotter came very close to the current understanding of the etiology of alcoholism when he suggested that the interaction of heredity and adverse early childhood experiences produces alcoholic drinkers. Given that the ideas of Rush and Trotter were advanced over two centuries ago, it is remarkable that so many continue to view pathological drinking as sin or moral weakness.

In 1960, Emil Jellinek promulgated a scientifically rigorous formulation of the *disease concept* of alcoholism. He radically redefined alcoholism as a disease characterized by progression and loss of control. Jellinek's reconceptualization has had a profound impact on the treatment of alcoholism. Alcoholics are now viewed as deserving medical treatment rather than recrimination. Although Jellinek's notion of alcoholism has had an enormously positive influence on attitudes toward and treatment of alcoholism, it has also had the unwitting effect of depsychologizing alcoholism, which underscores the importance of bringing the following contributions to the attention of mental health professionals.

DRIVE THEORY

If the salience of Rush, Trotter, and Jellinek lies in their progressively deepening understanding of alcoholism as a disease, the salience of the early analysts lies in their directing attention to the psychodynamic components of alcoholism. The classical theorists viewed psychopathology, including addiction, as the outcome of the dynamic struggle between the expression and repression of forbidden impulses. Freud suggested that all addictions are displacements and reenactments of the original addiction to masturbation. Later, he stressed the manner in which an addiction was simultaneously a symbolic gratification of oedipal wishes and a punishment for them. Karl Abraham was among the first to see how sociological and psychodynamic influences interact to promote drunkenness. Analyzing heavy male drinking in the *Bierstubbe*, Abraham postulated that many drink in order to disinhibit and express forbidden homosexual wishes.

If Freud and Abraham focused on expression of the sexual, Edward Glover was the first to highlight drinking as an aggressive act. According to Glover, alcohol unbinds repressed oral aggression so that all objects are colored by it, while the drinking itself is an expression of that aggression. Karl Menninger, a believer in the reality of Freud's death instinct, views alcoholism as progressive suicide as a punishment for death wishes against the father. Menninger stresses the seriousness of alcohol addiction and the depth of the underlying psychopathology.

Otto Fenichel sees the psychodynamic correlative of alcoholism as regression to the narcissistic stage of psychosexual development. He was the first to highlight the narcissistic component in addiction.

Thomas Szasz moved toward an ego psychological account of addiction. Szasz describes the alcoholic's anxiety toward and struggle against drive expression manifested in a counterphobic exposure to tantalizing and dangerous substances in an attempt to gain mastery. In Szasz's view, it is the attempt to master the anxiety and resist succumbing to the urges, rather than the pharmacological effects of the drug, that motivates the addict.

EGO PSYCHOLOGICAL FORMULATIONS

If the drive theorists stress the use of alcohol to enable the expression of and punishment for the "forbidden," the ego psychologists stress the adaptive function of addiction. They ask, What does the drinker believe, however falsely, drinking is doing for him or her? Sándor Radó gives an unequaled account of the phenomenology of addiction, demonstrating how ego weakness leads to the excessive use of alcohol in a quest for elation. This quest, however, doomed to failure by the pharmacology of alcohol, eventuates in progressively deeper depression. Radó was the first to see the isomorphism between the addictive cycle and the dynamics of manic depression. Paul Schilder, who worked at Bellevue with what we would now call dual diagnosis patients, demonstrated the relationship between the ego defects of his patients and dysfunction in their families of origin. As a result of harsh treatment during childhood, these patients suffered social lesions and sought relief in alcohol as a futile attempt to restore their egos to health. Schilder saw that the impact of the social system on ego deficits made group therapy a powerful vehicle for ego restitution in alcoholics who had been abused as children.

Harry Tiebout, a psychiatrist who treated Bill Wilson, cofounder of Alcoholics Anonymous, focused on the reactive grandiosity of the alcoholic and the necessity of relinquishing that grandiosity for recovery to be possible. Tiebout quoted the phrase "his majesty the baby" from Freud's essay "On Narcissism," which Wilson incorporated into the AA literature.

Henry Krystal and Herbert Raskin offer a developmental theory of affect with direct consequences for technique in helping alcoholics build affect tolerance. They see affect regression as the operative dynamic in addiction.

Leon Wurmser builds on the work of Radó and Krystal and Raskin, outlining the impact of narcissistic crisis and overwhelming affects on the addict. Wurmser expands earlier work by elaborating the defenses used to manage affects, particularly denial, splitting, and externalization. He sees compulsive drug users as suffering from the sort of borderline personality organization described by Otto Kernberg, with the addiction an example of a primitive mechanism of defense. The idea that alcoholism overlaps with borderline and narcissistic disorders was furthered by Peter Hartocollis and Pitsa Hartocollis. They described alcoholism as a developmental disorder akin to borderline states, showing how repressed affects such as rage find their expression under the influence of alcohol.

John Wallace appreciates the adaptive function of the alcoholic's defenses, recommending that they be supported in the initial stages of recovery. This is crucial so that the patient is not overwhelmed in early recovery by unmanageable affects, guilt, and traumatic memories. This departure from drive theory is deepened by Edward Khantzian. Khantzian views alcohol use not as a reflection of unconscious intentions or oral fixation and dependency but rather as an attempt to remediate ego deficits. The alcoholic is radically impaired in basic ego function, such as self-care, a point that resonates with clinicians. Furthermore, alcoholics are impaired in affect regulation, which leaves them helpless in managing debilitating depression and anxiety. For Khantzian, alcoholic dependency is a result of defects in psychological structure prompting the alcoholic to attach to alcohol to compensate for internal deficits.

OBJECT RELATIONAL FORMULATIONS

The object relations theorists describe both the relationships of the inner world of representations and family dynamics. Robert Knight described the family constellations of alcoholic men and demonstrated their internalization. Recommending psychoanalysis within a hospital setting, Knight viewed the goal of treatment as repair of pathological object relations.

Ernst Simmel ran the first alcohol rehabilitation unit in suburban Berlin in the 1920s. Ironically, Freud stayed at Simmel's sanitarium when he was treated for the malignancy stemming from his cigar addiction. Simmel later advocated cooperation between AA and psychoanalysis at a time when professionals did not know AA existed. He correctly predicted an explosion of addictive behavior in the wake of the destructiveness of the Second World War, powerfully demonstrating the relationship between individual and social pathology.

Giorgio Lolli saw the alcoholic as striving for psychosomatic unity, a quest driven by developmental arrest consequent upon childhood disturbance. He gives us another angle on splitting and the attempt to heal it through drinking.

Henry Krystal sees the object world of the alcoholic as radically impaired by repression, splitting, and projection, all of which are consequent upon pathological early object relations. He sees the self-representation of the alcoholic as distorted by repression of the good aspects of the self. Alcohol is used to perform the ego functions that were never the possession of the alcoholic as a result of failures of internalization consequent on disturbances in the mother–infant relationship.

SELF PSYCHOLOGICAL FORMULATIONS

Gregory Bateson brings the perspective of a social anthropologist and information theorist to the dilemma of self-destruction through drinking. He sees the alcoholic as suffering from an exaggerated version of the characteristic epistemological error of Western culture, which sees such radical disjunction between subject and object that it leaves no possibility for a nonexploitive relationship between humanity and its environment or between people. Bateson sees alcoholism as an attempt to correct this false epistemology through drinking; tragically, the pharmacology of alcohol exacerbates that which it attempts to cure. Bateson sees AA's Twelve Steps as a vehicle for correcting this epistemology through the surrender experience. He sees the key transformation in recovery as a shift in self-perception from an isolated self doing battle with an externalized addiction to a noncombatant self that is part of an interactive interpersonal feedback loop.

Literary critic Alfred Kazin reviews the striking incidence of alcoholism in great writers. He debunks the myth that their drinking was intrinsic to their creativity. He sees these writers as highly vulnerable—caught between their allegiance to their art and their public personas. In his own way, he is saying that their alcoholism is a narcissistic disturbance.

Heinz Kohut, the founder of self psychology, compares addiction to a futile attempt to cure a gastric fistula by eating. The hoped-for cure just runs through. It is only through relationship that the building of psychic structure—that is, remediation of self deficits in anxiety modulation, self-soothing, and self-esteem regulation—becomes possible. The terrible emptiness of the addict's unmirrored self cannot be filled by booze or other drugs, no matter how desperately the addict may try to do so. For Kohut, alcoholism is an attempt at self-medication, which can only worsen the condition it tries to treat.

Edward Khantizian and John Mack, seeing the self as always a social self, elucidate the dynamics of AA, stressing its unique ability to remediate the alcoholic's problems in self-governance. Mack's notion of self-governance holds that interdependence is essential in the governance of the individual and that AA acts as a matrix for that interdependence.

Jerome Levin develops Kohut's notions into a metapsychological model of alcoholism as a regression/fixation to the stage of the archaic nuclear self, a stage correlative with pathological narcissism. Levin also makes explicit the selfobject (mirror and idealizing) transferences to alcohol and shows how successful treatment replaces these bonds to alcohol with bonds to the therapist. In short, rum is replaced with relationship.

TREATMENT: ISSUES AND TECHNIQUE

Although Arnold Ludwig and Abraham Wikler's paper is a behavioral one, we include it in this psychodynamic book because it is a seminal one on the eliciting of drink signals to prevent relapse. The contributions of Ronna Weiss and Howard Shaffer highlight the significance of countertransference, which, although endemic to alcoholism treatment, is not sufficiently addressed. Weiss's article demonstrates how countertransference reverberates in health care systems that provide services to alcoholics. Weiss also outlines common countertransference reactions in the relationship between therapist and patient and examines unconscious anxieties aroused in the therapist by the phenomenon of addiction. Shaffer further discusses the issues most difficult for the therapist: the patient's denial and ambivalence and the therapist's negative countertransference. Shaffer's proposed stage model of recovery from addiction further provides a useful context for understanding the unfolding transference and countertransference reactions in the patient and therapist.

HISTORICAL PAPERS
Part II

1: AN INQUIRY INTO THE EFFECTS OF ARDENT SPIRITS UPON THE HUMAN BODY AND MIND

Benjamin Rush, Surgeon General,
American Revolutionary Army

PART I

By ardent spirits, I mean those liquors only which are obtained by distillation from fermented substances of any kind. To their effects upon the bodies and minds of men, the following inquiry shall be exclusively confined. Fermented liquors contain so little spirit, and that so intimately combined with other matters, that they can seldom be drunken in sufficient quantities to produce intoxication, and its subsequent effects, without exciting a disrelish to their taste, or pain, from their distending the stomach. They are moreover, when taken in a moderate quantity, generally innocent, and often have a friendly influence upon health and life.

The effects of ardent spirits divide themselves into such as are of a prompt, and such as are of a chronic nature. The former discover themselves in drunkenness; and the latter in a numerous train of diseases and vices of the body and mind.

I shall begin by briefly describing their prompt, or immediate, effects in a fit of drunkenness.

This odious disease (for by that name it should be called) appears with more or less of the following symptoms, and most commonly in the order in which I shall enumerate them.

1. Unusual garrulity.
2. Unusual silence.
3. Captiousness, and a disposition to quarrel.
4. Uncommon good humour, and an insipid simpering, or laugh.
5. Profane swearing, and cursing.
6. A disclosure of their own or other people's secrets.

7. A rude disposition to tell those persons in company whom they know their faults.

8. Certain immodest actions. I am sorry to say, this sign of the first stage of drunkenness sometimes appears in women, who, when sober, are uniformly remarkable for chaste and decent manners.

9. A clipping of words.

10. Fighting; a black eye, or a swelled nose, often marks, this grade of drunkenness.

11. Certain extravagant acts which indicate a temporary fit of madness. These are singing, hallooing, roaring, imitating the noises of brute animals, jumping, tearing off clothes, dancing naked, breaking glasses and china, and dashing other articles of household furniture upon the ground, or floor. After a while the paroxysm of drunkenness is completely formed. The face now becomes flushed, the eyes project, and are somewhat watery, winking is less frequent than is natural; the under lip is protruded, the head inclines a little to one shoulder; the jaw falls; belchings and hickup take place; the limbs totter; the whole body staggers. The unfortunate subject of this history next falls on his seat; he looks around him with a vacant countenance, and mutters inarticulate sounds to himself; he attempts to rise and walk. In this attempt, he falls upon his side, from which he gradually turns upon his back. He now closes his eyes, and falls into a profound sleep, frequently attended with snoring, and profuse sweats, and sometimes with such a relaxation of the muscles which confine the bladder and the lower bowels, as to produce a symptom which delicacy forbids me to mention. In this condition, he often lies from ten, twelve, and twenty-four hours, to two, three, four, and five days, an object of pity and disgust to his family and friends. His recovery from this fit of intoxication is marked with several peculiar appearances. He opens his eyes, and closes them again; he gapes and stretches his limbs, he then coughs and pukes, his voice is hoarse, he rises with difficulty, and staggers to a chair; his eyes resemble balls of fire, his hands tremble, he loathes the sight of food; he calls for a glass of spirits to compose his stomach—now and then he emits a deep-fetched sigh, or groan, from a transient twinge of conscience, but he more frequently scolds, and curses every thing around him. In this state of languor and stupidity, he remains for two or three days, before he is able to resume his former habits of business and conversation.

Pythagoras, we are told, maintained that the souls of men after death expiated the crimes committed by them in this world, by animating certain brute animals; and that the souls of those animals, in their turns, entered into men, and carried with them all their peculiar qualities and vices. This doctrine of one of the wisest and best of the Greek Philosophers was probably intended only to convey a lively idea of the changes which are induced in the body and mind of man by a fit of drunkenness. In folly, it causes him to resemble a calf; in stupidity, an ass; in roaring, a mad bull; in quarrelling and fighting, a dog; in cruelty, a tyger; in fetor, a skunk; in filthiness, a hog; and in obscenity, a he-goat.

It belongs to the history of drunkenness to remark that its paroxysms occur, like the paroxysms of many diseases, at certain periods, and after longer or shorter intervals. They often begin with annual, and gradually increase in their frequency, until they appear in quarterly, monthly, weekly, and quotidian or daily periods. Finally they afford scarcely any marks of remission either during the day or the night. There was a citizen of Philadelphia many years ago, in whom drunkenness appeared in this protracted form. In speaking of him to one of his neighbours, I said, "Does he not *sometimes* get drunk?" "You mean," said his neighbour, "is he not *sometimes* sober?"

It is further remarkable that drunkenness resembles certain hereditary, family and contagious diseases. I have once known it to descend from a father to four out of five of his children. I have seen three, and once four, brothers who were born of sober ancestors affected by it, and I have heard of its spreading through a whole family composed of members not originally related to each other. These facts are important, and should not be over-looked by parents, in deciding upon the matrimonial connexions of their children.

Let us next attend to the chronic effects of ardent spirits upon the body and mind. In the body, they dispose to every form of acute disease; they moreover *excite* fevers in persons predisposed to them, from other causes. This has been remarked in all the yellow fevers which have visited the cities of the United States. Hard drinkers seldom escape, and rarely recover from them. The following diseases are the usual consequences of the habitual use of ardent spirits, namely:

1. A decay of appetite, sickness at stomach, and a puking of bile or a discharge of a frothy and viscid phlegm by hawking, in the morning.

2. Obstructions of the liver. The fable of Prometheus, on whose liver a vulture was said to prey constantly, as a punishment for his stealing fire from heaven, was intended to illustrate the painful effects of ardent spirits upon that organ of the body.

3. Jaundice and dropsy of the belly and limbs, and finally of every cavity in the body. A swelling in the feet and legs is so characteristic a mark of habits of intemperance, that the merchants in Charleston, I have been told, cease to trust the planters of South Carolina, as soon as they perceive it. They very naturally conclude industry and virtue to be extinct in that man, in whom that symptom of disease has been produced by the intemperate use of distilled spirits.

4. Hoarseness, and a husky cough, which often terminate in consumption, and sometimes in an acute and fatal disease of the lungs.

5. Diabetes, that is, a frequent and weakening discharge of pale or sweetish urine.

6. Redness, and eruptions on different parts of the body. They generally begin on the nose, and after gradually extending all over the face, sometimes descend to the limbs in the form of leprosy. They have been called "Rum-buds," when they appear in the face. In persons who have occasionally survived these

effects of ardent spirits on the skin, the face after a while becomes bloated, and its redness is succeeded by a death-like paleness. Thus the same fire which produces a red colour in iron, when urged to a more intense degree, produces what has been called a white heat.

7. A fetid breath, composed of every thing, that is offensive in putrid animal matter.

8. Frequent and disgusting belchings. Dr. Haller relates the case of a notorious drunkard having been suddenly destroyed in consequence of the vapour discharged from his stomach by belching, accidentally taking fire by coming in contact with the flame of a candle.

9. Epilepsy.

10. Gout, in all its various forms of swelled limbs, colic, palsy, and apoplexy.

Lastly, 11. Madness. The late Dr. Waters, while he acted as house pupil and apothecary of the Pennsylvania Hospital, assured me that in one third of the patients confined by this terrible disease, it had been induced by ardent spirits.

Most of the diseases which have been enumerated are of a mortal nature. They are more certainly induced, and terminate more speedily in death, when spirits are taken in such quantities, and at such times, as to produce frequent intoxication; but it may serve to remove an error with which some intemperate people console themselves, to remark that ardent spirits often bring on fatal diseases without producing drunkenness. I have known many persons destroyed by them who were never completely intoxicated during the whole course of their lives. The solitary instances of longevity which are now and then met with in hard drinkers no more disprove the deadly effects of ardent spirits than the solitary instances of recoveries from apparent death by drowning prove that there is no danger to life from a human body lying an hour or two under water.

The body after its death from the use of distilled spirits, exhibits by dissection certain appearances which are of a peculiar nature. The fibres of the stomach and bowels are contracted; abscesses, gangrene, and schirri are found in the viscera. The bronchial vessels are contracted, the blood-vessels and tendons in many parts of the body are more or less ossified, and even the hair of the head possesses a crispness which renders it less valuable to wig-makers than the hair of sober people.

Not less destructive are the effects of ardent spirits upon the human mind. They impair the memory, debilitate the understanding, and pervert the moral faculties. It was probably from observing these effects of intemperance in drinking upon the mind that a law was formerly passed in Spain, which excluded drunkards from being witnesses in a court of justice. But the demoralizing effects of distilled spirits do not stop here. They produce not only falsehood, but fraud, theft, uncleanliness, and murder. Like the demoniac mentioned in the New Testament, their name is "legion," for they convey into the soul a host of vices and crimes.

A more affecting spectacle cannot be exhibited than a person into whom this infernal spirit, generated by habits of intemperance, has entered. It is more or less affecting according to the station the person fills in a family, or in society, who is possessed by it. Is he a husband? How deep the anguish which rends the bosom of his wife! Is she a wife? Who can measure the shame and aversion which she excites in her husband? Is he the father, or is she the mother, of a family of children? See their averted looks from their parent, and their blushing looks at each other! Is he a magistrate or has he been chosen to fill a high and respectable station in the councils of his country? What humiliating fears of corruption in the administration of the laws, and of the subversion of public order and happiness, appear in the countenances of all who see him! Is he a minister of the gospel? Here language fails me. If angels weep, it is at such a sight.

In pointing out the evils produced by ardent spirits, let us not pass by their effects upon the estates of the persons who are addicted to them. Are they inhabitants of cities? Behold! their houses stripped gradually of their furniture, and pawned, or sold by a constable, to pay tavern debts. See! their names upon record in the dockets of every court, and whole pages of newspapers filled with advertisements of their estates for public sale. Are they inhabitants of country places? Behold! their houses with shattered windows, their barns with leaky roofs, their garden overrun with weeds, their fields with broken fences, their hogs without yokes, their sheep without wool, their cattle and horses without fat, and their children filthy and half clad, without manners, principles, and morals. This picture of agricultural wretchedness is seldom of long duration. The farms and property thus neglected, and depreciated, are seized and sold for the benefit of a group of creditors. The children that were born with the prospect of inheriting them are bound out to service in the neighbourhood; while their parents, the unworthy authors of their misfortunes, ramble into new and distant settlements, alternately fed on their way by the hand of charity, or a little casual labour.

Thus we see poverty and misery, crimes and infamy, diseases and death, are all the natural and usual consequences of the intemperate use of ardent spirits.

I have classed death among the consequences of hard drinking. But it is not death from the immediate hand of the Deity, nor from any of the instruments of it which were created by him. It is death from *suicide*. Yes—thou poor degraded creature, who art daily lifting the poisoned bowl to thy lips—cease to avoid the unhallowed ground in which the self-murderer is interred, and wonder no longer that the sun should shine, and the rain fall, and the grass look green upon his grave. Thou art perpetrating gradually, by the use of ardent spirits, what he has effected suddenly by opium—or a halter. Considering how many circumstances from surprise, or derangement, may palliate his guilt, or that (unlike yours) it was not preceded and accompanied by any other crime, it is probable his condemnation will be less than yours at the day of judgment.

I shall now take notice of the occasions and circumstances which are supposed to render the use of ardent spirits necessary, and endeavour to shew that the arguments in favour of their use in such cases are founded in error, and that in each of them, ardent spirits, instead of affording strength to the body, increase the evils they are intended to relieve.

1. They are said to be necessary in very cold weather. This is far from being true; for the temporary warmth they produce is always succeeded by a greater disposition in the body to be affected by cold. Warm dresses, a plentiful meal just before exposure to the cold, and eating occasionally a little ginger-bread, or any other cordial food, is a much more durable method of preserving the heat of the body in cold weather.

2. They are said to be necessary in very warm weather. Experience proves that they increase, instead of lessen, the effects of heat upon the body, and thereby dispose to diseases of all kinds. Even in the warm climate of the West-Indies, Dr. Bell asserts this to be true. "Rum (says this author), whether used habitually, moderately, or in excessive quantities in the West-Indies, always diminishes the strength of the body, and renders men more susceptible of disease, and unfit for any service in which vigour or activity is required."[1] As well might we throw oil into a house, the roof of which was on fire, in order to prevent the flames from extending to its inside, as pour ardent spirits into the stomach, to lessen the effects of a hot sun upon the skin.

3. Nor do ardent spirits lessen the effects of hard labour upon the body. Look at the horse; with every muscle of his body swelled from the morning till night in the plough, or a team; does he make signs for a draught of toddy, or a glass of spirits to enable him to cleave the ground, or to climb a hill? No — he requires nothing but cool water and substantial food. There is no nourishment in ardent spirits. The strength they produce in labour is of a transient nature, and is always followed by a sense of weakness and fatigue.

But are there no conditions of the human body in which ardent spirits may be given? I answer — there are. 1st. When the body has been suddenly exhausted of its strength, and a disposition to faintness has been induced. Here a few spoonfuls, or a wine-glass full of spirits, with or without water, may be administered with safety and advantage. In this case we comply strictly with the advice of Solomon, who restricts the use of "strong drink" only "to him who is ready to perish." 2d. When the body has been exposed for a long time to wet weather, more especially, if it be combined with cold. Here a moderate quantity of spirits is not only safe, but highly proper to obviate debility, and to prevent a fever. They will more certainly have those salutary effects if the feet are at the same time bathed with them, or a half pint of them poured into the shoes or boots. These I believe are the only two cases in which distilled spirits are useful or necessary to persons in health.

---

[1]Inquiry into the causes which produce and the means of preventing diseases among British officers, soliders and others in the West-Indies.

PART II

But it may be said, if we reject spirits from being a part of our drinks, what liquors shall we substitute in their room? I answer in the first place,

1. *Simple water.* I have known many instances of persons who have followed the most laborious employments for many years, in the open air, and in warm and cold weather, who never drank any thing but water, and enjoyed uninterrupted good health. Dr. Mosely, who resided many years in the West-Indies, confirms this remark. "I aver (says the Doctor) from my own knowledge and custom, as well as the custom and observations of many other people, that those who drink nothing but water, or make it their principal drink, are little affected by the climate, and can undergo the greatest fatigue without inconvenience, and are never subject to troublesome or dangerous diseases."

Persons who are unable to relish this simple beverage of nature, may drink some one, or of all the following liquors, in preference to ardent spirits.

2. *Cyder.* This excellent liquor contains a small quantity of spirit, but so diluted, and blunted by being combined with a large quantity of sugar matter, and water, as to be perfectly wholesome. It sometimes disagrees with persons subject to the rheumatism, but it may be made inoffensive to such people, by extinguishing a red hot iron in it, or by mixing it with water. It is to be lamented that the late frosts in the spring so often deprive us of the fruit which affords this liquor. The effects of these frosts have been in some measure obviated by giving an orchard a north-west exposure, so as to check too early vegetation, and by kindling two or three large fires of brush, or straw, to the windward of the orchard, the evening before we expect a night of frost. This last expedient has in many instances preserved the fruit of an orchard to the great joy and emolument of the ingenious husbandman.

3. *Malt liquors.* The grain from which these liquors are obtained, is not liable, like the apple, to be affected by frost, and therefore they can be procured, at all times, and at a moderate price. They contain a good deal of nourishment; hence we find many of the poor people in Great Britain endure hard labour with no other food than a quart or three pints of beer with a few pounds of bread in a day. As it will be difficult to prevent small beer from becoming sour in warm weather, an excellent substitute may be made for it by mixing bottled porter, ale, or strong beer with an equal quantity of water; or a pleasant beer may be made by adding to a bottle of porter ten quarts of water, and a pound of brown sugar or a pint of molasses. After they have been well mixed, pour the liquor into bottles and place them loosely corked in a cool cellar. In two or three days, it will be fit for use. A spoonful of ginger added to the mixture renders it more lively and agreeable to the taste.

4. *Wines.* These fermented liquors are composed of the same ingredients as cyder, and are both cordial and nourishing. The peasants of France who drink them in large quantities are a sober and healthy body of people. Unlike ardent spirits, which render the temper irritable, wines generally inspire cheerfulness and good humour. It is to be lamented that the grape has not as yet been

sufficiently cultivated in our country, to afford wine for our citizens; but many excellent substitutes may be made for it, from the native fruits of all the States. If two barrels of cyder fresh from the press are boiled into one, and afterwards fermented, and kept for two or three years in a dry cellar, it affords a liquor which, according to the quality of the apple from which the cyder is made, has the taste of Malaga, or Rhenish wine. It affords, when mixed with water, a most agreeable drink in summer. I have taken the liberty of calling it *Pomona wine*. There is another method of making a pleasant wine from the apple, by adding four and twenty gallons of new cyder to three gallons of syrup made from the expressed juice of sweet apples. When thoroughly fermented, and kept for a few years, it becomes fit for use. The blackberry of our fields, and the raspberry, and currant of our gardens, afford likewise an agreeable and wholesome wine, when pressed and mixed with certain proportions of sugar and water, and a little spirit, to counteract the disposition to an excessive fermentation. It is no objection to these cheap and home-made wines that they are unfit for use until they are two or three years old. The foreign wines in common use in our country require not only a much longer time to bring them to perfection, but to prevent their being disagreeable even to the taste.

5. *Molasses* and *water,* also *vinegar* and *water* sweetened with sugar or molasses, form an agreeable drink in warm weather. It is pleasant and cooling, and tends to keep up those gentle and uniform sweats on which health and life often depend. Vinegar and water constituted the only drink of the soldiers of the Roman republic, and it is well known they marched and fought in a warm climate, and beneath a load of arms which weighed sixty pounds. Boaz, a wealthy farmer in Palestine, we find treated his reapers with nothing but bread dipped in vinegar. To such persons as object to the taste of vinegar, sour milk, or buttermilk, or sweet milk diluted with water, may be given in its stead. I have known the labour of the longest and hottest days in summer supported by means of these pleasant and wholesome drinks with great firmness, and ended with scarcely a complaint of fatigue.

6. The *sugar maple* affords a thin juice which has long been used by the farmers in Connecticut as a cool and refreshing drink in the time of harvest. The settlers in the Western counties of the middle States will do well to let a few of the trees which yield this pleasant juice remain in all their fields. They may prove the means not only of saving their children and grand-children many hundred pounds, but of saving their bodies from disease and death, and their souls from misery beyond the grave.

7. *Coffee* possesses agreeable and exhilarating qualities, and might be used with great advantage to obviate the painful effects of heat, cold and fatigue upon the body. I once knew a country physician who made it a practice to drink a pint of strong coffee previous to his taking a long or cold ride. It was more cordial to him than spirits, in any of the forms in which they are commonly used.

The use of the cold bath in the morning, and of the warm bath in the evening, are happily calculated to strengthen the body the former part of the day, and to restore it in the latter from the languor and fatigue which are induced by heat and labour.

Let it not be said, ardent spirits have become necessary from habit in harvest, and in other seasons of uncommon and arduous labour. The habit is a bad one, and may be easily broken. Let but half a dozen farmers in a neighbourhood combine to allow higher wages to their labourers than are common, and a sufficient quantity of *any* of the pleasant and wholesome liquors I have recommended, and they may soon, by their example, abolish the practice of giving them spirits. In a little while they will be delighted with the good effects of their association. Their grain and hay will be gathered into their barns in less time, and in a better condition than formerly, and of course at a less expense, and a hundred disagreeable scenes from sickness, contention and accidents will be avoided, all of which follow, in a greater or lesser degree, the use of ardent spirits.

Nearly all diseases have their predisposing causes. The same thing may be said of the intemperate use of distilled spirits. It will, therefore, be useful to point out of the different employments, situations, and conditions of the body and mind which predispose to the love of those liquors, and to accompany them with directions to prevent persons being ignorantly and undesignedly seduced into the habitual and destructive use of them.

1. Labourers bear with great difficulty long intervals between their meals. To enable them to support the waste of their strength, their stomachs should be constantly but moderately stimulated by aliment, and this is best done by their eating four or five times in a day, during the seasons of great bodily exertion. The food at this time should be *solid*, consisting chiefly of salted meat. The vegetables used with it should possess some activity, or they should be made savoury by a mixture of spices. Onions and garlic are of a most cordial nature. They composed a part of the diet which enabled the Israelites to endure, in a warm climate, the heavy tasks imposed upon them by their Egyptian masters; and they were eaten, Horace and Virgil tell us, by the Roman farmers, to repair the waste of their strength, by the toils of harvest. There are likewise certain sweet substances which support the body under the pressure of labour. The negroes in the West-Indies become strong, and even fat, by drinking the juice of the sugar cane in the season of grinding it. The Jewish soldiers were invigorated by occasionally eating raisins and figs. A bread composed of wheat flour, molasses, and ginger (commonly called gingerbread) taken in small quantities during the day is happily calculated to obviate the debility induced upon the body by constant labour. All these substances, whether of an animal or vegetable nature, lessen the desire, as well as the necessity, for cordial drinks, and impart equable and durable strength to every part of the system.

2. Valetudinarians, especially those who are afflicted with diseases of the stomach and bowels, are very apt to seek relief from ardent spirits. Let such people be cautious how they make use of this dangerous remedy. I have known many men and women of excellent characters and principles, who have been

betrayed by occasional doses of gin and brandy, into a love of those liquors, and have afterwards fallen sacrifices to their fatal effects. The different preparations of opium are much more safe and efficatious than distilled cordials of any kind, in flatulent or spasmodic affections of the stomach and bowels. So great is the danger of contracting a love for distilled liquors by accustoming the stomach to their stimulus, that as few medicines as possible should be given in spiritous vehicles in chronic diseases. A physician of great eminence, and uncommon worth, who died towards the close of the last century, in London, in taking leave of a young physician of this city, who had finished his studies under his patronage, impressed this caution with peculiar force upon him, and lamented at the same time, in pathetic terms, that he had innocently made many sots by prescribing brandy and water in stomach complaints. It is difficult to tell how many persons have been destroyed by those physicians who have adopted Dr. Brown's indiscriminate practice in the use of stimulating remedies, the most popular of which is ardent spirits; but it is well known several of them have died of intemperance in this city, since the year 1790. They were probably led to it, by drinking brandy and water to relieve themselves from the frequent attacks of debility and indisposition to which the labours of a physician expose him, and for which rest, fasting, a gentle purge, or weak diluting drinks would have been more safe and more certain cures.

None of these remarks are intended to preclude the use of spirits in the low state of short, or what are called acute, diseases; for in such cases, they produce their effects too soon to create a habitual desire for them.

3. Some people, from living in countries subject to intermitting fevers, endeavour to fortify themselves against them, by taking two or three wine-glasses of bitters, made with spirits, every day. There is great danger of contracting habits of intemperance from this practice. Besides, this mode of preventing intermittents is far from being a certain one, a much better security against them is a tea-spoonful of the Jesuits bark, taken every morning during a sickly season. If this safe and excellent medicine cannot be had, a gill or half a pint of a strong watery infusion of centaury, camomile, wormwood, or rue, mixed with a little of the calamus of our meadows, may be taken every morning with nearly the same advantage as the Jesuits bark. Those persons who live in a sickly country, and cannot procure any of the preventatives of autumnal fevers, which have been mentioned, should avoid the morning and evening air, should kindle fires in their houses on damp days, and in cool evenings, throughout the whole summer, and put on winter clothes about the first week in September. The last part of these directions applies only to the inhabitants of the middle States.

4. Men who follow professions which require constant exercise of the faculties of their minds are very apt to seek relief, by the use of ardent spirits, from the fatigue which succeeds great mental exertions. To such persons it may be a discovery to know that *tea* is a much better remedy for that purpose. By its grateful and gentle stimulus, it removes fatigue, restores the excitement of the mind, and invigorates the whole system. I am no advocate for the excessive use of tea. When taken too strong, it is hurtful, especially to the female constitution;

but when taken of a moderate degree of strength and in moderate quantities, with sugar and cream, or milk, I believe it is in general innoxious, and at all times to be preferred to ardent spirits, as a cordial for studious men. The late Anthony Benezet, one of the most laborious schoolmasters I ever knew, informed me he had been prevented from the love of spirituous liquors, by acquiring a love for tea in early life. Three or four cups, taken in an afternoon, carried off the fatigue of a whole day's labour in his school. This worthy man lived to be seventy- one years of age, and died of an acute disease, with the full exercise of all the faculties of his mind. But the use of tea counteracts a desire for distilled spirits, during great *bodily* as well as mental exertions. Of this, Captain Forest has furnished us with a recent and remarkable proof, in his history of a voyage from Calcutta to the Marqui Archipelago. "I have always observed (says this ingenious mariner) when sailors drink tea, it weans them from the thoughts of drinking strong liquors, and pernicious grog; and with this, they are soon contented. Not so with whatever will intoxicate, be it what it will. This has always been my remark! I therefore always encourage it, without their knowing why."

5. Women have sometimes been led to seek relief from what is called breeding sickness, by the use of ardent spirits. A little gingerbread, or biscuit, taken occasionally, so as to prevent the stomach being empty, is a much better remedy for that disease.

6. Persons under the pressure of debt, disappointments in worldly pursuits, and guilt have sometimes sought to drown their sorrows in strong drink. The only radical cure for those evils, is to be found in Religion; but where its support is not resorted to, wine and opium should always be preferred to ardent spirits. They are far less injurious to the body and mind than spirits; and the habits of attachment to them are easily broken, after time and repentance have removed the evils they were taken to relieve.

7. The sociable and imitative nature of man often disposes him to adopt the most odious and destructive practices from his companions. The French soldiers who conquered Holland, in the year 1794, brought back with them the love and use of brandy, and thereby corrupted the inhabitants of several of the departments of France, who had been previously distinguished for their temperate and sober manners. Many other facts might be mentioned, to shew how important it is to avoid the company of persons addicted to the use of ardent spirits.

8. Smoking and chewing tobacco, by rendering water and simple liquors insipid to the taste, dispose very much to the stronger stimulus of ardent spirits. The practise of smoking segars, has, in every part of our country, been more followed by a general use of brandy and water, as a common drink, more especially by that class of citizens who have not been in the habit of drinking wine, or malt liquors. The less, therefore, tobacco is used in the above ways the better.

9. No man ever became suddenly a drunkard. It is by gradually accustoming the taste and stomach to ardent spirits, in the forms of *grog* and *toddy*, that men have been led to love them in their more destructive mixtures, and in their simple state. Under the impression of this truth, were it possible for me to

speak, with a voice so loud as to be heard from the river St.Croix, to the remotest shores of the Mississippi, which bound the territory of the United States, I would say, Friends and Fellow-Citizens! avoid the habitual use of those two seducing liquors, whether they be made with brandy, rum, gin, Jamaica spirits, whiskey, or what is called cherry bounce. It is true, some men, by limiting the strength of those drinks, by measuring the spirit and water, have drunken them for many years, and even during a long life, without acquiring habits of intemperance or intoxication; but many more have been insensibly led by drinking weak toddy, and grog first at their meals, to take them for their constant drink, in the intervals of their meals; afterwards to take them, of an increased strength, before breakfast in the morning, and finally to destroy themselves by drinking undiluted spirits, during every hour of the day and night. I am not singular in this remark. "The consequences of drinking rum and water, or *grog* as it is called, [says Dr. Mosely] is, that habit increases the desire of more spirit, and decreases its effects; and there are very few grog-drinkers, who long survive the practice of debauching with it without acquiring the odious nuisance of dram-drinkers breath, and downright stupidity and impotence."[2] To enforce the caution against the use of those two apparently innocent and popular liquors still further, I shall select one instance from among many, to shew the ordinary manner in which they beguile and destroy their votaries. A citizen of Philadelphia, once of a fair and sober character, drank toddy for many years, as his constant drink. From this he proceeded to drink grog. After a while, nothing would satisfy him, but slings made of equal parts of rum and water, with a little sugar. From slings, he advanced to raw rum, and from common rum, to Jamaica spirits. Here he rested for a few months, but at length finding even Jamaica spirits were not strong enough to warm his stomach, he made it a constant practice to throw a table-spoonful of ground pepper into each glass of his spirits, in order, to use his own words, "to take off their coldness." He soon afterwards died a martyr to his intemperance.

Ministers of the gospel, of every denomination in the United States! — aid me with all the weight you possess in society, from the dignity and usefulness of your sacred office, to save our fellow-men from being destroyed by the great destroyer of their lives and souls. In order more successfully to effect this purpose, permit me to suggest to you, to employ the same wise modes of instruction, which you use in your attempts to prevent their destruction by other vices. You expose the evils of covetousness, in order to prevent theft; you point out of the sinfulness of impure desires, in order to prevent adultery; and you dissuade from anger, and malice, in order to prevent murder. In like manner, denounce, by your preaching, conversation and examples, the seducing influence of toddy and grog, when you aim to prevent all the crimes and miseries which are the offspring of strong drink.

---

[2]Treatise on Tropical Diseases.

We have hitherto considered the effects of ardent spirits upon individuals, and the means of preventing them. I shall close this head of our inquiry, by a few remarks on their effects upon the population and welfare of our country, and the means of obviating them.

It is highly probable, not less than 4,000 people die annually, from the use of ardent spirits, in the United States. Should they continue to exert this deadly influence upon our population, where will their evils terminate? This question may be answered by asking, where are all the Indian tribes, whose numbers and arms formerly spread terror among their civilized neighbours? I answer in the words of the famous Mingo Chief, "the blood of many of them flows not in the veins of any human creature." They have perished, not by pestilence, nor war, but by a greater foe to human life than either of them—Ardent Spirits. The loss of 4,000 American citizens, by the yellow fever, in a single year, awakened general sympathy and terror, and called forth all the strength and ingenuity of laws, to prevent its recurrence. Why is not the same zeal manifested in protecting our citizens from the more general and consuming ravages of distilled spirits? Should the customs of civilized life preserve our nation from extinction, and even from an increase of mortality, by those liquors; they cannot prevent our country being governed by men chosen by intemperate and corrupted voters. From such legislators, the republic would soon be in danger. To avert this evil, let good men of every class unite and besiege the general and state governments, with petitions to limit the number of taverns—to impose heavy duties upon ardent spirits—to inflict a mark of disgrace, or a temporary abridgement of some civil right, upon every man convicted of drunkenness; and finally, to secure the property of habitual drunkards, for the benefit of their families, by placing it in the hands of trustees, appointed for that purpose, by a court of justice.

To aid the operation of these laws, would it not be extremely useful for the rulers of the different denominations of Christian churches to unite, and render the sale and consumption of ardent spirits a subject of ecclesiastical jurisdiction? The Methodists, and society of Friends, have for some time past viewed them as contraband articles, to the pure laws of the gospel, and have borne many public and private testimonies against making them the objects of commerce. Their success in this benevolent enterprise affords ample encouragement for all other religious societies to follow their example.

PART III

We come now to the third part of this Inquiry; that is, to mention the remedies for the evils which are brought on by the excessive use of distilled spirits. These remedies divide themselves into two kinds.

I. Such as are proper to cure a fit of drunkenness; and

II. Such as are proper to prevent its recurrence, and to destroy a desire for ardent spirits.

I. I am aware that the efforts of science and humanity, in applying their resources to the cure of a disease induced by an act of vice, will meet with a cold reception from many people. But let such people remember the subjects of our remedies are their fellow creatures, and that the miseries brought upon human nature, by its crimes, are as much the objects of divine compassion (which we are bound to imitate) as the distresses which are brought upon men, by the crimes of other people, or which they bring upon themselves, by ignorance or accidents. Let us not then pass by the prostrate sufferer from strong drink, but administer to him the same relief we would afford to a fellow creature, in a similar state, from an accidental and innocent cause.

1. The first thing to be done to cure a fit of drunkenness is to open the collar, if in a man, and remove all tight ligatures from every other part of the body. The head and shoulders should at the same time be elevated, so as to favour a more feeble determination of the blood to the brain.

2. The contents of the stomach should be discharged, by thrusting a feather down the throat. It often restores the patient immediately to his senses and feet. Should it fail of exciting a puking,

3. A napkin should be wrapped round the head, and wetted an hour or two with cold water, or cold water should be poured in a stream upon the head. In the latter way, I have sometimes seen it used when a boy, in the city of Philadelphia. It was applied, by dragging the patient, when found drunk in the street, to a pump, and pumping water upon his head for ten or fifteen minutes. The patient generally rose, and walked off, sober and sullen, after the use of this remedy.

Other remedies, less common, but not less effectual, for a fit of drunkenness are,

4. Plunging the whole-body into cold water. A number of gentlemen who had drunken to intoxication, on board of a ship in the stream near Fell's point, at Baltimore, in consequence of their reeling in a small boat, on their way to the shore, in the evening, overset it, and fell into the water. Several boats from the shore hurried to their relief. They were all picked up, and went home, perfectly sober, to their families.

5. Terror. A number of young merchants, who had drunken together, in a compting-house on James river, above thirty years ago, until they were intoxicated, were carried away by a sudden rise of the river, from an immense fall of rain. They floated several miles with the current, in their little cabin, half filled with water. An island in the river arrested it. When they reached the shore that saved their lives, they were all sober. It is probable terror assisted in the cure of the persons who fell into the water at Baltimore.

6. The excitement of a fit of anger. The late Dr. Witherspoon used to tell a story of a man in Scotland, who was always cured of a fit of drunkenness, by being made angry. The mean chosen for that purpose was a singular one. It was talking against religion.

7. A severe whipping. This remedy acts by exciting a revulsion of the blood from the brain, to the external parts of the body.

8. Profuse sweats. By means of this evacuation, nature sometimes cures a fit of drunkenness. Their good effects are obvious in labourers whom quarts of spirits taken in a day will seldom intoxicate, while they sweat freely. If the patient be unable to swallow warm drinks, in order to produce sweats, they may be excited by putting him in a warm bath, or wrapping his body in blankets, under which should be placed half a dozen hot bricks, or bottles filled with hot water.

9. Bleeding. This remedy should always be used where the former ones have been prescribed to no purpose, or where there is reason to fear from the long duration of the disease a material injury may be done to the brain.

It is hardly necessary to add that each of the above remedies should be regulated by the grade of drunkenness, and the greater or less degree in which the intellects are affected in it.

II. The remedies which are proper to prevent the recurrence of fits of drunkenness, and to destroy the desire for ardent spirits, are religious, metaphysical, and medical. I shall briefly mention them.

1. Many hundred drunkards have been cured of their desire for ardent spirits, by a practical belief in the doctrines of the Christian religion. Examples of the divine efficacy of Christianity for this purpose, have lately occurred in many parts of the United States.

2. A sudden sense of the guilt contracted by drunkenness, and of its punishment in a future world. It once cured a gentleman in Philadelphia, who, in a fit of drunkenness, attempted to murder a wife whom he loved. Upon being told of it when he was sober, he was so struck with the enormity of the crime he had nearly committed, that he never tasted spirituous liquors afterwards.

3. A sudden sense of shame. Of the efficacy of this deep-seated principle in the human bosom, in curing drunkenness, I shall relate three remarkable instances.

A farmer in England, who had been many years in the practice of coming home intoxicated, from a market town, one day observed appearances of rain, while he was in market. His hay was cut, and ready to be housed. To save it, he returned in haste to his farm, before he had taken his customary dose of grog. Upon coming into his house, one of his children, a boy of six years old, ran to his mother, and cried out, "O! mother, father is come home, and he is not drunk." The father, who heard this exclamation, was so severely rebuked by it, that he suddenly became a sober man.

A noted drunkard was once followed by a favourite goat, to a tavern, into which he was invited by his master, and drenched with some of his liquor. The poor animal staggered home with his master, a good deal intoxicated. The next day he followed him to his accustomed tavern. When the goat came to the door, he paused: his master made signs to him to follow him into the house. The goat stood still. An attempt was made to thrust him into the tavern. He resisted, as if struck with the recollection of what he suffered from being intoxicated the night before. His master was so much affected by a sense of shame, in observing the conduct of his goat to be so much more rational than his own, that he ceased from that time to drink spirituous liquors.

A gentleman in one of the southern states, who had nearly destroyed himself by strong drink, was remarkable for exhibiting the grossest marks of folly in his fits of intoxication. One evening, sitting in his parlour, he heard an uncommon noise in his kitchen. He went to the door, and he peeped through the key-hole, from whence he saw one of his negroes diverting his fellow-servants, by mimicking his master's gestures and conversation when he was drunk. The sight overwhelmed him with shame and distress, and instantly became the means of his reformation.

4. The association of the idea of ardent spirits, with a painful or disagreeable impression upon some part of the body, has sometimes cured the love of strong drink. I once tempted a negro man, who was habitually fond of ardent spirits, to drink some rum (which I placed in his way) and in which I had put a few grains of tartar emetic. The tartar sickened and puked him to such a degree, that he supposed himself to be poisoned. I was much gratified by observing he could not bear the sight nor smell of spirits for two years afterwards.

I have heard of a man, who was cured of the love of spirits, by working off a puke, by large draughts of brandy and water; and I know a gentleman, who, in consequence of being affected with a rheumatism, immediately after drinking some toddy, when overcome with fatigue and exposure to the rain, has ever since loathed that liquor, only because it was accidentally associated in his memory with the recollection of the pain he suffered from his disease.

This appeal to that operation of the human mind, which obliges it to associate ideas, accidentally or otherwise combined, for the cure of vice, is very ancient. It was resorted to by Moses, when he compelled the children of Israel to drink the solution of the golden calf (which they had idolized) in water. This solution, if made as it most probably was, by means of what is called hepar sulphuris, was extremely bitter, and nauseous, and could never be recollected afterwards, without bringing into equal detestation the sin which subjected them to the necessity of drinking it. Our knowledge of this principle of association upon the minds and conduct of men should lead us to destroy, by means of other impressions, the influence of all those circumstances, with which the recollection and desire of spirits are combined. Some men drink only in the *morning*, some at *noon*, and some at *night*. Some men drink only on a *market day*, some at *one* tavern only, and some only in *one kind* of company. Now by finding a new and interesting employment, or subject of conversation for drunkards at the usual times in which they have been accustomed to drink, and by restraining them by the same means from those places and companions, which suggested to them the idea of ardent spirits, their habits of intemperance may be completely destroyed. In the same way the periodical returns of appetite and a desire of sleep have been destroyed in a hundred instances. The desire for strong drink differs from each of them, in being of an artificial nature, and therefore not disposed to return, after being chased for a few weeks from the system.

5. The love of ardent spirits has sometimes been subdued, by exciting a counter passion in the mind. A citizen of Philadelphia had made many unsuccessful attempts to cure his wife of drunkenness. At length, despairing of her reformation, he purchased a hogshead of rum, and after tapping it, left the key in the door of the room in which it was placed, as if he had forgotten it. His design was to give his wife an opportunity of drinking herself to death. She suspected this to be his motive, in what he had done, and suddenly left off drinking. Resentment here became the antidote to intemperance.

6. A diet consisting wholly of vegetables cured a physician in Maryland of drunkenness, probably by lessening that thirst, which is always more or less excited by animal food.

7. Blisters to the ankles, which were followed by an unusual degree of inflammation, once suspended the love of ardent spirits, for one month, in a lady in this city. The degrees of her intemperance may be conceived of when I add that her grocer's accompt for brandy alone amounted annually to one hundred pounds, Pennsylvania currency, for several years.

8. A violent attack of an acute disease has sometimes destroyed a habit of drinking distilled liquors. I attended a notorious drunkard, in the yellow fever, in the year 1798, who recovered with the loss of his relish for spirits, which has, I believe, continued ever since.

9. A salivation has lately performed a cure of drunkenness in a person in Virginia. The new disease excited in the mouth and throat, while it rendered the action of the smallest quantity of spirits upon them painful, was happily calculated to destroy the disease in the stomach which prompts to drinking, as well as to render the recollection of them disagreeable, by the laws of association formerly mentioned.

10. I have known an oath taken before a magistrate, to drink no more spirits, produce a perfect cure of drunkenness. It is sometimes cured in this way in Ireland. Persons who take oaths for this purpose are called affidavit men.

11. An advantage would probably arise from frequent representations being made to drunkards, not only of the certainty, but of the *suddenness*, of death, from habits of intemperance. I have heard of two persons being cured of the love of ardent spirits, by seeing death suddenly induced by fits of intoxication; in the one case in a stranger, and in the other in an intimate friend.

12. It has been said that the disuse of spirits should be gradual; but my observations authorise me to say that persons who have been addicted to them should abstain from them *suddenly* and *entirely*. "Taste not, handle not, touch not," should be inscribed upon every vessel that contains spirits in the house of a man, who wishes to be cured of habits of intemperance. To obviate for a while, the debility which arises from the sudden abstraction of the stimulus of the spirits, laudanum, or bitters infused in water should be taken, and perhaps a larger quantity of beer or wine than is consistent with the strict rules of temperate living. By the temporary use of these substitutes for spirits, I have never known the transition to sober habits to be attended with any bad effects, but often with permanent health of body, and peace of mind.

2: HEREDITY AND PRE-MATURE WEANING: A DISCUSSION OF THE WORK OF THOMAS TROTTER, BRITISH NAVAL PHYSICIAN

Emil Jellinek

Many writers on inebriety have been credited with recognizing, for the first time, alcohol addiction as a disease. Earlier and earlier instances are mentioned in historical notes and perhaps the original coiner of the phrase will never be ascertained. Certainly Dr. Thomas Trotter was not the first writer to assert this, as a few years before him Benjamin Rush had referred to alcohol addiction as a disease. On the other hand, it was probably Trotter who was the first to go farther than merely stating the fact and who actually dealt with the question in a truly medical sense.

Thomas Trotter (1760–1832) studied medicine in Edinburgh and in 1778, at the age of 18, became a physician in the British Navy. He later returned to the University of Edinburgh where he worked for his medical degree which he received in 1788. His ambition was to submit a doctor's thesis on a subject "that had never been noticed by any former graduate." After much consideration he decided on the subject of "ebriety," but doubted "whether such a thesis was proper matter for an academic exercise." The subject was found acceptable by the faculty and in 1788 Trotter submitted his thesis, *De Ebrietate, ejusque Effectibus in Corpus humanum*. For this work he received the thanks of the Royal Humane Society. Dr. Hawes in transmitting the thanks of this institute observed that "the investigation of so important an inquiry, in a regular scientific manner, was never before thought of: it was a subject left, happily left, to be ingeniously executed and amplified by Dr. Trotter."

In 1804, after having served again in important positions in the Navy, Trotter greatly amplified and revised his inaugural dissertation and published it as a book of over 200 pages. The passages given below are quoted from the 1813 edition published by Bradford and Read of Boston and A. Finley of Philadelphia. This *Essay* dedicated to Dr. Jenner is an important document on the knowledge at the opening of the nineteenth century relative to the physical and chemical effects of alcohol. The book is even more important as representing an early medical view of alcohol addiction and as a first systematic consideration of psychotherapy of this disease.

Trotter gives the following definition of alcohol addiction:

> In medical language, I consider drunkenness, strictly speaking, to be a disease; produced by a remote cause, and giving birth to actions and movements in the living body, that disorder the functions of health.

The reason why it was not treated as a medical subject and why it should be treated so he explained in the introduction:

> Mankind, ever in pursuit of pleasure, have reluctantly admitted into the catalogue of their diseases, those evils which were the immediate offspring of their luxuries. Such a reserve is indeed natural to the human mind: for of all deviations from the paths of duty, there are none that so forcibly impeach their pretentions to the character of rational beings as the inordinate use of spirituous liquors. Hence, in the writings of medicine, we find drunkenness only cursorily mentioned among the powers that injure health, while the mode of action is entirely neglected and left unexplained. . . . The priesthood hath poured forth its anathemas from the pulpit; and the moralist, no less severe, hath declaimed against it as a vice degrading to our nature. Both have meant well; and becomingly opposed religious and moral arguments to the sinful indulgence of animal appetite. But the physical influence of custom, confirmed into habit, interwoven with the actions of our sentient system, and reacting on our mental part, have been entirely forgotten. The perfect knowledge of those remote causes which first induced the propensity to vinous liquors, whether they sprung from situation in life, or depended on any peculiar temperament of body, is also necessary for conducting the cure.

Trotter was fully cognizant of the medical literature dealing with the effects of alcohol on the body, but as far as medical discussion of addiction itself was concerned, his statement was in order.

There are various etiological remarks in the *Essay*. That alcohol addiction could be transmitted from father to son had been said before him, but the hereditary role was envisaged by Trotter in a much more modern sense.

> Drunkenness itself, is a temporary madness. But in constitutions where there is a predisposition to insanity and ideotism, these diseases are apt to succeed the paroxysm, and will often last weeks and months after it. Wounds and contusions of the brain and cranium, with other organic lesions, have a similar effect. I have known numberless instances of these kinds of *Mania* and *Amentia*.

He was a believer in psychogenesis of the habit:

> Again, are not habits of drunkenness more often produced by mental affections than corporeal diseases? I apprehend few people will doubt the truth of this. Does not the inebriate return to his potation rather to raise his spirits, and exhilarate the mind, than to support and strengthen the body? The diseases of body, if unattended with dejection, have no need of vinous stimulus; and three-fourths of the human race recover daily from all the stages of debility without ever having recourse to it.

Trotter had also some etiological ideas relating to early nutritional habits:

> The seeds of this disease, (the habit of ebriety,) I suspect, like many other, are often sown in infancy. I do not merely allude to the moral education. In the present stage of society, human kind are almost taken out of the hands of Nature: and a custom called *fashion*, a word which ought to have nothing to do with nursing, now rules

every thing. The early stages of our existence require a mild bland nourishment, that is suited to the delicate excitability of a tender subject. But it too often happens that the infant is deprived of the breast, long before the growth of the body has fitted the stomach for the reception of more stimulant food. Instead, therefore, of its mother's milk, the infant is fed on hot broth, spiced pudding, and, perhaps also, that enervating beverage tea. The taste is thus early vitiated, the stomach and bowels frequently disordered; and, to add to the mischief, the helpless child is forced to gulp down many a nauseous draught of medicine or bitter potion, that its unnatural mother may acquit her conscience of having done every thing in her power to recover its health. Dyspeptic affections are in this manner quickly induced: a constant recourse to medicine, wine, cordials, and spirits, must be the consequence; and the child of the fashionable lady becomes a certain *annuity* to physic; a drunkard at twenty, and an old man at thirty years of age.

Relative to the therapy of alcohol addiction Trotter expressed ideas which are still being reiterated by psychotherapists. Previous to Trotter, Benjamin Rush had presented some ideas on the therapy of addiction, such as religious conversion and even conditioning, but Rush's ideas on the subject were not systematic and did not show the psychiatric insight which is revealed in Trotter's discussion.

It is to be remembered that a bodily infirmity is not the only thing to be corrected. *The habit of drunkenness is a disease of the mind.* The soul itself has received impressions that are incompatible with its reasoning powers. The subject, in all respects, requires great address; and you must beware how you inveigh against the propensity; for the cravings of appetite for the poisonous draught are to the intemperate drinker as much the inclinations of nature, for the time, as a draught of cold water to a traveller panting with thirst in a desert. Much vigilence will often be required in watching these cravings; for they are sometimes attended with modes of deception, and a degree of cunning, not to be equaled. I have known them employ force in the rudest manner in order to gratify their longing after spirituous liquors. I firmly believe that the injudicious and ill-timed chastisement of officious friends have driven many unfortunate inebriate to ruin, that might have been reclaimed by a different treatment. Nay, if such corrections are applied when the mind is ruffled with nervous and hypochondrical feelings, and depressed with low spirits, which so frequently follow a last night's debauch, the consequences may be fatal; and it is well known that suicide has sometimes been first resolved upon after these ghostly admonitions.

When the physician has once gained the full confidence of his patient, he will find little difficulty in beginning his plan of cure. I have on several occasions wrought myself so much into the good graces of them, that nothing gave them so much alarm or uneasiness as the dread of declining my visits after they had been argued out of the pernicious practice. This confidence may sometimes be employed to great advantage when your regimen is in danger of being transgressed, for frequent relapses, and promises repeatedly broken, will, in such situations, render the physician's visits a work of great trial to his patience. This disease, I mean the habit of drunkenness, is like some other mental derangements; there is an ascendancy to be gained over the person committed to our care, which, when accomplished, brings him entirely under our control. Particular opportunities are therefore to be taken, to hold up a mirror as it were, that he may see the deformity of his conduct, and represent the incurable maladies which flow from perserverance in a course of intemperance. There are times when a picture of this kind will make a strong impression on the mind; but at the conclusion of every visit,

something consolatory must be left for amusement, and as food for his reflections. . . .

I have mentioned, above, the necessity of studying the patient's temper and
character, that we may acquire his confidence. These will lead us to the particular
cause, time and place of his love of the bottle. The danger of continuing his career
may be then calmly argued with him, and something proposed that will effectually
wean his affections from it, and strenuously engage his attention. This may be
varied according to circumstances, and must be left to the discretion of the
physician.

The modern principle of suiting the treatment to the individual was also
expressed by Trotter:

In treating these various descriptions of persons and characters, it will readily
appear to a discerning physician, that very different methods will be required. The
patient already knows, as well as the priest and moralist that the indulgence is
pernicious, and ultimately fatal: he is also aware, without the reasonings of the
physician, that the constant repetition will destroy health; but it is not so easy to
convince him that you posses a charm that can recompence his feelings for the want
of a grateful stimulus, or bestow on his nervous system sensations equally soothing
and agreeable as he has been accustomed to receive from the bewitching spirit. *Hic
labor, boc opus est:* this is the difficulty; this is the task, that is to prove your
discernment, patience, and address. That little has been done hitherto with success,
we may be assured, by very rarely meeting with a reformed drunkard. The habit,
carried to a certain length, is a gulph, from *whose bourne no traveller returns:* where
fame, fortune, hope, health, and life perish.

Trotter did not forget that the bodily diseases attendant upon inebriety had
to receive attention too.

In order to strengthen the body if debilitated, general remedies, as commonly
employed, may be resorted to; such as the cold bath, chalybeate waters, exercise in
the open air, condiments, vigorous diet, etc. . . .

The chief complaints which require medicine are of the dyspeptic kind. The
pain and uneasiness which they create is almost constant; and if accompanied with
a hypochondriacal disposition, nothing can be more harassing. It is always
necessary in such cases to correct the acidity prevailing in the stomach and bowels;
which may be done by Pulv. chel. comp. Pulv. cretæ comp. Mag. ust. Aq. calcis,
etc. Acidity with flatulence often produces spasmodic pains and twitches, as they
are called, as well as that irregular and tumultuous motion of the intestines called
borborrygmi. Bitters are readily combined with these anti-acids, such as colombo,
quassia, chamœmelum, etc.; they likewise impede fermentation in the stomach,
and also correct acidity. Iron, in its most suitable state, (for the form ought to be
studied) given in small quantity, and continued long, is justly celebrated in these
cases. I would have the belly preserved in a soluble condition by gentle laxatives;
but all the harsher purgatives must be avoided: if the diet can be so conducted as
to supersede the use of medicine in regulating this discharge, so much the better.
The cramps and spasms which so often attend the weakened stomach are readily
relieved by æther. vitr. and opium, with other stimulants; but these generally yield
when the acidity is overcome. The physician, in directing his *formula*, will cautiously
avoid every preparation that has ardent spirit in its composition. I have seen and
known many instances where the most nauseous and fetid tinctures were devoured
with an avidity not to be conceived, when it was found that they were compounded
of brandy. The taste of the mouth on such occasions has little to do in exciting the

desires of the patient; there is a *vacuum* in sensation, if I may so term it, that can be supplied with nothing but the vinous stimulus while the habit remains, and the mind not earnestly in pursuit of something that can engage it.

The treatment of dyspnea of drunkards and "schirrous liver" were also considered.

Relative to diet Trotter thought it best

to put him on food in direct opposition to his former modes of living, and consign him to the lap of nature as if his existence were to pass through a second infancy. Indeed the reformed drunkard must be considered as a regenerated being.

He advocated immediate withdrawal of alcohol in opposition to the contemporary ideas on the harmfulness of such procedure (ideas which even at present are occasionally expressed).

As far as my experience of mankind enables me to decide, I must give it as my opinion, that there is no safety in trusting the habitual inebriate with any limited portion of liquor. Wherever I have known the drunkard effectually reformed, he has at once abandoned his potation. That dangerous degree of debility which has been said to follow the subtraction of vinous stimulus, I have never met with, however universal the cry has been in its favour; it is the war-whoop of alarmists; the idle cant of arch theorists.

Trotter's ideas on physiology and biochemistry of alcohol are naturally reflections of the status of knowledge in those fields at his time. Historically his opinions are of considerable interest and they are given here without further comment.

The stimulant action of ardent spirit is first exerted on the stomach, and spread, by sympathy, from thence to the *sensorium commune,* and the rest of the system. But there can be no doubt that much of the liquor also enters the circulation, and gives there an additional stimulus: for we are acquainted with no particular appetency inherent in the lacteal vessels, that can confine the absorption only to mild and bland fluids. It is true that the urine, perspirable matter, and serum of inebriates have never yet been so carefully analyzed as to discover alkohol; but that vinous spirit mixes with the blood we know to a certainty, from the hydrogenous gas which escapes from the lungs, to be perceived in the fœtor of the breath. We are, however, ignorant what combinations the hydrogen, or other parts of the alkohol, may form with the human fluids. But, besides the effect which spirits may have, in directly exciting the nervous system, it would appear that intoxication and delirium are also much increased, by the force of the circulation in the blood vessels of the brain, and the mechanical compression as a consequence of their surcharged state. This being admitted, at once explains why so much comatose affection attends ebriety. It is also observed that some liquors, more than others, produce sopor: porter, and all strong malt liquors, are of this description, as characterized by the swoln and bloated countenance, stupor, sluggishness, drowsiness, and sleep: while gaiety and an immense flow of spirits distinguish the frisky delirium from drinking champaigne, and some other liquors. Obesity and fulness commonly follow the long indulgence of strong ale, strong beer, or porter: the blood vessels would appear to be clogged with a dense blood; and I have observed, in such cases, that the drunken paroxysm lasts much longer, than when it has been produced by any kind of wine, or even ardent spirit diluted or otherwise. The fixed air in champaigne must give but a temporary stimulus; and the tartar, which is an ingredient in all wines, probably facilitates their evacuation from the body, by its diuretic quality.

Indeed the only way of accounting for the solution of the drunken paroxysm, must be as follows: the ardent spirit must either be attenuated, diluted, neutralized, or evacuated, that it ceases to have effects. It probably partakes of all these. It is also peculiar to the living fibre, to remain a given time in the state of excitement only, unless a new portion of stimulus is supplied. But the body does not immediately return to the former condition after the solution of the disease. It has been weakened by excessive stimulation; and it is only by the exhibition of moderate stimuli, such as pure air, animal food, and mental exhilaration, that it can resume its former health and vigor. The head-ach, nausea, languor, and low-spirits, which follow a debauch, are so many proofs of a debilitated frame. . . .

That *alkohol*, independent of its intoxicating quality, possesses a *chemical* operation in the human body, cannot be doubted. Applied directly to the animal solid, it constringes and hardens it: and suspends its progress towards putrefaction when separated from the body. It coagulates the serum of the blood, and most of the secreted fluids.

Alcohol certainly, deoxygenates the blood in some degree; at least decompounds its floridity. The arterial blood of a professed drunkard approaches to the color of venous; it is darker than usual. The rosy colour of the eruptions about the nose and cheeks does not disprove this: for it is probable that these spots attract oxygen from the atmosphere through the cuticle that covers them, just as Dr. Priestly observed venous blood, confined in a bladder, to acquire a more florid colour from the exposure to his dephlogisticated air. In the sea scurvy, a disease, where, in the advanced stage, the blood is always found of a very dark colour, we know that spirituous liquors more than any thing else, have a manifest tendency to aggravate every symptom. This fact has often come under my observation; and a very correct statement of the kind is to be found in my first volume on the Diseases of the Fleet, page 410.

The component parts of alkohol are not sufficiently known; but it has a large proportion of hydrogen, which is proved by its combustion in pure air, when water is produced. Thus fourteen ounces of alkohol burnt in a proper apparatus, with a sufficient quantity of oxygen gas, yield sixteen ounces of pure water; hydrogen and oxygen being the component principles of water, as proved by modern chemistry. Alkohol has a strong attraction for water, and readily mixes with it, and it is the chief vehicle in which it is drank; but in what manner it is separated from the water within the body, would be difficult to find out. The evolution of hydrogenous gas is chiefly learned from the fœtor of the breath; it seems to be sent off from the surface of the lungs, in a disengaged state; and so pure in its kind from the expiration of a dram-drinker, that it is easily inflamed on the approach of a candle. The process of respiration probably effects this; and I should think at such a time there must be an unusual consumption of vital air. No experiments have been made on the blood of inebriates: and we are not informed, that in the circulating state, it exceeds the common temperature of the human body. But it is said, on the authority of Mr. Spalding, the celebrated diver, that after drinking spirits he always found the air in his bell consumed in a shorter time, than when he drank water. This gentleman was lost in Dublin bay in 1783, in attempting to take the treasure out of an imperial Indiaman that sunk there, on her passage from Liverpool where she was built: the misfortune, it appeared, was owing to the negligence of the attendants in not renewing the air.

If the blood of drunkards is strongly charged with hydrogen, must not that very much affect the quality of the biliary secretion, independent of any effect it may have on the liver itself? Might not the resinous matter which bile is found to contain, be greatly increased after spirituous potation? The liver is an organ very liable to be injured by hard drinking; this gives cause for suspicion, that the *chemical* operation of alkohol on the blood and the bile, has also some share in producing hepatic diseases. It may increase the generation of *biliary calculi*, and the disposition of dyspepsia, which prevail in the constitution of drunkards.

Trotter also enumerates and describes in great detail the bodily ailments of inebriety, but neither his lists nor his descriptions differ in any way from the well known lists of his times.

While Trotter's *Essay* is an indictment of excessive drinking, and while he even believed that moderate drinking was unnecessary for younger people, he conceded advisability of drinking from middle age on.

I am of opinion, that no man in health can need wine till he arrives at forty. He may then begin with two glasses in the day: at fifty he may add two more; and at sixty he may go to the length of six glasses *per diem*, but not to exceed that quantity even though he should live to an hundred.[1] Lewis Cornaro, the Venetian nobleman who lived upwards of a hundred, used fourteen ounces of wine in the day. The stimulus of wine is favourable to advanced age.

Further medical use of alcoholic beverages he saw in the case of typhoid fever, but generally he cautioned against the therapeutic administration of alcoholic beverages.

REFERENCE

Trotter, T. (1804). *Essay Medical, Philosophical, and Chemical on Drunkenness.* Boston: Bradford, Read, 1813.

---

[1] Let it be remembered that I only apply this quantity to the abstemious man who has never indulged in wine.

3: ALCOHOLISM AS A PROGRESSIVE DISEASE

Emil Jellinek

NOTE: In 1946 Emil Jellinek, on the basis of a questionnaire study of members of Alcoholics Anonymous, first formulated his concept of phases in the drinking history of alcoholics. With the original publication[1] of this concept Jellinek outlined a more detailed questionnaire, which in the intervening years has been administered to some 2,000 alcoholics. The elaboration of the phases concept resulting from analysis of these additional materials has been presented by Jellinek in lectures at the Yale Summer School of Alcohol Studies (July 1951 and July 1952) and at the European Seminar on Alcoholism (Copenhagen, October 1951). The summary of these lectures, as published under the auspices of the Alcoholism Subcommittee of the World Health Organization,[2] is reproduced here in full.

INTRODUCTION

Only certain forms of excessive drinking—those which in the present report are designated as alcoholism—are accessible to medical-psychiatric treatment. The other forms of excessive drinking, too, present more or less serious problems, but they can be managed only on the level of applied sociology, including law enforcement. Nevertheless, the medical profession may have an advisory role in the handling of these latter problems and must take an interest in them from the viewpoint of preventive medicine.

The conditions which have been briefly defined by the Subcommittee as alcoholism are described in the following pages in greater detail, in order to

---

[1]Jellinek, E. M. Phases in the drinking history of alcoholics. Analysis of a survey conducted by the official organ of Alcoholics Anonymous. (Memoirs of the Section of Studies on Alcohol, Yale University, No. 5.) *Quart. J. Stud. Alc.* 7:1-88, 1946. Published also as a monograph (Hillhouse Press, New Haven, 1946) under the same title; the monograph is now out of print.

[2]Expert Committee on Mental Health, Alcoholism Subcommittee, Second Report. Annex 2, The Phases of Alcohol Addiction. World Hlth Org. Techn. Rep. Ser., No. 48, Aug. 1952.

delimit more definitely those excessive drinkers whose rehabilitation primarily requires medical–psychiatric treatment.

Furthermore, such detailed description may serve to forestall a certain potential danger which attaches to the disease conception of alcoholism, or more precisely of addictive drinking.

With the exception of specialists in alcoholism, the broader medical profession and representatives of the biological and social sciences and the lay public use the term "alcoholism" as a designation for any form of excessive drinking instead of as a label for a limited and well-defined area of excessive drinking behaviors. Automatically, the disease conception of alcoholism becomes extended to all excessive drinking irrespective of whether or not there is any physical or psychological pathology involved in the drinking behavior.

Such an unwarranted extension of the disease conception can only be harmful, because sooner or later the misapplication will reflect on the legitimate use too and, more importantly, will tend to weaken the ethical basis of social sanctions against drunkenness.

The Disease Conception of Alcohol Addiction

The Subcommittee has distinguished two categories of alcoholics, namely, "alcohol addicts" and "habitual symptomatic excessive drinkers." For brevity's sake the latter will be referred to as nonaddictive alcoholics. Strictly speaking, the disease conception attaches to the alcohol addicts only, but not to the habitual symptomatic excessive drinkers.

In both groups the excessive drinking is symptomatic of underlying psychological or social pathology, but in one group after several years of excessive drinking "loss of control" over the alcohol intake occurs, while in the other group this phenomenon never develops. The group with the "loss of control" is designated as "alcohol addicts." (There are other differences between these two groups and these will be seen in the course of the description of the "phases.")

The disease conception of alcohol addiction does not apply to the excessive drinking, but solely to the "loss of control" which occurs in only one group of alcoholics and then only after many years of excessive drinking. There is no intention to deny that the nonaddictive alcoholic is a sick person; but his ailment is not the excessive drinking, but rather the psychological or social difficulties from which alcohol intoxication gives temporary surcease.

The "loss of control" is a disease condition per se which results from a process that superimposes itself upon those abnormal psychological conditions of which excessive drinking is a symptom. The fact that many excessive drinkers drink as much as or more than the addict for 30 or 40 years without developing loss of control indicates that in the group of "alcohol addicts" a superimposed process must occur.

Whether this superimposed process is of a psychopathological nature or whether some physical pathology is involved cannot be stated as yet with any degree of assurance, the claims of various investigators notwithstanding. Nor is it possible to go beyond conjecture concerning the question whether the "loss of control" originates in a predisposing factor (psychological or physical), or whether it is a factor acquired in the course of prolonged excessive drinking.

The fact that this "loss of control" does not occur in a large group of excessive drinkers would point towards a predisposing X factor in the addictive alcoholics. On the other hand this explanation is not indispensable as the difference between addictive and nonaddictive alcoholics could be a matter of acquired modes of living—for instance, a difference in acquired nutritional habits.

The Meaning of Symptomatic Drinking

The use of alcoholic beverages by society has primarily a symbolic meaning, and secondarily it achieves "function." Cultures which accept this custom differ in the nature and degree of the "functions" which they regard as legitimate. The differences in these "functions" are determined by the general pattern of the culture, for example, the need for the release and for the special control of aggression, the need and the ways and means of achieving identification, the nature and intensity of anxieties and the modus for their relief, and so forth. The more the original symbolic character of the custom is preserved, the less room will be granted by the culture to the "functions" of drinking.

Any drinking within the accepted ways is symptomatic of the culture of which the drinker is a member. Within that frame of cultural symptomatology there may be in addition individual symptoms expressed in the act of drinking. The fact that a given individual drinks a glass of beer with his meal may be the symptom of the culture which accepts such a use as a refreshment, or as a "nutritional supplement." That this individual drinks at this given moment may be a symptom of his fatigue, or his elation or some other mood, and thus an individual symptom, but if his culture accepts the use for these purposes it is at the same time a cultural symptom.

In this sense even the small or moderate use of alcoholic beverages is symptomatic, and it may be said that all drinkers are culturally symptomatic drinkers or, at least, started as such.

The vast majority of the users of alcoholic beverages stay within the limits of the culturally accepted drinking behaviors and drink predominantly as an expression of their culture, and while an individual expression may be present in these behaviors its role remains insignificant.

For the purpose of the present discussion the expression "symptomatic drinking" will be limited to the predominant use of alcoholic beverages for the relief of major individual stresses.

A certain unknown proportion of these users of alcoholic beverages, perhaps 20 per cent, are occasionally inclined to take advantage of the "functions" of alcohol which they have experienced in the course of its "cultural use." At least at times, the individual motivation becomes predominant and on those occasions alcohol loses its character as an ingredient of a beverage and is used as a drug.

The "occasional symptomatic excessive drinker" tends to take care of the stresses and strains of living in socially accepted—that is, "normal"—ways, and his drinking is most of the time within the cultural pattern. After a long accumulation of stresses, however, or because of some particularly heavy stress, his tolerance for tension is lowered and he takes recourse to heroic relief of his symptoms through alcoholic intoxication.[3] Under these circumstances the "relief" may take on an explosive character, and thus the occasional symptomatic excessive drinker may create serious problems. No psychological abnormality can be claimed for this type of drinker, although he does not represent a well-integrated personality.

Nevertheless, within the group of apparent "occasional symptomatic excessive drinkers" there is a certain proportion of definitely deviating personalities who after a shorter or longer period of occasional symptomatic relief take recourse to a constant alcoholic relief, and drinking becomes with them a "mode of living." These are the "alcoholics" of whom again a certain proportion suffer "loss of control," i.e., become "addictive alcoholics."

The proportion of alcoholics (addictive and nonaddictive) varies from country to country, but does not seem to exceed in any country 5 per cent or 6 per cent of all users of alcoholic beverages. The ratio of addictive to nonaddictive alcoholics is unknown.

THE CHART OF ALCOHOL ADDICTION

The course of alcohol addiction is represented graphically in Figure 3-1. The diagram is based on an analysis of more than two thousand drinking histories of male alcohol addicts. Not all symptoms shown in the diagram occur necessarily in all alcohol addicts, nor do they occur in every addict in the same sequence. The "phases" and the sequences of symptoms within the phases are characteristic, however, of the great majority of alcohol addicts and represent what may be called the average trend.

For alcoholic women the "phases" are not as clear-cut as in men and the development is frequently more rapid.

The "phases" vary in their duration according to individual characteristics and environmental factors. The "lengths" of the different phases on the diagram do not indicate differences in duration, but are determined by the number of symptoms which have to be shown in any given phase.

The chart of the phases of alcohol addiction serves as the basis of description, and the differences between addictive and nonaddictive alcoholics are indicated in the text.

---

[3]This group does not include the regular "periodic alcoholics."

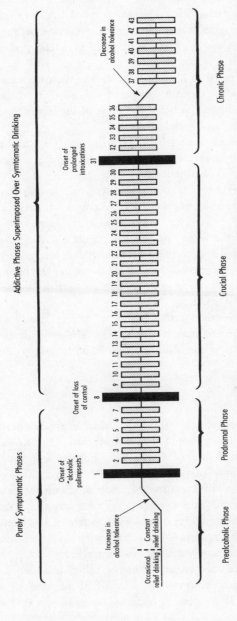

FIGURE 3-1. The Phases of Alcohol Addiction. The large bars denote the onset of major symptoms that initiate phases. The short bars denote the onset of symptoms within a phase. Reference to the numbering of the symptoms is made in the text. From "Phases of Alcohol Addiction." *Journal of Studies on Alcohol* 13 (4):673–684, 1952.

e Prealcoholic Symptomatic Phase

The very beginning of the use of alcoholic beverages is always socially motivated in the prospective addictive and nonaddictive alcoholic. In contrast to the average social drinker, however, the prospective alcoholic (together with the occasional symptomatic excessive drinker) soon experiences a rewarding relief in the drinking situation. The relief is strongly marked in his case because either his tensions are much greater than in other members of his social circle, or he has not learned to handle those tensions as others do.

Initially this drinker ascribes his relief to the situation rather than to the drinking and he seeks therefore those situations in which incidental drinking will occur. Sooner or later, of course, he becomes aware of the contingency between relief and drinking.

In the beginning he seeks this relief occasionally only, but in the course of 6 months to 2 years his tolerance for tension decreases to such a degree that he takes recourse to alcoholic relief practically daily.

Nevertheless his drinking does not result in overt intoxication, but he reaches toward the evening a stage of surcease from emotional stress. Even in the absence of intoxication this involves fairly heavy drinking, particularly in comparison to the use of alcoholic beverages by other members of his circle. The drinking is, nevertheless, not conspicuous either to his associates or to himself.

After a certain time an increase in alcohol tolerance may be noticed, that is, the drinker requires a somewhat larger amount of alcohol than formerly in order to reach the desired stage of sedation.

This type of drinking behavior may last from several months to 2 years according to circumstances and may be designated as the prealcoholic phase, which is divided into stages of occasional relief-drinking and constant relief-drinking.

The Prodromal Phase

The sudden onset of a behavior resembling the "blackouts" in anoxemia marks the beginning of the prodromal phase of alcohol addiction. The drinker who may have had not more than 50 to 60 g of absolute alcohol and who is not showing any signs of intoxication may carry on a reasonable conversation or may go through quite elaborate activities without a trace of memory the next day, although sometimes one or two minor details may be hazily remembered. This amnesia, which is not connected with loss of consciousness, has been called by Bonhoeffer the "alcoholic palimpsests," with reference to old Roman manuscripts superimposed over an incompletely erased manuscript.

"Alcoholic palimpsests" (1)[4] may occur on rare occasions in an average drinker when he drinks intoxicating amounts in a state of physical or emotional exhaustion. Nonaddictive alcoholics, of course, also may experience "palimp-

---

[4] The figures in parentheses following the designations of the individual symptoms represent their order as given in Figure 3-1.

sests," but infrequently and only following rather marked intoxication. Thus, the frequency of "palimpsests" and their occurrence after medium alcohol intake are characteristic of the prospective alcohol addict.

This would suggest heightened susceptibility to alcohol in the prospective addict. Such a susceptibility may be psychologically or physiologically determined. The analogy with the "blackouts" of anoxemia is tempting. Of course, an insufficient oxygen supply cannot be assumed, but a malutilization of oxygen may be involved. The present status of the knowledge of alcoholism does not permit of more than vague conjectures which, nevertheless, may constitute bases for experimental hypotheses.

The onset of "alcoholic palimpsests" is followed (in some instances preceded) by the onset of drinking behaviors which indicate that, for this drinker, beer, wine and spirits have practically ceased to be beverages and have become sources of a drug which he "needs." Some of these behaviors imply that this drinker has some vague realization that he drinks differently from others.

Surreptitious drinking (2) is one of these behaviors. At social gatherings the drinker seeks occasions for having a few drinks unknown to others, as he fears that if it were known that he drinks more than the others he would be misjudged: those to whom drinking is only a custom or a small pleasure would not understand that because he is different from them alcohol is for him a necessity, although he is not a drunkard.

Preoccupation with alcohol (3) is further evidence of this "need." When he prepares to go to a social gathering his first thought is whether there will be sufficient alcohol for his requirements, and he has several drinks in anticipation of a possible shortage.

Because of this increasing dependence upon alcohol, the onset of *avid drinking* (4) (gulping of the first or first two drinks) occurs at this time.

As the drinker realizes, at least vaguely, that his drinking is outside of the ordinary, he develops *guilt feelings about his drinking behavior* (5) and because of this he begins to *avoid reference to alcohol* (6) in conversation.

These behaviors, together with an *increasing frequency of "alcoholic palimpsests"* (7), foreshadow the development of alcohol addiction; they are premonitory signs, and this period may be called the prodromal phase of alcohol addiction.

The consumption of alcoholic beverages in the prodromal phase is "heavy," but not conspicuous, as it does not lead to marked, overt intoxications. The effect is that the prospective addict reaches towards evening a state which may be designated as emotional anesthesia. Nevertheless, this condition requires drinking well beyond the ordinary usage. The drinking is on a level which may begin to interfere with metabolic and nervous processes as evidenced by the frequent "alcoholic palimpsests."

The "covering-up" which is shown by the drinker in this stage is the first sign that his drinking might separate him from society, although initially the drinking may have served as a technique to overcome some lack of social integration.

As in the prodromal phase rationalizations of the drinking behavior are not strong and there is some insight as well as fear of possible consequences, it is feasible to intercept incipient alcohol addiction at this stage. In the United States of America, the publicity given to the prodromal symptoms begins to bring prospective alcoholics to clinics as well as to groups of Alcoholics Anonymous.

It goes without saying that even at this stage the only possible modus for this type of drinker is total abstinence.

The prodromal period may last anywhere from 6 months to 4 or 5 years according to the physical and psychological make-up of the drinker, his family ties, vocational relations, general interests, and so forth. The prodromal phase ends and the crucial or acute phase begins with the onset of loss of control, which is the critical symptom of alcohol addiction.

The Crucial Phase

Loss of control (8) means that any drinking of alcohol starts a chain reaction which is felt by the drinker as a physical demand for alcohol. This state, possibly a conversion phenomenon, may take hours or weeks for its full development; it lasts until the drinker is too intoxicated or too sick to ingest more alcohol. The physical discomfort following this drinking behavior is contrary to the object of the drinker, which is merely to feel "different." As a matter of fact, the bout may not even be started by any individual need of the moment, but by a "social drink."

After recovery from the intoxication, it is not the "loss of control"—that is, the physical demand, apparent or real—which leads to a new bout after several days or several weeks; the renewal of drinking is set off by the original psychological conflicts or by a simple social situation which involves drinking.

The "loss of control" is effective after the individual has started drinking, but it does not give rise to the beginning of a new drinking bout. The drinker has lost the ability to control the quantity once he has started, but he still can control whether he will drink on any given occasion or not. This is evidenced in the fact that after the onset of "loss of control" the drinker can go through a period of voluntary abstinence ("going on the water wagon").

The question of why the drinker returns to drinking after repeated disastrous experiences is often raised. Although he will not admit it, the alcohol addict believes that he has lost his will power and that he can and must regain it. He is not aware that he has undergone a process which makes it impossible for him to control his alcohol intake. To "master his will" becomes a matter of the greatest importance to him. When tensions rise, "a drink" is the natural remedy for him and he is convinced that this time it will be one or two drinks only.

Practically simultaneously with the onset of "loss of control" the alcohol addict begins to *rationalize his drinking behavior* (9): he produces the well-known alcoholic "alibis." He finds explanations which convince him that he did not lose control, but that he had a good reason to get intoxicated and that in the absence of such reasons he is able to handle alcohol as well as anybody else. These rationalizations are needed primarily for himself and only secondarily for his family and associates. The rationalizations make it possible for him to continue with his drinking, and this is of the greatest importance to him as he knows no alternative for handling his problems.

This is the beginning of an entire "system of rationalizations" which progressively spreads to every aspect of his life. While this system largely originates in inner needs, it also serves to counter *social pressures* (10) which arise at the time of the "loss of control." At this time, of course, the drinking behavior becomes conspicuous, and the parents, wife, friends and employer may begin to reprove and warn the drinker.

In spite of all the rationalizations there is a marked loss of self-esteem, and this of course demands compensations which in a certain sense are also rationalizations. One way of compensation is the *grandiose behavior* (11) which the addict begins to display at this time. Extravagant expenditures and grandiloquence convince him that he is not as bad as he had thought at times.

The rationalization system gives rise to another system, namely the "system of isolation." The rationalizations quite naturally lead to the idea that the fault lies not within himself but in others, and this results in a progressive withdrawal from the social environment. The first sign of this attitude is a *marked aggressive behavior* (12).

Inevitably, this latter behavior generates guilt. While even in the prodromal period remorse about the drinking arose from time to time, now *persistent remorse* (13) arises, and this added tension is a further source of drinking.

In compliance with social pressures the addict now goes on *periods of total abstinence* (14). There is, however, another modus of control of drinking which arises out of the rationalizations of the addict. He believes that his trouble arises from his not drinking the right kind of beverages or not in the right way. He now attempts to control his troubles by *changing the pattern of his drinking* (15), by setting up rules about not drinking before a certain hour of the day, in certain places only, and so forth.

The strain of the struggle increases his hostility towards his environment and he begins to *drop friends* (16) and *quit jobs* (17). It goes without saying that some associates drop him and that he loses some jobs, but more frequently he takes the initiative as an anticipatory defence.

The isolation becomes more pronounced as his entire *behavior becomes alcohol-centered* (18), that is, he begins to be concerned about how activities might interfere with his drinking instead of how his drinking may affect his activities. This, of course, involves a more marked egocentric outlook which leads to more rationalizations and more isolation. There ensues a *loss of outside interests* (19) and a *reinterpretation of interpersonal relations* (20) coupled with *marked self-pity* (21). The isolation and rationalizations have increased by this time in intensity and find their expression either in contemplated or actual *geographic escape* (22).

Under the impact of these events, a *change in family habits* (23) occurs. The wife and children, who may have had good social activities, may withdraw for fear of embarrassment or, quite contrarily, they may suddenly begin intensive outside activities in order to escape from the home environment. This and other events lead to the onset of *unreasonable resentments* (24) in the alcohol addict.

he predominance of concern with alcohol induces the addict to *protect his supply* (25), that is, to lay in a large stock of alcoholic beverages, hidden in the most unthought-of places. A fear of being deprived of the most necessary substance for his living is expressed in this behavior.

Neglect of proper nutrition (26) aggravates the beginnings of the effects of heavy drinking on the organism, and frequently the *first hospitalization* (27) for some alcoholic complaint occurs at this time.

One of the frequent organic effects is a *decrease of the sexual drive* (28) which increases hostility towards the wife and is rationalized into her extra-marital sex activities, which gives rise to the well-known *alcoholic jealousy* (29).

By this time remorse, resentment, struggle between alcoholic needs and duties, loss of self-esteem, and doubts and false reassurance have so disorganized the addict that he cannot start the day without steadying himself with alcohol immediately after arising or even before getting out of bed. This is the beginning of *regular matutinal drinking* (30), which previously had occurred on rare occasions only.

This behavior terminates the crucial phase and foreshadows the beginnings of the chronic phase.

During the crucial phase intoxication is the rule, but it is limited to the evening hours. For the most part of this phase drinking begins sometime in the afternoon and by the evening intoxication is reached. It should be noted that the "physical demand" involved in the "loss of control" results in continual rather than continuous drinking. Particularly the "matutinal drink" which occurs toward the end of the crucial phase shows the continual pattern. The first drink at rising, let us say at 7 A.M., is followed by another drink at 10 or 11 A.M., and another drink around 1 P.M., while the more intensive drinking hardly starts before 5 P.M.

Throughout, the crucial phase presents a great struggle of the addict against the complete loss of social footing. Occasionally the aftereffects of the evening's intoxication cause some loss of time, but generally the addict succeeds in looking after his job, although he neglects his family. He makes a particularly strong effort to avoid intoxication during the day. Progressively, however, his social motivations weaken more and more, and the "morning drink" jeopardizes his effort to comply with his vocational duties as this effort involves a conscious resistance against the apparent or real "physical demand" for alcohol.

The onset of the "loss of control" is the beginning of the "disease process" of alcohol addiction which is superimposed over the excessive symptomatic drinking. Progressively, this disease process undermines the morale and the physical resistance of the addict.

The Chronic Phase

The increasingly dominating role of alcohol, and the struggle against the demand set up by matutinal drinking, at last break down the resistance of the addict and he finds himself for the first time intoxicated in the daytime and on a weekday and continues in that state for several days until he is entirely incapacitated. This is the onset of *prolonged intoxications* (31), referred to in the vernacular as "benders."

This latter drinking behavior meets with such unanimous social rejection that it involves a grave social risk. Only an originally psychopathic personality or a person who has later in life undergone a psychopathological process would expose himself to that risk.

These long-drawn-out bouts commonly bring about *marked ethical deterioration* (32) and *impairment of thinking* (33), which, however, are not irreversible. True *alcoholic psychoses* (34) may occur at this time, but in not more than 10 per cent of all alcoholics.

The loss of morale is so heightened that the addict *drinks with persons far below his social level* (35) in preference to his usual associates—perhaps as an opportunity to appear superior—and, if nothing else is available, he will *take recourse to "technical products"* (36) such as bay rum or rubbing alcohol.

A *loss of alcohol tolerance* (37) is commonly noted at this time. Half of the previously required amount of alcohol may be sufficient to bring about a stuporous state.

Indefinable fears (38) and *tremors* (39) become persistent. Sporadically these symptoms occur also during the crucial phase, but in the chronic phase they are present as soon as alcohol disappears from the organism. In consequence, the addict "controls" the symptoms through alcohol. The same is true of *psychomotor inhibition* (40), the inability to initiate a simple mechanical act—such as winding a watch—in the absence of alcohol.

The need to control these symptoms of drinking exceeds the need of relieving the original underlying symptoms of the personality conflict, and the *drinking takes on an obsessive character* (41).

In many addicts, approximately 60 per cent, some *vague religious desires develop* (42) as the rationalizations become weaker. Finally, in the course of the frequently prolonged intoxications, the rationalizations become so frequently and so mercilessly tested against reality that the entire *rationalization system fails* (43) and the addict admits defeat. He now becomes spontaneously accessible to treatment. Nevertheless, his obsessive drinking continues as he does not see a way out.

Formerly it was thought that the addict must reach this stage of utter defeat in order to be treated successfully. Clinical experience has shown however, that this "defeat" can be induced long before it would occur of itself and that even incipient alcoholism can be intercepted. Since the incipient alcoholic can be easily recognized, it is possible to tackle the problem from the preventive angle.

The "Alcoholic Personality"

The aggressions, feelings of guilt, remorse, resentments, withdrawal, and so forth, which develop in the phases of alcohol addiction, are largely consequences of the excessive drinking. At the same time, however, they constitute sources of more excessive drinking.

In addition to relieving, through alcohol, symptoms of an underlying personality conflict, the addict now tends to relieve, through further drinking, the stresses created by his drinking behavior.

By and large, these reactions to excessive drinking—which have quite a neurotic appearance—give the impression of an "alcoholic personality," although they are secondary behaviors superimposed over a large variety of personality types which have a few traits in common, in particular a low capacity for coping with tensions. There does not emerge, however, any specific personality trait or physical characteristic which inevitably would lead to excessive symptomatic drinking. Apart from psychological and possibly physical liabilities, there must be a constellation of social and economic factors which facilitate the development of addictive and non-addictive alcoholism in a susceptible terrain.

THE NON-ADDICTIVE ALCOHOLIC

Some differences between the non-addictive alcoholic and the alcohol addict have previously been stated in this chapter. These differences may be recapitulated and elaborated, and additional differential features may be considered.

The main difference may be readily visualized by erasing the large bars of the diagram in Figure 3–1. This results in a diagram which suggests a progressive exacerbation of the use of alcohol for symptom relief and of the social and health consequences incumbent upon such use, but without any clear-cut phases.

The prealcoholic phase is the same for the non-addictive alcoholic as for the alcohol addict. That is to say, he progresses from occasional to constant relief of individual symptoms through alcohol.

The behaviors which denote that alcohol has become a drug rather than an ingredient of a beverage—symptoms (2) to (6)—occur also in the non-addictive drinker, but, as mentioned before, the alcoholic palimpsests occur rarely and only after overt intoxication.

Loss of control is not experienced by the non-addictive alcoholic, and this is the main differentiating criterion between the two categories of alcoholics. Initially, of course, it could not be said whether the drinker had yet reached the crucial phase. However, after 10 or 12 years of heavy drinking without loss of control, while symptoms (2) to (6) were persistent and palimpsests were rare and did not occur after a medium intake of alcohol, the differential diagnosis is rather safe.

The absence of loss of control has many involvements. First of all, as there is no inability to stop drinking within a given situation there is no need to rationalize the inability. Nevertheless, rationalizations are developed for justifying the excessive use of alcohol and some neglect of the family attendant upon such use. Likewise, there is no need to change the pattern of drinking, which in the addict is an attempt to overcome the loss of control. Periods of total abstinence, however, occur as responses to social pressure.

On the other hand, there is the same tendency toward isolation as in the addict, but the social repercussions are much less marked, as the non-addictive alcoholic can avoid drunken behavior whenever the social situation requires it.

The effects of prolonged heavy drinking on the organism may occur in the non-addictive alcoholic too; even delirium tremens may develop. The libido may be diminished and "alcoholic jealousy" may result.

Generally, there is a tendency toward a progressive dominance of alcohol resulting in greater psychological and bodily effects. In the absence of any grave underlying psychopathies a deteriorative process is speeded up by habitual alcoholic excess, and such a non-addictive drinker may slide to the bottom of society.

APPLYING DRIVE THEORY TO
ALCOHOLISM TREATMENT
Part III

4: MASTURBATION AS THE ORIGINAL ADDICTION

Sigmund Freud

Vienna, 22.12.97.

My dear Wilhelm,

I am in good spirits again, and keenly looking forward to Breslau–that is, to you and the fine new things you will have to tell me about life and its dependence on the world-process. I have always been curious about it, but hitherto I have never found anyone who could give me an answer. If there are now two people, one of whom can say what life is, and the other can say (nearly) what mind is, it is only right that they should see and talk to each other more often. I shall now jot down a few novelties for you, so that I shall not have to talk and shall be able to listen undisturbed.

It has occurred to me that masturbation is the one great habit that is a "primary addiction," and that the other addictions, for alcohol, morphine, tobacco, etc., only enter into life as a substitute and replacement for it.[1] Its part in hysteria is prodigious, and perhaps my great outstanding obstacle is, wholly or in part, to be found in it. The doubt of course arises whether such an addiction is curable, or whether analysis and therapy must stop short at this point and remain content with transforming a hysteria into a neurasthenia.

It is becoming confirmed that in obsessional neuroses the *verbal idea,* and not the concept dependent on it, is the point at which the repressed breaks through. (More accurately, it is the verbal memory.) Hence in the case of an obsessional idea the most disparate things tend to be brought together under a word with more than one meaning. Ambiguous words serve the break-through tendency as a way of killing several birds with one stone, as in the following case, for instance. A girl attending a sewing class which was soon coming to an end was

---

[1]Freud neglected this approach to the problem of addiction in the years that immediately followed, for example, in his *Three Essays* (1905), and did not return to it till "Dostoevsky and Parricide" (1928) in the course of an analysis of gambling.

troubled by the obsession: "No, you mustn't go yet, you haven't finished, you must *do*[2] still more, you must learn all that it's possible to learn." Behind this was the memory of childhood scenes; when she was put on the pot, she did not want to stay on it and was subjected to the same compulsion: "You mustn't go yet, you haven't finished, you must *do* some more." The word "do" permits identification of the later with the infantile situation. Obsessions often clothe themselves in a remarkable verbal vagueness in order to make possible manifold applications of this kind. Looked at more closely, the (conscious) content of this one yields: "You must go on learning." What, later, becomes the fixed, compulsive idea arises from such misinterpretation on the part of the conscious.

All this is not entirely arbitrary. The word *machen* [to "make" or "do"] has itself undergone a similar transformation of meaning.[3] An old phantasy of mine, which I should like to recommend to your linguistic perception, deals with the derivation of our verbs from such originally copro-erotic terms.

I can hardly tell you how many things I (a new Midas) turn into — filth.[4] This is in complete harmony with the theory of internal stinking. Above all, gold itself stinks. I think the association is that "miserliness" is "dirty." Similarly birth, miscarriage, and menstruation are all connected with the lavatory *via* the word Abort[5] (Abortus[6]). It is quite crazy, but completely analogous to the process by which words assume a transferred meaning as soon as new concepts appear requiring definition. . . .

Have you ever seen a foreign newspaper after it has passed the censorship[7] at the Russian frontier? Words, sentences and whole paragraphs are blacked out, with the result that the remainder is unintelligible. A "Russian censorship" occurs in the psychoses, and results in the apparently meaningless deliria.

Au revoir,

Your Sigm.

---

[2][In German, *machen*.]

[3]This discovery of Freud's in connection with obsessional neurosis was later recognized by him as a general property of the primary process.

[4][The German *Dreck* also means excrement.] These and many subsequent passages in the letters refer to the phenomena of the anal phases of libidinal development.

[5][Lavatory.]

[6][Abortion.]

[7]The first appearance of a conception made public in *The Interpretation of Dreams*. [See, however, *Studies on Hysteria* (1895), *Ges. Werke*, I, pp. 269 and 284; also "Further Remarks on the Neuro-Psychoses of Defence" (1896) *Ges. Werke*, I, p.402.]

5: THE PSYCHOLOGICAL RELATIONS BETWEEN SEXUALITY AND ALCOHOLISM

Karl Abraham

It is an undisputed fact that, generally speaking, men are more prone to taking alcohol than women. Even though in many countries women daily take alcohol as a matter of course just like men, and though in many places intoxicated women are often seen in the streets, still alcohol is never associated with the social life of women to anything like the extent that it is with that of men. There are wide circles in which to be a hard drinker is looked upon as a sign of manliness, even as a matter of honour. Society never demands in this way that women should take alcohol. It is the custom with us rather to condemn drinking as unwomanly; nor is drinking ever a matter of boasting among normal women as it is among men.

It seems to me worth inquiring whether this difference in the attitude of men and women towards alcohol rests on sexual differences. But such an inquiry must start from the newer conceptions of the psychosexual constitution of men and women as laid down in Freud's works in especial.

It is a biological fact that the human body contains the genital organs of both sexes in a rudimentary form. In the course of its normal development one of the two sets of organs is suppressed or takes over other activities, whilst the other goes on developing until it is capable of performing its true functions. An analogous process takes place in the psychosexual sphere. Here, too, the differentiation of the sexes proceeds from an original state of bi-sexuality. In childhood the expressions of the sexual instincts in boys and girls are still very much alike.

We have learned, particularly through Freud's investigations, that sexual activities are by no means lacking in childhood. Only the function of procreation does not as yet appear; that instinct only gradually finds its definitive form. According to Freud the infantile libido is without an object; it is "auto-erotic." It obtains gratification by the stimulation of certain parts of the body which serve as *erotogenic zones*. Nevertheless in the pre-pubertal period not the whole of the child's sexual energy is employed in auto-erotic pleasure-gain. A large part of it is repressed out of consciousness. It is no longer applied to sexual ends, but takes over important social functions. This concept of "repression," introduced by Freud, is indispensable for the understanding of many psychological processes, both normal and pathological. The deflection of repressed sexual ideas and feelings on to social spheres is termed by us, following Freud, "sublimation"; and this process serves to set up the barriers which restrain the sexual instincts of both sexes.

On arrival at maturity the boy, like the girl, acquires the marked bodily and physical characteristics of his sex; and in the psychosexual sphere the important process of object-finding commences. The libido is now directed on to the other sex. But the male and female libido is differentiated not only in this respect but in another, and one which especially interests us here. The female sexuality shows a greater tendency to repression and to the formation of resistances. The infantile sexual repression in women receives a strong reinforcement at puberty. This gives rise to the greater passivity of the sexual instinct in woman. The male libido is of a more active nature. It overcomes by means of its aggressive components the psychical resistances with which it meets in its sexual object. In the German language two expressions characterize the psychosexual differences of the sexes. The man is said to "make a conquest" in love; the woman, to "yield herself" up to it.

Alcohol acts on the sexual instinct by removing the resistances and increasing sexual activity. These facts are generally known, but their real nature is not inquired into as a rule.

The more we study the subject the more complicated does the sexual instinct appear. Besides "normal" heterosexual love, it includes a number of "perverse" impulses. In the child we see those impulses in a state of complete chaos; for the child is a "polymorpho-perverse" being (Freud). The "component-instincts" are only gradually subordinated to the single heterosexual one. They succumb to repression and sublimation, and from them originate shame and disgust, moral, æsthetic and social feelings, pity and horror, the child's filial devotion to its parents, and the parents' fond care of their child. Artistic and scientific activities, too, are based to a great extent on the sublimation of sexual energies. On these products of sublimation depend our social life and our entire civilization. There is not one among them which is not weakened or removed through the effect of alcohol.

In normal individuals the homosexual component of the sexual instinct undergoes sublimation. Between men, feelings of unity and friendship become divested of all conscious sexuality. The man of normal feelings is repelled by any physical contact implying tenderness with another of his own sex. And a number of similar feelings of repugnance or disgust originating in the same source could be mentioned. Alcohol suspends these feelings. When they are drinking, men will fall upon one another's necks and kiss one another; they feel that they are united by specially close bonds, and are easily moved to tears by this thought and very quick to use the intimate *Du* ("thou") in speaking. When sober, the same men will term such conduct "effeminate." Recent events have caused a lot of talk about "abnormal friendship" between men. The presence of such feelings, which are stigmatized as morbid or immoral in that connection, can be observed by anyone during a drinking bout. In every public-house there is an element of homosexuality. The homosexual components which have been repressed and sublimated by the influence of education become unmistakably evident under the influence of alcohol.

Freud was the first to give due importance to the pair of component-instincts which are manifested in *scopophilia* and *exhibitionism* respectively. They are closely associated with sexual curiosity, and their sublimation produces the feelings of shame. In the first years of its life the child has no such feelings; it has first to learn to feel "embarrassment." If sublimation does not take place then a perversion (*voyeurism* and exhibitionism) arises. Now the feeling of shame is not confined to the naked body only, but sets up important barriers in regard to social relations, conversation, and so forth. It is precisely these barriers which fall before alcohol. Obscene wit, which according to Freud's brilliant analysis represents an exposure in a psychological sense, is inseparably associated with the enjoyment of alcohol. Forel has described in a masterly manner how "flirting" assumes coarse and repugnant forms under the influence of alcohol.

There is another pair of component-instincts which also represent active and passive counterparts of each other. The one impels the individual to dominate his sexual object, the other to submit to its will. Feelings of pity, horror, and so forth, originate from the sublimation of these tendencies. If sublimation does not take place we get the perversions called *sadism* and *masochism* respectively. It is hardly necessary to mention that many brutal crimes are perpetrated in states of alcoholic intoxication. Nevertheless, the repressed component-instincts need not necessarily be expressed in such a crude way; we can recognize them in more disguised forms. Drinking customs and laws have existed since primitive times; the "drink king" at a carousal is absolute master. I might point to the German students' *Komment* of to-day with its rigorous obligation to drink, the proud satisfaction with which the older students compel the younger ones to do so, and the blind submission of the latter to the commands of their elders. I know that my view of these customs will meet with opposition. Let me therefore remark that these students' drinking laws have gradually developed their present more civilized forms out of incredibly gross customs in the past.

We have still to mention one more important limitation of the sexual instinct. As it grows up the normal child first transfers its libido on to the persons of the opposite sex in its immediate environment — the boy on to his mother or sister, the girl on to her father or brother. A long period of cultural development was required before the nearest blood relations were excluded as eligible objects. The repudiation of incest led to the sublimation of the child's love for his parents, which became converted into filial respect. Every child has to repeat this process of development. At a certain period it transfers its awakening sexual wishes on to the parent of the opposite sex. These impulses become repressed, in the same way as our moral code condemns an unsublimated inclination on the part of a father for his daughter. But alcohol does not spare even these sublimations. Lot's daughters knew that wine would break down the incest barriers, and they attained their object by making their father drunk.

It is generally said that alcohol removes mental inhibitions. We have now recognized the nature of these inhibitions: they are the products of the sublimation of sexual energy.

The re-emergence of repressed sexual impulses increases the individual's normal sexual activity so that he gets a feeling of increased sexual capacity. Alcohol acts as a stimulus to the "complex" of manliness.[1] We are familiar with the arrogance of the male from many examples in the animal kingdom. And we meet with the same phenomenon, *mutatis mutandis*, in human beings. The man feels proud of being the begetter, the giver; the woman "receives."[2] Analysis of the myths of Creation shows in a surprising manner how deeply rooted this grandiose complex is in the male. In a work I have in preparation[3] I hope to bring forward detailed evidence to show that the myths of Creation among different peoples originally represented a deification of the male power of procreation, thereby proclaiming it as the principle of all life. In myths the male power of reproduction and the divine power of creation are identified and the two are often used interchangeably. We meet here a psychological process of extraordinary importance, whose effects we can recognize in all forms of imaginative activity, whether normal or morbid, whether of the individual or of the group; and we term this process *identification*.

A question which has occupied mankind from the beginning, but which we are still unable to answer satisfactorily, is how "sexual excitement" arises. The assumption that in the male the stimulus proceeds from the semen was a very natural one; and, because intoxicating beverages are sexually exciting, the naïve mind of the common people went on to identify such beverages with semen or with that unknown substance which (in the absence of artificial stimulants) causes sexual excitement. This popular idea finds expression in the German word *Liebesrausch* ("intoxication of love").

The sphere of influence of this particular identification is very wide. Tales of the nectar of the gods and of its origin are found throughout the whole of Indo-Germanic mythology. This nectar, which is represented as an invigorating and inspiring drink, is identified with the intoxicating beverages of ordinary men. But the identification goes still further. In the above-mentioned work I have quoted the old Indian myths to show that the drink of the gods is considered

---

[1]In accordance with the nomenclature of the Psychiatric Clinic at Zürich, I use the shortened expression "complex" to denote a complex of images and ideas, together with the feelings accompanying them, that is repressed into unconsciousness in certain circumstances, but can, in others, force its way back into consciousness once more.

[2][German, *empfängt* also = "conceives." — *Trans.*]

[3]*Traum und Mythus* (1909).

equivalent to semen. This is because of the life-giving properties of semen. It is worth noting that stories about the begetting (Creation) of the first man, as found in the Prometheus Saga, stand in the closest possible relation to stories about the drink of the gods. It is not possible to make a deeper psychological analysis of these myths here. I will only mention that the Greek tales of the birth of the god of wine, Dionysus, show the same identification.

Love potions play a great part everywhere in myths. Undoubtedly the idea of their erotic effect is borrowed from the effect of alcoholic beverages. Here also intoxication and sexual excitement are identified. We meet the same idea in numerous customs. The banquets dedicated to the god of wine are always at the same time erotic in character. In many customs wine is used as a symbol of procreation or fertilization. Riklin[4] relates that in a certain locality it is customary at the Spring Festival to pour wine into girls' laps. Here the symbolic representation of semen by wine is quite manifest. Drinking healths in wine is a universal custom. The alcoholic beverage represents the vital force on account of its stimulating effect. If one drinks the health of another person it is equivalent to saying: "May the invigorating effect of the wine benefit you."

This identification must be an exceedingly firmly established one. There is a close association between the deference paid to prowess in drinking and prowess in the sexual field. He who does not drink is looked upon as a weakling. A man begins to take alcohol at puberty, at the time when he wishes to be looked upon as a man; and if he does not drink with his companions he is regarded as immature. Boasting about drinking is never so pronounced as in the period of commencing manhood. If in later years he loses his potency, a man will eagerly seize upon pleasure-bringing alcohol; and it becomes a surrogate for his diminishing power of procreation.

Men turn to alcohol because it gives them an increased feeling of manliness and flatters their complex of masculinity. The nature of her psychosexual constitution urges a woman far less to take alcohol. Her sexual instinct is less active and her resistance against its impulses greater. We traced this difference in her attitude to the new onset of repression at puberty. A woman stimulates a man through her psychical resistances, just as a man pleases her by his energetic initiative. The girl at puberty has no motive to turn to alcohol, for it would remove the effects of repression — the resistances — and if she relinquished these she would no longer attract the man. We should expect to find on closer observation that women who show a strong inclination for alcohol always have a marked homosexual component in them.

The results of alcohol — that is, the facilitating of sexual transference and the removal of the effects of repression — are not merely temporary but, as is well known, chronic as well. Chronic drinkers exhibit a characteristic excess of feelings; they are coarsely familiar, look upon every one as an old friend, indulge in unmanly sentimentality, and lose the feeling of shame. I need scarcely refer

[4]Riklin, *Wunscherfüllung und Symbolik im Märchen* (1908).

to the scenes that children of drinkers have to witness. In short, all the finer feelings which owe their origin to sublimation are destroyed in the habitual drunkard.

And it is not the sublimations alone of the sexual impulse that are destroyed. An acute alcoholic intoxication will, as we know, reduce a man's actual sexual capacity. And we are acquainted with the poisonous effect of alcohol on the embryonic cells (blastophthoria).[5] We know that a great number of drinkers become impotent. Alcohol has proved a false friend. They imagined that it increased their virility, because it gave them a feeling of sexual power; and instead, it has robbed them of that power. But even so they fail to recognize the fraud. They will not give up alcohol, and they continue to identify it with their sexuality and to use it as a surrogate of the latter. I see in this an analogy to certain sexual perversions in which a sexual stimulus, which might normally have served as an introduction to the sexual act, is put in the place of that act. Freud terms this "fixation of a temporary sexual aim." For instance, looking at the sexual object is under normal conditions a source of fore-pleasure merely, while the sexual act itself alone gives rise to satisfaction-pleasure. Certain perverts, however, are content with looking alone. And the alcoholic behaves in a similar manner. Alcohol excites the sexual feelings; this excitement the drinker seeks to capture and thereby loses his capacity for normal sexual activity.

There are yet other analogies between alcoholism and sexual perversions. The investigations of Freud have shown us the intimate relations that exist between the perversions and the neuroses, and that many neurotic symptoms are the expression of repressed perverse sexual phantasies,[6] and are therefore a kind of sexual activity on the part of the patient. The patient always opposes an extraordinary resistance to the analysis of his symptoms; this is connected with his repression of his sexual complexes. In attempting to discover and resolve the patient's symptoms by psycho-analytic means the only reply which the physician obtains is a "no," however much his inquiry may be justified. Instead of the real causes the patient brings forward cover-motives. In the same way the alcoholic will deny with his last breath facts which cannot possibly be disputed. He has a plentiful choice of cover-motives for his alcoholism and uses them to parry every attempt to get to the bottom of the matter. I think we must conclude that for the same reason that the neurotic protects his symptoms the drinker fights in defence of his alcoholism. It represents his sexual activity.

There is yet another point that seems to me worth mentioning. Certain ideas of an undoubtedly sexual nature play a prominent part in the morbid changes that take place in the mentality of the alcoholic. I refer to the well-known jealousy of the drinker—a jealousy which may increase until it becomes a delusion. The cause of this jealousy is, I believe, a feeling of diminishing potency on the subject's part (I base my conclusion on a wide range of experience which

---

[5]Cf. Forel and Juliusburger, "Über Blastophthorie" (1908), p. 346.
[6]Freud, "Hysterical Phantasies and their Relation to Bisexuality" (1908).

I cannot quote here in detail). The drinker makes use of alcohol as a means of obtaining pleasure without trouble. He gives up women and turns to alcohol. This state of affairs is exceedingly painful to his self-esteem; and he represses it, just like the neurotic, and at the same time effects a displacement such as we are accustomed to find in the mechanism of the neuroses and psychoses. He displaces his feelings of guilt on to his wife and accuses her of being unfaithful.

We see, therefore, that alcoholism, sexuality and neurosis are connected in many ways. It seems to me necessary to employ the psycho-analytic procedure developed by Freud, which enables us to penetrate into the structure of the neuroses, for the analysis of alcoholism as well. From the oral communications of colleagues, I know that in cases of morphinism psycho-analysis has demonstrated the existence of unexpected relations between sexuality and the use of narcotics. I may also mention the inexplicable behaviour of many nervous persons in regard to narcotics. Hysterical patients often beg their physician not to prescribe morphia or opium for them whatever he does, because they cannot stand it; and they go on to tell of the unpleasant experiences they have had with it. It looks very much as though the drug evokes sexual excitement in certain hysterical persons — an excitement which, in consequence of the hysteric's peculiar psychosexual constitution, is converted into physical symptoms and feelings of anxiety. Perhaps the intolerance of alcohol so frequently met with in nervous people has a similar cause. Finally, I might mention a remarkable fact which I have repeatedly observed in insane patients. When they are given a hypodermic injection of morphia, they regard it as a sexual assault, and they interpret the injection syringe and the fluid in a symbolic way.

As we see, the psychological investigation of alcoholism still offers many unsolved problems. External factors such as social influences, faulty education, hereditary taint, and so forth, are not by themselves sufficient to explain drunkenness. An individual factor must be present. Our first task is to investigate that factor; and it seems to me only possible to succeed in this if the connections between alcoholism and sexuality are constantly borne in mind.

6: DOSTOEVSKY AND PARRICIDE: ADDICTION AND GUILT

Sigmund Freud

Four facets may be distinguished in the rich personality of Dostoevksy: the creative artist, the neurotic, the moralist and the sinner. How is one to find one's way in this bewildering complexity?

The creative artist is the least doubtful: Dostoevsky's place is not far behind Shakespeare. *The Brothers Karamazov* is the most magnificent novel ever written; the episode of the Grand Inquisitor, one of the peaks in the literature of the world, can hardly be valued too highly. Before the problem of the creative artist analysis must, alas, lay down its arms.

The moralist in Dostoevsky is the most readily assailable. If we seek to rank him high as a moralist on the plea that only a man who has gone through the depths of sin can reach the highest summit of morality, we are neglecting a doubt that arises. A moral man is one who reacts to temptation as soon as he feels it in his heart, without yielding to it. A man who alternately sins and then in his remorse erects high moral standards lays himself open to the reproach that he has made things too easy for himself. He has not achieved the essence of morality, renunciation, for the moral conduct of life is a practical human interest. He reminds one of the barbarians of the great migrations, who murdered and did penance for it, till penance became an actual technique for enabling murder to be done. Ivan the Terrible behaved in exactly this way; indeed this compromise with morality is a characteristic Russian trait. Nor was the final outcome of Dostoevsky's moral strivings anything very glorious. After the most violent struggles to reconcile the instinctual demands of the individual with the claims of the community, he landed in the retrograde position of submission both to temporal and spiritual authority, of veneration both for the Tsar and for the God of the Christians, and of a narrow Russian nationalism — a position which lesser minds have reached with smaller effort. This is the weak point in that great personality. Dostoevsky threw away the chance of becoming a teacher and liberator of humanity and made himself one with their gaolers. The future of human civilization will have little to thank him for. It seems probable that he was condemned to this failure by his neurosis. The greatness of his intelligence and the strength of his love for humanity might have opened to him another, an apostolic, way of life.

To consider Dostoevsky as a sinner or a criminal rouses violent opposition, which need not be based upon a philistine assessment of criminals. The real motive for this opposition soon becomes apparent. Two traits are essential in a criminal: boundless egoism and a strong destructive urge. Common to both of these, and a necessary condition for their expression, is absence of love, lack of an emotional appreciation of (human) objects. One at once recalls the contrast to this presented by Dostoevsky—his great need of love and his enormous capacity for love, which is to be seen in manifestations of exaggerated kindness and caused him to love and to help where he had a right to hate and to be revengeful, as, for example, in his relations with his first wife and her lover. That being so, it must be asked why there is any temptation to reckon Dostoevsky among the criminals. The answer is that it comes from his choice of material, which singles out from all others violent, murderous and egoistic characters, thus pointing to the existence of similar tendencies within himself, and also from certain facts in his life, like his passion for gambling and his possible confession to a sexual assault upon a young girl.[1] The contradiction is resolved by the realization that Dostoevsky's very strong destructive instinct, which might easily have made him a criminal, was in his actual life directed mainly against his own person (inward instead of outward) and thus found expression as masochism and a sense of guilt. Nevertheless, his personality retained sadistic traits in plenty, which show themselves in his irritability, his love of tormenting and his intolerance even towards people he loved, and which appear also in the way in which, as an author, he treats his readers. Thus in little things he was a sadist towards others, and in bigger things a sadist towards himself, in fact a masochist—that is to say the mildest, kindliest, most helpful person possible.

We have selected three factors from Dostoevsky's complex personality, one quantitative and two qualitative: the extraordinary intensity of his emotional life, his perverse innate instinctual disposition, which inevitably marked him out to be a sado-masochist or a criminal, and his unanalysable artistic gift. This combination might very well exist without neurosis; there are people who are complete masochist without being neurotic. Nevertheless, the balance of forces

---

[1]See the discussion of this in Fülöp-Miller and Eckstein (1926). Stefan Zweig (1920) writes: "He was not halted by the barriers of bourgeois morality; and no one can say exactly how far he transgressed the bounds of law in his own life or how much of the criminal instincts of his heroes was realized in himself." For the intimate connection between Dostoevsky's characters and his own experiences, see René Fülöp-Miller's remarks in the introductory section of Fülöp-Miller and Eckstein (1926), which are based upon N. Strakhov [1921]. [The topic of a sexual assault on an immature girl appears several times in Dostoevsky's writings—especially in the posthumous *Stavrogin's Confession* and *The Life of a Great Sinner*.]

between his instinctual demands and the inhibitions opposing them (plus the available methods of sublimation) would even so make it necessary to classify Dostoevsky as what is known as an "instinctual character." But the position is obscured by the simultaneous presence of neurosis, which, as we have said, was not in the circumstances inevitable, but which comes into being the more readily, the richer the complication which has to be mastered by the ego. For neurosis is after all only a sign that the ego has not succeeded in making a synthesis, that in attempting to do so it has forfeited its unity.

How then, strictly speaking, does his neurosis show itself? Dostoevsky called himself an epileptic, and was regarded as such by other people, on account of his severe attacks, which were accompanied by loss of consciousness, muscular convulsions and subsequent depression. Now it is highly probable that this so-called epilepsy was only a symptom of his neurosis and must accordingly be classified as hystero-epilepsy—that is, as severe hysteria. We cannot be completely certain on this point for two reasons—firstly, because the anamnestic data on Dostoevsky's alleged epilepsy are defective and untrustworthy, and secondly, because our understanding of pathological states combined with epileptiform attacks is imperfect.

To take the second point first. It is unnecessary here to reproduce the whole pathology of epilepsy, for it would throw no decisive light on the problem. But this may be said. The old *morbus sacer* is still in evidence as an ostensible clinical entity, the uncanny disease with its incalculable, apparently unprovoked convulsive attacks, its changing of the character into irritability and aggressiveness, and its progressive lowering of all the mental faculties. But the outlines of this picture are quite lacking in precision. The attacks, so savage in their onset, accompanied by biting of the tongue and incontinence of urine and working up to the dangerous *status epilepticus* with its risk of severe self-injuries, may, nevertheless, be reduced to brief periods of *absence*, or rapidly passing fits of vertigo or may be replaced by short spaces of time during which the patient does something out of character, as though he were under the control of his unconscious. These attacks, though as a rule determined, in a way we do not understand, by purely physical causes, may nevertheless owe their first appearance to some purely mental cause (a fright, for instance) or may react in other respects to mental excitations. However characteristic intellectual impairment may be in the overwhelming majority of cases, at least *one* case is known to us (that of Helmholtz) in which the affliction did not interfere with the highest intellectual achievement. (Other cases of which the same assertion has been made are either disputable or open to the same doubts as the case of Dostoevsky himself.) People who are victims of epilepsy may give an impression of dullness and arrested development just as the disease often accompanies the most palpable idiocy and the grossest cerebral defects, even though not as a necessary component of the clinical picture. But these attacks, with all their variations, also occur in other people who display complete mental development and, if anything, an excessive and as a rule insufficiently controlled emotional life. It is no wonder in these circumstances that it has been found impossible to maintain that "epilepsy" is a single clinical entity. The similarity that we find in the manifest symptoms seems to call for a functional view of them. It is as though a mechanism for abnormal instinctual discharge had been laid down organically, which could be made use of in quite different circumstances—both in the case of disturbances of cerebral activity due to severe histolytic or toxic affections, and also in the case of inadequate control over the mental economy and at times when the activity of the energy operating in the mind reaches crisis-pitch. Behind this dichotomy we have a glimpse of the identity of the underlying mechanism of instinctual discharge. Nor can that mechanism stand remote from the sexual processes, which are fundamentally of toxic origin: the earliest physicians described coition as a minor epilepsy, and thus recognized in the sexual act a mitigation and adaptation of the epileptic method of discharging stimuli.[2]

The "epileptic reaction," as this common element may be called, is also undoubtedly at the disposal of the neurosis whose essence it is to get rid by somatic means of amounts of excitation which it cannot deal with psychically. Thus the epileptic attack becomes a symptom of hysteria and is adapted and modified by it just as it is by the normal sexual process of discharge. It is therefore quite right to distinguish between an organic and an "affective" epilepsy. The practical significance of this is that a person who suffers from the first kind has a disease of the brain, while a person who suffers from the second kind is a neurotic. In the first case his mental life is subjected to an alien disturbance from without, in the second case the disturbance is an expression of his mental life itself.

It is extremely probable that Dostoevsky's epilepsy was of the second kind. This cannot, strictly speaking, be proved. To do so we should have to be in a position to insert the first appearance of the attacks and their subsequent fluctuations into the thread of his mental life; and for that we know too little. The descriptions of the attacks themselves teach us nothing and our information about the relations between them and Dostoevsky's experiences is defective and often contradictory. The most probable assumption is that the attacks went back far into his childhood, that their place was taken to begin with by milder symptoms and that they did not assume an epileptic form until after the shattering experience of his eighteenth year—the murder of his father.[3] It would be very much to the point if it could be established that they ceased completely

---

[2][Cf. Freud's earlier paper on hysterical attacks (1909), *Standard Ed.*, 9. 234.]

[3]See René Fülöp-Miller (1924). [Cf. also the account given by Aimée Dostoevsky (1921) in her life of her father.] Of especial interest is the information that in the novelist's childhood "something terrible, unforgettable and agonizing" happened, to which the first signs of his illness were to be traced (from an article by Suvorin in the newspaper *Novoe Vremya*, 1881, quoted in the introduction to Fülöp-Miller and Eckstein, 1926, xlv). See also Orest Miller (1921, 140): "There is, however, another special piece of evidence about Fyodor Mikhailovich's illness, which relates to his earliest youth and brings the illness into connection with a tragic event in the family life of his parents. But, although this piece of evidence was given to me orally by one who was a close friend of Fyodor Mikhailovich, I cannot bring myself to reproduce it fully and precisely since I have had no confirmation of this rumour from any other quarter." Biographers and scientific research workers cannot feel grateful for this discretion.

during his exile in Siberia, but other accounts contradict this.[4]

The unmistakable connection between the murder of the father in *The Brothers Karamazov* and the fate of Dostoevsky's own father has struck more than one of his biographers, and has led them to refer to a "a certain modern school of psychology." From the standpoint of psycho-analysis (for that is what is meant), we are tempted to see in that event the severest trauma and to regard Dostoevsky's reaction to it as the turning-point of his neurosis. But if I undertake to substantiate this view psycho-analytically, I shall have to risk the danger of being unintelligible to all those readers who are unfamiliar with the language and theories of psycho-analysis.

We have one certain starting-point. We know the meaning of the first attacks from which Dostoevsky suffered in his early years, long before the incidence of the "epilepsy." These attacks had the significance of death: they were heralded by a fear of death and consisted of lethargic, somnolent states. The illness first came over him while he was still a boy, in the form of a sudden, groundless melancholy, a feeling, as he later told his friend Soloviev, as though he were going to die on the spot. And there in fact followed a state exactly similar to real death. His brother Andrey tells us that even when he was quite young Fyodor used to leave little notes about before he went to sleep, saying that he was afraid he might fall into this death-like sleep during the night and therefore begged that his burial should be postponed for five years (Fülöp-Miller and Eckstein, 1926, 1x.).

We know the meaning and intention of such deathlike attacks.[5] They signify an identification with a dead person, either with someone who is really dead or with someone who is still alive and whom the subject wishes dead. The latter case is the more significant. The attack then has the value of a punishment. One has wished another person dead, and now one *is* this other person and is dead oneself. At this point psycho-analytical theory brings in the assertion that for a boy this other person is usually his father and that the attack (which is termed hysterical) is thus a self-punishment for a death-wish against a hated father.

Parricide, according to a well-known view, is the principal and primal crime of humanity as well as of the individual. (See my *Totem and Taboo*, 1912–1913.) It is in any case the main source of the sense of guilt, though we do not know if it is the only one: researchers have not yet been able to establish with certainty the mental origin of guilt and the need for expiation. But it is not necessary for it to be the only one. The psychological situation is complicated and requires

---

[4]Most of the accounts, including Dostoevsky's own, assert on the contrary that the illness only assumed its final, epileptic character during the Siberian exile. Unfortunately there is reason to distrust the autobiographical statements of neurotics. Experience shows that their memories introduce falsifications which are designed to interrupt disagreeable causal connections. Neverthe-less,it appears certain that Dostoevsky's detention in the Siberian prison markedly altered his pathological condition. Cf. Fülöp-Miller (1924, 1186).

[5][The explanation was already given by Freud in a letter to Fliess of February 8, 1897 (Freud, 1950, letter 58).]

elucidation. The relation of a boy to his father is, as we say, an "ambivalent" one. In addition to the hate which seeks to get rid of the father as a rival, a measure of tenderness for him is also habitually present. The two attitudes of mind combine to produce identification with the father; the boy wants to be in his father's place because he admires him and wants to be like him, and also because he wants to put him out of the way. This whole development now comes up against a powerful obstacle. At a certain moment the child comes to understand that an attempt to remove his father as a rival would be punished by him with castration. So from fear of castration—that is, in the interests of preserving his masculinity—he gives up his wish to possess his mother and get rid of his father. In so far as this wish remains in the unconscious it forms the basis of the sense of guilt. We believe that what we have here been describing are normal processes, the normal fate of the so-called Oedipus complex; nevertheless it requires an important amplification.

A further complication arises when the constitutional factor we call bisexuality is comparatively strongly developed in a child. For then, under the threat to the boy's masculinity by castration, his inclination becomes strengthened to diverge in the direction of femininity, to put himself instead in his mother's place and take over her role as object of his father's love. But the fear of castration makes *this* solution impossible as well. The boy understands that he must also submit to castration if he wants to be loved by his father as a woman. Thus both impulses, hatred of the father and being in love with the father, undergo repression. There is a certain psychological distinction in the fact that the hatred of the father is given up on account of fear of an *external* danger (castration), while the being in love with the father is treated as an *internal* instinctual danger, though fundamentally it goes back to the same external danger.

What makes hatred of the father unacceptable is *fear* of the father; castration is terrible, whether as a punishment or as the price of love. Of the two factors which repress hatred of the father, the first, the direct fear of punishment and castration, may be called the normal one; its pathogenic intensification seems to come only with the addition of the second factor, the fear of the feminine attitude. Thus a strong innate bisexual disposition becomes one of the preconditions or reinforcements of neurosis. Such a disposition must certainly be assumed in Dostoevsky, and it shows itself in a viable form (as latent homosexuality) in the important part played by male friendships in his life, in his strangely tender attitude towards rivals in love and in his remarkable understanding of situations which are explicable only by repressed homosexuality, as many examples from his novels show.

I am sorry, though I cannot alter the facts, if this exposition of the attitudes of hatred and love towards the father and their transformations under the influence of the threat of castration seems to readers unfamiliar with psychoanalysis unsavoury and incredible. I should myself expect that it is precisely the castration complex that would be bound to arouse the most general repudiation. But I can only insist that psycho-analytic experience has put these matters in particular beyond the reach of doubt and has taught us to recognize in them the key to every neurosis. This key, then, we must apply to our author's so-called epilepsy. So alien to our consciousness are the things by which our unconscious mental life is governed!

But what has been said so far does not exhaust the consequences of the repression of the hatred of the father in the Oedipus complex. There is something fresh to be added: namely that in spite of everything the identification with the father finally makes a permanent place for itself in the ego. It is received into the ego, but establishes itself there as a separate agency in contrast to the rest of the content of the ego. We then give it the name of super-ego and ascribe to it, the inheritor of the parental influence, the most important functions. If the father was hard, violent and cruel, the super-ego takes over those attributes from him and, in the relations between the ego and it, the passivity which was supposed to have been repressed is reestablished. The super-ego has become sadistic, and the ego becomes masochistic—that is to say, at bottom passive in a feminine way. A great need for punishment develops in the ego, which in part offers itself as a victim to Fate, and in part finds satisfaction in ill-treatment by the super-ego (that is, in the sense of guilt). For every punishment is ultimately castration and, as such, a fulfilment of the old passive attitude towards the father. Even Fate is, in the last resort, only a later projection of the father.

The normal processes in the formation of conscience must be similar to the abnormal ones described here. We have not yet succeeded in fixing the boundary line between them. It will be observed that here the largest share in the outcome is ascribed to the passive component of repressed femininity. In addition, it must be of importance as an accidental factor whether the father, who is feared in any case, is also especially violent in reality. This was true in Dostoevsky's case, and we can trace back the fact of his extraordinary sense of guilt and of his masochistic conduct of life to a specially strong feminine component. Thus the formula for Dostoevsky is as follows: a person with a specially strong innate bisexual disposition, who can defend himself with special intensity against dependence on a specially severe father. This characteristic of bisexuality comes as an addition to the components of his nature that we have already recognized. His early symptoms of death-like attacks can thus be understood as a father-identification on the part of his ego, which is permitted by his super-ego as a punishment. "You wanted to kill your father in order to be your father yourself. Now you *are* your father, but a dead father"—the regular mechanism of hysterical symptoms. And further: "Now your father is killing *you*." For the ego the death symptom is a satisfaction in phantasy of the masculine wish and at the same time a masochistic satisfaction; for the super-ego it is a punitive satisfaction—that is, a sadistic satisfaction. Both of them, the ego and the super-ego, carry on the role of father.

To sum up, the relation between the subject and his father-object, while retaining its content, has been transformed into a relation between the ego and the super-ego—a new setting on a fresh stage. Infantile reactions from the Oedipus complex such as these may disappear if reality gives them no further nourishment. But the father's character remained the same, or rather, it deteriorated with the years, and thus Dostoevsky's hatred for his father and his death-wish against that wicked father were maintained. Now it is a dangerous thing if reality fulfils such repressed wishes. The phantasy has become reality and all defensive measures are thereupon reinforced. Dostoevsky's attacks now assumed an epileptic character; they still undoubtedly signified an identification with his father as a punishment, but they had become terrible, like his father's frightful death itself. What further content they had absorbed, particularly what sexual content, escapes conjecture.

One thing is remarkable: in the aura of the epileptic attack, one moment of supreme bliss is experienced. This may very well be a record of the triumph and sense of liberation felt on hearing the news of the death, to be followed immediately by an all the more cruel punishment. We have divined just such a sequence of triumph and mourning, of festive joy and mourning, in the brothers of the primal horde who murdered their father, and we find it repeated in the ceremony of the totem meal.[6] If it proved to be the case that Dostoevsky was free from his attacks in Siberia, that would merely substantiate the view that they were his punishment. He did not need them any longer when he was being punished in another way. But that cannot be proved. Rather does this necessity for punishment on the part of Dostoevsky's mental economy explain the fact that he passed unbroken through these years of misery and humiliation. Dostoevsky's condemnation as a political prisoner was unjust and he must have known it, but he accepted the undeserved punishment at the hands of the Little Father, the Tsar, as a substitute for the punishment he deserved for his sin against his real father. Instead of punishing himself, he got himself punished by his father's deputy. Here we have a glimpse of the psychological justification of the punishments inflicted by society. It is a fact that large groups of criminals want to be punished. Their super-ego demands it and so saves itself the necessity for inflicting the punishment itself.[7]

Everyone who is familiar with the complicated transformation of meaning undergone by hysterical symptoms will understand that no attempt can be made here to follow out the meaning of Dostoevsky's attacks beyond this beginning.[8] It is enough that we may assume that their original meaning remained unchanged behind all later accretions. We can safely say that Dostoevsky never got free from the feelings of guilt arising from his intention of murdering his father. They also determined his attitude in the two other spheres in which the

---

[6]See *Totem and Taboo* [(1912–13), Section 5 of Essay IV, *Standard Ed.* **13**, 140].

[7][Cf. "Criminals from a Sense of Guilt," the third essay in Freud's "Some Character-Types Met with in Psycho-Analytic Work" (1916), *Standard Ed.,* **14**, 332.]

[8]The best account of the meaning and content of his attacks was given by Dostoevsky himself, when he told his friend Strakhov that his irritability and depression after an epileptic attack were due to the fact that he seemed to himself a criminal and could not get rid of the feeling that he had a burden of unknown guilt upon him, that he had committed some great misdeed, which oppressed him (Fülöp-Miller, 1924, 1188). On self-accusations like these psycho-analysis sees signs of a recognition of "psychical reality," and it endeavours to make the unknown guilt known to consciousness. S.F. XXI—N.

father-relation is the decisive factor, his attitude towards the authority of the State and towards belief in God. In the first of these he ended up with complete submission to his Little Father, the Tsar, who had once performed with him in *reality* the comedy of killing which his attacks had so often represented in *play*. Here penitence gained the upper hand. In the religious sphere he retained more freedom: according to apparently trustworthy reports he wavered, up to the last moment of his life, between faith and atheism. His great intellect made it impossible for him to overlook any of the intellectual difficulties to which faith leads. By an individual recapitulation of a development in world-history he hoped to find a way out and a liberation from guilt in the Christ ideal, and even to make use of his sufferings as a claim to be playing a Christ-like role. If on the whole he did not achieve freedom and became a reactionary, that was because the filial guilt, which is present in human beings generally and on which religious feeling is built, had in him attained a super-individual intensity and remained insurmountable even to his great intelligence. In writing this we are laying ourselves open to the charge of having abandoned the impartiality of analysis and of subjecting Dostoevsky to judgements that can only be justified from the partisan standpoint of a particular *Weltanschauung*. A conservative would take the side of the Grand Inquisitor and would judge Dostoevsky differently. The objection is just; and one can only say in extenuation that Dostoevsky's decision has every appearance of having been determined by an intellectual inhibition due to his neurosis.

It can scarcely be owing to chance that three of the master-pieces of the literature of all time—the *Oedipus Rex* of Sophocles, Shakespeare's *Hamlet* and Dostoevsky's *The Brothers Karamazov*—should all deal with the same subject, parricide. In all three, moreover, the motive for the deed, sexual rivalry for a woman, is laid bare.

The most straightforward is certainly the representation in the drama derived from the Greek legend. In this it is still the hero himself who commits the crime. But poetic treatment is impossible without softening and disguise. The naked admission of an intention to commit parricide, as we arrive at it in analysis, seems intolerable without analytic preparation. The Greek drama, while retaining the crime, introduces the indispensable toning-down in a masterly fashion by projecting the hero's unconscious motive into reality in the form of a compulsion by a destiny which is alien to him. The hero commits the deed unintentionally and apparently uninfluenced by the woman; this latter element is however taken into account in the circumstance that the hero can only obtain possession of the queen mother after he has repeated his deed upon the monster who symbolizes the father. After his guilt has been revealed and made conscious, the hero makes no attempt to exculpate himself by appealing to the artificial expedient of the compulsion of destiny. His crime is acknowledged and punished as though it were a full and conscious one—which is bound to appear unjust to our reason, but which psychologically is perfectly correct.

In the English play the presentation is more indirect; the hero does not commit the crime himself; it is carried out by someone else, for whom it is not parricide. The forbidden motive of sexual rivalry for the woman does not need, therefore, to be disguised. Moreover, we see the hero's Oedipus complex, as it were, in a reflected light, by learning the effect upon him of the other's crime. He ought to avenge the crime, but finds himself, strangely enough, incapable of doing so. We know that it is his sense of guilt that is paralysing him; but, in a manner entirely in keeping with neurotic processes, the sense of guilt is displaced on to the perception of his inadequacy for fulfilling his task. There are signs that the hero feels this guilt as a super-individual one. He despises others no less than himself: "Use every man after his desert, and who should 'scape whipping?"

The Russian novel goes a step further in the same direction. There also the murder is committed by someone else. This other person, however, stands to the murdered man in the same filial relation as the hero, Dmitri; in this other person's case the motive of sexual rivalry is openly admitted; he is a brother of the hero's, and it is a remarkable fact that Dostoevsky has attributed to him his own illness, the alleged epilepsy, as though he were seeking to confess that the epileptic, the neurotic, in himself was a parricide. Then, again, in the speech for the defence at the trial, there is the famous mockery of psychology — it is a "knife that cuts both ways":[9] a splendid piece of disguise, for we have only to reverse it in order to discover the deepest meaning of Dostoevsky's view of things. It is not psychology that deserves the mockery, but the procedure of judicial enquiry. It is a matter of indifference who actually committed the crime; psychology is only concerned to know who desired it emotionally and who welcomed it when it was done.[10] And for that reason all of the brothers, except the contrasted figure of Alyosha, are equally guilty — the impulsive sensualist, the sceptical cynic and the epileptic criminal. In *The Brothers Karamazov* there is one particularly revealing scene. In the course of his talk with Dmitri, Father Zossima recognizes that Dmitri is prepared to commit parricide, and he bows down at his feet. It is impossible that this can be meant as an expression of admiration; it must mean that the holy man is rejecting the temptation to despise or detest the murderer and for that reason humbles himself before him. Dostoevksy's sympathy for the criminal is, in fact, boundless; it goes far beyond the pity which the unhappy wretch has a right to, and reminds us of the "holy awe" with which epileptics and lunatics were regarded in the past. A criminal is to him almost a Redeemer, who has taken on himself the guilt which must else have been borne by others. There is no longer any need for one to murder, since *he* has already murdered; and one must be grateful to him, for, except for him, one would have been obliged oneself to murder. That is not kindly pity alone, it is identification on the basis of similar murderous impulses — in fact, a slightly displaced narcissism. (In saying this, we are not disputing the ethical value of this kindliness.) This may perhaps be quite generally the mechanism of kindly

---

[9][In the German (and in the original Russian) the simile is "a stick with two ends." The "knife that cuts both ways" is derived from Constance Garnett's English translation. The phrase occurs in Book XII, Chapter X, of the novel.]

[10][A practical application of this to an actual criminal case is to be found in Freud's comments on the Halsmann Case (1931), p. 251 below, where *The Brothers Karamazov* is again discussed.]

sympathy with other people, a mechanism which one can discern with especial ease in this extreme case of a guilt-ridden novelist. There is no doubt that this sympathy by identification was a decisive factor in determining Dostoevsky's choice of material. He dealt first with the common criminal (whose motives are egotistical) and the political and religious criminal; and not until the end of his life did he come back to the primal criminal, the parricide, and use him, in a work of art, for making his confession.

The publication of Dostoevsky's posthumous papers and of his wife's diaries has thrown a glaring light on one episode in his life, namely the period in Germany when he was obsessed with a mania for gambling (cf. Fülöp-Miller and Eckstein 1926), which no one could regard as anything but an unmistakable fit of pathological passion. There was no lack of rationalizations for this remarkable and unworthy behaviour. As often happens with neurotics, Dostoevsky's sense of guilt had taken a tangible shape as a burden of debt, and he was able to take refuge behind the pretext that he was trying by his winnings at the tables to make it possible for him to return to Russia without being arrested by his creditors. But this was no more than a pretext and Dostoevsky was acute enough to recognize the fact and honest enough to admit it. He knew that the chief thing was gambling for its own sake — le jeu pour le jeu.[11] All the details of his impulsively irrational conduct show this and something more besides. He never rested until he had lost everything. For him gambling was a method of self-punishment as well. Time after time he gave his young wife his promise or his word of honour not to play any more or not to play any more on that particular day; and, as she says, he almost always broke it. When his losses had reduced himself and her to the direst need, he derived a second pathological satisfaction from that. He could then scold and humiliate himself before her, invite her to despise him and to feel sorry that she had married such an old sinner; and when he had thus unburdened his conscience, the whole business would begin again next day. His young wife accustomed herself to this cycle, for she had noticed that the one thing which offered any real hope of salvation — his literary production — never went better than when they had lost everything and pawned their last possessions. Naturally she did not understand the connection. When his sense of guilt was satisfied by the punishments he had inflicted on himself, the inhibition upon his work became less severe and he allowed himself to take a few steps along the road to success.[12]

What part of a gambler's long-buried childhood is it that forces its way to repetition in his obsession for play? The answer may be divined without difficulty from a story by one of our younger writers. Stefan Zweig, who has incidentally devoted a study to Dostoevsky himself (1920), has included in his collection of three stories Die Verwirrung der Gefühle [Confusion of Feelings] (1927)

---

[11]"The main thing is the play itself," he writes in one of his letters. "I swear that greed for money has nothing to do with it, although Heaven knows I am sorely in need of money."

[12]"He always remained at the gaming tables till he had lost everything and was totally ruined. It was only when the damage was quite complete that the demon at last retired from his soul and made way for the creative genius" (Fülöp-Miller and Eckstein 1925, lxxxvi).

one which he calls "Vierundzwanzig Stunden aus dem Leben einer Frau" ["Four-and-Twenty Hours in a Woman's Life"]. This little masterpiece ostensibly sets out only to show what an irresponsible creature woman is, and to what excesses, surprising even to herself, an unexpected experience may drive her. But the story tells far more than this. If it is subjected to an analytical interpretation, it will be found to represent (without any apologetic intent) something quite different, something universally human, or rather something masculine. And such an interpretation is so extremely obvious that it cannot be resisted. It is characteristic of the nature of artistic creation that the author, who is a personal friend of mine, was able to assure me, when I asked him, that the interpretation which I put to him had been completely strange to his knowledge and intention, although some of the details woven into the narrative seemed expressly designed to give a clue to the hidden secret.

In this story, an elderly lady of distinction tells the author about an experience she has had more than twenty years earlier. She has been left a widow when still young and is the mother of two sons, who no longer need her. In her forty-second year, expecting nothing further of life, she happens, on one of her aimless journeyings, to visit the Rooms at Monte Carlo. There, among all the remarkable impressions which the place produces, she is soon fascinated by the sight of a pair of hands which seem to betray all the feelings of the unlucky gambler with terrifying sincerity and intensity. These hands belong to a handsome young man — the author, as though unintentionally, makes him of the same age as the narrator's elder son — who, after losing everything, leaves the Rooms in the depth of despair, with the evident intention of ending his hopeless life in the Casino gardens. An inexplicable feeling of sympathy compels her to follow him and make every effort to save him. He takes her for one of the importunate women so common there and tries to shake her off; but she stays with him and finds herself obliged, in the most natural way possible, to join him in his apartment at the hotel, and finally to share his bed. After this improvised night of love, she exacts a most solemn vow from the young man, who has now apparently calmed down, that he will never play again, provides him with money for his journey home and promises to meet him at the station before the departure of his train. Now, however, she begins to feel a great tenderness for him, is ready to sacrifice all she has in order to keep him and makes up her mind to go with him instead of saying goodbye. Various mischances delay her, so that she misses the train. In her longing for the lost one she returns once more to the Rooms and there, to her horror, sees once more the hands which had first excited her sympathy: the faithless youth had gone back to his play. She reminds him of his promise, but, obsessed by his passion, he calls her a spoil-sport, tells her to go, and flings back the money with which she has tried to rescue him. She hurries away in deep mortification and learns later that she has not succeeded in saving him from suicide.

The brilliantly told, faultlessly motivated story is of course complete in itself and is certain to make a deep effect upon the reader. But analysis shows us that its invention is based fundamentally upon a wishful phantasy belonging to the period of puberty, which a number of people actually remember consciously. The phantasy embodies a boy's wish that his mother should herself initiate him into sexual life in order to save him from the dreaded injuries caused by masturbation. (The numerous creative works that deal with the theme of redemption have the same origin.) The "vice" of masturbation is replaced by the addiction to gambling[13]; and the emphasis laid upon the passionate activity of the hands betrays this derivation. Indeed, the passion for play is an equivalent of the old compulsion to masturbate; "playing" is the actual word used in the nursery to describe the activity of the hands upon the genitals. The irresistible nature of the temptation, the solemn resolutions, which are nevertheless invariably broken, never to do it again, the stupefying pleasure and the bad conscience which tells the subject that he is ruining himself (committing suicide)—all these elements remain unaltered in the process of substitution. It is true that Zweig's story is told by the mother, not by the son. It must flatter the son to think: "if my mother only knew what dangers masturbation involves me in, she would certainly save me from them by allowing me to lavish all my tenderness on her own body." The equation of the mother with a prostitute, which is made by the young man in the story, is linked up with the same phantasy. It brings the unattainable woman within easy reach. The bad conscience which accompanies the phantasy brings about the unhappy ending of the story. It is also interesting to notice how the *façade* given to the story by its author seeks to disguise its analytic meaning. For it is extremely questionable whether the erotic life of women is dominated by sudden and mysterious impulses. On the contrary, analysis reveals an adequate motivation for the surprising behaviour of this woman who had hitherto turned away from love. Faithful to the memory of her dead husband, she had armed herself against all similar attractions; but—and here the son's phantasy is right—she did not, as a mother, escape her quite unconscious transference of love on to her son, and Fate was able to catch her at this undefended spot.

If the addiction to gambling, with the unsuccessful struggles to break the habit and the opportunities it affords for self-punishment, is a repetition of the compulsion to masturbate, we shall not be surprised to find that it occupied such a large space in Dostoevsky's life. After all, we find no cases of severe neurosis in which the auto-erotic satisfaction of early childhood and of puberty has not played a part; and the relation between efforts to suppress it and fear of the father are too well known to need more than a mention.[14]

REFERENCES

Freud, S. (1909). Some general remarks on hysterical attacks. *Standard Edition* 9: 229.

———— (1931). The expert opinion in the Halsmann case. *Standard Edition* 21: 251.

———— (1950). *The Origins of Psychoanalysis*. London: Hogarth.

Fülöp-Miller, R. (1924). Dostojewski's Heilige Krankheit. In *Wissen und Leben*, pp. 19–20. Zurich.

---

[13][In a letter to Fliess of December 22, 1897, Freud suggested that masturbation is the "primal addiction," for which all later addictions are substitutes (Freud, 1950, Letter 79).]

[14]Most of the views which are here expressed are also contained in an excellent book by Jolan Neufeld (1923).

Fülöp-Miller, R., and Eckstein, F. (1926). *Der unbekannte Dostojewski*. Munich.

Miller, O. (1921). Zur Lebensgeschicte Dostojewski's. In *Autobiographische Schriften*. Munich.

Neufeld, J. (1923). *Dostojewski: Skizze Zu Seiner Psychoanalyse*. Vienna.

Strakhov, N. (1921). Uber Dostojewski Leben und literachishe Tätlgkeit. In *Literachishe Schriften*. Munich.

Zweig, S. (1920). *Drei Meister*. Leipzig.

7: THE AETIOLOGY OF ALCOHOLISM

Edward G. Glover

When psycho-pathologists discuss with psychiatrists "the aetiology of alcoholism," both parties must realize clearly the differences in their methods of approach. The psycho-pathologist approaches his problem with a roving commission. His interest in "diseases" is largely secondary, dictated by considerations of convenience in discussion; he prefers to describe as *maladaptations* the various groups of neurotic and associated disorder which come to his notice. He abandons the term "patient" and starts work with a conception of the ego as a psychic organ developed to sample stimuli from the external world and to register inner psychic stimuli (instincts). The alterations effected by the ego in response to these stimuli are described as adaptations, and may take the form of alterations in the individual or in environment. When the individual alteration is detrimental to the interests of the ego it is termed a "maladaptation."

In approaching alcoholism, the psycho-pathologist asks: To what development of instinct life is this a response? Secondly, How does it affect the individual's relation to environment? Thirdly, What individual and environmental factors contribute to the choice of alcoholism as a (mal) adaptation? His problem is primarily one of individual psychology. He is concerned less with statistics of age-incidence than with the reason why any individual should become alcoholic at a particular age. If the alcoholism is uncomplicated he desires to find out why the instinctual difficulties were capable of such direct solution: if the alcoholism is part of a wider symptom complex he wishes to know how the alcoholic response dovetails into other precautions. He then considers certain social factors, to see how far they obscure the individual problem, and the distillate of his combined observations may be regarded as a valid contribution to the psycho-pathology of the condition.

GENERAL PSYCHO-PATHOLOGICAL ASPECTS

No sooner do we consider the case material than a second difference in approach becomes apparent. The clinician wants to distinguish entities and to show his skill in differential diagnosis. The psycho-pathologist is concerned to discover, for example, what *psychic mechanisms* are common to chronic alcoholism, dipsomania and Korsakow's psychosis, and *then* to discover the mechanisms causing clinical differences.

If we consider clinical manifestations from the point of view of an individual caught between his instinctual urges and the pressure of reality, it becomes apparent that all the primary features of alcoholism represent fundamentally the individual's attempt to extricate himself from an impasse. As far as environment is concerned they are attempts at *flight from reality*, whilst as far as instincts are concerned, this flight coincides with an obvious *increase in phantasy formation*. Clinical differences can then be related to the *completeness* of the withdrawal and to its *periodicity*. The habitual drunkard adopts continuous flight, in contrast to the periodic bouts of the dipsomaniac: neither can compare with the flights in alcoholic hallucinosis of delirium tremens. There is one subjective factor which hinders adequate appreciation of the extent of phantasy activity. The investigator is apt to describe much of the drunkard's phantasy life by calling him an "inveterate liar" and at the same time to obscure the significance of phantasy in psychotic states by calling it "confabulation." Lying, romancing, boasting, obscene wit, illusion, confabulation, hallucination and delusion, all are results of overcharged phantasy.

But hallucinations and delusions also indicate an attempt to *substitute a new reality for the old,* or at least to *project* into reality the more painful elements of phantasy life. So we must inquire to what extent the alcoholic's overcharge of phantasy life leads to *actual gratification* in *real* life. What is generally called weakness of will, lack of decency, and moral deterioration in the chronic alcoholic can then be described in psycho-pathological terminology as the gratification of previously inhibited impulse. In any case terms such as "weakness of will" combine diagnosis with moral judgment in much the same way that the phrase "obstinate constipation" combines an accurate psycho-physiological diagnosis with an expression of the diagnostician's annoyance.

But it is not enough to say that withdrawal from reality increases or activates phantasy; it activates phantasy corresponding to definite *layers of psychic development*. This element of *regression* can be studied behaviouristically over years in chronic alcoholism, or over a few hours in acute intoxication. The regression of intoxication is plainly heading towards an infantile end, and the ultimate picture is scarcely distinguishable from that of a suckling, who, after an ample feed, might be described as "blind to the world."

The next step in investigation is to catalogue the *instincts* or *component instincts* gratified in alcoholic regression. Impulses of *aggression* with their accompanying attitudes of hate are freely expressed (irritation, quarrelsomeness, assault). Again, there is accentuation of *sexual impulse* and especially of *component sexual impulses*. Exhibitionism (lack of decency, exposure, obscene wit), scoptophilia (sexual curiosity), sadism (acts of sexual violence), fetishistic activities, manifest expressions of homosexuality can all obtain representation in alcoholism. On the other hand, in simple intoxication it is easy to find not only direct but *displaced* (and) or *rationalized* expressions of the same impulses (vanity, boasting, anecdotage, exchange of confidences, argumentation, sociability and general "heartiness" towards members of the same sex). Moreover, in alcoholic hallucinosis or paranoia, we see the same impulses in the form of accusations of sexual perversion or delusions of infidelity.

To the *mechanism of projection* involved in the latter instances we will return: meanwhile we may note that it is characteristic of all alcoholic states. The chronic alcoholic shelves responsibility, attributes his drink habits to social or marital difficulties, is suspicious, distrustful and generally "on guard," especially against non-drinkers; the sufferer from delirium tremens may even attack his anxiety hallucinations in environment.

SOCIAL ASPECTS

Coming to the social aspects of the problem, not all psycho-pathologists are agreed on the aetiology of alcoholism. Some authorities consider that in many instances the unconscious factors can be ignored; they regard social drinking customs, habit, idiosyncrasy, or economic conditions as prime aetiological factors, but the Freudian school holds that external frustration owes its apparent pathogenicity to internal (instinctual) frustrations. Social drinking habits have the same aetiological relation to alcoholism as a pandemic of mild itch would have to acute eczema: moreover, if we examine them closely we can scarcely resist the conclusion that they are socially sanctioned measures of instinctual gratification or defence: witness the joviality of a "stag party" with its scarcely concealed bonds of homosexual interest (Abraham 1927a, Boehm 1920).

The true pioneers of behaviouristic aetiology are the alcoholics themselves, who are always ready to give rationalistic explanations of their habits. If diagnosticians are to avoid the charge of unconscious collusion, they should be prepared to pay attention to the unconscious significance of *rationalizations,* to say nothing of the language of *symbolism* (compare the homosexual significance of "snake" hallucinations in delirium tremens).

SYSTEMATIC PSYCHO-PATHOLOGY

The results of psycho-analytical investigation must be considered from three points of view: (a) the modification of instinct, (b) the Ego's relation to instinct, and (c) the relation of instincts and Ego to environment.

The Modification of Instinct

A main feature of analyses of alcoholics, drug addicts and manic-depressive insanity is intense preoccupation with *oral* images and phantasies (Abraham 1927b, Freud 1905, 1917, Glover 1924); these are concerned with mouth–breast gratification, or with scenes of frustration accompanied with rage affect. They may be finally expanded into fellatio, cunnilingual, coprophagic or cannibalistic phantasies. The unconscious preoccupations and character traits of the alcoholic indicate either that he has brought about an unobstructed *oral regression* or that his libido has never completely abandoned the oral stage, that is, that he is *orally fixated*. This fixation is rarely complete even in manic-depressive cases, but we are safe in saying that the alcoholic is *partially fixated*. But since all individuals have oral erotic interests and undergo oral frustration, why are these of special importance in alcoholism? The first reason is that, apart from the gratification of self-preservative urges, oral activities represent the earliest form of libidinal gratification and are associated with the earliest form of aggression and destruction. This particular combination, described as *oral sadism,* is specially accentuated in the alcoholic. The second reason is that excessive frustration in this primitive phase makes the relations to objects (primarily nipple–mother) exceedingly difficult, and *all future relations to objects tend to be coloured by this oral ambivalence.*

The alcoholic then has made a bad start, and whether this is exaggerated by *constitutional* factors or not, he is hampered thenceforward by a tendency to psychic *regression* which produces inertia in development. But matters go from bad to worse. The next stage of libidinal development, the *anal* stage, has more severe frustrations in store. In the alcoholic, *anal erotism* is heightened, again owing to partial fixation, whilst *anal sadism* is correspondingly increased. The result is that when the potential alcoholic reaches the third or infantile genital stage he is faced with a double difficulty: his genital impulses towards objects preserve an archaic sadistic quality, and his reaction to thwarting and disappointment is appropriately severe. His genital libido is impoverished and when the incestuous climax to infantile sexuality is shipwrecked on castration anxiety, the *tendency to regression is fully established.* The ground is thus prepared for miscarriages of sexual instinct in adult life. Most characteristics of alcoholism depend on the *distribution* of this regressional interest. Anal sadistic fixation and regression supply the driving power to *homosexual* impulses (Abraham 1927b, Clark 1919, Ferenczi 1916, Freud 1915, Juliusburger 1912), which play so large a part in the analysis of alcoholism. Together with other fixations on component sexual instincts, these help us to understand in part the close relation between alcoholism and *perversion*. Finally, the accentuation of genital (castration) anxiety in the alcoholic sheds light on the acute anxieties of alcoholic deliria and psychoses. *One of the dire necessities which drives the individual to alcohol is the need to overcome these excessive charges of castration anxiety.* In the early stages of chronic alcoholism it is partly overcome; the drunkard's boastfulness affords compensation for inner insufficience or impotence (symbolic castration): when, however, the Ego is temporarily or permanently damaged the anxiety breaks through in massive charges.

The Development of the Ego

When the real Ego begins to develop and become consolidated, a large part of libidinal interest is directed on the self as object (narcissism). Each thwarting produces narcissistic injury, increases ambivalence to objects and makes it more difficult to establish object relations. The most advanced pleasure-producing zone (genital) becomes the centre of narcissistic interest. But this is the zone thwarted in primitive object relations. So between narcissistic fixation, anxiety and regression, the Ego of the alcoholic is overcharged with narcissistic libido. Relations with objects are of course established, but the Ego hardly dares love anyone who cannot be identified with the self. In some cases identification depends upon the object possessing the same genital, incidentally another clue to the homosexual fixations of the alcoholic. When a true object is chosen it is more often than not for revenge, as witness the misery of the alcoholic's marital life.

A second factor in the variety of alcoholic manifestations is therefore *the stage at which the Ego began to lag in development.* Evidence of narcissistic regression is found in the increased use of the defence mechanism of *projection.* The Ego overworks that primitive method of flight from painful excitations which it cannot master, projecting them into a "painful" outer world. This is characteristic of all alcoholic states, although the manifestations vary from vague suspicion to hallucinatory certitude. Some subjects go so far as to pursue these excitations in the outer world and attempt to destroy them (assault, homicide).

The Ego and Environment

Many of the guilts and anxieties of alcoholics indicate interference with the function of conscience. The constant use of projection makes it appear as if their consciences were turned inside out. The alcoholic paranoiac detects malignant influences outside himself and rushes to destroy (punish) them; the chronic drunkard feels that everyone else is to blame, especially the virtuous members of his group. Again, the euphoria of alcoholism suggests that relief has been obtained from an intolerable burden, whilst the disregard of social usages indicates temporary suspension of conscience.

Analytic investigation of both normal and alcoholic types shows that what we recognize as conscious conscience is only the peak of a more *primitive conscience,* which operates unconsciously. This archaic conscience (super ego) (Freud 1923, Rickman 1925) is a protective organ developed during the gradual wrecking of infantile sexuality: it instigates inside the ego the inhibiting activities at first associated with the parents. Built up when the child's reality sense is weakly developed and when its instincts are exceedingly primitive, this super-ego has primitive characteristics; it demands the repression of incestuous impulse and failing successful repression exacts primitive punishments. Now as the alcoholic tends to remain fixated or to regress to primitive impulses, we must expect to find *either that he has a more severe primitive conscience than normal or that he is unable to cope with the drive of primitive impulse and lands himself in situations of self-punishment.* Both difficulties can be observed in alcoholics. The former is seen in the depressed secret drinker and in more psychotic types whose bout may end in suicide. Up to a point alcohol counters the depression by inducing relative euphoria. This cycle reminds us of the manic-depressive states, and the labile moods of alcoholics are well known. The second mechanism, where inhibition fails and punishments are instituted, is still more obvious. The chronic alcoholic gratifies tendencies which previously may have been foreign to consciousness, and the punitive response elicited from environment varies from moral reprobation to capital punishment. *With the collusion of society the alcoholic has established and for a time reinforced the function of primitive conscience.* The abuse of alcoholism leads inevitably to self-punishment (organic illness, economic failure); it promotes projected self-punishment (aggression towards environment) and this ultimately provokes punishment of the self by environment. In this sense *alcoholism is a disastrous attempt to cure abnormalities of primitive conscience.* Should the alcoholic attempt to break through primitive inhibitions he risks the integrity of his ego (compare the sequence, latent homosexuality, alcoholism, abstinence, paranoia) (Ferenczi 1911, 1916); if he maintains an uneasy balance by means of alcohol he is compelled to keep to a course which also ends in physical and mental disintegration.

WHY ALCOHOL?

To answer this question we must recall (1) the compulsive element in alcoholism; (2) its close connexion with sexual instincts and their components, in particular its compensatory relation to impotence; (3) the fact that sexual instincts are to a large extent capable of displacement; (4) that alcohol is unconsciously identified with bodily secretions and excretions (milk, urine, saliva, semen and blood), and plays a part in unconscious imagery as a medium of sexual assault and as a procreative fluid. It is not too much to say then that *alcohol is chosen as a surrogate of sexuality or, at the least, as a method of short-circuiting sexuality, a method which at the same time releases the pressure of repression and reverses processes of sublimation* (Abraham 1927b, Freud 1923).

INTER-RELATIONS OF ALCOHOLIC STATES

To sum up: three main aetiological factors have to be considered in alcoholism: (a) The partial fixation of libido at oral or anal sadistic levels of development; the alcoholic maintains ambivalent object relations at the price of alcoholism (E. Glover 1924, J. Glover 1927). (b) The constant tendency to regress to a narcissistic Ego organization which automatically sets primitive mechanisms (projection) in action. (c) The disorders of primitive conscience which lead to a fruitless exploitation of the same mechanism of projection. We have already noted the resemblance between alcoholic lability and manic-depressive insanity; some forms of alcoholism might be called artificial manic-depressive states. The manic-depressive, however, has a more severe oral fixation of libido, his super-ego is more disordered and his sadism is completely inverted. On the other hand, with a stronger anal-sadistic element, a more primitive narcissistic regression and a disintegrated super-ego the picture becomes one of paranoia; alcoholic paranoia, however, has originally maintained slightly stronger object relations than non-alcoholic. In the next place the dipsomaniac exhibits some of the characteristics of an obsessional neurotic, although alcoholic ceremonial is more apparent in the social drinker. Again, although alcohol brings out many "perverse" sexual tendencies it may itself function as a surrogate of component sexuality. As we know, the essential mechanism of perversion depends on the canonization of one or more component sexual impulses in order that the remainder of infantile sexuality can remain repressed. Alcoholism is in this sense a "pseudo-perversion" (Glover 1924, Glover 1927, Keilholz 1926, Radó 1926, 1927). Finally its close relation to psycho-sexual impotence brings us back to the fundamental significance of castration anxiety. We must not forget that the essential problem in depressive states, in obsessional neurosis, fetishism, homosexuality and impotence, is one of infantile guilt and anxiety. Alcohol owes most of its attraction to the fact that it is primarily well adapted to overcome castration anxiety, although in the long run it defeats its own end by bringing about impotence and death (symbolic castration).

REFERENCES

Abraham, K. (1927a). The psychological relations between sexuality and alcoholism. In *Selected Papers*. London: Hogarth.

——— (1927b). *Selected Papers*. London: Hogarth.

Boehm, F. (1920). Beiträge zur Psychologie der Homosexualität. *Internationale Zeitschrift für Psychoanalyse* 6, issue 4.

Clark, L. P. (1919). A psychologic study of some alcoholics. *Psychoanalytic Review* 6.

Ferenczi, S. (1911). Alkohol und neurosen. *Jahrbuch. für psychoanalytische Forschungen* 3.

——— (1916). Homosexuality in the pathogenesis of paranoia. In *Contributions to Psycho-analysis*.

Freud, S. (1905). Three essays on the theory of sexuality. *Standard Edition* 7:1–243.

——— (1915). A case of paranoia running counter to the psycho-analytic theory of the disease. *Standard Edition* 14:261–272.

——— (1917). Mourning and melancholia. *Standard Edition* 14:237–258.

——— (1923). The ego and the id. *Standard Edition* 19:1–62.

Glover, E. (1924). The significance of the mouth in psycho-analysis. *British Journ. Med. Psych.* 4.

Glover, J. (1927). Notes on an unusual form of perversion. *International Journal of Psycho-Analysis* 8.

Juliusburger, O. (1912). Beitrag zur Psychologie der sogennanten Dipsomanie. *Zentralblatt für Psychoanalyse* 2.

Keilholz, A. (1924). *Internationale Zeitschrift für Psychanalyse* 70.

——— (1926). Analyseversuch bei Delirium Tremens. *Internationale Zeitschrift für Psychoanalyse* 7, Issue 3.

Radó, S. (1926). Die psychischen Wirkungen der Rauschgifte. *Internationale Zeitschrift für Psychoanalyse*.

——— (1927). Das problem der melancholie. *Internationale Zietschrift für Psychoanalyse* 13, issue 4.

Rickman, J. (1925). Alcoholism and psycho-analysis. *British Journal of Inebriety* 23.

Sachs, H. (1925). Zur Genese der Perversionen. *Internationale Zeitschrift für Psychoanalyse* 9.

Wholey, C. C. (unknown). Revelations of the unconscious in a toxic (alcoholic) psychosis. *American Journal of Insanity* 74.

8: ALCOHOLISM AS CHRONIC SUICIDE

Karl Menninger

Only a few years ago, were a psychiatrist to approach the subject of alcohol, it would be assumed immediately that he would deal chiefly with the celebrated syndrome, delirium tremens. As a student at Harvard Medical School twenty years ago, I was minutely instructed, along with my classmates, in the details of differential diagnosis that would distinguish delirium tremens from a half dozen other psychotic pictures that somewhat resembled it. And this is all I learned of alcohol and its function in the disruption of mental health.

Today, in the active practice of psychiatry, with patients before my eyes daily, including many whom alcohol has ruined or nearly ruined, I have not seen three cases of delirium tremens in as many years. Not that this affliction has disappeared from the earth, for in the wards of public hospitals or behind the bars of city jails new cases are, I am sure, admitted daily. But they do not interest psychiatrists now so much as those cases which give a better opportunity to discover why they drink rather than the results of their drinking.

I do not think this represents any change in the effects of alcohol on the human being. I think, rather, that it is the best possible illustration of the change in emphasis, interest, and concept in psychiatry. Once we looked curiously — and, to be sure, tenderly and humanely as well — at the end-results of men whose brains were finally reacting in a dramatic spectacle to a cumulative over-dose of poison. Those inestimably more numerous persons whose self-poisoning produced symptoms less vividly tinctured with hallucinations and terrors were regarded as sociological — not psychiatric — problems. The psychology of the man impelled to ruin himself by self-poisoning, in spite of disaster, remorse, and resolutions to abandon it, some way or other escaped the consideration of the psychiatrists and was left to the clergy, the social workers, the prohibitionists, or to the devil.

Drunkenness is as old as Noah, but drunkenness is not alcohol addiction. Many become drunk who never become addicts. Furthermore, an occasional alcoholic addict is seen who is never, or rarely, "drunk" in the popular sense (because he is partially intoxicated all the time, and the effects are concealed for want of a comparative background). It is not my intention to discuss the function of alcohol in the life of a normal person, or the amenities of social drinking. There is much to indicate that in our civilization alcohol has a very useful function to perform, and may be a source of increased happiness and decreased hostilities.

But there remains the phenomenon of self-destruction by irresistible addiction to repeated, excessive drinking of alcohol.[1] Everyone knows examples of this — individuals who suffer from what seems to be an irresistible impulse to throw away all obligations and opportunities and bring their house of cards tumbling about their heads by getting drunk. Every social worker could testify to homes filled with bitterness and despair because of an addiction to alcohol on the part of a father, husband, son, or even a mother. Furthermore, every psychiatrist (and others, too, of course) could, with the author, cite case after case of prominent and formerly successful men, together with many others who are potentially successful, whose lives are literally ruined in this peculiar way. I say "peculiar" because it is paradoxical that a substance which gives and has for centuries given pleasure, relief, and stimulation to man, should, for a few, become an instrument of self-destruction.

Someone may be tempted here to make a jocular response, that if, indeed, it be self-destruction, it is at least a pleasant form of it. With this no one intimately acquainted with the suffering of an alcoholic addict or his family could agree. Funny it may seem to the casual observer, but to the drinker's family and ultimately to him, too, it is a tragedy past jocularity.

Yet, at the same time, there is a little truth in that joke. It is an example of what has been called "gallows humor" — as in the case of the condemned man who remarked, on the way to his execution, "This is certainly going to be a lesson to me."

Since it is true that alcohol has the quality of giving some degree of relief from the pain of facing reality and also from other psychic pain resulting from emotional conflicts, to the extent that it is sought for the purpose of relieving pain, the use of alcohol can be regarded as an attempt at self-cure. Some alcoholics recognize this but many others cannot be persuaded that their periodic bouts are more than jolly little affairs which, for all they may end in a rather untidy and tiresome mess, with a few disappointments all around, no one should hold against them. This wish to be treated like a child and to have one's most serious aggressions overlooked is very characteristic of the type of personality which finds excessive indulgence in alcohol so irresistible.

This leads us to wonder what type of personality or what predisposing experiences in any personality lead to the election of this kind of suicide. In order to arrive at some conclusions about this let me describe some of the typical situations.

---

[1]Addiction to drugs is psychologically similar, but differs in that all narcotic habituation is socially taboo, while alcohol ingestion is socially approved and hence immensely more dangerous and frequent as a basis of addiction.

In tracing back the history of drinking in those individuals who later become its victims, we usually find it difficult to say when socially and relatively harmless drinking was superseded by a more malignant and compulsive type of drinking. In fact, this is one of the insidious dangers of alcohol for unstable individuals. A typical history of the early period would run somewhat as follows: George is the oldest son in a prominent family. He is successful in high school, both socially and in athletics. He is not brilliant but his teachers like him as do all the students. He is sent to the state university. Up to this time he had little to do with alcohol; his parents were opposed to it in any form. At the university he sees considerable drinking but takes little part in it, at first; then, with increasing frequency, he finds one or another group of companions with whom he can spend the evening or the week-end and drink more and more. His parents get wind of this and there is a family scene. He is very humble and penitent, promises not to do it any more. Three months later there are reports of repeated drunkenness and threats of suspension, and there is another family scene and more penitence and promises.

Occasionally (actually rather rarely) parents will at this point consult a psychiatrist and what they say, if their words, gestures, attitudes, and behavior can be synthesized and summarized, is something like this: "We are rather important people, you know, and we have a very fine son, in fact, an extraordinary fellow, now attending the university, who has been in a little trouble recently about drinking. Of course, we realize that it is somewhat absurd to regard this as anything serious or anything in which a psychiatrist might have any interest, because the boy isn't crazy; in fact, there's really nothing the matter with him but bad companions. We don't think he needs any treatment but maybe you could scare him a little, and perhaps threaten to lock him up for a day or two if he doesn't quit drinking. Tell him he will get delirium tremens. He has just been spoiled by too much fun down at the university."

Although there are exceptions, as a general rule the parents of alcoholics, for reasons that we shall understand better later, are peculiarly unseeing with regard to the sufferings of their children. They think because their child is popular in high school or because he makes a fraternity or an athletic team in college that all is well with him, that peace and contentment fill his heart. Such parents little realize the suffering silently endured (often unconsciously) by well-appearing, well-regarded children. Once let these sufferers discover the temporary assuaging powers of alcohol, and it will take more than family scenes, reproaches, and threats to deter a repetition. We psychiatrists know this from repeated experiences but most of us have discovered that it is totally useless to convince such parents that we are other than alarmists who want to frighten them into a more radical treatment program than they see the slightest necessity for. They align us with the most rabid prohibitionists whose sweeping denunciations of alcohol have probably done more harm than good in deterring people from its expedient use.

Usually the parents do not consult us; they do not consult anyone. The boy shortly leaves the university and gets a job. The parents may hear some rumors of week-end sprees but these are discounted. News that the son has lost his position because of drinking comes then as a great shock.

Very likely he comes home, then, very disheartened. His father is provoked, denounces such behavior, and expresses himself as disgusted. The mother weeps. The son is thoroughly humiliated, obviously remorseful, resembles nothing so much as an overgrown child, and knows it. Again he makes apologies, resolutions, and promises. A few months pass and again the relatives feel justified in assuming that their good boy is relinquishing his bad habit and will live happily ever afterwards.

Of course he does not. I could pile case history on case history and make a composite record which would show that the career of the alcoholic is one such episode after another. More jobs, more drinking, more dismissals, more scenes, more promises, more disappointments. To be sure, there are many variations. Marriage usually occurs early and often involves financial help from the parents. There may be children to complicate the picture. Sometimes the wife is helpful, more often not; frequently she herself joins in the alcoholic sprees. I remember one instance in which the wife of an alcoholic patient went on a spree while her husband was taking treatment for alcoholism, and taking her two frightened little girls with her, drove five hundred miles to the sanitarium where her husband was confined to demand that he abandon his treatment and join her.

There is another complication to be mentioned, that in spite of their addiction to occasional orgies these victims sometimes do fairly well, even surprisingly well. Some only begin to drink seriously after they have achieved considerable success. This the reader will recall is exactly what we have observed in connection with suicide; some only kill themselves or attempt to do so or feel like doing so after success or reward. We will not repeat the explanation but only mention the parallelism here.

Sooner or later, however, most alcoholics get themselves into a hopeless impasse. They lose all their friends, they estrange their wives, they drive their parents to repudiate them,[2] or they come into conflict with the law, because of automobile accidents while drunk, sexual scandals while drunk, check forging, indecent exposure, and so on (the latter, *of course*, are not necessarily impasses, but there is usually an accumulation of circumstances which make it so). Novelists have described this—Ernest Hemingway, F. Scott Fitzgerald, John O'Hara, John Dos Passos.

I don't know what usually happens after that. Naturally the psychiatrist sees only a small proportion of them. We know that some land in jail, some in the asylum, and that some commit suicide. We also know that many others go from one sanitarium or so-called "cure" to another. Those whom we finally do see have generally come to us because relatives and friends have become exasperated and provoked beyond endurance. It is very rare indeed that an alcoholic addict comes to a psychiatrist voluntarily. It is usually by reason of medical, legal, or moral—

---

[2]One father, in exasperation at innumerable attempts to help his son, said in my hearing, "He can lie in the gutter and rot before I lift a finger to help him again!"

sometimes physical — compulsion from without. The spasmodic attempts to save themselves, to relinquish their intemperate demands for periods of drunken insensibility, are usually bogus; they are insincere, half-hearted, often flagrantly hypocritical. The reason for this does not lie in some wicked perverseness but in the deep hopelessness and despair from which every alcoholic secretly suffers. For him the efforts of any person or institution to relieve him of his alcohol habit is as if they would rob him of the only relief he has from unendurable suffering — expensive, disastrous, and disappointing as the relief has been to him. For this reason these patients usually dodge psychiatrists and psychiatric hospitals, where the underlying basis of the alcoholism might be approached, and play with the idea that a fishing trip, a dude ranch, a nursing home, a so-called "cure" or just "a rest" will do the trick.

If and when alcoholics do come to a psychiatric hospital, their admission is regularly accompanied by certain peculiar circumstances. In the first place they are apt to be drunk, even though they were sobering up from a previous bout at the time of the decision to take psychiatric treatment. The anticipation of deprival pain, the "last chance" philosophy and sometimes a wave of resentment against "well-meaning but mistaken friends" impels a final fling. This is apt to be followed by a period of remorseful shamefacedness. In this the patient shares, on the one hand, the attitude of the stricter religious groups that drinking is a sin to be abstained from on the basis of moral conviction, and, on the other hand, the mixture of resentment, disappointment and pity manifested by his relatives and friends.

At such a time the patient will promise anything and comply with any rules or expectations. This, however, gradually gives way to increasing assertiveness and truculency — everything about the hospital is "terrible" and the patient is "entirely cured and ready to return to work immediately" (this even when no work exists any longer, the patient having completely destroyed all of his opportunities).

In this connection, I must mention another curious but almost invariable phenomenon. This is the characteristic pathological optimism from which both the patient and all members of his family seem regularly to suffer. The word "suffer" is chosen advisedly because as a rule this attitude is the most serious obstacle to the successful treatment of the affliction. No matter how desperate the case may seem at first or how dismal or tragic the history, it is usually only a matter of a few weeks or months until the patient and (what is really much more strange) his relatives are convinced that he is now perfectly well, has made a radical change in his psychology, will never fall into such a habit again, and should accordingly be trusted and expected to resume his full share of responsibilities in life. Even when this same trick, this same formula of promise and disappointment, has been repeated over and over, it still works because the members of the family *want* to believe it. It is the vicious circle of interaction between the mutual aggressions of patient and family.

It would seem almost too obvious to require mention that such an optimism and such a false sense of security are only self-deception used for the purpose of escaping the necessity of effecting a thoroughgoing change in the underlying psychopathology. The alcoholic suffers secretly from unspeakable terror which he cannot bear to face. He knows only the device of drowning the fear by drinking and this "cure" (drinking) then becomes worse than the disease, at least so far as outside evidences are concerned. When his hand is called he temporarily repudiates the attempt at self-cure rather than confess or face the reason for the need of it and accepts a more promising scientifically applied cure which he soon runs away from, as described.

Some alcoholic patients, however, if properly approached can be engaged in an attempt to discover what lies back of the alcoholic compulsion, what great anxiety drives them to this suicidal comfort. That it arises from external life difficulties is an alibi no alcoholic patient gives to a psychiatrist who has won his confidence. Troubles there are in the world, to be sure, and some insoluble problems that would vex the soul of the most enduring, but it is not these, or at least not these alone, which impel alcoholic solution. (If it were so, we should all become alcoholics.) No, the victim of alcohol addiction knows what most of his critics do not know, namely, that alcoholism is not a disease, or at least not the principal disease from which he suffers; furthermore, *he knows that he does not know* the origin or nature of the dreadful pain and fear within him which impel him, blindly, to alcoholic self-destruction. It is like some poor beast who has been poisoned or set on fire, and runs blindly into the sea to court one death in fleeing another.

Indeed, we frequently see patients who start out with *conscious* suicidal intentions and end up by getting drunk (or who get drunk first in order to make a suicidal attempt), as if this was (as it is!) a less certain death than shooting. Many of the patients treated for alcohol addiction are preoccupied in their sober moments with thoughts of self-destruction, sometimes coupled with realization of their own unworthiness, sinfulness, and incompetence. Some patients partially carry out these suicidal intentions even, as it were, in spite of getting drunk. One, for example, slashed his face repeatedly with a razor. Another jabbed himself with a knife. Several jumped or attempted to jump off high places and it scarcely seems necessary to speak of the thousands of instances of persons who head for suicide by getting drunk and then attempting to drive their own cars.

Thus alcohol addiction can be thought of not as a disease, but as a suicidal *flight from* disease, a disastrous attempt at the self-cure of an unseen inner conflict, aggravated but not primarily caused (as many think) by external conflict. It is literally true that the alcoholic, as he himself says, does not know why he drinks.

We do know now, however, from painstaking psychoanalytic investigations into the unconscious mental life of a goodly number of alcoholics by numerous psychoanalytic workers,[3] why some of them drink. Why is it?

---

[3] Radó, Sandor, "The Psychic Effects of Intoxicants," *International Journal of Psychoanalysis*, 1926, vol. VII, pp. 396–402; Radó, Sandor, "The Psychoanalysis of Pharmacothymia" (Drug Addiction),

Let us begin with the more superficial aspects. "Alcoholics" are almost invariably jolly, sociable, talkative fellows who make themselves very popular, who indeed seem *obliged* to make themselves well liked and are very skillful at doing so. It takes very little penetration to discover, however, that this inordinate wish to be loved which compels them to be at such pains to be charming and to win popularity in one circle or another bespeaks a great underlying feeling of insecurity, a feeling which must constantly be denied, compensated for, or anesthetized.

From clinical experience also we know that such feelings of insecurity and inferiority depend less upon actual reality comparisons than upon unconscious, "irrational" reasons — generally feelings of great frustration and rage, and the fear and guilt which the rage induces. All this is, of course, now unconscious. But once it was *fully* conscious, only too conscious. In fact, a supplementary function of the alcohol-drinking is the further repression of such feelings and memories which threaten to emerge, to become again conscious. Such individuals, as children, have endured bitter disappointment, *unforgettable* disappointment, *unforgivable* disappointment! They feel, with justification, that they have been betrayed, and their entire subsequent life is a prolonged, disguised reaction to this feeling.

It is true that every child meets with disappointment and frustration; this is inevitable in the nature of reality. We are born into a world where we must change from directing our existence according to the pleasure principle to a program of directing our existence according to a reality principle which we discover by painful testing, step by step. We all had to be weaned, we all had to give up our dependence on our parents, we all had to relinquish our belief in Santa Claus. In this respect, then, the alcoholic probably does not suffer in childhood anything qualitatively different from what the rest of us suffer, but apparently there is a quantitative difference. In the case of the alcoholic the disappointment has actually been greater than he could bear. It was so great that it definitely affected his personality development so that in certain respects he remains all his life what we call an "oral character." We have already referred to this in the discussion of melancholia; I shall only repeat that an oral character is one characterized by conspicuous residua of the stage of psychological development in which the child's attitude toward the world was determined by his wish

Psychoanalytic Quarterly, vol. II, pp. 1–23, 1933; Simmel, Ernst, *Zum Problem von Zwang und Sucht*, Bericht V. allg. ärztl. Kongress f. Psychotherapie, 1930; Knight, Robert, P., *The Dynamics and Treatment of Alcohol Addiction*, read at the Fourteenth Congress of the International Psychoanalytic Association, Marienbad, Czechoslovakia, Aug. 4, 1936, and published in the *Bulletin of the Menninger Clinic*, vol. I, pp. 233–50, 1937; Knight, Robert P., "The Psychodynamics of Chronic Alcoholism," *Journal of Nervous and Mental Diseases*, Nov., 1937, pp. 538–48.

Knight believes that there are at least two main clinical varieties of alcohol addiction: (1) That in which alcohol addiction appears to be a reactive symptom in the course of a neurotic illness developing in adult life, and (2) that in which alcoholism is the most conspicuous of numerous devices utilized by a developmentally deformed character arising from earliest childhood. Such a distinction is extremely valuable clinically. The former naturally has a much better prognosis; but while the total personality development is quite different, the psychological motives are essentially the same in both types.

to take it in through the mouth and to destroy with his mouth anything which resisted his demands.

Drinking (in the sense in which we are now using it) is a typical infantile revenge reaction. In the first place, it is performed with the mouth; in the second place, it places a fictitiously high value upon the magical virtues of the substance desired; more important still, its practical aggressive values are indirect. An adult reaction of revenge would be more directly aggressive. For example, a mature person, angry for good reason at his father, would state the issue and discontinue further dealings instead of grieving and embittering his father by debauches. But the alcoholic cannot risk giving up the love objects to which he clings, angry and resentful as he may feel toward them, consciously or unconsciously. Furthermore, like all neurotics he confuses his friends and his (theoretical) enemies and treats those whom he thinks he loves as if they were identical with those whom he hates or whom he *once* hated. Thus, the alcoholic suffers at the same time from the wish to destroy his love-objects and the fear that he will lose them. He also fears the consequences of the aggressions which he is constantly impelled to make against them and from which he deters himself only by fierce internal restraint which in time accumulates to the point of leading him to seek a form of anesthetization which indirectly achieves the very aggressions and other consequences which he so feared he would succumb to.

In this strong ambivalence of the alcoholic, this conflictual and confusing attitude of love and hate, one sees an epitome and therefore a partial explanation of the nature of the great disappointment which he once suffered. Rather than derive it logically, let me depend again on empirical observations. We have noted time after time in those cases which have been subjected to penetrating anamnestic and psychological investigations that the parents of alcoholics increased the inevitable disappointment of the child tremendously by artificial, however unintentional, means. Apparently they did this usually by leading the child to expect more gratification than they were prepared to give or than reality made it possible to give. A few examples of this will illustrate specifically what I mean. The mother of one alcoholic nursed her child until he was nearly three years old because she herself was so fond of the experience; she then became desperate because of the difficulty she encountered in weaning him and achieved her aim finally by painting her breasts with stove blacking in order to frighten and repel the child. The mother of another alcoholic made of her child a pet and darling, almost ignoring the other children, a role which naturally had to be relinquished when he grew a little older. The father of still another alcoholic habitually did such things as this: he sent his son to the corner drug store repeatedly for cigars and household supplies, instructing him to say to the clerk only the magic words, "Charge it." One day the son used this same formula to obtain some candy, seeing nothing wrong in extending his knowledge to this new need. When his father learned of it he whipped the boy severely to the child's astonishment and resentment. Still another father encouraged his son to work and develop a savings account; then he, the father, appropriated the account.

This inconsistency in attitude toward the child bespeaks an ambivalence on the parents' part and explains why these patients are so often described by their friends and relatives as "spoiled"; "a spoiled child that never grew up," and similar expressions which imply reproach to both the "child" and his parents. Such appellations are partially correct, but err in the assumption that such children are "spoiled" by having been given too much love. I doubt very much if any child is ever spoiled by too much love. What passes for excessive "love" on the part of the parents is often only thinly disguised hate or guilt, and this fact is perceived by the child, if not by the neighbors. Over-solicitous, over-protective mothers and fathers who bestow large gifts to avoid the necessity of spending time and thought on the child; parents who exploit, promote, or smother their children with their own personalities, for the gratification of their own narcissism, cannot be said to be said to be "loving" their children however much they themselves may think so. And for all these aggressions against him the child will certainly some day, perhaps at great cost to himself, take full and terrible revenge.

All this theory becomes very much more understandable when studied in a particular case:

Jonathan Richardson was the son of one of the most distinguished men in the United States in his generation and in his particular field. We saw him — the patient — first at the age of thirty-five. The preceding fifteen years of his life had consisted of a dismal series of failures and the decimation of an opportunity for a career such as is offered to few men. The ostensible cause of all his failure was alcohol; indeed, the tragedy of his life was of just the sort which those opposed to the sale and use of alcohol use as an example with telling effect.

He was a very handsome man both in feature and in figure. He had perfect manners and good, if not superior, intelligence. These things, with his family's prestige and money, combined to make him exceedingly popular wherever he went. He had been a leading socialite, a prominent athlete, and a popular leader in the student body of the large and well-known eastern university to which he was sent. Nor did he carry his popularity with a bad grace; he was not arrogant, snobbish, or ostentatious. Indeed, his only fault during the earlier years of his life might be said to have lain in a certain passive acceptance of his good fortune rather than any energetic effort to gain it or make the best of it. He did not drink at all during his freshman year.

He left the university, where his father thought he was not working hard enough, and went to another school to obtain training in his father's business specialty in order to be equipped to take over the large responsibilities that would devolve upon him as the ultimate head of the firm — his father's great ambition for him. But here he showed a strange reaction to his opportunities which no one could understand. It was first a lack of enthusiasm about the work and later an out-and-out aversion to it. Finally, in spite of what seemed to be a conscientious effort, he failed completely in all the subjects related to the professional course.

It was in connection with this failure that he began drinking. Repeatedly, on nights when he should have been studying, he would go out for a few hours' relaxation and end up by becoming dead-drunk, and would then miss his classes the next day. In desperation his father insisted that he transfer to still another school but here the same thing happened. He had decided by now that he did not want to go into his father's business, that he had no interest in it or liking for it, that the apparently great opportunity meant nothing to him. His father could out-argue him and he would always admit that his father was probably right and then lapse into silence and (at the first opportunity) into another drunken spree.

He had some talent for drawing and pleaded that he be allowed to cultivate this talent, but his father thought it ridiculous that a son with his opportunities in the business world should dabble in art, for which, moreover, he seemed to have at best only a mediocre gift.

Then several things happened almost simultaneously: The World War broke out, and disregarding the opportunity for advancement which his father's prestige would have given him, he enlisted as a private and worked his own way up to the rank of commissioned officer. He married a beautiful woman and one who subsequently turned out to be as intelligent, levelheaded, and patient as she was beautiful. At that time, however, she was the cause of repeated penalization for him because he would absent himself from the army without leave in order to see her. He continued to drink surreptitiously and after his discharge more than ever.

The father in the meantime had become fully reconciled to the fact that his son would never come into his business and was anxious only to have him stop drinking and get into some work at which he would be self-supporting. During the next ten years he financed project after project, lending the son thousands of dollars, setting him up in one business after another, only to have him make a failure of every one of them. In each case the failure would be of the same character. There would be a burst of enthusiasm, an initial spurt of hard work, the establishment of many contacts, a period of good will and popularity and the promise of success, then increasing disappointments of customers on account of absences from the store (drinking), increasing drinking, and decreasing sales, the latter causing discouragement and thus more drinking, the whole thing ending up in bankruptcy, arrest and threatened or actual imprisonment, sudden disappearance, or some other dramatic finale. Throughout all this he would preserve an amiable, conciliatory, earnest manner that had the effect of convincing everyone that surely he had repented all his dissolute ways and had turned the corner toward reform.

"I have thrown away everything," he would say. "I have broken my mother's heart, turned down the best business opportunity a man ever had, wasted my youth, neglected opportunities for education, encumbered myself with the responsibilities of a loving wife and children whom I can't support, and what have I got out of it? Nothing! A lot of drunken brawls which I didn't even enjoy at the time."

Now to look into the psychology of this boy's drinking. He had what we feel to be the typical set-up for alcoholism. He had a powerful, money-bestowing, but vacillating (i.e., ambivalent) father; he had an indulgent and undiscriminating (therefore also ambivalent) mother; he had a sister whom the parents definitely preferred.

A word of explanation about these. The father, whom every son unconsciously strives to emulate, was in this instance on a very high pinnacle. This alone made a difficulty for the boy, because the greatness of his father seemed to him to be unattainable. But added to this was the fact that the father used his position cruelly. He was high and mighty with his son, at times savage with him, and at other times sentimental to the point of being maudlin. A consistently harsh father gives his son something to fight against. A father who, as this one, ridicules and humiliates the son with sarcasm until he leaves the table sobbing, and at other times boasts of him to others in his presence and overwhelms him with gifts, excites terrific antagonism and at the same time inspires its suppression. The son is not only embittered by the harshness but forestalled by the occasional kindness from normal attempts at retaliation.

Another resentment of this son against the father was the father's preference for the sister. Normal as this may have been on the part of the father, it aroused in the son — as it always does — unconscious envy of the feminine position because the father's attitude toward her was more consistently kind. The normal solution of the emotional conflict caused by this family set-up would be for the boy to turn toward his mother for such help as he needed during his growing years and then graduate from the family to more hospitable and less conflictual fields. But there are certain difficulties about this. The wives of such superior men as this boy's father are apt to have their own private neuroses, a very common one being the tendency to turn from the husband to the son as a love-object. This leads to further complications; it overwhelms the son with love from a source which either tends in the direction of keeping him a spoiled child who need make no manly effort to win love, or increases his fear of the powerful father in whose domain he is trespassing. One might say that such boys, incensed at being slighted by their fathers and by the preference shown their sisters (or someone else), turn toward the mothers for affection inordinately, but because of the fear of the powerful father, accept this love from her only in the infantile mode and remain sucklings.

Exactly this happened in the patient I have been describing. How it was reflected in later life can be clearly seen in the brief history of him given above. The boy was forced by his feelings of inferiority toward his father, his envy of the sister, and his oral dependence upon the mother into the acceptance of an extremely passive role in life. All the characteristics of the typical alcoholic which I described above can be related to his essential passivity and the wish to win love from people by excessive friendliness and essential subservience rather than by masculine achievement. But while passive in method, alcoholics are by no means lacking in aggressiveness.[4] Indeed, they use their passivity in the most aggressive

---

[4]It is a common error to think of passivity as the opposite of aggressiveness. Passivity is often very aggressive in intention and effect.

way against those who thwart them. It is for this reason that alcoholism so often develops or increases to a pathological degree shortly after marriage. The predisposed individual seeks more maternal gratification from the wife than the average or normal woman is prepared to give, characteristically accuses her of not being affectionate enough, and is himself reluctant to assume his masculine responsibilities toward her. The result of this feeling of thwarting is a return to the bottle which serves at the same time as a gratification to him and as an aggression against her.

In the case of Jonathan Richardson, it will be recalled that the drinking began before marriage at a time when the father insisted upon a change in universities. He wanted the son to follow in his business. This the son could not do for many reasons. It implied an undesired identification with his father. Moreover, it would have put him in an unendurable position of comparison and rivalry with his father of whom he was so afraid. (It is characteristic of oral characters that they are poor winners and poor losers; they cannot bear to do either and hence usually sidestep competitive activities of all sorts.) Jonathan wanted rather to be an artist, another feminine identification (no aspersion upon artists is intended; I refer now to art as *he* conceived of it, which was in imitation of his mother). In this his father tried to thwart him and he tried in turn to thwart his father's ambition for him. He did so, however, in the way characteristic of alcoholics. He went through the motions of trying to comply with his father's wishes and appeared to fail only through succumbing to the temptation of drink (which is symbolically equivalent to the childhood retreat to his mother).

There is one other element in this case not invariably characteristic of alcoholics but very common. That is the fact that the patient's father himself drank very heavily. The older psychiatrists regarded this as a very important point because they considered alcoholism to be a hereditary trait. Of course, scarcely any scientist believes so today, although it is still a popular theory. Alcoholism cannot possibly be a hereditary trait, but for a father to be alcoholic is an easy way for the son to learn *how* to effect the retaliation he later feels compelled to inflict. Many alcoholics, as everyone knows, have parents distinguished for their sobriety and self-restraint. Of course, in such homes the alcoholism of the son carries the greater power as a weapon.

Such a case illustrates as well as any one case can some of the various psychological functions of alcohol addiction. What strikes some as most apparent in such cases is the feeling of inferiority which the alcoholism seems to relieve; many people have made this observation introspectively and the case just cited seems to be a good example of it. However, one should remember that such a great sense of inferiority usually depends upon guilt feelings arising from envy and hostility. The mild elation which releases inhibitions after a few drinks of an alcoholic beverage cannot be compared directly with the feelings of a person addicted to alcohol. For one thing, the alcoholic never stops in the stage where such feelings of release can be advantageously enjoyed but carries the drinking to a point where these feelings are annulled, and usually to a point where his behavior is such as to actually increase rather than decrease his social or intellectual disability or "inferiority." This, plus the most casual observation of the behavior of such individuals, is sufficient to convince anyone of the unconsciously aggressive function of the drinking. It would seem scarcely necessary to prove this point; everyone is familiar with the obnoxious behavior of drunken boors at parties, public gatherings, and in private life. Alcoholic patients give psychiatric hospitals more trouble than any others, not because of any consistent disagreeableness or belligerency but rather because of the contrast between their superficial attitude of amiable, courteous compliance and the petty grumbling and occasional impulsive and unexpected obstreperousness which any denial of their incessant importunacy evokes. They simply cannot endure the privations incident to life in a real world (or even in the specially modified world of the sanitarium). Indeed, an alcoholic may be considered as beginning to "get well" when he discovers that getting drunk is not the only way in which he habitually makes himself disagreeable. William Seabrook[5] in his amazingly candid account of his experiences while under treatment for alcoholism describes this faithfully and accurately. For anyone interested in the problem this book is an indispensable source of material in spite of the fact that what the author may have regarded as a deep psychological study of himself was quite obviously interrupted at a relatively superficial stage, at least so far as the recorded account goes.

I have stated that the inferiority feelings of the alcoholic frequently arise from a sense of guilt. In some individuals this consciously precedes the drinking but in the majority of instances it is often erroneously ascribed (by them and by some physicians) to the physiological effects of the drinking (hangover, katzen-jammer, etc.). But this sense of guilt pertains not so much to the immediate aggressiveness implicit in the drinking as to the fundamental aggressiveness back of it, the partially but never successfully repressed hostility which, I believe, is one of the chief determinants of the alcoholic neurosis. This is apparent in some cases only after considerable study but in others, as in one now to be cited, it strikes one immediately.

This was a thoughtful, intelligent young fellow of twenty-three who looked and acted as if he were thirty and who, after outstanding success in the preparatory school from which he graduated with honors, was dismissed from the university on account of excessive drinking. Subsequent to this he lost position after position on account of drinking and dissipation with women. He came to the clinic in a serious frame of mind, determined that he must get help or face the consequences of becoming a hopeless drunkard. He was the more thoughtful and earnest about it because his father had recently died, throwing considerable responsibility upon his shoulders as well as increasing feelings of remorse which had never been entirely absent but which, on the other hand, had never been effective in inhibiting his drinking.

He was considerably disturbed by recurrent dreams of being in the penitentiary. He recalled that shortly after his father's death he had been

---

[5]Seabrook, William, *Asylum,* Harcourt, Brace, 1935.

awakened several times by a nightmare in which he saw his father's corpse arise from the dead, angry and threatening. His father, a successful, intelligent, far-seeing man, had been greatly disappointed in this son, and had been stern and reproachful with him. The patient admitted that he could not escape the conviction that his drinking had so distressed the father as to have actually been a contributing factor in causing his death. This explains the patient's nightmare dream and penitentiary dream. "I realize I killed my father," said he; "small wonder I dream of going to the penitentiary."

The patient continued to dream of being hanged or put in the penitentiary which disturbed him so much that he would get drunk and then remorseful again. "I am nothing but a drunken bum and a degenerate," he said. "Let me drink myself to death. I am not worth saving."

He broke off his treatment and left the institution (toward which, however, he retained the kindliest feelings) in a determined effort to carry out this intention of self-destruction. He continued to drink, became involved in an automobile accident in which a man *was* killed (as in his "prophetic" dream) and he was actually put on trial for manslaughter (also conforming to his dreams) but was acquitted.

He went to another psychoanalyst for a while but again broke off the treatment and entered business, in which he was moderately successful. He had meanwhile discontinued drinking as the result of his fright in connection with the automobile accident but in its place he suffered now from an array of almost paralyzing neurotic symptoms, fears, anxieties, inhibitions, physical symptoms, and morbid ideas. The substitution of one type of neurosis for another is here strikingly illustrated.

This case also demonstrates the rather typical sexual pattern in alcoholism relating the aggressiveness and guilt-feelings to the erotic value of the drinking. The terrific sense of guilt with reference to the father, the almost studied provocativeness toward him combined with a deep attraction to him led to a conflict between his wish for passive erotic dependence upon him, and his rejection of this wish. It is almost axiomatic that alcoholics in spite of a great show of heterosexual activity have secretly a great fear of women and of heterosexuality in general, apparently regarding it as fraught with much danger. They often realize that they do not posses normal sexual powers or interests, frankly avowing that it is not sexual gratification they seek from women so much as affection, care, love — by which they mean maternal solicitude. This, ultimately, the normal wife rebels against giving to a grown man supposedly her protector and master. The outcome is inevitable. The patient then assumes a grieved or contemptuous or utilitarian or even consciously hostile attitude toward her and all women and turns toward men with a mixture of friendly and provocative behavior, with temporary jollity and popularity but ultimate misery and personal loss. At the same time that he is drinking with boon companions who appear to be substitutes for his father, he is defying and grieving his real father and rejecting his real mother or her substitute. This, in turn, gives rise to remorse which leads to self-depreciation and self-injury. Meanwhile the exasperated wife considers or applies for divorce. Immediately, the little-boy husband rushes back to her with tears, prayers, and promises to which she very likely succumbs and the whole cycle begins again.

The self-destructive consequences of alcoholism which are so obvious would seem to be in part incidental, that is, they are the untoward consequences of self-administered efforts at obtaining relief from internal dangers. As soon as these internal dangers threaten the destruction of the individual by his own impulses, alcoholism is chosen or substituted as a kind of lesser self-destruction serving to avert a greater self-destruction.

We have commented that the same problem faces many if not all people and the same solution is also available to everyone. The question is, what particular problems obsess the potential alcoholic and why is this particular method chosen by him to solve them. The cases recited illustrate some of the conditioning experiences which favor the development of the alcoholic's emotional problems and also favor this method of attempted solution. They relate to the thwarting of the early oral receptive cravings of these individuals, that is, their need of love and the fearful resentments which these thwartings create with a corresponding anticipation of punishment or annihilation as the consequence of indulging or even fantasying these retaliations.

The alcoholism solves the problem neatly because it enables the individual to carry out these retaliations and aggressions, often against the very person toward whom they were originally directed; in addition, however, it incurs liability for a certain amount of punishment which is not so dreadful as that feared under the original circumstances.

Furthermore, it supplies the oral love — *symbolically,* in the form of a precious liquor taken by mouth, the "mother's milk" which was so much craved; and *actually,* in the form of conviviality and sentimentality which accompany social drinking. To be sure, this sometimes seems to be a substitute for heterosexual object love, but the alcoholic, like all oral characters, is not very discriminating between the sexes. Indeed, his chief resentment may be against women rather than men on account of thwarting propensities ascribed to his mother so that he discriminates against them, not so much on account of their sex, as on account of their similarity to her, that is, not so much on a sexual basis as on a personal basis. Many alcoholics indulge in homosexual (or in heterosexual) relations only when they are drunk but these various facts confirm our proposition that all forms of self-destruction are partially (incompletely) eroticized, that is, used as a source of pleasure.

The general problems of treatment I have consistently deferred for special consideration in the final section. Alcohol addiction is, however, such a widespread affliction and one in which present modes of treatment are so notoriously inadequate that I have thought it worthwhile to insert a brief summary of the treatment methods indicated by the conception of it as a form of self-destruction as outlined above.

Given this view of the problem of alcohol addiction, one can see that the general principles of its successful treatment must necessarily follow very different lines from those based upon the old conception that it represents a bad habit or an unfortunate inheritance. The effective treatment of alcohol addiction is, of course, the treatment of that which impels it. This means the gradual elimination of the tendency of over-reaction to frustration, and the progressive relief of those deep, inner feelings of anxiety, insecurity, and of childlike expectation and resentment which so regularly determine it.

Inasmuch, however, as the persistence of these traits represents a definite character deformity of very long standing, the modified results of childhood injuries, the accomplishment of their elimination implies a complete and thoroughgoing reconstruction of the entire personality.

So far as I know, there is only one treatment technique which even attempts to accomplish this, and that is psychoanalysis. I do not say that alcoholism cannot be cured by any other means. I have seen it happen in one instance as the result of a prolonged vigil of several years in a lonely spot by a very intelligent and determined man; I have known it to occur as the result of religious conversion; and I am sure it is occasionally possible in not too severe cases as the result of psychiatric conferences and counsel. We all know that "cure" is occasionally accomplished as the result of substituting another neurosis for the alcoholism; alcoholics, for example, sometimes cease to be alcoholics and become hypochondriacs or religious fanatics. And, finally, in justice to the facts, one must add that it sometimes happens suddenly following intense emotional experiences and also following apparently trivial incidents; the explanation of the metamorphosis in these cases remains entirely obscure.

But, on the other hand, I have never seen an alcoholic addict cured by confinement alone, even though alcohol is withdrawn completely during that period. This applies to long-time commitments as well as short-time "cures." I have talked to superintendents of numerous state hospitals where alcoholics have been treated and their observations have been the same as mine. In fact, one of our friends, who is the superintendent of such an institution, has recently refused to approve the admission of any more alcoholics to his hospital, not because of any scientific disinterest in them, but because of his conviction that residence in a state hospital is a state expense which accomplishes nothing for them or for the state.

It is not difficult to see why such treatment does not change the character or allay the underlying desires. Just as soon as the alcoholic is released he is once more exposed to the same opportunities for relief with just as much inner distress clamoring to be relieved.

To bring about the character revision necessary to relieve alcohol addiction requires psychological "surgery," that is, psychoanalysis. *Theoretically,* it is the treatment of choice. *Practically,* there are many serious difficulties in the way. In the first place, psychoanalytic treatment cannot be accomplished in a few months. It is a typical alcoholic fantasy that the reconstruction of a character which has been thirty-odd years in forming (or, rather, deforming) can be accomplished in three, six, or even twelve months. The treatment of alcohol addiction, like the treatment of tuberculosis, is a long-time affair. This means that it is expensive in money as well as time. This is unfortunate but it is true. To encourage relatives or patients to believe that a few weeks or months are likely to bring about a fundamental change (with or without analysis) is only to disappoint them with certain failure.

Furthermore, most persons addicted to alcohol are too "far gone," too far removed from loyalty to the reality principle, to be treated by psychoanalysis under the ordinary circumstances. In other words, they must be treated in a specially adapted environment and for practical purposes this means that they must be confined, and opportunities for alcohol removed from immediate availability. Provision for increasing freedom, as their general behavior justifies it, is implicit in this plan. The proper direction of the aggressive tendencies as they become more and more direct and less and less circumvented by the neurotic inhibitions can be made to contribute to the therapeutic effectiveness of the treatment regime. Athletic and competitive tendencies are encouraged, and as soon as possible business or other sublimated aggressions engaged in.

Hence, confinement, *plus* psychoanalysis, *plus* the proper direction of the increasing capacity for externally directed aggressions constitute in our opinion and experience the best program of therapy for this affliction. Even this is not always successful but by means of it a few individuals have been cured and have stayed cured, not only of drinking but of the infantilism which accompanies it and the character deformities which produce it. This cannot be said, so far as I know, of any other treatment of alcohol addiction at the present time.

SUMMARY

Alcohol addiction, then, can be considered a form of self-destruction used to avert a greater self-destruction, deriving from elements of aggressiveness excited by thwarting, ungratified eroticism, and the feeling of a need for punishment from a sense of guilt related to the aggressiveness. Its further quality is that in a practical sense the self-destruction is accomplished *in spite of* and at the same time *by means of* the very device used by the sufferer to relieve his pain and avert this feared destruction.

9: DYNAMICS OF ADDICTION

Otto Fenichel

The same urge that governs other pathological impulses is operative in addicts: the need to get something that is not merely sexual satisfaction but also security and assurance of self-assertion, and as such essential to the person's very existence. Addicts represent the most clear-cut type of "impulsives."

Certain cleptomaniacs get into fatal vicious circles because their stealing gradually becomes insufficient to give relief. They have to steal more and more. These persons could be called theft addicts. Other persons are compelled violently and impulsively to devour whatever food is in reach at the moment; they are food addicts. The word addiction hints at the urgency of the need and the final insufficiency of all attempts to satisfy it. Drug addictions differ in one point from these "addictions without drugs," a point that makes them much more complicated, that is, the chemical effects of the drugs.

The usual effects of drugs used by addicts are either sedative or stimulating ones. There are many occasions in human life in which the longing for these effects may be very legitimate. If a person in such a situation uses drugs, and ceases to use them when he is out of the situation, he is not called an addict. A person suffering from pain who gets an injection of morphine has received necessary protection. Similarly, the euphoric drugs are protections against painful mental states, for example, against depressions, and are indeed often very effective. As long as the use of drugs remains purely a protective measure, there is no addiction. An addict, in contradistinction, is a person to whom the effect of a drug has a subtle, imperative significance. Initially the patient might have sought nothing but consolation; but he comes to use (or try to use) the effect of the drug for the satisfaction of another inner need. The person becomes dependent on this effect, and this dependence eventually becomes so overwhelming as to nullify all other interests. Thus the problem of addiction reduces itself to the question of the nature of the specific gratification which persons of this type receive or try to receive from their chemically induced sedation or stimulation, and the conditions that determine the origin of the wish for such a gratification.

In other words, addicts are persons who have a disposition to react to the effects of alcohol, morphine, or other drugs in a specific way, namely, in such a way that they try to use these effects to satisfy the archaic oral longing which is sexual longing, a need for security, and a need for the maintenance of self-esteem simultaneously (Radó 1926, 1933). Thus the origin and the nature of the addiction are not determined by the chemical effect of the drug but by the psychological structure of the patient (Glover 1931, 1932).

The pre-morbid personality, therefore, is the decisive factor. Those persons become drug addicts for whom the effect of the drug has a specific significance. For them it means the fulfillment, or at least the hope of fulfillment, of a deep and primitive desire, more urgently felt by them than are sexual or other instinctual longings by normal persons. This pleasure or the hope for it makes genital sexuality uninteresting for them. The genital organization breaks up, and an extraordinary regression begins. The various points of fixation determine which fields of infantile sexuality — Oedipus complex, masturbation conflicts, and especially pregenital impulses — come to the fore, and in the end the libido remains in the form of an "amorphous erotic tension energy" without "differential characteristics or forms of organization" (Radó 1926).

The previous study of impulsive behavior makes it easy to understand what kind of pleasure the addicts are seeking. Patients who are ready to give up all object libido necessarily are persons who never estimated object relationships very highly. They are fixated to a passive-narcissistic aim and are interested solely in getting their gratification, never in satisfying their partners nor, for that matter, in the specific personalities of their partners. Objects are nothing else for them but deliverers of supplies. Erogenously, the leading zones are the oral zone and the skin; self-esteem, even existence, is dependent on getting food and warmth.

The effect of the drug rests on the fact that it is felt as this food and warmth. Persons of this kind react to situations that create the need for sedation or stimulation differently from others. They are intolerant of tension. They cannot endure pain, frustration, situations of waiting. They seize any opportunity for escape more readily and may experience the effect of the drug as something much more gratifying than the original situation that had been interrupted by the precipitating pain or frustration. After the elation, pain or frustration becomes all the more unbearable, inducing a heightened use of the drug. All other strivings become gradually more and more replaced by the "pharmocotoxic longing" (Radó 1933). Interests in reality gradually disappear, except those having to do with procuring the drug. In the end, all of reality may come to reside in the hypodermic needle. The tendency toward such a development, rooted in an oral dependence on outer supplies, is the essence of drug addiction. All other features are incidental.

Analysis of drug addicts shows that genital primacy tends to collapse in those persons whose genital primacy always has been unstable. In analysis, all kinds of pregenital wishes and conflicts may reveal themselves in a confusing manner. The final stages are more instructive than the confusing pictures that appear during the process. The eventual "amorphous tension" actually resembles the very earliest stage in libidinal development, before there was any organization at all, namely, the oral orientation of the infant, who asked for gratification without any capacity for giving and without any consideration of reality. Oral and cutaneous tendencies are manifest in those cases where the drug is taken by mouth or by hypodermic injection; the syringe, it is true, may also have a genital symbolic quality; the pleasure, nevertheless, is secured through the skin and is a passive-receptive one. More important than any erogenous pleasure in drug elation, however, is the extraordinary elevation in self-esteem. During the drug elation, erotic and narcissistic satisfactions visibly coincide again. And this is the decisive point.

Various findings of other writers (Crowley 1939) can easily be brought into harmony with this formulation. According to Simmel (1930) the use of drugs at first represents genital masturbation accompanied by appropriate fantasies and contents; but later, conflicts from deeper levels of development appear, extending back to the oral stage. This corresponds to the gradual regressive disintegration of sexuality, the terminal point of which is certainly more significant than the mid-way positions. Simmel also showed that for drug addicts, the organs may represent introjected objects, which also is in accordance with an oral regression. Similarly the findings of Gross (1935), that in the addict there is a dysfunction of the superego and of other identification, are in keeping with the same point of view, for identification is the object relationship of the oral stage.

The identity of the decisive conflict explains the relation between drug addiction and the manic-depressive states. Simmel (1930) correctly designated the elation due to drugs as "artificial mania." In the final stages of their illness, drug addicts live in objectless alternating states of elation and "morning after" depression which, in the last analysis, correspond to the alternation of hunger and satiation in the mentally still undifferentiated infant.

The "morning after" depressions begin more and more to prevail in the later development of addictions. The decisive complication in the psychology of addicts is represented by the increasing insufficiency of the elation achieved. Physiological and psychological conditions, still to be investigated, negate the sufficiency or even the appearance of elation. The patient must resort to larger doses at shorter intervals. The lack of effect increases the longing. The tension, when the longing is not gratified, becomes more unbearable. Now the hypodermic needle is employed less for the purpose of obtaining pleasure but rather as an inadequate protection against an unbearable tension, related to hunger and guilt feeling.

The decrease of the effect of the drug certainly has a physiological root. But there are also psychological ones. If, after a drug elation, the same misery that initiated the use of the drug has to be faced again, it necessarily appears still more unbearable, necessitating more frequent and more intense escapes. It has also been mentioned that impulsive actions carried out for the purpose of protection against supposed dangers may become dangerous themselves, and thus a vicious circle may be created. This is what happens to addicts also. If addicts become aware of their progressive mental disintegration, they certainly perceive it as a danger; but they have no other means of meeting this danger than by increasing the amount of the drug. The idea that forcing the gods to give protection may be dangerous, and that because of this danger one has to force the gods still more, is valid for any impulse neurosis. In drug addiction, however, the idea that the protective measure may be dangerous is, for physiological reasons, a very real one. It *is* a danger; the patients become aware of it and get into an unsolvable vicious circle. The manic-depressive circle between elation and "morning after" becomes more and more irregular, the elation being shorter and shorter and eventually disappearing, the depression becoming permanent.

As to the specific effects of various individual drugs on the personality structure, the problem of a psychoanalytic supplement to their special pharmacology, in spite of Schilder's (1928) program of a "pharmacopsychoanalysis," has as yet hardly been attacked (Hartmann 1925).

The specific elation from alcohol is characterized by the fact that inhibitions and limiting considerations of reality are removed from consciousness before the instinctual impulses are, so that a person who does not dare to perform instinctual acts may gain both satisfaction and relief with the help of alcohol. The superego has been defined as the "part of the mind that is soluble in alcohol." Therefore, alcohol has always been extolled for its power to banish care; obstacles appear smaller and wish fulfillments nearer, in some persons through the diminishing of inhibitions, in others through withdrawal from reality to pleasurable daydreams.

Correspondingly the reasons for reverting to alcohol are either the existence of external frustrations, that is, states of misery one would like to forget and to replace by pleasurable fantasies, or internal inhibitions, that is, states in which one dare not act against the superego without such artificial help; among these inhibitions, depressive inclinations are of the greatest importance

When the (external or internal) misery is at an end, the drinking may or may not be at an end. Persons in whom it is not are called alcoholics. They are characterized by their oral and narcissistic pre-morbid personalities, as described above for addictions in general. However, there are a few points that are specific for alcoholism. Knight (1936, 1937, 1938) and others (Abraham 1908, Bleuler 1911, Chassell 1938, Clark 1919, Daniels 1933, Ferenczi 1911, Glover 1928, Hoch 1940, Jelliffe 1917, Juliusburger 1912, 1941, Kielholz 1930, Menninger 1938, Moore 1941, 1943, Rickman 1925, Weijl 1928) showed that in chronic alcoholics difficult family constellations created specific oral frustrations in childhood. These frustrations gave rise to oral fixations, with all the consequences of such fixations for the structure of the personality. In boys the frustrations resulted also in a turning away from the frustrating mother to the father, that is, to—more or less repressed—homosexual tendencies. The uncon scious impulses in alcoholics typically are not only oral but also homosexual in nature.

It is only necessary to call to mind the numerous drinking customs to find confirmation of this fact. That latent homosexuals, seduced by social frustrations, are particularly fond of alcohol is more probable than that alcohol through its toxic effectiveness would be conducive to homosexuality.

It is very important to determine whether a person resorts to alcohol from external or internal (depressive) distress, leaving off when he ceases to need it for this purpose, or whether his entire psychosexuality and self-esteem are governed by a desire to be elatedly drunk, or whether, finally, this desire for elated drunkenness is in danger of breaking down and the patient in "pharmacotoxic impotence" is trying to pursue an unattainable happiness.

Decisive also is whether the necessary supply is still demanded of an object, and the alcohol thus used as a means to facilitate the winning of this object, or whether the alcohol has become the supply in itself, the interest in alcohol supplanting any interest in objects.

With some degree of certainty the general behavior of the patient in relation to the environment gives an index of the extent to which his object relationships have disintegrated. Those who drink convivially with friends have a better prognosis than lone drinkers.

The periodic drinkers' disorder is constructed along the same lines as the periodicity of the manic-depressive states. When alcohol has been used for an escape from external or internal misery this misery, after the elation, seems worse.

Whereas alcohol in general helps to get rid of depressive moods that return only in "morning after" effects, in some persons it may immediately precipitate depressions. Analysis sometimes succeeds in explaining this failure of the drinker's intention in terms of his history. Any actual procurement of the needed supplies becomes a new danger or guilt. Drinking then plays the role of the "pathognomonic introjection," precipitating depressions.

Psychoses in addicts, especially alcoholic psychoses, have been but little studied by psychoanalysts (Bromberg and Schilder 1933, Kielholz 1926, Read 1920, Schilder 1928, Tausk 1915, Wholey 1917). In so far as they are of a manic-depressive nature, the psychological relationship of the two conditions suffices as an explanation; when the addiction can be looked upon as a last means to avoid a depressive breakdown, it is understandable that the breakdown occurs when the addiction becomes definitely insufficient. The uselessness of the objective world, rendered superfluous by the pharmacotoxic orientation, evidently facilitates an eventual psychotic "break with reality." Psychoses frequently begin during a period of abstinence, due to the fact that the withdrawal itself made the remainders of reality still more unbearable. In psychoses other than manic-depressive ones, it is not definitely established where the clinical symptoms originate, to what extent they are psychogenic, and to what extent organic or toxic.

In a very instructive article, Tausk interpreted alcoholic occupational delirium as the expression of sexual excitement in patients who are erotically stimulated and at the same time rendered impotent by alcohol, and who are, on deeper levels, homosexual and narcissistic.

REFERENCES

Abraham, K. (1908). The psychological relations between sexuality and alcoholism. In *Selected Papers*. London: Hogarth, 1927.

Bleuler, E. (1911). Alkohol und neurosen. *Jahrbuch für Psychoanalytische Forschungen* 3.

Bromberg, W., and Schilder, P. (1933). Psychological considerations in alcoholic hallucinations. *International Journal of Psycho-Analysis* 14.

Chassell, J. (1938). Family constellation in the etiology of essential alcoholism. *Psychiatry* 1.

Clark, L. P. (1919). A psychological study of some alcoholics. *Psychoanalytic Review* 6.

Crowley, R. M. (1939). Psychoanalytic literature on drug addiction and alcoholism. *Psychoanalytic Review* 26.

Daniels, G. E. (1933). Turning points in the analysis of a case of alcoholism. *Psychoanalytic Quarterly* 2.

Ferenczi, S. (1911). Alkohol und neurosen. *Jahrbuch für Psychoanalytische Forschungen* 3.

Glover, E. (1928). The etiology of alcoholism. *Proceedings of the Royal Society of Medicine* 21.

_____ (1931). The prevention and treatment of drug addiction. *Lancet*.

_____ (1932). On the aetiology of drug addiction. *International Journal of Psycho-Analysis* 13.

Gross, A. (1935). The psychic effects of toxic and toxoid substances. *International Journal of Psycho-Analysis* 16.

Hartmann, H. (1925). Kokainismus und homosexualitaet. *Zeitschrift für die Gesamte Neurologie und Psychiatrie* 95.

Hoch, P. H. (1940). Personality factors on alcoholic psychoses. *Psychiatric Quarterly* 14.

Jelliffe, S. E. (1917). Alcohol in some of its social compensatory aspects. *New York Medical Journal* 105.

Juliusburger, O. (1912). Beitrag zur psychologie der sogenannten. *Centralblatt für Psychoanalyse* 2.

_____ (1941). The chronic alcoholic as a neurotic and a dreamer. *Journal of Nervous and Mental Disease* 94.

Kielholz, A. (1926). Analyseversuch bei delirium tremens. *Internationale Zeitschrift für Psychoanalyse* 7.

_____ (1930). Seelische hintergruende der trunksucht. *Psychoanalytische Bewegung* 2.

Knight, R. (1936). The psychodynamics of chronic alcoholism. *Journal of Nervous and Mental Disease* 86.

_____ (1937). The dynamics and treatment of chronic alcohol addiction. *Bulletin of the Menninger Clinic* 1.

_____ (1938). The psychoanalytic treatment in a sanatorium of chronic addiction to alcohol. *Journal of the American Medical Association* 3.

Menninger, W. C. (1938). The treatment of chronic alcohol addiction. *Bulletin of the Menninger Clinic* 2.

Moore, M. (1941). Alcoholism: some contemporary opinions. *American Journal of Psychiatry* 97.

_____ (1943). A didactic note on alcoholism. *Journal of Nervous and Mental Disease* 97.

Rado, S. (1926). The psychic effects of intoxicants. *International Journal of Psycho-Analysis* 7.

_____ (1933). The psychoanalysis of parmacothymia. *Psychoanalytic Quarterly* 2.

Read, C. S. (1920). The psychopathology of alcoholism and some so-called alcoholic psychoses. *Journal of Mental Science* 66.

Rickman, J. (1925). Alcoholism and psychoanalysis. *British Journal of Inebriety* 23.

Schilder, P. (1928). *Introduction to Psychoanalytic Psychiatry*. New York: Nervous and Mental Disease Publishing.

Simmel, E. (1930). Zum problem von Swang und Sucht. Bericht uber den V. allegemeinen arzlichen. Kongress für Psychotherapie in Baden-Baden, pp. 26–29.

Tausk, V. (1915). Zur psychologie des alkoholischen Beschdefigungsdeeiirs. *Internationale Zeitschrift für psychoanalyse* 3.

Weijl, S. (1928). On the psychology of alcoholism. *Psychoanalytic Review* 15.

Wholey, C. C. (1917). Revelations of the unconscious in an alcoholic psychosis. *American Journal of Insanity* 74.

10: THE ROLE OF THE COUNTERPHOBIC
MECHANISM IN ADDICTION

Thomas S. Szasz

"Things won are done; joy's soul lies in the doing."
— William Shakespeare

INTRODUCTION

The Scope of This Contribution

A comprehensive approach to the problem of addiction would require the careful evaluation of personal constitution, genetic-and ego-psychological factors, sociological considerations and knowledge of the pharmacological effects of the drug. This breadth and complexity of the phenomenon suggests that no single "etiological factor" can reasonably be expected to "explain" addiction.

The scope of this paper is restricted to an examination of the role and significance of the counterphobic mechanism (Fenichel 1939) in some cases of addiction and to a discussion of the possible implications of this mechanism which may add to our understanding of addiction in general. Accordingly, the aim of this contribution is not to explain the "etiology" of any particular form of addiction, nor is it to attempt to present a general "theory" of this phenomenon.

Comments on the Literature on Addiction

Since we are not concerned with confirming or refuting previous suggestions about the psychological nature of addiction, no comprehensive review of the literature will be presented. Psychoanalytic contributions on this subject, for the most part, have emphasized the early history of the addict (Crowley 1939, Lorand 1945). From a metapsychological viewpoint, most attention has centered on the importance and meaning of the instinctual gratifications (i.e., the "pleasure") provided by the drug (Abraham 1908, Simmel 1948). The role of the ego in the formation and function of the symptom has received less attention. The present study represents an attempt to contribute to the latter aspect of the problem.

In the psychoanalytic literature, the ego's participation in addiction has been interpreted generally in terms of regression to primitive levels of ego development, characterized by "passive-narcissistic aims." From the viewpoint of libido development, addicts have most often been described as predominately orally fixated and thus vulnerable to regression from genital to oral mechanisms of tension discharge. Fenichel (1945) stated:

> Those persons become drug addicts for whom the effect of the drug has a specific significance. For them it means the fulfillment, or at least the hope of fulfillment, of a deep and primitive desire, more urgently felt by them than are sexual or other instinctual longings by normal persons. This pleasure or the hope for it makes genital sexuality uninteresting for them. The genital organization breaks up and an extraordinary regression begins. The various points of fixation determine which fields of infantile sexuality — Oedipus complex, masturbation conflicts, and especially pregenital impulses — come to the fore, and in the end the libido remains in the form of an "amorphous erotic tension energy" without "differential characteristics or forms of organization." . . .
>
> In the end, all of reality may come to reside in the hypodermic needle. The tendency toward such a development, rooted in an oral dependence on outer supplies, is the essence of drug addiction. All other features are incidental. [pp. 376, 377]

In addition to the erogenous pleasure (elation) provided by the drug, Fenichel also emphasized its importance in producing an elevation in the feeling of self-esteem. Similar considerations are mentioned by Lewin (1950) in his recent work on elation. He comments that: " . . .whatever the permutations in development may be, the basic identity of the manic-depressive states and pharmacothymia is now generally accepted" (p.40).

These views draw heavily on Rado's two classical papers on addiction (1926, 1933), the first of which was published fully thirty years ago.

It is important to note, however, that in his discussion of "addictions without drugs," Fenichel (1945) added that "All morbid impulses as well as addictions (with and without drugs) are, it may be stated again, unsuccessful attempts to master guilt, depression or anxiety by activity. As such they are related to counterphobic attitudes" (p. 382). Fenichel did not develop this theme. To do so is the purpose of this paper.

Source of Material and Nature of Study

The observational material of this study was derived from psychoanalytic work with three patients. One patient was an impulse-driven personality whose symptoms, among others, included addiction to alcohol and to barbiturates. The two others possessed essentially well-developed egos and showed no disturbance in their social behavior. They came for analysis because of "personal" ("characterological") difficulties. In the course of their treatment it appeared, to patient as well as therapist, that their orientation to smoking was important to them and to the work of the analysis. The clinical observations pertaining to these two patients relate therefore more to "socially acceptable" smoking than to "socially condemned" drug addiction. It may be noted that because of our interest in a particular mechanism which appeared to play a significant part in all of these patients' addictions, we have deliberately neglected (in this paper) to consider the differences between these two types of addictions.

In addition to the clinical material (to be cited), this study is based on theoretical considerations of a psychoanalytic and sociological nature. We will comment specifically on cultural orientations to drugs and to drug addiction as factors to be considered in our psychiatric theory-building relative to these phenomena.

CLINICAL OBSERVATIONS

Addiction To Alcohol and to Barbiturates

The following remarks are based on observations made during the analysis of a patient severely addicted to both alcohol and barbiturates. He did not claim to know why he took these drugs but asserted that they made him feel better. Drinking, in particular, appeared to him to be an "escape" from some of the vicissitudes of his life, much as is the general view of this matter. The general mood and pattern which characterized his use of these drugs, however, did not suggest (at least to me) that he "enjoyed" them. It appeared, rather, as if he acted under a tense compulsion, as if driven to drink by some invisible master to whom he was enslaved. It is, of course, not uncommon for patients to describe their experiences about drinking in this way. My patient never verbalized this but rather seemed to act it out.

He often drank heavily at night and also took barbiturates in order, he said, to help him fall asleep. In the course of the analysis it gradually became apparent that the facts, so to speak, were different. It should be emphasized, however, that the patient himself was not initially aware of some of the following aspects of his drinking behavior.

What we discovered in the course of the analysis was that while he thought he drank and took barbiturates in order to sleep, his behavior indicated that he *tried to resist* the natural pharmacological effects of the drugs. He would not go to bed or lie down; instead he would remain dressed, sit on the toilet, and so forth. He engaged in various activities designed to help him *fight off* sleep. Without going into further details, suffice it to say that a pattern of activity emerged which seemed to have the *meaning* of a battle: It was as if the patient was engaged in a silent struggle, testing his "strength" or "will power" against the effects of the drug. If he could stay awake, he was strong; if he fell asleep, it meant he had succumbed to his adversary, and he was weak. The most crucial aspect of the drinking and the taking of barbiturates thus appeared to lie in the very opposite of what could be called the naive conception of "wanting to forget"; *the patient took these drugs not to secure their effects but, on the contrary, in order to expose himself repetitively to their (dangerous) effects and then to resist succumbing to them.* The fear of inner weakness was one of this patient's important problems in life. He attempted to master this anxiety by varied *counterphobic* maneuvers, exposing himself to dangerous situations, hoping thereby to prove his strength.

The foregoing is not intended to imply that the patient did not derive important instinctual gratifications from alcohol and barbiturates. Without doubt, he did. I think, however, that this component of alcoholism is related to much deeper layers of the personality, that is to say, it is much more deeply unconscious or repressed than is the mechanism discussed in this paper. While it is a time-honored psychoanalytic concept that dreams and neurotic symptoms are compromise formations, in relation to the problem of addiction the weight of emphasis has tended to be one-sided, with the focus on the fulfillment of instinctual wishes. This paper may be thought of as focusing on the other half of the compromise, that is, on the ego's participation in the conflict. This aspect of the symptom lies closer to consciousness and is probably more important for therapeutic work than is the instinctual component.

From the point of view of the ego, therefore, the goal of drinking was to drink and yet to resist its effect. The anxiety which the patient tried to master related to a feeling of weakness on the part of the ego vis-à-vis the instincts, in particular the sexual drive.[1] Parallel with this feeling of weakness and fear in relation to an inner danger, the patient developed similar feelings and attitudes toward external obstacles and stresses. He dreaded being ill, being unaccepted, being thought of as a "sissy" or being a "sucker." But since he could not fight the enemy, the fear," of which he was not conscious, he displaced the battle to external situations, in the manner of counterphobic symptoms (Fenichel 1945, p. 480).

Addiction to Smoking

The smoking habits of two men in analysis for matters unrelated to smoking form the basis of the following remarks. One smoked a pipe, not to excess in the ordinary social sense, and he had no conscious preoccupation with smoking prior to his analysis. The other smoked cigarettes, averaging about one pack a day, but on some days he smoked twice as many. For some time he had felt that this was too much for him and that it resulted in anorexia, tension and coughing. He had

---

[1] I omit a psychologically more refined description of the patient's unconscious organization, particularly with respect to certain primitive aspects of the drives toward which his ego felt so feeble. The fantasies associated with sexual (and aggressive) acts, originating — generally speaking — from his childhood development, unsupported by adequate parental "care," are probably of considerable significance in accounting for the question of why the fear of inner drives was displaced and handled in the manner described. I want to emphasize again that for the sake of clarity (and brevity) I restrict my comments in this paper to observations on the *function* of addiction and omit considerations of its *origin*. In other words, I try to answer the question: "How does the symptom of addiction work?" (or, "At what does it aim? How is this achieved? And what are the implications of the success and failure of the mechanism?"). The important question, "How did the symptom *originate?*" (or, "Why specifically did this mode of behavior take place?") is touched upon but is not specifically considered.

tried to "cut down" and switched to filter cigarettes some time before coming for treatment.

The pipe smoker had a number of anxieties about his body and these formed, in part, his original motivation for seeking analysis. In the course of our work it became apparent that he regarded tobacco and smoking in a very ambivalent light: it was something at once appealing (adult, sophisticated, etc.) and dangerous. The latter thoughts were associated with the burning—and at first distinctly unpleasant—taste of the pipe and more significantly with fears of the effect of the smoking on his body (health). When he smoked he enacted what may be regarded as a symbolic drama consisting of exposing himself to a dangerous situation and feeling reassured afterwards when he "saw" that he was still uninjured. The danger to which he exposed himself was experienced and expressed in a number of different ways. They were, briefly, the following: (1) the danger associated with excessive heat (burning) and unpleasant taste; (2) the danger of tissue damage locally and generally, inside the body; the fear of inducing cancer (the patient was a well-educated person and knew of the traditional connection between pipe-smoking and oral cancer from sources long antedating the recent newspaper publicity on a related subject); (3) the symbolic danger associated with smoking, such as becoming pregnant. The foregoing three concepts of "danger" are listed in order proceeding from the most concrete and conscious to the most abstract and least conscious. I will comment further about this subsequently.

There was an abundance of clinical material, consisting both of the patient's fantasies and smoking behavior, which pointed to the conclusion that these activities formed a counterphobic mode of attempted mastery of an unconscious danger. Illustrative of the material interpreted in the aforementioned manner are the following incidents. His distaste of the burning heat of the pipe became conscious during the analysis, and this was followed by fears of leukoplakia and cancer. He attempted to stop smoking by scaring himself with fantasies of what would happen if he did not stop. This phobic attempt at control is, of course, a familiar one in patients addicted to alcohol. Hypochondriacal anxieties about the mouth and the inside of the body emerged during this phase of the analysis. It was my impression that at least some of these had been "bound" previously by the smoking. Here again the original source of the danger which was displaced onto smoking (as well as into other areas of conduct) need not concern us. What I wish to stress is simply that in this case, much as in the previous one of alcohol and drug addiction, the "symptom" did not seem to relieve tension simply by providing "oral gratification," as is often assumed and asserted.[2]

---

[2]The interpretations of addiction as instinctual gratification on the one hand and as counterphobic mastery on the other are not mutually exclusive. Which of these is more relevant may vary; the issue of mastery, for example, will probably be more important in so-called early cases of addiction or in individuals who are relatively well integrated and whose egos are still actively engaged in a struggle for mastery. In so-called deteriorated cases this mechanism may be completely absent. Furthermore, inferences from the success or failure of the symptom will provide the most valuable clues about the nature of the mechanism which activates it.

The patient who smoked cigarettes displayed an orientation to this habit which was similar in most ways to the observations noted above. In this case, the "dangerousness" of smoking as an "object" was manifested by the patient's conscious thoughts that the cigarettes were making him fatigued, interfered with his appetite and caused a cough. The need for mastery, at times in an exaggerated and counterphobic manner, was not limited to this man's relationship to cigarettes but was expressed in several other areas of conduct as well. Prominent among these was his exaggerated work pattern, which in the analysis appeared fused with the smoking in the following anxious preoccupation: "What is ruining my health—too much work or too much smoking?"

Comments

The following features are shared by all three of the foregoing cases with respect to the symptom of "addiction." The object of addiction is consciously "liked" and craved. At the same time, in part consciously but in larger part without such awareness, this object is feared since it represents (by displacement) a "phobic *object*" whose power and fearful qualities derive from other sources. The essence of the "addiction," at least in these cases, appeared to lie in the ego's *deliberate exposure to the dreaded* situation—albeit in a symbolically displaced and disguised manner—in the hope of *thus achieving mastery over it* (Fenichel 1939, Freud 1948). This mechanism is capable of accounting rather adequately for both the temporary success of the addiction and the pleasure resulting from it, as well as for its frequent ultimate failure, deriving from the splitting off of the symptom from the original source of the danger.[3] The continued unconscious activity of the latter, as in other neurotic symptoms, could be looked upon as the "cause" for the persistence of the symptom.

SOCIOLOGICAL CONSIDERATIONS

Observations from sources other than the cases cited suggest that emphasis on the importance of instinctual gratification as the central determinant in addiction may be misleading. For example, stressing the great pleasure which the addict derives from alcohol or other drugs is reminiscent of the popular belief about the unusual pleasure which "perverts" obtain from their practices. We recognize in this belief a distortion created by the observer, who reacts as does the child in the face of forbidden adult activities, like smoking, drinking and sexual activity. Not only does this result in an overestimation of the pleasure component ("forbidden fruit tastes sweeter"), but it also tends to obscure any other meaning and function of the particular activity. In the case of perversions, for example, we know that the symptom not only serves to discharge and gratify pregenital sexual impulses, but also that it functions as a defense against certain aspects of genital sexuality. Or, we could say that the patient is sexual in one way, in order not to be sexual

---

[3]Consider in this connection the insight of the poet: "Who overcomes by force hath overcome but half his foe" (John Milton, *Paradise Lost*).

in another way. Exclusive emphasis on the sexual gratification afforded by the symptom would be misleading.

Not only does the observer often bring childhood attitudes to his view of alcoholism, but so does the alcoholic, too. His relationship to the drug often is phenomenologically indistinguishable from the relationship of the child to certain types of activity, such as eating ice cream or candy. The latter foodstuffs are regarded in our culture as unusually pleasure-producing. This idea is communicated to every child, and accordingly he develops a special craving for candy. The adult world then tries to counterbalance this by admonitions about the *deleterious effects* of candy ("It's not good for you"), or by emphasis on eating it only *in moderation*. The cultural orientation to alcohol, and to narcotics in general, is clearly very similar. While we know that these notions about "pleasure" or "harmfulness" have no objective relationship to the food substances or drugs in question,[4] we recognize that in these instances we witness a struggle between the developing ego of the child on one hand and the demands of the instincts on the other. Accordingly, any control or moderation of the instinctual desire is regarded as "good" and any compliance with the need as "bad." At the same time, the child learns to feel "strong" if he can control his cravings and "weak" if he gratifies them. While these processes are experienced by all of us as children, as we grow up in the European or American culture, we sooner or later become aware of many of these fictitious notions about adult prerogatives. When the ego becomes sufficiently secure vis-à-vis the instincts, it no longer has to create such myths of temptations. Accordingly, many adults neither drink to excess nor advocate prohibition, but have an essentially neutral ("take it or leave it") attitude toward alcohol. The same may be said of such things as smoking, gambling, mountain climbing, and the like.

If the child feels threatened by a forbidden craving, one solution is to avoid it. He then develops a *phobic attitude* toward the object (of his craving); that great and evil power is attributed to the feared object is, of course, implicit in the phobic attitude. Another solution lies in denying the whole conflict, repudiating both that a craving exists and that failure to resist it is feared. The chronic alcoholic manifests both of these attitudes. He may try to deny that he has a "problem" about drinking. Even more strikingly and more often, he has a phobic attitude, revealed by resolutions to "lick this thing" (as in a fight), and "never touch it again" or to "go on the wagon."

The alleged need on the part of the alcoholic to abstain altogether from alcohol or risk a relapse is worthy of special emphasis and comment. This belief

---

[4]See in this connection the recent work of Beecher and his associates (Lasagna, von Felsinger, and Beecher 1955, von Felsinger, Lasagna, and Beecher 1955) demonstrating quite clearly that opiates, for example, do *not* invariably produce "pleasure," as commonly believed and described in textbooks of pharmacology. Glover came to a similar conclusion many years ago. He wrote: "There is now no doubt that the pharmacotoxic effects of drugs do not play such a specific part in dangerous drug-addictions as is supposed in extra-psychological circles. In certain addiction-cases where a harmless substitute was established (in one case sugar was used in this way), I have observed the same slavish compulsion attach itself to the substitute. And deprivation of the substitute loosened massive charges of anxiety" (Glover 1932, p.316).

is shared by the alcoholic, the lay public and the medical (and most of the psychiatric) profession. I wonder if this is a rational therapeutic notion, or whether it is an irrational expression of our unconscious reaction to excessive drinking. In other words, I am suggesting that the generally accepted idea that an alcoholic must not touch liquor condenses and expresses the same unconscious emotional attitudes in the general public as are reflected in the alcoholic's struggles with his symptom. This belief expresses, with the official sanction of the group (culture), the view that the alcoholic is, indeed, engaged in a mortal battle with the drug. Moreover, it acknowledges the superior strength of the adversary and abandons all hope of "winning" the battle. The only remaining solution is to strengthen the phobic defense: "If you never engage in this fight, then you will not lose; otherwise you will be defeated."

Many of the therapeutic techniques used with alcoholics, such as the conditioned reflex treatment or Alcoholics Anonymous, aim at reinforcing the phobic defense against the drug with the aid of authoritative reassurance about the value of this attitude. Prohibition, the Federal law, expressed the same attempt at a defense. At the same time it represented a reaction formation against a more subtly expressed cultural demand, namely that one is not a "real man" unless one can drink and "take it" without showing undue effects. These therapeutic orientations only serve to increase the conviction of the alcoholic, and of the general public, in the potent nature of alcohol and the myths surrounding it, mentioned earlier. While such an orientation may be helpful in achieving the desired goal, that is, abstinence, it must perforce exert an antitherapeutic bias for treatment aimed at increased insight and increased ability of the ego to deal with the conflicts.[5]

Finally, we may note that the idea that alcohol is somehow an adversary with whom one is engaged in a struggle is neither novel nor limited to our present culture. Among the nobility of medieval Europe, drinking was used much like a duel. Two or more men would drink with the explicit purpose of drinking the other fellow(s) under the table. The one who could resist the effects of alcohol the longest was considered the strongest (most masculine, etc.). In this custom, the test of strength was displaced from direct bodily contact to the intermediary of alcohol. The mechanism of addiction described in this paper is analogous to this, except that the object of addiction is used as a substitute (symbolic

---

[5]This consideration raises the question of the manner in which the therapist's understanding of the meaning and function of any symptom may influence the treatment and its outcome. While I believe there is general agreement among analysts that this is an important issue in psychoanalytic treatment, it has not received the detailed attention it deserves. Regarding the analyst's orientation toward the symptom, we may note that there are two predominant *directions*. The first tends to regard symptoms predominantly as *gratifications*, as if they aimed at *pleasure*. The other emphasizes the role of *defense against anxiety* (stimulated either by instincts or by object relationships), as if the symptom aimed at *mastery*. It appears that these divergent orientations refer to more than what is customarily thought of as the id and ego (superego) components of the symptoms. They probably reflect cultural (moral) attitudes in the analyst as well. Clarification of these issues may lead to a better understanding of the therapeutic problems traditionally associated with so-called psychopathic personalities or impulse-ridden characters.

equivalent) for an internal (instinctual) danger. The persistence of the symptom is thus inherent in the periodic recurrence of the "danger" of instinctual stimulation in the ordinary course of living.

Most of these comments apply to our orientation to alcohol and drugs rather than to tobacco. In our culture, smoking is fully "accepted" just as certain drugs are "accepted" in other cultures. A detailed consideration of the sociology of drugs is not within the scope of this paper. In this connection, it should be noted, however, that the terms "addiction" and "habit" have both technical and moral meanings: the former is used in psychiatry not only to describe certain mechanisms but it also carries the connotation of something "bad," and *ipso facto* it is more "pathological" than a "habit." This distinction, like the use of words which carry value judgments in any area of inquiry, tends to prevent a clear and unbiased analysis of the problem. In this essay, I have tried to avoid the distinction between "habit" and "addiction." I have used these terms only descriptively in order to identify certain phenomena, and I have tried to present certain psychological and sociological considerations which may further our understanding of man's relationship to smoking, to alcohol and to certain drugs.

While it probably does not require "objective" evidence to show that smoking, drinking, and taking various drugs represent, so to speak, some of the most important "object relationships" in our culture, the following documentation is of interest. According to a recent survey (What Americans spend 1955), Americans spend $8.8 billion annually on alcohol and $5.3 billion on tobacco (a total of $14.1 billion). In contrast to this huge figure for these two items alone, the total expenditure for four items related to "health" was $9.9 billion ($1.6 billion for drugs, $2.6 billion for hospital expenses, $2.8 billion for physicians' services, and $2.9 billion for "all other health care").

The object of addiction — as noted earlier — may be either culturally accepted as "normal" or it may be prohibited as "dangerous" and "morally evil." Prohibition reinforces the unconscious fantasies about the power and dreadfulness of the object and tends to make "mastery" over it more desired. Thus the very measures which are designed to combat the use of the allegedly addictive substances make their social control, in actual practice, more difficult. Social acceptance of the object, on the other hand, makes its function and its analysis more elusive, since "addiction" then constitutes one of the "normal ways of living." Various degrees and mixtures of acceptance and repudiation of different objects of addiction may be found in different societies. Our present culture, for example, completely accepts smoking and fully rejects opium, while it simultaneously stimulates, accepts and repudiates the use of alcohol. Such a multivalued and vacillating social position vis-à-vis an "addiction" renders attempts at social control practically impossible. Effective social control must, under such circumstances, wait for prior resolution of such ambivalent social orientations, in much the same way as a man must *want* to have his inflamed appendix removed before he will engage a surgeon.

These considerations, finally, lend support to the thesis that when moral judgments are disguised as psychological "knowledge," they may exert a powerfully inhibiting influence on a scientific understanding of the phenomena in question. Thus, if psychiatrists accept the socially given meaning of "addiction" and focus their studies only at the socially repudiated objects of addiction, they lend the scientific prestige of their profession in support of what would otherwise be only a social (moral) judgment (Szasz 1956).

DISCUSSION

The specific symbolic (unconscious) meaning of the object of addiction (e.g., pipe-smoking, alcohol, etc.) is, of course, determined by the historical experiences of a person together with the cultural milieu in which he lives (Menninger 1938, Thorner 1953). Still, while the fantasies concerning the "object" are in a sense unique for each person, they can be said to *represent* certain ubiquitous phenomena and processes. The chief symbolic meanings of the object of addiction seem to be the following: (1) *fear of the instincts* (or drives) (i.e., of inner excitation and helplessness) in a manner familiar to us from the theory of phobias; (2) *fantasy and fear of pregnancy*. In this context, the object of addiction represents, so to speak, the penis or "semen" and the body of the self stands for the recipient (female) object in the sexual act. Notions of being poisoned (alcohol, barbiturates, etc.) or of developing cancer (smoking) signify the dangers of mysterious processes in the depth of the body ("pregnancy"). These factors may be particularly important in men, whereas similar phobic-counterphobic oscillations with regard to food (and "being fat") may more commonly symbolize similar fantasies in women.

The basic position toward these danger situations is considered to be that of phobic avoidance. Superimposed upon it is the counterphobic mechanism which is an attempt to master the danger. The essence of this mechanism was described by Fenichel (1939) as follows: "The experience that imaginary ideas connected with a certain situation actually do not prove true, is precisely the basis of most counterphobic attitudes. The situation must be sought again and again, because although, owing to this experience, reassurance is obtained that on this occasion the imaginary expectations are not realized, it is not a final proof that they never will be realized."

At this point I would like to suggest a connection between two basic, but previously unrelated, psychological observations. One pertains to the counterphobic mechanism, which is a psychoanalytic construct embodying the idea of the persistence of the "memory" of an unmastered danger situation, together with its sequel and corollary, a chronic characterological "attitude" (or "symptom") which represents — metaphorically speaking — a frozen and equally persistent attempt to achieve belated mastery. The other observation is Zeigarnik's (1927) classic psychological work in which she showed that a person's ability to recall unfinished tasks is very much greater than his ability to recall tasks which have been successfully completed. Zeigarnik's study, it seems to me, is an incisive experimental demonstration of the same phenomenon as that formulated by psychoanalysis in the more complex clinical conception of the counterphobic attitude. The latter, however, is not only consistent with Zeigarnik's fundamental observations but also furnishes a theoretically sound and useful framework for them.[6]

In conclusion, I shall comment briefly on some inferences which may be drawn — specifically in the light of the present hypothesis — from the sequelae which often ensue from the interruption of the "symptom" of addiction.

In a general way, the functional value of alcoholism, as a defense on the part of the ego, is well appreciated by analysts and needs no special emphasis (Glover 1955). Eloquent testimony to the economic role and importance of this symptom is found in some of the consequences which follow upon its interruption. For example, the emergence of an overt psychosis is a relatively common occurrence after the use of Antabuse (Bennett, McKeever, and Turk 1951, Macklin, Simon, and Crook 1953, Usdin and Robinson 1951). It would seem that when the patient can no longer prove — even though sometimes quite unsatisfactorily — his strength against the sham adversary, the drug, he is suddenly confronted with the full force of his feelings and fears of weakness and inadequacy (passivity, femininity, etc.). The real threat (the unconscious instincts or bad internal objects) now emerges since it can no longer be held in even faulty repression, and the ego is overwhelmed and temporarily put out of action: this is the acute psychosis which was held in abeyance by the addiction.

Fenichel's (1945) interpretation of this phenomenon is as follows: "Psychoses frequently begin during a period of abstinence, due to the fact that the withdrawal itself made the remainders of reality still more unbearable. In psychoses other than manic-depressive ones, *it is not definitely established where the clinical symptoms originate,* to what extent they are psychogenic, and to what extent organic or toxic" (p. 380; my italics).

The hypothesis here proposed permits one to dispense with the postulating of unknown "organic" factors in an effort to account for the overt psychosis, as well as with the psychologically naive idea that "unbearable reality" is a cause of "psychosis." The counterphobic mechanism thus furnishes an economical (in the sense of "frugal") interpretation not only of many facets of addictive behavior but also of some of the common consequences which occur when such behavior is blocked.

SUMMARY

1. The purpose of this paper is to identify and to demonstrate the role and significance of the counterphobic mechanism in addiction. The latter term is

---

[6]Following a careful review and discussion of this work, Hilgard (1948) commented that: "The practical implications of Mrs. Zeigarnik's findings are somewhat obscure" (p. 228). There seem to be numerous aspects of psychoanalytic theory for which this work appears relevant and useful. From among these, I will mention only one, namely, that in psychoanalytic work really first-hand observations are gathered only about *unmastered* ("traumatic") situations. Observations about the past "positive" influences on the analysand's personality are, by necessity, more indirect and inferential.

used in a primarily descriptive sense and includes phenomena which are both socially accepted and repudiated.

2. The observations reported herein are based on the analytic treatment of one patient who was an alcohol and drug addict in the traditional sense of this term, as well as on observations of two men who used tobacco in a socially approved manner. In addition to the clinical material, some cultural phenomena pertaining to this problem are discussed.

3. The nature and function of the counterphobic mechanism in addiction is illustrated. The sources of the "danger" which is displaced unto, and is symbolized by, the object of addiction are discussed.

4. According to the view put forward, an important mechanism (at least in some cases) of addiction lies in the following. The symptom represents a repetitive ("dramatic") re-enactment of a situation of danger (e.g., fear of instinct, of helplessness or fearful fantasies of bodily damage in connection with pregnancy). The ego deliberately exposes itself to this situation in the hope of achieving mastery. The gratification associated with this process derives from the knowledge that one has been through the danger and has emerged unharmed. Interference with the symptom exposes the ego more directly to the underlying phobic, hypochondriacal and paranoid anxieties.

REFERENCES

Abraham, K. (1908). The psychological relations between sexuality and alcoholism. In *Selected Papers*, pp. 80–89. London: Hogarth, 1927.

Bennett, A. E., McKeever, L. G., and Turk, R. E. (1951). Psychotic reactions during tetraethyl-thiuramdisulfide (Antabuse) therapy. *Journal of the American Medical Association* 145:483–484.

Crowley, R. M. (1939). Psychoanalytic literature on drug addiction and alcoholism. *Psychoanalytic Review* 26:39–54.

Fenichel, O. (1939). The counter-phobic attitude. *International Journal of Psycho-Analysis* 20:263–274.

_____ (1945). *The Psychoanalytic Theory of Neurosis*. New York: W. W. Norton.

Freud, S. (1905). Three essays on the theory of sexuality. *Standard Edition* 7:123–243.

_____ (1920). *Beyond the Pleasure Principle*. London: Hogarth, 1948.

Glover, E. (1932). On the aetiology of drug addiction. *International Journal of Psycho-Analysis* 13:298–328.

_____ (1955). *The Technique of Psycho-Analysis*. New York: International Universities Press.

Hilgard, E. R. (1948). *Theories of Learning*. New York: Appleton-Century-Crofts.

Lasagna, L., von Felsinger, J. M., and Beecher, H. K. (1955). Drug-induced mood changes in man. 1. Observations on healthy subjects, chronically ill patients, and "postaddicts." *Journal of the American Medical Association* 157:1006–1020.

Lewin, B. (1950). *The Psychoanalysis of Elation*. New York: W. W. Norton.

Lorand, S. (1945). A survey of psychoanalytic literature on problems of alcohol: bibliography. In *The Yearbook of Psychoanalysis* 1:359–370. New York: International Universities Press.

Macklin, E. A., Simon, A., and Crook, G. H. (1953). Psychotic reactions in problem drinkers treated with Disulfiram (Antabuse). *Archives of Neurology and Psychiatry* 69:415–426.

Menninger, K. A. (1938). *Man Against Himself*. New York: Harcourt, Brace and Co.

Radó, S. (1926). The psychic effects of intoxicants: an attempt to evolve a psycho-analytical theory of morbid cravings. *International Journal of Psycho-Analysis* 7:396–402.

_____ (1933). The psychoanalysis of pharmacothymia (drug addiction). *Psychoanalytic Quarterly* 2:1–23.

Simmel, E. (1948). Alcoholism and addiction. *Psychoanalytic Quarterly* 17:6-31.

Szasz, T. S. (1956). Malingering: "diagnosis" or social condemnation? *Archives of Neurology and Psychiatry* 76:432-441.

Thorner, I. (1953). Ascetic Protestantism and alcoholism. *Psychiatry* 16:167-176.

Usdin, G. L., and Robinson, K. E. (1951). Psychosis occurring during Antabuse administration. *Archives of Neurology and Psychiatry* 66:38-43.

von Felsinger, J. M., Lasagna, L., and Beecher, H. K. (1955). Drug-induced mood changes in man. 2. Personality and reactions to drugs. *Journal of the American Medical Association* 157:1113-1119.

What Americans spend (1955). *Medical Economics*, October, p. 48.

Zeigarnik, B. (1927). Das Behalten erledigter and unerledigter Hanlungen. *Psychol. Forsch.* 9:1. (Cited by Hilgard [1948].)

APPLYING EGO PSYCHOLOGY TO
ALCOHOLISM TREATMENT
Part IV

11: THE PSYCHOANALYSIS OF PHARMACOTHYMIA (DRUG ADDICTION)

Sándor Radó

THE CLINICAL PICTURE

Clinical psychiatry regards the disorders known as alcoholism, morphinism, cocainism, and so forth — for which, as an inclusive designation, we may provisionally use the term "drug addiction" — as *somatic intoxications*, and places them in the classificatory group "mental disorders of exogenous origin." From this point of view, the process of mental dilapidation presented in the clinical picture of the addiction would appear to be the mental manifestation of the injury to the brain produced by the poisons. The investigation of the addictions has imposed upon it by this theory, as its first task, the determination in detail of the cerebral effect of the noxious substance. Ultimately, its goal would be the exact correlation of the course of the mental disorder with the toxic processes in the brain. But this investigation, especially in its experimental aspects, is disturbingly complicated by the fact that the poisons in question attack not only the brain but the rest of the organism as well; therefore, injurious effects may be exerted upon the brain by changes in other organs through an impairment of the general metabolism. The problem thus includes not only the direct influence of the poison on the brain, but also its indirect influence. It is, consequently, not remarkable that the notion that the problem of addiction is a problem of somatic intoxication has borne so little fruit.

How did it happen, then, that psychiatry became so wedded to this idea? The obvious answer is that the idea was developed because infectious diseases were used as paradigms. To be sure, one could not ignore the fact that alcohol, for example, does not "cause" alcoholism in the same sense as the spirochæte causes luetic infection. The pathogenic microörganisms attack a person quite regardless of what his wishes or purposes in the matter may be. But the drugs in question attack him only if he purposely introduces them into his body. This distinction, however, has not sufficiently affected psychiatric thinking. In psychiatry, the idea was promulgated that a certain type of "uninhibited," "weak-willed" or "psychopathic" individual happens to develop a passion for using these drugs—which means, to read between the lines, that how these substances get into the body is of no importance: the problem is scientific and worth touching only after they are inside. It must be admitted that after the drugs have made their entry, there is, unquestionably, a certain similarity to the infections. But in so far as psychological questions, such as the susceptibility of an individual to develop a craving for drugs, were broached at all, one was groping in the dark. The intoxication theory furnished no point of departure for any solution of this type of problem. Indeed, even if all the problems relating to somatic intoxication were solved, there would still be no answer to this type of question.

The psychoanalytic study of the problem of addiction begins at this point. It begins with the recognition of the fact that not the toxic agent, but the impulse to use it, makes an addict of a given individual. We see that this unprejudiced description focuses our attention on the very feature, which, under the influence of premature analogical reasoning, was permitted to fall by the wayside. The problem then presents a different appearance. The drug addictions are seen to be psychically determined, artificially induced illnesses; they can exist because drugs exist; and they are brought into being for psychic reasons.

With the adoption of the psychogenetic standpoint, the emphasis shifts from the manifoldness of the drugs used to the singleness of the impulse which unleashes the craving. The ease with which an addict exchanges one drug for another immediately comes to mind; so that we feel impelled to regard all types of drug cravings as varieties of *one single* disease. To crystallize this theory, let me introduce the term "pharmacothymia" to designate the illness characterized by the craving for drugs. We shall have occasion later to explain our selection of this term.

The older psychoanalytic literature contains many valuable contributions and references, particularly on alcoholism and morphinism, which attempt essentially to explain the relationship of these states to disturbances in the development of the libido function. Reports of this type we owe to Freud, Abraham, Tausk, Schilder, Hartmann and others in Europe, and in this country, Brill, Jelliffe, Oberndorf and others. Two definite conclusions could be drawn from these studies, namely, the etiological importance of the erotogenic oral zone and a close relationship to homosexuality. Several years ago, I outlined the beginnings of a psychoanalytic theory which aimed to include the whole scope of the problem of drug addiction.[1] Further, as yet unpublished, studies

---

[1] *The Psychic Effects of Intoxicants: An Attempt to Evolve a Psycho-Analytical Theory of Morbid Cravings.* Int. J. Ps-A. VII, 1926. Since this, I have reported the progress of my views in a number of addresses: "Drug Addiction" at the First Congress for Mental Hygiene, at Washington D.C., May 1930; "Intoxication and 'The Morning After'" at a meeting of the German Psychoanalytic Society in Berlin, November 1930; "Depressive and Elated States in Neuroses and in Drug Addiction," a lecture course at the Berlin Psychoanalytic Institute, Spring 1931.

have led me to introduce the conception of pharmacothymia, to the preliminary description of which the present paper is devoted.

Since, for our purposes, suggestions derived from the theory of somatic intoxication are of no avail, we ourselves must select a suitable point of departure, taking our bearings from psychoanalysis. Our notion that despite the many drugs there is only one disease suggests where we may begin. We must separate out of the abundant clinical findings those elements which are *constant* and determine their interrelationships empirically, and then from this material, formulate the general psychopathology, that is to say, the *schematic structure* of pharmacothymia. Generalizations which we can make in this way concerning the nature of the illness will discover for us the viewpoints and conceptions needed for the study of individual phenomena. If our outline is well founded, the more new details are added, the more will it reproduce living reality.

Pharmacothymia can occur because there are certain drugs, the "elatants," to give them an inclusive designation, which a human being in psychic distress can utilize to influence his emotional life. I have given a description of this influence in a previous communication (*loc. cit.*). Here I need only say that there are two types of effects. First, the analgesic, sedative, hypnotic and narcotic effects—their function is easily characterized: they allay and *prevent "pain."* Secondly, the stimulant and euphoria-producing effects—these promote or *generate pleasure.* Both types of effect, the pain-removing and the pleasure-giving, serve the pleasure principle; together they both constitute what may be called "the pharmacogenic pleasure-effect." The capriciousness of the pharmacogenic pleasure-effect is well known; it vitiates the best part of the experimental work of the pharmacologists. I have found that in addition to the pharmacological factors (nature, dose and mode of administration of the substance), the pleasure-effect depends essentially on a *psychological* factor—a certain active preparedness with which the individual approaches the pleasure-effect.

The thing which the pharmacothymic patient wishes the toxic agent to give him is the pleasure-effect. But this is not to be obtained without cost. The patient must pay for his enjoyment with severe suffering and self-injury—often, indeed, with self-destruction. These are assuredly not the effects desired. If, notwithstanding this fact, he clings to the use of drugs, it must be either because the pleasure gained is worth the sacrifice of suffering, or he is in a trap and is forced to act as he does.

Then we must ask: What is the nature of the psychic situation which makes acute the demand for elatants? What is the effect of this indulgence upon the mental life? What is there in it that makes the patient suffer? And why, in spite of the suffering, can he not cease from doing as he does?

The previous history of those individuals who take to the use of elatants reveals, in a general way, the following. There is a group of human beings who respond to frustrations in life with a special type of emotional alteration, which might be designated "tense depression." It sometimes happens, too, that the first reaction to the frustration takes the form of other types of neurotic symptoms, and that the "tense depression" appears only later. The intense, persistent suffering due to a severe physical illness may also lead to the same emotional state. The tense depression may change into other forms of depression; since pharmacothymia originates from the tense depression, let us designate it the "initial depression." It is marked by great "painful" tension and, at the same time, by a high degree of intolerance to pain. In this state of mind, psychic interest is concentrated upon the need for relief. If the patient finds relief in a drug, in this state he is properly prepared to be susceptible to its effects. The role of the initial depression, then, is to *sensitize* the patient for the pharmacogenic pleasure-effect. It is immaterial whether the drug comes into his hands by accident or whether it is prescribed by his physician for therapeutic purposes, whether he was induced to use it or made the experiment on his own responsibility: he experiences a pharmacogenic pleasure-effect, which is in proportion to his longing for relief, and this event frequently, therefore, determines his future fate. If the substance and the dose were well chosen, the first pharmacogenic pleasure-effect remains as a rule the most impressive event of its kind in the whole course of the illness.

We must consider the pharmacogenic pleasure-effect, particularly this maiden one, more intensively. That which makes it so outstanding, when viewed from without, is the sharp rise in self-regard and the elevation of the mood—that is to say, elation.[2] It is useful to distinguish conceptually between the pharmacogenic elation and the pharmacogenic pleasure-effect, although they merge in the course of the emotional process. The elation would then represent the reaction of the ego to the pleasure-effect. After therapeutic medication, we observe countless instances of the pharmacogenic pleasure-effect which do *not* set up an elation in the patient. It is evident that in the evolution of a pharmacothymia, it is essential that an elation should be developed. In our outline, we must confine ourselves to a description of the outspoken forms, yet we should like to emphasize that the pharmacogenic elation is a protean phenomenon. It may remain so inconspicuous, externally viewed, that a casual observer could overlook it, and nevertheless be an experience which is psychologically an elation. The elation also need not appear immediately after the first contact with the poison. The important thing is not when it is experienced, but whether it is experienced.

What happens in a pharmacogenic elation can be understood only on the basis of further circumstantial discussion.

This individual's ego was not always so miserable a creature as we judge it to be when we encounter it in its "tense depression." Once it was a baby, radiant with self-esteem, full of belief in the omnipotence of its wishes, of its thoughts, gestures and words.[3] But the child's megalomania melted away under the inexorable pressure of experience. Its sense of its own sovereignty had to make room for a more modest self-evaluation. This process, first described by Freud,[4]

---

[2]"Elation" = *Rausch*. "Elatant" = *Rauschgift*. — TR
[3]Ferenczi, S.: *Development of the Sense of Reality*. Trans. by Jones, in *Contributions to Ps-A*.
[4]Freud: *On Narcissism, an Introduction. Coll. Papers* IV.

may be designated the reduction in size of the original ego; it is a painful procedure and one that is possibly never completely carried out. Now, to be sure, the path to achievement opens for the growing child: he can work and base his self-regard on his own achievements. Two things become evident. In the first place, self-regard is the expression of self-love — that is to say, of narcissistic gratification.[5] Secondly, narcissism, which at the start was gratified "at command" with no labor (thanks to the care of the infant by the adults), is later compelled to cope more and more laboriously with the environment. Or we might put it, the ego must make over its psychology from that of a supercilious parasite into that of a well adjusted self-sustaining creature. Therefore, a complete recognition of the necessity to fend for itself becomes the guiding principle of the mature ego in satisfying its narcissistic needs, that is to say, in maintaining its self-regard. This developmental stage of the "narcissistic system" we may call the "realistic regime of the ego."[6]

There is no complete certainty that one can attain one's objectives in life by means of this realistic regime; there is always such a thing as bad luck or adversity. It is even worse, certainly, if the functional capacity of the ego is reduced through disturbances in the development of the libido function, which never fail to impair the realistic regime of the ego. The maladapted libido can wrest a substitute satisfaction from the ego in the shape of a neurosis, but then the self-regard usually suffers. An ego whose narcissism insists on the best value in its satisfactions is not to be deceived in regard to the painfulness of real frustration. When it perceives the frustration, it reacts with the change in feeling we have described as "tense depression." Of interest to us in the deep psychology of this condition is the fact that the ego secretly compares its current helplessness with its original narcissistic stature,[7] which persists as an ideal for the ego, torments itself with self-reproaches and aspires to leave its tribulations and regain its old magnitude.

At this pass, as if from heaven, comes the miracle of the pharmacogenic pleasure-effect. Or rather, the important thing is that it does not come from heaven at all, but is *brought about by the ego itself.* A magical movement of the hand introduces a magical substance, and behold, pain and suffering are exorcized, the sense of misery disappears and the body is suffused by waves of pleasure. It is as though the distress and pettiness of the ego had been only a nightmare; for it now seems that the ego is, after all, the omnipotent giant it had always fundamentally thought it was.

In the pharmacogenic elation the ego regains its original narcissistic stature. Did not the ego obtain a tremendous *real* satisfaction by mere wishing, that is, without effort, as only that narcissistic image can?

Furthermore, it is not only an infantile wish but an ancient dream of mankind which finds fulfillment in the state of elation. It is generally known that

---

[5]Cf. my article, "An Anxious Mother." *Int. J. Ps-A.* IX, 1928.

[6]"Regime of the ego" = *Steuerung des Ichs.* — TR.

[7]"Original narcissistic stature" = *narzisstische Urgestalt* — TR.

the ancient Greeks used the word "φάπμαον" to mean "drug" and "magical substance." This double meaning legitimates our designation; for the term "pharmacothymia," combining the significations of "craving for drugs" and "craving for magic," expresses aptly the nature of this illness.

At the height of the elation, interest in reality disappears, and with it any respect for reality. All the ego's devices which work in the service of reality — the ascertainment of the environment, mental elaboration of its data, instinctual inhibitions imposed by reality — are neglected; and there erupts the striving to bring to the surface and satisfy — either by fantasies or by floundering activity — all the unsatisfied instincts which are lurking in the background. Who could doubt that an experience of this sort leaves the deepest impression on the mental life?

It is generally said that a miracle never lasts longer than three days. The miracle of the elation lasts only a few hours. Then, in accordance with the laws of nature, comes sleep, and a gray and sober awakening, "the morning after." We are not so much referring to the possible discomfort due to symptoms from individual organs as to the *inevitable alteration of mood.* The emotional situation which obtained in the initial depression has again returned, but exacerbated, evidently by new factors. The elation had augmented the ego to gigantic dimensions and had almost eliminated reality; now just the reverse state appears, sharpened by the contrast. The ego is shrunken, and reality appears exaggerated in its dimensions. To turn again to real tasks would be the next step, but meanwhile this has become all the more difficult. In the previous depression there may have been remorse for having disregarded one's activities, but now there is in addition a sense of guilt for having been completely disdainful of real requirements, and an increased fear of reality. There is a storm of reproaches from all sides for the dereliction of duty toward family and work. But from yesterday comes the enticing memory of the elation. All in all, because of additional increments in "pain" the ego has become more irritable and, because of the increased anxiety and bad conscience, weaker; at the final accounting, there is an even greater deficit. What can be done, then? The ego grieves for its lost bliss and longs for its reappearance. This longing is destined to be victorious, for every argument is in its favor. What the pains of the pharmacogenic depression give birth to is, with the most rigorous psychological consistency, the craving for elation.

We obtain, thus, a certain insight into fundamental relationships. The transitoriness of the elation determines the return of the depression; the latter, the renewed craving for elation, and so on. We discover that there is a cyclic course, and its regularity demonstrates that the ego is now maintaining its self-regard by means of an artificial technique. This step involves an alteration in the individual's entire mode of life; it means a change from the "realistic regime" to a *"pharmacothymic regime"* of the ego. A pharmacothymic, therefore, may be defined as an individual who has betaken himself to this type of regime; the ensuing consequences make up the scope of the manifestations of pharmacothymia. In other words, this illness is a narcissistic disorder, a destruction through artificial means of the natural ego organization.[8] Later we shall learn in what way the erotic pleasure function is involved in this process, and how the appreciation of its role changes the appearance of the pathological picture.

Comparing life under the pharmacothymic regime with life oriented towards reality, the impoverishment becomes evident. The pharmacothymic regime has a definite course and increasingly restricts the ego's freedom of action. This regime is interested in only one problem: depression, and in only one method of attacking it, the administration of the drug.

The insufficiency of this method, which the ego at first believes infallible, is soon demonstrated by sad experience. It is not at all the case that elation and depression always recur with unfailing regularity in a cyclic course. The part that puts in its appearance punctually is the depression; the elation becomes increasingly more undependable and in the end threatens complete non-appearance. It is a fact of great importance that the pharmacogenic pleasure-effect, and particularly the elation induced by repeated medication, rapidly wanes. Thus, we encounter here the phenomenon of "diminishing return" in terms of elation. I cannot promise to explain the dynamics of this fall. It is doubtless ultimately dependent on organic processes, which are referred to as the "development of a tolerance" but which cannot as yet be given an accurate physiological interpretation. During the past years an extensive study of this problem was initiated in this country. A comprehensive report of the results arrived at so far has been published recently by the pharmacologists A. L. Fatum and M. H. Seevers in *Physiological Reviews* (Vol. XI, no. 2., 1931). A reading of this report shows that such an explanation has not yet been found. I should like to contribute a point in relation to this problem from the psychological side; namely, the assurance that in the phenomenon of "diminishing return" in elation a *psychological* factor is involved: the patient's fear that the drug will be inefficacious. This fear is analogous to the fear of impotent persons, and, similarly, reduces the chances of success even more. We shall learn, below, which deeper sources give sustenance to this fear.

The phenomenon of "diminishing return" intensifies the phase of depression, inasmuch as it adds to the tension the pain of disappointment and a new fear. The attempt to compensate the reduction of the effect by increasing the dosage proves to be worthwhile in the case of many drugs; a good example of this is morphine-pharmacothymia. With this develops the mad pursuit of the patients after the constantly increasing doses which become necessary. Moral obligations, life interests of other kinds are thrown to the winds, when it is a question of pursuing the satisfaction of this need—a process of moral disintegration second to none.

Meanwhile, crucial alterations occur in the sexual life of the patient. In order to remain within the limits of this presentation, I must restrict my remarks to the most fundamental ones. All elatants poison sexual potency. After a

---

[8]In my article, *The Problem of Melancholia* (Int. J. Ps.-A IX, 1928), I first alluded to the narcissistic nature of drug addictions.

transient augmentation of genital libido, the patient soon turns away from sexual activity and disregards more and more even his affectionate relationships. In lieu of genital pleasure appears the pharmacogenic pleasure-effect, which gradually comes to be the dominant sexual aim. From the ease with which this remarkable substitution is effected, we must conclude that pharmacogenic pleasure depends upon genetically preformed, elementary paths, and that old sensory material is utilized to create a new combination. This, however, is a problem which can be postponed. What is immediately evident is the fact that the pharmacogenic attainment of pleasure initiates an artificial sexual organization which is autoerotic and modeled on infantile masturbation. Objects of love are no longer needed but are retained for a time in fantasy. Later the activity of fantasy returns, regressively, to the emotional attachments of childhood, that is to say, to the Oedipus complex. The pharmacogenic pleasure instigates a rich fantasy life; this feature seems especially characteristic of opium-pharmacothymia. Indeed, struck by this fact, the pharmacologist Lewin suggested that the "elatants" should be named "phantastica." The crux of the matter is, that it is the pharmacogenic pleasure-effect which discharges the libidinal tension associated with these fantasies. The pharmacogenic pleasure process thus comes to replace the natural sexual executive. The genital apparatus with its extensive auxiliary ramifications in the erotogenic zones falls into desuetude and is overtaken by a sort of mental atrophy of disuse. The fire of life is gradually extinguished at that point where it should glow most intensely according to nature and is kindled at a site contrary to nature. Pharmacothymia destroys the psychic structure of the individual long before it inflicts any damage on the physical substrate.

The ego responds to this devaluation of the natural sexual organization with a fear of castration only too justifiable in this instance. This warning signal is due to the narcissistic investment of the genital; anxiety about the genital should then compel abstention from the dangerous practice, just as, at one time, it compelled abstention from masturbation. But the ego has sold itself to the elatant drugs and cannot heed this warning. The ego, to be sure, is not able to suppress the fear itself, but it perceives the fear consciously as a dread of pharmacogenic failure. This switching of the anxiety is, psychologically, entirely correct. Whoever secretly desires to fail because he is afraid of succeeding is quite right in being in dread of failure. The effect of the fear is naturally in accordance with its original intent; as we have learned, it reduces the pleasure-effect and the intensity of the elation.

By frivolously cutting itself off from its social and sexual activities the ego conjures up an instinctual danger, the extent of which it does not suspect. It delivers itself over to that antagonistic instinctual power within, which we call masochism, and following Freud, interpret as a death instinct. The ego had an opportunity to feel the dark power of this instinct in the initial depression; partly for fear of it then, the ego took flight into the pharmacothymic regime. The ego can defend itself successfully against the dangers of masochistic self-injury only by vigorously developing its vitality and thus entrenching its narcissism. What the pharmacothymic regime bestowed upon the ego was, however, a valueless inflation of narcissism. The ego lives, then, in a period of pseudo-prosperity, and is not aware that it has played into the hands of its self-destruction. The ego, in every neurosis, is driven into harmful complications by masochism; but of all methods of combating masochism, the pharmacothymic regime is assuredly the most hopeless.

It is impossible for the patient not to perceive what is happening. His friends and relatives deluge him with warnings to "pull himself together" if he does not wish to ruin himself and his family. And at the same time, the elation diminishes in intensity continuously and the depression becomes more severe. Physical illnesses, unmistakably due to the use of the poison, afflict him with pains. Since the first temptation the picture has completely changed. Then, everything was in favor of the elation, whereas now the hopes set upon it have been revealed as deluding. It might be supposed that the patient would reflect on this and give up the drug—but, no; he continues on his way. I must admit that for many years I could not grasp the economics of this state of mind until a patient himself gave me the explanation. He said: "I know all the things that people say when they upbraid me. But, mark my words, doctor, *nothing* can happen to *me*." This, then, is the patient's position. The elation has reactivated his narcissistic belief in his *invulnerability*, and all of his better insight and all of his sense of guilt are shattered on this bulwark.

Benumbed by this illusion, the ego's adherence to the pharmacothymic regime is strengthened all the more. The pharmacothymic regime still seems to be *the* way out of all difficulties. One day, things have progressed so far that an elation can no longer be provided to combat the misery of the depression. The regime has collapsed, and we are confronted by the phenomenon of the *pharmacothymic crisis*.

There are three ways out of this crisis: flight into a free interval, suicide and psychosis.

By voluntarily submitting to withdrawal therapy, the patient undertakes a flight into a free interval. It is out of the question that he is actuated by any real desire to recover his health. In those rare instances in which the patient really wishes to be delivered from his pharmacothymia, as I have occasionally been able to observe in my analytic practice, he sets great store upon executing his resolve by himself, and it does not occur to him to seek aid from others. But, if he submits to a withdrawal cure, as a rule, he wishes only to rehabilitate the depreciated value of the poison. It may be that he can no longer afford the money for the enormous quantity of the drug that he needs; after the withdrawal treatment he can begin anew with much less expense.

Since the withdrawal of the drug divests the ego of its elation—its protection against masochism—the latter can now invade the ego. There it seizes upon the physical symptoms due to abstinence and exploits them, frequently to the point of a true masochistic orgy, naturally with the opposition of the ego, which is not grateful for this type of pleasure. As a result, we have the familiar scenes which patients produce during the withdrawal period.

Suicide is the work of self-destructive masochism. But to say that the patient kills himself because of a masochistic need for punishment would be too one-sided a statement. The analysis of the suicidal fantasies and attempts of which our patients tell us, reveals the narcissistic aspect of the experience. The patient takes the lethal dose because he wishes to dispel the depression for good by an elation which will last *forever*. He does not kill himself; he believes in his *immortality*. Once the demon of infantile narcissism is unchained, he can send the ego to its death.

Furthermore, in suicide through drugs, masochism is victorious under the banner of a "feminine" instinctual demand. Remarkably enough, it is the deeply rooted high estimation which the male has for his sexual organ, his genital narcissism, which brings about this transformation and transmutes masochism into a feminine phenomenon. This sounds paradoxical but can readily be understood as a compromise. The ingestion of drugs, it is well known, in infantile archaic thinking represents an oral insemination; planning to die from poisoning is a cover for the wish to become pregnant in this fashion. We see, therefore, that after the pharmacothymia has paralyzed the ego's virility, the hurt pride in genitality, forced into passivity because of masochism, desires as a substitute the satisfaction of child bearing. Freud recognized the replacement of the wish to possess a penis by the wish to have a child as a turning point in the normal sexual development of women. In the case we are discussing, the male takes this female path in order to illude himself concerning his masochistic self-destruction by appealing to his genital narcissism. It is as though the ego, worried about the male genital, told itself: "Be comforted. You are getting a new genital." To this idea, inferred from empirical findings, we may add that impregnation biologically initiates a new life cycle: the wish to be pregnant is a mute appeal to the function of reproduction, to "divine Eros," to testify to the immortality of the ego.

The *psychotic episode* as an outcome of the crisis is known to us chiefly — though by no means exclusively — in alcohol-pharmacothymia. This is a large chapter. I can only indicate the framework around which its contents may be arranged.

The failure of the pharmacothymic regime has robbed the ego of its protective elation. Masochism then crowds into the foreground. The terrible hallucinations and deliria, in which the patient believes that he is being persecuted, or threatened — particularly by the danger of castration or a sexual attack — and the like are fantasies that gratify masochistic wishes. The masochism desires to place the ego in a situation where it will suffer, in order to obtain pleasure from the painful stimulation. The narcissistic ego offers opposition to this "pain-pleasure"; it desires the pleasure *without* pain. The wishes of its masochism inspire the ego with fear and horror. It can, to be sure, no longer prevent the eruption of the masochistic fantasies, yet it looks upon them through its own eyes. Thus, the latent *wish* fantasies of masochism are transformed into the manifest *terror*-fantasies of the ego. Now it is as though the danger proceeded from without; there, at least, it can be combated, and the terrified patient attempts to do this in the imaginations of his psychosis.

It is even worse if the anxiety which protects the ego from masochism breaks down. Then, the ego must accede to masochism. If the patient has arrived at this point, he suddenly announces his intention of destroying his genital organ or—substitutively—inflicting some other injury upon himself. He actually takes measures towards the blind execution of the biddings of his masochism; the patient's narcissism, defeated, can only insure that he will literally act blindly. It dims his gaze by means of delusion: the patient is not aware of the true nature of his masochism and refuses to recognize it. Instead, he asserts that he must rid himself of his organ because this organ is a nuisance to him, or has been a source of harm, or the like. If we read, for this statement, "because this organ has sinned against him," a path opens for the clarification of the latent meaning of this delusion. We may now compare it with another type of delusion of self-injury, in which the patient is well aware that he is engaged in harming himself yet persists in his designs nonetheless. This variant of the delusion usually appears in the guise of the moral idea of sin; the ego believes that it must inflict a merited punishment upon itself, in order to purify its conscience. The central feature in this "moralizing" type of delusional state is self-reproach. It may be assumed that in the "unconcerned" type of delusional state, previously described, the ego institutes a displacement of the guilt and directs its reproaches, not against itself, but against its genital organ. Primitive thought finds displacements of this sort very easy. We often hear small children say: "I didn't do it. My hand did it." The life of primitive peoples is replete with instances of this sort. The patient, then, is incensed with his genital organ, dispossesses it of the esteem previously lavished upon it (its narcissistic investment), and wishes to part with it. It is as though the ego said to the genital organ: "You are to blame for it all. First you tempted me to sin." (Bad conscience for infantile masturbation.) "Then your inefficiency brought me disappointment." (Lowering of self-esteem through later disturbances of potency.) "And therefore you drove me into my ill-omened drug addiction. I do not love you any more; away with you!" The ego does not castrate itself; it wrecks vengeance on its genital.[9]

In the "unconcerned" form of delusion of self-injury, the ego obviously is still experiencing an after-effect of the continuous elation; it is still "beclouded by original narcissism." To masochism—that is, to knowledge that it wishes to injure itself and that this is its sole objective—the ego is blind and deaf. It is as though, in the ego's state of grandeur, whether or not it has a genital is of no moment. The genital offended the ego—away with it!

The unconcerned type of delusion of self-injury occurs more frequently in

---

[9]In Ferenczi's ingenious theory of genitality (*Versuch einer Genitaltheorie* 1923), the author calls attention to the fact that the relationship of the ego and the genital, in spite of all interests held in common, reflects profound biological antagonisms. The ego is, after all, the representative of the interests of the "soma"; and the genital, the representative of those of the "germ plasm." In so far as the ego feels itself at one with its genital libido, its genital organ impresses it as its most prolific source of pleasure; but for an ego that wishes peace, the genital becomes merely the bearer of oppressive tensions, which the ego wishes to shake off. From these and like premises, Ferenczi infers that—in the male—the act of procreation includes among its psychic qualities a "tendency towards autonomy of the genital."

schizophrenia than in pharmacothymia. In schizophrenia, the megalomania is responsible for the fact that the ego, under pressure of masochism, undertakes so easily to inflict the most horrible mutilations upon itself, such as amputations, enucleation of the eyeball, etc. The megalomania of schizophrenia and the megalomania of pharmacothymic elation are related manifestations of narcissistic regression. The former pursues a chronic course, the latter an acute, and they differ in regard to intellectual content and emotional tone; nevertheless, they both are based upon a regression to the "original narcissistic stature" of the ego.

Masochism in pharmacothymia may be attenuated into the passivity of a homosexual attitude. This fact gives us deep insight into the dynamics of homosexuality. The pharmacothymic regime has driven eroticism from its active positions and thereby, as a reaction, encouraged masochism. The genital eroticism which is on the retreat can then with the masochism enter into a compromise which will combine the genital aim of painless pleasure with the passive behavior of masochism, and the result of this combination, in men, is a homosexual choice of object. The danger proceeding from the masochistic wish to be castrated, naturally remains extant. if it is of sufficient magnitude, the ego reacts to it with a fear of castration and represses the homosexual impulse, which afterwards in the psychosis may become manifest as a delusion of jealousy, or in the feminine erotic quality of the delusions of persecution.

The advantage of homosexuality as compared to masochism is its more ready acceptability to the ego. In overt homosexuality, the ego combats the masochistic danger of castration by denying the existence, in general, of any such thing as a danger of castration. Its position is: there is no such thing as castration, for there are no castrated persons; even the sexual partner possesses a penis. If the ego in pharmacothymia or after the withdrawal of the drug accepts homosexuality, this turn must be regarded as an attempt at autotherapy. The recrudescence of the genital function with a new aim, more readily attainable, psychologically speaking, permits the ego to return to, or fortify, the "realistic regime." After being reconciled to its homosexuality, the ego can subsequently take a new reparative step toward masculinity by progressing from a passive homosexual to an active homosexual attitude. Thus, male heterosexual normality is changed into active homosexuality by a three-stage process: (1) weakening of genital masculinity (because of intimidation due to threats of castration, diversion of the libido into the pharmacothymia, etc.) and a corresponding reactive increase in the antagonistic masochism; (2) the confluence of genital pleasure and masochism in the compromise, passive homosexuality; and (3) the development of homosexuality from the passive to the active form as the result of a vigorous reparative action on the part of the ego. In corroboration of this idea is the finding, hitherto neglected, that the homosexuality which the ego rejects and combats by the formation of delusions (symptoms) is always passive homosexuality. These facts help to clarify clinical manifestations that appeared obscure and complex. Obviously, the ego may have become homosexual, because of analogous circumstances, even before the pharmacothymia began.

These views, as I have presented them here, seem to me to throw new light upon the problem of the relationship between homosexuality and pharmacothymia. The homosexual background became evident to psychoanalysis, first in alcoholism, later in cocainism, and finally in morphinism. Since I attribute homosexuality to the influence of masochism, and since, furthermore, every type of pharmacothymia attacks genitality and by reaction strengthens masochism, the opportunity to effect this compromise must naturally be present in every case of pharmacothymia.

The love life of pharmacothymics may present pathological features other than homosexuality. These all derive from the basic situation described above, in my outline of the development of homosexuality, as "stage (1)." The pharmacothymic whose potency is debilitated by masochism may find ways of preserving his heterosexuality. In the first place, he may choose another compromise solution and become oriented passively towards *women*. This erotic position is quite unstable; but it can be reenforced, by an infusion of fetishism, to withstand the onslaught of castration anxiety. With the aid of the fetishistic mechanism, the beloved woman is in imagination transmuted into the possessor of a penis and elevated to take the place of the "phallic mother."[10]

With this alignment of the instincts, the persons chosen as objects are, by preference, women who have a prominent nose, large breasts, an imposing figure, or, too, a good deal of money, and the like. Correlated with this, the emotional tone in regard to the genital region of women is disturbed by a sort of discomfort, and the patient assiduously avoids looking at it or touching it. In mild cases of pharmacothymia, this passive orientation towards women with its fetishistic ingredient often plays a major role, but its distribution is by no means restricted to pharmacothymia. A further intensification of the masochistic wish to be castrated, or better, of the fear of castration aroused by this wish, then forces the patient either to be abstinent or to follow the homosexual course and exchange the partner without a penis for one who possesses a penis. (See "stage (2)" described above.) In the second place, the ego may refuse to adopt as a solution the compromise of any passive orientation; it may respond to the danger proceeding from the masochistic instinct by a reaction formation. It is no easy task to divine what special conditions enable the ego to react in this way. But at any rate, the means used by the ego are the strained exertion of its pleasure in aggression. Sadism is rushed to the rescue of imperiled masculinity, to shout down, by its vehemence, fear of castration and masochistic temptation. In this case, too, heterosexuality is preserved, but the ego must pay for this by entering the path of sadistic perversion. In the dynamics of the perversion of sadism, the *vis a tergo* of masochism is the crucial factor; in its construction, infantile and recent experiences are jointly effective, in the usual familiar manner. The appearance of this variant, that is, the production of a true sadistic perversion, is not, to be sure, promoted by the pharmacothymia. I recognized this mechanism in non-pharmacothymic cases, and I have mentioned it here only

---

[10]Freud: "Fetishism." *Int. J. Ps-A.* IX, 1928.

because it may furnish us with the explanation of a conspicuous deformation of the character, which may be considered a counterpart of the perversion of sadism, and which often may be found in pharmacothymia. Particularly in drunkards, we are familiar with aggressive irritability, with unprovoked outbursts of hate or rage against women, and the like, which in apparently unpredictable fashion, alternate with states of touching mollification. We can now understand that the accesses of brutality are the substitutes for potency of the pharmacothymic who is fighting for his masculinity, and that his sentimental seizures are eruptions of the masochism which his pharmacothymia has reactively intensified.

Pharmacothymia is not ineluctably bound to this basic course with its terminal crisis. Many drugs, especially alcohol, admit of combating the recurrent depression by overlapping dosage. The patient takes a fresh dose before the effect of the previous one has ceased. If he does so, he renounces "elation" in the narrower sense of this word; for elation is a phenomenon dependent on contrast. Instead, he lives in a sort of "subdued continuous elation" which differs from simple stupefaction probably only because of its narcissistically pleasurable quality. This modified course leads through a progressive reduction of the ego to the terminal state of pharmacogenic stupor. A flaring up of the desire for a real elation or other reasons may at any time bring the patient back to the basic course with its critical complications.

This sketch of the theoretical picture of pharmacothymia roughly outlines the broad field of its symptomatology. One thing remains to be added. In more severe, advanced cases, symptoms appear which are the result of cerebral damage, and which are consequently to be interpreted with due consideration of the point of view of brain pathology. In this, we may expediently make use of the psycho-physiological point of view introduced into psychopathology by Schilder with the concept of "inroad of the somatic" ("somatischer Einbruch"). If the poisons consumed have damaged the brain substance, and permanently impaired cerebral activity, this is perceived in the mental sphere as a disturbance of the elementary psychological functions. The psychic organization reacts with an effort to adapt to this fact and correct the result. It is well to differentiate the phenomena which originate in this way, as the "secondary symptoms" of pharmacothymia, from those "primary" ones which we have been considering. The secondary symptoms are more characteristic of the brain lesions which determine them than of the illness in which they appear. This can be seen in the example of the Korsakoff syndrome, which occurs in other conditions as well as in pharmacothymia.

Finally, it might be pointed out that in addition to full-blown pharmacothymia there are obviously abortive forms of this illness. The patient may, generally speaking, retain the realistic regime, and use his pharmacothymic regime only as an auxiliary and corrective. He desires in this way to make up for the uncertainty in his realistic attitude and cover a deficit by means of counterfeit. By easy transitions we arrive at the normal person who makes daily use of stimulants in the form of coffee, tea, tobacco, and the like.

12: THE PSYCHOGENESIS OF ALCOHOLISM

Paul Schilder

In order to understand the psychogenesis and the psychodynamics of alcoholism, one has to understand the effects of alcoholic intoxication. What happens when an individual is intoxicated? The experimental literature has lately been reviewed by Jellinek and McFarland (1940), who come to the conclusion that alcohol has a depressing effect on all psychological functions yet measured and that such stimulation as has been reported for some psychological variables is a pseudostimulation. The psychological picture of the effect of alcohol is one of reduced efficiency. The simple psychological functions are less affected than the complex ones. Their ability to judge relations and to grasp contents suffers greatly under the influence of alcohol. The associations are impoverished and there is a tendency toward egocentric forms. The authors come to the conclusion that the main effect of alcohol is cortical with an added peripheral effect. The experimental results concerning the influence on volition, emotion and personality are very meager.

However, people do not drink in order to produce an impairment in cortical function or to reduce their critical faculty, but they drink in order to feel differently. We are accordingly chiefly interested in the emotional manifestations of alcoholic intoxication. We have to turn to clinical experience. Fleming (1935) has collected the material on acute alcoholic intoxication. There is no question that the higher degrees impair perception, judgment and motor function. With the increase of intoxication the functions of perception and judgment become more and more outspoken. However, the fundamental change is the change in mood. There is, at first, euphoria and increased confidence in one's mental and physical powers. If the intoxication progresses, lack of judgment combines with the increased feeling of one's own importance and actions occur which show the weakening of inhibitions.

A description like this leads to the fundamental problem. In acute alcoholic intoxication one can love oneself. One has the feeling that one is good, both morally and intellectually. Accordingly, one is ready to receive the love of others and one feels loved more. The term "love" means not only sexual desirability but also admiration and appreciation. One becomes a valuable citizen. Hand in hand with this increased esteem of one's own person goes an increased love toward others to whom one is ready to grant love, appreciation and admiration. The appreciation of one's own conversation and intelligence increases irrespective of the objective impairment of judgment. When the individual feels so valuable, there is no need of controlling one's activities. Free rein is given to impulses, especially the sexual ones. There is no doubt that the individual who is drunk has not completely lost the awareness that his claims for eminence and gratification are not justified in reality. There is an underlying anxiety which leads to an increased emphasis on one's claims and even to irritability and pugnaciousness. There is clinical evidence of a fundamental change in sexual attitudes. The sexual desire is increased. Sexual wishes, otherwise hidden, come into the foreground and find more or less open expression. The forms of sexuality that appear are very often of a more or less primitive character. There is no interest in finer differentiations and even infantile forms of sexuality may prevail.

It is vain to speculate whether the impairment of judgment and reality sense in general, with the lessening of one's critical faculty, liberates the sexual tendencies, or whether alcohol as such has a direct influence on the sexual structure. Dynamically speaking, alcohol produces a change in the relation between the ego and the id. One may say that the function of the superego is impaired. Simmel (1929) is credited with the remark that alcohol dissolves the superego. However, such formulations are very unsatisfactory since they neglect the finer psychological structures and lead especially away from the all-important concrete situations of life. With the progress of the intoxication and its aftereffects, the individual is more and more overcome by the insight that he really does not deserve love and appreciation. The euphoria changes into the feeling of depression and worthlessness.

The intoxications vary, not only in degree but also in quality, according to individual differences and according to the changes of the total situation in a single individual. However, it seems that we always deal with the same basic picture and that merely the accent on the different facets of the intoxication varies. The same is true about the problem of tolerance. There is no doubt that besides the psychological factors, physiological factors are of importance for the difference in the pictures of acute alcoholic intoxication.

The so-called pathological intoxication occurs in individuals with labile perceptive (cortical) mechanisms. Difficulties in perception, memory disturbances and violent outbursts resulting from confusion are in the foreground. These types have a close clinical relation to epilepsy and head injury. The intoxication releases a dissociation in cortical function. The effects of alcoholism will be different in such a change of the total situation. This is by no means merely a sum of two psychopathological disturbances, but an interaction which forms a new unit.

The so-called pathological intoxication is merely an exaggerated expression of the fact that alcoholic intoxication does not occur in the ideal average person, who obviously does not exist, but in a specific individual who lives in a specific life situation. One may expect that a tendency to self-depreciation, and a feeling of not being loved and not deserving love, will enhance the pleasure of feeling sure of one's own esteem and of the esteem of others in the acute intoxication. This surmise is amply substantiated by clinical experience. The return to soberness will be particularly bitter in such cases—the "blues."

One may expect that individuals with reasonable self-assurance will enjoy the intoxication without having a definite need for it.

One will expect that people of cyclothymic temperament as well as many depressives will show a comparatively strong reaction in the intoxication since their basic psychology has so many relations to the problems of love and self-esteem.

There is no deeper relation between the paranoid attitudes of individuals who live in tense relations with the outside world and the psychological effects of alcohol. The alcoholic intoxication is therefore generally uneventful. The same is true regarding the fantastic dreamer and the schizophrenic.

Individuals who are accustomed to fight against their drives and urges, and who have repressed strong sexual urges persistently, will enjoy the release offered by intoxication and will express sexuality with gusto. One can make similar statements about those who have been persistently careful not to experience hate and have otherwise conformed to social properties such as tact, cleanliness and orderliness. However, it seems that obsessional types with their deeper destructive hate do not find any particular gratification in the alcoholic intoxication. The hate to which I have alluded is a hate closely related to the fight of social ambitions and maintenance of prestige.

The general principle involved allows, therefore, a unified approach to the problem of individual differences in the acute intoxication.

Acute alcoholic intoxication in the individual who drinks regularly, and in the individual who generally does not drink, is certainly not identical. We have very little evidence as to what happens psychologically in an individual who is intoxicated often and intensively. We may surmise that we deal then with an individual whose perceptive and thinking apparatus is dulled and whose emotions are more and more pressed into a pattern of striving for admiration and appreciation which he can gain subjectively and objectively only by being intoxicated. The underlying insight of this very deficiency will make him crude, irritable and overbearing and the characteristics of the bully will come more and more into the foreground.[1] I may also mention that the physical signs of acute alcoholic intoxication are different in persons who are chronic alcoholics. There exists, for instance, the type of coarse tremor which occurs only in the acute intoxications of the severe chronic alcoholic.

---

[1] It is not our problem to decide whether this progressive "alcoholic deterioration" is due to the cumulative effect of alcohol on the brain, or whether the varied vitamin deficiencies play an important role here.

I cite here three cases of so-called alcoholic hallucinosis.[2]

The first one is a forty-year-old man who has been repeatedly admitted to psychiatric institutions because of alcoholism. He has been drinking for twenty years. His childhood was sheltered and strictly supervised. His marriage was unsatisfactory. There was a passing episode of impotency. In the course of heavy drinking he saw himself in a bus surrounded by men and women trying to stab one another. He himself felt threatened and hit them over the head with a bottle thus defending himself until the Naval Intelligence Service would arrive. This was an optic dreamlike experience which faded indeed from reality as a dreamlike memory. It seems that the patient had some concern regarding his regained potency which he wanted to utilize in a second marriage. The problem, which should be an individual one, becomes the problem of a general mix-up in which persons of the same sex participate as well as persons of the opposite sex. The social situation is obviously filled with fear and he maintains the role of the eminent hero with some difficulty. One has the impression that there is always some correlation between the problems of social prestige and physical attachments to persons of the same sex.

The second case is a thirty-one-year-old man who heard that a daughter in the apartment nearby had sex relations with a boy and was surprised by her mother, who felt that the patient was responsible for it. The patient, a chronic alcoholic for ten years, had been on a spree since his sister's marriage several weeks before. The hallucinatory episode expresses seemingly incestuous desires concerning his sister, otherwise hidden before himself. The patient is very proud that he has so many friends. His sex activity, however, is limited. The psychotic episode can just as well be termed a pathological intoxication as an alcoholic hallucinosis and helps to a distorted breaking through of incestuous impulses.

The third case is a thirty-nine-year-old alcoholic of long standing who had attempted to jump into the East River. He had heard voices threatening to shoot him in the chest and in the legs; the President and the Mayor were talking about him, discussing a plan for his execution. He was also supposed to meet President Roosevelt on a boat where he was to get his final citizenship papers. This is more or less a typical case of alcoholic hallucinosis. He is in the center of the social situation and goes through something which is comparable to a distorted and terrifying initiation rite. The community insists upon shooting him or, in the terminology of Bromberg and myself (1933), he is about to be dismembered. Interestingly the shots are aimed all around his genitals, but not at the genitals themselves. This is somewhat contrary to the usual picture in which the castration is very often the main motive. Nevertheless, it is the same problem which can be characterized as the idea that the community will demand the sacrifice of the integrity of the body and especially of the sex parts which have sinned. Indeed, the alcoholic has not reached the sexuality socially demanded, the durable heterosexual attachment. Caught in problems of prestige, inferiority

---

[2]These cases were presented by Dr. Leo L. Orenstein at the Society of Clinical Psychiatry, November 12, 1940.

and superiority, self-esteem and social esteem, he has often found himself in close relation to persons of the same sex with whom he may even have had sexual contact in early childhood and later. He may at least have wished so. His early education may have deterred him from sexuality in general. This has led him to an insufficient heterosexual adjustment. This is followed by impulses of a lower sexual order, urethral, anal, oral, sadistic and homosexual, which obviously cannot be tolerated by an individual conscious of his social obligations. The newly gained insight that heterosexual adaptation is demanded is not strong enough to overcome the severe feelings of guilt which were connected in childhood with every sexual activity due to faulty education. The description of these processes is rather uniform in the modern literature on alcoholism which has been collected by Crowley (1929). The studies by Wall (1936, 1937) and Curran (1937) are of particular importance from our point of view. Curran formulates as follows:

A strong attachment to the parent of the same sex, strong Narcissism and strong inner tensions making the social contact difficult, are the outstanding features in alcoholic women. Alcoholic women are always striving for social recognition and fear that this will not be given. In their acute psychosis they often experience an attack of criticism from others, which is a projection of the self-criticism which is at the base of their social shyness. The alcoholism also influences their aggressive and sadistic tendencies, so that in the acute hallucinosis they believe relatives or others have been killed off. The alcoholics experience feelings of sexual inferiority and project it in hallucinations to the outside world.

The results of Wall are basically similar. It is obvious that the correlation between these findings concerning the character structure of alcoholics and the experiences in the acute intoxication is a very close one, if we put the increased wish for admiration and love which is increased in the potential alcoholic into the foreground. The alcoholic intoxication gives to the socially insecure individual the fulfillment which he desires. With these statements we have already approached the central problem in the psychodynamics of the chronic alcoholic. It becomes obvious that the central social problem of an alcoholic transgresses the boundaries of homosexuality. The struggle for prestige and the close attachment to the person of the same sex, especially the parent of the same sex, also evokes sexual repercussions. Sexual attachments of this type will lead in turn to prestige problems even if the homosexual attachment came from other sources. However, as mentioned above, the possibility that the alcoholism, as such, disturbs the libidinous balance must be very seriously considered. It is an interesting thought, which cannot be substantiated at the present time, that human beings choose for addiction drugs which physiologically will increase tendencies previously present. Homosexuality can be almost experimentally produced by cocaine intoxication which in turn is mostly resorted to by those with latent homosexual cravings. Hartmann (1925) presents clinical evidence which makes a similar relation between the organic influence of alcohol in sexuality and the so-called psychological processes appear plausible. The formulations given so far make it clear that placing the emphasis in alcohol on oral and anal libidinous trends cannot exhaust the problem. It seems more or less accidental that the alcoholic ingests the alcohol by mouth and the satisfaction received from drinking has no deeper relation to the oral gratification of eating. Radó (1926) has spoken of alimentary orgasm. This concept does not only overrate the oral libidinous gratification of alcoholics, but also the libidinous gratification connected with the process of eating. However, in a later paper (1933) he justly stresses the complicated dynamics of the tense depression which results from frustration and drives the ego to a desire to return to a stage of magic omnipotence. This formulation considers the problem too much from the point of view of the isolated individual and neglects the social aspects. The social aspects occur twice in the psychology of alcoholism. The alcoholic primarily has deep relations to the society around him and is at least psychologically in continuous contact with it. I think this is even true concerning the lonely drinker, although I have never had the opportunity of analyzing one. He furthermore commits a social act in drinking and is fully aware that he needs an agent which acts in reality, namely the drug, for the fulfillment of his desires. To stress the self-destructive tendencies of alcoholism, as Karl Menninger (1938) does, overlooks the deep striving of the alcoholic to be loved and appreciated by society, which would grant to him the integrity of his body and his sex parts. He merely feels that without alcohol he will also be exposed to criticism and destruction. It is true, however, that in the deeper layers the alcoholic experiences the striving for prestige as a struggle for life and death. He may feel that by incapacitating himself by alcohol he may gain a greater claim for mercy.

The problem remains, which are the forces which give to the individual the feeling of such a deep-seated social insecurity? The answer has always been sought in the individual history of the patient. Knight (1937a,b) and Chassell (1938) discuss similarly, like Wall and Curran, the family situation of the alcoholic. They stress the inner need to be loved by the parent of the other sex, if the parent of the same sex is overaggressive and severe. The alcoholic strives to restore his sex value and his strength in connection with the restoration of his prestige. However, we have less evidence in this respect concerning women. According to the material of Curran (1937) it seems that they maintain great pride in their body, not only concerning strength, but also concerning general function and beauty.

These general remarks may help us in the understanding of cases which have been studied from the point of view of psychogenesis.

Frank R. is a man of forty-one of Irish descent and a Catholic. He is married; has a boy of five and a girl of ten. He is particularly attached to the boy. The sex relations with his wife are satisfactory. However, he is not enthusiastic about them. He is a lawyer of great capacities who worked at first in a firm where the somewhat older employees used to drink. He finally decided that he would not drink continually, but would merely have an alcoholic bout in space intervals. However, these bouts became more and more frequent, until they finally impaired his position and drove him into an independent position in which he was successful until he endangered it again by periods of drinking.

After laborious work, failure or success, more often after failure in court, he decided to refresh himself by only one drink. Having once started, he drank continually, did not come home, drove wildly, picked up women without caring very much what they were like, was rather reckless in having sex relations with them and finally had to be picked up in hotels, completely drunk, psychotic or stuporous. He was generally a very meticulous and clean person and an overcareful dresser. He was very polite and was overcareful in everything. When he had sex relations with his wife he was very careful that he should not be disturbed by the least suggestion of uncleanliness either on his or her part. The preparations for this took almost an hour and he was very often too tired to go through the somewhat complicated procedure. There is no question that his sexual and social behavior during the alcoholic intoxication were the complete reversal of his usual attitudes. In the psychotic episodes he dreamed of machinery falling on one of his children and of big horses jumping on him. One of the dreams which he had after such a spree is remarkable. He saw colored laughing faces which looked like little artists' models in red and yellow. "They were grotesque and in different shapes. They came close to my bed. There were scattered colors and movements. A theatrical village appeared. There were phony Chinese and Italians with hatchets and beams battling each other. People were cut up; horses and a big bull ran away. I ran up a flight of stairs, afraid to be crushed." The patient had been afraid throughout his whole childhood. He was afraid of being attacked by others who were fighting. He was afraid of horses. He was afraid of fights in general. This was partially due to the fact that he was always very tall and felt that he would not gain any social prestige if he were to win and that he would lose prestige if he did not win. In addition to this, he was continuously cautioned by his father to be careful, and he was beaten by his father whenever he had an accident. He practiced the same method with his own children. The motive of prestige was one of the leading motives in his entire life. He came from a very large family in which he was the second oldest. His father was strict and his mother also enforced discipline. He was beaten, for instance, by his mother when he was five when he left a smaller child alone. He saw his father drunk rather often. He had to start working very early; responsibilities were very soon thrust upon him. However, due to his intelligence, he assumed leadership, inside and outside of the family, very early and even threatened to hit a younger brother with a hammer when he resisted him. He very often induced other children in school to do what he organized. At the time of treatment he was also very active in all kinds of organizations. In spite of this he was always a failure in dramatic plays and in debating societies. In spite of being an excellent talker at the present time he always had to take careful notes when he talked and felt rather insecure. He always wanted to be a good baseball and football player. However, he was always afraid of getting hurt. It is interesting that in spite of his fear of accidents from earliest childhood on, he is decidedly traumatophil and has had a great number of minor as well as major accidents. He was always afraid of criticism and when a teacher proved to be unsympathetic to him, he started with long periods of truancy. It may be worth-while mentioning that during his sober periods he was also very particular concerning food. Since he was not allowed to eat candies as a child he had an enormous urge for them and overate them whenever he had the opportunity. He had some disgust concerning food which was shiny, such as butter.

The details of this case history could be easily multiplied. However, the basic pattern is obvious. A child rather harshly treated and restricted in sex develops a particular interest in prestige, shows outbursts in fighting against everything which he is supposed to do, but feels threatened continually, taking over some of the fears of his father whom he later on also imitates in drinking. Prestige and fight, particularly with persons of the same sex, and the change between the utmost consideration for social order and a complete neglect of it, are the outstanding features. His interest in women is restricted to rather a primitive type of sexual gratification. Psychogenesis of his alcoholism out of the family constellation and the social constellation is obvious. In the single bout he rebels against the restriction imposed upon him. There is fighting in some of the psychotic episodes; there is no breaking through of homosexuality in the libidinous sense and there is very little indication of an increase of homosexual tendencies in early childhood. Alcohol is here a release. He feels that he will not be condemned even if he does let out his reckless and sexual tendencies. The family factors and the social factors are of equal importance. It is remarkable that his father and his superiors were alcoholics. The alcoholic is socially sensitive and for this reason the social customs change the type of drinking. It is also in connection with this fact that there are fewer women alcoholics and fewer Jewish alcoholics.

I have observed a similar type of drinking in a thirty-year-old lawyer of good intelligence in whom social shyness was in the foreground. He has a very severe conscience, which is due to a very rigid education, especially in relation to sex problems. His feelings of inferiority extend particularly to his body. Drinking relieves him from an ever present social tension and allows a casual sex contact of which he would otherwise be afraid. In his early sex history, urination and defecation played an important part (the previous patient had continued bed-wetting for a long time). He urinated with other children repeatedly and was discovered and punished. He wets the bed when he is drunk.

The punishment consisted of spanking the bare buttocks. They said it hurt them more than it did him. He yelled loudly when spanked. Everything was forgiven after the punishment. He always felt that he was socially not popular enough. He always wanted to be praised for his looks, wanted to be well built and wanted to stand out in sports. He wanted to be intellectually brilliant and to be praised for this. He felt that he was disliked in high school as a sissy. His parents warned him particularly against drinking. He was always afraid to look into the eyes of people, particularly his mother's, after masturbation or intercourse. He prefers to blame himself for his drinking and for his sex activities and blames the alcohol for his sexuality. He is very much concerned about his body. He was always worried that his parents lacked social graces. In this patient, the alcoholism was less important than his social fears. However, unquestionably the social neurosis has a close relation to alcoholism since alcohol is, as mentioned, specific in relieving social tensions.

It seems doubtful whether drinking may not serve different purposes. Berm, a man of thirty-one years, drinks rather heavily; he always had a very high opinion of himself. However, he felt continually mistreated by his father, who also mistreated his mother. Both father and mother showed, from his earliest childhood on, an enormous interest in the alleged masturbation of the boy. Since he was born after a mentally deficient sister, his mother gave him an extraordinary amount of attention. However, he was beaten by his mother as well as by his father; he was especially threatened repeatedly by the latter. Around puberty his sexuality developed, a decidedly masochistic trend which persisted. He is intellectually vain and wanted to be considered as intelligent. He worked only very irregularly and drank excessively without being strictly an alcoholic. One may expect that his drinking allows him to maintain his feeling of intellectual superiority and gives him the feeling that he can hold his own in relation to his father and mother. The sexual conflict is more manifest in this case. However, even in such a case, which seems to differ so much in structure from the other cases, the prestige problem in relation to his family plays the leading part in his drinking. This prestige seeking is the counterpart of a deeply masochistic attitude acquired by the family situation.

We deal with variations of the same basic motive and it does not seem necessary, from our point of view, to assume as varied a genesis of alcoholism as Seliger (1938) has stated. One may, of course, list many apparent reasons for drinking. From a general point of view, I would not think that such a well-characterized picture as chronic alcoholism should not have a psychogenesis in which basic features are common in spite of all kinds of variations. I have observed, with Dr. Keiser, the following case, which I report in the formulation of Dr. Keiser.

L. R. is a white man of thirty-five, married twice (divorced from his first and separated from his second wife), and an artist by occupation. On admission he was acutely alcoholic and had a three inch laceration at the base of the penis with two healed scars distal to it. The history revealed that he had been drinking and on awakening had found his penis cut. This had happened on two previous occasions and he believed they were self-inflicted since he had been alone. There was a persistent denial of ever having had a delirious or hallucinatory episode. No signs of such a state were ever found despite several subsequent admissions for alcoholism. No explanation was ever offered by him for his actions.

When sober he was shy and ill at ease and had a tremendous sense of guilt. This sense of guilt had been with him since early childhood and arose out of his father's harsh and punishing attitude toward him. When alcoholic he was witty and friendly and would lose all his self-consciousness. However, he would seduce the wives of his friends, for which he would suffer with a great intensification of his guilty feelings. He relates many memories concerning feelings of inferiority, both physically and mentally. Following intercourse with his wife he invariably felt ashamed and guilty, though he claimed to have satisfactory potency.

There had never been any special preoccupation with sex, death or suicide.

The patient had written a detailed report about his early memories. They consisted mostly of being slapped or scolded or derided by his father. The following is typical. (Age five or six): "I had a whistle and I allowed a colored boy to blow it. My father whipped me for this. I was always punished bodily; never sent to bed or deprived of meals. My father would slap my face with his open hand. I did not resent it, but accepted it as a matter of course." When asked about his feelings of guilt, he wrote: "This is difficult for me to write about or explain. Neither can I determine if the feeling is of guilt, or shame, or embarrassment, or a sense of inferiority, or of a combination of these. As far back as I can remember I was never free of this feeling. Punishment does not seem to have had as much to do with this feeling as being ridiculed or laughed at, which my parents and others often did. When very young, I was ridiculed for physical weakness, cowardice, misfit clothing, and many other things. I made good marks in school, so my schoolmates called me 'teacher's pet.' This made me feel guilty."

It would appear that his attempt at self-castration was a gesture to regain the passive state into which his father had forced him. At the same time it satisfied his guilt feelings toward his father in regard to his homosexual love for him. It also serves as a punishment for his incestuous desires as indicated in his repeated seductions of his friends' wives.

In contrast to the other patients this patient gives in to his desire for passivity in his alcoholic state. However, the family problems of prestige and social shyness are again outstanding. He owes his success with his friends' wives to the increased self-confidence in the first stages of his alcoholism.

In men and women the fear of loss of sexual prestige may become of paramount importance. In Edith, a thirty-three-year-old very good looking woman alcoholic, this motive comes out in voices which call her hermaphrodite, "which would be the same thing as homosexual, which certainly would be one form of split-personality unless it was natural." This patient reported that she remembers that at four or five she hid under a woodpile and masturbated. However, she told that her mother had always told her that she had masturbated since her birth. She had a very extensive and promiscuous sex life and "I have not fulfilled my duties as a citizen. I feel sometimes not worthy to talk to others. It is exactly like when my mother told me at the age of five that I would be like a defective woman who could not walk and floundered along with the help of one or more nuns." The mother accused her father very often. She had separated from him when the patient was around seven. It is not necessary to add further details since sufficient material can be found in the case histories reported by Curran.

There is a tendency to believe that the drinking of psychotics has mechanisms fundamentally different from the mechanisms discussed here. However, the drinking of psychotics, even of schizophrenics, is comparatively rare and can be understood on the basis of mechanisms very similar to the mechanisms discussed here, which are in connection with the particular personality structure of the psychotic individual. This at least is the impression I have received from the clinical observation of schizophrenic alcoholics. However, I have never analyzed cases of this type deeply.

I cannot believe that alcoholism consists, in some cases, of an attempt to get over the effects of previous drinking by new imbibing. I am much more inclined to believe that those who suffer from occasionally drinking too much are persons who have a very low opinion of themselves and suffer from social tensions. [Compare Moore (1939).]

SUMMARY AND CONCLUSIONS

An acute alcoholic intoxication gives to the individual the desire to be loved and appreciated. He feels as an individual accepted by others because of his capacities, appearance and sexual qualities. At the same time he feels ready and willing to give the same appreciation to others. The perceptive and intellectual spheres are impaired.

Hand in hand with this impairment and increased self-confidence goes a lack of inhibition which leads to a breaking through of sexual striving otherwise repressed.

This basic pattern varies with the total situation. There may be a lability of the perceptive and intellectual inhibitory (cortical) mechanism. This may lead to more or less dissociated breaking through of sexual and aggressive impulses. The social situation may demand particular drinking habits. Early experiences in childhood may have enforced one or the other variation in sexuality which then appears during the intoxication. For similar reasons violence may break through. The total situation will determine the psychological picture of the acute alcoholic intoxication, the basic pattern of which, however, is a heightened feeling of one's being connected in love and admiration with other human beings so that one can even allow oneself the breaking through of one's sexual impulses. An underlying anxiety that one's social perfection may merely be assumed unjustly is never completely absent and may lead to self-assertion, irritability, aggressiveness and the attempt to bully others. The psychological gain by intoxication points to the personality structure of those who need this psychological gain badly. These are human beings with feelings of great social insecurity and social tension.

The acute alcoholic intoxication is different in persons who are chronic alcoholics than in those who are intoxicated for the first time. It seems that in the chronic alcoholic the acute intoxication brings forward more primitive material with a corresponding increase in anxiety. Such an acute intoxication in the chronic alcoholic leads him imperceptibly to delirious and hallucinatory episodes in which he experiences primitive sexuality in a distorted form and feels particularly threatened in his social function. The threat does not remain in the sphere of social insecurity but extends from there to sexual threats and even to the threat of dismemberment and castration. Society has become completely hostile and destructive and the patient may not even blame his community for the attempt at destroying him.

The chronic alcoholic person is one who, from his earliest childhood on, has lived in a state of insecurity. This insecurity in childhood is necessarily insecurity in relation to parents and siblings. The child has felt ridiculed and pushed into a passive position, sometimes by threat, sometimes by corporal punishment and sometimes by deprivation. This threat may come from both parents or from one parent only. In men the threat by the father seems to be more effective. It seems that help and consideration from the other parent cannot counteract the tendency to submission and the direction of a severe superego which takes over the part of the punishing and repressing parent. The punishing parent is particularly intolerant toward sex in any form. The community is experienced as an agent similar to the restrictive parents. Individuals are generally ready to submit to these influences in a passive and masochistic way. Men generally blame themselves for their "femininity" and have to seek redress in ideals of heightened masculinity and strength. In women, paradoxically, this process may be similar or the women feel that they are not capable of fulfilling their feminine functions. The characteristic of the alcoholic is social tension, with the tendency to give in passively to the assumed pressure or to react by overcompensation.

Alcoholism reverses this process. It gives social security and acceptance as long as the intoxication lasts. With the wearing off of the intoxication the underlying tensions and terrors reappear in increased form and demand renewed drinking.

The alcoholic is dependent upon his society, since he has a striving for social acceptance beyond the norm. The sociological and economic factors in alcoholism should therefore not be underrated. To be sure no problem is merely an individual problem. Human beings live in communities. However, alcoholism is, even beyond this, a problem of society. There is not only the problem of social competition, in which the alcoholic does badly, but society continually exposes the socially insecure individual to the temptation of a seemingly easy escape by encouraging drunkenness. Alcoholism is not only a problem of individual treatment but of social attitudes and it seems, therefore, that individual treatment has to be complemented by offering to the alcoholic a social group in which competition is diminished and in which the use of alcoholic beverages is not foisted upon the patient. It seems, indeed, that all modern treatments of alcoholism stress the community factor. However, beyond that, the alcoholic needs a deeper understanding of his problem, which very often is only possible by continued and intensive psychoanalytic work. The basic psychology of the alcoholic is preordained by the psychological effect of the acute intoxication and all forms of alcoholic intoxication and patterns of chronic alcoholism center around the psychological effect of the drug. In some types of chronic alcoholism the personality difficulty is chiefly in the sphere of sexual adaptation. In others, the family situation or community situation seems to offer the chief difficulty. However, these variations are merely facets of the same basic problem. The best prevention of alcoholism will lie in an attitude of the parents which does not increase the insecurity and passivity of the child and guarantees a reasonably free development of sexual adaptation. If the family, and later on the community, does not stress superiority, perfection and blamelessness and offers beyond that friendly help and understanding, individuals will not need alcohol as an escape for insecurities, but may be able to enjoy it as a method of heightening one's appreciation of oneself and of others on rare occasions of festivity.

REFERENCES

Bromberg, W., and Schilder, P. (1933). *International Journal of Psycho-Analysis* 14:206.

Chassell, J. (1938). *Psychiatry* 1:473.

Crowley, R. M. (1929). *Psychoanalytic Review* 76:37.

Curran, F. J. (1937). *Journal of Nervous and Mental Disease* 86:645.

Fleming, R. (1935). *American Journal of Psychiatry* 92:89.

Hartmann, H. (1925). *Z. ges. Neurol. Psychiat.* 95:415.

Jellinek, E. M., and McFarland, R. A. (1940). *Quarterly Journal of Studies on Alcohol* 1:272.

Knight, R. P. (1937a). *Bulletin of the Menninger Clinic* 1:233.

———— (1937b). *Journal of Nervous and Mental Disease* 86:538.

Menninger, K. A. (1938). *Man Against Himself.* New York: Harcourt, Brace & Co.

Moore, M. (1939). *New England Journal of Medicine* 221:489.

Radó, S. (1926). *International Journal of Psycho-Analysis* 7:396.

———— (1933). *Psychoanalytic Quarterly* 2:1.

Seliger, R. V. (1938). *American Journal of Psychiatry* 95:701.

Simmel, E. (1929). *International Journal of Psycho-Analysis* 10:83.

Wall, J. H. (1936). *American Journal of Psychiatry* 92:1389.

———— (1937). *American Journal of Psychiatry* 93:943.

13: THE EGO FACTORS IN SURRENDER IN ALCOHOLISM

Harry M. Tiebout

In the past 15 years, my understanding of the nature of alcoholism as a disease has been influenced largely by insight into the mechanisms at work in the Alcoholics Anonymous process. Some years ago I stated that A.A., to succeed, must induce a surrender on the part of the individual (Tiebout 1949). More recently, I discussed the idea of compliance (Tiebout 1953) acting as a barrier to that real acceptance which a surrender produces. On this occasion I propose to extend my observations by discussing (a) what factors in the individual must surrender, and (b) how the surrender reaction changes the inner psychic picture.

The first question, what factors in the individual must surrender, received passing attention in the article on compliance. There, relative to the difficulty of surrender, I noted that "the presence of an apparently unconquerable ego became evident. It was this ego which had to become humble." The first part of the present communication will be devoted to an elaboration of the nature of this ego factor.

Use of the word ego involves always the possibility of confusion of meaning. For a time, therefore, I considered a substitute term. That idea was set aside because, despite possible misinterpretation, the word ego is current in everyday language in exactly the sense in which it will be employed in this discussion. The expression, "he has an inflated ego," is self-explanatory. It evokes the picture of a pompous, self-important, strutting individual whose inferiorities are masked by a surface assurance. Such a person appears thick-skinned, insensitive, nearly impervious to the existence of others, a completely self-centered individual who plows unthinkingly through life, intent on gathering unto himself all the comforts and satisfactions available. He is generally considered the epitome of selfishness, and there the matter rests.

This popular view of ego, while it may not have scientific foundation, has one decided value: it possesses a meaning and can convey a concept which the average person can grasp. This concept of the inflated ego recognizes the common ancestor of a whole series of traits, namely, that they are all manifestations of an underlying feeling state in which personal considerations are first and foremost.

The existence of this ego has long been recognized but a difficulty in terminology still remains. Part of the difficulty arises from the use of the word ego, in psychiatric and psychological circles, to designate those elements of the psyche which are supposed to rule psychic life. Freud divided mental life into three major subdivisions, the id, the ego and the superego. The first, he stated, contains the feeling life on a deep, instinctual level; the third is occupied by the conscience, whose function is to put brakes on the impulses arising within the id. The ego should act as mediator between the demands of the id and the restraints of the superego, which might be overzealous and bigoted. Freud's own research was concerned mainly with the activities of the id and the superego. The void he left with respect to the ego is one that his followers are endeavoring to fill, but as yet with no generally accepted conclusions.

The word ego, however, has been preempted by the psychiatrists and psychologists, although they do not always agree among themselves about the meaning to be attached to it. The resulting confusion is the more lamentable because almost everyone, layman or scientist, would agree on the concept of the inflated ego. It would be helpful if other terms were found for the ego concepts about which there are differing views.

The solution for this dilemma here will be to indicate with a capital E the big Ego, and without a capital to identify the personality aspect which Freud had in mind when he placed ego between id and superego.[1]

With this disposition of the problem of terminology, it is now possible to consider the first issue, namely, the Ego factors in the alcoholic which, through surrender, become humble. The concept of the enlarged Ego, as noted previously, is available to common observation. Those who do not recognize it in themselves can always see it in some member of their family or among friends and acquaintances — not to mention patients. Everyone knows egotistical people and has a perfectly clear idea of what the word means. Besides egotistical, and the series of words mentioned earlier, adjectives which help to round out the portrait of the egotistical person are prideful, arrogant, pushing, dominating, attention-seeking, aggressive, opinionated, headstrong, stubborn, determined and impatient.

All these terms are inadequate, however, because they describe only surface features without conveying any feeling of the inner essence from which the Ego springs. Unless some appreciation of the source of the Ego is gained, the dynamic import is lost and the term may seem merely a form of name-calling. It is easy to say someone is a big Ego without awareness of what is really happening in the deep layers of that person's mind, without perception of the

---

[1]To see the capitalization or not at once clarifies the concept. In presenting this material as a lecture, however, it was necessary to clarify which ego was meant each time the word was used.

Ego. Nor is it a matter of intellect. The need here is to lay hold of the inner feeling elements upon which the activity of the Ego rests. Only when these elements become clear can the fundamental basis of the Ego also be clarified.

It is convenient, for the exposition of this inner functioning, to reverse the usual sequence and to present a conclusion in advance of the evidence on which it is based. This is, briefly, that the Ego is made up of the persisting elements, in the adult psyche, of the original nature of the child.

Certain aspects of the infant's psyche may be usefully examined. There are three factors which should receive mention. The first is, as Freud observed in his priceless phrase "His Majesty the Baby," that the infant is born ruler of all he surveys. He comes from the Nirvana of the womb, where he is usually the sole occupant, and he clings to that omnipotence with an innocence, yet determination, which baffles parent after parent. The second, stemming directly from the monarch within, is that the infant tolerates frustration poorly and lets the world know it readily. The third significant aspect of the child's original psyche is its tendency to do everything in a hurry. Observe youngsters on the beach: they run rather than walk. Observe them coming on a visit: the younger ones tear from the car while their elder siblings adopt a more leisurely pace. The three-year-olds, and more so the twos, cannot engage in play requiring long periods of concentration. Whatever they are doing must be done quickly. As the same children age, they gradually become able to stick to one activity for longer times.

Thus at the start of life the psyche (1) assumes its own omnipotence, (2) cannot accept frustrations and (3) functions at a tempo allegretto with a good deal of staccato and vivace thrown in.

Now the question is, "If this infantile psyche persists into adult life, how will its presence be manifested?"

In general, when infantile traits continue into adulthood, the person is spoken of as immature, a label often applied with little comprehension of the reason for its accuracy. It is necessary to link these three traits from the original psyche with immaturity and, at the same time, show how they affect the adult psyche. If this is done, not only will the correctness of the appellation "immature" be apparent but, moreover, a feeling for the nature of the unconscious underpinnings of the Ego will have been created.

Two steps can aid in recognizing the relationship between immaturity and a continuance of the infantile elements. The first is, by an act of imagination, to set these original traits into an adult unconscious. The validity of this procedure is founded upon modern knowledge of the nature of the forces operating in the unconscious of people of mature age. The second step is to estimate the effect that the prolongation of these infantile qualities will have upon the adult individual.

This attempt should not strain the imagination severely. Take, for instance, the third of the qualities common to the original psychic state, namely, the tendency to act hurriedly. If that tendency prevails in the unconscious, what must the result be? The individual will certainly do everything in a hurry. He will think fast, talk fast and live fast, or he will spend an inordinate amount of time and energy holding his fast-driving proclivities in check.

Often the net result will be an oscillation between periods of speeding ahead followed by periods during which the direction of the force is reversed, the brakes (superego) being applied in equally vigorous fashion. The parallel of this in the behavior of the alcoholic will not be lost on those who have had experience with this class of patients.

Let us take the same trait of doing everything in a hurry and apply it to the word "immature." Few will deny that jumping at conclusions, doing things as speedily as possible, gives evidence of immaturity. It is youth that drives fast, thinks fast, feels fast, moves fast, acts hastily in most situations. There can be little question that one of the hallmarks of the immature is the proneness to be under inner pressure for accomplishment. Big plans, big schemes, big hopes abound, unfortunately not matched by an ability to produce. But the effect upon the adult of the persisting infantile quality to do everything in less than sufficient time can now be seen in a clearer light. The adult trait is surely a survival from the original psyche of the infant.

The two other surviving qualities of the infantile psyche similarly contribute to the picture of immaturity and also, indirectly, help to clarify the nature of the Ego with a capital E. The first of these, the feeling of omnipotence, when carried over into adult life affects the individual in ways easily anticipated. Omnipotence is of course associated with royalty, if not divinity. The unconscious result of the persistence of this trait is that its bearer harbors a belief of his own special role and in his own exceptional rights. Such a person finds it well-nigh impossible to function happily on an ordinary level. Obsessed with divine afflatus, the thought of operating in the lowly and humble areas of life is most distressing to him. The very idea that such a place is all one is capable of occupying is in itself a blow to the Ego, which reacts with a sense of inferiority at its failure to fill a more distinguished position. Moreover, any success becomes merely Ego fodder, boosting the individual's rating of himself to increasingly unrealistic proportions as the king side eagerly drinks in this evidence of special worth.

The ability to administer the affairs of state, both large and small, is taken for granted. The belief that he is a natural executive placed in the wrong job merely confirms his conviction that, at best, he is the victim of lack of appreciation, and at worst, of sabotage by jealous people who set up roadblocks to his progress. The world is inhabited by selfish people, intent only on their own advancement.

The genesis of all this is beyond his perception. To tell him that his reactions spring from the demands of an inner unsatisfied king is to invite incredulity and disbelief, so far from the conscious mind are any such thoughts or feelings. People who openly continue to cling to their claims of divine prerogative usually end up in a world especially constructed for their care. In others, the omnipotence pressures are rather better buried. The individual may admit that, in many ways, he acts like a spoiled brat, but he is scarcely conscious of the extent of the tendency, nor how deeply rooted it may be. He, like most people, resolutely avoids a careful look because the recognition of any such inner attitudes is highly disturbing. The unconscious credence in one's special prerogatives savors too much of straight selfishness to be anything but unpleasant to contemplate.

And so, for the most part, people remain happily ignorant of the unconscious drives which push them around. They may wonder why they tend to boil inside and wish they could free themselves from a constant sense of uneasiness and unsettlement. They may recognize that they seem jittery and easily excited and long for the time when they can meet life more calmly and maturely; they may hate their tendency to become rattled. But their insight into the origin of all this is next to nothing if not a complete blank. The king lies deep below the surface, far out of sight.

The last trait carried over from infancy is the inability to accept frustration. In an obvious sense this inability is another aspect of the king within, since one of the prerogatives of royalty is to proceed without interruption. For the king to wait is an affront to the royal rank, a slap at his majesty. The ramifications of this inability to endure frustration are so widespread and the significance of much that occurs in the behavior of the alcoholic is so far-reaching that it seems advisable to discuss this trait under a separate heading.

As already indicated, on the surface the inability of the king to accept frustration is absolutely logical. The wish of the king is the law of the land, and especially in the land of infancy. Any frustration is clearly a direct threat to the status of his majesty, whose whole being is challenged by the untoward interruption.

Even more significant is another aspect of this inner imperiousness. Behind it lies the assumption that the individual should not be stopped. Again, this is logical if one considers how an absolute monarch operates. He simply does not expect to be stopped; as he wills, so will he do. This trait, persisting in the unconscious, furnishes a constant pressure driving the individual forward. It says, in essence, "I am unstoppable!"

The unconscious which cannot be stopped views life entirely from the angle of whether or not a stopping is likely, imminent, or not at all in the picture. When a stopping is likely, there is worry and perhaps depression. When it seems imminent, there is anxiety bordering on panic, and when the threat is removed, there is relief and gaiety. Health is equated with a feeling of buoyancy and smooth sailing ahead, a sense of "I feel wonderful!" Sickness, contrariwise, means lacking vim, vigor and vitality, and is burdened with a sense of "I'm not getting anywhere." The need to "get somewhere," to "be on the go," and the consequent suffering from eternal restlessness, is still another direct effect of an inner inability to be stopped or, expressed otherwise, to accept the fact that one is limited. The king not only cannot accept the normal frustrations of life but, because of his inordinate driving ahead, is constantly creating unnecessary roadblocks by virtue of his own insistence on barging ahead, thus causing added trouble for himself.

Of course, on some occasions, the king gets stopped and stopped totally.

Illness, arrest, sometimes the rules and regulations of life, will halt him. Then he marks time, complies if need be, waiting for the return of freedom, which he celebrates in the time-honored fashion if he is an alcoholic: he gets drunk, initiating a phase when there is no stopping him.

The immaturity of such a person is readily evident. He is impatient of delay, can never let matters evolve; he must have a blueprint to follow outlining clearly a path through the jungle of life. The wisdom of the ages is merely shackling tradition which should make way for the freshness, the insouciance of youth. The value of staying where one is and working out one's destiny in the here and now is not suspected. The 24-hour principle would be confining for one whose inner life brooks no confinement. The unstoppable person seeks life, fun, adventure, excitement, and discovers he is on a perpetual whirligig which carries him continuously ahead — but, of course, in a circle. The unstoppable person has no time for growth. He must always inwardly feel immature.

This, then, is how the carry-over of infantile traits affects the adult so encumbered. He is possessed by an inner king who not only must do things in a hurry but has no capacity for taking frustration in stride. He seeks a life which will not stop him and finds himself in a ceaseless rat race.

All this is part and parcel of the big Ego. The individual has no choice. He cannot select one characteristic and hang on to that, shedding other more obviously undesirable traits. It is all or nothing. For example, the driving person usually has plenty of energy, sparkle, vivacity. He stands out as a most attractive human being. Clinging to that quality, however, merely insures the continuance of excessive drive and Ego, with all the pains attendant upon a life based on those qualities. The sacrifice of the Ego elements must be total or they will soon regain their ascendancy.

Those who view the prospect of life without abundant drive as unutterably dull and boring should examine the life of members of Alcoholics Anonymous who have truly adopted the A.A. program. They will see people who have been stopped and who, therefore, do not have to go anywhere — but people who are learning, for the first time in their lives, to live. They are neither dull nor wishy-washy. Quite the contrary, they are alive and interested in the realities about them. They see things in the large, are tolerant, open-minded, not close-mindedly bulling ahead. They are receptive to the wonders in the world about them, including the presence of a Deity who makes all this possible. They are the ones who are really living. The attainment of such a way of life is no mean accomplishment.

Preliminary to this discussion the conclusion was offered that the Ego was a residual of the initial feeling life of the infant. It should be evident that the immaturity characteristically found in the make-up of the alcoholic is a persistence of the original state of the child. In connection with the description of the manifestations which denote a large and active Ego, it should be recalled that the presence in the unconscious of such Ego forces may be quite out of reach of conscious observation. Only through the acting and feeling of the individual can their existence be suspected.

Now the answer to the first question raised herein, namely, what part of the alcoholic must surrender, is obvious: it is the Ego elements.

Life without Ego is no new conception. Two thousand years ago, Christ preached the necessity of losing one's life in order to find it again. He did not say Ego but that was what He had in mind. The analysts of our time recognize the same truth; they talk also about ego reduction. Freud saw therapy as a running battle between the original narcissism of the infant (his term for Ego) and the therapist whose task it was to reduce that original state to more manageable proportions. Since Freud could not conceive of life without some measure of Ego, he never resolved the riddle of how contentment is achieved; for him man to the end was doomed to strife and unhappiness, his dearest desires sure to be frustrated by an unfriendly world.

In his studies on the addictions Radó (1933) more explicitly asserts that the Ego must be reduced. He first portrays the Ego as follows: "Once it was a baby, radiant with self-esteem, full of belief in the omnipotence of its wishes, of its thoughts, gestures and words." Then, on the process of Ego-reduction: "But the child's megalomania melted away under the inexorable pressure of experience. Its sense of its own sovereignty had to make room for a more modest self-evaluation. This process, first described by Freud, may be designated the reduction in size of the original ego; it is a painful procedure and one that is possibly never completely carried out."

Like Freud, Radó thinks only in terms of reduction; the need for the complete elimination of Ego is a stand which they cannot bring themselves to assume. Hence they unwittingly advocate the retention of some infantile traits, with no clear awareness that trading with the devil, the Ego, no matter how carefully safeguarded, merely keeps him alive and likely at any occasion to erupt full force into action. There can be no successful compromise with Ego, a fact not sufficiently appreciated by many if not most therapists.

Thus the dilemma encountered in ego-reduction would be best resolved by recognizing that the old Ego must go and a new one take its place. Then no issue would arise about how much of the earliest elements may be retained. The answer, theoretically, is none. Actually the total banishment of the initial state is difficult to achieve. Man can only grow in the direction of its complete elimination. Its final expulsion is a goal which can only be hoped for.

The second question raised here is, How does the surrender reaction change the inner psychic picture? This question is based on a presupposition, namely, that surrender is an emotional step in which the Ego, at least for the time being, acknowledges that it is no longer supreme. This acknowledgement is valueless if limited to consciousness; it must be accompanied by similar feelings in the unconscious. For the alcoholic, surrender is marked by the admission of being powerless over alcohol. His sobriety has that quality of peace and tranquility which makes for a lasting quiet within only if the surrender is effective in the unconscious and permanent as well.

The effects of surrender upon the psyche are extremely logical: The traits listed as characteristic of the Ego influence are canceled out. The opposite of king is the commoner. Appropriately, Alcoholics Anonymous stresses humility. The opposite of impatience is the ability to take things in stride, to make an inner reality of the slogan, "Easy does it." The opposite of drive is staying in one position, where one can be open-minded, receptive and responsive.

This picture of the non-Ego type of person might be amplified in many directions but to do so would serve no immediate purpose. To have discussed the effect of the Ego upon behavior, and to have pointed out what may happen when the Ego is at least temporarily knocked out of action, is sufficient to make the point of this communication: It is the Ego which is the arch-enemy of sobriety, and it is the Ego which must be disposed of if the individual is to attain a new way of life.

Up to this point no clinical material has been submitted to confirm the ideas presented. Their validity will be apparent to many therapists. One brief citation from clinical experience will be offered, however, in the hope that it may serve as a concrete illustration of these ideas.

The patient, a man in his late thirties, had a long history of alcoholism, with 7 years of futile attempts to recover through Alcoholics Anonymous, interspersed with countless admissions to "drying out" places. Then, for reasons not completely clear, he decided to take a drastic step. He determined to enter a sanitarium and place himself in the hands of a psychiatrist, a hitherto unheard of venture. He telephoned to arrange for a limited stay at a sanitarium where he could have regular interviews with me.

From the outset he was undeniably in earnest, although it was only after the first interview that he really let go and could talk freely about himself and the things that were going on inside him. After the usual preliminaries, the first interview started with a discussion of feelings and how they operate. The patient was questioned about the word Ego as used at A.A. meetings. He confessed his ignorance of its true meaning and listened with interest to brief remarks on how it works. Before long, he was locating in himself some of the Ego forces which hitherto he had been vigorously denying because they savored too much of vanity and selfishness. With that recognition, the patient made a revealing remark. He said, in all sincerity, "My goodness, I never knew that. You don't do your thinking up here [pointing to his head], you think down here where you feel [placing his hands on his stomach]." He was learning that his feelings had a "mind" of their own and that unless he heeded what they were saying, he could easily get into trouble. He was facing the actuality of his Ego as a feeling element in his life, a step he was able to take because he was no longer going at full steam ahead. His decision to place himself under care, a surrender of a sort, had quieted him and made him receptive, able to observe what was going on in himself. It was the beginning of a real inventory.

The next insight he uncovered was even more startling. He had been requested routinely to report any dreams he would have. Much to his surprise, they appeared regularly during the period of contact. In his fifth dream, the patient found himself locked up in an institution because of his drinking. The interpretation offered, based upon relevant materials, was that the patient equated any kind of stopping with being locked up; that his real difficulty lay in the fact that he could not tolerate being stopped, and abstaining was merely another stopping he could not take. The patient's reaction to the interpretation was most significant. He remained silent for some little time; then he began to talk, saying, "I tell you, Doc, it was like this. I'd get drunk, maybe stay on it 2 or 3 days, then I'd go into one of those drying out places where I'd stay 5 or 6 days and I'd be all over wanting a drink. Then I'd come out and stay sober, maybe a week, maybe a month, but pretty soon the thought would come into my mind, I want to drink! Maybe I'd go into a tavern and maybe not, but sooner or later I'd go and I'd order a drink, but I wouldn't drink it right off. I'd put it on the bar and I'd look at it and I'd think and then I'd look and think: King for a day!" The connection between Ego and his own conduct had become explicit, as well as the relationship between not being stopped and Ego. He saw clearly that when he took that drink, he was the boss once more. Any previous reduction of Ego had been only temporary.

In treatment, the problem is to make that reduction permanent. Therapy is centered on the ways and means, first, of bringing the Ego to earth, and second, keeping it there. The discussion of this methodology would be out of place here, but it is relevant to emphasize one point, namely, the astonishing capacity of the Ego to pass out of the picture and then reenter it, blithe and intact. A patient's dream neatly depicted this quality. This patient dreamt that he was on the twelfth-floor balcony of a New York hotel. He threw a rubber ball to the pavement below and saw it rebound to the level of the balcony. Much to his amazement, the ball again dropped and again rebounded to the same height. This continued for an indefinite period and, as he was watching, a clock in a neighboring church spire struck 9. Like the cat with nine lives, the Ego has a marvelous capacity to scramble back to safety — a little ruffled, perhaps, but soon operating with all its former aplomb, convinced once more that now it, the Ego, can master all events and push on ahead.

The capacity of the Ego to bypass experience is astounding and would be humorous were it not so tragic in its consequences. Cutting the individual down to size and making the results last is a task never completely accomplished. The possibility of a return of his Ego must be faced by every alcoholic. If it does return, he may refrain from drinking but he will surely go on a "dry drunk," with all the old feelings and attitudes once more asserting themselves and making sobriety a shambles of discontent and restlessness. Not until the ego is decisively retired can peace and quiet again prevail. As one sees this struggle in process, the need for the helping hand of a Deity becomes clearer. Mere man alone all too often seems powerless to stay the force of his Ego. He needs outside assistance and needs it urgently.

SUMMARY

In the process of surrender which the alcoholic necessarily undergoes before his alcoholism can be arrested, the part of the personality which must surrender is the inflated Ego. This aspect of personality was identified as immature traits carried over from infancy into adulthood, specifically, a feeling of omnipotence, inability to tolerate frustration, and excessive drive, exhibited in the need to do all things precipitously. The manner in which surrender affects the Ego was discussed and illustrated briefly from clinical experience. The object of therapy is permanently to reduce the Ego and its activity.

REFERENCES

Radó, S. (1933). The psychoanalysis of pharmacothymia (drug addiction). The clinical picture. *Psychoanalytic Quarterly* 2:1-23.

Tiebout, H. M. (1949). The act of surrender in the therapeutic process. With special reference to alcoholism. *Quart. J. Stud. Alc.* 10:48-58.

———— (1953). Surrender versus compliance in therapy. With special reference to alcoholism. *Quart. J. Stud. Alc.* 14:58-68.

14: AFFECT TOLERANCE

Henry Krystal and Herbert Raskin

There are few generalizations which can be stated to be applicable to drug dependence. A striking exception is that the drug dependent person invariably is seeking relief, modification or avoidance of a painful state. In his drug he has found something that he knows will put an end to unbearable tensions and pain. His own ego resources, organization, and functions suffer from impairments and defects which produce an insidious and inexorable helplessness to deal with pain and tension without his drug. But pain and painful affects are very complex phenomena. Preliminary to our study of painful affects will be a review of some work on pain.

A GENETIC VIEW OF AFFECTS

It is generally assumed that the degree of physical pain experienced is proportional to the extent of the injury. Such is not the case, however, even in those body areas adequately supplied with pain fibers. Physiological and psychological studies made since World War II have shown that the experience of pain is inseparable from anxiety, pain anticipation anxiety and fear of destruction of one's self (Szasz 1957). The relation of anxiety to problems of aggression, object-representations (benign introject), and the development of the ability to desomatize and verbalize affect seems to be closely related to the development of drug dependence.

Pain and Anxiety

It is the anxiety associated with pain that provides its unbearable quality (Livingston 1953, Melzack 1961). It is the anxiety mobilized which threatens to overwhelm all other perceptions and functions of the entire self, but especially to overwhelm conscious ego functions. Anxiety and pain are very closely related. Each state is modified and influenced by the other. Exposure to much pain is

likely to produce excessive anxiety, and the presence of anxiety almost inva__
predisposes to and increases pain response.

Pertinent here is Melzack's (1961) observation that before a surgical procedure people will rarely ask, "how deeply, how extensively will you cut me?" but rather, "how much will it hurt?" Here anxiety is motivated by the fear of pain, rather than of the injury for which the pain stands. The close and persistent connection between pain and anxiety can also be illustrated by a unique disturbance in individuals with congenital pain agnosia, in their ability to anticipate danger.

A review of the literature on the subject indicates that many such individuals keep hurting themselves accidentally, or perform in side-shows and have various sharp articles driven into their flesh. Their psychic reality is devoid of fear and pain and they generally show a lack of normal anxiety reactions or empathy with other people's anxiety. An interesting example is that of a famous performer who regularly had nails and pins driven into his tongue and other parts of his body. He arranged for "a spectacular," his own crucifixion. After a couple of gold-plated nails had been hammered into his hands and feet, the show had to be discontinued because of the massive incidence of fainting in the audience. The performer was totally surprised (Critchley 1956).

In "congenital analgesic indifference" there is a hyporeactivity to pain, apparently an underestimation of danger and subsequently inadequate utilization and function of anxiety as a signal. The opposite is ordinarily true of severely traumatized individuals. They often show intensity as a permanent character trait plus chronic anxiety states (Weiss 1959). Additionally, studies on concentration camp survivors found that many of them hyperreact to pain in a practically hypochondriacal fashion. Pain mobilizes dream-screens of their trauma. If they develop pain while asleep, they dream of the return of the trauma (e.g., of being in a concentration camp in a situation of great peril). This is the result of the formation of a type of screen memory, the traumatic screen (Krystal 1968). Once a traumatic screen is established, pain mobilizes all the anxiety of impending traumatization, and as the dreams of the concentration camp survivors show, pain is experienced as the return of the traumatic situation. We can also add that in *massive* psychic traumatization a reaction is established similar to that described by Greenacre (1952) regarding traumatization in infancy and the prenatal period. The result is that pain and/or danger mobilize excessive amounts of anxiety, especially its somatic component (Krystal 1968).

In normal people the introduction of small amounts of anxiety (e.g., preoperatively) raises the threshold of trauma resistance. There has been extensive experimentation in desensitizing soldiers to fears provoked by front-line explosions and by dangers in war-games (Rees 1945). But in both of these situations, an excess of anxiety, noise or pain will panic and demoralize the patient or trainee, rendering him later incapable of tolerating even small quantities of pain or anxiety.

Physicians especially tend to think of the problem of pain in terms of the pain threshold, with the idea that neurotic, anxious patients perceive pain where others do not. Besides the fact that it is simpler to measure pain threshold, the attitude reflects the doctor's experience and belief that only the patients who complain of pain have it. The fact is that the problem is that of the ability to *tolerate* pain, and it is in this sphere that the amount of anxiety accompanying the pain is the essential factor. This applies to physical pain, "mental pain," which indicates the pain experience not generated in a diseased organ, and painful affects (Romzy and Wallerstein 1958). Perhaps only in a lobotomized patient (or one chemically lobotomized) is the experience of pain not associated with anxiety, and therefore does not become unbearable.

From studies in the use of narcotic analgesics it is now quite evident that they do not provide relief from pain but from the attending anxiety. In experimental subjects, if pain is experienced without the feeling of danger (anxiety), no relief is obtained from narcotics (Beecher 1959). In clinical patients the relief of pain with narcotics is abolished by the injection of sympatho-mimetic drugs (Wolf et al. 1940). Morphine was shown to reduce the disruptive effect of pain upon performance which was associated with anxiety produced by the anticipation of pain (Hill et al. 1952). The studies of Goldstein indicate that even aspirin has an anxiety relieving effect, "similar to those of minor tranquilizing drugs and small doses of phenobarbital" (Goldstein 1966).

What then is the genesis of this close relationship between pain and anxiety; what are its genetic antecedents? Anna Freud (1952) commented:

> Where the direct observation of infants in the first year of life is concerned, the relative proportion of physiological and psychological elements in the experience of pain is an open question. At this stage, any tension, need or frustration is probably felt as "pain," no real distinction being made yet between the diffuse experience of discomfort and the sharper and more circumscribed one of real pain arising from specific sources. In the first months of life, the threshold of resistance against stimulation is low and painful sensations assume quickly the dignity of traumatic events.

Traumatization at this early stage, before physical pain is recognized and identified as a specific kind of disturbance, also poses some questions regarding the effect of trauma prior to the development of adequate reflective self-awareness. The point is the trauma may interfere with the very development of a fine discrimination between what is truly dangerous and what is not, what is external and what is internal. Khan (1963) has pointed out that the mother supplements the infant's stimulus barrier in her protective function. When pain develops, the child's security is threatened with a failure of the magical protection from the omnipotent love object. The reactions here are complex, and include aggression and guilt. Pain thereafter retains the ability to mobilize the threat of failure of the remnants and transferences of the maternal protection.

Theory of the Developmental History of Affects

Krystal's (1962) studies of drug withdrawal states led him to suggest that anxiety and depression evolve from a common precursor (Ur-affect). In a drug dependent person there is a regression in regard to affects; anxiety and depression are again de-differentiated and show other attributes of primitivisation of affects, such as resomatization, and deverbalization. The ideational component of the affect is isolated from its expressive aspects (glandular and muscular responses). The affects are experienced as threatening and therefore excluded from conscious awareness whenever possible. All of these characteristics, especially the regression to the "all or none" affective responses, impair their use as signals. We will presently attempt to discuss these in detail.

Prior to the "discovery" of the love object, the infant's response to distress takes a single form: totally somatic and uncontrollable. The establishment of the nuclei of self-representation and object-representation facilitates the separation of pain from the painful affects, which remain as a single, totally somatic reaction to the absence and threat of loss of the love object. In addition, the infant's physiological balance is so precarious, and lability so great, that affective disturbance produces immediate physical changes and pain. Anxiety in the infant may produce instant colic and hence be converted into severe pain. Other affects can similarly be converted into painful physical symptoms, because the infant lacks the adult's protective ego functions and is more readily thrown into psychogenic shock which may be lethal. This type of reaction accounts for the child's confrontation with mortal fear, not fear of dying, but an enormous, overwhelming, deadly anxiety of being eaten up, swallowed, and so forth. This death anxiety is linked with the feeling of helplessness, immobility, suffocation, and remains the core of that overwhelming anxiety which in the adult we refer to as the "automatic anxiety" in trauma: castration anxiety, fear of dismemberment, losing one's mind (Engel 1962). Perhaps it is also what Melanie Klein called "psychotic anxiety" linked with the ideational component of the fear of falling to bits. This feeling is unbearable, and is the thing that causes, or more properly is, the traumatic situation. It initiates a series of unconscious pathogenic reactions which represent the trauma syndrome.

Out of the infant's general state of distress, several states and feelings evolve. The "discovery" of the mother and her power to nurture and give relief shifts the ideational component of it from physical distress to the fear of the loss of the object. This shift establishes the basis for the object-representation in the child's mind which we will discuss in detail in Chapter II.

With the increased acuity of perception and the maturation of the ego apparatuses of proprioception, the body image is gradually built up. Pain is separated from the general distress pattern, albeit it is never completely separated from anxiety. Still, the normal adult does not obtain automatic relief from physical pain by oral gratification. Some of this potential, however, is retained, as we shall demonstrate in our discussion of the placebo. This type of reaction is one of the remnants of infantile function which becomes important in drug dependence.

As to other affects, anxiety becomes separated from depression primarily in the fact that anxiety is the reaction to the expectation of danger, whereas depression represents a hopeless giving up and resignation. The "agitation" in anxiety serves an expressive function, and when the situation is hopeless, a flaccid or tense-immobile catatonoid, inhibited reaction develops (Schur 1955). Depression and anxiety not only become separated but also become in a way antagonistic because of their physiologic association with opposing parts of the autonomic nervous system. Thus, it happens that sometimes either on order of physicians or in drug self-medication, people can stimulate the anxiety-agitation response (with amphetamine drugs or fear-producing thrills) as a way to combat the parasympathetic aspects of depression.

Affect Disturbance in Drug Dependence

However, in many drug dependent persons we find an affect combining depression and anxiety, a disturbance in which the de-differentiation of anxiety and depression takes place or a state in which the differentiation was never successfully accomplished. Thus, in Krystal's (1962) studies of drug withdrawal states, the affect seemed to approximate the infantile "total" and somatic distress pattern rather than a clear-cut adult affect pattern. Radó (1935) was the first to describe this condition clinically, calling it "the anxious depression" of alcoholics. He did not, however, pursue in detail the nature and consequences of this regression. Engel (1962) considers "anxiety and depression withdrawal" to be the "primary affect of unpleasure." His excellent and scholarly work traces the development of the Ur-affects in the infant in relation to drives and object representations, and confirms the expressive attitudes of anxiety ("flight or fight") and depression ("to give up") to be a psychological continuum, although they "represent two basic physiological states." He pointed out that depressions may become "maladaptive or unsuccessful in which case they seem to be potent provoking conditions for major psychic and somatic disorganizations, sometimes leading to death."

Perhaps Freud (1926) also hinted at this developmental history of the painful affects when he said about the infant's reaction to loss, in the "Problems of Anxiety," that "some things were fused together which later will be separated. He is not yet able to distinguish temporary absence from permanent loss." Schur has come to similar conclusions about the development of affects and has drawn our attention to the fact that affects, like other aspects of mental function, are subject to regression. Schur's work on the metapsychology of fear contributed the observation of a type of *physiological regression* in patients with dermatoses, which allows us to add another dimension to our knowledge of some drug dependent individuals. We gain an appreciation of a regression manifest in the words of Schur in "a regressive evaluation of danger and an ego which responds with deneutralized energy. This corresponds to the re-emerging somatic discharge phenomena." Upon observing that some patients developed symptoms representing anxiety equivalents instead of becoming conscious of their anxiety, Schur (1955) postulated that there was an "interdependence" between the ego's faculty to use secondary processes and neutralized energy, and the desomatization response. This implies an inverse relation between an individual's consciousness of his affect and the intensity of physiological (stress) responses and affect equivalents. The relevance of the regression vis-à-vis the problem of pain consists in the nature of pain, which is a complex conscious phenomenon composed of the perception of injury associated with disturbing affects. Commonly the affect involved is that of anxiety. However, in the regressed state the impact of the resomatized Ur-affect presents a complex danger. One of the results, which will be discussed in detail later, is the inability to tolerate even small amounts of anxiety, hence the failure of its signal function. This creates the threat of trauma, to which we shall return.

A reconsideration of the mode of development of the affect of anxiety from the infantile, that is, totally somatic, to the adult form suggests that the original pattern is modified by later experiences and developments. Verbalization and desomatization of affect represent one aspect of ego development (Schur 1955). Learned responses to pain as the representative of danger represent another and important aspect. We will pursue the story of development of pain tolerance in the child, because it can serve us as a pattern and prototype for the development of individual resources for dealing with painful states and affects.

Pain is a perceptive process in which the possibility of injury is evaluated in terms of one's psychic reality. Anna Freud (1952), in considering the effect of pain on children, observed:

> According to the child's interpretation of the event, young children react to pain not only with anxiety but with other affects appropriate to the contents of the unconscious phantasies, i.e., on the one hand with anger, rage and revenge feelings, on the other with masochistic submission, guilt or depression . . . and . . . where anxiety derived from phantasy plays a minor or no part, even severe pain is borne well and forgotten quickly. Pain augmented by anxiety, on the other hand, even if slight in itself, represents a major event in the child's life and is remembered long afterward, the memory being frequently accompanied by phobic defenses against its possible return.

Here, Anna Freud treats pain as an absolute perception, indicating that the child's responses to it are modified by the factors stated. We would maintain, however, that the very perception of pain, and hence its memory traces, is influenced by the child's interpretation of the experience. It is not really "pain" until the child, sometimes by looking at his parents and estimating their mood, decides whether he has received a spanking (been hurt) or a love-pat. Theresa Benedek discussed in some detail the child's need, upon perceiving pain, to appeal to his mother to find out whether he has been injured. She pointed out that the mother may respond to the child's need and reassure him by talking to him gently. The mother, responding to her own needs at the moment, may lose control of her own fears and express panic, or scold the child for getting hurt, adding guilt to fear—literally adding insult to injury (Benedek 1956). The child thus is deprived of an opportunity to observe, imitate and learn modes of behavior which he can use to increase his tolerance of anxiety and pain. He may be driven to repeat the pain in an attempt to master it and/or force magically a "better" response from his parent. In some drug dependent patients the drug represented a slightly improved version of the parent's response in regard to pain—the drug did give relief, but only postponed the anxiety *because it was itself experienced as dangerous.*

Identification and imitation of parental patterns of dealing with pain (physical and mental) are important. In some cultures patterns for dealing with pain are quite prominent. For instance, one may be expected to drink alcohol whenever one is upset, especially during the period of mourning, to the point of complete numbing. In other cultures the noisy expression of grief and pain is encouraged and accepted both as conscious experience and as a method of dealing with the feelings involved. In yet others, the males are required to tolerate pain, grief, and so forth, stoically, without even an outward response. The patterns for handling pain and unpleasant affects are usually the same for the given culture. Pain can be a part of depression or a substitute for it (Bradley 1963). We have had the opportunity to observe a number of so-called iatrogenic addicts who used narcotics primarily for the relief of physical pain (e.g., headaches or abdominal pains). With remarkable consistency we found a severe latent depression warded off by massive denial, hypomanic or obsessive-compulsive mechanism. Pain, like depression or anxiety, can be the direct symptom of intersystemic intrapsychic tension.

The relationship of this formulation to the state of drug dependence is well stated by Chessick (1960). The drug dependent person frequently shows little awareness of his affects. Especially in the group of "medically addicted" individuals, there is a conspicuous absence of anxiety or depression, along with a great frequency of anxiety-equivalent symptoms. In psychoanalysis or psychotherapy with narcotic and alcohol dependent persons, the discovery and verbalization of the nature of affect is an important step toward making possible the giving up of regressive symptoms.

The perception of pain, or any discomfort, tension or stimulus, is a complex process of interpretation and association. The studies by Ostow (1957) on temporal lobe function suggest that the association paths of special importance are related to memory traces of an unpleasant nature concerned with avoidance patterns. Perhaps this fashion of perception of pain is predestined by the anatomical structure of pain fibers in such a way that we have a quick signal at first, via the unmyelinated pain fibers, and perception of the "pain" as such arrives only some time later, permitting an evaluation of it in the meantime. Sherrington, Livingston, and others have concluded that pain is a conscious and complex process, rather than a primary perception (Krystal 1968, Livingston 1953, Melzack 1961).

Physiologists have found that higher brain centers can suppress or modify the perceptual quality of pain (Beecher 1956a,b). This seems to be the anatomical framework for the hysterical phenomena we discussed above. The time interval between the signal-perception and the full consciousness of pain can be utilized for the associative interpretation and modification of the pain experience. In the secure individual the infantile (total) fear response to pain is suppressed. This is attributable to the predominance of the secondary process, and the relatively lesser prevalence of destructive fantasies and wishes.

Inadequately understood is the mechanism by which the perception of pain is terminated psychically, as in the numbing which follows a crushing or cutting wound, or in the phenomenon of depersonalization. Our experience has been that depersonalization, *as a defense against anxiety or pain*, functions in a way exactly analogous to tissue-numbness. For instance, victims of Nazi torture very frequently became depersonalized when the torture became unbearable. Studies on convalescence by Krystal and Petty (1961) showed that either the onset of illness, development of pain, or the awareness of being ill or injured may be handled by depersonalization in normal subjects. One might say that either the depersonalization or the "numbing" represented a hysterical conversion symptom. Since it requires a quantity of counter-cathectic energy and ability to use it for a reversible splitting of the ego, we begin to appreciate the variety of ego functions involved in the mastery and tolerance of pain.

Of unusual research interest is the old method of managing pain by "counter-irritation." It acts as if pain tracts, a mental apparatus of perception, can be "overloaded" by other messages, such as heat or cold stimulation (from the same dermatomes), thus making the perception of pain indistinct. A host of pain relievers function on the basis of "overloading the lines" of an affected area with perception of heat, cold, sound, and so forth, thus muffling the conscious experience of pain.

Psychic pain can be handled in a similar manner. Freud (1917) has noted that counter-irritations or distractions are utilized to cope with physical and psychic pain, as in mourning. The mourner distracts himself, and only periodically returns to perceive the pain of loss, and to rework the loss piecemeal. The ability for such self-distraction, vis-à-vis pain of psychic or somatic origin, requires adequate energy and diversified object investments of the ego, which *clinically* can be seen to be impaired in many drug dependent persons. This is shown by the paucity and primitive nature of their object relations and gratifications. This is another mechanism involved in utilization and tolerance of pain. Tolerance for pain is a complex of ego functions which, when impaired, may create a greater than usual need of (and therefore a tendency to) drugs for the relief from the pain of physical or psychic origin, in order to be able to tolerate the stresses of everyday living.

It is our contention that the very same ego functions which are utilized in the reaction to physical pain become involved in the *handling of unpleasant (painful) affects,* and that these functions may be deficient, causing the organism to be less able to tolerate pain, anxiety, and so on, as signals. The individual who cannot deal with the unpleasant states becomes subject to stress and trauma. Szasz (1957) pointed out that anxiety is analogous in the ego–object orientation to the role of pain in self-perception in the ego–body plane of reference. Furthermore, there are parts of all those ego functions which together are referred to as the "stimulus barrier." In the conscious experience of "pain," anxiety is an indispensable part of its urgent quality.

THE PROBLEM OF TRAUMA

Closely related to the subject of pain and painful affects, and perhaps even constituting only a variant of the same theme, is the concept of trauma. Freud

(1926) stated that "the essence of a traumatic situation is an experience of helplessness on the part of the ego in the face of accumulation of excitation, whether of external or internal origin." Dorsey (1969) indicates that the term trauma introduces an economic concept. "It means my inability to sustain and keep my mental balance when the exertion I am undergoing, the mental excitation I am suffering, is more than I can tolerate and, at the same moment, arouse my awareness for my identity." The phenomenon of trauma includes "paralysing, immobilizing, or rendering to a state of helplessness, ranging from numbness to an emotional storm in affect behavior"; also "disorganization of feelings, thoughts and behavior, as well as physical symptoms reflecting autonomic dysfunction" (Rangell 1967). We would prefer to emphasize that this autonomic overaction is actually part of overwhelming and overflowing affect and that the affect disorganization represents a regression in which the affects are de-differentiated and discharged in a total excitation pattern like the infant. By definition, once the traumatic process is initiated, it represents a chain of unconscious reactions, which may result in a variety of specific and lasting psychopathological states. Among these, increased susceptibility to future traumatization and decreased ability to tolerate affects, and to utilize them as signals, are virtually unavoidable (Solnit and Kris 1967).

Raskin, Petty, and Warren (1957) related the question of trauma to drug dependence (addiction) in the following manner:

> Through every stage of the development of the addiction the person we are dealing with is helpless to make an adequate adjustment by himself. His personality is characterized by serious defects in its development and pathological tendencies inherent in its structure. He is intolerant of anxiety. He avoids or escapes experiencing it through impulsive action. Before discovering the effect of drugs, his sense of security and well-being are dependent upon the immediate gratification of his needs and wants. The ordinary delays and inconveniences of daily living are experienced by him as intolerable frustrations. He cannot escape them. Unbearable tensions are experienced which he feels the environment should relieve. When the relief is not forthcoming, he feels that his inalienable right to happiness as a human being has been abrogated. Thus, simultaneously confronted with the irresistible need for immediate gratification and an ungratifying environment, it is inevitable that he will feel justified in employing any measure to rectify his deprivation.

The drug dependent personality as such does not exist. There are a variety of factors and influences, however, which make drug use, abuse, and dependence more likely. Among the factors discussed so far, several suggest that drugs are used to avoid impending psychic trauma in circumstances which would not be potentially traumatic to other people. Such potential sources are regression vis-à-vis affect, the inability to utilize anxiety or affects as a signal, and the inability to tolerate pain and painful affects, especially the Ur-affects or predecessors of depression and anxiety. Since this Ur-affect is conceptualized as the infant's reaction to loss, it begs the question of object relations, which will be taken up later.

The point to be made is that the resistance to trauma, the stimulus barrier, is defective in drug dependent persons.

The Stimulus Barrier

The stimulus barrier has usually been visualized as a wall, or as Freud (1920) put it, a "crust" or "protective shield," analogous to the hornified layer of the skin:

> It acquires the shield in this way: its outmost surface ceases to have structure proper to living matter, becomes to some degree inorganic and thenceforward functions as a special envelope or membrane resistant to stimuli. In consequence, the energies of the external world are able to pass into the next underlying layers which have remained living, with only a fragment of their original intensity; and these layers can devote themselves behind the protective shield to the reception of the amounts of stimulus which have been allowed through it. By its death, the outer layer has saved all the deeper ones from a similar fate, unless, that is to say, stimuli reach it which are so strong that they break through the protective shield.

This model of the stimulus barrier, derived from the function of the skin and the sensory organs, is inadequate in that it does not acknowledge that dealing with stimuli and affects is an active process. This analogy does not view the protection of the organism against trauma as an active ego function but as a sort of sieve or dam which performs entirely passively, unselectively, and whose function is not subject to variation. We would prefer to define the stimulus barrier as the sum total of all the individual's resources which prevent or work toward the prevention of the syndrome of traumatization.

Stimulus Barrier and Affect Tolerance

In meeting and coping with perceptions, affects, and ideas, many methods and ego functions are employed. The development of a crust might be effective in raising the stimulus threshold, but not the stimulus tolerance. Especially in relation to painful states, it is essential to distinguish between the acuity of perception of the stimulus and the affects arising from dealing with the perception. We are concerned with pain tolerance and not pain threshold. We wish to make explicit our view that the mastery of affects involves the same problems as that of external stimuli, and that the failure to master, to keep within bounds of tolerance, or to ward off affects can produce psychic trauma. Similarly, memories and unconscious memory traces pose a danger of overwhelming the ego with the intensity of stimulation related to previous perceptions (including those understood only later), memories of trauma in the past, and traumatic screens (Glover 1929, Rangell 1967). We conceptualize the drug dependent patient's plight as living in the dread of being overwhelmed with the primary unpleasure affects as a result of the after affects of trauma in infancy. These persons function as though they had an unconscious memory of this danger of trauma by being overwhelmed with the Ur-affect of anxiety–depression, and must ward it off by the mechanism of denial and their dependence upon drug effects.

An interesting correlate at this point is a clinical observation so frequently experienced in meeting with opiate dependent persons. The deficit in the integrity of their psychic stimulus barrier almost seems to be unconsciously perceived by these persons. Their inability to deal adequately and effectively with the stimulus and its provoked affectual response is eloquently expressed by their consciously stated desire and aim to gain a status of "oblivion" through the use of the drug. This same goal in relation to dealing with potential traumatizing affects is reflected by Chein (1964) in his considerations of drug dependence and Nirvana. The opiate dependent person is stated to be seeking Nirvana rather than Paradise. The latter represents an ideal situation in which all desires are easily and immediately satisfied; Nirvana constitutes the ideal of fulfillment through the absence of desire, and desire itself is viewed as an inherently frustrated state that cannot be compensated for through the pleasure of its gratification.

Use of Drugs in Augmenting Stimulus Barrier

The traumatic situation, however, is difficult to recognize because of the multiplicity of functions involved. For one, the threat is not exactly from the intensity of stimuli but, as Murphy (1961) pointed out, "the specific intensity of meaning." In fact, the absence of stimuli can be just as disturbing. Also, intense stimulation or affect may be preferred, sought by drug users in warding off that which is threatening. This might be the way the amphetamine and other stimulant drug users prefer to tolerate excitement, hypomania, sensory hyperacuity, and the physiological aspects of anxiety (jitters, etc.) rather than the threatening depression or boredom. One might say that the stimulus barrier in this instance is augmented by drugs, exciting perceptions and affects against the specific threatening perception. The analogy that fits this picture better is the "living" action at cell membranes selectively absorbing some ions and using the exertion of others in the process, and at the same time the balance between the two for maintaining the pH, and the electrochemical charge at the surface — and who knows how many other functions at the same time?

Even the function of perception is subject to modification. Petrie (1967) showed that experimental subjects consistently decreased or increased the quantity of perceptions. The former also "reduced" the amount of pain they experienced, while under the same circumstances they later "augmented" it. Among the groups tested, alcoholics were consistently "average augmenters" and none were "reducers." Alcohol, aspirin, or placebos decreased the degree to which they augmented their perception, including pain. At the same time, we have commented on the drug dependent person's selective lack of or awareness of the one Ur-affect for the relief of which they take the drug. This is a selective "numbing" and blocking.

The ego functions that guard the integrity of the psyche (and therefore the organism) are complex and interrelated. Keiser (1967) has pointed out:

> The loss of any one function must necessarily affect all the functions of the ego, since the ego must compensate, or find other means of satisfaction, for those drives or partial drives that can no longer be discharged or gratified through their accustomed pathways. Furthermore energy must be expended on the alteration of

the ego function. Hence, it can be postulated that whenever the barrier surrounding a specific ego function is threatened with extinction, a feeling of psychic helplessness is generated. The clinical results of this feeling of helplessness may then be manifest primarily in the area of the damaged ego function.

What we are observing with drug dependent individuals in regard to ego functions may have a prehistory in terms of disturbances of drives and affects (Krystal 1962), a resulting disturbance of the ability to deal with the affects, and consequently all the variety of abnormalities of ego functions we are describing here. Finally, as we shall discuss later, drugs themselves are used to produce yet other (temporary) changes in ego functions and consciousness as a means of dealing with or relieving the dysphoric states produced by the disturbed functions.

Case Illustration

A man dependent upon narcotics and other drugs utilized them in major part to control anxiety. Daily he would confront the excessive load of work he had arranged. He would then think that he could not possibly handle it, and this thought would further frighten him that he could not possibly face his public—hence he had to take his drug. Besides anxiety-depression, he also dreaded other affects; helplessness most of all, anger, boredom, and without having been aware of it until the analysis, sexual excitement. He managed to avoid discovering his fear of sexual excitement because of the use of the drugs, and before that a counterphobic promiscuity and transvesticism.

The fear of sexual excitement was related to a childhood strain-trauma[1] of a seductive older sister who, in her acting as a substitute mother for years, used to arouse more excitement in him than he could handle. The primary trauma, however, was unsatisfactory mothering by his depressed mother. This man lived in constant danger of return of his traumatization, now by his own affect. His experience of his affects, especially the dysphoric ones, was that they threatened to overwhelm him. While fearful of affects and taking drugs "for them," after taking the drug he was able to experience the physiological expressive parts of them, especially of anxiety, without being panicked by the experience, and in fact with enjoyment, betraying the erotization (deneutralization) of the affects.

Effect of Trauma on Affect Tolerance

This patient illustrates a disturbance in regard to the handling of most affects, related to a dysfunction of his maternal love objects. Boyer (1956) has pointed out that it is a part of the maternal function to provide a barrier against endogenous and exogenous stimuli for the baby, and excessive stimulation or

---

[1] In Kris's (1956) sense it related not to a single seduction but to a continuously seductive and frustrating relationship with his sister.

deprivation from the maternal love object as well. The failure of this protective function would threaten the overwhelming of the child with his affect, threatening his survival, and interfering with his ability to handle affects as only one of the resulting ego disturbances. Greenacre (1958) has implied that this type of maternal failure may result in the establishment of character trait disturbances and even establish the physical patterns of responses to affects; these people would be thus threatened with more violent reactions.

Krystal has pointed out in connection with studies of withdrawal phenomena that there is a "rebound" of the somatic aspects of affects suppressed by drugs on a subcortical level (Krystal 1962), and that whenever psychotropic drugs are used, some "break-through" of the expressive aspects of the drugs allows the maintenance of their effectiveness (Krystal 1966). The ability to alleviate some withdrawal symptoms representing a rebound of the feeling of anxiety and depression is a protection against the development of drug dependence. Conversely, an over-reactivity to these affects, and an inability to handle them in small quantities, increases the probability of addiction. In drug dependent persons there is evidence of both phenomena, and hypercathexis of those parts of the body related to affect expression—namely, the muscular and visceral organs. Chodorkoff (1964, 1967) has demonstrated corresponding changes in body-image in psychological studies of alcoholics.

We are dealing, then, with a disturbance in the handling of unpleasant affects, resulting from a failure of the protective and guiding role of the mother in providing what Winnicott (1958) called a "good enough holding environment." Khan's (1963) concept of cumulative trauma fits this situation well. As he puts it, "cumulative trauma is the result of the breaches in the mother's role as a protective shield over the whole course of the child's development, from infancy to adolescence—that is to say, in all those areas of experience where the child continues to need the mother as an auxiliary ego to support his immature and unstable ego functions."

While Khan (1963) discusses a variety of disturbances that result from the mother's failure to provide the shielding function as needed, he also points out that she "sponsors the capacity for toleration of tensions and unpleasure, thus promoting structural development." If this process fails, and the individual has an inadequate ability to tolerate tension and unpleasant affects, the differentiation of the forerunners of these affects into depression and anxiety is impaired, the signal function of anxiety does not develop, and the threat of psychic trauma looms large through life, making the use of drugs necessary.

DRUGS AND THE PLEASURE-PAIN PRINCIPLE

In previous discussions of the ways drugs are used for relief of the unpleasant Ur-affects, we have generally referred to their blocking. We have, however, noted in one case that upon taking the drug, some somatic experiencing of the affect became possible, and was experienced with excitement and pleasure. This situation must prevail in the use of the amphetamine-like drugs, which stimulate the release of norepinephrine, and thus initiate the somatic changes of anxiety.

Thrills and Regressions of Affect

In the use of barbiturates, while the ideational perception of danger is minimized, it often becomes possible to experience some anxiety equivalents (e.g., heart-pounding, chills, and various skin and mucous membrane sensations), while the breathing takes on a sighing character. Thus the libidinization of anxiety may be an important aspect of some drug dependence. Some barbiturate users experience their anxiety equivalents as "thrills." The anxiety provoking experience of becoming aware of the narcotic effect of a drug is sometimes related by the patient to the return of fear first experienced while being anesthetized for a surgical procedure. The fear of "going under" may be reexperienced, even though fleetingly, while the patient is conscious of becoming sedated by, say, a sleeping pill. However, our observation of some patients, especially those who tend to develop "pathological intoxication" with alcohol or other drugs, suggests that the allegedly insensible overactivity of the anesthesiologist's "first plane of anesthesia" may, in fact, represent the expression of anxiety experienced by the partly narcotized individual in terms of loss of self-control, fear of inability to recover consciousness, or fear of death. Thus the source of "thrill" in drug use may be a source of panic, and seems to be related to the repetition compulsion.

Szasz (1958) has noted the importance of counter-phobic attitudes in addiction, as well as the importance of allowing a mastery-through-play of ambivalent object substitutes. This will be discussed in relation to placebo studies.

The Principle of Constancy

We can no longer assume that the relief from conscious anxiety provided by the drug comes only from its analgesic action directly, that is, by a chemical blockage of the function of conscious perception of intersystemic tensions. We must add to this its ability to permit regression, and thus allow discharge of impulses, affording relief in terms of the constancy principle. At other times drugs are used for the very opposite purpose—to prevent regression, as brilliantly described by Glover (1932), thus avoiding this particular dread.

Studies on sensory deprivation show that a total lack of stimuli is anxiety provoking and suggest the necessity of objects for normal ego function. Pertinent here is Freud's (1920) quotation of the work of Fechner in *Beyond the Pleasure Principle:*

> Insofar as conscious impulses always have some relation to pleasure and unpleasure having a psycho-physical relation to conditions of stability and instability . . .every psycho-physical movement crossing the threshold of consciousness is attended by pleasure in proportion as, beyond a certain limit, it deviates from complete stability; while between the two limits, which may be described as qualitative thresholds of pleasure and unpleasure, there is a certain margin of aesthetic indifference.

The recent work of Bowlby (1961) on mourning stresses the dependence of normal ego function on one's love objects. The *disorganization* attending the object loss and the cathectic shifts in mourning are seen as a most painful and anxiety-laden experience. An added dimension in the pleasure–pain series is the ego's perception of self control or organization. We believe anxiety is not caused by the pressure of undischarged drives alone, but also *involves the conception of the danger and unpleasure of disorganization.* This aspect becomes important in the consideration of schizoid personality types who seem to live in constant danger of disorganization. Many alcoholics and other drug dependent persons fall into this category. They seem to be unable to give up or change libidinal positions, but tend to try to preserve the relations in phantasy through regression.

Studies utilizing the newer drugs affecting the central nervous system (CNS) suggest that some of them depress certain brain functions while selectively stimulating others. The newer anatomical knowledge of inhibitor areas of the cortex and reticular formation gives rise to practically unlimited combinations of ways of modifying an organism's drives and their controls. The work of Olds (1956), for instance, seems to be pertinent to the concept of pharmacogenic orgasm as formulated by Radó (1935). On the one hand, a drug can give relief by depressing the whole brain, thus dulling all consciousness and perception. Drugs may facilitate drive expression by suppressing inhibitor areas or functions concerned with conscious self-control. Finally, drugs may cause drive discharge by the direct stimulation of appropriate brain centers.

"Corruption" of Life Enhancing Functions of the Erotogenic Zones

Olds, working with rats which had permanently implanted electrodes in their CNS that made possible electrical self-stimulation of distinct areas of the brain, showed that the animal quickly became "addicted" to self-stimulation of certain brain centers. The stimulation of "reward systems" at the midline tracts to the rhinencephalon produced an apparently pleasurable response that the animal preferred to food. It gave up all survival or sexual activities, and self-stimulated itself several thousand times a day. When the self-stimulatory circuit was disconnected, the animal became apathetic and fell asleep (Olds 1956). This recalls the effect on humans of intravenously-given opiates, especially heroin. The possibility is raised that narcotics, by a direct effect on the CNS, perhaps on specific brain centers, allow an orgasm-like discharge. This dependence upon an artificially-induced drive discharge and the consequent pharmacotoxic orgasm imply a modification of the pleasure principle, its "corruption," in the sense that it no longer serves survival or supports adaptive activity.[2]

Our psychoanalytic work with drug dependent individuals raises the question of the constancy principle as the exclusive principle in gratification. The idea of the accumulation of tension and its discharge in an orgasm was

---

[2]Incidentally, a similar corruption of the biological function of the pleasure principle takes place in counter-phobic reactions, in which the dominant goal is to master the anxiety at the cost of repeated exposure to danger.

developed on the model of the male orgasm, and supported in observations on convulsive phenomena and some "thrills."

While the orgasm mode of discharge is one valid model, we must acknowledge another type of gratification: the relief from unpleasant stimuli or states (e.g., eating stops the tension of hunger). Satiety is pleasant in itself, but only allegedly in infants may feeding culminate in an orgasm. If the eating is pleasing, that is, stimulating by itself (*Mit dem Essen kommt der Appetit*), we are dealing with a gratification different from foreplay, as it does not lead to an orgiastic discharge. Chewing coca-leaves anesthetizes the stomach and gives gratification neurologically similar to being nourished, but certainly is different in regard to the general function and survival of the organism (Lewin 1929). And does not a full and digesting stomach send proprioceptive signals, albeit of a different kind, just as an empty or anesthetized one does? The implications of these observations are very important to our understanding of the metapsychology of anxiety, pleasure, and the various affects in the unpleasure series as well.

The economic principle becomes involved here. To the concept of accumulation of tension from instinctual needs is added the tension produced by pain and unpleasant states, such as hunger and anger. The relief of tension, then, will be produced by a discharge of drive or relief from the painful stimulus.

The Relief Principle

Very pertinent here are some observations reported to the American Psychoanalytic Association Panel on Female Frigidity, 1961. Helene Deutsch, especially, made the point that the phenomenon of orgasm as patterned on the male ejaculatory and orgiastic experience (as well as phenomenological observation of infants) may not apply to the sexual function of some normal women (Moore 1961). Certainly, it does not apply to the pleasure obtainable in erotogenic zones other than the genitals. This modification of our concept of gratification has important implications in our approach to drug dependent persons. It is possible that a desired endpoint of gratification is the relief or blocking of feelings of unpleasure, which may be produced not only by instinctual tensions, but also by pain, painful affects, or unpleasant states. What seems applicable here is Freud's (1920) concept of the relief principle which he described in *Beyond the Pleasure Principle*, in relation to traumatization, as "to obtain control, or bind the excitation, not in opposition to the pleasure principle but independently of it, and in part without regard to it."

The function of the pleasure principle is further affected by the fact that the use of drugs prevents the drug dependent person from building up psychic tension which can be released in normal activities experienced as pleasurable. This general lowering of tension, which makes the usual pleasure discharge impossible for the drug dependent person, is another side effect of this type of self medication. With it, tension-tolerance and consciousness are also impaired.

In dealing with drug dependence, therefore, it becomes dynamically and therapeutically relevant to pinpoint the specific effect sought by the particular person. The therapist has to be aware of the specific type of relief the patient craves. The pharmacogenic effect is of no less importance than the meaning of the act to the patient in terms of its symbolic wish-fulfillment. Yet, the *meaning* to the patient of the use of the drug remains of great intrinsic importance.

REFERENCES

Beecher, H. K. (1956a). The relationship of wounds to pain experienced. *J.A.M.A.* 197:1609–1613.
_____ (1956b). The subjective response and reaction to sensation. *Am. J. Med.* 20:107–113.
_____ (1959). The measurement of subjective response. In *Qualitative Effects of Drugs*, p. 123. New York: Oxford University Press.
Benedek, T. (1956). Towards a biology of a depressive constellation. *J. Am. Psychoan. Assn.* 4:389–427.
Bowlby, J. (1961). Processes of mourning. *Int. J. Psycho-An.* 42:317–340.
Boyer, L. B. (1956). On maternal overstimulation and ego defects. *Psychoan. St. Child* 11:236–256. New York: International Universities Press.
Bradley, J. J. (1963). Pain associated with depression. *Brit. J. Psych.* 109:741–745.
Chein, I., Gerald, D. L., Lee, R. S., and Rosenfeld, S. (1964). *The Road to H.* New York: Basic Books.
Chessick, R. D. (1960). The pharmacogenic orgasm in drug addicts. *Arch. Gen. Psych.* 3: 545–556.
Chodorkoff, B. (1964). Alcoholism and ego function. *Quarterly Journal of Studies on Alcohol* 25:292–299.
_____ (1967). Body image characteristics of the alcoholics. Mimeographed. Detroit Psychiatric Institute.
Critchley, M. (1956). Congenital indifference to pain. *Arch. Int. Med.* 45:735–747.
Dorsey, J. M. (1969). Opening remarks to second workshop. In *Massive Psychic Trauma*, ed. H. Krystal, p. 48. New York: International Universities Press.
Engel, G. L. (1962). Anxiety and depression—withdrawal: the primary affect of unpleasure. *Int. J. Psycho-An.* 43:89–98.
Freud, A. (1952). The role of bodily illness in the mental life of children. *Psychoan. St. Child* 7:69–81. New York: International Universities Press.
Freud, S. (1917). Mourning and melancholia. *Standard Edition* 14:245.
_____ (1920). Beyond the pleasure principle. *Standard Edition* 18:27.
_____ (1926). Inhibitions, symptoms and anxiety. *Standard Edition* 20.
Glover, E. (1929). The screening function of traumatic memories. *Int. J. Psycho-An.* 10:90–93.
_____ (1932). On the etiology of drug addiction. *Int. J. Psycho-An.* 13:298–328.
Goldstein, L. (1966). Aspirin vs. anxiety. Reported at 1966 convention of American societies for experimental biology. Quoted in *Modern Medicine*, p. 39, May 23.
Greenacre, P. (1952). *Trauma, Growth and Personality*. New York: Norton.
_____ (1958). Towards an understanding of the physical nucleus of some defense mechanisms. *Int. J. Psycho-An.* 39:69–76.
Hill, H. E., Koznetsky, C. H., Flannery, H. J., and Wikler, A. (1952). Studies on anxiety associated with anticipation of pain. *A.M.A. Arch Neur. & Psych.* 67:612–619.
Keiser, S. (1967). Freud's concept of trauma and a specific ego function. *J. Am. Psychoan. Assn.* 15:781–794.
Khan, M. M. (1963). The concept of cumulative trauma. *Psychoan. St. Child* 18:286–307. New York: International Universities Press.
Kris, E. (1956). The recovery of childhood memories in psychoanalysis. *Psychoan. St. Child* 11:54–88. New York: International Universities Press.
Krystal, H. (1962). The study of withdrawal from narcotics as a state of stress. *Psych. Quart. Suppl.* 36:53–65.
_____ (1966). Withdrawal from drugs. *Psychosomatics* 7:299–302.

_____ , ed. (1968). *Massive Psychic Trauma*. New York: International Universities Press.

Krystal, H., and Petty, T. A. (1961). The psychological aspects of normal convalescence. *Psychosomatics* 2:1–7.

Lewin, K. (1929). *Phantastica: Die betaubenden und erregenden Genussmittel*. Berlin: Kluge & Co.

Livingston, W. K. (1953). What is pain? *Sc. Amer.* 407:3–9.

Melzack, R. (1961). The perception of pain. *Sc. Amer.* 457: 3–12.

Moore, B. E. (1961). Frigidity in women. Report of Panel, *J. Am. Psychoan. Assn.* 9:511–585.

Murphy, W. F. (1961). Trauma and loss. *J. Am. Psychoan. Assn.* 9:519–532.

Olds, J. (1956). Pleasure centers in the brain. *Sc. Amer.* 30:1–8.

Ostow, M. (1957). Psychic function of temporal lobes as inferred from seizure phenomena. *Arch. Neur. & Psych.* 77:79–85.

Petrie, A. (1967). *Individuality in Pain and Suffering*. Chicago: University of Chicago Press.

Radó, S. (1935). The psychoanalysis of pharmacothymia. *Psych. Quart.* 2:2–23.

Ramzy, I., and Wallerstein, R. S. (1958). Pain, fear and anxiety: a study in their interrelationship. *Psychoan. St. Child.* 13:147–189. New York: International Universities Press.

Rangell, L. (1967). The metapsychology of trauma. In *Psychic Trauma*, ed. S. Furst, pp. 51–85. New York: Basic Books.

Raskin, H. A., Petty, T. A., and Warren, M. (1957). A suggested approach to the problem of narcotic addiction. *Am. J. Psych.* 113:1089–1094.

Rees, J. R. (1945). *The Shaping of Psychiatry by War*. New York: Norton.

Schur, M. (1955). Comments on the metapsychology of somatization. *Psychoan. St. Child* 10:119–64. New York: International Universities Press.

Solnit, A., and Kris, M. (1967). Trauma and infantile experiences: a longitudinal perspective. In *Psychic Trauma*, ed. S. Furst, pp. 175–221. New York: Basic Books.

Szasz, T. (1957). *Pain and Pleasure*. London: Tavistock.

_____ (1958). The counterphobic mechanism in addiction. *J. Am. Psychoan. Assn.* 6:309–325.

Weiss, J. (1959). Intensity as a character trait. *Psychoan. Quart.* 28:64–72.

Winnicott, D. W. (1958). Mind and its relation to psyche-soma. In *Collected Papers*. New York: Basic Books, 1949.

Wolf, H. G., Hardy, J. P., and Goodell, H. (1940). Studies in pain. *J. Clin. Invest.* 19:659–688.

15: PSYCHODYNAMICS IN COMPULSIVE DRUG USE

Leon Wurmser

THE SHIFT IN FOCUS

The starting point of my reevaluation of some of the common preconceptions about compulsive drug users in general and narcotic addicts in particular was the following distressing experience, repeated many times over the last 12 years since I started working intensively and systematically with all types of what is too loosely called "drug abuse."

At first I was provoked by the habits and attitudes of these patients, feeling that I was dealing indeed with the scum of mankind, feeling anger about being lied to and manipulated, feeling scorn for their flaunting of being "high" and their flouting of all efforts to help them and of all rules we live by.

Yet the more I got to know them, anger, disdain, frustration vanished, and a deep sense of despair and pity broke through. I could hardly find better words than what Faust said entering the dungeons where Margarete was awaiting the dawn and her execution, his almost untranslatable: "The whole depth of human misery grips me" ("Der Menschheit ganzer Jammer fasst mich an"). Often I felt a sense of helplessness, a wish to help, and an ignorance of how to help. The problems of drugs, drug effects, drug prohibition receded, paled compared with the overwhelming problems posed by these patients who sought help, were forced to be treated, fled from help, died.

When I followed the literature, the discussions at scientific conventions, the opinions expressed by friends, in audiences, by lawyers, no suggestions, no help were offered. A vast *terra incognita* was lying before me, covered by such expressions as: "They are just sociopaths!" or "They are not motivated," "the living dead," "the dope friends." Thus the problem posed itself with glaring sharpness: How can drug abuse be understood from the context of the individual's life experience, from his wishes and fears, from his deficiencies and efficiencies, from his conflicts in past and present — in short, from a psychological point of view. How can these deeper problems be treated?

Thus on the one side we have a relative plethora of pharmacological studies and sociological inquiries, although I do not imply these are redundant, and much more work in these fields should be done. Moreover, the politics and the legal aspects of illegal drug use fill the columns of our newspapers and tax the exegetical skills of self-styled experts of all kinds: lawyers, politicians, policemen and administrators. Many deal seriously and compassionately with the problems, many others make cheap hay from them, but most skim just the surface.

On the other side, drug abuse has remained off the beaten track, where many psychiatric and psychological explorers will not tread. There are good reasons for this: one is precisely the complexity of the problem, namely that psychological factors are so tightly interwoven with sociological, economic, political, and legal factors. Where the values of power, expediency, public success, and cost efficiency are uppermost, the required strategies of manipulation and control become so intermingled with therapeutic considerations that the value of insight, inner change and control, and the methods of introspection and empathy, have perforce to take a back seat. Yet, in all these years that I have consistently devoted a large part of my professional work to these patients I have been struck by this overriding impression: that severe psychopathology was a preexisting condition in those people for whom "drug abuse" became a real problem; that these inner problems were indeed of crucial explanatory importance.

At the same time I noticed resistance against this view, resistance of different content, from different walks of life, of various intensity and origin. Medical colleagues frowned upon it. Psychiatrists doubted it. Even some psychoanalytic friends felt I exaggerated the role of intrapsychic and family problems as compared with social, cultural and political influences. My co-workers in the drug abuse programs were often quite negative about recognizing the psychological problems and—sometimes with some derision—emphasized instead the value of manipulation and exhortation in the form of counseling, the value of external change. The patients themselves very often—though by no means always—put their problems on friends, "bad environment," "curiosity" and "society." Their families regularly did, nearly without fail.

A large role in this negation is played by an antipsychiatric bias on many levels, a prejudice against looking at one's inner life (problems or potentialities), at times so strong that we might call it "psychophobia"—a deep-seated fear of taking emotional factors seriously, *a denial of the importance of emotional conflict*, which haunts drug abusers as well as those dealing with it.

Thus, I decided to collect as much evidence for the importance of psychopathology as I could muster and put it in a reasonable perspective. Obviously many other factors—social, cultural, etc.—are involved, cannot be neglected, have to be weighed, put in relation to the rather crushing weight of personal clinical experience.

This leads to a rather radical refocusing which has only a few precedents, mainly, the work of Krystal and Raskin, Wieder and Kaplan, Khantzian, Frosch.

These reformulations can be summarized in the following five points:

1. The focus of inquiry and intervention is shifted *from drugs to personality,* from drug use as a social phenomenon which might be relatively easily manipulated, deterred, cured by external means (such as threats, counseling, laws and jails), to drug use as a symptom of a psychological depth dimension which has been up to now only rarely investigated or treated. This implies that psychoanalysis and psychotherapy have to contribute a vastly neglected component to the study and treatment of this mass phenomenon.

At a time when both psychoanalysis and psychiatry are under fire for being irrelevant, moribund or dead, this study is grounded in the *psychoanalytic process of inquiry* in regard to both observation and abstraction. Hence it is no part of the current stampede to get "nothing but Facts . . .imperial gallons of facts," the flight from theoretical constructions and hierarchies of abstractions. Nor does it take any theory as dogma, as more than a form of symbolic representation. Symbols are not facts, but ways to order them—indispensable, but on a different plane of understanding.

2. Yet this reorientation does not lead to a one-way street. Rather, psychoanalysis as *theory* may in turn benefit from new observations gained in this field. Therefore, the investigation underlying this brief essay, by examining in depth a number of individual cases, tries to deepen, to question and to enlarge some common (and a few less common) psychoanalytic and psychiatric concepts. For example, the phenomena and theories of narcissism and aggression are reevaluated in the light of these experiences. The defense "mechanisms" of denial and externalization and the problems of splitting are examined. Such investigation may lead to a deeper understanding of the quite complex nature of "simple" defense mechanisms and eventually to a hierarchical ordering of them. At the same time these defense mechanisms have to be viewed as patterns of drive gratification, as cognitive forms and basic elements of symbolization, and as fundamental action patterns. [In addition to new thoughts about forms of defense, the book at large, though not this excerpt, attempts, perhaps most importantly, to reexamine the concept of *boundaries and limits,* a notion which proves to be crucial for an understanding of these patients, and attempts to integrate the concept more solidly with current psychoanalytic theory.] Throughout, the affects of guilt and shame, and their archaic precursors, have proven to be of special help for deeper understanding.

3. By merely differentiating non-intensive from heavy drug use, the sociolegal definition of drug abuse is woefully inadequate for a psychotherapeutic approach. Instead, the concept of compulsiveness is chosen as operationally most meaningful, both for this particular field and for psychopathology in general. It serves as *the* criterion for "emotionally sick," as proposed by Kubie, not primarily to adjudge whole persons, but single mental acts. To select this specific "elementary particle" as criterion, with its practical, theoretical and axiological implications, appears especially useful and fulfils the crucial criteria for scientific knowledge as set down by Cassirer (1958).

Moreover, compulsiveness emerges as a *relative* property of mental processes: acts (thoughts, feelings, actions, etc., and their sequences and patterns) may be *more or less* compulsive, varying from person to person, and within an individual from time to time; acts felt to be absolutely compulsive or absolutely free either do not occur at all or are very rare. Since it is to a large extent observable, this criterion may prove to be particularly helpful for research.

4. Since drug abuse always involves pharmacological and social factors, it is strategically placed on the crossroads of psychoanalysis and pharmacology, of somatic medicine and general psychiatry. Indeed, the long shadow of drug abuse in human history lies across the crossroads of sociology and politics, of history and philosophy, even of literature and anthropology.

No look at the "hidden dimension" of drug abuse psychodynamics can fail to notice the connections between leading underlying problems in the individual (and this holds true not merely for the drug use itself) and sociocultural and philosophical antitheses, conflicts, contradictions. In a more comprehensive study than presented here much thought will therefore have to be devoted to tracing such lines from the individual to the surrounding circles of etiology, no matter how unspecific such connections remain.

Of particular importance among these connecting threads is the one between various aspects of the superego and axiology. The pathology of ideal formation in compulsive drug abusers reflects a deeper, more general "betrayal of philosophy." Again, there may be mutual illumination between the psychoanalysis of the superego and value philosophical conflicts and hierarchies.

More concretely this leads inevitably into considerations of ethics and legal philosophy. The experiences garnered in psychoanalytic and psychotherapeutic work cast new light on many central questions of these two philosophical fields and hence on the practice of legislation and law enforcement as well.

The psychoanalyst is in a delicate position: she/he cannot advocate specific ethical values but has to remain, even in clinical work, primarily a scientist who is beholden to one leading value system, namely, that inherent in every scientific method. Yet, as this system applies to psychoanalytic values (integration, freedom of compulsions, integrity and honesty, etc.), it has ineluctable effects upon specific decisions of an ethical nature. His central value system is beyond ethics in a narrow sense, but not beyond value philosophy. It also has a most profound influence on ethics, probably as no other area of scientific inquiry.

5. From all this it becomes obvious that there are, on no level, any simple, quick, easy solutions. The answers to many of the questions lie at this time still out of reach. Glib "either–or" reactions inevitably founder on this *complexity*.

An implication of this complexity is that in no case of severe drug use will one form of treatment suffice. It is typical (quite similar to severe chronic physical illnesses, like leukemia or tuberculosis) that one method of therapy is not enough, that *four to seven (or more) "modalities"* may have to be employed, *concomitantly or sequentially*. It is not at all rare that a therapeutic advance becomes possible only when individual-, group-and family-therapy are combined and often supported by medication or hospitalization, and vocational (and other forms of social) counseling.

The "one-track mentality" is very common and often a cardinal error in the treatment of these patients. Still, even a modality orientation does not do justice to the complexity and quite often may prove disastrous. Not only may it impede the tackling of a patient's severe inner problems, but it may exacerbate a severe "pathology" of treatment programs and systems themselves. In the administration of such programs one often witnesses an "insolence of office," a kind of pathology from people expected to treat it. Further, from insufficient command of complexity, treatment is often "penny wise and pound foolish." By saving in the short run, expenditures grow in the long run massively and outrageously, manifested, for example, in enormous costs of crimes committed by compulsive drug users and due, I believe, mostly to irrational approaches to their problems.

Even individual psychotherapy needs new methods, new parameters, to cope with the peculiar problems of this important group of patients. Conventional psychoanalysis quickly runs into insurmountable difficulties. At the same time some of the basic conditions of psychoanalysis (analysis of transference, countertransference, resistance) remain indispensable.

Recommendations made on the basis of recognizing this hidden, often negated or circumvented issue of compulsive drug use may strike many as revolutionary or puzzling—by those who have not struggled themselves with these patients' problems for many years, who have not been burned many times trying to build up programs for them, and who have not been called to help by the families of these patients in despair.

Yet I consider this type of effort very important. A considerable proportion of the population in our culture is involved in mild or severe forms of drug abuse: it may be one-fourth to more than half of the population. Of these, a very large proportion is undoubtedly involved in compulsive forms of drug use (at least between 5 and 10 percent of the population in Western countries) if we include, as we must, alcohol. Therefore, systematic in-depth studies should be considered with the seriousness a social and health problem of such magnitude demands, a problem probably affecting far more people than schizophrenia or most forms of somatic illness.

In addition, the social consequences of this symptom are enormous—another dimension dealt with by a legal system as ill-suited to deal with the problem as with plague, cholera or depressions.

I hear a loud protest, "You use a medical model; how inappropriate!" My answer is, "Yes, it is primarily a problem of illness and medicine, and more specifically of psychopathology and therefore of psychiatry and psychoanalysis. Logically and historically this makes more sense than any other current claim. It is the only approach which is both humane, seeing and treating this illness like all others, as part of the human condition, and still takes it very seriously—not merely as a social and legal deviance nor as a part of politics and economics, dehumanized to some statistics, nor as a part of physiology, magically overcome by some enzyme repairs and powerful potions." We ought to condemn less and try to understand more.

ANALYSIS OF THE DIRECT ANTECEDENTS

The Vicious Circle

Before the beginning of compulsive drug use, there are clear signs of a serious emotional disorder, one which may be called "the addictive illness" or the signs for an addictive career. We are confronted with the very difficult question how to analyze this complex of phenomena leading to the overt outbreak of the illness. This outbreak especially takes the form of compulsive drug use, but is not always restricted to this symptom. A few equivalents to drug dependency which precede or replace this symptom can be observed repeatedly (violence, other forms of criminality, depression, anxiety attacks, eating disturbances).

The following distinctions emerge: (a) A *horizontal plane* ("what goes on in the here and now when I start taking drugs for inner needs") should be distinguished from what we glean from the *vertical plane,* which includes the history, the depth dimension, the predisposition. (b) Even on this horizontal level, however, we clearly can distinguish that there are *covert events* which gradually emerge in detailed probing beneath the overt phenomena; these covert processes are partly *preconscious* and relatively easily retrievable, partly *unconscious* and, due to the particular difficulties of psychotherapy or psychoanalysis with these patients, almost inaccessible. (c) The conscious and preconscious processes can, without undue problems, be arranged in a fairly regular sequence, a vicious circle, which will be presently outlined. This vicious circle has, as all psychopathology to some extent, a particularly strong self-perpetuating quality, a feeding on itself. (d) When we explore the underlying dynamics of the single elements of such a cycle, we discover that all of them are themselves already *compromise formations*, partial conflict solutions. The entire vicious circle thus presents itself as a *complex series of compromise solutions.* (e) Next we need to recognize and define distinctly the underlying constituent components: What exactly are the unconscious impulses, wishes, drive components? What exactly are the defenses? How do the defenses themselves reflect instinctual processes? And: What are structural defects — neither defense nor instinctual drive? (f) In answering some of these questions we get onto very slippery terrain and are in danger of sliding into pseudoexplanatory concepts. We come face to face with something which Roy Schafer (1968) rightly complained about: "many of the familiar descriptive and explanatory terms of psychoanalysis are global terms, and, if used without further specification and qualification, they limit or distort perception and conceptualization of the phenomena" (p. 100). The notions of narcissism, denial, splitting, aggression proved to become names that were called by Szasz (1957) "panchresta," catch-all terms, too broad, playing into the need for complaisance and a sense of knowledge, but becoming imprecise, even contradictory cliches.

At the same time they could not be discarded by any means. They are, as the term "panchreston" connotes, overly general; they need further specifications, redefinitions, and occasionally new contents. At times the attempts to do this are provisional first trials at differentiating what seems well covered with the broad notions.

But to start we have to examine the more overt, less arcane vicious circle which is accessible to any careful ("microscopic") inspection. To illustrate, I use the near verbatim account by a patient of how he experienced his going to the Bowery at age 19 and getting drunk, and how this was identical with many events with alcohol before, with drugs later on, a sequence which I could witness as well right in the sessions.

1. It starts out with "any big event whether I succeed or I fail; it has the same aftermath: sadness, letdown, loneliness." In all patients it is some form of disappointment—realistic or in fantasy, a letdown from an expectation which may be justified or, more often, vastly exaggerated, an expectation usually of one's own grandeur, far less commonly a disappointment about someone else. This sudden plummeting of self-esteem is best called a *narcissistic crisis*.

2. The next step is that the feelings become overwhelming, global, archaic, physically felt, cannot be articulated in words. "I feel a foreign power in me which I cannot name; all barriers are gone." The patients describe an uncontrollable, intense sense of rage or shame or despair, and so forth. This is clearly an *affect regression* and brings a generalization and totalization of these very archaic, often preverbal affects (cf. especially Krystal). It is a *breakdown of affect defense.*

3. What happens next is least clear. The affect disappears; only a vague, but unbearable tension remains; there may be a longing, a frantic search for excitement and relief, a sense of aimless, intolerable restlessness, a craving (not unlike the one later seen in acute withdrawal). Instead of the prior feeling we hear: "I thought about myself as something else, as an object, as a character in a book, that I was creating the story about myself, a novel. I am not even actually aware of the pain anymore; it is not you, it is a character in a book you are creating. My whole life is so: a part who acts and a part who observes." The intellectual, observing part is not really alive, whereas the acting one lives. Like Alexander the Great comparing Achilles with Homer, our patient states: "It is better to *be* the character than to *write* about him in a novel"—better to act than to observe. It is important for us to notice the *split*, reminiscent of the one observed in severe states of depersonalization. This splitting recurs in many forms in our patients. In the passage just quoted it is between observing (and controlling) versus acting in a particular way, which we shall study shortly. More typically it is between the most troublesome feelings held down, suppressed, disregarded, the inner problems in general, and a facade, an illusion of being all right. Or: the problem lies in the body, outside. I believe the split necessitates above all a *massive denial* of inner reality, specifically of the overwhelming affects. Other defenses—for example, negation, avoidance, repression and projection—

seem to operate as well, but they pale beside the role of denial in the exact sense: "Disavowal or denial as originally described by Freud involves, not an absence or distortion of actual perception, but rather a failure to fully appreciate the significance or implications of what is perceived"—especially of affects (Trunnell and Holt 1974). What is important for us is the phenomenological evidence of many forms of massive splits, accompanied by unconscious denial, by an "invalidating fantasy," and by a partial acknowledgment.

4. There is a wild drivenness for *action*, for seeking an external *concrete* solution to the internal (and denied) conflict. "It was unbearable; I had to do something external to change the situation—no matter what." Violence, arrest, drugs—the specific *modus* of this *defense by externalization* is actually not even terribly relevant at a given moment for the patient: *the defense by concrete action on the outside which magically changes life* is what counts.

5. "It was something fascinating when I went to the Bowery. The position was appealing: to destroy myself, to be a bum. It was sheer *self-destructiveness.*" In other moments it was murderous anger. Again, as Anna Freud and many others observed: aggression, especially directed against the self, becomes an inevitable link in the chain. Our paradigmatic case also notes: "I progress, and suddenly I have the urge to break out, to destroy everything I have built up, and then I am completely down for a month and slowly build it (self-esteem, social accomplishment) up again."

This fifth step is the involvement of *aggression*, usually by "breaking out," transgressing boundaries, violating social limits, attacking others, destroying oneself, hurting and being hurt, humiliating others and being shamed.

6. "When despair takes over, the question of honesty becomes ridiculous." The drowning man has commonly little regard for questions of ethics, of integrity. Conscience becomes utterly irrelevant. Trustworthiness, reliability, commitments to others are acknowledged, and yet made meaningless, treated as if of absolutely no importance whatsoever. Again I believe there is a *profound splitting of the superego,* usually accompanied above all by denial, but also by projection and externalization.

No compulsive drug use (except perhaps for one commonly not recognized as such, like compulsive smoking) goes without this superego split.

7. "When I have broken out, there is so much enjoyment and excitement, that everything appears okay. I am satisfied then: I feel sheltered. I am acknowledged: the world owes me a living. I get something for nothing, and I deserve it." It is pleasure of many forms—*entitlement* above all—which forms the end point of the cycle.

Let us summarize what we have found so far: It is a series of conflicts, actuated in an acute crisis, which forms *the* specific cause. This specific cause is the following circular constellation: It starts out with (1) the *narcissistic crisis,* leading to (2) overwhelming affects, to an *affect regression,* a totalization and radicalization of these feelings. (3) As directed affect defenses the closely related phenomena of *splitting* ("ego splits") and fragmentation are deployed: the defense, mainly in the form of *denial*, but also of repression and other "mechanisms," is carried out partly by psychological means alone, partly and secondarily by pharmacological propping up (pharmacogenic defense). (4) Denial requires an additional form of defense, the element most specific in this series of seven, defense by *externalization,* the importance of reasserting magical (narcissistic) power by external action — including taking magical "things" such as drugs. (5) This reassertion of power by externalization requires the use of archaic forms of *aggression,* of outwardly attacking and self-destructive forms of sado-masochism. (6) In most cases this is only possible by a sudden *splitting of the superego* and other defenses against superego functions. (7) The final point is the enormous *pleasure* and gratification which this complex of compromise solutions of various instinctual drives with various defenses brings about. Most importantly the acute narcissistic conflict appears resolved — for the moment. But, as Radó described, the patient is caught in a vicious circle: "The elation had augmented the ego [now we would say the self] to gigantic dimensions and had almost eliminated reality; now just the reverse state appears, sharpened by the contrast. The ego is shrunken, and reality appears exaggerated in its dimensions" (1933). The patient is not merely back where he started, but on a yet much lower level of self-esteem.

What I have called "the vicious circle" is represented in the following model, Figure 15-1.

It is important to consider the probability that *each of the seven* components of the circle is already in itself a *compromise formation, a derivative of impulse, defense and defect (or deficiency).*

We have to keep this in mind and try to analyze this unconscious substratum as well. That part is most difficult and uncertain in its outcome.

Here still another objection will be raised: What is so distinctive about this League of Seven to make them the culprits in the problem posed? Do we not all undergo narcissistic crises, and are severe narcissistic disorders not even the daily

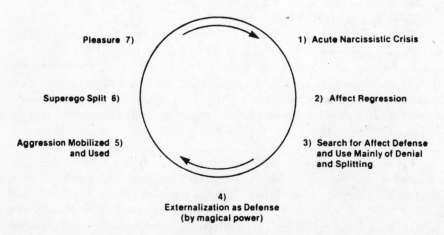

FIGURE 15-1.   The Vicious Circle in Compulsive Drug Use

bread of all psychiatrists and many psychoanalysts? Or to turn to the next objection: Are the internal and external structures and safeguards against these affects not often in many other people very brittle, just like the ground around a geyser: apparently firm, but breaking in at smallest weights and letting the boiling water flood over; is affect regression not a very common occurrence? And thus we can march down the list together and eliminate all distinctiveness. It appears to me, and I cannot be more than hypothetical, that the *combination is distinctive. Defective affect defense* (of those inner structures that channel affects, eventually becoming part of the predisposing personality structure) combines with the two most specific and most important factors: (a) deep-going and *labile, rapidly shifting splits,* largely resulting from the *all-pervasive* use of the defense mechanism of *denial,* especially against affects, and (b) the *massive defensive use of externalization* in its characteristic *concreteness of action.* This combination in its severity and massivity marks these patients and sets them apart from all others. This bold claim is based on a careful comparison in my mind of my toxicomanic patients with a number of neurotic patients having ostensibly somewhat similar problems whom I see in analysis, but who have never developed any drug problems. Whether this specification will hold up, however, only further comparative scrutiny will show.

Affect Regression and Breakdown of Affect Defense

This phenomenon which is shared by *all* toxicomanics and by many other borderline patients is also described as generalization, radicalization, totalization of affects, or, as Krystal and Raskin (1970) did, as dedifferentiation, resomatization, deverbalization. The terms are ponderous, the facts simple: The feelings become suddenly and irresistibly overwhelming, fearfully out of control. Words cannot do justice to them, nor can they be clearly differentiated from each other: Anxiety, anger, despair, pain, and so on — all flow into each other. Henry Krystal (1974) devoted a special and excellent article to this concept, which had been developed by M. Schur (1953, 1966).

All compulsive drug users have the following affects in common, which have to be warded off by all means (not only by drugs). All these feelings are the direct outcome of narcissistic frustration. Some of them are more prevalent in one type of drug use, others in another form, but basically they are all there. These basic moods and affects are: *disappointment, disillusionment, rage, shame, loneliness and a panicky mixture of terror and despair.*

In a short survey we can glance at the correlation of specific affects denied, the nature of the narcissistic wish fulfillment attained, and the preference for certain types of drugs.

a. The narcotics user has to cope with the emotional *pain and anxiety* flowing from the entire array of affects mentioned above. Among them *rage, shame and loneliness* seem particularly prominent. What he attains on the side of wish fulfillment is a sense of *protection, warmth and union,* of *heightened self-esteem and self-control.*

b. The user of barbiturates and other sedatives has to deal with nearly the same task. Perhaps the feelings of *humiliation, shame and rage* are particularly prominent and need the most powerful form of denial: that contained in *estrangement* (partial or total depersonalization and derealization). Thus, a study of the barbiturate addict has to pay particular attention to that peculiar form of compromise formation; depersonalization is not simply a defense. Particular wish fulfillments are contained in this symptom and need to be studied in depth. (However, this does not mean that we shall not meet in most other toxicomanics hints of this very important symptom, although it is most prominent in the user of hypnotics.)

c. In psychedelic users the major affects to be denied are the moods of *boredom, emptiness, lack of meaning;* from the primary list too, it is mostly *disillusionment and loneliness* which is walled off with the drug's help. What is attained—as gratification—is a sense of *meaning, of value, of admiration* and of *passive merger*—concerning the self as well as ideals.

d. The users of stimulants, again beyond the primary list, fight against a particularly intense *form of depression, despair, sadness, loss. Shame about weakness and vulnerability, boredom and emptiness,* are quite prominent. The narcissistic gain lies in the feelings of *strength, victory, triumph, invincibility and invulnerability* that reach in some nearly a manic state. The importance of *magical control,* ubiquitous in all categories, is particularly marked in this group.

e. Alcoholics are less subject to the primary feelings listed above; the main feelings denied appear to be *guilt and loneliness,* also in many, shyness, shame, social isolation. The narcissistic gratification lies in the expression, not in the denial, of *anger* which had been so long suppressed or repressed. In many there is also the feeling of *company and togetherness,* of *shared regression* and *acceptance in a childlike status,* the overcoming of being an outcast, when alcoholized.

These manifold negative affects break through with unrestrained force when archaic narcissistic demands are thwarted. Many of them are already expressions of aggression, the twin brother of narcissism (cf. Freud 1930, Eissler 1971, 1975, Rochlin 1973). In the section on predisposition the connection of the two will be studied in a new light.

We have seriously to ask ourselves, however, whether this *radicalization and totalization* is simply a breakdown of deficient inner structures, of primitive defenses, or may be in itself a form of defense. Clinical experience with borderline characters (not solely compulsive drug users) leads me to presume that it can be both: manifestation of a structural defect as well as a defense.

This becomes clearer when we see how this *affect regression* leads to a regressive generalization of perception and cognition. It is the exaggeration of a correct perception, for example, its *generalization* from one injustice and unfairness or hurt to the whole life. This *global* spread, like oil on water, I have often witnessed during sessions.

This affect regression is of central importance for the character structure of all patients with severe drug problems; and it is a totalization not restricted to some minor areas and choices; it permeates the whole world view for certain periods, until they can make it relative again. If they cannot do this, I think we deal with a *paranoid* deepening of the character pathology already outlined.

Very often it is experienced merely as a vague, but overwhelming physical *tension and restlessness*.

This entire phenomenon of affect regression is intertwined with a factor of the underlying personality, of the predisposition: the factor of *hyposymbolization*, the stunting of symbolic processes (for a brief note, cf. below). In regard to the question of compromise formation: All this stormy boiling up of affects is an outlet of regressed instinctual drives, mainly many forms of aggression. Simultaneously we have already remarked how this "totalization" serves as a defense, a flight from all too painful, all too limiting, crushing reality.

The Search for an Affect Defense

This third step is the most difficult to conceptualize. The patient is, as we saw, overwhelmed and flooded with unmanageable affects and often also most intense wishes, mostly destructive ones. His usual defenses have proven deficient. It is here that the drug enters — as memory or fantasy, then as sought-after means of solution, and finally as *found* help and protection, as a discovered coping mechanism (Khantzian et al. 1974).

When Dorian Gray recalled the murder of his (homosexual) admirer, mentor and father substitute, Basil Hallward, the morning after, he felt: "It was a thing to be driven out of the mind, to be drugged with poppies, to be strangled lest it might strangle one itself." Many observers have noted that all compulsive drug use is to be considered an *attempt at self-treatment*, and that the specific importance of the drug effect can be best explained as an *artificial or surrogate defense against overwhelming affects,* at least on a par with the aspect of wish fulfillment. Moreover it was already noted that there evidently exists some specificity in the choice of the drug for this purpose. But then the problems become so difficult and complex that one is tempted to exclaim with one of Dickens's characters: " 'Tis a muddle, and that's aw." And yet it is perhaps the most crucial issue to be solved if we want to gain a deeper comprehension of compulsive drug use.

What is the nature of the defenses employed in these patients and propped up or instituted with the help of the pharmacological effect? The answer to this question is difficult and complicated.

When we examine the nature and order of defense "mechanisms," we should keep in mind what was briefly touched upon earlier — that the same processes we encounter as defense mechanisms can also serve as instinctual drive derivatives, as controlling processes of perception and cognition, and as basic action patterns (beyond drive-motivated ones). Moreover we can arrange them in several continua.

These continua stretch from highly differentiated, subtle, usually mostly preconscious-conscious ones, to defenses operating on an archaic, undifferentiated level, functioning in a state of low integration, of global overinclusive-ness, and, as processes, carried by a most peremptory, that is, unconscious force. As to the latter I refer to Kubie's (1954) and Sandler's (1969) hypothesis: the more preemptory, compelling, rigid, inflexible, the more pushed by uncon-scious motivation (even if the process itself appears on the surface to be conscious).

Despite the current onslaught against the energy concept in psychoanalytic theory formation I find it, also in this context, a most useful, albeit metaphor-ical, one. The defenses on the more mature end of the continua operate with "neutralized," sublimated "energies," those toward the primitive end are, even experientially, when analyzed, of quite archaic instinctual, mainly directly aggressive quality.

I suggest to consider these defenses as lying on four continua:

a. A first continuum, the *avoidance type of defenses,* stretches from *conscious and preconscious proclamations* and wishes: "I do not want to know" (in Trunnell and Holt's paper: "denial" in the vernacular sense: "a 'declaring' not to be true") over *neurotic (unconscious) forms of denial* (keeping the affective significance of percep-tions and entire parts of percepts unconscious) and *repression* (directed against drive derivatives) to very regressive, much more *global forms of denial* (of psychotic or near psychotic proportions).

This first continuum is artificially instituted or, far more likely, massively *reinforced by depressant drugs:* narcotics, hypnotics, minor sedatives and alcohol. The *other two types* (psychedelics and stimulants) sometimes support especially denial, sometimes *lift* these defenses; their major action lies, however, in what follows.

Amongst all these defenses lying on the continuum, conscious "disavowal" and *massive unconscious denial* are by far the most prominent — immediately prior to drug use and then part of the drug effect.

Cognitively we find, for example, the averting of attention versus the focusing of attention.

b. The second continuum pertains to the *dissociation type of defenses,* the breaking of connections. It stretches again from conscious and preconscious versions, as described by Eissler (1959) and also in the Glossary (Moore and Fine 1968): *conscious isolation* in concentrated thinking, the *conscious ego split and superego split* in the psychoanalytic situation, to unconscious *isolation,* and the various forms of *splitting accompanying denial* (denial of loss, of castration), to more regressive types (Kohut's "vertical" splitting and the limited, *partial forms of fragmentation*), and, beyond: to very severe, erratic, *labile* forms of *dissociation and pervasive splitting,* and to the two most extreme forms of *global splitting* into all-good and all-bad and of radical, *psychotic fragmentation.*

Dissociation's cognitive usefulness in concentration was commented upon by Freud (1926). In all compulsive drug users severe forms of splitting and fragmentation can be encountered. The *depressant* drugs usually *reduce* the dissociations and indeed thus help to synthesize, whereas particularly the *psychedelic drugs massively deepen the dissociation.* Whoever prefers splitting chooses psychedelic drugs.

c. The third continuum pertains to the *action or fight type of defenses:* again from conscious, controlled use (alloplastic change, creative use of externalization, outright aggression as defense) to unconscious *externalization,* turning *passive into active,* possibly even identification with the *attacker* and *reaction formation,* turning aggression *against the self,* and magical *undoing,* all on various levels of primitiveness. From all these, *archaic forms of externalization* will loom up as an omnipresent, massive form of defense in all compulsive drug users and will be treated separately. *Stimulants* are the one category of drugs which particularly *supports* the defenses on this continuum, especially *externalization and aggression, turning passive into active,* often in a very primitive form.

d. A fourth continuum of far more cognitive and action-oriented significance than for defenses is the continuum of the *boundary and limitation type of defenses,* stretching again from highly differentiated and preconscious forms of boundary forming and limit-setting "mechanisms," of boundary creation and breaking, to the most archaic forms of fusion, boundary and limit blurring and transgressing. Instinctually the continuum reaches from extreme merger to full separateness, cognitively from the archaic *syncretistic* thinking (Werner 1948) to full *differentiation and integration* (Hartmann, Kris, and Loewenstein 1946; Wynne and Singer 1963; also cf. Cassirer 1923), in action patterns in Piaget's sense, from "original reflex or global schemata" to schemata based on "generalizing assimilation" and differentiation (cf. Wolff 1960). In regard to the defenses on the one end we have largely preconscious identifying, learning and once again externalizing, also conscious detaching, separating and transgressing, whereas at the more primitive end we would encounter well-known archaic defenses like introjection and projection, radical idealizing and devaluing, primitive forms of externalization and identification.

I presume that the placing of one well-known defense "mechanism" (e.g., externalization) on several continua is quite justifiable, because the processes contained are often of multiple significance, and thus, multidetermining. I hold that in all drug abuse this fourth continuum of defenses (and beyond: of gratification, cognition and action) is used throughout and has particular importance. Since I presume that all four continua reach back into earliest childhood, I doubt whether any drug type by itself evokes a more or less regressive form of defense "mechanism" (and with that of conflict solution). Usually severity of preexisting pathology plus massivity of drug effect (usually dependent upon the dosage and the setting) determines the depth of regression on each of the four continua.

I do not pretend that I have encompassed all defense "mechanisms." It is quite conceivable that more forms and different lines can be found. It appears to me too that, as Hartmann postulated (Hartmann, Kris, and Loewenstein 1949), all defenses operate mostly with aggressive energies, often in very archaic, not "neutralized" versions. "It is likely that defense against the drives (counter-cathexis) retains an element (fight) that allows of their description as being mostly fed by one mode of aggressive energy, and that this mode is not full neutralization" (Hartmann 1955, p. 232). This reference, including the indispensable energy metaphors, is amply demonstrated by the observations in drug patients: The pharmacogenic deepening of a defense is blatantly aggressive in nature, the pharmacogenic lifting unleashes overt conscious forms of aggressive defense (e.g., conscious disavowal and invalidation, use of direct violence for defensive purposes).

Thus the very deepening of the major defenses (denial, splitting, externalization) with the help of drugs is an act of destructive aggression, albeit intensely libidinous, especially narcissistic gains are also attained by the intensification of these defenses: the very muting of severely disruptive affects itself can lead to overwhelming feelings of joy, warmth, "good vibes" and, of course, as we will see in due course, much heightened self-esteem. Patients often become more sociable, friendly, accepting, harmonious, at peace, especially with depressant and psychedelic drugs.

This then leads to the conclusion that again this step, the pharmacogenic defense, is in truth a *compromise formation, in these patients, between their major affect defenses (denial, splitting, and externalization)* and *gratifications of aggression and libido,* in narcissistic and object related forms.

Splitting

When I use the term "splitting," I shall refer to it in three meanings, largely (though not fully concordant) with Lichtenberg and Slap's (1973) distinction: (a) as disjunction and fragmentations of representations, (b) in their extreme form as polarization into all-good and all-bad, and (c) very importantly, as "splits" in the entire personality organization, what Schafer (1968), Lichtenberg and Slap called "pathological *intersystemic suborganizations*" or "*persistent drive-defense-prohibition couplings.*"

Lichtenberg and Slap describe these couplings, "manifestations of *defensive* activity become connected with a specific *drive* and with *superego* structures. . . . Associated with such drive-defense-prohibition couplings are elaborate networks of memories and displacements. These networks are built around the ideational contents of the developmental disturbance" (1973, p. 786).

Since these latter theoretical expositions are very abstract and difficult to understand, I try first to put them into somewhat simpler language: We observe in many, particularly borderline, patients a kind of "split personality."

In all forms I consider *splitting* a defense "mechanism" and the resultant *splits* experienced or observed as more complex phenomena, combining the *process* of splitting with hidden, unconscious gratifications, and filled with emotional and ideational *content.* When we now return to the three radical forms of splitting encountered in all compulsive drug users three features stand out: What I am most impressed with is the *lability* of these splits, the steady shifting of them, the *sudden flipflops.* Now there is synthesis—now there is a split. This pertains to feelings, to external limits, to self-image, the value of others, to ideals and to the conscience (cf. also Lucy Kirkman's test results [Wurmser 1977]). It is an utter unreliability of structures, an iridescence of denials and of experienced and often-described and observed "splits."

Secondly, these splits are very often covered over by depressants, exacerbated by stimulants and psychedelics. In the former instance (use of narcotics, hypnotics, alcohol) they become particularly evident during withdrawal and abstinence.

Thirdly, these splits always involve cognition. At the least it is what Freud described, the rending of the ego between two functions: For example, the *acknowledgement* of the standing structures of the object world and the largely unconscious *disavowal* of such cognitive entities. Beyond this, in much broader terms, these splits profoundly affect the *cognition of objects and self, of time and space,* of all representations of self and object world, of one large part of the personality versus another massive part.

If we look back over what we have found, especially the prominence of denial and splitting, we are not surprised about the frequency with which these patients describe phenomena of depersonalization and derealization (see above). These twin symptoms occur either spontaneously or pharmacogenically. The more I study the material the stronger my suspicion becomes that if we only observe carefully enough we would find at least bits and pieces, if not the panoply, of the estrangement syndrome, in these patients.

Drug abuse thus seems like an artificial depersonalization state coupled with the next defense, externalization, which is so characteristic for "sociopaths."

Are drug abusers perhaps nosologically a *group uniting near psychotic estrangement with "sociopathy"?*

Externalization — The Neglected Defense

I set externalization apart, because it does not only function as a direct pharmacogenic affect defense (e.g., in stimulants, alcohol), but it has an overriding importance in *all* drug users in the form of seeking the solution to an inner problem on the *outside*, by *action* and in *concrete* form, quite apart from the eventually successful or failing function as affect defense.

This crucially important defense is the *action of taking magical, omnipotent control over the uncontrollable.* Everything else appears less specific compared with this peculiar and I think rather novel form of defense, valid for all compulsive drug taking. The anxiety is always there: "The various affects, like rage and depression, are going to overwhelm me." This fear of the traumatic state is powerfully warded off by the potent substance which is eaten, injected, snorted, or smoked: "I have the power — via this magical substance — to 'master' the rage, the pain, the boredom, etcetera." It is a specialized form of *defense by acting* — just as many analytic patients feel they solve an inner problem by an outer action (or avoidance of action), instead of by exploring, understanding and remembering. Moreover, since the Archimedean standpoint we have to take in psychoanalytic theorizing, after all, always addresses the inner stream of feelings and thought, any such act as utilizing an external help to "cope" with the frightening feeling, is a form of *externalization*—just like the picking of a fight by a guilt-laden patient or the carrying around of the powerful protecting lion by the boy who is afraid of his own aggression.

Now all the rest falls into place too. Of course, one who *magically externalizes as a defense* against being overpowered by frightening affects uses the same defense in form of "concretization." He says, "It's not I who feels, it's society or the body which makes me suffer from this unnameable tension"—what was already referred to as *hyposymbolization*. One who thus externalizes by massive action cannot form the guiding values and ideals—again abstract, symbolic versions of early feelings toward persons. Instead the drug is a concrete, external, sought after vehicle of action. It stands in the place of the group of the most potent symbols: values and ideals—and the powerful drug effect replaces the power which values have for us, thus the chemical mythology!

Archaic guilt and shame are all over the place anyhow in these patients—the drug is both a magical protection, a *talisman* against them—from the outside—and an implementation of this *double Nemesis*—again from the outside. In other words: The drug tries to ward off externalized (mostly not yet internalized) retribution and humiliation, but simultaneously it functions itself as a punishment and as a shaming, a shameful proof of weakness and failure. The drug dependency is both a matter for boasting: the conquest of shame, and a cause for shame: an obvious weakness and failure, exposed for all to see, though anxiously hidden. The same interpretation holds for the *archaic dependency* and ties Kohut's and Anna Freud's views, which seemed to contradict each other, together: the *defect in inner structures* lets the patient *seek an external object* of magical power to depend on for this all pervasive control. Again it is defense by externalization. *Externalization thus proves the magical key* for understanding not only all the proposed predispositions, but also so much of the external bluster. I have spoken sometimes—in connection with some cases—of the "Quadrangle of Fire" as a metaphor: All four "corners" are forms of externalization. It is the yearning for total unbound freedom, yet fatally abused; it is the need for security-lending structures, sought even as jail, but violently fought and rebelled against; it is the continuous search for adoration, the external confirmation of self-infatuation, the parading of phallic self-glorification; and it is the self-destruction by external means, the continuous arrangement of life that the patient has to flee like a hunted animal from police, mafia, vindictive whores—or imaginary enemies.

In contrast to paranoid states *the crucial "mechanism" of defense is not projection, it is externalization.*

And of course "society" falls in with it: "they"—police, politicians, physicians, parents, public (these five external powers)—go right along with the compulsive *drug user's demand for externalization:* They punish, prosecute, shame, hunt, prohibit, set up structures—inadvertently feeding this demand and becoming victims of it themselves.

In a sense the addict—like the paranoid—has been most successful in making the world serve his inner defense. Just as paranoid leaders influence world history by their terror-ridden projections, the addicts influence social history by their incessant demand for externalization. The success of both lies in forcing their surroundings near and far to play necessary roles in what is originally an internal conflict. The world goes along in this game of externalization, just as it does all too often with the projections of the totalitarian terrorists (whose concrete ideologies are but icing on their cake). These games of projection and externalization must have a potent lure for the "masses" to fall in so willingly.

But to return to the defense of externalization. That is surely not restricted to compulsive drug users? Do we not find it in many other patients (and nonpatients)? What then is specific for the form externalization assumes in the addicted person (even in its extensions—the TV addict, the gambler, the food addict, the compulsive smoker, the alcoholic)? It is the *magical* power invested *in a thing*; the *"thing" is endowed with control over the self*, over the inner life, over the feelings. The solution for any inner problem is sought in this one magical thing or type of things. The parallel case of endowing a *person* with such a magical power—very akin to the addictions—is the symbiotic surrender (and domination) in very regressed, often paranoid, but not necessarily psychotic patients. On the other, healthier side are those neurotics who externalize all over the place, but do not endow *one* thing (or type of things) with any of this exclusive magical power.

Kazin put this dynamic fact excellently: "the addict to alcohol, like the addict to anything else, believes that he can *will* a change within himself by ingesting some material substance. Like so many of the things we do to ourselves in this pill-happy culture, drinking is a form of technology. . . . Drinking cuts the connections that keep us anxious" (1976, p. 45).

It is also blatantly obvious that externalization is thus not solely a defense mechanism, but also a wish fulfillment, above all the *wish for magical power*, the subcategory of narcissism stressed earlier—so again a *compromise* formation.

A few theoretical addenda to the concept of externalization (cf. Anna Freud [1965]) are in order here.

It is rather difficult to separate cleanly and clearly externalization from projection. The way I conceive the difference is that the emphasis in externalization as a defense lies on *action* (including and especially provocation), whereas in the case of projection as defense the emphasis is put on emotionally distorted *perception*. Obviously both often go hand in glove together.

We also can distinguish various modes of *defensive externalization:*

a. by use of a *magically* powerful, mind altering, especially self-esteem increasing and affect-dampening *substance or thing*

b. by use of another *impersonal agent* as internal problem solver, like *television, gambling, money, food*

c. by use of an all-powerful, all-giving *personal agent* in *symbiotic* bonds or by fight against a *totally evil enemy* (here the projections are particularly prominent)

d. by *lying,* manipulating and evading all personal commitments

e. by *transgressing* in grandiose "acting out" the limits set by nature and society (in what the Greeks called *hubris*, a specific characteristic of the "tragic character")

f. by *provoking retaliation* in the form of shaming, of angry punishment or of diffuse attack

g. by outright *violence:* to destroy a symbolic representative of part of oneself, or, as in the just described mode, to bring about punishment

h. by *action as exciting risk,* especially if forbidden and dangerous, in an attempt to get rid of an almost somatic uneasiness and pressure, felt as primitive "discharge," a *breaking out of being closed in,* trapped, with undifferentiated but deeply frightening tension within. We saw how very typically the affect regression is experienced as a vague but broad, all-permeating *tension,* a drivenness and restlessness, a longing for risk and excitement. This tension is perhaps the prototype for all other modes of externalization.

In all these examples an external conflict situation and action ward off the internal conflict and the archaic overwhelming affects stemming from it. It is a very primitive group of defense modes. Also in all patients, this defense is combined with other defenses, above all — as we saw already — with splitting, regression and of course most massive denial, often with projection. All compulsive drug users show all or most of the eight modes of externalization described, concomitantly or alternatively.

As a general characteristic of all defensive externalization, we discern its *dehumanizing quality.* With the defensive use of action, this action itself is relevant, not the needs, qualities, properties of the persons "used," unless they happen to fit totally into this doing in the service of the denial. It is mainly this dehumanizing use of others which strikes us as so infuriating in all "sociopaths."

Another aspect of it has been described again by Eissler (1950): "their tendency to accept only the concrete part of external reality as valid and valuable." He adds that "The tendency toward concreteness is mainly based on oral fixation and is also the result of the comparative deficiency in the ability to sublimate, which is significant of so many delinquents." This last remark, however, would lead us clearly into the question of predisposition and will be touched upon in that section.

But it is important that this fourth stage in our sequence is marked by the predominance of a magical, global form of externalization directed toward impersonal, concrete, dehumanized objects and action for action's sake.

An important aspect of externalization, in these patients at least, is so obvious that it is almost omitted. The defense of externalization reestablishes the illusion of *narcissistic power and control.* Most prominently in compulsive amphetamine users, but to an only slightly lesser extent in all toxicomanics we find fulfilled a *feverish wish for autonomy, for being in control,* an escape from the panicky fear of not being in charge of one's destiny, especially the most ominous "ghosts," the haunting representatives of one's inner life.

And since it is action, frenetic action, it always must *perforce use aggression in the service of this narcissism.* Externalization is obviously the exact opposite of inhibition: the blocking of the feared and wished action. Thus again this stage can be comprehended as a compromise formation.

Summary of the Direct Antecedents

When we summarize this section and repeat its main points we have to ask: "What is now the specific constellation, the final common pathway, immediately preceding acute beginning or resumption of compulsive drug use? What is essential and present every time?" It is the following group of indispensable phenomena:

a. We noticed the externally precipitated, internally strongly experienced crisis in self-esteem, the severe narcissistic crisis, the collapse of expectations and valuations of the self and of others, and the reactivation of archaic narcissistic conflicts in an acute form. Their contents vary, from case to case, from time to time, appear isolated or in combination; but the acute precipitation of a conflict about self-esteem, valuation, meaning, in other words of an *acute narcissistic conflict,* remains.

b. This is followed by *affect regression,* a totalization and radicalization of feelings. The narcissistic conflict is either accompanied by *overwhelming feelings* of anger and rage, of shame and guilt, or boredom and emptiness, of loneliness and depression, or by a vague sense of wanting "excitement," adventure, to feel alive, oneself, awake, not estranged any more, a broad ill-defined tension, and sense of emptiness. This totalization serves at least partly defensive functions.

c. The third component is the urgent, again acute, need to defend against these overflooding, overbearing affects — above all by *denial* and *dissociation;* these two are the major *affect defenses,* now *pharmacogenically supported,* because insufficient in their own right. They affect not solely the emotional life and the underlying instinctual drives, mobilized in the crisis (most prominently intense sado-masochistic impulses, often of uncontrollable intensity), but all of reality testing. It is an acute, pervasive, and characteristically varying, labile, but *very destructive ego split.* The splitting up may be of varied severity: in fetishism, a narrow one, or more extensive disjunctions and partial fragmentations or an overall polarization into all-good and all-bad. The combination of denial and splitting very often leads to typical states of depersonalization and derealization, with and without drugs.

d. The fourth, most specific, most intense component is the use of *externalization* as defense: "I have to find an external solution for the unbearable internal problem which I do not want to see, cannot cope with, and yet am not able to avoid entirely either. I have several ways of external action: If I cannot find the *magical substance*, I choose one of the other avenues" — one of the other seven modes described. They are initially exchangeable and typically combined. The crux is: *action, "excitement," risk* — as a lightning rod for what is mobilized and denied.

e. This defense by externalization carries intense *sado-masochistic* impulses with it; very often these aggressive intents are most vehemently repressed and denied, feared to the extreme, and yet palpably and indispensably present.

f. There is not merely an ego split; there is a characteristic sudden "inoperativeness," a collapse of the superego, and an appearance of much more primitive forms of superego functions, a surprising, abrupt change from more mature, more integrated functioning of conscience, responsibility, ideals, to a much more primitive one, very often even a side-by-side existence of the two forms of superego. This superego with a suddenly unmasked Janus head is the *split in the superego*. This sixth constituent, ineluctable part of the specific cause, the *acute splitting of the superego*, occurs under the onslaught of the urge for externalization, for impetuous, impulsive, seemingly redeeming action.

g. Finally, the end goal is getting "high" or at least finding relief — the euphoria, the regressive pleasure, usually of a combined narcissistic, oral, object-dependent nature, and, as part of the narcissistic fulfillment, a sense of being a cohesive, bounded self again. Furthermore, claustrophilia wins out over claustrophobia.

This is the *heptad of compulsive drug use*, which we have called the "vicious circle" and now described psychoanalytically as a series of complex compromise formations, appearing in this order, in this sequence, each dependent on its predecessor, a vicious circle of mutual reinforcement and malignancy.

SOME COMMENTS ABOUT PREDISPOSITION

We have described a perspective on a *horizontal* plane, which encompassed mainly a microanalysis of the structural, dynamic, topographic and some economic and adaptational factors as they are needed to understand the historically closest and logically most specific antecedents directly leading up to the addictive syndrome. We should add a *vertical* perspective — a look into the historical depth of the personality, an attempt to see the aforementioned factors in their genesis and unfolding.

Skepticism is particularly justified in our field. What Eissler (1969) wrote in regard to treatment holds true no less for theory:

> Strangely enough, psychoanalysis is not able to provide the tools with which to combat the majority of forms in which drug addiction is now making its appearance among the younger generation in the United States. It seems that, just as psychoanalysis is, with few exceptions, not the method of choice in acute conditions, so it is not prepared to stem the tide of that form of psychopathology that is provoked by *anomie*. The dissolution of societal structures does not travel solely the path of lessening the strength of institutions and finally abolishing them entirely (at least for the time being), but also the path of *reducing structure in individuals*. The structure of the *ensuing psychopathology seems to be quite different* from

the psychopathology whose treatment led to the evolvement of psychoanalysis. [p. 463; my italics]

Thus we face the following obstacles to a genetic exploration:

a. The methods of psychoanalytic inquiry have to be modified to such an extent in the treatment of these patients that the observations gained do not lend themselves easily to simple and minor modifications of the theoretical abstractions gained by the classical method.

b. Very few patients stick to psychotherapy long enough to allow us sufficient genetic reconstructions which would give us the security of empirical probability.

c. As Eissler noted there is such an intertwining of intrapsychic with familial, societal, cultural pathology that we cannot investigate and understand one without at least trying to do this for the others.

d. The drug user himself is crippled by his very symptom in some of the core processes of judgment and self-recognition. Retrospective falsification is an ever-looming danger.

e. The main tool of recognition in psychoanalysis, the transference neurosis, only most rarely becomes clear in treatment. The therapist has to assume so much of a reality role, the patient is so intolerant of deprivation, that very little indeed remains of the "as-if" nature needed to explore in a systematic way the transference aspects (Tarachow 1963)—no matter how hard a good, conscientious therapist and analyst tries to keep these parameters to a minimum. Very often the choice is between keeping the patient in treatment or even alive versus maintaining a therapeutic relationship allowing a maximum of theoretic insight.

In favor of our efforts are, however, a few clear insights:

a. The heptad (see Figure 15–1) gives us plentiful clues to tie very many processes, seen in our patients as an ensemble, together with similar processes in other patients where they may appear "in single file."

b. There is no question that most or all of these patients suffered very massive traumatization all through their childhood, mostly in the form of gross violence and crass seduction and indulgence. What neurotics show mainly as intrapsychic conflicts with preponderance of fantasy, these patients experienced as massive *external* conflicts of overwhelming dimensions from early childhood right through adolescence.

c. Thus drug use is not simply an adolescent crisis gone awry (as the parents regularly want us to believe).

All compulsive drug users whom I ever got to know show what Kernberg so excellently described and studied as "borderline personality organization" (Kernberg 1967, 1970a, b, 1971, 1975). Here I stress mainly the predominance of primitive mechanisms of defense, that is, of splitting, of primitive idealization, of early forms of projection ("projective identifications": "They have to attack and control the object before [as they fear] they themselves are attacked and destroyed"), of primitive manifestations of denial ("'mutual denial' of two emotionally independent areas of consciousness"), and of omnipotence and devaluation. Kernberg also points to the lack of superego integration and easy reprojection of superego functions, the protective shallowness of their emotional relationships, their demandingness and exploitiveness, the chameleonlike quality of their adaptability and "as-if" quality.

But any such excerpt does injustice to the depth and richness of Kernberg's concepts.

Suffice it to note here that the toxicomanic patient allows us a detailed study of some of the traits shared by all "borderline" patients — especially splitting, denial and idealization (let alone the intolerance to anxiety and impulse, the blurring of ego boundaries) — but also permits us to gain rather novel insights into the role of manifold externalizations, the problems of affect tolerance and affect regression in general (not just anxiety), the important role of depersonalization, and especially the broad spectrum of various forms of boundaries and limits.

d. As Eissler and Kohut in particular emphasized: These archaic personality organizations reflect a lack of inner structures which early damage and family and societal pathology conspire to bring about. A fourth aspect, usually omitted, may play a very important role in this lack of inner structures: heredity. How important a role, we have no way of knowing today, but this is a scientific problem open to experimental solution.

e. The seven factors enumerated in the heptad all point to very archaic fixations — to problems in the first 2–3 years of life, to severe damage suffered at the time when these inner structures need to be built, when the child has to come to terms with frustrations to his omnipotence, to oral gratification, when boundaries between self and others are established, when he gradually learns to establish his own regulations of self-esteem, and, most importantly, when his affects become differentiated, put in symbols (including words, but not restricted to them) and slowly become manageable (cf. Schur 1953, 1966, especially Krystal 1974). There is no question that the severest damages in our patients lie in these early, largely preverbal times, though perpetuated on and on, as massive narcissistic conflicts and primitive aggressions directed with little differentiation against others and the self, as a general problem about boundaries and limitations, as archaic forms of defenses, as structural deficiencies of manifold nature.

Although we need particularly in this area far more specificity than our current theory provides us, I restrict myself to a cursory summary of the extensive findings presented in my full-length study.

If I try to select the one trait in the personality of the compulsive drug user which is most specific, it is the *overall lability of inner structures and of boundaries*. Not only are the emotions inconsistent and overwhelming, but so are the defenses, the self-other boundaries, generally the perceptual boundaries, and the limitations and boundaries watched over by the superego. Clinical experience, social and administrative observations and the test findings described especially by L. Kirkman (Wurmser 1977) all converge on that one point: the inner *"anomia,"* lawlessness, *the lack of consistency, structure, boundaries.* As Kohut so rightly remarks: This is the expression of a profound narcissistic defect. On the one side it is the outcome of acute and chronic narcissistic conflicts; therefore, the archaic, peculiarly narcissistic affects are overwhelming and unrestrained. But on the other side there is also a profound deficit *in structures* to cope in any consistent way with the help of a reliable defense constellation, with such conflicts and ensuing affects. Withal we encounter this peculiar *shift of boundaries and limits of all sorts,* concretely and metaphorically.

The analysis regarding structure formation comes down to the cycle shown in the accompanying figure 15-2. One may separate the five elements into different defenses or defects; it is perhaps more accurate to view them as different parts of the same phenomenon which appear as defenses and as defects. When we look at it as denial, we emphasize the defensive aspect; when we stress splitting, we view the double nature of disavowal or denial and acceptance or acknowledgment, especially from a cognitive point of view; and finally when we focus on the boundaries, structures, and lack of effective affect defense, we seek mainly the "defect" nature of the phenomenon.

Again, as on the level of the immediate antecedents, we see the entire constellation of the predisposition as *necessary* preconditions. Among them I consider this element of an inner "anomia," this peculiar lability in structures, as the most specific one.

The pathogenic conflicts probably reach, as in schizophrenics, very far back: to *the most archaic conflicts in perception and expression* and, with that, to the original forming of any boundaries and self-nuclei. These conflicts are postulated to form a specific part of what is too loosely and broadly known as the oral stage.

The massivity of other (though closely related and overlapping) problems, especially of severe and archaic narcissistic conflicts in the patient and the gravity of inconsistency, aggression and promotion of externalization and

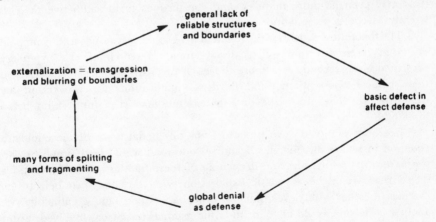

FIGURE 15-2. Cycle of Structure Formation in the Personality of the Compulsive Drug User

deception in the family, are invariably present. These other necessary parts of the precondition are: hyposymbolization; labile, often externalized superego; defect in ideal and value formation; prevalence of shame; massive aggression, mainly of the rage and contempt type, more self-directed than against others (cf. Wurmser 1974).

Even in the predisposition of the patient himself usually the entire heptad described as the "final common pathway" can be discerned throughout life and becomes usually very prominent in adolescence.

If we compare this predisposition, the personality, the "set," with other nosological categories, the work with patients who are not compulsive drug users (e.g., psychoanalytic patients) allows a strong contradistinction: Above all, the intensity and archaic nature of narcissistic conflicts are usually much more pronounced in toxicomanics. The extent of boundary problems and the prevalence of the very archaic defenses of denial, splitting and externalization are most striking. Neurotics use, instead, much more repression, introjection, or the obsessional defenses. Projection appears in both to a moderate extent. The superego pathology is far deeper in addicts than in all types of neurosis. Finally, a strong case can be made that the peculiar form of aggression which is evident in shame, namely *contempt, disdain, scorn,* plus undifferentiated rage, but less anger and hatred, are the one which are particularly prominently used in the service of externalization in these patients, and this even more in a self-directed, masochistic version, than against the outer world.

In contrast to the various psychoses the extent of ego split and superego split and, more generally, of fragmentation of cognition and perception is less strong in addicts. Projection, dehumanization, depersonalization are much stronger in psychotics during the acute phase than in addicts. Recompensated psychotics have much in common with recompensated addicts: If anything, the propensity to the characteristic splits, fragmentation, denial and externalization, even projection, the extent and massivity of narcissistic and sado-masochistic problems may even be more manifest and conspicuous in the addictive than the latently psychotic personality.

The theoretical conclusions presented here could serve us as a starting point to go in three directions—first, to systematic research of the hypotheses presented here, second, to a more thorough metapsychological exploration of these clinical observations, and third, to applications for prevention and treatment which would go beyond the present mad rush into action before thinking.

Research would have to proceed from this nodal point of the etiological equation in severe directions. Of course, one road would lead simply toward *confirmation* (or refutation) and deepening of these findings. Another even less paved road would be a genetic exploration tying the described defects and conflicts together with developmental disturbances and family pathology. On another path, one would have to study the *constitutional* factors involved; at this point, we have no way of knowing how much of the underlying problems are of hereditary nature. Yet study beyond speculation is particularly tantalizing in this area. Still another route goes in an altogether different direction: The defects in ideal formation may open a deeper understanding for *value psychological* and value philosophical questions; thus such a study would assist us in a more thorough theoretical superego analysis than has been known hitherto.

TREATMENT

A few fragmentary thoughts about treatment need to be added, first, regarding psychotherapy and then regarding large-scale treatment policy.

Psychotherapy

One thing is clear above all: One cannot do "business as usual" with this type of patient. They resemble in many regards psychotic patients. Despite the usually dismal prognosis, I have seen a number of very severe chronic drug abusers successfully in long-term therapy. I think in particular of several patients who had been dependent for 10–20 years on very high doses of amphetamines (100 mg and more, or similar stimulants) or of narcotics (with dosages of 100–800 mg of methadone daily), whom I saw for one or several years. Looking back over these experiences, I single out one precondition of treatment which has facilitated successful treatment in several instances: the readiness on both sides for intensive, analytically oriented work and to stick it out no matter what. By "intensive" I mean often, in times of crises, three to seven sessions a week, and sometimes much longer than 1 hour, plus telephone availability in times of lesser urgency. I have had cases who decompensated repeatedly and required brief hospitalizations (e.g., for suicidality in the case of amphetamine abstinence — often many months after withdrawal), but were able to work out their problems sufficiently in such very intensive psychotherapy that they were not only capable of assuming highly responsible positions, but eventually also to enter psychoanalysis proper. Given the severely regressive nature of the entire personality organization, it gradually became clear to me that the treatment situation has to encompass the following built-in transference elements:

a. It has to have strongly *nurturing, supportive* elements without, however, feeding into the often overwhelming fears in the toxicomanic patient of *engulfment*. The therapist has to be far more *active*, warm, interested, personally involved, yet again without becoming *intrusive*, as very often the mother was.

b. Also in all instances the exact counterpart has to be observed as well: to maintain *distance*, to be very patient, not pressuring, almost detached, without, however, supporting the profound sense of *abandonment and despair* so deep in these patients. One has to create a clear boundary of separateness, an atmosphere of nonsymbiosis and respect for individuality while still allowing symbiotic conflicts to be expressed and to become interpretable. The patient must not feel exploited and treated as a nonhuman object, no matter how much he may try to do that to the therapist.

Clinical experience appears to indicate that there may be indeed two basic types of compulsive drug users, one far more afraid of engulfment (a preponderantly *claustrophobic* type), the other fearing much more isolation and loneliness (in whom *claustrophilic* needs prevail).

In the first type the distance needs to be preserved far more and far longer for trust to arise, whereas in the second type far more direct support is needed, making up for a traumatic sense of object loss.

In most cases, though a delicate balance needs to be found somewhere in the middle, a constant empathetic weighing is required of whether more nurturing or more distance is needed at the given moment.

c. *Limit setting:* external structure is absolutely crucial. Time and again the patient needs to be faced with the alternative of curtailing some particularly noxious form of acting out or of forfeiting any true benefit from therapy and even the gains already attained. Each time of such an intervention is a crisis for the therapy. The patient may concur and work on the intense anger this limit setting evokes, with additional gain in self-control and with that in the ability to observe himself and in the working alliance. Or he may bolt, revolt, vanish, seeing the therapist's guardianship of boundaries and limits as yet a new form of entrapment, of intrusion, of enclosure. Therefore such interventions have to be used very sparingly and without any moralistic implication: Transgression of ethical or of any other boundaries has to be treated strictly as a symptom with severe self-destructive potential, the compulsiveness of which is the sole concern, not its antisocial (or socially positive) valence.

d. This leads naturally to problems of *countertransference*. Outrageous disregard of limits is often enacted precisely to *provoke rage*, punishment and scorn from the therapist and thus to reconfirm the *masochistic triumph:* "No one can ever be trusted. I am suffering again betrayal and degradation, and thus I prove the basic unworth of human relationships; I can rely only on my actions and on nonhuman substances."

Or in turn the therapist becomes a masochistic partner, forced by the ostentatious suffering of the patient into endless giving and giving-in, or into going along with and thus once again *indulging* the severest, most pernicious regressions.

Again the therapist has to find a golden mean: actively to set limits, but without anger, sadism, shaming, and vindictiveness, and yet to be very flexible, patient, always oriented not toward ethical values in a narrow sense, but toward the central psychoanalytic value outlined.

e. This *demand for giving* and indulgence may in some cases be overwhelming, especially in massively spoiled or severely neglected patients. The transference-countertransference bind may turn into a *sado-masochistic nightmare,* a severe negative therapeutic reaction and hence into defeat: rage, pain, hopelessness alternate with insatiable demands. Here the *dilution* of the dyadic therapy relationship may save both treatment and life. In a number of cases the splitting up of the therapeutic approaches, for example, into a combination of individual, family and group therapy, carried out by different therapists, proved far superior to individual psychotherapy alone. This is again an approach directly contravening the one-track mentality already criticized (cf. also E. Khantzian).

f. Whereas the transference-countertransference constellation is a kind of perversion of intimacy, the next is a type of distancing which can reach extreme proportions. In many patients it may take a real *therapeutic moratorium* of months, even years, of passive drifting, boredom, interrupted treatment, apparent endless stagnation, of a deep gloom of despair and hopelessness in the patient, at times effectively transmitted to the therapist, until a solid basis of trust has grown to start therapy in earnest.

This *moratorium of passivity* might be necessary not just because of the deep fear of intimacy, of the claustrum and thus the devouring, englutting mother, but also (and connected with it) because of dread of murderous aggression unleashed in submission to the power of the stronger "other."

In order to tolerate such a lengthy moratorium the therapist has not only to be patient and rather at peace with his own narcissistic needs, but I believe it likely that he needs two additional traits: First, he has to see in the patient strongly *redeeming features,* for example, in the case described (pp. 182ff), there was an intense feeling in me, through the years of despair: "What a waste of a capable, likeable, highly gifted, basically honest person!" In this feeling of *respect* and esteem for him, there was of course a lot of *hope,* which kept outweighing nearly always the massive despair. Second, the therapist has, as Freud stressed, to subordinate his therapeutic zeal to *scientific curiosity:* to understand and to help to understand must take precedence over the wish to heal, to mold according to one's own value priorities. To wait may mean to build up trust and to show caring; but then to step in and to set the right limits at the right moment (the "kairós") may be critically important.

g. The *working alliance* was defined by R. Greenson (1967) as "the relatively nonneurotic, rational rapport which the patient has with his analyst" (p. 192). I believe this concept to be equally applicable to the analytically oriented psychotherapy commonly chosen with these patients. In most instances these patients are too sick, too self-destructive, too demanding to leave much room for such rational cooperation. At first their attitude merely consists of a gut reaction: "I have suffered enough; I want to start anew. The price I paid in the past I am not willing to pay in the future." Thus, it is not so much the value of rationality which attracts them, but the *fear of further pain* and suffering which pushes them from behind. But as the time passes (again often years) an *identification* with the value of inner freedom, of self-mastery, of non-condemning exploration and knowledge, as represented by the therapist, may replace the more archaic ego ideals, and gradually lend more and more force to rationality and thus to the working alliance. Hence, shame and guilt may become associated with such a standard of reason instead of the grandiose self-image which had ruled supreme.

Large-Scale Treatment Policy

Heavy (compulsive) drug use is *coextensive with moderate to severe psychopathology underlying the drug use, not caused by it.* The crisis in the treatment of these patients who are either rejected or inadequately treated by the currently existing programs is also *coextensive with the crisis in the treatment of* emotionally disturbed or outright mentally ill patients in general. Innovative facilities should be created employing the gamut of already known psychiatric techniques to this class of patients; it appears imperative to develop and implement *innovative psychotherapeutic techniques* specifically for this type of pathology—combining in-depth dynamic (psychoanalytic) understanding and leadership, structure building and limit setting, family treatment, vocational retraining (or new training), opening up of creative or recreational avenues of gratification, and the flexible use of psychopharmacological agents. In other words: *Instead of one-track modalities* we need *combinations* of four to seven methods for each individual patient in a methodical, specific way.

Such a plan calls for the *avoidance* of many of the current faddish "short-cuts" and fashionable new "simplistic" techniques, because of their destructive potential with these severely ill patients. It requests a deeper involvement in the positions of *leadership* by psychiatrists and psychoanalysts in dealing with the majority of the problems of compulsive drug use. The current debunking of a thorough training in psychiatry and especially in *intensive individual psychotherapy,* and with that the nearly *total lack of understanding for the psychodynamics of these patients and their families,* has been devastating for psychiatry in general; but it has left the field of treatment of these patients almost entirely to paraprofessionals and to specialists from other fields who are naive as to the gravity and nature of the psychopathology in the majority of these cases and as to measures for devising rational treatment strategies for each individual case.

Most specifically, it calls for a *deeper involvement of psychoanalysis in such a leadership role,* not as a treatment method, but as the only accredited institution which has set itself the goals of a deeper systematic understanding of the human mind and of a methodical, thorough, well-structured and supervised training of its practitioners. Despite its current external and even internal crisis, its factual contribution to the huge problem at hand could perhaps be the *most innovative suggestion* this report can make—as old-fashioned as it may sound to many readers.

Reluctantly, I have to break off. What I have presented is, naturally, condensed, fragmentary, but I believe it may give some hints whither the new developments evolving from intensive therapy have led us so far and may point onward.

To finish, suffice it to say that we cannot remain, in this field which often appears to me beset by ponderous rhetoric and fatuous motion, like Mr. Pecksniff's horse (in Dickens's *Martin Chuzzlewit*), "full of promise, but of no performance. He was always, in a manner, going to go, and never going."

REFERENCES

Cassirer, E. (1923). *Philosophie der Symbolischen Formen.* Darmstadt: I: Buchges, 1958.
Eissler, K. R. (1950). Ego-psychological implications of the psychoanalytic treatment of delinquents. *Psychoanal Study Child* 5:97–121. New York: International Universities Press.

_____ (1959). On isolation. *Psychoanal Study Child* 14:29-60. New York: International Universities Press.

_____ (1969). Irreverent remarks about the present and the future of psychoanalysis. *Int J Psycho-Anal* 50:461-471.

_____ (1971). Death drive, ambivalence, and narcissism. *Psychoanal Study Child* 26:25-78. New Haven, CT: Yale University Press.

_____ (1975). The fall of man. *Idem* 30:589-646.

Freud, A. (1965). Normality and pathology in childhood. In *The Writings of A. Freud,* vol. 6. New York: International Universities Press.

Freud, S. (1926). Inhibitions, symptoms and anxiety. *Standard Edition* 20:75-174.

_____ (1930). Civilization and its discontents. *Standard Edition* 21:57-145.

Greenson, R. R. (1967). *The Technique and Practice of Psychoanalysis.* New York: International Universities Press.

Hartmann, H. (1964). Notes on the theory of sublimation (1955). In *Essays on Ego Psychology,* pp. 215-240. New York: International Universities Press.

Hartmann, H., Kris, E., and Loewenstein, R. M. (1946). Comments on the formation of psychic structure. *Psychoanal Study Child* 2:11-38. New York: International Universities Press.

_____ (1949). Notes on the theory of aggression. 3/4:9-36. In *Essays on Ego Psychology.* New York: International Universities Press, 1964.

Kazin, A. (1976). "The Giant Killer": drink and the American writer. *Commentary* 61:44-50.

Kernberg, O. F. (1967). Borderline personality organization. *J Am Psychoanal Assoc* 15(3): 641-685.

_____ (1970). Factors in the psychoanalytic treatment of narcissistic personalities. *J Am Psychoanal Assoc.* 18(1):51-85.

_____ (1970). A psychoanalytic classification of character pathology. *J Am Psychoanal Assoc* 18(4): 800-822.

_____ (1971). Prognostic considerations regarding borderline personality organization. *J Am Psychoanal Assoc.* 19(4):595-635.

_____ (1975). *Borderline Conditions and Pathological Narcissism.* New York: Jason Aronson.

Khantzian, E. J., Mack, J. E., and Schatzberg, A. F. (1974). Heroin use as an attempt to cope: clinical observations. *Am J Psychiatry* 131:160-164.

Krystal, U. (1974). The genetic development of affects and affect regression. *Ann Psychoanal* 2:93-126.

Krystal, H., and Raskin, H. A. (1970). *Drug Dependence. Aspects of Ego Functions.* Detroit: Wayne State University Press.

Kubie, L. S. (1954). The fundamental nature of the distinction between normality and neurosis. *Psychoanal Q* 23:167-204.

Lichtenberg, J. D., and Slap, J. W. (1973). Notes on the concept of splitting and the defense mechanism of the splitting of representations. *J Am Psychoanal Assoc* 21:772-787.

Moore, B. E., and Fine, B. D. (1968). *Glossary of Psychoanalytic Terms and Concepts.* New York: American Psychoanalytic Association.

Radó, S. (1933). The psychoanalysis of pharmacothymia (drug addiction). *Psychoanal Q* 2:1-23.

Rochlin, G. (1973). *Man's Aggression. The Defense of the Self.* Boston: Gambil.

Sandler, J., and Joffe, W. G. (1969). Towards a basic psychoanalytic model. *Int J Psychoanal* 50:79-90.

Schafer, R. (1968). *Aspects of Internalization.* New York: International Universities Press.

Schur, M. (1953). The ego in anxiety. In *Drives, Affects, Behavior,* pp. 67-100. New York: International Universities Press.

_____ (1966). *The Id and the Regulatory Principles of Mental Functioning.* New York: International Universities Press.

Szasz, T. S. (1957). The problem of psychiatric nosology. *Am J Psychiatry* 114:405.

Tarachow, S. (1963). *An Introduction to Psychotherapy.* New York: International Universities Press.

Trunnell, E. E., and Holt, W. E. (1974). The concept of denial or disavowal. *J Am Psychoanal Assoc* 22:769-784.

Werner, H. (1948). *Comparative Psychology of Mental Development.* New York: International Universities Press.

Wolff, P. H. (1960). (Psychol. Issues. No. 5) *The Developmental Psychologies of Jean Piaget and Psychoanalysis.* New York: International Universities Press.

Wurmser, L. (1974). Psychoanalytic considerations of the etiology of compulsive drug use. *J Am Psychoanal Assoc* 32:820–843.

———— (1977). *The Hidden Dimension: Psychopathology of Compulsive Drug Use.* New York: Jason Aronson.

Wynne, L. C., and Singer, M. T. (1963). Thought disorder and family relations of schizophrenics. *Arch. Gen Psychiatry* 9:191–206.

16: ALCOHOLISM, BORDERLINE AND NARCISSISTIC DISORDERS

Peter Hartocollis
Pitsa C. Hartocollis

On the basis of a systematic review of the psychoanalytic literature, we will attempt in this chapter to draw a composite picture of alcoholism and, in the process, show that the condition greatly overlaps with what psychoanalysts and others, clinicians as well as researchers, describe as borderline states or, more broadly, borderline and narcissistic personality disorders (Hartocollis 1977). Such a diagnostic coincidence may be particular to psychoanalytic practice or experience with alcoholic patients — the kind of alcoholic patients psychoanalysts are familiar with. It should be also pointed out that psychoanalysts tend to discuss alcoholism concurrently, indeed interchangeably, with drug addiction — the implication being that both conditions represent manifestations of the same basic psychopathology.

That alcoholics may be heavy users of drugs, and vice versa, enhances the impression that the two conditions are governed by similar dynamics. Nevertheless, there are obvious differences in both the use of the two categories of addictive (chemical) substances and their psychophysiology. The abuse of alcohol usually precedes drug addiction. And, characteristically, drug addiction involves more violence than alcoholism, a difference that may be related to sociocultural factors, which undoubtedly play an important role in the development of both conditions (Zinberg 1975).

EARLY PSYCHOANALYTIC FORMULATIONS: REGRESSION AND BORDERLINE PSYCHOSIS

The first psychoanalytic conceptualization of alcoholism (and drug addiction in general) was made by Abraham (1908). He suggested that alcoholics are struggling against latent homosexual wishes — an idea obviously related to

Freud's theory of paranoia, with alcoholic delusional jealousy serving as the connecting link. Others stressed the importance of oral narcissistic and depressive personality traits. Pointing out that exhibitionistic and sadomasochistic tendencies might be even more crucial than unconscious homosexuality, Sachs, as reported by Yorke (1970), saw addiction to alcohol as a compromise between the perversions and compulsive neurosis. Radó (1933), on the other hand, described alcoholism as a hypomanic attempt to escape the awareness of narcissistic pain or depression. He proposed the term "pharmacothymia" to describe the mood-lifting effects of chemical substances for a "group of human beings who respond to frustrations in life with a special type of emotional alteration, which might be designated 'tense depression' . . .or 'initial depression' marked by great 'painful' tension and, at the same time, by a high degree of intolerance to pain" (Glover 1932, 1949).

In considering the dynamics of alcoholism. Glover stressed the importance of sadism and aggression in general. He pointed out that, while orally gratifying, alcohol unbinds aggression so that all object relations are colored by it—oral aggression or, rather, oral ambivalence, but also anal erotism and sadism—and he suggested that such disorders as alcoholism and drug addiction might represent "transitional states," clinically and developmentally related to both the neuroses and the psychoses. Clearly, the characteristics Glover attributed to alcoholics—namely, a "localized" or transient disturbance in reality testing; object relations invested with pre-oedipal aggression, frustration and disappointment; and an archaic, severe and inconsistent superego—coincide with those attributed by contemporary authors, Kernberg (1967) in particular, to patients with a borderline personality organization.

Espousing the idea of repressed aggression as its central dynamic, Simmel (1929) saw in alcoholism a latent "narcissistic neurosis" controlled by means of obsessional mechanisms. Simmel's ideas, derived from his experience with hospitalized alcoholics and drug addicts in Tegel/Berlin, were developed further by Will Menninger (1937) and his brother Karl (1938) in Topeka. It was at the Menninger Clinic that Knight (1937) explored the early object relations of alcoholics, reconstructing the personality characteristics of parental figures and the developmental determinants of the alcoholic condition from the analysis of adult male patients. He described two types of alcoholism, "essential" and "reactive" —the former, earlier in its onset, often polysymptomatic, involving as a rule serious behavioral maladjustment and responding poorly to psychoanalysis or psychoanalytic psychotherapy; the latter appearing after a more or less successful social and family adjustment, as a reaction to some recognizable external or internal stress, and responding favorably to psychoanalytic treatment.[1] In agreement with Glover, Knight (1937) declared: "alcohol addic-

---

[1]On the basis of genetic research, Winokur and his co-workers (1970) have more recently identified two types of male alcoholism, "sociopathic" and "primary," entities phenomenologically equivalent to Knight's "essential" and "reactive" alcoholism, respectively. A third type, "depression-alcoholism," was ascribed primarily to women (Winokur et al. 1971).

tion, along with other drug addictions, constitutes a borderline condition psychiatrically."

Curiously, Knight did not follow up on his seminal ideas concerning the dynamics and treatment of alcoholism. Instead, he turned his attention to borderline disorders or, more specifically, "borderline schizophenia"—a development that may be related to his earlier interest in alcoholics in more than a coincidental way. Significantly, it seems to us, in discussing Knight's (1938) work in alcoholism, Karl Menninger declared: "I regard it as near a psychosis . . .I think that addiction to alcohol is more serious than any neurosis and should be thought of along with the psychoses."

Knight's (1937) description of "essential alcoholics" is worth quoting in part, as it unmistakably applies to patients with typical borderline pathology:

> They are completely dependent economically and emotionally. . . . Also one finds lacking the character traits which derive from the second anal stage—those of perseverance, retention and mastery of the object. . . . The character traits are essentially oral derivatives—oral dependence, oral demanding, pleasure seeking with small regard to reality requirements or possibilities. This lack of reality sense is evidenced by their unreliability, irresponsibility and especially by their lying and general lack of sincerity.

Fifteen years later, Knight (1953a) conceptualized the "borderline case" as "one in which normal ego functions of secondary process thinking, integration, realistic planning, adaptation to the environment, maintenance of object relationships, and defenses against primitive unconscious impulses are severely weakened."[2]

CONTEMPORARY VIEWS: AFFECT-TOLERANCE AND STRUCTURAL DEFICIT

The ability of alcohol and drugs, in general, to relieve bad feelings almost instantaneously has led to the hypothesis that addiction is an attempt at self-healing. According to this view, advanced first by Rado (1933), the peremptory nature of the drug use is a reflection of the intensity of the addict's affects; addiction to chemical substances is presumably a defense against affects that have lost the capacity to serve as signals of inner distress or danger, affects that have reverted to their primitive, massive, psychosomatic form normally experienced in a traumatic situation, particularly in early childhood before the establishment of an effective ego structure (Krystal and Raskin 1970, Schur 1955, Wurmser 1974). The idea is implicit in Kohut's (1959) assertion that drugs are not symbolic substitutes for missing love objects as traditionally assumed, but replacements for "psychological structure." According to Kohut (1977), drug

---

[2]W. Menninger (1937) referred to two more groups of patients who habitually abuse drinking: "neurotic characters" as described by Alexander, and "psychotic personalities" in whom "alcoholism represents only a symptom in a paranoid or schizoid or otherwise psychotic system." Clearly, these represent borderline patients.

addiction, and presumably alcoholism, is similar to the narcissistic personality disorders in that both conditions share a developmental defect in the self.

As Khantzian (1977) has pointed out in reviewing the contemporary literature on addictive personalities, the emphasis is on ego functions and ego impairments, with attention focused on the areas of affect tolerance and drive defense. Rather than delving into the regressive, acting out aspects of addictive behavior, contemporary workers stress its adaptive functions, the dynamic interaction of the psychopharmacologic effect of chemical substances and the personality organization of the addicted individual in his present environment. In describing the personality of the alcoholic or drug addict, these workers borrow heavily from the literature of borderline and narcissistic disorders. Characteristically, Wurmser (1974) concluded that the psychopathology of such patients is "most frequently of the borderline type." His description of their subjective experience corresponds closely to the typical feelings of borderline patients; namely, loneliness, emptiness and depression, meaninglessness and pervasive boredom or hurt, rejection, shame and murderous rage. Alcohol or drugs help to alleviate such feelings or to make them more bearable. The following account of an alcoholic patient, diagnosed also as depressed, underscores the point:

> I took pills and became drunk deliberately at times—one, when I could no longer carry on my facade; two, when anger at my mother or father overwhelmed me and I feared I'd express it; three, when I feared my husband would approach me sexually. . . . When my feelings of frustration, guilt, futility—to cite a few—became too intense to endure, I drank to alleviate the pain. I did not then identify any of the diffuse misery I felt as anger, at least not consciously, and I had no idea that the capacity for hostility is at least as great in a human being as is the capacity for love. This is perhaps not surprising in view of the fact that I had certainly not properly developed the capacity to love; I was emotionally starved because I was unable to express affection in any of the normally acceptable ways—not even to my husband, who naturally misinterpreted this and subsequently rejected me completely.

This patient had been through Alcoholics Anonymous and many attempts at psychotherapy before she came to our hospital. But she still felt that she was not an alcoholic. She said:

> I am not—and never have been—powerless over alcohol. Again, morally this makes my apparent behavior all the more reprehensible, but I cannot in good faith pray for God's intervention when I acted deliberately and willfully. I can pray for self-knowledge, strength, and the wisdom to avoid wallowing in remorse or self-pity. I see now that my means of escape was a potentially suicidal act of self-destruction—a "plea for help" just as "sick" as lacerating one's wrists or taking an overdose of pills. I am ashamed to say that my drinking also expressed an element of hate—of lashing out at those I loved and hated most in a vicious "I'll show you I don't care" gesture, which I must have known would offend, hurt and displease them, I, who had spent a misguided lifetime desperately seeking *approval*, could become despicable in the eyes of the world and thereby increase my self-punishment.

Two of the most characteristic clinical features of alcoholism, at least of the global, most commonly encountered type in this country described by Jellinek (1960) as *delta* alcoholism— "loss of control" and "craving" —are as typical of borderline patients. "Loss of control," referring to a person's inability to regulate his drinking, is what the literature of borderline disorders describes as "weak impulse control." The symptom of "craving" corresponds to a pervasive experience of unpleasure—what borderline patients describe as emptiness or inner badness—and the urge to obliterate it by compulsively indulging in alloplastic behavior, such as self-mutilation, sexual promiscuity, repeated masturbation, over-eating, or drinking to excess. In this respect, Little (1966) has observed that patients with a single pattern of addiction are probably closer to the border of psychosis than patients who can have any one of several objects or modes of gratification, even when they may need them all at once.

BORDERLINE PERSONALITY ORGANIZATION AND PATHOLOGICAL NARCISSISM

Even though by no means universally accepted, the belief that typical personality traits establish themselves before the development of alcoholic addiction is supported by observation of formerly addicted patients after prolonged abstinence, especially in the absence of psychodynamic treatment (Armstrong 1958, Blane 1968, McCord et al. 1960). Put in terms of Kernberg's (1970b) classificatory system of character pathology, alcoholics display a severe disturbance in object relationships, reflecting inadequate object constancy and identity diffusion; a pathological condensation of genital and pre-genital instinctual strivings with a predominance of pre-genital aggression; a primitive, poorly integrated and largely insufficient superego; and a developmentally mixed picture of ego defenses, predominantly denial, splitting,[3] projection, and omnipotence. Such structural characteristics, defining Kernberg's lower level of character pathology, are pathognomonic of borderline patients, characterizing as well Knight's "essential" alcoholics.

Whether "reactive" or, in Winokur's more recent terminology (Winokur et al. 1970), "primary" alcoholics fall within the spectrum of borderline disorders is more difficult to decide. We could imagine someone asking Knight to comment on his later thinking about alcoholism and receiving something like the following response: "But of course, there are no alcoholics, only borderlines who happen to share a common symptom—drinking to excess." He might or might not have limited such a statement to the group of "essential" alcoholics; and that, as far as we are concerned, is a crucial question.

Some persons become publicly identified as alcoholics relatively late in life, following what appears to be a successful personal and social adjustment, their primary problem seemingly being excessive drinking and its debilitating effects.

---

[3]The importance of the primitive mechanism of splitting in the psychopathology of drug addiction has been stressed by Rosenfeld (1959).

In this connection Kernberg's (1970a) remarks about a paradoxical discrepancy in the degree of disturbance between the actual interpersonal functioning and the level of character organization that some borderline patients display seem to us relevant. "Reactive" ("primary") alcoholics may for a long time manage to function in an apparently normal way. Narcissistic character traits, obsessive defenses, and a massive use of denial provide such individuals with a protective shield of self-deception, which isolates them from close personal contact with people whom they depend on but cannot trust. They feel empty and angry inside, very much like people with an "as-if personality" (Deutsch 1965), but so far as anyone else is concerned they are pleasant and function adequately. Gradually, however, as the cumulative impact of internal and external frustrations undermines the effectiveness of their protective devices, the level of their functioning begins to suffer. And, wishing to maintain their precarious emotional equilibrium, they resort to increasing amounts of alcohol, which has the power to reenforce denial, even though not performance, which continues to deteriorate, exposing further their borderline pathology.

On the other hand, such patients may be classified more accurately as narcissistic rather than borderline. As Settlage (1977) has pointed out, the distinction between the two conditions is not very clear in the literature. In fact, according to Kernberg (1970b), a large proportion of narcissistic individuals, if not all of them, share the same borderline personality organization. But narcissistic disorders are generally considered less severe than borderline disorders. Like "reactive" ("primary") alcoholics, narcissistic patients are, according to Settlage again (1977), "usually capable of functioning quite well in the area of work responsibilities. Yet they have major difficulty in regulating affects and self-esteem, in maintaining a cohesive sense of self, and in their capacity for intimacy in full object relations."

The following case illustrates the problem of distinguishing between a narcissistic and a borderline disorder in a patient clearly identified as alcoholic:

A 42-year-old, moderately successful executive came to treatment complaining about obsessive thoughts of a homosexual nature. In addition, he called himself an "alcoholic," even though he had totally abstained from drinking for the past seven years. Handsome, well dressed and well mannered, he expressed himself in a soft-spoken, friendly, articulate but somber way, giving the impression of being mildly depressed. He described his mother as self-centered, domineering and sadistic. Even though feeling better about her now, he still held her responsible for his becoming an alcoholic, recalling that when at the age of 14 he went home drunk, she reacted with indifference, saying nothing about it. He described his father as cold, distant and ineffectual. In spite of his early dependence on drinking, the patient went through high school and managed to finish college; but he could not hold a job for any length of time, invariably being fired because of his drinking behavior. While on a drinking spree, he married a woman he had met only a few days earlier and divorced her as soon as he was sober, a few days later. At the age of 33, he sought a psychiatrist and had once-a-week psychotherapy for two years, until he was offered a promotion to an office in another city. With the consent of his therapist, he accepted the offer, was placed on disulfiram, joined Alcoholics Anonymous, and quit psychotherapy. Thereafter, for nearly seven years, he was able to maintain a stable work adjustment, with a marginal social life revolving around AA meetings and heterosexual relationships of short duration.

His new therapist made the diagnosis of narcissistic personality with obsessive-compulsive features and started him in psychoanalysis, five times a week. Two months later, as he was describing the loneliness of the past weekend, during which he had experienced an intense longing for his analyst, the patient became agitated, got up from the couch and declared that he was going to kill the analyst if he did not take him in his hands. At the analyst's firm suggestion that he could manage to contain himself if he sat on the chair across from him, the patient calmed down and, shortly afterwards, was able to return to the couch. Subsequently, he described feelings of admiration and complete trust for the analyst, only to revert to hateful, murderous fantasies a few days later, but without coming near the point of losing control or abandoning his sense of reality testing again. He revealed perverse sexual fantasies about other men as well as women and wondered about his identity, asking repeatedly the question, "Who am I," and "What do I want from life?" In short, he presented the classical symptoms and signs of a patient with a borderline personality organization.

DRINKING IN THE SERVICE OF DENIAL

The fact that a person is addicted to alcohol indicates that his primary defenses have been weakened on one level, yet strengthened on another. Drinking comes to the rescue of a person whose basic mental mechanisms have begun to lose their adaptive power, being helpful not only by providing relief from psychic pain (literally anesthesia), but by stimulating these mechanisms or defenses as well. The alcoholic whose premorbid personality is typically maintained by denial, splitting, rationalization and projection finds himself compelled to use these defenses even more extensively, more openly and more or less exclusively after he becomes a heavy drinker (Hartocollis 1969). Secondary defenses are built within the context of his premorbid character traits, typically identified as the alcoholic personality and representing a superficial, fragile and maladaptive form of reaction formation and obsessiveness, which shield the individual from the experience of negative, difficult to tolerate affects.

In listing the alcoholic's typical ego defenses, we placed denial first in order to emphasize its uniqueness in the case. Students of alcoholism have observed that denial is one of its more striking features (Hartocollis 1968). We believe that the content of his denial is important in understanding the alcoholic patient and his personality development. There is something particular about the alcoholic's denial. On the surface, it is a denial of problems — primarily a denial of the idea that drinking may reflect a personal problem, except for the problem that other people's reaction to it creates. More careful examination, however, will reveal that what the alcoholic denies is a problem for which he needs any help. He may very well admit that he has problems so long as he can deny the idea that he needs help. What he denies is in essence the notion of help, the idea that he needs help. As Kernberg (1970a) observed with regard to narcissistic individuals, "The greatest fear of these patients is to be dependent on anybody else." And yet, behind this denial there lies a strong wish for help — only that this wish is fraught with anxiety.

The following letter of a woman alcoholic, expressing feelings of distress at the idea that her family did not like her because she was sick, reads like an echo from the past, a revival of childhood feelings regarding her place in the family:

> Mother, you wouldn't believe what a rotten opinion I have of myself—now that I can see it just a little I can hardly believe it myself. The way I appear to others has been the most colossal hoax imaginable. The creation of the bright, charming, witty, efficient and talented personality that you know is the product of a near genius brain with the emotional maturity of a six-year-old. When I start really thinking about how I really, *really* feel about everything—people, situations, achievements, effort, everything—two things come through loud and clear: I'm absolutely frightened to death, and I feel as though I'm such a disappointment to everyone, including myself. . . . I seem to be *so* sharp and intelligent and yet *no one* could be more naive or guileless than I am when it comes to knowing the difference between how things really are and how I want them to be. I'm so afraid I'll fail. Then I think of you all at home so *angry* with me because I'm sick and bitter because I don't appear to be making any progress—the agony is too much— and up goes the phony mask and I become again the person I created and I hate myself even more.

The same patient returned to the hospital from a town trip late and drunk. However, she secreted herself in her room, skillfully avoiding the nursing staff the next day. She also failed to appear for her appointed session with the therapist. Then she became quite angry, blamed the nursing staff for not finding her and wrestling from her the secret of her being upset and drunk.

What makes an alcoholic, especially of the "reactive" type, different from the typical borderline patient is his or her apparent lack of anger. Even though psychological testing invariably points to a great deal of inner aggression and suppressed anger, the alcoholic patient is typically affable, and denies feelings of anger about anyone. Alcoholics have an extremely low tolerance for the direct expression of anger and hence they are constantly leaning over backwards to deny any hostile or aggressive impulses. Denial is also used extensively in connection with sexual problems. Drinking serves the purpose of strengthening the denial of anger or of sexual impulses when the denial becomes weak and the anger or the sexual impulses come close to awareness.

A DEVELOPMENTAL HYPOTHESIS

In describing his patients' early object relations, Knight (1937) speculated that the future alcoholic is likely to become overindulged by his mother and to react with rage when faced with the moment of weaning. Aggressive fantasies, prompted by the mother's efforts to control his insatiable needs for oral gratification, make him fear that she will retaliate in anger, hurt him or abandon him. Such a fear prompts him to deny his oral aggressive needs and to seek satisfaction in omnipotent but passive fantasies and neurotic behavior, which eventually lead to problem drinking and alcoholism. Mother's own relationship to the child, on the other hand, is determined by feeling anxious and resentful in facing her child's needs, because she perceives them as demands on herself when she feels deprived in her own need for emotional attention. It is significant that several investigators describe the fathers of alcoholic patients as cold and distant and by implication unable to fulfill not only the child's emotional needs, but those of the mother as well (Knight 1937, Strecker and Chambers 1938).

A survey of over 300 long-term alcoholic patients by the authors confirmed the impression, derived from personal clinical work with such patients, that alcoholics have had a child–mother relationship that discouraged the communication of the normal developmental need for help. In a majority of cases, we found that alcoholic patients had more or less serious problems in childhood, including bedwetting, sleep-walking, shyness and withdrawal or excessive aggressiveness. The patients themselves reported having had fewer problems in childhood than what their relatives indicated — a finding that underscores the alcoholic's propensity to deny the existence of psychological difficulties whether in the present or in the past. In the course of treatment, alcoholics will more readily recall having experienced serious emotional problems as children — problems, however, for which they could not find satisfactory help. Alcoholic patients recall asking for help and not finding it, or not asking at all because of the impression that they could not find it. This inability to ask for help, present since childhood, seems to be a function of the personality of the alcoholic's mother. Thus, in a high proportion of our cases, patients described their parents in negative terms, remembering them as aggressive, domineering, possessive, unfriendly, inconsistent, cold or distant. Both men and women alcoholics were more critical of their mothers than of their fathers, men slightly more than women. Such findings point to a mother–child relationship that discouraged the admission of problems and rewarded their denial. The mother lets the child know that what she really wishes is to get rid of his needs, which she perceives as demands upon and complaints against her. Then, rather than helping him satisfy such needs, she encourages him to deny them. She welcomes him with a show of happiness and gestures of love whenever he appears or claims to be happy. She is nice to him so long as he does not voice any wishes for help or any resentment for not getting what he wishes to have from her, the tender unsolicited care that she would like to have for herself.

The following are excerpts from psychotherapy reports, referring to the feelings of chronic alcoholic patients about their parents in childhood:

In a highly intellectualized, sarcastic, cynical way, the patient, a 37-year-old journalist with at least 15 years of alcoholic abuse, family, and social maladjustment, heaped a barrage of accusations at his mother for being hypocritical, rejecting, and cold, and on his father for being domineering, punitive, and tyrannical. His anger was directed most intensely toward his mother, whom he perceived as expecting him to make up for the frustrations she experienced in her relations with his father.

A 43-year-old man, a successful writer with a long history of heavy drinking and brief depressive episodes, described his mother as a woman who felt very sorry for herself, who constantly complained that no one loved her, and who made incessant demands on the patient that he "take care of her."

Another alcoholic patient, a 36-year-old college graduate and mother of four children, acknowledged that, in spite of three years in analysis, she was still unable to experience feelings — except for "knowing" that the feelings were "really there." Yet, she reasoned, if she did something about it, about making contact with her feelings, "even worse hell would break out." It was better to let things go on this way, even if to her own destruction. Referring to herself in the third person, as if talking about someone else (possibly the analyst and ultimately mother), she said: "I can see what she must be feeling, but I can't feel it." She talked about being "encased." She couldn't trust anyone, she never had, she didn't dare to. "Should I want to dare?" she wondered. But if she did trust her analyst, he would find out that there was nothing to her, nothing to be trusted about. And he would ridicule her.

The same patient awakened one morning crying from an unremembered dream, to which she could only associate her lifelong terror and hatred of mother. She wondered, could she, would she talk with her mother about herself and her difficulties in her relationship with mother in all her growing-up years? Would mother attempt to deny it all? Would she herself accept mother's denial?

Following Masterson and Rinsley's (1975) suggestion regarding the development of a "split-mother image" in borderline patients, we presume that the origin of the alcoholic's pathognomonic denial is to be found during the "rapprochement" subphase of the "separation-individuation" period of infantile development described by Mahler (1968, 1971). During this crucial phase in the formation of an autonomous identity, mother and child reach a tacit agreement not to disturb each other with their personal problems — a relationship characterized by a mutual attitude of denial. Regressing to the hypomanic mode of functioning that characterizes the preceding developmental subphase of "practicing," the child denies having any problems that may involve any wish for help; and, in a reciprocal fashion, the mother denies any awareness of such problems on the part of the child. The child's needs may express themselves in psychosomatic symptoms, but these are dissociated from his wishes and treated medically. The child then grows up looking happy and brave, or at least quiet and unassuming, until internal and external pressures begin mounting, family and social responsibilities, competitive strivings and libidinal longings become too heavy to cope with by means of his favorite defense of denial and its superego appeasing variants of rationalization and externalization. At a certain point, he may discover that something so easy to get and so perfectly normal to use in our society — alcohol — can reinforce these defenses and help him carry on with a semblance of competence. And eventually he or she becomes addicted.

What seems to be unique with alcoholics, especially the characterologically more advanced "reactive" ("primary") types, is their ability to suppress the negative side of ambivalence — angry, hateful, depressive and, in short, aggressive tendencies — in favor of a pleasant, friendly, cheerful facade. Such behavior corresponds to the positive "split-mother image" that borderline patients carry within. In fact, one may say that "reactive" alcoholics cannot get openly angry or hurtful unless they get drunk. Alcohol, soothing or not, is the magic potion that converts the Dr. Jekyl-like identity of the "reactive" alcoholic into that of Mr. Hyde's. The same mechanism holds generally true with regard to the alcoholic's sexual identity, which becomes clearly and aggressively homosexual or aggressively seductive, homosexually or otherwise, when he or she becomes drunk.

TREATMENT CONSIDERATIONS

In tracing the psychoanalytic literature on the subject, we have tried to show that inherent in old and new views lies the notion that alcoholism is a developmental disorder akin to borderline states. According to the same literature, treatment should be modified psychoanalysis or expressive-supportive psychotherapy, individually or in groups.

Indications for psychoanalysis should be virtually the same as for borderline patients in general, and more specifically for passive-aggressive personalities, sadomasochistic personalities, the better functioning infantile or hysteroid personalities, and narcissistic personalities that fall into what Kernberg (1970a) has described as the intermediate level of organization of character pathology, or what Knight (1937) classified as "reactive" alcoholics. Modified psychoanalysis, or expressive-supportive psychotherapy, is indicated for the more severe borderline personality disorders, most patients with infantile and severe narcissistic personalities who were never able to make a stable adjustment in their life, whose drinking becomes habitual and is combined with drug addiction or sexual deviation or some other form of antisocial behavior, "as-if personalities," schizoid and paranoid character disorders which more or less coincide with Knight's type of "essential" alcoholism. In addition to modified psychoanalysis or expressive psychotherapy, such patients need a supportive, firmly structured environment that in most cases only a hospital can provide. This point was emphasized quite early by psychoanalysts, beginning with Simmel (1929) and Knight (1937, 1978) who, along with William Menninger (1937), devised a meticulous treatment milieu and defined a special working relationship between the psychotherapist and the hospital doctor, which, in its essentials, is still in effect at the Menninger Clinic, as one of us has described elsewhere (Hartocollis 1967). Knight's (1953b) description of treatment for borderline patients is but a variant of his earlier description of treatment for alcoholics, and it may apply to them as well.

The basic requirement is to uncover and remove the patient's crippling defenses, beginning with his drinking, which both relieves psychic pain and necessitates the redoubled employment of denial, splitting, rationalization, and projection, which characterize the alcoholic's premorbid personality. The alcoholic's actual or potential wish to drink—appearing more or less undisguised in fantasies and dreams—should be considered, initially at least, within the context of the therapeutic alliance rather than in connection with its putative genetic origin. The point should be made that alcohol is not a substitute for mother or love as the patient may claim, but an end in itself, a primary object affording discharge of tension and signifying the patient's inability to tolerate his feelings of frustration, narcissistic hurt, or loneliness, and to accept the therapist as his helper. Confrontation of the patient's typical defenses is not only the first step in the treatment of alcoholics, but also essential to maintain throughout treatment; for, if exercised consistently, with concern and patience, it promotes and safeguards the therapeutic alliance, which is always fragile with alcoholics, and with borderline patients, in general, full of mistrust and anxiety.

Dealing with the patient's defenses should be in terms of their current, adaptational meaning rather than their genetic content. The alcoholic's defenses aim at sparing his vulnerable self-esteem. Specifically, they protect him from the experience of anxiety, depression, guilt or, in the more severe, clearly borderline cases, anger, fear, emptiness, self-contempt and other such negative affects, narcissistic in origin. To interpret the patient's defenses—or resistances, including the transference—beyond the here-and-now, to attempt to reconstruct the traumatic oedipal or preoedipal childhood, makes little difference to the alcoholic patient, if not making it worse. In one of the cases cited earlier, the patient was able to acknowledge that she had real feelings even though she could still not experience them as such, and she knew that in hating her analyst she was transferring onto him the hatred she harbored for her childhood mother. Yet, in spite of three years in classical analysis, she was not at all ready to give up her alcoholic illness. As her analyst put it, "all [my] interpretative work 'made sense' to her but did not 'click.' " In fact, the analyst's interpretative "pressures" upset the patient to the point that she became delusional for the first time in her life. This bit of psychotic transference, typical of borderline patients in analysis, was also interpreted, and it promptly cleared. Soon afterwards, however, the patient began drinking again. When she was brought back to the hospital she indicated that the analyst was the first one she wanted to see, but also the last one who could help her.

Defenses should be further analyzed within the context of the patient's character traits, typically identified as the alcoholic personality and representing a superficial, fragile and maladaptive form of reaction formation and obsessiveness, which again shields the individual from the experience of unpleasant affects, predominantly anger, boredom, emptiness and sheer narcissistic hurt.

The way an analyst and, in general, a psychotherapist approaches his patient's defenses is bound to determine the kind of transference that develops in the process of treatment. When core defenses are under attack, the patient's aggressiveness is going to surface in the transference, alone or fused with homosexual potential. Oral aggressive and paranoid tendencies may drive the patient back to drinking, and for this reason firm setting of limits and the ready availability of a hospital have been advocated by those who prescribe psychoanalytic psychotherapy or analysis to alcoholic patients (Hartocollis 1967, Knight 1937, 1938, Menninger 1937).

On the other hand, the alcoholic's oral dependent proclivity to behave properly without complaining can make him look like an ideal patient, resulting in relaxation of vigilance on the part of those concerned with his well-being and of the therapist himself, who may feel that his help is superfluous or no longer necessary. Caught in a transference-countertransference bind, the therapist comes to feel like the patient's childhood mother, all too ready to let him go his own way and forget him, while the patient feels secretly inadequate, misunderstood and deprived of the love and protection that he does not dare demand for the fear that it may be experienced as insatiable, bothersome, or rejectable. And the mere probability of rejection, along with the secret craving of "love" — experienced as emptiness, badness, or alienation—tends to make him angry and revengeful, ready to drive him back to drinking, away from treatment.

The slightest indication of rejection on the therapist's part, a long weekend, a canceled appointment or spending more time with another patient, may become the fatal trigger point. That is why firmness and limit setting should be combined with empathic attention, personal warmth and encouraging comments, even active advice on occasion — what Winnicott (1965), in referring to the normal early mother–child relationship, has described as "the holding environment." As Knight (1953b) put it in discussing the treatment of borderline states, "[the patient] needs *proofs* of emotional support, of trusting and trustworthiness, and of genuine human interest rather than merely detached professional interest." Or, as Kohut (1959) wrote with reference to addicts, "[their dependence] must be recognized and acknowledged. In fact, it is a clinical experience that the major psychoanalytic task in such instances is the analysis of the denial of the real need; the patient must first learn to replace a set of unconscious grandiose fantasies that are kept up with the aid of social isolation by the, for him, painful acceptance of the reality of being dependent."

Once committed to treatment — or rather to the therapist, to whom he or she is likely to become very dependent, virtually addicted — the patient should be guided along in expanding his or her capacity for genuine object relations beyond the therapeutic situation. The process is inevitably long and arduous, involving the use of transitional objects (Little 1966), inanimate ones like disulfiram, a job, or a hobby; and live people, who may or may not be the ones — spouse, lover, mother — the patient had available at the beginning of treatment.

SUMMARY

This paper traces the psychoanalytic literature on alcoholism from its early conceptualization as a manifestation of oral narcissism, latent homosexuality and repressed aggression, to the current view that defines it in terms of ego deficit and low affect-tolerance. Implicit in old and newer views seems to be the notion that, generally, alcoholism is a developmental disorder of a borderline nature. On evidence from current psychoanalytic reports and our own research, we propose that most alcoholic patients are borderline, narcissistic or both. That some alcoholic patients recover from their dependence on alcohol, with or without treatment, means no more than that some borderline and narcissistic individuals can function indefinitely without apparent need for psychiatric help.

REFERENCES

Abraham, K. (1908). The psychological relations between sexuality and alcoholism. In *Selected Papers*, pp. 80–89. London: Hogarth.

Armstrong, J. D. (1958). The search for the alcoholic personality. *Ann. Amer. Acad. Polit. Soc. Science* 315:40–47.

Blane, H. T. (1968). *The Personality of the Alcoholic: Guises of Dependency*. New York: Harper & Row.

Deutsch, H. (1965). Some forms of emotional disturbance and their relationship to schizophrenia. In *Neuroses and Character Types*, pp. 262–281. New York: International Universities Press.

Glover, E. (1932). On the etiology of drug-addiction. *Int. J. Psycho-Anal.* 13:298–328.

―――― (1949). *Psychoanalysis*. 2nd ed. New York: Staples.

Hartocollis, P. (1967). Psychotherapy and the alcoholic. In *Opportunities and Limitations in the Treatment of Alcoholics*, ed. J. Hirsch, pp. 53–75. Springfield, IL.: Charles C Thomas.

———— (1968). Denial of illness in alcoholism. *Bull. Menn. Clinic* 32:47–53.

———— (1969). A dynamic view of alcoholism: drinking in the service of denial. *Dynam. Psychiat.* 2:173–182.

———— (1977). *Borderline Personality Disorders.* New York: International Universities Press.

Jellinek, E. (1960). *The Disease Concept of Alcoholism.* New Brunswick, NJ: Hillhouse.

Kernberg. O. (1967). Borderline personality organization. *J. Amer. Psychoan. Assoc.* 15:641–685.

———— (1970a). Factors in the psychoanalytic treatment of narcissistic personalities. *J. Amer. Psychoan. Assoc.* 18:51–85.

———— (1970b). A psychoanalytic classification of character pathology. *J. Amer. Psychoan. Assoc.* 18:800–822.

Khantzian, E. J. (1977). The ego, the self, and opiate addiction: theoretical and treatment considerations. In *Psychodynamics of Drug Dependence* (NIDA Research Monograph 12), ed. J. D. Blaine and D. A. Julius, pp.l 101–117. Washington, DC: U.S. Dept. of Health, Education and Welfare.

Knight, R. P. (1937). The dynamics and treatment of chronic alcohol addiction. *Bull. Menn. Clinic* 1:233–250.

———— (1938). The psychoanalytic treatment in a sanatorium of chronic addiction in alcohol. *JAMA* 111:1443–1448.

———— (1953a). Borderline states. *Bull. Menn. Clinic* 17:1–12.

———— (1953b). Management and psychotherapy of the borderline schizophrenic patient. *Bull. Menn. Clinic* 17:139–150.

Kohut, H. (1959). Introspection, empathy, and psychoanalysis. *J. Amer. Psychoan. Assoc.* 7:459–483.

———— (1977). Preface. In *Psychodynamics of Drug Dependence* (NIDA Research Monograph 12), ed. J. D. Blaine and D. A. Julius, pp. VII–IX. Washington, DC: U.S. Dept. of Health, Education and Welfare.

Krystal, H., and Raskin, H. A. (1970). *Drug Dependence. Aspects of Ego Functions.* Detroit: Wayne State University Press.

Little, N. (1966). Transference in borderline states. *Int. J. Psycho-Anal.* 47:476–485.

Mahler, M. S. (1968). *On Human Symbiosis and the Vicissitudes of Individuation.* Vol. I: *Infantile Psychosis.* New York: International Universities Press.

———— (1971). A study of the separation-individuation process and its possible application to borderline phenomena in the psychoanalytic situation. *Psychoan. Stud. Child* 26:403–424. New York: International Universities Press.

Masterson, J. F., and Rinsley, D. B. (1975). The borderline syndrome: the role of the mother in the genesis and psychic structure of the borderline personality. *Int. J. Psycho-Anal.* 56:163–177.

McCord, W., McCord, J., and Gudeman, J. (1960). *Origins of Alcoholism.* Stanford, CA: Stanford University Press.

Menninger, K. A. (1938). *Man Against Himself.* New York: Harcourt, Brace & Co.

Menninger, W. (1937). The treatment of chronic alcohol addiction. *Bull. Menn. Clinic* 1:101–112.

Radó, S. (1933). The Psychoanalysis of pharmacothymia. *Psychoanal. Quart.* 2:2–23.

Rosenfeld, H. A. (1959). On drug addiction. *Int. J. Psycho-Anal.* 41:467–475.

Schur, M. (1955). Comments on the metapsychology of somatization. *Psychoan. Stud. Child* 10:119–164. New Haven, CT: Yale University Press.

Settlage, C. F. (1977). The psychoanalytic understanding of narcissistic and borderline personality disorders: advances in developmental theory. *J. Amer. Psychoanal. Assoc.* 25:805–833.

Simmel, E. (1929). Psycho-analytic treatment in a sanatorium. *Int. J. Psycho-Anal.* 10:70–89.

Strecker, E. A., and Chambers, F. T. (1938). *Alcohol, One Man's Meat.* New York: MacMillan.

Winnicott, D. W. (1965). *The Maturational Processes and the Facilitating Environment.* New York: International Universities Press.

Winokur, G., Reich, T., Rimmer, J., and Pitts, F. N., Jr. (1970). Alcoholism III: diagnosis and familiar psychiatric illness in 259 alcoholic probands. *Arch. Gen. Psychiat.* 23:104–111.

Winokur, G., Rimmer, J., and Reich, T. (1971). Alcoholism IV: is there more than one type of alcoholism? *Brit. J. Psychiat.* 118:525–531.

Wurmser, L. (1974). Psychoanalytic considerations of the etiology of compulsive drug use. *J. Amer. Psychoan. Assoc.* 22:820–843.

Yorke, C. (1970). A critical review of some psychoanalytic literature on drug addiction. *Brit. J. Med. Psych.* 43:41–159.

Zinberg, N. E. (1975). Addiction and ego function. *Psychoan. Stud. Child* 30: 567–588. New York: International Universities Press.

17: WORKING WITH THE PREFERRED DEFENSE STRUCTURE OF THE RECOVERING ALCOHOLIC

John Wallace

INTRODUCTION

Despite the increasing concentration of effort upon rehabilitation of alcoholic drinkers, a systematic and specific theory of alcoholism therapy remains to be formulated. Alcoholism therapy today seems largely a grab bag of tricks, slogans, techniques, assumptions, and ideological stances derived from common sense, implicit theories of personality, and formal theories of behavior developed for other purposes. Although *seemingly* reasonable, these generalizations of therapeutic principles are proving unreasonable and, in many cases, detrimental to the progress of the alcoholic client.

But is it any wonder that current approaches to alcoholism therapy leave much to be desired? The majority have been developed for purposes other than alcoholism. Few, if any, have been developed from the perspective of the alcoholic client. None has taken into account the attributes, characteristics, and common situational elements of the alcoholic and the alcoholic career. And, most important, none has recognized the fact that intelligent treatment of the recovering alcoholic is a *time-dependent process*. That is, alcoholism therapy must be viewed in terms of a long time span. A particular therapeutic intervention for a recently drinking alcoholic may be entirely inappropriate for one who has managed to achieve several years of sobriety and vice versa.

The purpose of this chapter is indeed an ambitious one. It is my aim to develop a theory of therapy specific to alcoholism, a theory that takes into account the nature of the disease, the characteristics of the client, and the time-dependent nature of intelligent therapeutic intervention.

In the following pages, my arguments will include the following major ideas:

1. Alcoholics can be described in terms of a preferred defense structure. This preferred defense structure (PDS) need not be cast in negative terms. In fact, it need not be construed at all in terms of the classical language of defense mechanisms. The alcoholic PDS can be thought of as a collection of skills or abilities — tactics and strategies, if you will — for achieving one's ends.

2. Therapy with alcoholics as it is currently practiced too often attempts to remove the alcoholic PDS instead of utilizing it effectively to facilitate the achievement of abstinence. Therapeutic efforts that confront the alcoholic PDS prematurely and too heavily will increase rather than reduce the probability of further drinking.

3. Recovery programs successful in producing abstinence, such as Alcoholics Anonymous, partially owe their success to the intuitive recognition of the fact that the alcoholic PDS is to be protected and capitalized upon rather than confronted and radically altered.

4. Paradoxically, the very same defenses that the alcoholic used to maintain his drinking can be used effectively to achieve abstinence.

5. Equally paradoxically, the very same defenses that enabled the alcoholic to drink, as well as achieve abstinence, must ultimately be removed if long-term sobriety is to be maintained. However, in many cases such growth must take place over periods of time ranging from two to five years of abstinence.

THE PREFERRED DEFENSE STRUCTURE (PDS) OF THE RECOVERING ALCOHOLIC

Enough controversy has been generated around the question of the existence of something called an "alcoholic personality" to caution me not to engage that particular battle. It is curious to note, however, that the strength of belief in something called "the alcoholic personality" is a direct function of degree of actual involvement with alcoholics on a sustained and continuing basis. Thus, in the fellowship of Alcoholics Anonymous, the reification is so intense as to fix the concept in concrete. Persons are said to be "alcoholic in personality long before the first drink," they are alcoholic in personality and behavior "whether they are drinking or not," and the alcoholic personality can return at any time for no apparent reason in the form of the "dry drunk." These and other exotic beliefs that abound in AA are not without enormous therapeutic value.

On the other hand, the concept of an alcoholic personality has not fared well at all among those whose acquaintance with alcoholics is merely passing and whose knowledge about them flows from their own and other persons' research laboratories.

Hence, the data of experience and of folk wisdom urge us in one direction while the data of the research laboratory caution us to choose a different one. The situation is not unusual. In truth, both accounts of reality are biased. The sober member of AA *needs* his ideological base. He can ill afford the dispassionate, disinterested, and, indeed, almost casual play upon words and ideas of the inquiring academic intellectual. The alcoholic recognizes intuitively that he needs a stable and enduring *belief system* if he is to stay sober.

The academician's equally biased view of reality is often more difficult to discern. Hidden neatly beneath the rhetoric of science and "scientism" are the actualities of dreadfully inadequate personality-measuring instruments, inappropriate sampling procedures, inadequate measuring operations, improper choice of variables for study, grossly violated statistical assumptions, data-gathering, recording, and analyzing errors, and so on and so forth. Is it any wonder then that the most outstanding quality of most academic research is "now you see it, now you don't"? Are we really amazed to find sober alcoholics clinging to their belief systems like poets to their metaphors, drowning in a sea of uncertainty?

For my purposes, I assume that an alcoholic PDS exists and that it is the *outcome* of alcoholism, not an antecedent condition. In the following, I do not mean to suggest a single, unvarying profile — one that is characteristic of each and every alcoholic drinker. I am assuming, however, that *some* of these are found in *some* combinatorial pattern in virtually every alcoholic drinker at *some* point in his drinking and recovery from alcoholism.

Denial

Enough has been written about denial as a major defense in alcoholism as to require little in the way of further elaboration here. What has *not* been observed, however, is that aside from the obvious destructive nature of denial in matters concerned with drinking, denial is not without merit. Tactical denial or, if you will, *deliberate* denial of certain life difficulties or problems is a useful and extremely valuable temporary adjustive and coping device. In the case of the alcoholic well-practiced in such behavior, denial as a general tactical mechanism should not be discarded totally. That would be rather like throwing out the baby with the bath water.

But, of course, the recovering alcoholic must stop denying the impact of alcohol upon his major life concerns. That is an obvious truism in alcoholism therapy that need not be altered. Simply because that statement is true, however, it does not follow that the recovering alcoholic must immediately, thoroughly, and completely root out all evidence of denial generally in his personality and behavior. First of all, he can't. Second, he rather likes the tactic of denial — he should, he's leaned heavily upon it for years. Third, at some level or another, he recognizes that tactical denial is a coping strategy he simply cannot do without. Whatever else do sober AA's mean when they say, "turn it over"? Despite the spiritual origins of that phrase, its meaning is more commonly understood in practice as "don't worry about it," "let it go," "don't think about it," "don't talk about it," "don't focus on it because you really can't do anything about it anyway."

But, in any case, the important point is as follows: alcoholism may very well be referred to aptly as "the merry-go-round of denial." If my analysis is correct, however, with regard to denial generally, the alcoholic is going to keep going round and round, *long after his drinking stops*. And the very worst thing a therapist could ever possibly do is try to jam the mechanism and block the use of tactical denial entirely.

Projection

While much has been written about *disowning* projection (the tendency to attribute unwanted and unacceptable aspects of self to others), there has been very little appreciation of other types of projection in the field of alcoholism. This is most surprising since *assimilative* projection is perhaps the most outstanding characteristic of both drinking and sober alcoholics. Assimilative projection is the tendency to assume that others are very much like oneself and to perceive them as such. Negative or socially unacceptable impulses and traits need not be seen in others. In fact, much of assimilative projection involves many desirable and socially admirable characteristics. As we shall see, the tendency toward assimilative projection has great significance, both for the illusion and substance of identification and also for the understanding of therapeutic communities.

All-or-None Thinking

It is often the case that the alcoholic will exhibit a strong preference for certainty. Judgments of people, events, and situations are often extreme. Decision-making does not often seem to take into account the realistically probable. Decision rules are often inflexible, narrow in scope, and simplistic. Perceived alternatives are few, consisting largely of yes-no, go-no go, black-white, dichotomized categories. It is in this sense that the thinking is said to be "all or none" in character. This aspect of the alcoholic PDS has obvious implications for the nature of persuasive communications in therapy as well as for the manner in which information is structured and presented.

In general, it is my experience with alcoholics in a variety of therapeutic contexts that they prefer large amounts of structure. While the drinking alcoholic may certainly appear to prefer uncertainty and unpredictability bordering on chaos, the recovering alcoholic seems to like things to move along in a fairly predictable and structured manner. Meetings of AA, for example, are certainly among the most structured of social encounters. True, the setting is informal and nonbureaucratic, but the actual content of an AA meeting is most predictable. In southern California, for example, virtually every meeting begins with a reading of Chapter 5 of the book *Alcoholics Anonymous*. Hence, for example, an alcoholic from Anaheim, sober for ten years, attending three meetings of AA a week, has heard the same thing read 1560 times!

The qualities of all-or-none thinking, preference for highly certain communications, simple decision-making rules, restricted choices, and highly structured social encounters all have obvious implications for the conduct of therapy and the structuring of therapeutic environments.

Conflict Minimization and Avoidance

Although their behavior while drinking may suggest otherwise, alcoholics do not like interpersonal conflict, nor do they handle it well; nor do they thrive in competitive relationships. As others have suggested, alcoholics do best in relationships characterized by complementarity rather than competition. Complementary relationships are those based upon satisfaction of reciprocally balanced needs. For example, a dominant person and submissive person would constitute a complementary relationship. These attributes concerning conflict minimization and conflict avoidance have obvious implications for both the nature and depth of therapeutic confrontation with the alcoholic. Confrontation tactics should be used by only the most skillful of therapists and only at carefully selected times in the therapeutic process. Angry and hostile confrontation with the alcoholic client is rarely, if ever, appropriate. Moreover, the group therapist working with alcoholics should exercise extreme caution in utilizing the resources of the group to confront a resistant member.

Rationalization

As anybody with only passing acquaintance with alcoholism can testify readily, alcoholics are often masters of rationalization. Many have developed the art and science of wishful thinking to its ultimate form of expression. They have had to. Anybody who can continue to drink in the face of the steadily accumulating disastrous consequences of active alcoholism must surely have learned a trick or two in order to make his drinking appear perfectly reasonable to himself and to others. But, as we have already seen with denial, rationalization can be a useful tactic in dealing with otherwise difficult situations, anxiety-laden happenings, and guilt-provoking personal actions. Perhaps the most extreme example of naked rationalization known to mankind is apparent in the phrase, "Well, what the hell, at least I'm sober today!"

After years of making the procuring and drinking of alcohol his number one priority, the alcoholic understands very well how ultimate priorities can be maintained. Paradoxically, it is a relatively straightforward shift from rationalizing drinking to rationalizing other less than desirable behaviors *with sobriety*. That is, in the early stages of abstinence, the recovering alcoholic may quickly discover that while drinking was a crutch, sobriety is an even better one! "Why, I can't do that, I might get drunk!" "I had to have an affair—my sobriety was in jeopardy." "I had to choose between her and my sobriety." In essence, the recovering alcoholic may discover that he has a freedom of personal action that few others can enjoy. But such rationalization can be an invaluable tactic in avoiding the reexperiencing of painful emotional cues that previously served as triggers to drinking, for example, guilt, remorse, anxiety, resentment, and anger. Eventually, of course, the recovering alcoholic must face up to his *sober* rationalizations. However, the word to be stressed in that sentence is *eventually*. What the alcoholic very definitely does not need early in his sobriety is a therapist dedicated to immediate rigorous honesty—especially one devoted to immediate rigorous honestly in *others*, or even what he imagines rigorous honesty to be in others.

Self-Centered Selective Attention

Alcoholics, for the most part, tend to look at things from a single perspective— *theirs*. Even in some alcoholics with considerable sobriety, there is often a curious lack of true empathy, a seeming inability to grasp the position of the other. This is not to say that alcoholics are "selfish." The facts are often to the contrary. But an alcoholic can be generous to a fault and still show extreme self-centeredness. As used here the term *self-centered selective attention* refers to the fact that alcoholics tend to be obsessed with self, to perceive the happenings around them largely as they impinge upon self. They attend selectively to information relevant to self, ignore other information not relevant to self, screen out information that is discrepant with their views of themselves, and distort other information that does not fit their preferred self-image.

In a very real sense, alcoholics are often resistant to feedback from others as well as from their own life experiences. This characteristic "blindness" can prove severely distressing and, in fact, maddening to those whose lives are linked to the alcoholic in important ways. It is often the case that drinking alcoholics (as well as recently sober ones) can maintain views of reality in the face of even massively disconfirming feedback. Faced with these obvious contradictions, the therapist may feel that it is his responsibility to apply immediate corrective feedback. Unfortunately, with the alcoholic client that is surely the very worst thing that the therapist could do. One must never forget that the characteristic blindness of the alcoholic is there for reasons, that it is dynamically linked to chronically low self-esteem, feelings of worthlessness, guilt, fear, and what might otherwise prove to be overwhelming anxiety. It is not that the therapist and his client are uninterested in the "truth," whatever that might be. It is really more a matter of *when* "truths" get revealed and also what "truths" need to be invented if the client is to get sober.

Preference for Nonanalytical Modes of Thinking and Perceiving

It often seems to be the case that alcoholics are influenced more by the emotional persuasive appeal than the "rational." Leadership styles that are likely to work with the alcoholic are often charismatic, inspirational, and "spiritual." It is not that alcoholics cannot operate in logical–analytical modes. That would be patently false since alcoholics are as capable as nonalcoholics in approaching matters in a linear, logical, and analytical manner. In terms of preference, however, the alcoholic is more often drawn to the warmth of magic rather than the cold objectivity of science.

Passivity versus Assertion

Although the intoxicated individual may often appear aggressive, assertive, and even frankly hostile, it is often the case that the alcoholic in the initial stages of abstinence prefers passivity over active coping as a general adjustive strategy. Assertion and active coping tend to bring the person into normal conflict with others, and, as we have seen, alcoholics do not thrive in situations characterized by conflict, competition, and win–lose outcomes. In fact, it is precisely in these situations that they tend to pick up a drink.

In actuality, despite the surface picture, the preferences of the alcoholic are for a general life attitude of passivity rather than active assertion.

Obsessional Focusing

Alcoholics are, for the most part, intense people, and, as nearly everyone knows, they are often obsessed people. Intense obsession is no stranger to the alcoholic. In addition to the obsession with alcohol during periods of active drinking, it is not uncommon to find obsessions with work, money, success, sexuality, and so forth. Contrary to popular stereotype, the alcoholic, sober and drinking, is often so obsessed with work as to fully deserve the label "work-aholic."

In general, the alcoholic seems to prefer a state characterized by a moderate-to-high activation level. Witness the enormous amounts of stimulating drugs, for example, caffeine and nicotine, consumed by sober alcoholics. Even the so-called states of serenity of many sober alcoholics are intensely focused states of moderate-to-high activation rather than low.

The therapeutic problem in alcoholism therapy is not to alter directly this level of intense obsession, but to *redirect* it. Along these lines, it is interesting to note how the obsession with alcohol, previous drinking, and sobriety continues in the *sober* alcoholic. Recovering alcoholics in AA, for example, often seem obsessed with their programs, with meetings, and with alcoholism generally. Curiously, this same obsession with the problem is what enables them to remain sober when previously it served to maintain drinking.

In essence, the problem in alcoholism therapy is not to reduce obsessional energy, an often impossible task, but to switch the focus of the obsession.

TACTICAL AND STRATEGIC USE OF THE PDS

In the preceding material, I described the alcoholic PDS and hinted at how it might be used effectively to help the alcoholic client achieve abstinence. I do not wish to imply that the above is an exhaustive description of the PDS. However, the major features of that structure have now been considered. We are in a position now to restate the central thesis of this chapter. An alcoholic preferred defense structure exists. It is not only ineffectual but therapeutically disastrous to confront this structure prematurely. The therapist knowledgeable about alcoholics will turn this structure to the advantage of his client and himself by selectively reinforcing and encouraging the defenses of the alcoholic client. The central problem in therapy with the alcoholic is learning how to swing the PDS into the service of abstinence rather than continued drinking.

Eventually, the alcoholic preferred defense structure must be dealt with directly if real changes in personality are to be achieved. When and to what extent such changes should be attempted, however, depends upon characteristics of individual alcoholics as well as upon years of continuous sobriety. In my opinion, in the majority of recovering alcoholics, such changes should not be attempted until several years of sobriety have been achieved.

The therapeutic task in alcoholism therapy at the early stages of abstinence differs radically from that of other psychotherapies. The role of the therapist is not to expose, confront, and modify the defenses of the alcoholic client. Rather, the role of the therapist is to teach the alcoholic client how to use these very defenses to achieve and maintain abstinence. Denial, rationalization, projection, and so forth have for too long been construed in moralistic terms by psychotherapists. In actuality, such mechanisms are perfectly acceptable *tactics* when used deliberately and selectively for particular purposes. In the case of the alcoholic, these tactics have become part of a preferred defense structure throughout years of alcoholic drinking. For a therapist to try to remove these is equivalent to trying to force water to flow uphill.

Little therapeutic imagination is required to see how tactics such as denial and rationalization can be used effectively with the recovering alcoholic. Once the denial and rationalization associated with drinking have been confronted and dealt with, the recovering alcoholic typically is faced with many very real and difficult life problems. A list of these may serve to remind us of the intolerable internal and external stressors the recovering alcoholic may be required to face. He may have to deal with very serious malfunctions of physical health. His marital situation may remain complicated for many years after his last drink. His finances are often in alarmingly poor condition. He may have alienated everybody who ever meant anything to him. He may be facing nontrivial legal and criminal proceedings, unemployment, disturbed interpersonal relationships, parent–child complexities of unbearable proportions, personal emotional problems of serious dimensions, and so on. What can we do for the person in not one serious life crisis, but in a host of them all at once? It is precisely here that variants of denial and rationalization become important. Through direct tuition, we can help the alcoholic to the position that things will work out if he just will stay sober, that even though his life is complicated at the moment, at least he is sober, that sobriety is his number one priority, and so on and so forth. In other words, we as therapists are appealing to his preferred use of denial and rationalization to give him a toehold on abstinence.

Similarly, by appealing to the alcoholic's preference for assimilative projection, we can get him to identify with other persons whose problems seem to center around something called "alcoholism." If the alcoholic comes to construe himself in these terms, then all of the benefits that can flow from such a self-attribution are his. The label "alcoholic" or "alcoholism" provides the person with a convenient explanatory system for much of his behavior. Moreover, by listening to the experiences of others who make the same self-attribution and who also conveniently explain their behavior by this attribution, the person has a ready source of social reinforcement for his changing belief system. Furthermore, he is now open to considerable positive social influence. And he has been given the key to dealing with otherwise overwhelming anxiety, remorse, guilt, and confusion. In addition, by fixing his lifeline in terms of two clearly demarcated points, that is, when you were drinking and now that you are sober, we have provided the client with reference points for a belief system that includes the possibility of dealing with the negativity of previous behavior and the possibility of hope for desired future behaviors.

In a very real sense, helping the client to achieve a self-attribution of "alcoholic" and, hence, an explanatory system for his behaviors is a central role of the therapist. It should not be done directly. In fact, the guiding principle of work at this phase of therapy should be, "as little external force as necessary for the attribution to be made." If the therapist literally tries to force the attribution upon the client, one of two things will happen: The client will become defiant and reject the therapist's attribution, or the client will publicly acquiesce but privately disagree.

In truth, psychotherapy with the client at this point is very much the teaching of an "exotic belief." The often heard phrase, "your life was a mess because you were drinking, you weren't drinking because your life was a mess," and the many variants of this phrase are, in actuality, efforts to teach the client the convenient fiction that all of his problems are or were attributable to alcoholism. The truth value of this assertion is irrelevant. If it enables the client to (1) explain his past behavior in a way that gives him hope for the future, (2) cope with his guilt, anxiety, remorse, and confusion, and (3) provide himself with a specific behavior (staying sober) that will change his life in a desired direction, then the assertion is valuable despite its questionable truth. *The therapist must remember that the recovering alcoholic has a lifetime of sobriety in which to gradually recognize the fact that not all of his personal and social difficulties can be attributed to alcoholism.* In the meantime, the intelligent therapist will make very good use of assertions that have their basis in denial and rationalization. In effect, the therapeutic task is one of helping the client to construct a belief system. The fact that this belief system may at the beginning of sobriety contain strong elements of denial and rationalization should not trouble us. One must remember that the recovering alcoholic in initial stages of sobriety is faced with so many serious life problems that he will need a healthy dose of denial and rationalization if he is to survive at all.

SUMMARY AND CONCLUSIONS

Throughout this chapter, I have argued for the existence of a preferred defense structure in the alcoholic client. I have further maintained that traditional and even contemporary psychotherapies are largely inappropriate for the recovering alcoholic precisely because they have failed to recognize the *value* of the alcoholic's preferred defense structure. Therapeutic ideologies that consist largely of disguised moralistic stances concerning certain behaviors called "defenses" are likely to do more harm than good in alcoholism therapy.

The central problem in alcoholism psychotherapy is not one of exposing, uncovering, and modifying the alcoholic PDS. The central problem is one of discovering ways of swinging the PDS into the service of achieving and maintaining sobriety.

Finally, psychotherapists must recognize that alcoholism therapy is a time-dependent process. We must begin to see the obvious fact that entirely different therapeutic behaviors are called for in various stages of the long recovery period from active alcoholism.

18:   SOME TREATMENT IMPLICATIONS OF THE EGO
AND SELF DISTURBANCES IN ALCOHOLISM

Edward J. Khantzian

Effective treatment of alcoholism must address the core problems of the alcoholic, namely, the enormous difficulties that such people have had in controlling and regulating their behavior, feelings, and self-esteem. Although psychoanalysis is rarely the treatment of choice for alcoholics, it does offer a special understanding of many of the alcoholic's problems and a rationale for the treatment choices and decisions that must be made to help the alcoholic.

Although in its early application to alcoholism[1] psychoanalysis stressed the instinctual and regressive-pleasurable aspects of alcohol use (Abraham 1908, Freud 1905, Knight 1937, Radó 1933, Simmel 1948), many investigators also appreciated other contributing factors such as mood disturbance, particularly depression, diminished self-esteem, faulty ego ideal formation, and other forms of narcissistic disturbance. Blum (1966), Blum and Blum (1967), Rosenfeld (1965), and Yorke (1970) have published excellent reviews and critiques of these trends in the literature. In this chapter I shall elaborate on more recent psychoanalytic explanations which have attempted to identify more precisely impairments and disturbances in the ego and self, especially involving problems in self-care, affect management, and self–other relationships and related problems in coping. I shall then review through case examples some important implications for treatment of these ego and self disturbances in alcoholics.

Some of the distinctions made in this presentation between "ego" and "self" are arbitrary and artificial. Although structure and function are stressed in relation to the ego, and subjective attitudes and states in relation to the self, clearly the ego has subjective elements associated with it, and the self has

---

[1]For the purposes of this presentation, "alcoholism" refers to a frequency and amount of alcohol consumption sufficient to result in significant physical-psychological, social, legal, or employment difficulties for the individual.

structural and functional aspects. The distinctions are made for heuristic purposes and to delineate more precisely the nature and qualities of the alcoholic's psychological disturbances.

EGO FUNCTIONS AND THE ALCOHOLIC

As already indicated, early formulations of alcoholism were heavily influenced by an instinct psychology that stressed the oral dependency and fixation of the alcoholic. More recent attempts to explain alcoholism from a psychoanalytic point of view have understandably focused on the ego to delineate better the nature of the structural impairments that cause alcohol to become such a compelling and devastating influence in an individual's life. The nature of the ego disturbances and impairments in the alcoholic are varied and manifold. I shall selectively focus on and explore some of those that seem to me most germane in understanding a person's problems with alcohol.

In the broadest terms, it seems to me that the alcoholic has been most vulnerable and impaired in two areas of ego functioning. One area involves functions of self-care; whether sober or drunk, the alcoholic demonstrates a repeated tendency to revert to or persist in drinking behavior despite all the apparent indications that such behavior is self-damaging and dangerous. The second area of obvious difficulty has been in the alcoholic's inability to regulate his or her feelings. When sober, he or she often denies or is unable to identify or verbalize feelings. At other times he or she experiences nameless fears and suffers with depression that might be vaguely perceived or experienced as overwhelming and unbearable, even leading to suicide.

THE EGO AND SELF-CARE

The defense mechanism of denial is frequently invoked to explain why or how alcoholics persist in their self-defeating behavior. In such instances the presence of conscious and unconscious destructive impulses, intentions, and behavior is assumed; presumably there is awareness of real or potential danger, but the individual resorts to an active process or defense against such awareness. Although there is probably a reasonable basis for these assumptions, such explanations are excessively influenced by early instinct theory that stressed pleasure seeking and life–death instincts to the exclusion of other considerations. In contradistinction to such a formulation, I am of the opinion that the self-damaging aspects of alcoholism can be better accounted for by considering a deficiency or impairment in development of an ego function we have designated as "self-care."[2]

The self-destructiveness apparent in alcoholism is not willed or unconsciously motivated by suicidal wishes (i.e., the model of the nemeses) as often as it is the result of impairments and deficiencies in ego functions whereby an individual fails to be aware, cautious, worried, or frightened enough

---

[2] I am indebted to Dr. John E. Mack for the germinal idea of self-care as an ego f

desist in behavior that has damaging consequences. This function originates in the early child–mother relationship when the caring and protective functions of the mother are gradually internalized so that the individual can eventually take care of and adequately protect himself/herself from harm and dangerous situations (Khantzian 1978, Khantzian et al. 1974). Extremes of parental deprivation or indulgence may have devastating subsequent effects, and it is not surprising that both patterns are frequently identified in the background of alcoholics (Blum 1966, Knight 1937, Simmel 1948).

Self-care is a generic or global function and is related to ego functions such as signal anxiety, reality testing, judgment, and synthesis. When self-care is impaired, certain other ego mechanisms of defense are prominent or exaggerated. In fact I suspect such mechanisms might be related to and perhaps even secondary to impairments in self-care. That is, in working with individuals who have self-care problems I have been impressed by how they are vaguely aware of their susceptibility to mishaps and danger and they sense in themselves the lack of a self-protective or self-caring ability and thus need and depend on others to protect them and to help in making judgments about dangerous situations. The ill-defined fears of vulnerability and feelings of helplessness associated with such states compel those who are so affected to counteract these feelings and to externalize their problem by resorting to such mechanisms as justification, projection, and phobic and counterphobic avoidance. In the absence of self-care, such defenses are prominent in alcoholics.

I believe that self-care is deficient, impaired, or absent in many if not most alcoholics and that this accounts for much of the disastrous and destructive behavior in their lives, in addition to the malignant involvement with alcohol. In studying over fifty alcoholics, I have observed the problem of self-care in their histories of poor attendance to preventable medical and dental problems, patterns of delinquent, accidental, and violent behavior, and other forms of impulsivity that predate their alcoholism. It is most obvious in their apparent disregard for the consequences of drinking; there is little evidence of fear, anxiety, or realistic evaluation of the deterioration and danger when they revert to or persist in drinking. Although much of this is secondary to the regression and deterioration in judgment as a function of continued drinking, I have been impressed by the presence and persistence of these tendencies in such individuals both prior to their becoming alcoholic and subsequent to detoxification and stabilization (Khantzian 1978, 1979b).

The Ego and Regulation of Feelings

Whereas self-care serves to warn and protect against external dangers and the consequences of careless behavior, the ego functions involved in regulation of feelings serve as signals and guides in managing and protecting against instability and chaos in our internal emotional life. Many of the same processes which establish self-care functions and originate from the nurturing and protective role of the mother in infancy are involved in the development of ego functions that serve to regulate feelings. It is not surprising, then, that alcoholics also suffer from a range of ego impairments that affect their capacity to regulate their feeling life. These impairments take such forms as an inability to identify and verbalize feelings, an incapacity to tolerate painful feelings such as anxiety and depression, an inability to modulate feelings, problems in activation and initiative, and a tendency to exhibit extreme manifestations of feelings including hypomania, phobic-anxious states, panic attacks, and labile emotional outbursts.

As has been suggested for other mental processes and functions, affects develop along certain lines and are subject to fixation, distortions, and regression. Krystal and Raskin (1970) have helpfully traced and formulated how the affects of anxiety and depression develop out of a common undifferentiated matrix. At the outset feelings are undifferentiated, somatized, and not verbalized. Normally, the tendency is for feelings to become differentiated, desomatized, and verbalized. If this process proceeds optimally, it contributes significantly to the development of an effective stimulus barrier. As used here, "stimulus barrier" refers to aspects of ego function that maintain minimal levels of unpleasant feelings through appropriate action and mechanisms of defense when they reach high or intolerable levels (Khantzian 1978, Krystal and Raskin 1970). In such instances, feelings act as a guide or signal to mobilize ego mechanisms of defense in response to internal emotions and external stimuli. Either as a result of developmental arrest or because of regression caused by traumatic events later in life, alcoholics fail to differentiate successfully, with the consequence that they are unable to use feelings as signals or guides because they are unable to identify affects or their feelings are unbearable or overwhelming. Because of defects in the stimulus barrier, alcoholics use denial and/or the effects of alcohol to ward off overwhelming affects (e.g., undifferentiated anxiety-depression). That is, in lieu of an affective stimulus barrier, "drugs or alcohol are used to avoid impending psychic trauma in circumstances which would not be potentially traumatic to other people" (Krystal and Raskin 1970, p. 31).

Borderline and narcissistic pathology has been implicated in alcoholism (Kernberg 1975, Klein 1975, Kohut 1971), but there has been little systematic attempt to understand the relationship between the structural impairments of such pathology and alcoholism. Kernberg has emphasized ego weakness in borderline conditions and has singled out lack of anxiety tolerance and impulse control, primitive defensive operations including rigid walling off of good and bad introjects, and splitting and denial in the service of preventing anxiety related to aggression (pp. 25–45). Kernberg fails to make it clear whether he believes that such borderline symptomatology is at the root of alcohol problems or that borderline conditions and alcoholism have similar processes operating that affect both conditions. Presumably, the borderline processes delineated by Kernberg are consistent with those identified by Krystal and Raskin, who have detailed more precisely how such problems in coping with feelings affect alcoholics.

Taking a somewhat more descriptive approach, Klein has similarly focused on unpleasant dysphoric affect states associated with borderline conditions and alcoholism. He discounts the role of "ego defects" in borderline conditions and instead emphasizes the importance of a descriptive approach for purposes of diagnosis and classification. Klein stresses the ubiquity of labile, anxious, and depressive states associated with so-called borderline pathology. He believes the "border" in such conditions is more with affective disorders than with neurosis, character pathology, or schizophrenia, and that it is on such a basis that certain individuals welcome the effects of alcohol. He has singled out several syndromes of which alcohol and antianxiety agents are sought for relief, namely hysteroid ("rejection sensitive") dysphoria, chronic anxiety-tension states, and phobic neurosis with panic attacks. Despite his disclaimer about ego defects in such conditions, I believe his own description of these problems as an "affective or activation disorder, or a stereotyped affective overresponse" (Klein 1975, p. 369) speaks for an impairment in the ego's capacity to regulate feelings in such individuals. This is further supported by his observation that psychoactive drugs are effective with such patients because "they modify states of dysregulation of affect and activation." Along these lines, Quitkin and colleagues (1972) have impressively demonstrated that a small but significant proportion of alcoholics suffer from a phobic-anxious syndrome and respond to imipramine with marked symptomatic improvement and elimination of their dependence on alcohol.

In brief, then, I believe there is convincing evidence from several convergent lines of inquiry to support the point of view that significant impairments in ego structure predispose to alcoholism. Impairments in self-care leave individuals ill equipped to properly weigh, anticipate, and assess the consequences of risky and self-damaging behavior, but particularly in relation to the consequences of their alcohol involvement. The other area of ego impairment in alcoholics involves problems in recognizing, regulating, and harnessing feeling states to the point that conditions of immobilization or being overwhelmed with affects result, and alcohol is sought to overcome or relieve such dilemmas.

THE SELF AND THE ALCOHOLIC

Alcoholics suffer not only because of impairments in their ego. They also suffer because of impairments and injury in their sense of self. As in ego disturbances, developmental problems loom large in the self disturbances of alcoholics. Both the development of the ego and the sense of self are results of internalization processes. Optimally, the developing child acquires qualities and functions from the caring parents such that the individual can eventually take care of himself. When successful, the process of internalization establishes within the person a coherent sense of the self, an appreciation of the separate existence of others, and adequate ego functions that serve purposes of defense and adaptation (Khantzian 1978).

In the previous sections we focused on how alcohol problems were related to impairments in ego function which resulted in a deficiency and/or inability to appreciate consequences of dangerous behavior and to regulate emotion. In this section I will emphasize and explore how alcohol problems are also the result of impairments in the sense of self whereby the individual is unable or ill equipped to value, comfort, soothe, care for, and express himself or herself. Although I have designated the impairments around self-care and affect regulation as ego disturbances, such problems are not entirely distinguishable from self disturbances. As indicated at the outset of this chapter, some of these distinctions are arbitrary. It is likely that the nature of the self disturbances I will delineate in this section significantly impact upon and interact with ego disturbances involving self-care and (affect) regulation.

Dependency and the Self

Alcoholics are desperately dependent people. Formulations about the nature of this dependency have, however, been overly simplistic and reductionistic, placing undue emphasis on the symbolic, oral, regressive aspects of the alcoholic's dependency on the substance itself. Similarly, the personal relationships of the alcoholic are characterized as infantile and clinging (Khantzian 1979b). The dependency of alcoholics is not primarily the result of oral fixations and oral cravings. The dependency has more to do with deficits and defects in psychological structure and sense of self whereby the alcoholic depends on the effects of alcohol and attaches himself to others to compensate for deficiencies in self-care, affect regulation, self-esteem, and subjective sense of well-being.

Balint (1968) has characterized the alcoholic's dependency as a "basic fault." He emphasizes that it does not have the form of an instinct or of conflict, but is "something wrong in the mind, a kind of deficiency which must be put right." According to Balint, the alcoholic seeks the effects of alcohol to establish a feeling of "harmony — a feeling that everything is now well between them and their environment — and . . . the yearning for this feeling of harmony is the most important cause of alcoholism or, for that matter, any form of addiction" (p. 56). Along these same lines, Kohut (1971) has observed that dependency of such people on substances (Kohut does not distinguish between alcohol and other substances) says less about the person's attachment to substances and/or people as loved or loving objects than about the search for "a replacement for a defect in psychological structure" (p. 46).

The "fault" or "defect" that alcoholics experience in their psychological-self structure is the result of developmental failures in ego ideal formation. The developing child and adolescent insufficiently experience admired and admiring feelings in response to parents and other adult figures. Because of this deficiency in the relationship with parents and others, such individuals fail to internalize and identify with the encouraging, valued, and idealized qualities of important adults.

Although alcoholics indeed suffer as a result of conscience or superego and seek to drown their guilt and self-condemnation in alcohol, I am impressed that they suffer more from the lack of an adequate ego ideal that would otherwise help them to evaluate themselves as worthwhile and good enough in a whole range of human involvements and activities. Because of faulty ego ideal formation, self-esteem suffers and there is an inability or failure to judge one's relationships, work, or play as sufficient or satisfactory. As a result, individuals so afflicted constantly seek external sources of reassurance, recognition, solace, and approval. Such individuals feel especially wanting from within for an approved self by an approving ego ideal, and it is in this respect that they are so desperately dependent. They seek out alcohol, people, and activities not primarily for gratification of oral, infantile drives and wishes, but more in an attempt to feel better or good about themselves, as they are almost totally unable to achieve this feeling for themselves from within.

Corollary to the disturbance in ego ideal formation are disturbances related to the capacity to comfort, soothe, and care for oneself. Alcoholics seem to adopt modes of polar extremes with regard to such needs and functions. Alcoholics' search for "external supplies" and their dependency on alcohol and leaning on others are the result of a failure to internalize adequately and to develop capacities for nurturance within the self, which causes them to turn primarily outside themselves for comfort, soothing and caring, or defensively to deny such needs or wants.

Pathological Self-Formations

One of the main consequences of the ego and self disturbances in alcoholics is that such individuals have developed and display troublesome and self-defeating compensatory defenses and pathological self-structures in response to underlying conflicts around need satisfaction and dependency. In some instances the defenses that are employed serve to compensate for and counteract the sense of incompleteness such people feel as a result of deficits in affect defense and self-esteem. In other instances the more rigid and primitive defenses that are employed seem to be the result of pathological internalizations, identifications, and self-structures. The alcoholic seeks the releasing effect of alcohol to overcome rigid and overdrawn defenses and to facilitate and regulate the experiencing and expression of affectionate or aggressive feelings in the absense of ego and self structure that helps to modulate such affects and drives (Khantzian 1979a).

Some of the recent elaborations on self-pathology are probably pertinent with regard to the facilitating and regulating influences of alcohol and help to explain why alcoholics need to depend on such effects. Kernberg (1975) has emphasized the importance of pathological self-structures in borderline conditions and has also implicated them in alcoholism. He believes that rigid and primitive defenses of splitting, denial, and projection serve to cause the repression, splitting off, and dissociation of parts of the self, and that the effect of alcohol acts to "refuel" the grandiose self and to activate the "all good" self and object images and to deny the "all bad" internalized objects (p. 222). Despite the emphasis on a deficit psychology, Kohut places equal if not greater emphasis on compensatory and defensive reactions such as massive repression, self-disavowal, and denial of needs. According to Kohut, substance users resort to the effects of substances to lift these defenses in order to feel the soothing and resurgence of self-esteem they are otherwise unable to experience (Kohut 1977). Although Kohut does not specify any particular drugs or substance, in my experience it is precisely this effect that the alcoholic seeks to achieve with the use of alcohol.

On a similar basis, Krystal and Raskin (1970) and Krystal (1977) stress the special and exaggerated defenses of denial and splitting that are adopted by individuals dependent on alcohol. These defenses serve to "wall off" and suppress aggressive and loving feelings in relation to the self and others. Krystal emphasizes the great difficulty alcoholics have with ambivalence, and how they prefer to use the short-acting effect of alcohol to experience and give vent to such feelings briefly, and therefore "safely."

Finally, on a somewhat different basis, Silber (1970, 1974) has focused on the developmental impairments of alcoholics that have been the result of pathological and destructive identifications with psychotic and/or very disturbed parents. The self-damaging and destructive aspects of alcohol involvement parallel and represent identifications with self-neglecting, self-destructive aspects of the parents.

TREATMENT IMPLICATIONS

As I have indicated, alcoholics suffer tremendously in their attempts to regulate their behavior, feelings, and relationships with other people. Effective treatment of these problems must be based on a more precise identification of the disturbances in the ego and self structures of alcoholics, and our psychotherapeutic and psychopharmacological interventions should be based on such an appreciation. In this final section, using case material, I will explore some treatment implications of the alcoholic's ego and self disturbances.

Implications For Initial Care

At the outset, the most urgent and often life-threatening aspect of alcoholism must be faced, namely, the impulsive unbridled use of alcohol. Alcoholics Anonymous has been most effective in helping alcoholics gain control over their drinking; "They have become experts in sobriety" (Mack, personal communication). It is little wonder that A.A.'s success rests upon an emphasis on abstinence as the single most important goal to be achieved by the alcoholic. A.A. has often worked because it skillfully manages and compensates for the impairments in self-care. A.A. also works because it contains and partly satisfies some of the other determinants of alcoholism, namely, problems in regulating emotions and maintaining self-esteem and related dependency problems.

Unfortunately, A.A. is unacceptable for many if not a majority of alcoholics. For many alcoholics, psychiatric and psychological approaches become a logical if not necessary alternative. If such becomes the case, it remains critical that the clinician appreciate, as much as A.A. has, the urgency and dangers of the uncontrolled drinking, as the equally important determinants and causes of the alcoholism are explored and understood. Clearly, until control over the drinking is established, exploration of predisposing causes is of little value.

I have evolved an approach that has proved to be surprisingly useful and effective in dealing with uncontrolled drinking when contact is first made with the alcoholic. As indicated, it is in regard to the uncontrolled drinking that impairments in self-care are most alarmingly and dangerously apparent, and this must become the first focus of any treatment intervention. Rather than stress abstinence or sobriety, I immediately attempt to ascertain the amount and pattern of drinking and ask the patient respectfully and empathically to share with me his or her own reasons for drinking, especially what the drinking does for him or her. I also ask patients as tactfully as I can to reflect on how much danger and harm they have caused themselves as a result of their drinking. Such an approach helps a patient to ease into a treatment relationship where his or her enormous shame about and desperate dependence on alcohol are not immediately challenged or threatened, but which at the same time begins to focus early on some of the important determinants of the uncontrolled drinking.

Once satisfied that the drinking is out of control, I emphatically point this out with undisguised concern and stress that it is the single most immediate problem to be faced. Unrecognized impairments and evident rationalizations are identified as well as the unacknowledged physical and behavioral consequences of the drinking. I openly discuss how difficult it will be to stop drinking, but share with the patient my conviction about the urgency for control and an intention to keep this the main focus for both of us until it is achieved. Keeping the focus on control allows a strategy to develop that avoids premature insistence on permanent abstinence, or an equally untenable permissive acceptance of uncontrolled drinking. Alternative models and methods of control are described explicitly, such as gradual curtailment or abrupt cessation with short-term drug substitution if physiological dependence is evident. If the latter is the case, or if deterioration is evident and/or there is need for external support and control, hospitalization is recommended. In some cases I insist upon it if it seems necessary. Surprisingly, this is rarely the case, and often there is a margin and opportunity in such an approach for the therapist to share with the patient information, experiences, and knowledge about how others have gained control over their drinking. In most instances then, the emphasis in this approach is on establishing control and giving the patient a chance to make a choice.

In one case the discovery that a choice about one's drinking can be made in collaboration with the therapist evolved over several months.

Case 1

This patient was a fifty-one-year-old tradesman who had worked successfully at his job and consumed large amounts of distilled alcohol daily dating back to his late teenage years. He was considered a leader among his peers and until four years prior to seeking treatment had functioned effectively as the elected shop steward for his union. His drinking usually began at mid-day, and he continued drinking from the end of the workday at 4:00 P.M. until supper. He drank with his co-workers in a local pub which was also a gathering place for people of his own nationality. He insisted and his wife confirmed that he never was drunk or reacted adversely to alcohol until four years before, when his shoe shop went out of business and he was unable to find employment because most of the other shoe shops in the area were also going out of business.

At the time of evaluation he indicated that over the past year and a half his drinking had been totally out of control, stating, "I wouldn't dare count how much I was drinking a day this past year or so — all I know is I needed it to start the day and finish the day." He stated that during this period he was experiencing "shakes" every morning. I immediately shared with him my sense that his drinking was out of control and agreed with him that it probably dated back to the loss of his job. I indicated that it would be extremely important to gain control, but I avoided explaining then what this would entail. During the initial sessions he alternated between being garrulous, expansive, and bantering and being irritable and defensive, especially about his drinking. According to the patient — again confirmed by his wife, who was reliable — he made significant but only moderately successful efforts to curtail his drinking over the first two months of weekly contacts with me. After his ninth session I felt he was more at ease with me as he was sharing both pleasant and troubling reminiscences from his childhood years, as well as his challenges and experiences as a union steward. In this context of a more relaxed treatment relationship with me I expressed my concern that he was not sufficiently controlling his drinking. I told him that I was not sure he could take one or two drinks and then leave it alone. I told him that curtailment could be one form of control but I suspected it was not working for him. I shared with him my own discovery that I could not control my use of cigarettes and that smoking one cigarette inevitably led to my resuming smoking a pack a day and how after much experimentation I had learned that abstinence from cigarettes (and the occasional substitution of a cigar) worked best for me. I reviewed with him my knowledge of A.A. and my experience with other patients for whom abstinence from alcohol seemed to work best as a form of control, but I said it remained to be seen what would work for him.

In an interview one month later he reported being discouraged in his efforts to modify his drinking and appeared dejected and depressed. In this context I told him that he seemed to be least able to control his drinking when he felt "lousy." Shortly after this session he stopped drinking. In an interview another month later in which he was evidently feeling much better, he indicated he was not craving alcohol at all. After a thoughtful review on his part of how he planned to approach finding a new job, I puzzled out loud with him how he had managed to gain control over his drinking. He told me that he had thought about my comment two months previously about whether he could have one or two drinks and then stop. He said he decided to try it out and he discovered he couldn't. Again he stressed that once he had stopped drinking, he didn't crave alcohol at all. Reflecting out loud, he reminded me again how much alcohol he needed to get a "little high," an amount that would make others "go staggering." Not without significance and characteristic of this man, he made a playful reference to my example of substituting cigars for cigarettes and revealed some successful substitutions of his own—he said he was "drinking lots of Moxie [a bittersweet, pungent carbonated beverage] and milk." He also added that he was eating well. Over two years of follow-up this man has remained totally sober and abstinent, and he has resumed working in a supervisory capacity. He has also considerably improved his relationship with his wife.

Taking an approach such as the one I have presented here, I have now had the experience of seeing several patients significantly modify and ultimately gain control over their drinking behavior. However, in the majority of the cases I have treated, the patients have *chosen* abstinence as the most reliable means of control. For some, this occurs at the outset; for others, after some tentative experimentation and attempts at continued drinking, such as those I described in Case 1. What has been most impressive has been the salutary discovery by the patient and myself that some choice can be exercised in achieving the goal of control over drinking behavior. In taking such an approach, struggles tend to be avoided, the patient feels a gradual sense of mastery over his or her own problems, and the joint effort to solve a problem fosters a healthy alliance rather than an adversary role between patient and therapist (Khantzian 1980).

As the urgency and danger of the destructive drinking behavior recede and the patient begins to develop an alliance with the therapist, examination and treatment of the predisposing disturbances can and should be considered. Although psychotherapeutic and psychopharmacological treatment of alcoholics has often been dismissed as ineffective and possibly even dangerous, I believe growing clinical understanding and experience with alcoholics suggest that alcoholics are eminently suitable for such treatment. In the preliminary phases of treatment it is most important that decisions about treatment alternatives (psychotherapy and/or drug therapy) be based on identifying more precisely the particular qualities and extent of the ego and self disturbances and other target symptoms that are ascertained. Although I have stressed certain ego and self disturbances in this chapter, it should be apparent that a whole range of psychiatric problems may contribute to or be a part of an alcohol problem, and specific treatment modalities should be tailored to the particular psychopathology or symptoms that may be identified. Of course allowances should also be made in the early phases of treatment, especially with psychotherapy, for cognitive impairments due to toxic aftereffects of prolonged drinking (usually reversible) that make integration of information and interpretations more difficult for the patient.

Implications For Psychotherapy

Critics of psychotherapy for alcoholism have focused on the impulsive, dependent, demanding characteristics and lack of introspection of alcoholics which make them ill suited for therapy, and others have stressed the destructive and unworkable regressive transferences that develop in psychotherapeutic relationships with alcoholics (Canter 1969, Hill and Blane 1967, Pattison 1972). These accounts give an unnecessarily pessimistic view of the alcoholic and do not consider how such reactions surface as a result of passivity on the part of the therapist and an outmoded model of therapy that emphasizes uncovering techniques alone. These approaches reflect once again the influences of an early instinct psychology that is based on the assumption that recovery and cure take place by making the unconscious conscious, reconstructing the past, and uncovering feelings. More recent approaches have better taken into account the alcoholic's impairments and disturbances in identifying and tolerating painful feelings, and have a clearer appreciation of the nature of alcoholics' dependency needs and major problems around self-esteem. In contrast to early psychotherapeutic models, more recent approaches have appreciated the importance of structure, continuity, activity, and empathy in engaging and retaining alcoholics in treatment (Chafetz and Demone 1962, Khantzian 1980, Krystal and Raskin 1970, Silber 1970).

For some, the initial work of therapy becomes that of gradually discovering and identifying states of anxiety and/or depression that have been relieved by drinking. For others, a gradual identification of the forms their dependency has taken, such as a denial of their needs or counterdependent attitudes, becomes important. In early phases of treatment there is a need for the therapist to be active, and to share openly his understanding of the alcoholic's problems, particularly how his use of alcohol has interacted with the particular ego and self disturbances that have been identified.

Some of the alcoholic's disturbances in identifying and experiencing his feelings and rigidly defending against affects have particular psychotherapeutic implications. Krystal has suggested that a "pre-therapy" phase of psychotherapy (personal communication) may be necessary with such patients to teach them about their feelings by helping them to identify and label them, particularly feelings of anxiety, fear, and depression. Krystal (1977) has also focused on alcoholics' use of splitting and other rigid defenses to wall off their ambivalent feelings. He has emphasized that effective therapy with such individuals hinges on helping them to master their fear of closeness with the therapist (related to reactivated childhood longings and feelings of aggression), to learn to grieve effectively, to take responsibility for their destructive feelings, and, perhaps most important, to overcome the barriers (i.e., rigid defenses) that prevent effective comforting of themselves. In my own work with alcoholics I have been impressed with how the affect disturbances significantly contribute to the self-care impairments of alcoholics and how necessary and useful it is to help such patients realize how feelings can be used as a guide for one's behavior and actions.

Case 2

Psychotherapeutic interaction with a fifty-one-year-old man who had a combined alcohol–drug problem nicely demonstrated elements of such affect disturbance, and how such disturbances may be psychotherapeutically managed and brought into the patient's awareness. This patient also gave dramatic evidence of impairments in self-care and some of the more extreme and primitive defenses that are adopted in the absence of self-care, namely denial, counterphobia, and massive repression.

This man had achieved a significant amount of success in his life and his work despite an early childhood in which he suffered much traumatic neglect as a result of his mother's alcoholism and father's chronic depression and absorption with his wife's alcoholism.

Subsequent to the patient's eleven-year-old son's contracting a severe illness, the patient had recently become more withdrawn, depending increasingly on alcohol and drugs himself, and he had been mandated for treatment as a result of indiscriminate behavior at work as a result of his drug–alcohol use. The two most outstanding features of this man, not unrelated to each other, were (a) the direction his interests took starting in early adolescence, and (b) his almost total inability to talk about his feelings. Starting at around age ten he precociously and actively became sexually involved with the opposite sex. Early in his teenage years he turned to and became involved with hobbies that he has continued up until the present which have definite danger and/or violence associated with them. Except for his quick wit (sometimes biting) he displays very little emotion, usually appearing indifferent or apathetic in his facial expressions. Attempts to elicit or draw out feelings are met with either frank denial or, at best, tentative acknowledgment that he might be feeling something.

During one group therapy session the patient reviewed some of his recent indiscretions in his work situation that resulted in possibly jeopardizing his job. He went into great detail about the events, which could have resulted in harm to himself and others. He appeared to be strikingly devoid of feelings as he elaborated on his behavior. A group member immediately exclaimed, "Didn't you realize how vulnerable you were leaving yourself?" The patient insisted that he never gave the situation a thought and denied being fearful about dangerous consequences for himself or others. Other members of the group persisted in inferring an unconscious self-destructive motive. I chose to comment on the patient's insistence that he had neither thought about the danger nor experienced any fear in relation to his behavior. I shared with him and the group my sense of his reluctance and inability to "fuss" over himself or to admit to any worry or fear. I suggested that this difficulty was perhaps a reflection of insufficient "fussing" over him earlier in his life when his parents were too tied up with themselves and their own problems.

As the group meeting continued, a curious and revealing exchange developed between myself and the patient in which he gave further evidence of his deficiencies in signal affects (i.e., feelings in the service of mobilizing mechanisms of defense and/or restraint over impulses). This exchange also demonstrated the necessity for the therapist to be ready to use his/her own feelings and reactions with such patients as an object lesson in helping them to use feelings to better serve and care for themselves. The patient commented on and inquired about my seemingly gruff response in a recent individual psychotherapy hour when he had corrected me on some technicality. I hesitantly acknowledged that he might have been correct in his impression, and I indicated that I knew this was a trait of mine when I am worried and I believed it reflected my worrying about his problem. I subsequently offered that I was worrying for him when he was not sufficiently worrying about himself. He next disclosed to the group and myself how at times in our individual sessions he often deliberately "eyeballed" me and stared me down and that he was surprised that I repeatedly looked away, and again he asked why I reacted in that way. I was surprised again and somewhat caught off guard (perhaps I should not have been) that a man who was so unaware of his own reactions could be so fined tuned to my reactions. Pausing for a moment to get over my surprise, I answered him by acknowledging once again that he was most likely correct in his observation and that my reaction was probably a function of some self-consciousness as a result of his staring at me. I told him that I thought his puzzlement and surprise were some indication that he was unable to admit to any such part of himself, but that if he could continue to watch for other people's self-consciousness, especially in group therapy, he might better develop this in himself to his own benefit. I emphasized how my self-consciousness and others' can actually act as a guide and that being insufficiently self-conscious caused him to get into trouble. Toward the end of the group meeting he began mildly to taunt one of the patients on the number of cups of coffee he drank during the group meeting. Piecing this together with his uncharacteristic confrontations about my behavior, I interpreted his provocativeness to be a function of having overexposed himself and his behavioral difficulties early in the meeting. I pointed out that it was to his credit that he was courageous enough to share his problems with the group, but that I was also equally concerned that he might have overexposed himself; I told him that someone else might not have been as open and as explicit, leading to so much exposure, but that in his case he was not sufficiently self-conscious to protect himself from overexposure.

Duration and Goals of Psychotherapy

Decisions about the duration and goals of psychotherapy with alcoholics should remain flexible and should be based on a consideration of the patient's wishes and a judgment by the therapist, weighing the indications and necessity for continued treatment against the hazards and risks. Many patients feel great relief and appreciation when they are able to control their drinking and know that someone who understands and accepts their problems is available. Such patients often decide for themselves that this is enough of a goal. If the patient is out of immediate danger, I often agree to stop, albeit my decision at times might be based as much on my clinical judgments about the patient as simply on what the patient wants to do, or even based more on my judgment. The following case illustrates how clinical judgments to stop treatment and what the patient wants are not mutually exclusive.

Case 3

This patient, a forty-two-year-old, very intense and conscientious man, gave me good reasons pragmatically and clinically to take him seriously when he proposed that it was best to settle for the initial gains we had made and to discontinue his individual psychotherapy with me after a brief intervention that lasted about three months.

His initial meeting with me was prompted by a crisis that had been precipitated in his second marriage as a result of continued, recurrent alcoholic binges. He had recently remarried, entered into a new small business venture and relocated on the East Coast — all in an attempt to build a new life. He was originally from an extremely wealthy Midwestern family. After attending an exclusive college and doing a tour of duty as a jet pilot in the military, he joined his family's large corporate business. From his late college years and through the military he was a heavy social drinker. Upon joining the family business and over the subsequent ten years, his drinking became increasingly heavy, which ultimately led to a decline and deterioration in his social standing, his marriage, and his job.

By the time he came for his first interview he had rejoined Alcoholics Anonymous (he belonged once before) and was having some success in abstaining from alcohol. In the first visit with me he reviewed how success, ambition, and achievement had always been tremendously important. He went back and forth from examining my professional certificates on the wall to discussing his father's great business success (despite being an extremely heavy drinker himself) to his own lack of achievement and his alcoholic decline. He then went on to express in a most poignant way how there had been a lifelong strained relationship of aloofness and distance between his father and himself and how he had always longed for a better relationship. In this and subsequent interviews it was quickly evident that his longings for a closer relationship with his father coexisted with feelings of just as much bitterness and hatred. Strikingly and in contrast, during the same initial interview he reviewed with me some of his work in Alcoholics Anonymous and how it was helping him. He said the people there were "real — and seeking alternatives to destructiveness." He stressed how they were able to get into the issues of alcohol, and that the feelings of "warmness, camaraderie, and family" were very important to him. At the end of the first hour we agreed that there was a "cauldron of issues bubbling inside" with which he struggled, but that for a while we would focus on his marital problems and he would continue to work on his sobriety through Alcoholics Anonymous. He agreed to join a couples group in which a common denominator was that the life of one of the spouses in each couple had been affected by drug or alcohol dependence. He also agreed to see me for individual psychotherapy.

Over the next several months his ambivalence toward me became evident. On the one hand he admired my achievements and how I seemed to be able to understand him. However, he also regularly made it clear that psychiatrists understood little about alcoholism or alcoholics. In his first interview with me he said, "My [previous] psychiatrist never even asked about the alcohol—he gave me medicine saying it might help to deal with some of the underlying feelings so that I wouldn't have to use alcohol—and that when we got to the root of the problem, then maybe I wouldn't need to drink. I liked him, but I don't think he understood anything about alcohol." In subsequent visits he either would totally accept my clarifications and interpretations or just as arbitrarily would argue a point based on "strict principles" and a conviction that A.A. could serve him better, adding, furthermore, that it didn't cost anything.

After two months of individual and couples group meetings he became more clear and explicit about the reasons for his reluctance to continue in individual and ultimately group psychotherapy. He worried that his dependency on me and my ideas might be too consuming emotionally and financially (despite relatively unlimited financial backing from his family). References to competitive situations and stories where someone or an animal was killed or hurt only thinly masked concerns about his relationship with me. In one group meeting someone asked him about his tendency to avoid people with whom he identified. He responded that he tended to become anxious and then resort to "impulsive and compulsive behavior." About six weeks into the treatment (in association with a drinking setback) he sent a letter to me stating he would not see me anymore, indicating he did "not want to go back into the 'cauldron of issues' anymore." With one phone call from me he agreed to return, but he persisted in his ambivalence about continuing in individual psychotherapy. I told him I respected his wishes, and we met a few more times. In one of his final regularly scheduled meetings he once again spoke with concern about his tendency to adopt and depend upon others wholesale but said that he wanted and intended to continue group because he could "sample" other people's ideas and thoughts with "a little more protection." In this hour he made a reference to "symbiotic relationships" and commented on some stories about the Pharaoh and the "tooth scraper" and a crocodile who had a bird picking his teeth.

Considering that his drinking was under control, that he had by then joined several A.A. groups in which he felt comfortable, and the help obtained from the couples group, I decided that he had gained enough personal support and control over his drinking to stop his individual meetings. He also asked if he might periodically see me if he felt the need (which he has since done). I felt that the limited goals and involvement of obtaining support, clarification, and sobriety for this man were sufficient and outweighed the risks that were possible, given the intensity of his ambivalence toward me.

As the above case demonstrates, the risks of ongoing psychotherapy with certain alcoholics outweigh the advantages that might be achieved, and limited goals of clarification and support are preferable. However, in many other cases disabilities and problems surface for which psychoanalytic psychotherapy should be considered, and in fact might be the treatment of choice. Many patients continue to evidence considerable impairment and vulnerability, and the constant threat of reversion to alcohol and other forms of impulsivity remains apparent. In still other instances, despite considerable stability and improvement the patient and the therapist begin to sense and identify the persistence of subtle indications that things are not right: dissatisfactions in relationships or feelings of loneliness, isolation, and unhappiness emerge; or vague feelings of tension, anxiety, and depression continue; or self-defeating personality characteristics continue to plague a person, and related complaints and conflicts previously masked by the alcohol and associated acting out become more apparent. Qualities and characteristics often emerge in the treatment relationship that are symptomatic of ego and self impairments and become the basis for judgments about continued, long-term treatment.

In some cases more definitive long-term analysis-treatment of the determinants of the ego and self disturbances is not only possible but indicated. In my experience there is no basis to conclude categorically that a person with an alcohol problem lacks the requisite ego strength and capacity for an alliance to do such psychotherapeutic work. In such cases it is important for the therapist to combine elements of empathy and ego analysis to help patients gain an understanding of their dilemmas, as the following case illustrates.

Case 4

Taking such an approach with a twenty-nine-year-old resident internist was particularly useful. Worried that he might be prone to alcoholism, he described a drinking pattern that involved regular, daily consumption of moderate to heavy amounts of beer interspersed with periodic episodes of extremely heavy drinking at various social get-togethers in which he might become amnesic for part of or all the episode.

The developments over the course of a particular treatment hour demonstrated how empathy with the patient's embarrassment and shame over his need to be appreciated, reassured, and understood led to a better elucidation and understanding of certain ego traits (cynicism and suspiciousness) and the uneven and self-defeating ways in which he satisfied his dependency including his use of alcohol. At the beginning of the hour he mentioned that he had to present a problem case to a senior attending physician at grand rounds. With a certain degree of detachment he observed that it would be interesting to see what the attending physician had to say on the case. He quickly became aware of and commented on his own "cynicism" and then conceded that the attending physician might also feel under pressure to do a good job. He wondered out loud some more as to the meaning of his cynicism. He speculated that it had to do with feeling "on the outside" and trying to get "in" himself. In an aside he complained of feeling "hung over" from the previous evening, when he had drunk a considerable amount of beer. He then joked about a new symptom of bruxism and lightly reviewed in the same vein how he frequently washed his hands, drank a lot, and "twiddled" his fingers. At this point I observed that he began to be self-conscious and wonder about his own cynicism and then to make light of his symptoms at the point where he indicated his more sympathetic appreciation that both the attending physician and myself might feel pressure to do a good job. He quickly agreed and volunteered that he was quick to disbelieve the intentions of people. He gave the example of people in medicine professing a motive of wanting to help when he suspected the motive of wanting money and prestige. He went on to say that he became defensive when a consultant such as the attending physician "delivers on what I implicitly ask for — or want." He also indicated he felt the same with me when I delivered on what he wanted. Among the forms his "defensiveness" might take he listed cynicism, humor, and a "carping anger." He reflected that he might be self-defeating, for example, with the attending physician at grand rounds, and he might become obsequious, and he then questioned whether there might be a parallel pattern with me. I gently confirmed that such alternating patterns had occurred with me.

After a slight pause he began quietly to review how he thought a lot went into his reactions. He said, "Part of me wants to make repair of the things that are bad; part of me wants to exaggerate and make too much or the most of things. Somewhere in here there is a part of me that emerges that I don't know very well — it reminds me of how I recently told you I didn't know what my father thought of me. I still wonder how people see me."

He then began to address himself more directly to me. "Although you don't see me in action, I think you know me pretty well and have a pretty fair idea of how I interact with people. But I don't know how you see me — so I wonder what I am." His mood shifted abruptly and with a hint of embarrassment and some more evident impatience with himself he protested. "This is getting too complicated for this hour of the morning." I told him that I thought he was talking about something important but that he became uncomfortable when he approached a part of himself that he wanted me to know and understand better; he had become embarrassed as he did so, as we evident when he tried to dismiss his thoughts by commenting on the hour of the morning. He then associated to wanting to have children but returned to his embarrassment reaction and the wishes behind such reactions that I had been "able to pick up." He said, "You will think, how self-centered of me." I responded that he not only was embarrassed, but even more, he was ashamed of his wishes towards me. I suggested that he was experiencing in a small way with me the ways he got stuck in his life with his defensiveness, wherein he went from one extreme or the other, so that he couldn't allow himself anything he wanted or indulged himself too much. He quickly interjected that drinking was his main "self-indulgence" and then chastised himself, saying twice, "God, I wish I didn't drink!" He promptly qualified this, reassuring me and himself me had been doing better. He then just as promptly castigated himself for reassuring himself. I ended the hour by pointing out that he berated and put himself down for reassuring himself. I said that reassuring himself was important and that if he could not allow that kind of indulgence for himself it was understandable how he could continue to resort to more extreme, self-defeating indulgences.

This case demonstrates how certain patients adopt exaggerated postures of indifference and self-sufficiency to defend against their dependent longings and needs. Empathically focusing on the patient's discomfort, shame, and embarrassment reactions allowed the therapist to analyze with the patient how he repeatedly and characteristically denied and avoided his wish for recognition and approbation. Taking such an approach also makes extreme and alternating patterns of self-indulgence and denial more understandable, and thus more controllable — patterns that are otherwise driven, repetitious, and self-defeating. Such reactions suggest the operation of narcissistic resistances analogous to neurotic transference resistances, and represent opportunities for the patient and therapist to understand together, in the treatment relationship, the nature and origins of core conflicts around need satisfaction and dependency problems.

Many of the defenses and reactive patterns of alcoholics, including those of the patient just reviewed, resemble aspects and features of borderline and narcissistic conditions described by Kohut and Kernberg. Although they differ in their theoretical understanding and clinical application of these problems, they have both implicated such processes in drug–alcohol problems, and certain of their observations and approaches to such patients seem worth considering. In my opinion it is not clear whether borderline and narcissistic conditions share in common with alcoholics processes that are similar though not necessarily the same, or whether borderline and narcissistic pathology is at the root of alcoholism. However, the more recent emphasis on treatment of the deficits and pathology in ego and self structures is a promising and hopeful development for alcoholism treatment. I also believe we are still in a discovery phase of understanding narcissistic pathology in general, and how such pathology and its treatment applies in cases of alcoholism.

Implications for Psychopharmacological Treatment

The use of psychotropic drugs has a legitimate place among the treatment alternatives for alcohol problems and alcoholism. However, the literature on the efficacy of psychotropic agents in the treatment of alcoholism is for the most part confusing and discouraging. Part of the problem in drawing conclusions from these reports is that few if any of the studies are comparable. First, standard criteria for diagnosis of the alcoholism or the presumed underlying condition which is being treated are lacking. Another problem is related to the fact that depending on the study, different facets of the problem are studied to judge the usefulness of various psychopharmacological agents. In some reports relief of target symptoms such as sleeplessness, anorexia, and anergia is studied, in others whether abstinence is achieved, and in others overall improvement of depression. Reviews by Mottin (1973), Viamontes (1972), and Greenblatt and Shader (1973) are generally pessimistic about all classes of psychopharmacological agents in the treatment of alcoholism. Mottin is most negative with regard to drug therapy. Viamontes's review reveals that the majority of uncontrolled clinical trials using antidepressants, phenothiazines, and benzodiazepines are effective in the treatment of alcoholism. Mottin, Viamontes, and Greenblatt and Shader uniformly emphasize the methodological problems of clinical trials with these drugs and cite the lack of double-blind controlled studies that might better establish the efficacy of these drugs.

Notwithstanding these methodological inconsistencies and shortcomings, a number of carefully controlled and executed studies over the past decade have proved to be promising and hopeful with regard to the use of drug therapy in alcoholism. Bliding (1973) demonstrated the benzodiazepine oxazepam to be more effective than chlorprothixene or placebo in the treatment of chronic alcoholism. Kissin and Gross (1968) showed chlordiazepoxide combined with imipramine to be effective in controlling drinking behavior and furthering overall improvement. In studies by Butterworth (1971) and Overall and colleagues (1973), the use of tricyclic antidepressants and to a lesser extent phenothiazines has proved effective in relieving symptoms of underlying depression (also anxiety in the Overall et al. study). In another important study conducted by Quitkin and colleagues (1972) target symptoms of phobia and anxiety in a subsegment of alcoholics were dramatically relieved by imipramine with significant improvement of drinking behavior. More recently, reports by Wren and colleagues (1974), Klein and colleagues (1974), and Merry and colleagues (1976) suggest that lithium is effective in cases of alcoholism associated with depression.

What is to be made of these often confusing and contradictory findings? What should guide the practitioner in the decision to treat or not treat the alcoholic with these pharmacological agents? Do the findings of a dynamic approach that identifies structural impairments have any relevance to a descriptive approach that suggests such individuals might have pharmacologically treatable problems? Most if not all of the drug studies with alcoholics have been based on descriptive approaches in which target symptoms and psychopathology are identified. Nevertheless, I believe there is a basis for speculation that such target symptoms and psychopathology are the result of failures and deficits in ego and self structures, particularly those involving regulation of affects. I expect that these drugs work with alcoholics because they serve, support, and augment otherwise impaired ego capacities and disturbances in self-regulation.

The findings of descriptive psychiatry complement an approach aimed at identifying the ego and self disturbances in alcoholics. This is particularly so given recent trends in both descriptive psychiatry and psychoanalysis to state more explicitly the criteria for diagnosis and identify more precisely the nature of the psychopathology. Such approaches are consistently demonstrating the ubiquity of depression, phobia, anxiety, and panic states in association with alcoholism (Behar and Winokur 1979, Klein 1975, Quitkin et al. 1972, Weisman and Meyers 1980, Weisman et al. 1980, Winokur et al. 1970). There is evidence that these conditions are as treatable in alcoholics as they are in other patients and that they are contributory to the alcoholism (Behar and Winokur 1979, Klein 1975, Quitkin et al. 1972). Although the incidence of depression in alcoholism has ranged from 3 to 98 percent in different studies, the application of precise diagnostic criteria for depression and phobic anxious states has produced more uniform results when attempts have been made more recently to identify these conditions in alcoholics (Keeler et al. 1979, Weisman et al. 1980). Moreover, when considered from a point of view taken by Klein (1975), where a more generic view of affective disturbance is considered symptoms of dysphoria, anergia, anxiety, and depression become interacting, overlapping, and on a continuum and seem more to be evidence of the "dysregulation of affects" and "disorders of activation" to which Klein refers.

In the first part of this chapter I explored how self-care disturbances and disturbances in affect regulation predisposed individuals to alcoholism. I speculated that in the absence of adequate self-care functions, the individuals' vague sense of vulnerability might contribute to phobias in alcoholics. I also suggested that because of developmental failures alcoholics either overregulated or underregulated their affects and depended on the effects of alcohol to release or submerge their "good and bad" feelings. In my estimation, many of the symptomatic features of alcoholics, including, for example, anxiety, depression, dysphoria, and sleeplessness, are indicators and the result of more fundamental and serious disturbances in the ego and self structures that are responsible for affect regulation and the achievement of subjective states of well-being, including the maintenance of self-esteem. These disturbances seriously incapacitate the alcoholic and are not easily or readily influenced by psychotherapeutic interventions alone, especially early in treatment. It is exactly in this respect that many alcoholics need assistance with the intolerable and overwhelming feeling states with which they suffer and why psychopharmacological agents might be considered useful if not necessary.

The common and prevalent distrust of alcoholics' suitability for drug therapy is unwarranted, in my opinion. Much of the controversy over drug use in alcoholism stems from a misunderstanding of the alcoholic's dependency problems. When considering psychopharmacological treatment of the alcoholic, it is understandable that we remain apprehensive about the "regressive-oral" needs and inclinations of the alcoholic. However, when we consider the structural impairments with which alcoholics suffer, the use of psychoactive drugs becomes a logical alternative that should be seriously considered. In my own experience, using predominantly tricyclic antidepressants and/or benzodiazepines (particularly oxazepam), I have very rarely had patients abuse or misuse these drugs. On the other hand, I have seen several alcoholic patients in consultation who had overused prescribed benzodiazepines, and it has been my clinical impression that this was more likely to occur when they were prescribed in lieu of a treatment relationship that considered and tried to understand all aspects of the physiological and psychological disturbances associated with alcohol problems.

For some the duration of need for these psychopharmacologic agents is short, and for others the need continues for longer periods. For many others there is no need for medication at all. The timing, duration, and choice of these agents should be based on clinical observations and judgments about each patient as he or she gains or attempts to gain control over drinking. I believe the cases requiring no medication or only short-term use of medication are those in which the disturbances are less severe and/or the regression is more readily reversible. The more usual case in my experience involves situations where as control is gained over the drinking, depressive anxious syndromes, including phobias, surface, which are evident and are most often quite disabling. For some, the severity of these symptoms seems to be secondary and related to regressive states associated with protracted drinking, but the symptoms nevertheless respond to antidepressants and/or benzodiazepines. In my experience the decision as to which of the two drugs to use or whether to combine them should be based on clinical judgment as to the predominant symptomatology. Perhaps Klein has properly elaborated on what one rationale might be for using these drugs in combination, namely that the phobic and panic states often involved with alcohol problems respond to imipramine, but the anticipatory anxiety associated with the phobic states is unresponsive to this drug. The anticipatory anxiety does, however, respond to antianxiety drugs, and therefore these drugs might be indicated in alcohol problems associated with phobic states. In many instances the disturbances I have outlined are severe, ubiquitous, and persistent. The buffering, supporting action of these drugs in helping to manage affects is needed, and the need for a longer and more indefinite period of drug therapy is indicated. In those instances where the patient was slow to abstain or curtail his/her drinking, where all other efforts on the part of myself, A.A., the family, and others had failed, and where continued drinking threatened to be disastrous, I deliberately chose to initiate the use of antianxiety agents or antidepressants to help contain and cope with painful affects of anxiety and/or depression. This is admittedly risky, and I have in such cases involved family members for supervision and dispensed only small amounts of the medication. Fortunately these instances are rare.

In summary, I would suggest that it is often the combination of psychotherapeutic and psychopharmacologic interventions, especially early in treatment, that is critical in helping alcoholics overcome their dependence on alcohol and assisting them with their enormous problems with self-care and affect regulation. In some instances the psychopharmacologic intervention may be time-limited and an adjunct to psychotherapy and other approaches, but in other instances it may be a definitive treatment for identified target symptoms and psychopathology.

REFERENCES

Abraham, K. (1908). The psychological relation between sexuality and alcoholism. In *Selected papers on psychoanalysis*. New York: Basic Books, 1960.

Balint, M. (1968). *The Basic Fault*. London: Tavistock.

Behar, D., and Winokur, G. (1979). Research in alcoholism and depression: a two-way street under construction. In *Psychiatric Factors in Drug Abuse*, ed. R. W. Pickens and L. H. Heston. New York: Grune & Stratton.

Bliding, A. (1973). Efficacy of anti-anxiety drug therapy in alcoholic post-intoxication symptoms: A double-blind study of chlorpromazine, oxazepam and placebo. *British Journal of Psychiatry* 122:465–468.

Blum, E. M. (1966). Psychoanalytic views of alcoholism. *Quarterly Journal of Studies on Alcohol* 27:259–299.

Blum, E. M., and Blum, R. H. (1967). *Alcoholism*. San Francisco: Jossey-Bass.

Butterworth, A. T. (1971). Depression associated with alcoholic withdrawal: Imipramine therapy compared with placebo. *Quarterly Journal of Studies on Alcohol* 32:343–348.

Canter, F. M. (1969). The future of psychotherapy with alcoholics. In *The Future of Psychotherapy*. Boston: Little, Brown.

Chafetz, M., and Demone, H. W., Jr. (1962). *Alcoholism and Society*. New York: Oxford University Press.

Freud, S. (1905). Three essays on the theory of sexuality. *Standard Edition* 7.

Greenblatt, D. J., and Shader, R. I. (1973). *Benzodiazepines in Clinical Practice*. New York: Raven.

Hill, M., and Blane, H. T. (1967). Evaluation of psychotherapy with alcoholics: a critical review. *Quarterly Journal of Studies on Alcohol* 28: 76–104.

Keeler, M. H., Taylor, I. C., and Miller, W. C. (1979). Are all recently detoxified alcoholics depressed? *American Journal of Psychiatry* 136: 586–588.

Kernberg, O. F. (1975). *Borderline Conditions and Pathological Narcissism*. New York: Jason Aronson.

Khantzian, E. J. (1978). The ego, the self and opiate addiction: theoretical and treatment considerations. *International Review of Psycho-Analysis* 5:189–199.

———— (1979a). Impulse problems in addiction: cause and effect relationships. In *Clinical Approaches to Impulsive Patients*, ed. H. Wishnie and J. Nevis-Olesen. New York: Plenum.

———— (1979b). On the nature of the dependency and denial problems of alcoholics. *Journal of Geriatric Psychiatry* 11:191–202.

———— (1980). The alcoholic patient: an overview and perspective. *American Journal of Psychotherapy* 34:4–19.

Khantzian, E. J., Mack, J. E., and Schatzberg., A. F. (1974). Heroin use as an attempt to cope: Clinical observations. *American Journal of Psychiatry* 131:160–164.

Kissin, B., and Gross, M. M. (1968). Drug therapy in alcoholism. *American Journal of Psychiatry* 125:31–41.

Klein, D. F. (1975). Psychopharmacology and the borderline patient. In *Borderline States in Psychiatry*, ed. P. Hartocollis. New York: Grune & Stratton.

Klein, N. S., Wren, J. C., Cooper, T. B., et al. (1974). Evaluation of lithium therapy in chronic and periodic alcoholism. *American Journal of Medical Science* 268: 15–22.

Knight, R. P. (1937). The dynamics and treatment of chronic alcohol addiction. *Bulletin of the Menninger Clinic* 1:233–250.

Kohut, H. (1971). *The Analysis of the Self*. New York: International Universities Press.

_____ (1977). Preface. In *Psychodynamics of Drug Dependence*. Research monograph 12, pp. vii–ix. Rockville, MD: National Institute on Drug Abuse.

Krystal, H. (1977). Self- and object-representation in alcoholism and other drug dependence: implications for therapy. In *Psychodynamics of Drug Dependence*. Research monograph 12, pp. 88–100. Rockville, MD: National Institute on Drug Abuse.

Krystal, H., and Raskin, H. A. (1970). *Drug Dependence: Aspects of Ego Functions*. Detroit: Wayne State University Press.

Merry, J., Reynolds, C. M., Bailey, J., and Coppen, A. (1976). Prophylactic treatment of alcoholism by lithium carbonate. *Lancet* 2:481–482.

Mottin, J. L. (1973). Drug-induced attenuation of alcohol consumption. *Quarterly Journal of Studies on Alcohol* 34:444–463.

Overall, J. E., Brown, D., Williams, J. D., and Neill, L. (1973). Drug treatment of anxiety and depression in detoxified alcoholic patients. *Archives of General Psychiatry* 29:218–221.

Pattison, E. M. (1972). The rehabilitation of the chronic alcoholic. In *The Biology of Alcoholism*. Vol. 2. *Physiology and Behavior,* ed. B. Kissin and H. Begleiter. New York: Plenum.

Quitkin, F. M., Rifkin, A., Kaplan, J., and Klein, D. F. (1972). Phobic anxiety syndrome complicated by drug dependence and addiction. *Archives of General Psychiatry* 27:159–162.

Radó, S. (1933). The psychoanalysis of pharmacothymia (drug addiction). *Psychoanalytic Quarterly* 2:1–23.

Rosenfeld, H. A. (1965). The psychopathology of drug addiction and alcoholism: a critical review of the psychoanalytic literature. In *Psychotic States*. London: Hogarth.

Silber, A. (1970). An addendum to the technique of psychotherapy with alcoholics. *Journal of Nervous and Mental Diseases* 150:423–437.

_____ (1974). Rationale for the technique of psychotherapy with alcoholics. *International Journal of Psychoanalytic Psychotherapy* 28:47.

Simmel, E. (1948). Alcoholism and addiction. *Psychoanalytic Quarterly* 17:6–31.

Viamontes, J. A. (1972). Review of drug effectiveness in the treatment of alcoholism. *American Journal of Psychiatry* 128:1570–1571.

Weisman, M. M., and Meyers, J. K. (1980). Clinical depression in alcoholism. *American Journal of Psychiatry* 137:372–373.

Weisman, M. M., Meyers, J. K., and Harding, P. S. (1980). The prevalence rates and psychiatric heterogeneity of alcoholism in a United States urban community. *Quarterly Journal of Studies on Alcohol* 41:672–681.

Winokur, G., Reich, T., Rimmer, J., and Pitts, G. (1970). Alcoholism: III. Diagnosis and familial psychiatric illness in 259 alcoholic probands. *Archives of General Psychiatry* 23:104–111.

Wren, J., Kline, N., and Cooper, T. (1974). Evaluation of lithium therapy in chronic alcoholism. *Clinical Medicine* 81:33–36.

Yorke, C. (1970). A critical review of some psychoanalytic literature on drug addiction. *British Journal of Medical Psychology* 43:141.

APPLYING OBJECT RELATIONS THEORY
IN ALCOHOLISM TREATMENT
Part V

19: THE DYNAMICS AND TREATMENT OF CHRONIC ALCOHOL ADDICTION

Robert P. Knight

Abraham, in 1908, published a paper on "The Psychological Relations between Sexuality and Alcoholism," which was the first evidence of psychoanalytic interest in the problem of chronic alcohol addiction. His comments and interpretations in this paper are still regarded as correct. Since this time, however, analysts have written comparatively little about this condition. In the past ten years, several articles by Radó (1933), Simmel (1930), and Glover (1932) constitute practically the only attempts to formulate etiologic and dynamic concepts of alcohol and other drug addictions. Single case studies by Daniels (1933) and Robbins (1935) are to be found in the literature in English, but aside from the general implications contained in these case studies, the literature of psychoanalysis is singularly free from discourses on the therapeutic techniques in chronic alcohol addiction. The psychiatric literature, on the other hand, contains many statistical studies and other articles on alcoholism, with especial emphasis perhaps on the psychoses which complicate excessive drinking. Perhaps the small number of articles on this subject is due to the fact that comparatively few alcoholics have come to analysis, in either Europe or America and, especially in America, many other forms of treatment are better known and more widely utilized than psychoanalytic treatment.

In the past two and a half years my colleagues at the Menninger Clinic and I have had the opportunity to observe and study 30 cases of alcohol addiction in men. All cases have been studied intensively by the staff, and were under observation for periods of from one to nine or ten months, the conferences with the physician being supplemented by detailed observational notes during the other twenty-three hours of the day by nurses and therapists. I propose on the basis of experience thus far gained to discuss the etiology, dynamics, classification, prognostic appraisal and technique of treatment in cases of chronic addiction. This discussion of dynamics and technique of treatment is to be regarded only as a preliminary report.

CASE MATERIAL

Although the twenty cases not directly under the writer's care have been observed and studied in conjunction with other staff members, and although the psychological material from these cases substantiates the theories and conclusions as to treatment set forth in this paper, I shall in this preliminary paper limit my material to the ten cases personally studied and treated by psychoanalysis.

All of the cases were brought to the Clinic by desperate relatives, in most cases against the patient's will, and, in the majority of cases, the patients arrived heavily intoxicated, some being brought in ambulances. In many of the cases there was a history of from one or two to ten or twelve previous attempts at treatment by the Keeley cure, banishment to remote ranches, confinement in jail, confinement in athletic resorts on the Hudson, and various attempts at psychotherapy. In most cases the responsible relative stated when the patient was admitted that this was the final desperate attempt to get the patient cured, and that if our treatment failed, the patient was to be permitted to "go to the dogs" as he seemed to want to.

ETIOLOGY

Alcohol addiction is a symptom, rather than a disease, and is used here as a diagnostic category only because the excessive drinking is the outstanding presenting complaint. In spite of the conviction of most alcoholics that they would be quite normal if only they could stop drinking, one never finds an alcoholic who is a psychologically healthy person when sober. There is always an underlying personality disorder evidenced by obvious maladjustment, neurotic character traits, emotional immaturity or infantilism, an often by other neurotic symptoms. In some cases, if not in all, thinly veiled psychotic trends — especially paranoid and schizoid features — are discovered. In the symptom of excessive drinking, one sees both the regressive acting out of unconscious libidinal and sadistic drives and the progressive attempt at solution or cure of the conflict by means of the ingestion of a pharmacologically potent substance, which is thus exploited both as a means of obtaining forbidden gratifications and carrying out of otherwise repressed hostilities (ego-alien impulses) and as a dissolver of inhibitions and anxieties (ego-protective impulses). Because it is so apparent with most alcoholics that they are able to purchase temporary freedom from reality considerations and embark upon a temporary psychosis (which sometimes becomes a genuine psychosis) one feels justified in agreeing with Glover that alcohol addiction, along with other drug addictions, constitutes a borderline condition psychiatrically.

We become aware, from these considerations, that the etiological roots of the addiction arise in the deepest layers of the unconscious. Since the actual drinking usually has its onset in the early twenties, occasionally as early as the mid-adolescent period, it becomes necessary also to evaluate the factors surrounding the onset of this symptom, as well as to correlate these factors with the infantile, unconscious roots which may be said to constitute the predisposing etiology.

In the papers by Radó and Glover on the etiology of drug addiction, there is no mention of the parental constellation in which the addict grew up. Glover dwells mainly on the patient's infantile sadism, and points out that other papers on addiction tend too much to attempt an understanding of the dynamics on the basis of the distortions and compromise formations of the libidinal components. Radó, in his earlier papers, promulgates the theory of the alimentary orgasm, pharmacogenically induced, but in his more recent paper he too is concerned with the sado-masochistic elements in the addiction. However, Radó contends that the addiction can arise in any type of neurotic conflict, that any person suffering from unresolved emotional conflict may turn to the magic elatant drug for a solution of his conflict. With this statement there can be no essential disagreement, since we see such a diversity of superficial neurotic conflictual situations among addicts studied, even though certain common features are evident in all cases. However, it seems that the one common feature to all, namely the excessive drinking, itself needs to be explained etiologically. In other words, why do these persons drink excessively instead of developing some other form of neurotic or psychotic picture? Although alcoholics exhibit types of conflict seen in other neuroses where addiction plays a small part or no part at all, still there must be definite and discoverable reasons why this particular solution is attempted in those who become addicts. Radó and Glover are not oblivious to this consideration, but their formulations do not relate at all to the actual characteristics and attitudes of the addict's parents toward him in infancy and childhood, and to the child's reaction to these attitudes and management.

At the risk of generalizing from too little material, I wish to present some observations and theories which I and my colleagues at the Menninger Clinic have made along this line which seem to us to have a very important bearing on the etiology of alcohol addiction.

With a frequency that was startling at first and then became almost a monotonous repetition as more cases were studied, we found a certain typical parental constellation. In each of the ten cases personally treated as well as in most of the other cases studied and treated by other staff members, there has been an over-indulgent, over-protective mother. Repeatedly in the histories we find incidents in which the mother constantly indulged the child by granting special favors or else acted as the child's advocate with the father and persuaded him to grant the indulgences. The child would, then, quite naturally, play the mother off against the father and would in many cases plan his campaign of obtaining something from the father by appealing to the mother first and letting her plead his case with the father. A number of the patients stated, "I could get anything out of my mother." Before analyzing this mother–son relationship further, permit me to make a further observation about the typical father.

This observation must first be qualified. I realize that alcoholic patients that are, finally, in desperation brought to a modern private sanitarium for protracted treatment must come from fairly well-to-do families, and this implies that the father has been financially successful, and hence is usually an aggressive, dominating individual, at least in the business world. Therefore, our observation about the typical father applies in the main to cases from a certain economic and social level. However, I shall not be concerned so much in this discussion with the father's wealth and economic achievement as with his emotional attitude toward his family. We have found such fathers to be almost invariably cold and unaffectionate, rather dominating toward their families, and inconsistently *severe* and *indulgent* toward their sons, to say nothing of their attitude toward their wives.

Let us see what the implications of such a regular parental pattern are for the child who later turns out to be an alcohol addict. We know from psychoanalytic experience that the first method the infant finds at his disposal for allaying distress and anxiety is through oral pacification. Therefore, if an individual later in life resorts to this same technique, it must mean that this infantile nursing experience was especially exploited by him. Since the infant cannot exploit his oral cravings without cooperation from his parents, especially from his mother, it seems that one is justified in assuming certain methods of management of him in infancy, even though the actual nursing experiences are unobtainable in the history and can only be hypothesized from the known material of later childhood. Hence, you will perhaps pardon me for indulging in a little speculation on this point.

Such a mother as I have described—over-indulgent and over-protective— would certainly have given her infant son ample opportunity to exploit the nursing situation. By over-responding to his natural demands for oral satisfaction she would encourage further demands, with the natural expectation on his part that these demands would be complied with. We also know from our analytic experience that such demands, if encouraged, always come to exceed the reality possibilities for gratification, so that in the end even the over-indulgent mother finds herself unable to keep up with the demands made on her and the child inevitably feels thwarted. The consequent rage at frustration may cause the mother to redouble her efforts to comply, until finally the pattern of excessive dependence and passivity, excessive claims and outbursts of rage at necessary thwartings is built into the child's personality. Weaning such a child becomes extremely difficult and, when accomplished, must be traumatic. Furthermore, whether or not a younger sibling is born to displace him and further increase his resentment, the child's ambivalence is greatly heightened, with much hostility toward the mother. There is one further point, which is highly speculative, but which I hope eventually to prove by means of actual material, and this has to do with the mother's own ambivalence toward her son. We are accustomed in psychoanalysis to view with suspicion the over-reactions we note in such a mother, and to perceive under the cloak of this over-compensation, as well as in the nature of her possessive, smothering type of love, her own hostility to and rejection of her child. It may be that this attitude of the mother is caused or at least enhanced by the coldness and lack of affection in her husband. In any case it is quite probable that the son unconsciously perceives and reacts to this rejection.

When the son who unconsciously feels thwarted, rejected and betrayed by his mother turns to his father for love and indulgence, he is bound to be increasingly frustrated. This type of father—independent, dominating, often severe—tries to force his son into independence by holding him too rigidly to reality requirements, to make up for the mother's indulgent attitude of which he has disapproved. The son can't stand this frustration, the mother intercedes, begs for leniency, shields the son from the father's punishments for forbidden indulgences which the son has taken anyway, and then, often enough, the father yields. One alcoholic told me that he never knew what to expect from his father when he asked him for money. His father might hand it over without question, much to the son's surprise and elation, he might refuse arbitrarily and with finality, or he might grant the request after a long harangue in which he reviewed past indulgences and past misuse by the son of those indulgences. However, in spite of the father's obvious attempt to force his son out of his passivity into independence, we find on investigation that he unconsciously did not want his son to grow up and become a threat to him. Many incidents could be cited from practically every case to show how these fathers, either by their (to the child) bewildering inconsistency or by their granting of apparent equality and masculinity and then suddenly withdrawing it, themselves contributed much toward perpetuating the trait of oral dependence and passivity in their sons. For example, one of my patients who was associated with his father in business had the experience innumerable times of being delighted at having some special new authority in the business bestowed upon him only to find later that his father was still giving his own orders and countermanding the son's without any discussion with the son about it. This same father had given his son several thousand dollars worth of securities in the boom period, and when the crash came he called his son in and laconically instructed him to sign a prepared paper which recalled all of these securities to the father's possession. The father of another patient seemed, during his son's adolescence, to be building him up into independence and masculinity by asking the son's advice on business matters, taking him around with him, and by paying for his time until the son had a bank account of several hundred dollars of which he was quite proud. Then the family moved to another city; the father transferred the accounts to a bank in the new city and simply absorbed his son's account in his own, saying nothing about it, and leaving the son bewildered, resentful, but silent. Such incidents furnish us with material on which to base presumably valid theories about the paternal attitudes under which the sons were expected to grow into independence and masculinity.

A psychological situation which makes it almost impossible for the son to overcome his passivity is thus created and perpetuated by both parents—quite unintentionally, since they both consciously want the son to grow up. Thus a pattern of oral dependence, oral demanding, suppressed rage at frustration, a feeling of being rejected by both parents, yet an intense desire for indulgence and affection in oral terms have been built into the son's personality. And along with this pattern there has arisen in the son a sense of guilt for his hatred, and a deep feeling of inferiority for his dependence and passivity. As the son now comes to puberty, all of these feelings are intensified, especially those of inferiority, envy of masculine potency as exemplified by the father, and fears of being regarded effeminate by his companions. Such a boy is psychologically predisposed and easily susceptible to drinking. When, in the late teens or early twenties, he almost inevitably comes in contact with liquor, he also encounters a special social situation, more or less peculiar to this country. He finds that it is regarded as not grown up, as "sissyfied," *not* to drink, and that to drink heavily and "hell around" with the boys is regarded as proof of manliness and potency. It becomes a very easy over-compensation for his feelings of inferiority, passivity, and effeminacy to espouse drinking as his salvation. Early hetero-sexual experiences, especially with prostitutes, are often a part of this reaction, but it is easy to see that the boy is developing a spurious masculinity. However, he is not at all able to evaluate this, and the drinking acts not only in the service of his masculine protest, but also helps to overcome inhibitions, dissolve anxieties and furnish a medium for expression of adolescent defiance and revolt. With a few drinks he can feel quite potent, can restore his injured self-esteem, can regain for a time his infantile sense of omnipotence, and his progress into chronic alcohol addiction usually proceeds apace, interrupted only by abortive attempts, doomed to failure, to establish independence and masculinity on a reality level.

DYNAMICS

It must be borne in mind that I have been attempting to trace the origins and causative factors in the symptom of drinking itself, realizing that there may still be some other X-factor which contributes to or determines the specificity of the drinking. Certainly it does not always develop according to the pattern described, and in many cases the parental attributes which, for purposes of making a point, I have set forth in bold relief, vary a great deal in their expression and effect.[1] As a matter of fact, in spite of such a predisposition as has been described, the son may not take up drinking at the usual age, or may indulge awhile and then abandon it, only to resort to it later when certain reality circumstances are too intolerable for him to handle and drinking appears as a sort of regressive retreat. Later in the paper, under the heading of "Classification and Prognostic Appraisal" I intend to deal with these variables in the onset and intensity of the drinking. Now, however, I wish to discuss the dynamic picture as it appears in the more severe cases.

The foregoing etiological account has already led us into the psychodyna-

---

[1]In some cases the parental constellation is reversed, that is, the father is the over-indulgent parent and the mother is severe, nagging and inconsistent.

mics involved. The typical adult alcoholic, although passive and dependent in his relationships, is usually a very personable, friendly, likeable fellow. His inner need to be loved, and to have his demands on people satisfied, has often caused him unconsciously to develop a technique of making himself liked. He is a good talker, often a salesman. He has many fair-weather friends, but few close, long-time friends, for he inevitably ruins his friendships sooner or later on account of his excessive demands and his strong homosexual conflict. Almost invariably with the severe cases one finds him still dependent economically at 30, 35, or 40. His excessive drinking and consequent unreliability have lost him many jobs, have alienated many friends, have usually wrecked one or more marriages, and have rendered his parents and friends desperate about him. He seems bound to destroy himself completely, although he is aware, in sober moments, that he is doing so.

His sexual life may seem superficially normal, for he is usually quite active heterosexually. But it requires only a superficial inquiry to discover grave maladjustments and sexual immaturity. There is often a conscious or almost conscious fear of being regarded effeminate. One alcoholic told me, for example, that he always wondered, after a spree, if perhaps he really had been overtly homosexual during the carousal. Associated with this fear of being effeminate is the inner, reluctantly admitted, conviction that he is essentially a physical coward and would quail in a physical encounter. Furthermore, in spite of his active heterosexuality, which we have seen to be only a masculine over-compensation, nearly every alcoholic patient is afraid of being impotent, and in fact, most of them are troubled with ejaculatio praecox or other symptoms of impotence. Because of the early significant disturbance in his relationship to his mother, he seems unable to fuse his tender and grossly sexual strivings toward the same woman. As a result, his premarital or extramarital sexual experiences are usually degrading in nature, carried out with prostitute types, and associated with heavy drinking and such aberrant sexual behavior as frequent desire for having women perform fellatio on him, having two couples in the same bed, having another man along to join him in sexual pleasures with the same woman, watching another couple during intercourse, and so on.

In these sexual characteristics and behavior we perceive a deep identification with the mother — but usually with the bad mother, the hated mother image. The patient becomes as unreliable as he considered his mother — and father — to be in their inconsistent attitudes toward him. There is also a partial, abortive identification with the — to him — super-potent father. The result of these conflicting identifications in his own marital life is that he usually seeks out for his wife a girl who is especially attractive to many men, hoping to demonstrate his own potency by winning her from them, but also feeling intensely jealous of her social relationships with other men, which relationships, however, he also unconsciously enjoys vicariously. Having picked a girl whom other men will continue to pursue, he is in the position of demonstrating to them and to himself his own potency in possessing her, but also in vicariously enjoying the attentions they pay her, this unconscious enjoyment being over-reacted to by intense jealousy. In his actual sexuality with his wife, his deep unconscious hostility toward her inhibits his own potency and leads him to fear injury by her.

When we consider how he disposes of his aggressions, we discover that in his sober periods he is capable only of suppressed resentment and rage at slights and frustrations, for he was never able to revolt successfully against the powerful father figure. He displays only childish rebellion or passive aggressivity. In his drunken periods, however, he often goes into a sort of sado-masochistic orgy. The drinking itself, being anti-social and a defiance of his parents' hopeful wishes for him, is a part of his unresolved adolescent revolt and, once the inhibitions are loosened by the pharmacological effect of alcohol, he carries out all sort of aggressions against his parents, his own family and his friends. He spends his father's money wildly, he speeds recklessly in his car endangering the lives of the other passengers as well as his own, he insults men and women acquaintances, he breaks up furniture and other private property, and at the same time the self-punitive, self-destructive behavior can be seen as an outcome of his sadistic behavior and guilt feelings. Through the degradation and humiliation of his debauch, and through the reality reprisals for his provocative behavior he gradually destroys himself. Four of the ten patients have had serious automobile accidents while drunk resulting in bodily injury. One has a long scar from his eye to his ear, another had his jaw and nose broken, his sinus crushed and his skull fractured.

I wish now to describe the rather typical vicious circle of neurotic behavior, complicated by excessive drinking, which the more severe patient exhibits and from which he apparently cannot extricate himself. Over a period of time the picture has become quite complicated, since the alcohol has become enmeshed in his entire emotional life and serves many psychological purposes. Let us start with the sense of frustration, the feelings of inferiority and inadequacy which proceed from his oral dependence and passivity, and the suppressed hostilities and accompanying guilt feelings for past and present hates and aggressions, for this is where the drinking often starts. He wants to feel better and freer and the illusion of the feeling of well-being that can be secured through drinking seems intensely attractive. He has forgotten or pushes down any memories of the past distress, remorse and disgust of the last hangover, and remembers only that he has, a few times in the past, been able to achieve and maintain for a while this marvelous sense of relief, well-being, and restored self-esteem. It may be that he is determined this time not to continue drinking past the time when he recaptures this glorious feeling. This is, as we have seen, the old infantile craving for the breast. He *needs* a drink, he says. In spite of a few forebodings, he begins to drink, for this craving is reinforced by his defiance of society (his parents) and by his masculine protest. The warm feeling in his stomach reassures him and he feels relieved before any pharmacological effect could possibly take place. His self-esteem and self-confidence return as anxiety leaves. But there is still some additional anxiety and guilt for having thus defiantly taken the forbidden bottle (breast, penis), and he feels that another drink or two will make him feel still better. He continues to drink and his fears and feelings of inadequacy and inferiority vanish. He begins to act out repressed impulses, as I have described above. The homosexual disguise thins out and his convivial behavior with his men companions becomes more obviously homoerotic. As the pharmacological effect sets in, paralyzing the higher faculties of judgment, discrimination and perspective on reality, he becomes entirely irresponsible. He finally ends up completely passive and symbolically dead. Having revolted against the world for thwarting him, he now forces somebody to take care of him through his ultimate passivity, the drunken stupor. One alcoholic, for example, typically woke up from a drunk in a hotel where his friends had taken him instead of taking him home, then by phone hired a nurse to be with him night and day and called in a doctor to look after him. He would remain in their care for several days while sobering up, then return to his family. As the patient awakens from his drunk he returns to his former neurotic state with a vengeance. He is depressed, intensely remorseful, disgusted with himself, and, as one patient always says, "If I had a gun I would have blown my brains out." He is now really terrified by the dangerously destructive behavior in which he has indulged. All sorts of terrors assail him as to what all he did for the period of his spree for which he is amnesic. Now is the time, he feels, to swear off completely, forever. But first, just one or two drinks to ease up the hangover and get him through the day. And now having sobered up enough finally to feel more inferior, guilty and inadequate again, with his situation much worse on account of his being depleted financially and his having to get himself out of whatever scrapes he has gotten himself into, he has completed the vicious circle and is ready to start another spell of drinking. His sublime confidence in the magic of the alcoholic potion, in spite of the fact that during his hangover he realized fully how alcohol always betrays him, is reminiscent of his similar attachment to both parents, but especially to his mother. She also led him on only to betray him, yet he could not free himself from her.

As to the question of why there are so few female alcoholics, one might suggest that women, although they may have in infancy experienced the same oral pacification and thwarting, have many more socially acceptable ways of indulging their passivity than men do and hence are not driven to drinking as the only solution. Furthermore, the element of masculine protest is absent. As Abraham pointed out, however, if there is a strong active homosexual component, the masculine protest factor may be there and they may drink to emulate masculinity.

CLASSIFICATION AND PROGNOSTIC APPRAISAL

It is probably evident to all who have had experience with alcoholics that the above description of the drinking and dynamics does not apply to all cases. The writer himself has one patient whose drinking bouts follow a stereotyped pattern which is quite different from the one described. He takes a bottle of liquor and a good book to his room, and quite alone, drinks and reads until he can just get himself to bed. He has no interest in "raising hell," nor in seeking either women or men companions. Many other variations, both in the character and severity of the drinking could be mentioned, and it should be recalled that the most severe type of drinking was being described.

Since there exist these wide variations in severity and character of the drinking, as well as in the personality characteristics of the drinker, it seems advisable to attempt to set up certain criteria in evaluating the case for purposes of classification and prognosis as well as to permit early orientation to the individual case on the part of the analyst. All excessive drinkers are called alcoholics, yet some are much more mature than others, some can be analyzed in office practice, some as outpatients with the institution handy in case of necessary confinement, and some can be analyzed only as institutional patients.

This evaluation of the case can be made to a large extent from the history and from one's early observations of the patient during preliminary interviews. As in other types of cases, it is helpful to estimate how far the patient progressed in his psychosexual development. While, by the very nature of the case, the evidence of oral fixation will be obvious, on close study of a number of cases one sees that there are many gradations in severity. The above descriptions of the alcoholic's personality and his drinking applied to the severest cases in the group. In these cases, there is almost no evidence of psychosexual development beyond the oral stage. They are completely dependent economically and emotionally, and there is no history of anything more than temporary, if any, financial independence. Also one finds lacking the character traits which derive from the second anal stage—those of perseverance, retention and mastery of the object. In other words, they have never applied themselves persistently to reality tasks, such as finishing college, following through on a job, saving money earned, and so on. Their drinking has started in the teens and is not related to significant precipitating factors in reality. They seldom keep friends over a long period or have any deep relationship with them—except an oral, dependent one. The character traits are essentially oral derivatives—oral dependence, oral demanding, pleasure seeking with small regard to reality requirements or possibilities. This lack of reality sense is evidenced by their unreliability, irresponsibility and especially by their lying and general lack of sincerity. Another feature which seems frequently to be found in cases in this group is the presence of gastrointestinal symptoms and multiform oral gratifications. These are the patients who seek the warm, glowing sensation in the stomach—who *crave* a drink. Their eating habits are easily upset, special values are put on certain foods for certain purposes, and they consume many beverages and foods for demonstrable psychological reasons. They are not particular about what they have to drink and will imbibe anything that has the desired pharmacological effect. Often various liquid medications or hypnotic drugs are consumed with regularity and seem really to be a part of the drinking. One patient regularly took a heavy dose of sal hepatica after a spree to clean himself out well. This same patient drank a quart of sauerkraut juice the morning of his wedding because he had heard it would insure his potency. He knew a few drinks of whiskey also would dispel his fear about his potency, but he dared not go to the altar smelling of liquor.

One feels justified in putting these cases in a separate category which has a much more doubtful prognosis, even with thorough analysis. One might label them "fixation addiction," or "true or essential alcohol addiction." I prefer the latter term. Another appropriate label might be the "alcohol personality." Prognostically, it is very doubtful if such patients ever will be able to drink moderately. They must become total abstainers, and one must not hold out to them the hope of drinking like a gentleman after the analysis is over. The saying, "Once an alcoholic always an alcoholic, or else a teetotaler" applies to them. Furthermore, they are practically impossible to deal with outside an institution. As outpatients, they miss appointments because of being drunk, come to the hour intoxicated, and while they may impart important material during such an hour, they do not remember afterwards what they said nor do they recall what comments or interpretations the analyst made. In our studies, this group fortunately forms a small percentage — two of my ten cases, and about four or five of the other twenty cases observed.

In contrast to this group of "essential alcoholics" one finds many individuals who drink excessively and who are usually thrown into the common classification of chronic alcoholics, but with whom closer study reveals certain significant features of further psychosexual maturity. Of especial importance is evidence of their having reached the second anal stage. This will be manifested in some by a compulsive type of personality, so that the occasional drinking seems to be in the nature of a temporary decompensation and regression to passivity. In others one can arrive at this estimation on the basis of character traits of reliability and responsibility which are apparent except when the patient is on a drinking bout. In the history will be evidence of some achievement, of some degree of independence having been reached. These patients have usually finished their schooling, have held down jobs over a fairly long period, often in spite of excessive week-end drinking. There will rarely be any associated gastrointestinal symptoms, aside from occasional chronic constipation. There is little or no emphasis by them on the warm glow in the stomach, little evidence of over-erotization of eating, little or no associated consumption of drugs and other medications. Furthermore, one finds usually that their drinking started later in their careers — after 21, for example, and in some cases as late as the early thirties, in one case at 55. Another factor which improves the prognosis, when found in association with the other characteristics mentioned, is the presence of a precipitating event or situation whether the patient recognizes it as such or not. For example, one alcoholic, apparently independent, aggressive, and successful in business, began to drink heavily the night his wife gave birth to their first child. His drinking continued for several years until he was brought for treatment.

This group might be labeled "reactive alcohol addiction" or "regressive alcoholism," and includes perhaps the majority of cases that come to psychiatrists or analysts for treatment. There will naturally be a number of gradations in severity and perhaps further subdivisions in classification could be made even in this group, but in general the prognosis is better, and the chances are that patients in this group will be able to drink in moderation after the analysis. Also, the less severe cases, at least, of this group, can be analyzed as out-patients, or by an analyst in office practice.

TECHNIQUE OF TREATMENT

Under this heading I do not intend to discuss the institutional management of alcohol addicts who are under analysis, nor to discuss exhaustively the technique of analysis as applied to these cases, but merely to emphasize a few points which I have discovered through my own mistakes and successes or have learned from private discussions with other analysts.

The so-called orthodox technique, to which analysts sometimes compulsively adhere, often means only the resolute maintenance of a quite impersonal, passive and withdrawn attitude by the analyst. Alcoholics cannot stand this attitude, and the more severe the case the less able is he to stand it. The close relationship of alcoholics to schizophrenics becomes apparent before one has studied them very long, and like schizophrenics, they have a deep-seated feeling of rejection, and are constantly super-sensitive to any evidence of rejection on the part of the analyst. Therefore, the analyst must be much more active and must not show any criticism or condemnation of their past drinking nor of any debauches which occur during the analysis. Always when the patient is remorseful about his drinking, the analyst must maintain a consistently uncritical, kindly, and friendly attitude toward him. The analyst's endurance and patience will frequently be tried to the utmost, but even when the drinking and acting out have been especially flagrant and one feels that it is imperative to point out certain reality values to which the patient seems oblivious, this criticism must be softened and must be made in tones and phrases which do not imply condemnation or rejection. On a few such occasions I have tried the experiment of calling the patient by his first name or by his nickname when addressing my remarks to him, and have found so far that this helps to avoid the rejection implications which would only drive him into further despair and increased drinking.

It is important from the outset, when the patient is looking for and is especially sensitive to any slightest evidence of condemnation, that the analyst not concentrate his questioning and attention on the drinking *per se*. In fact, throughout the analysis, the importance of the drinking itself should not be enhanced by focusing too much attention and interpretation on it. The drinking has many symbolic sexual values for the patient which one does not want to condemn but wishes to draw out so that they can be analyzed. Also, if one does condemn it the patient is likely to react masochistically with severe debauches. It is helpful, in getting the analysis in motion, to have quite a number of friendly, "get-acquainted" anamnestic interviews, with the patient sitting up. During these occasions one can establish the initial rapport, bring out into the open and into the patient's awareness much important material by skillful questioning, and then gradually maneuver the patient onto the couch to proceed with the analysis.

With some patients who were brought to the sanitarium by police officers or were brought forcibly, while intoxicated, by relatives, and who were uncooperative and rebellious at the idea of psychoanalytic treatment, protesting that they were "not sold on it at all," I have made no effort at all to convince them of its value or necessity but have continued to see them for interviews and have even played tennis, bridge, and golf with them at the sanitarium. One patient who said he would rot before he would begin an analysis unless he were first permitted to live in town melted before this friendly attitude and has now been in analysis six months and did not move to town until several months after he began the analysis.

The alcoholic's need for indulgence and for affection is so great, that one must meet some of these needs rather than simply analyze and interpret them. If the patient can at the outset be led to establish a relationship of tender dependence on a mildly indulgent analyst, this emotional relationship itself will act as a partial substitute for his drinking and will lessen his need for alcohol. A corollary point is that there should be no initial demands or deprivations by the analyst. It is helpful instead to suggest to the patient that because of the pharmacological effect of the alcohol, he should try drinking milk, orange juice, malted milk or coca cola when he feels the need for liquor. In this way one gives him something, a harmless substitute, instead of making demands upon him or depriving him of some gratification. For the same reason, one must be exceedingly chary about suggesting that he cut down his drinking or stop drinking. It is a mistake to tell a patient at the outset that after analysis he will be able to drink moderately. One does not know about this until much later on, and if the patient asks this question directly, the reply should be that one does not know yet, whether or not this will be possible for him. Later on, if the analyst becomes convinced that the patient is an "essential alcoholic," it will probably be necessary to tell him that he will never be able to imbibe any alcoholic drink, not even beer, and that he must reconcile himself to this outlook.

If the patient has regressed into prolonged drunken disability from a level of moderate achievement, and feels hopeless about ever rehabilitating himself, it is valuable to build up his ego by reminding him frequently of his capabilities and potentialities as demonstrated by past achievement and by expressing confidence that these potentialities are still there and that he will be able to reestablish himself. Also it is helpful to compliment and encourage him when he really does achieve anything, however small.

As to the thinly disguised homosexuality, one is even more cautious than in the ordinary case about analyzing this as such until the patient is well along in the analysis and comes to it of his own accord. It is easy to frighten an alcoholic away from analysis or drive him into difficult resistance if one too early mentions homosexuality or points out the homosexual implications in his material or behavior. For this reason it is advisable not to hurry him into the reclining position before he feels fairly secure with the analyst.

None of the above technical points are intended as substitutes for actual analysis, but only as modifications or aids in dealing with the severe cases which otherwise (i.e., with a strictly orthodox technique) would not begin analysis or else would not continue long. In proportion, as the case is less severe, one can use more readily the orthodox technique.

CONCLUSION

I have attempted, on the basis of experience with ten assorted, unfinished cases of chronic alcohol addiction, to set forth certain observations about the etiology, dynamics, prognostic appraisal and technique of treatment which seem to me so far to be valid. This is a preliminary report which I hope later to expand into a comprehensive paper on this subject.

REFERENCES

Abraham, K. (1908). The psychological relations between sexuality and alcoholism. In *Selected Papers on Psychoanalysis*, pp. 80–89. London: Hogarth.

Daniels, G. (1933). Turning points in the analysis of a case of chronic alcoholism. *Psychoanalytic Quarterly* 2:123–130.

Glover, E. (1932). On the etiology of drug addiction. *International Journal of Psycho-Analysis* 13:298–328.

Radó, S. (1926). The psychic effect of intoxicants. *International Journal of Psycho-Analysis* 7:396–413.

Robbins, B. (1935). A note on the significance of infantile nutritional disturbances in the development of alcoholism. *Psychoanalytic Review* 22:53–59.

20:   ALCOHOLISM AND ADDICTION

Ernst Simmel

We may expect as an aftermath of World War II the same psychological sequelæ which followed World War I. After the first World War there was noted an enormous increase in character disorders, particularly in addictions. Postwar mental disorders document the failure of the "war ego" to reconvert into a "peace ego" because of a shattering of ego and superego relationships. In war superego functions are disrupted, ego regressions enforced, and barriers of repression thus removed. If no neurotic or psychotic mechanisms are evoked as defenses, criminality results as the direct continuation of the war ego in civilian life.

During the war, working and fighting for victory was the common goal for civilians and soldiers alike, serving as a collective ego ideal, counteracting the blunting of the individual superego. Postwar disillusionment with the ideal of victory robs it of its significance and effectiveness as a stabilizing factor within individual psychological systems, thus depriving the individual egos of the supporting superstructure of a community spirit. The unified nation again disintegrates into dissenting groups with disparate aims of self-interest. The cessation of armed conflict is a narcissistic trauma for all; deprived of the protective participation in an inspiriting brotherhood of man, no longer able to identify himself with the nation as a whole, the disenchanted citizen finds that the bitter fruit of victory is a return to individual, social, and economic insecurity.

The less the individual ego is capable of reconstructing itself by a withdrawal of aggressive energies (increasingly precipitated by frustration), the greater the need that the nation as an entity undergo a process of structuralization. Failing this, the individual forms or joins groups which provide him with a new protective communion of spirit with a common goal for the discharge of aggressive energies.

Addictions offer a perfect subterfuge for the postwar ego which finds itself hopelessly entangled in a conflict between frustrating realities and impulses — particularly aggression — from the id, the controlling power of the superego having been rendered incapable of intermediating. In addiction the ego finds a way of denying painful reality by re-establishing the infantile pleasure principle, as a release from superego prohibitions, through artificial pharmacotoxic elation. *Pharmacotoxic elimination of superego interferences spares the ego the mental expenditure* of energy involved in neurotic or psychotic defenses, and in genuine addiction under certain conditions serves also as a preventive against criminality.

Since in the United States the sale of narcotic drugs is prohibited and drug addiction is a crime punishable by law, and because alcoholic drinks are generally socially approved, alcoholism becomes the common American addiction.

The psychoanalytic psychiatrist differentiates between genuine addiction to alcohol, which makes the individual asocial, and other forms which, by substituting other ego-impairing defenses, keep up or renew periodically the individual's contact with society. Such differentiation is of theoretical interest as well as of practical therapeutic importance. It helps to determine whether psychotherapy other than treatment of individual alcoholics is at our disposal, to treat alcoholism as a mass social disease.

The experience that some alcoholics can be successfully treated through any of a variety of approaches, while others cannot be influenced by any, is very often considered justifiable evidence for classifying alcoholics as mild or severe cases. However, amenability to treatment is by no means a criterion of the severity of this mental disorder unless the degree and quality of the disintegration of the ego of the alcoholic are taken into consideration; moreover, it must be determined whether the disintegration of the ego is the cause or the result of the alcoholic's chronic consumption of liquor.

That the need to drink alcoholic beverages serves one person as a means of escape from reality, whereas it serves another as a means of mastering reality, proves that the biochemical effect of alcohol is not the decisive factor for its use but the psychological effect which the ego derives from it. Our first effort, therefore, must be directed towards a psychodynamic classification of alcoholic mental disorders before we study alcoholic addiction in greater detail.

From observing alcoholics for many years, some in a hospital, some as ambulatory patients, I have differentiated four classes of chronic drinkers: the social drinker, the reactive drinker, the neurotic drinker and the alcoholic addict.

In each of these four interrelated categories the consumption of alcohol serves as a means of balancing an impaired mental equilibrium. In the first two groups, alcohol defends the ego against the mental impact of external circumstances; in the last two groups, it defends the ego against the threat of inner unconscious conflicts which only secondarily impair the ego's capacity for coping with reality.

By "social drinker" I refer to those who are chronically *dependent* upon the consumption of more or less moderate amounts of liquor, without which they cannot enjoy association with people. They cannot converse with others without having a drink, or cannot do business without drinking or offering drinks to those with whom they must deal.

From the standpoint of group psychology it is, briefly, my opinion that this kind of social drinking is a by-product of our civilization. People are capable of living together and submitting to common standards of ethics only by renouncing a certain amount of individual instinctual gratification. Such renunciation, without sufficient opportunity to achieve instinctual sublimation, is what Freud called "living beyond one's mental means" from which is derived the feeling of "discontent" in our civilization. The social drinker seeks in the effect of alcohol a means of disposing of this feeling of discontent, which he feels particularly strongly when in the company of his fellow men.

Drinking helps make congenial and convivial people who would otherwise dislike each other because of their mutually imposed instinctual renunciations. The perception of common discontent — sometimes felt only as common boredom — is substituted by and shared as a common feeling of alcoholic elation. If people are absolutely dependent upon social drinking in order to be convivial, we must conclude that there is something wrong not only with civilization, the collective character, but also with the individual characters. The superego obviously has not appreciably augmented its power, as a result of instinctual renunciations of the ego, which it should do in the normal process of sublimation. The sensation of increased self-esteem is not cherished if it has to be derived from diminishing returns of instinctual satisfactions. It is a minus of spirituality which must be compensated for by a surplus of spirits.

The reactive drinker is not necessarily a neurotic individual either, and it is not the demands of community life that promote his need for release from stress; it is his personal life which imposes too much deprivation from suppression of instinctual desires: for instance, someone who suffers from an unhappy marriage, or from an unhappy work situation which he is unable to change. For him drinking is an escape from unbearable reality. It helps him temporarily to forget, to suppress what he cannot repress, and to find a substitutive happiness in the artificially elated condition of drunkenness. Since such individuals are forced to live psychologically beyond their means, their habitual drinking excesses — by rendering powerless any still possible functioning of the superego — provide them with the possibility of balancing their mental budgets through temporarily unrestricted discharges of pent-up aggressive or erotic instinctual energies. The underprivileged of society belong in this group. They feel, however correctly, unjustly treated by society. Under the influence of alcohol they find an artificial happiness which they cannot achieve in reality. Under the veil of drunkenness they find a way to discharge their aggressions against the frustrating world, and eventually they become criminals. Such people do not commit crimes because they are drunk; they get drunk in order to commit crimes. Freud must have made reference to the reactive drinker when he stated that "alcohol does away with sublimations."

Of particular interest to the psychoanalyst is neurotic alcoholism. Freud's statement that alcohol disposes of inhibitions applies specifically to the alcoholic neurotic.

The neurotic alcoholic drinks not because he is entangled in an insoluble conflict with his environment, but because he is in need of an escape from himself, although he quite often believes that it is his unhappy life situation which drives him to drink. His is the neurotic character which, under the spell of repetition compulsion, recreates endlessly the same conflicts with people. For him drinking is not an escape from realistic unhappiness but from self-inflicted neurotic misery. It depends on the extent of his neurotic disturbance, on the morbidity of his ego, whether alcohol helps him to find an artificial adaptation to external reality, or whether his ego is doomed to disintegrate regressively and to lose its superego guidance in a clash between infantile instinctual cravings and the demands of reality. For these neurotic characters the business of living, loving, working, always has an unconscious connotation which brings an irrational trend into their pursuit of happiness. Ultimately, the unfulfilled infantile instinctual urges derive from the Oedipus conflict which they are still striving to gratify in their adult lives.

Instances are numerous of a man whose drinking begins either when his wife becomes pregnant or gives birth to his child. In becoming a mother, the wife approaches the unconscious image of his mother and tends to become sexually taboo. He feels anxious because unconsciously he is haunted by incestuous guilt and fear of castration. He feels estranged from his own child because to his unconscious this child is his brother or sister. Alcohol dissolves the anxiety and triumphs over the interference of his superego, liberating him from his sexual inhibition, possibly restoring his potency. For others drinking proves to be the opportunity for fleeing from the threatening female by bringing them into the community of fellow drinkers of men only.

For these neurotic alcoholics the self-induced sensation of elation through drinking has an unconscious autoerotic connotation. It revives and replaces orgastic sensations previously experienced in infantile or adolescent masturbation. The wish to bring about the alcoholic elation has become a compulsion because it is dominated by and has been elaborated upon by the process of the unconscious. It is a substitute for the repressed infantile wish to enjoy autoerotic pleasure which once served as a defense against insoluble conflicts by providing release for pent-up instinctual energies withdrawn from the objects.

It is striking how often we find that the struggle of the alcoholic with himself or with his environment in combating or indulging the forbidden enjoyment of drinking is an actual repetition of his original fight for or against masturbation. A patient who always made resolutions that today's drink would be the last, kept a book in which he made notations on the frequency of his taking drinks in a vain attempt to reduce the frequency to three times a week. He had kept a similar book when he once tried to cut down on his masturbatory activities, and still had the book in his possession. After some interval of abstinence, two of my patients felt impelled to start drinking again "in order to prove" to themselves that they could stop—the identical way in which during puberty they had rationalized their relapses into masturbation. The way an alcoholic lies to his wife or his father, the way he hides the bottles (particularly in the bathroom), is very often an exact repetition of the way he used to hide his masturbatory enjoyments against interference by a parent.

Neurotic alcoholism appears to be a mixture of a compulsion neurosis and a perversion. With the latter the alcoholic has in common the achievement of being able to gratify infantile sexual demands by excluding the danger of castration; but because the symptomatic drinking is a degenitalized masturbatory substitute, it is much closer to a compulsion neurosis in which the symptom at the same time is a substitute for and against infantile masturbation. The alcoholic's one great advantage over the compulsive neurotic is that his ego has also found a way to eliminate its fear of the superego. In the struggle of the alcoholic ego between the id and reality, the superego does not take sides in favor of reality and against the id; on the contrary, it helps subordinate the demands of reality to those of the id. The reason for this is that from the standpoint of reality, drinking alcohol is a socially acceptable enjoyment, and from the standpoint of the id the superego is inclined to favor this infantile satisfaction because of the characteristics of the parents, the prototypes of the alcoholics' superegos. The parents of most alcoholics I have studied, father or mother or both, were usually emotionally immature, unstable persons. They permitted themselves indulgences and enjoyments which they prohibited their children. For such parents it is a kind of ego defense against their own superego protests to suppress in their children manifestations of instinctual reactions which they themselves are unable to repress. They themselves may indulge in temper tantrums but strictly prohibit an outbreak of temper in their children. The mother may betray all the signs of indulgence in anal erotism by being sloppy and careless in conducting the household, but be tyrannical in enforcing the cleanliness of her children. The most severely traumatic effect on the children in creating a two-faced superego which sometimes prohibits, at other times encourages the same instinctual gratifications, comes from parents who combine attitudes of manifest incestuous seductiveness towards their children with an overpuritanical education in sex matters. Such parents, directly or indirectly, attempt to derive sexual gratification from their children, but if the child responds by showing signs of sexual excitement or reacts to stimulation by masturbation, the parents will punish it severely.

The stepmother of one of my patients, considerably younger than her husband, would regularly allow her four-year-old boy to caress her leg from the foot up to near the vagina, but she would beat him and threaten him with castration when he wet his bed, or when she found him playing with his penis. The father of a woman patient, himself an alcoholic, would attack sexually all the female members of the family, including this daughter, but he beat her whenever he found her playing with her genitals. When, in adolescence, she made her first attempts to get away from him by having dates with boys, he forbade such "indecency," and punished her drastically for overstepping his prohibitions.

It is no wonder that such parental prototypes help to create multiple superegos which can be opposed to instinctual demands of the id but can also be bribed by it.[1] This, as I once called it, is a form of resexualization of the superego relationship, a return to the once more or less latently incestuous parent–child relationship within the ego. The ego is thus enabled to bribe the superego into indulgence, in this way giving it a share of its id gratifications. There is much truth in the facetious statement that has become current to the effect that "The alcoholic's superego is soluble in alcohol."

Alcoholic euphoria, as degenitalized sexuality, constitutes a great triumph in the psychic economy of a neurotic. It is the successful transformation of the painful experiences accompanying infantile masturbation (fear of castration, anxious feelings of guilt) into pleasurable feelings which re-establish the orgastic sensation once denied in infancy.

An actor felt compelled to overcome his stage fright by becoming inebriated. Drinking resolved his inhibition. This proved to mean to his unconscious that acting on the stage (dependence on the applause of the audience) was the equivalent of exposing and playing with his penis in front of his mother in the hope of seducing her and winning her love. Acting for him was "acting out" infantile incestuous demands, which were taboo to his superego. The actor was unconsciously afraid of re-experiencing the rejection and the threat of castration he had once experienced when he attempted such "acting" in front of his mother. In enjoying his alcoholic elation, his "reality function" had not only become erotized, but it had also become degenitalized and thus freed from the impending doom of guilt and castration by his mother, displaced to the fear of being rejected by his audience.

The alcoholic ego's achievement of degenitalizing activities which have latent infantile sexual connotations is of fateful consequence. The character of this mechanism of ego defense determines whether the potential alcoholic can remain a neurotic or whether he must become an alcoholic addict; for the defense of degenitalization is a mechanism of infantile regression to pregenital stages of ego development. If the ego regresses beyond the phallic, the anal and the oral stages to its earliest pre-ego stage (which I have termed the gastrointestinal stage[2]) the alcoholic becomes an addict. Then the structure and dynamics of alcohol addiction are no different from any other pharmacotoxic drug addiction. It is understandable that the degree of premorbidity of the ego, due to pregenital fixation, is decisive for such an outcome; however, it is certainly true that the psychotoxic effects of alcohol or other drugs can push an ego on the path of these regressions if reality is too difficult to comprehend or too painful to bear. It is, as always in psychopathology, "a complemental series of external and internal factors" (Freud) which determine the final outcome of an instinctual conflict.

---

[1] Dr. Robert P. Knight referred explicitly in a paper to the multiple superego of the alcoholic. In his cases he found that what was mainly responsible for people becoming alcoholics was a constant disagreement between the parents concerning the instinctual education of the child.

[2] Simmel, Ernst: *Self-Preservation and the Death Instinct. Psychoanalytic Quarterly*, XIII, 1944, pp. 160–183.

The artificially created sensation of elation re-establishes the infantile pleasure principle within the *conscious* mind of the alcoholic. This weakens the ego's object strivings and contributes to throwing it back to the level of secondary narcissism, to the developmental stage of the infant that has discovered its ego and is in love with it—which explains much of the attractive charm of the autoerotic alcoholic personality. From here the way is open to a regressive splitting of this narcissistic self-love into partial erotic demands on the object. As we know, the process of instinctual regression is associated with the process of instinctual defusion, with an increasing subordination of the erotic instinct to the destructive instinct. This defusion is nothing but the process of regression itself: a gradual retreat from the genital stage to the gastrointestinal stage at which the mouth appears to be the only mediator between the instinctual demands of the pre-ego and the world of objects. The urge for sexual contact with the object is transformed into the desire for inner contact with it by devouring it. Love is replaced by hate; the process of identification reverts to a tendency towards actually devouring. The drink itself becomes interchangeable with the hated object, well expressed in a drinkers' joke: "I hate that stuff [liquor]. I seize every opportunity to get rid of it—by swallowing it." In accordance with the impulse to devour, this joke appears to tell the true meaning of alcoholic addiction. In addition, the physical incorporation (devouring) replaces psychological repression because it makes the object disappear from outer perception. The alcoholic addict in drinking strives ultimately for oblivion: the repression of reality.

I wish to state in connection with the example of the actor that in treating addicts it became clear to me what determines the neurotic-acting-out quality of a professional activity. Such professional activity is not the sublimation of a surplus of instinctual energy but is neurotic acting out if this activity is discovered to represent repressed infantile masturbatory fantasies.

In the stage of developing its object relationships, masturbation may be regarded as the infant's first social activity. For through this activity the child withdraws from the disappointing object which rejects its love and stimulates aggressive destructive reactions. In its own body, the child finds a substitutive gratification for the narcissistic trauma, replacing the object by its own genital as an object, and finding in itself a way of discharging object-directed erotic and aggressive tendencies. It has thus renounced direct instinctual gratification from the real objects, but keeps an ideational relationship with them in masturbatory fantasies. Through masturbating the child begins to resolve its instinctual conflicts within itself without, I might say, bothering the objects; but it is forced again secondarily into conflict with them if the parents interfere with this masturbation which is the child's struggle for a pleasurable release of instinctual tension. I have found in psychoanalyses that the child is often caught and interrupted in the midst of an orgastic elation; its reaction against the intruder is rage and hatred. The introversion of this hate and its destructive energies sets the individual on the path of self-destruction as a direct consequence of the latent masturbatory conflict.

One of my alcoholic patients, who became completely inhibited and unable to fulfill his professional duties as a physician, remembered that when he was four years old he once put in his mouth a cigar stolen from his father, and played with his penis, thinking of his mother. When he was just "feeling fine," his father trapped him, shook him and shouted literal threats that he would castrate him. It is understandable that such individuals experience a triumphant feeling of happiness when by drinking, they can recapture this infantile "feeling fine." This pleasure reconciles them with an object world which was violently hostile to their reasonable instinctual needs in childhood; but, as happens too often, it eventually causes narcissistic withdrawal from objects because infantile masturbatory activities and fantasies, prohibited at the genital level, have acquired pregenital regressive aims. These masturbatory fantasies then strive to satisfy instinctual demands from the anal and oral or gastrointestinal (aggressively devouring) stages of libidinal development. The chronic alcoholic progressively loses his grip on objects and reality of which he had maintained a semblance as a neurotic character by transferences, and by pleasantly dulling his sensorium through the toxically induced equivalent of infantile masturbatory elation. Eventually he develops the single craving to act out these infantile masturbatory fantasies directly. This acting out of unconscious infantile masturbatory fantasies is incorporated into his daily life and acquires the character of rebellion and protest against a frustrating world, repeating his protest against the unbearable conflict between the Oedipus complex and the prohibition against infantile masturbatory relief. In bouts of drinking he becomes again a baby with yearnings (anal, oral, gastrointestinal) for *one* object only: his mother.

There is a typical way in which such a chronic alcoholic starts his sprees, and how he ends them. He stays away from his home, and starts with the resolve to have only a few drinks; however, progressively he loses self-control and seems to come to have the one aim of becoming *insensibly* drunk. In this condition, he is dragged home by friends or strangers, having squandered all of his or other people's money, and losing all his valuables in the process of getting drunk. He is mentally and physically in a most deplorable condition, dirty and unkempt. Completely helpless, he must be taken care of by his wife or other members of his family, or in a sanitarium. He stops drinking for a while, voluble with good resolutions that this will never recur; and then he starts it all over again. During the abstemious interludes, he is quite aware that he is torturing his relatives and destroying himself, but he cannot prevent it.

In his sober intervals the alcoholic cannot hold any job because unconsciously he does not want to earn his living, wanting to remain dependent upon his mother or her equivalent. I have known several alcoholics who made all arrangements in advance for ending their drinking in a typical fashion. One of my patients cultivated a relationship with a nurse who always had to live with him in a hotel room to sober him up, to "wean" him from liquor by feeding him milk, and clean him up. Another of my patients always secured a prostitute for the same purpose as a mother substitute.

In my sanitarium[3] one of my patients was brought in on a stretcher in a state of stupor, cyanotic, unkempt and filthy to an extreme. He made a quick physical recovery, under the loving care of friendly nurses who bathed him and fed him warm milk. When he was completely sober, he readily agreed not to get any liquor, but he begged for a sleeping potion in the evening. I first sought to deny this, arguing that he would only be substituting one toxin for another. Finally I agreed to put it at his disposal, for him to use at his own discretion in the event he could not do without it. I filled a liquor glass, such as he was accustomed to using, with sleeping medicine and put it on his night table. The feeling that he could have it, that this mother substitute was within his reach, was enough to make him feel secure and he slept soundly without taking it that night, and, similarly, on three successive nights. The fourth day, sober, clean and well-fed, he left the sanitarium, declaring himself cured of alcoholism (an opinion which I did not share).

The alcoholics called dipsomaniacs have drunken sprees only sporadically, sometimes periodically, with relatively long intervals of pseudonormality. Their orgies begin like the others, but they often remain away from their homes for weeks or months and, remaining drunk, engage in all kinds of activities until they wind up in the routine desolate state of helplessness in accordance with the established custom of alcoholics. The dipsomaniac, however, has a complete amnesia for what happened during the preceding weeks or months of inebriation. One of my patients, after creating all kinds of embarrassing inconveniences for his older brother, used to travel through the country by train, always arriving sooner or later in the city in which his married sister lived. It was this sister, who during his childhood had substituted for his mother, to whom fell the task of sobering him up and caring for him. The addict thus acts out his pregenital masturbatory fantasies by returning in effect to his mother as her baby to be nursed and taken care of.

The pharmacotoxic effect of liquor psychologically re-establishes the dipsomaniac's infantile masturbatory elation of "feeling fine" by releasing barriers of repression which allow unconscious infantile impulses access to motor innervations. Dipsomania is a sort of alcoholic somnambulism, the effect of the alcohol protecting "sleep." The superego takes no part in these regressive symbolic actions of the alcoholic because the ego has temporarily regressed to the stage when the prohibitive authority (superego) was still an external object. Being a sick, helpless, dirty infant seems the only possible means of acquiring the kind of love he seeks, or of aggressively dominating the world around him.

In treating addicts, particularly under observation in a sanitarium, I have found that almost everything connected with acting out their addiction has a symbolic meaning: for instance, drinking his liquor from a *glass* or from a *bottle* has a specific meaning to the addict. One of my patients, upon missing his whiskey, would lie in bed crying bitterly, repeating over and over: "I want my bottle, my bottle." Another reported a compulsion to drain his bottles of whiskey

---

[3]Schloss Tegel, Berlin, Germany.

to the last drop, recalling the while that he was imitating what he had once long ago seen his baby brother do when being fed from a bottle by their mother.

Addiction to beer rather than to whiskey often has the special meaning of being especially the drink of the urethral erotic—giving him, as it does, the opportunity to fill himself with great quantities of liquid with the special pleasure of discharging them exhibitionistically, often in competition with other men. The substance he drinks sometimes has an equivalence to urine itself. Two of my alcoholic women patients, in states of abstinence under treatment, developed the compulsion to drink their own urine which brought about a condition of inebriation as from drinking alcohol.

For others, alcohol is unconsciously equivalent to their own feces. These people drink liquors of disgusting flavor, or abhor the taste of what they drink; they perform a real ceremonial in preparation for forcing themselves to swallow each drink. The pregenital masturbatory fantasies which these addicts strive to satisfy are what I once called "reciprocal autoerotism."[4] In these fantasies the various erogenous zones of the body serve to satisfy each other for want of satisfaction from the mother. These are wishful fantasies of urinating or defecating into one's own mouth.

For one of my patients, liquor signified castor oil which his mother used to force down his throat. The money which alcoholics squander has a symbolic meaning; also the habit of many drinkers of getting away without paying for their drinks I have found, on several occasions, to be unconsciously determined. To them, the bartender is a mother image from whom they want to get something (milk) without giving anything in return (feces). For one of my patients, drunken staggering invariably reminded him of the time when he had difficulties in learning to walk and held on to his mother's hands.

The few examples suffice to illustrate the most important trauma at the root of every addiction: the mothers, for whom these addicts long, provided them with no security whatever. They are mothers who indulged themselves without consideration for the child's needs. Such mothers may overindulge the child during the process of nursing and become tyrannically strict about toilet training and cleanliness. Mothers of three of my patients were hypocritically kind, never punishing the children themselves, but briefing the fathers to do the beating. One mother, to impress her husband, the father, enacted suicide by putting poison in a glass of liquor, inviting the boy to die with her. Such a child wants to love his mother, but she will not let him; therefore he must hate her. All my alcoholic patients had deeply seated hatreds for their mothers. This hatred is deeply repressed as an impulse to incorporate, to destroy by devouring the mother.

All addictions, and especially alcoholic addiction, are protections against depression (melancholia). The melancholia has introjected a disappointing object of love (basically his mother) and tends to attack and destroy the

---

[4]Simmel, Ernst: *Die Psycho-physische Bedeusamkeit des Intestinalorgans für die Urvendrängung.* Int. Ztschr. f. Psa. X. 1924, p. 219.

introjected object within himself. The alcoholic addict has only pseudo object-libidinous relationships with people, his drink increasingly representing his only external object. In his struggle for and against abstinence, he fights an endless, indissoluble object fixation and conflict: to draw life (love) from his mother by devouring her; to murder the one person on whose very existence his only hope for security depends.

The feelings of guilt and despair which torment the alcoholic after he has become sober may be partially the pharmacotoxic effect of alcohol, but it is essentially and much more significantly a clinical depression (melancholia) which follows the alcoholic mania. I always considered it progress in the psychoanalytic treatment of alcoholism when the consumption of alcohol not only ceased providing this manic effect, but produced instead misery, depression and guilt. That the alcoholic can react with a hangover during drinking instead of afterwards proves that the psychoanalytic process has succeeded in unmasking alcoholic elation as a defense against depression, although there are some alcoholics who have this depressive reaction while drinking without treatment.

The unconscious conflicts of the wish to destroy the mother on whom he depends, and the need to hate when he wants to love, are of the deepest significance to the alcoholic addict's fight for and against his drinking. By his alcoholism he tortures those who care for him, tending to destroy them, and with them, to destroy himself. His addiction is chronic murder and chronic suicide.

Identification with his mother within the ego is substituted by drinking as the physical introjective prototype of incorporation.[5] By drinking her, as it were, he becomes one with her and thus approximates psychologically a return to her womb. Death has a great attraction to his unconscious; it signifies Nirvana, pre-existence in the mother's womb, complete oneness with her, where love and hate do not exist. The alcoholic drinks himself into oblivion, the mental state of prenatal Nirvana; emergence from this stupor is a rebirth, with mother in attendance ready with milk to nurse him back to life.[6]

In psychoanalyzing patients in my sanitarium, I observed a form of supplementary and two forms of substitutive addictions. In the first, the alcoholic addict is impelled to seduce others into sharing the addiction with him. This was only seemingly determined by the wish for companionate enjoyment of elation. Unconsciously, the intent was to destroy the other person as he destroys himself: to drink him, to drink from him, devour him, and drown together in the same element. An alcoholic who consulted me had lived with a woman several years his senior — an obvious mother image — both doing nothing but mutually drinking themselves into destitution. His mother had to support them. The young man rejected my suggestion that he separate from the woman with signs of great anxiety. I asked him why. He answered: "She helps me. She gives me

---

[5]Simmel, Ernst: *Self-Preservation and the Death Instinct. Loc. cit.*

[6]Of all the addictions, the alcoholic addict shows most clearly that the addicted ego tends to realize the same unconscious regressive psychological strivings as the psychotic ego, an indication that an addiction may be a defense against a psychosis. A study of alcoholic psychoses might provide more insight into this speculation.

drinks and drinks with me." By drinking with someone the alcoholic addict achieves just what the social drinker seeks to avoid by the same means: mutual, orally aggressive, introjective, destruction.

A secondary, substitute addiction, I observed, was an identification addiction. The addict, under psychoanalytic treatment and abstinence, develops the compulsion to imitate others, particularly of course his psychoanalyst, often very clearly with the intent of doing damage to the person whom he imitates. One of my patients was seriously offended because I did not entrust him with the management of my sanitarium when I went on vacation. This same patient went on a drinking spree after a period of abstinence, and landed in a café close to the sanitarium. There he gave a big speech to an audience of fellow drinkers, telling them his name was Dr. Ernst Simmel, chief of the sanitarium for the cure of alcoholism. This patient revealed to me the deeper meaning of this hostile identification in a state of abstinence. He found a cat which he kept in his room. The cat slept with him, and regularly he fed it milk from a bottle, even at night, thus demonstrating how a good mother should love and feed him. But that he was also an evil mother (his own mother he hated) he proved by the way he would talk to the cat: "Now be a good baby: first you get milk, later on you will get coffee — and then liquor." The "good baby" gets poisoned by a hostile mother. In identifying himself with the hostile mother, he consumes his hatred towards her but, being the baby, he also destroys himself. This patient, in periods of abstinence, used to consume enormous amounts of coffee.

In one instance, I was able to observe directly and in *statu nascendi* the transformation of the process of identification into its physical prototype, incorporation, and vice versa. A young alcoholic, in the course of psychoanalysis, had reached in his regressive transference a stage of passive feminine submission to me. He tried to ward off castration anxieties resulting from unconscious passive feminine fantasies by a very aggressive rebellious attitude. His continuous attempts to provoke my counterhostility and counteraggression failed. Eventually his anxiety reached the proportions of panic and he shouted that he wanted to run away from the sanitarium and drink. I told him that drinking would do him no good but that no one would prevent him from doing what he thought he must do. He rushed out of doors through the park to the gate leading from the grounds of the sanitarium where he broke down writhing in pain with abdominal cramps. He was carried back on a stretcher and was brought to the treatment couch. Here he raged against "the pain you brought upon me." He pounded his painful abdomen with his fists, exclaiming, "This goddamned thing in here prevented me from getting my drink. This is you. Now I have you in my stomach." And, after a while, pounding his head, "Now I have you in my head too — twice." Later when I saw him, he said to me solemnly, "A strange thing has happened to me; for the first time in many years I can think and ponder about drinking and I really think it is no good."

It is clear to me that the patient had demonstrated his aggression from the fantasy of devouring an object to identifying himself with it. Instead of being identified with the mother who submits to the father, he regresses to infancy when he wanted actually to devour his mother, thus attempting to consume his hatred against both parents; then, after having transmitted the introjected parental object from the somatic to the psychic ego, he restructuralizes it by elevating the somatically introjected parental object into his superego. The "aggressive energies withdrawn from the object, introjected and made over to the superego" (Freud) enabled his ego to put restrictions upon itself, to interpolate the processes of thought and judgment between impulse and action.

The third substitute observed to occur, during a state of abstinence under psychoanalysis in a hospital, substituting the addiction to alcohol or drugs, was an overt suicidal addiction or an overt addiction to homicide.[7] During this stage the addict's only compulsion is to kill: himself or others. Usually he does not rationalize this urge; he just wants to die or, at other times, he just wants to kill.

In observing the process of becoming a compulsory killer under the influence of abstinence, we find a striking difference between the alcoholic addict and the reactive alcoholic; for the reactive alcoholic becomes homicidal only when he is intoxicated because then his superego is paralyzed and the barriers of suppression and repression are released. The alcoholic addict, however, would kill when he has to refrain from drinking because he is failing then to satisfy his homicidal impulse symbolically through drinking. One of my patients, in a state of abstinence, once exclaimed: "I must kill people—I hate them—or I must drink; then my hate is gone."

It is beyond the scope of this paper to discuss under what conditions committing murder can be a compulsory defense against suicidal depression, a re-extroversion of the object to be killed outside instead of inside the ego. What is germane to the discussion of alcoholic addiction is the apparent identity between the depression and the elation of the alcoholic, and the self-destructive significance of both.

This psychological constellation throws some light on the senseless and yet tragic fact that the alcoholic addict must drink in order to rid himself of his feelings of guilt caused by drinking. When after a period of contrite sobriety the alcoholic relapses into drinking, the world shrinks for him to one object: drink. This drink unconsciously symbolizes his mother at the time when he was afraid of her, and when she still was the external prototype of his superego. He relapses into drinking from a crushing feeling of guilt towards the mother (or substitute) who takes care of him. He devours in drink this reexternalized superego and thus disposes of his fear of punishment (infantile feelings of guilt). In thus condensing crime and punishment into the one act of drinking, the alcoholic addict

---

[7]I have noticed a difference between the alcohol and morphine addict with regard to these obsessional impulses to kill or commit suicide. The morphinist appeared to be more driven by the impulse to commit suicide, whereas the alcoholic addict is more driven by the impulse to commit homicide. It seems to me that the consumption of alcohol keeps the addicted ego longer object-related in its destructive tendencies than the consumption of morphine, possibly because alcohol is a socially accepted mother surrogate, whereas morphine is socially taboo.

achieves what he was denied as a child when he was prevented from introverting his aggression and converting it into the pleasurable "autoplastic" act of masturbation.

That the crime and punishment are identical for the alcoholic addict and that drinking is the crime of enjoying self-punishment was proven to me by a typical recurrent dream of the majority of my patients: dreams of drowning. In these dreams the alcoholic drowns himself, is drowned, or struggles to rescue someone who is in danger of drowning with him. Let me cite such a dream of an alcoholic being treated by psychoanalysis.

> I was on trial for murder, accused of having attempted to poison myself. I felt amused [cf. "feeling fine"] and was not at all cooperative with my defense counsel. Finally, I was sentenced to death by drowning. I was taken to a large pool and ordered to jump into the water, which I did. My body went to the bottom of the water and I intentionally opened my mouth to fill my lungs with water. I wanted to hurry the process of drowning, but I had to cough and I expelled water which caused me to come back to the surface. This process repeated itself several times until I was finally ordered to get out of the water because it seemed impossible for me to drown myself.

It is interesting to note that this dream directly represents the phenomenon of repetition compulsion. I think the fact that someone "orders him to stop" the repeated suicide by drowning does not make it less so, because the drinker repeats his debauches again and again in order "to be ordered" to stop, thus repeating the interferences in his masturbatory activity by his parent. Of course, the man in the dream who interrupts this chronic self-punishment is the psychoanalyst. The analyst's therapeutic task is to interrupt the vicious cycle by combining psychoanalytic therapy with temporary initial indulgences, satisfying the deepest instinctual needs of the addict and then lead him into occupational therapy, based on metapsychological principles with special outlets for aggression, and so back to mature reality. Without some such interruption the alcoholic will compulsively follow his regressive trend (also symbolized in dreams of drowning) and drown himself in liquor, returning to the mother's womb, to the stage of primary narcissism and complete oblivion.

CONCLUSIONS

Having completed the theoretical discussion of the psychopathology of alcoholism, we turn to the practical question of how to meet the danger which the chronic consumption of alcohol signifies for the individual, as well as for public mental health. As an aftermath of war, alcoholism has become a social disease and therefore has not only psychological but also sociological implications which must be taken into consideration, but whose correction is beyond the domain of the psychotherapist. However, a theoretical basis for improving therapy for the individual might help to understand and to further attempts at group treatments which already exist. I am of the opinion that the prognosis for the individual alcoholic may become most favorable if we select our psychotherapy in accordance with the proper classification of the case.

The alcoholic addict needs hospital care during psychoanalytic treatment. It should be combined with occupational therapy based on metapsychological principles which, for example, gives the patient an opportunity to discharge his aggressive, destructive tendencies before he is able to sublimate them in constructive activity. What these patients need, in addition to psychoanalysis, is the concerted therapeutic effort of the entire hospital personnel, which aims at rebuilding and reconstructing the alcoholic's ego,[8] gradually restricting his hostile, introjective, devouring impulses in favor of an ultimate healthy identification. Psychotherapy in a hospital furnishes a sound basis for a process of maturation of the ego because it begins with the active aim of remedying the fundamental narcissistic wound of the addict's ego: compensation for the loss of the drink, and its symbolical value, by gratifying the patient's unconscious infantile need for the loving and understanding care of a nursing mother. In the process of becoming sober, the alcoholic is "reborn." From then on, by psychoanalysis combined with careful management, he must be helped to develop a mature ego to replace the infantile narcissistic pleasure principle with the reality principle.

The neurotic alcoholic can be treated psychoanalytically without hospitalization; however, it seems advisable here also to intersperse periods of psychoanalytic treatment under hospital supervision. This becomes necessary when a tendency to relapse into drinking is precipitated by transference difficulties, or by impulses to maintain repression of emergent unconscious material sensitized by the psychoanalytic process. Experience has taught me that a phase of withdrawal symptoms under abstinence can yield very productive analytic results. For such temporary hospital treatments, the psychoanalyst should have access to the same facilities as other specialists have in treating their patients. There should be small hospital units in cities where alcoholic patients can be placed temporarily with adequate care and supervision. These units should have psychoanalytic treatment rooms.

The reactive alcoholic is not in need of a specific psychotherapy. He benefits from psychotherapeutic aid based on factual help and a metapsychological understanding of his unsolved inner and environmental conflicts. The reactive alcoholic needs supportive psychoanalytic therapy. It is mainly the preconscious which must be made conscious and integrated in his ego. He must become aware of and verbalize his conflicts and thus learn to interpolate thinking, instead of drinking, between impulse and action ("experimental way of acting" — Freud).

One last question of utmost practical importance remains to be discussed: does our theory, derived from psychoanalytic research, provide any possibility of

---

[8]The sanitarium, Schloss Tegel, in Berlin, Germany, had no closed wards, no locked doors. Any time an alcoholic seemed unable to endure his abstinence, and showed signs of breaking away to some bar, the entire personnel was informed of this situation and whoever saw the patient about to leave the hospital grounds was instructed to talk to him, induce him to stay within the grounds, and call his doctor immediately. The aim was to instigate and keep alive an inner mental conflict in the patient before he relapsed.

application to the therapy of groups of patients to meet the universal danger which alcoholism signifies for the mental health of the country? The answer is affirmative because, strangely enough, it has already been applied intuitively and successfully in a mass psychological experiment—Alcoholics Anonymous.

In studying a pamphlet of Alcoholics Anonymous, I was struck by the fact that the therapeutic principles employed in its psychotherapeutic endeavor correspond basically to psychoanalytic findings. This is not surprising because Alcoholics Anonymous was created by alcoholics for alcoholics and therefore originated from an unconscious awareness of the latent id drives in alcoholism, and the tendency of the alcoholic ego to preserve itself against them. It cannot be a mere coincidence that the creator of Alcoholics Anonymous was a doctor who found a cure for himself by helping a fellow alcoholic to get cured.

The therapy of Alcoholics Anonymous is based on three fundamental principles:

1. The alcoholic is treated by an exalcoholic not only in order to be cured but also in order to cure others.
2. Through being cured and becoming a healer, the alcoholic becomes a member of a society of exalcoholics in which, in contrast to our so-called "normal" society, alcohol is socially not accepted, but taboo.
3. The alcoholic must become capable of accepting two beliefs: one, which introduces the treatment; the other, which brings about the final curative achievement.

The first belief is for the alcoholic to accept the fact that he is powerless against alcohol. It is useless for him to struggle against it because he is forced to drink by an inner compulsion. The second belief is that there is a "Power greater than himself" in the Universe; if he submits to this Power, his compulsion will be broken. The first belief is easily accepted by the alcoholic because he realizes it is the first basic step in every cure. For the first time in his life of neurotic misery, the alcoholic finds himself understood, and by this learns to understand himself. His therapist is not a professional man, but his helper just because he is an exalcoholic. Before this experience,

The clergyman has said: "Your drinking is a sin."
The employer: "Quit this monkey business or get out."
The wife: "Your drinking is breaking my heart."
And everyone: "Why don't you exercise some will power—and be a man?"

He knows he cannot exert sufficient will power to counteract the overwhelming driving power which emanates from his unconscious. "But," the alcoholic whispers in his heart, "no one but me knows that I must drink to kill worry and suffering too great to stand." To achieve belief in a Universal Power which, if accepted emotionally, is capable of expelling the alcoholic compulsion, is the essence of the treatment. This achievement is based on what is called a spiritual experience, and he learns to see clearly "that he must have a spiritual experience or be destroyed by alcohol."

> This dilemma brings about a crisis in the patient's life. He finds himself in a situation which, he believes, cannot be untangled by human means. He has been placed in this position by another alcoholic who has recovered through a spiritual experience. This peculiar ability, which an alcoholic who has recovered exercises upon one who has not recovered, is the main secret of the unprecedented success which these men and women are having. . . . Under these conditions, the patient turns to religion with an entire willingness and readily accepts without reservation a simple religious proposal. He is then able to acquire much more than a set of religious beliefs; he undergoes the profound mental and emotional change common to religious "experience." Then, too, the patient's hope is renewed and his imagination is fired by the idea of membership in a group of exalcoholics where he will be enabled to save the lives and homes of those who have suffered as he has suffered.

It is always stressed that the core of the therapy of Alcoholics Anonymous is religiosity but not religion. The exalcoholic brotherhood consists of "Catholics, Protestants, Jews, near-agnostics, and near-atheists." It is emphasized that "the core of the technique by which Alcoholics Anonymous has worked . . .is not religious, but spiritual. . . ." It is "the recognition of a power higher than man . . .the Creative Spirit over all. The name is immaterial . . .it will simplify matters to use the familiar terminology employed in the Christian religion, calling this Power 'God'. . . ." The alcoholic gets hold of this Power "by a simple 'act of faith.' " In order to give this faith the power to revolutionize the mental self of the alcoholic, he must have a "spiritual experience" which "reaches the inner man." "It is surrender to the Higher Power. . . . In non-religious terms, the experience is like the realization that sometimes comes to a person who has never appreciated good music or good books, and who all of a sudden 'gets' the idea of the pleasure, the value to be found in them. Thenceforth he proceeds with delight to enjoy that in which he formerly had found no charm, no meaning." It is "the recognition of human helplessness and complete reliance on the Supreme Power as the one way out."

"These exalcoholics frequently find that unless they spend time in helping others to health, they cannot stay sober themselves. Strenuous, almost sacrificial work for other sufferers is often imperative in the early days of their recovery. This effort proceeds entirely on a good will basis. It is an avocation."

"A missionary with what a difference! What missionary to the savage was ever a savage?"

The formal typescript ends at this point. Following are Dr. Simmel's notes written in longhand on the last page of the manuscript. (Ed.)

Alcoholics Anonymous is a defense and a substitute formation. It is a new community spirit in a different but artificial society. It is a society not only of nondrinkers, but also a society of healers.

The alcoholic's psychopathological formula of destroy and be destroyed is changed to save and be saved.

The spiritual experience serves to undo wrongs, resolve guilt. Reinforcement of the superego, externally (prohibition) and internally (religion, introjection). Verbalizing preconscious material (ego-building).

The cure aims at becoming a healer through identification. Substitution of identification for addiction during abstinence makes the formation of this new society possible. Devouring is replaced by identification with the group.

Possibilities for Alcoholics Anonymous from the collaboration of psychoanalysts.

How much can be achieved for the increasing number of addicts by psychoanalytic therapy alone?

21:   THE ADDICTIVE DRINKER

Giorgio Lolli

Unhappiness stems from the inability of the individual to avail himself of what the environment offers, from the failure of the environment to provide what the individual needs, or, more often than not, from a combination of both. The individual for whom alcohol represents the main answer to unhappiness—the most cherished source of pleasure and the surest means of dulling pain—is usually carrying the load of deviant personality traits and fostering resentments against an increasingly hostile world. He is the addictive drinker. He is the one who, despite advancing years, remains infantile in many of his drives and in the ways he finds of satisfying them. The word "addictive" suggests the irresistible urge—and also the inevitable frustration growing out of the inadequacy of the agent used to satisfy the urge.

Alcohol, as an agent, performs its role through its immediate effect upon bodily functions, especially those of the central nervous system. Its pharmacological properties explain the dramatic psychological changes which it produces—changes which, however short-lived and subjective, allow the individual momentarily to reinterpret himself and his environment in a more satisfactory light.

Addiction to alcohol is an expression of lopsided growth; infantile traits in one part of the personality coexist with mature traits in another. But because of the interdependence of mental functions, those which are stunted often affect adversely the functions which have developed normally. The factors responsible for this uneven development are the same which operate in all human behavior—heredity and the early and late relationships of the individual to his environment.

The etiological emphasis which is usually given to environmental factors is justified by the impressive evidence of childhood and adult difficulties antedating the onset of addiction. The fact that these difficulties are sometimes observed in individuals who are not addicted to alcohol suggests the necessary, although minor, role played by heredity, which now can be interpreted only as a genetic transmission of an ill-defined susceptibility to difficult life experiences. The respective impacts of heredity and environment may vary greatly from person to person, with a probable preponderance of "nurture" over "nature" in all cases.

An appraisal of "nurture" necessitates a distinction between early and late experiences. Despite marked variations in their respective significance, the former usually play a more important role than the latter; witness the fact that addiction to alcohol often develops in individuals whose adult lives have been relatively untroubled but whose problems are largely determined by the perpetuation of infantile neuroticism.

In the rare cases when addiction sets in as the sequel of overwhelming new problems in individuals previously well adjusted, quiescent but unsolved childhood difficulties can almost always be uncovered. Once they are reignited, their explosive contribution to the development of addiction is just as significant as in the more numerous instances when their operation was obvious throughout.

The importance of the childhood background is confirmed by clinical experience. From this emerges a concept of alcohol addiction which maximizes the role played by the prealcoholic personality at the expense of the role played by alcohol. The quality which characterizes the addict is his "disposition" to react to the effects of alcohol in such a way that some of his anomalous and pressing needs are satisfied, albeit briefly and inadequately.

The dominant physiological connotations of this disposition are instability and a limited capacity for enduring stress. Prerequisite to normality and efficiency is the ability of the living organism to maintain a constant physiological equilibrium in the presence of conditions which might prove disturbing. This constancy is not stillness, but rather the expression of continuous, well-regulated readjustments.

The addictive drinker seems to display unsteadiness in some of his biological constants as evidenced, for instance, by wider than average fluctuations in the values of blood pressure and of blood sugar concentrations, and in the emptying time of the stomach. This unsteadiness is probably related to the low stress tolerance of the addict, to his limited ability to withstand physical and mental pain, with the consequence that unusual physiological deviations occur whenever stimuli cannot be discharged as soon as they arise.

The initial pangs of physiological hunger, for instance, are poorly tolerated by the addictive drinker and felt as keen pain earlier than by the average man. Hence the impulsive search for food and satiation, lest unbearable tension arise. Similar reactions are observed in the presence of stimuli arising within (as urination, evacuation) or without the organism. These deviant physiological regulations may be determined, in part, by dysfunctions of the pituitary–adrenal cortex system whose thorough investigation in addictive drinkers is long overdue.

More obvious than the physiological, however, are the psychological connotations of the prealcoholic personality. The latter seem to be caused to a great extent by anomalous family constellations which created serious difficulties in childhood. The fixations and regressions growing out of such experiences can be interpreted by means of widely accepted principles of dynamic psychology which apply to both normal and deviant mental development.

The critical phases of human life — early infancy included — are highlighted by pleasurable and painful experiences. A normal proportion of both generally results in a satisfactory adult adjustment. An excess of either kind, however, tends to halt the individual at that particular phase of his emotional development at which the excess is felt — as though in one case he hated to relinquish what was so gratifying, or in the other case he hoped eventually to discover the gratifications thus far denied to him (fixation).

He who pauses thus along the road may or may not be able to recover from the experience and to reach an adequate adjustment to adult life. In any event he is more susceptible than the average person to the impact of later difficulties. He may react to these just as he did during that earlier period of his life when pleasure or pain was unusually predominant (regression).

The addictive drinker, as has been noted, is an impulsive person who faces great difficulty in resisting his instinctual drives. Impulsiveness dominated his psychological as well as physiological behavior long before he first resorted to alcohol — indeed, throughout his life — and is only a perpetuation of behavior patterns which are normal in the infant. A baby experiences hunger as unbearable tension and at the same time as a dreadful threat to his existence. The acuity of his discomfort motivates the "impulsive" (and, in him, entirely normal) search for satiation, which for him represents supreme pleasure inextricably united with the feeling of unchallenged security.

With sharp contrasts between states of pain and pleasure, with swift, reversible shifts from one to the other, physiological and psychological phenomena are inseparable in the life of the infant. He experiences that unity of body and mind from which the maturing individual progressively and painfully disengages himself as a result of the ever-sharpening differentiations of growth.

Unlike the well-adjusted adult, the addictive drinker is still chained to this unity when he suffers from the intolerable pressure of his unconscious (and, to a certain extent, conscious) longings for physical warmth, pleasurable skin sensations, maternal coddling, liquid and warm filling of his stomach. For him these are undifferentiated from longings for security, assurance, self-respect, independence, omnipotence, and total oblivion. In contrast to the infant, the addictive drinker is denied in real life the experience of undifferentiated pleasure for which he is hopelessly yearning as a compensation for his undifferentiated pain. The revelation that alcohol is able to provide a blended pleasure of body and mind, and at the same time to satisfy most of his specific longings, marks the beginning of addiction. The satisfaction, however, is temporary and incomplete. Because of its chemical action on the central nervous system, with related psychological repercussions, alcohol only magnifies the addict's infantile longings, rendering attempts at their gratification increasingly unsuccessful.

Thus the life of the addictive drinker is governed by a vicious circle: real failures are compensated for by illusory alcoholic "successes." If not broken, this circle ultimately leads to alternations of ever-lengthening euphoric stupors and ever-shortening periods of painful awareness of reality. As the addiction progresses, these alternations resemble more and more the rhythm of hunger and sleep at the very dawn of the infant's life until they are concluded by the irreversible stillness of death.

The persistence of infantile psychological traits is, of course, common to all human beings in varying degrees, contributing in an exaggerated form to the maladjusted behavior of many a neurotic who will never become an addict. What characterizes the addictive drinker is not the survival of these drives but rather their peculiar grouping, their intensity (which is sustained and even aggravated by alcohol itself), and—preeminently—the fact that alcohol satisfies these strivings in a *unitary* way.

Milk, which quenches the infant's thirst, satisfies his hunger, gives him the security and power of mother's love, and eventually leads to the oblivion of sleep, causes predominantly alimentary reactions in the adult and satisfies predominantly physiological needs. In the irrationally controlled life of the infant, milk and the emotional feeling attached to it are one and the same thing; but in the life of reason of the ego-governed adult the reality of an object is quite distinct from its symbolic significance: milk mainly means milk, not supreme pleasure or eternal glory. Not even for the individual with excessively persistent infantile strivings do the psychological outweigh the physiological connotations. In the same way the psychological needs of the reality-adjusted adult are mainly satisfied by psychological means whose physiological overtones are minor though present occasionally. Honors which may come to him through achievement, power stemming from financial success, the love of another individual, the consolations of religion—these cannot supply pleasurable skin sensations or the soothing feeling of an adequately replenished bowel.

The physiological and psychological realms begin to merge when the adult bears the lineaments of an addictive drinker. Then some of his tensions no longer respond to purely psychological or purely physiological gratification. It is alcohol alone which can facilitate a simultaneous psycho–physiological fulfillment of his innermost urges. Under its influence the addictive drinker first disregards and finally denies the reality of the world he lives in. Under its influence he eventually unmasks and upholds the reality of his unconscious so that he himself becomes witness to the dialectical identity of opposite drives: dependence, independence; love, hate; self-depreciation, self-aggrandizement.

To unmask and to uphold the reality of his unconscious versus the reality of the world in which he lives means that the unitary fulfillment of his infantile promptings is reached through the detour of an alcohol-induced severe mental disorder—a real, though brief, psychosis. This fulfillment, found in the episode of acute intoxication, is seldom consciously sought in the preintoxication period. The causes precipitating a drinking episode are more likely to be derivative: perhaps conflicts with the environment arising from primitive impulses, physiological deviations which are sources of pain, or any neurotic reaction pattern (unrelated to addiction) which might lead to complications with the environment. In short, either mental or physical discomfort, rather than addictive conflicts themselves, usually impels the desire for alcohol, for its anesthetic more than for its euphoric properties. This assertion is valid if by discomfort we mean any sudden or slow accumulation of tension. The latter is early felt as pain by the addict because of his limited capacity for enduring stress.

Seldom does the addictive drinker plan a long spree. Like any other individual he decides to have a drink or two and, surprisingly enough, is sometimes able to stop there, although for him occasions of controlled drinking are infrequent. The addictive drinker can stop only if the amount of alcohol ingested and the conditions under which it is taken (full stomach, fractioned ingestion) do not allow the alcohol concentration in his blood to reach the minimum level requisite for psycho–physiological unity, or, in rare instances, if repressions are operating to such an extent that the urge for such unity goes unfelt. In either case the margin of safety is so narrow that inevitably the controlled phase terminates in new episodes of acute intoxication. The explosiveness of the situation is enhanced by the fact that the controlled phase magnifies the addictive drinker's grandiose confidence, encourages him to test himself anew against increasing amounts of alcohol, until the relapse occurs.

If addiction is a striving for psychosomatic unity, and if this striving is fulfilled in alcohol, it is understandable why the nonaddictive drinker is able to stop with a moderate amount of alcohol, or rather is hardly ever able to ingest an immoderate amount. More often than not, the infantile type of gratification offered by immoderate amounts of alcohol has no appeal for the well-adjusted or for the nonaddictive neurotic person. Even if he occasionally enjoys this type of regression, the pleasure involved is brief and constantly threatened by those distortions of external and internal perceptions which the reality-adjusted adult abhors. The adequate individual interrupts his drinking in good time because its disadvantages tip the scale. In the addictive drinker, however, disadvantages do not outweigh advantages until much later.

Having once achieved a state of psychosomatic unity, usually early in the spree, the addict's personality favors his clinging to this infantile regression, unlike the well-adjusted individual who tends to pull out of it once the stress is over. Maturity does not mean denial to the individual of infantile gratification, but rather the ability not to over-indulge, so that temporary and normal retreats can be followed by further advances.

The addict's rigidity fosters a continuing retreat. His goal is to maintain his blood alcohol concentration at a point where this unity will not be disturbed—a well-nigh impossible task. In most episodes of acute intoxication the psychosomatic unity is lost and regained countless times. Yet this elusive pleasure is still the crucial phase of the drinking pattern, the one that makes for its perpetuation. The end of a spree does not come until the unity is broken beyond repair, whether by dwindling supplies of liquor or serious miscalculation of the amount needed.

The psychological phase of this unity is characterized by the paradoxical satisfaction of contradictory emotions which, against the rules of reason, are tolerated and enjoyed despite—perhaps because of—diametrically opposite connotations. For example, the addictive drinker, who is torn between his longings for passive dependence and equally strong cravings for rebellious independence, cannot in his sober moments satisfy either drive without experiencing a frustrating and painful magnification of its opposite. But with the optimal blood alcohol concentration he can simultaneously gratify both and be witness to the fact that in a fleeting phase of his intoxication opposites are the same, just as they are all the time in one's unconscious life.

It thus appears that in this pleasurable, if short and illusory, synthesis of opposite pairs of emotions, *combined with physiological gratification,* is the basic difference between addictive and nonaddictive drinkers. In the example of the conflict between dependent versus independent drives, for instance, the peculiarity is not its presence (shared by all human beings), nor its abnormal pressure (shared by many nonaddictive neurotics), but rather the way it is unrealistically solved by means of alcohol. To hurt and to be hurt, to be secure and to be in danger, to be great and to be meek, to be generous and to be stingy, to reject and to be rejected, to be masculine and to be feminine, to be a child and to be an adult—all these and other pairs of opposites, unreconciled in sobriety, contributing to the mounting tension of the addict, find expression and gratification in one phase of intoxication.

The fleeting instants of unified and unadulterated pleasure are overshadowed during the episode of intoxication by longer phases when pain predominates and the over-all simplification of mental processes induced by alcohol is most obvious. The highest brain centers, whose normal operation underlies the intricacies of adult mental life, are the first to be affected by alcohol; then, with mounting concentration in the blood, its sedative action spreads downward to progressively lower nervous centers. As a result of this chemically induced, impermanent return to a simpler functioning of the central nervous system, the intoxicated person is enabled to interpret himself and his world with a clarity which, although false, is often more appealing than the real complications of sobriety. The bold relief of primitive drives, keenly felt inside and freely expressed outside, takes the place of subtleties and differentiations, so that the issues of man with himself and his environment become clear-cut.

Even more than in the solitary drinker this process of simplification is obvious in the actions and reactions of groups of drinkers, addictive or otherwise. Their attitudes and patterns of behavior bear striking resemblance to those observed in groups of children—in the elementary emotions displayed, in extremes of friendliness and hostility, in monotonous repetitions, and in the fact that the game is never up until exhaustion sets in or forces outside the group intervene.

In this sense alcohol is a real social lubricant whose operation in some ways resembles the socializing effects of art.

The free expression of elementary—and often objectionable—emotions shared by individuals drinking in groups invites mutual repulsion but also, and more often, mutual understandings which would be difficult to achieve when sober (and hence more complex) personalities meet. Underlying this process is an alcohol-induced suspension of those critical functions with which the individual discriminates between reality and fantasy, guilty and guiltless behavior.

In art also—especially tragedy—there is a communion of emotions shared by the artist and his audience. All those participating, however, are aware of the unreality of the experience. Knowing that they live momentarily in a world of fantasy, they can tolerate, share, and release guilt-laden emotions. The plots of Oedipus or Hamlet will be eternally "socializing" because they make mankind aware of one basic truth, the universality of guilt.

Alike in their ability to release shared emotions, art experiences and intoxication are nevertheless poles apart. The distinction between reality and fantasy is upheld in art, denied in intoxication. And art boldly faces morality; "guiltless," or rather amoral, the opaque emotional release in intoxication is infinitely removed from the elevating catharsis of great art.

Behavior during the non-unitary phases of intoxication, although tending always toward a simpler, more primitive level, varies greatly because of the endless possibilities resulting from the interaction of at least three factors: the amount of alcohol acting on the central nervous system, the impact of the environment during intoxication, and the addict's total personality which affects his reactions to alcohol. This last factor, which largely determines the first two, casts light on the apparent paradox of addiction: the individual resorts to alcohol because of his nonaddictive rather than his addictive traits. The latter perpetuate but do not precipitate the drinking episode.

There is practically no case of alcohol addiction isolated from other neurotic disorders or body illnesses. Alcohol addiction can be set apart from an intricate personality frame for descriptive purposes only and because an understanding of what is and what is not addictive is prerequisite to prognosis and treatment. This knowledge permits an evaluation, in a given patient, of how addictive and other neurotic reaction patterns interact. The fact that deviations other than addiction usually operate in the direction of precipitating or prolonging an addictive pattern of drinking has led to the dubious conclusion that excessive and uncontrolled drinking may be only the "symptom" of an unspecific variety of mental and physical deviations, from latent homosexuality to manic-depressive disorders, from so-called spontaneous hypoglycemia to the hormonal disorders of menopause.

If the definition of a symptom as "a phenomenon which arises from and accompanies a particular disease or disorder and serves as an indication of it,"[1] is accepted, the conclusion emerges that the condition dealt with is addiction itself, whose physiognomy colors the individual's sobriety as well as his drinking

---

[1]The American College Dictionary.

behavior with "addictive" traits. Moreover, what distinguishes addictive drinking from most symptoms is the fact that, although indicating an underlying disorder, the "symptom" in this case magnifies the disorder which leads, in turn, to a magnification of the "symptom."

That conditions other than addiction are not the ultimate cause of uncontrolled drinking, but only factors which precipitate or perpetuate it, can be illustrated. There is little doubt, for example, that the incidence of latent homosexual trends is high in addictive drinkers of both sexes and that what is latent in sobriety becomes, in many instances, patent in intoxication. The fact that an addictive pattern of drinking may be precipitated by mounting homosexual tensions and that the tensions, in turn, can be enhanced by drinking, contributing thus to its perpetuation, can hardly be challenged. This fact does not explain, however, why so many individuals suffering from homosexual anxieties do not resort to alcohol or are controlled drinkers. Only those homosexuals who exhibit addictive traits resort to an addictive pattern of drinking. Evidence that successful therapy aimed mostly at the homosexual anxieties may lead to an interruption of the drinking pattern proves only that to free emotional energies which were tied to the homosexual conflicts makes those energies available again for holding in check the addictive urge to drink.

In the field of physiopathology it has been observed that a limited number of women develop an addictive pattern of drinking after the onset of menopause. The link between hormonal changes, depression, and the addictive use of alcohol as a weapon against depression, is clear. Here again medication combined with psychotherapy aiming mostly at the menopausal syndrome may lead to sobriety. Here again it is noteworthy that only a few women in the throes of a menopausal upheaval resort to alcohol in an addictive way—only those whose histories have betrayed addictive-impulsive traits. In these cases a stormy menopause precipitates but does not cause the addiction, which otherwise might not have developed. Once brought into operation, however, the addiction unfavorably affects the menopausal syndrome. The same principles apply to a variety of disorders whose enumeration would cover the whole field of medicine with all its branches.

Although alike in the stage of unitary pleasure, the latent homosexual and the menopausal woman differ widely during other phases of intoxication. Alcohol offers to the former the possibility of expressing his anomalous drives without guilt; to the latter it gives a rosier vision of the present and the future. Infinite variations in the physiognomy, length, depth and frequency of the episodes of intoxication correspond to the infinite shades of human personality. The hysterical girl for whom sex is "guilt" in sobriety can turn promiscuous when intoxicated, while the girl who is promiscuous in sobriety, and so "suffers" in order to atone for her ill-repressed aggression, may reject and beat the male when intoxicated, thus fulfilling some of her deepest desires. Similar examples could be multiplied; they would only corroborate the fact that alcohol tips the emotional balance of the individual in directions favoring the expression of drives which are more or less controlled during sobriety. The nature and pressure of these drives vary from person to person and at different times in a given individual. These variations, together with variations in the amount of alcohol ingested and in the reactions of the environment, account for the physiognomy of the episode of intoxication.

Alcohol, then, favors a return of the repressed. A study of the individual when intoxicated gives clues to a better understanding of his sober personality. It is this return of the repressed, the release of primitive drives, which sets the addictive drinker at odds with the world. If the workings of civilization consist in taming the beast in man, the workings of addictive drinking are characterized by the reverse process with resulting asocial or antisocial behavior.

More is unknown than is known about the addictive drinker. What is already known breeds a more tolerant attitude toward him and favors a shift of attention from his objectionable deeds to those unfortunate experiences that determined them. The moral issue is not denied but reinterpreted in the light of medical, psychiatric and sociological facts. This reinterpretation helps considerably in efforts to free the addict from his ties to alcohol.

Because the addictive drinker cannot revert to controlled drinking, his goal must be permanent abstinence; this is prerequisite to and at the same time the outcome of favorable changes within the individual and in his relations to his environment. While therapeutic successes are highly rewarding, failures should not be considered fruitless efforts. They still add to the moral values of a civilized society earnestly striving for improvement.

22: SELF- AND OBJECT-REPRESENTATION IN ALCOHOLISM AND OTHER DRUG-DEPENDENCE: IMPLICATIONS FOR THERAPY

Henry Krystal

For years, there was an anomaly in applying the psychoanalytic approach to addictions. On the one hand it appeared that the studies of some analysts, especially Abraham (1926), Simmel (1930, 1948) and Radó (1926, 1933), contributed insight into the psychodynamics of the drug-dependent individual. Although as analysts we continued to find evidence in psychotherapy with alcoholics that these early formulations regarding the nature of important unconscious fantasies of the patients were basically correct, the degree of success in analytic treatment of addicts was minimal. One simply could not proceed to treat the drug-dependent person in the classical psychoanalytic fashion by simply amending the list of one's interpretations with those pertaining to the oral character. The patients did not stay in treatment.

In my previous study of this problem, I came to the conclusion that there were two major areas in which drug-dependent individuals required special consideration and modification of treatment: the problems of regression in the nature of affects and affect tolerance, and certain characteristics of the drug-dependent individual's self-representations and object-representations (Krystal and Raskin 1970). Elsewhere I have discussed the modifications of psychotherapy which are necessary to help the drug-dependent person to improve his affect tolerance, and start the process of affect verbalization (Krystal 1973a). I consider this to be an indispensable preliminary phase of treatment for drug-dependent individuals.

This paper is concerned with the transferences, and therefore also the nature of self- and object-representations in the drug-dependent patient. First, let us look at the commonplace statement: "The object-relations of the addict are ambivalent." What is the effect of this situation on the psychotherapy? Aggression is difficult for such a patient to handle. Because of the prevalence of magical thinking, fortified by the wish for magical powers, and in harmony with a grandiose self-representation, alcoholics in psychotherapy become terrified of their death wishes directed toward the therapist. At some point in treatment they are confronted with their extraordinary envy and have the need to deal with their poorly mastered narcissistic rages. At this point, they flee from treatment, because they fear that their death wishes will destroy their therapist. Alternately, they tend to turn their aggression against themselves, and act it out in an accidental injury, suicide attempt or relapse of drinking (Simmel 1948). This may be one of the major reasons why alcoholics and drug abusers do poorly in *individual* therapy. For those alcoholics with whom individual therapy is desirable, a clinical situation works better in which auxiliary therapists are made available. As additional contacts are usually readily available in a clinic, they may be observed to be spontaneously sought by some patients with addictive problems.

The idea of using a team to manage the alcoholic patient is not new. One of the successful psychoanalytic treatment centers was Simmel's Schloss Tegel Clinic (Simmel 1948). Simmel was concerned with the alcoholic's tendency to self-punishing ideas and suicide attempts after withdrawal. The patient who was being withdrawn from alcohol was permitted to stay in bed, and a special nurse was assigned to look after him, including his diet. This was a conscious attempt to provide the patient with passive gratification, to provide a gentle "weaning" and prepare the patient for his "regular analysis" (Szasz 1958).

It has been my observation that when highly ambivalent patients have a therapeutic team available, they will use it for the purpose of "splitting" their transferences. In this way they experience their angry and destructive wishes toward one member of the team while presenting a basically loving relationship toward another, preferably the chief therapist (Krystal 1973b). I believe that this happens all the time in treatment clinics and groups. However, most of the time the transferences acted out with various clinic employees will be unrecorded in a description of the therapeutic process unless a special effort is made to "gather" these. If everyone in the clinic reports to the chief therapist about every contact and communication with the patient, the picture of the nature of the patient's transference may then be put together. It will be found that the patient is not experiencing a simple splitting of the transference into one love and one hate relation. The picture will be quite complex, and quickly changing. At one moment, the chief therapist may be experienced as the idealized mother whose love and admiration he yearns for, while another staff member may be experienced as a rejecting, condemning parental image whom the patient dreads and hates; and still another staff member may be experienced as seductive, intrusive, destructive or other parental transference object. When the patient feels frustrated by the chief therapist, and needs to experience his rage toward him, instantly he will experience one of the other members of the team as an idealized parent, while he experiences other partial transferences with yet another clinic staff member — anybody around, whether in a therapeutic role or not. In order to demonstrate to the patient the ambivalent nature of his transference, it is necessary to bring his projections together and show that all of these transferences represent various object-representations, which he needs to experience toward the *one* therapist. The patient's vacillations and changes in attitudes toward the various staff members can be used to demonstrate his dilemma. Demonstrating the ambivalence in the transference is the crucial step in working with alcoholics, because one of the major forces which propels individuals toward addiction is that they can displace their ambivalence toward the drug. Szasz (1958) has emphasized this aspect of drug problems in his paper on the counterphobic attitude in drug dependence.

A special instance of transference splitting may occur when an alcoholic is sent to the clinic by a court. The probation officer assigned to the patient may become the object of transference of a very significant type. The fact that this type of a patient has a characterological defect, which requires that he "externalize" (that is, fail to integrate) his superego function so that others enforce controls for him, indicates that these transferences cannot be left out of the treatment (Margolis et al. 1964).

In 1931, Glover commented that drug-addicted patients are able to give up the drugs up to the very last drop. This "last drop" however, becomes virtually impossible to give up, because it contains the symbolic expression of the fantasy of taking in the love object (Glover 1931). The external object is experienced as containing the indispensable life-power which the patient wants to but cannot "internalize." This is the basic dilemma dominating the psychic reality of this type of patient. This externalizing tendency applies to his conscience as well, so that he is unable to experience it as being a part of himself but arranges for others to exercise it for him. In the use of Antabuse, we see that the fantasy solution of swallowing the object refers not only to "goodness" or narcissistic supplies, but swallowing an external source of impulse control in quite a concrete way. The failure to integrate one's own functions and aspects such as conscience, and attributing it to others, such as parents, spouses or probation officers, makes the drug-dependent individual experience the world in a paranoid way. Thus, Glover remarks that drug addicts are inverted paranoids, and that they are both the persecuting and persecuted ones (1931). Whether there is a probation officer or Antabuse or similar substances (or procedures) used by the therapist, the transferences, involved in the patient's failure to see his projection of his own superego onto the external object, have to be brought into the treatment by interpretation. Otherwise the patient is never going to be able to accept himself as a whole person.

I have been talking about what I consider to be the basic defect, the basic dilemma in the life of the drug-dependent individual, such as the alcoholic. It is that he is unable to claim, own up to and exercise various parts of himself. He experiences some vital parts and functions of his own as being part of the object-representation and not self-representation. Without being consciously aware of it, he experiences himself unable to carry out these functions because he feels that this is prohibited for him, and reserved for the parental objects. I have studied and described the clinical evidence for these views elsewhere

(Krystal 1975, Krystal and Raskin 1970). Let me illustrate with something that is familiar to all of us: All of us experience similarly those parts of ourselves under the control of the autonomic nervous system, which includes all of our affective expressions. We all consider these huge areas of ourselves as not being under our own control. Numerous experiments in recent years have demonstrated that through biofeedback devices one can learn to acquire conscious control of these parts. However, a surprising finding came up in our work with biofeedback combined with psychotherapy. In the psychotherapeutic relationship, we received information ordinarily lost in the biofeedback situation. Some patients experienced great anxiety over gaining control over these parts of themselves which they experienced as not meant for them. Their unconscious scheme of things was that organs such as their hearts were under the special care of God (or fate, doctor, hospital and the like) who guaranteed their survival. This is illustrated in an old-time, primitive theory of sleep—namely that God causes it by taking away the soul, which He may by His grace return to us, the next morning. This theory of sleep is a transference of the maternal image for whom lifegiving powers, as well as nursing, are reserved. This view has its roots in infancy, and even phylogeny, for certain newborn mammals will not even void unless licked by the mother (Kirk 1968). Thus, the mothering includes a permission to live by exercising certain vital functions. When the patients were told that they could be taught to control their autonomic functions, some experienced fears that taking over such maternal prerogatives would cause them to destroy themselves. Of course, even dying is viewed by some as being regulated by the mother who takes back her child (e.g., Mother Earth, or the Pieta theme) and it is a sin for one to usurp the right to end one's own life.

The reader may think I am jumping to conclusions and that biofeedback simply demonstrates a process of learning. Once the preceptive range is augmented by the apparatus, one can control extended parts of oneself. This is, of course, the learning theory as applied to biofeedback activities (DiCara 1972, Krystal 1975). But let us reexamine this premise. Experiences with hypnosis and placebo show that a subject has the potential to exercise these autonomic functions *right away* and that they are therefore not learned but are unutilized existing capacities. What happens under the influence of the hypnotist or the placebo which gives an individual the ability to exercise control over parts of himself he has hitherto reserved for his maternal transference objects?

There is a temporary lifting of internal barriers between the self-representation and the object-representation, thereby permitting access to, and control of, parts of oneself previously "walled-off." The walls curtain repressed parts of one's self, deprived of the conscious recognition of selfhood. This does not pertain just to parts of one's body but much more so to spheres of functions. Thus, just as biofeedback subjects may be reluctant to control autonomic nervous system functions even when they consciously desire it, so drug-dependents may not *want* control of appropriate self-functions.

Repressions take place at various times in childhood in connection with the various conflicts centered in psychosexual development. A boy who finds himself frightened of his competitive strivings with his father because of his fantasies and theories of destroying his father and taking his place (becoming the father) may repress these wishes and fantasies. Thereafter he may see himself as a boy, with adult masculine modes of action reserved for the father. Unless he finds some way to overcome or get around these repressions, he may never be able to fulfill his masculine ambitions, or consciously own up to, or exercise his masculinity. This would lead to the kind of inhibition in occupational and sexual goals, with a rise to prominence of homosexual striving which the early psychoanalytic writers described many times in their observations of alcoholics (Abraham 1926, Hartmann 1925, Juliusberger 1913, Radó 1926, 1933, Simmel 1930, 1948). In some homosexuals, the fantasy is that through the sexual act one will regain an alienated masculinity attributed to one's "others."

However, in drug-dependent individuals it is the "walling-off" of the maternal object-representation, and within it self-helping and comforting modes, which is the specific disturbance. Thereby, the alcoholic loses his capacity to take care of himself, to attend to his needs, to "baby" or nurse himself when tired, ill or hurt narcissistically.

In the relationship between the infant and the mother, the child gradually takes over certain functions from the mother by identification with her. Where the relationship with the mother is very troubled for the child, the maternal function becomes rigidly reserved for the mother and is experienced as prohibited for him. Some drug-dependent individuals fall into this category. But even where the relationship with the mother is good, the mother must, in addition to providing the model, communicate to the child the permission to take over these functions. An example of a type of mother who has difficulty in permitting this can be observed in the nursery where some mothers become "jealous" of the child's transitional object, and punish the child or prevent its use for self-comforting. Those things which the child does to comfort himself, from thumbsucking to masturbation, each provide an occasion for communication of the permissibility of utilizing self-comforting modes of behavior. When a person feels that he cannot (actually may not) exercise these functions, he feels envious of his mother, and other women, and transference objects, for example, doctors, and yearns to gain them symbolically or magically.

Therein is the source of the drive by the alcoholic to use the drug, both as a pharmacological means to manipulate his affective states and as a placebo, to gain surcease from his feelings of depletion resulting from the repression[1] of self-helping attributes and functions of his own by making it part of a rigidly walled-off object-representation. We must recognize and acknowledge that the kind of person who is likely to become drug dependent is one who uses the drug to help him carry out basic survival functions which he otherwise cannot do. People who drink in order to be able to continue to work thus gain access to their

---

[1] I have discussed elsewhere the concept of repression as referred to in this context. It extends the definition of elements repressed from those rendered unconscious, to include those alienated: not consciously recognizable as part of one's self and one's own living (Krystal 1973b).

assertive, masculine, paternal modes of behavior. People who drink for the purpose of surcease and comfort obtain their goal, in addition to the pharmacological effects, by gaining access and ability to exercise their maternal functions. The longing to regain alienated parts of oneself is the real meaning behind the fantasies of fusion with the good mother so clearly discernible in drug-dependent individuals (Chessick 1960, Savitt 1963).

These yearnings make their appearance in the transference in psychotherapy with alcoholics and other drug-dependent individuals, and in this phase of the treatment, the phenomenon has been termed by Fenichel "object addiction" (1945). This transference needs to be interpreted in psychotherapy for the same reason that all transferences need to be interpreted: So that the patient will discover that the characteristics which he attributes to the analyst (psychotherapist) are actually his own mental representations which he first perceived as being part of his mother, and now reexperiences again, attributing them to the therapist. The healing principle of psychoanalysis consists in the patients, claiming their own mind, restoring the inviolable unity of their own selves.

But, as we know too well, patients do not feel free to do this. They fight it with all the means at their disposal, as if their lives depended on maintaining the repressions. And of all patients, drug-dependent individuals have the worst struggle with this part of treatment. When we try to understand the nature of their psychic reality, which made the removal of repression of their maternal object-representations so difficult for them, we discover that it leads to care of their emotional problems derived from infantile traumata.

However, first let us step back and take another look at one aspect of drug addiction so obvious that we take it for granted, and thereby miss an essential clue to the nature of the intrapsychic conflict in alcoholism as well as other related states. Drug abuse consists in fact not only of taking drugs but, equally important, being deprived of drug effect. Drugs which are addicting are short acting. The longer acting the drug, the greater the likelihood of the user panicking and developing a "bum trip" (Krystal and Raskin 1970).

Withdrawal from drugs is an integral part of the process of addiction (Krystal 1962). The development of ever-increasing tolerance for the drug is greater and faster in drug-dependent individuals because they have the need to deprive the drug of its power (Krystal 1966); at the same time, the moment it does lose its force, they panic (Krystal 1962, Radó 1933).

What is the meaning of all of these apparent contradictions? It is that *while the drug-dependent yearns for the union with his maternal love object (representation), he also dreads it.* He really can't stand it either way. Schizophrenic patients and some borderline individuals yearn for union with their love object (representation) and once they achieve it (in fantasy), they cling to it passionately, giving up conscious registration of all contacts with whatever might spoil it.

Drug-dependent individuals are very busy getting the drug, but can feel themselves reunited with the idealized love object only rarely for short periods of time, and only at moments when they are virtually totally anesthetized. And even then, one finds with amazement that many of them—at the very moment of the climactic action of the drug—indulge in acts of riddance, such as moving bowels, vomiting, cleaning their bodies, cutting their nails, or even house cleaning (Chessick 1960). It may be said that they are *addicted to the process of taking in and losing the drug rather than to having it.* The seemingly bizarre behavior of the drug addict who plays with the drug by "regurgitating" it back and forth between the syringe and vein suddenly falls into place here.

Drug-dependent individuals dread fusion with the love object representations because of the way they experienced them in the formative period of their lives. Their mothering was unsatisfactory, with resulting severe psychic traumatization in infancy, and many and wide-ranging damaging effects to their personalities. As a result, whatever one looks for, one finds.

When the early analysts were fascinated by their discovery of the psychosexual development, they found that alcoholics were fixated on the oral level (Abraham 1954). When they paid attention to the nature of unconscious fantasies, they discovered yearning for union, as well as persecutory fears (Radó 1926, Simmel 1948, Szasz 1958). When they became aware of the role of homosexual striving in the genesis of emotional problems, alcoholics were found to have them and dread them (Hartmann 1925). When they became aware of characterology, alcoholics were found to be schizoid characters (Simmel 1930), in addition to the earlier classification of them as oral characters. When they started paying attention to ego functions, these were found to be impaired as well (Savitt 1963).

I have made two additions to this wealth of views of the nature of psychological disturbances of drug-dependent individuals:

1. I have found that as a result of massive childhood psychic trauma, these individuals experienced arrest in affect development and an impairment of affect tolerance (Krystal 1974, 1975, Krystal and Raskin 1970). These produce, in effect, a fear of feelings, and need to block them.

2. I found that in order to survive, some drug-dependent individuals had to repress their rage and destructive wishes toward their maternal love object. This manifests itself in a rigid "walling-off" of the maternal love object representation, especially with an idealization of it, and an attribution of most of life-supporting and nurturing functions to it. By doing this, the patient manages (in his fantasy) to protect the love object from his fantasied destructive powers, and assure that "someone *out there*" loved him and would take care of him (Krystal and Raskin 1970).

But the repressed aggression never disappears, and so the alcoholic and other drug addicts dread that if they accomplish fusion with the love object they will destroy it, and thereby return themselves to a traumatic situation, which they dread. One clinical observation well known to every worker in this field supports the accuracy of these constructions: Patients are unable to accomplish normally the work of mourning and the feeling of "introjecting" the lost love object. The introjection fantasy is a form of partial union of the self-representation and object-representation, which most people achieve at the end of mourning. It is a clinical commonplace to say that alcoholics and other drug-dependent individuals cannot tolerate object losses (and that includes therapists) without being so threatened with their own affects that they have a virtually unavoidable relapse to self-destructive drug use.

This is the dimension of the problem of ambivalence which makes its appearance in psychotherapy with alcoholics. In the early stages of therapy the very availability of an object creates serious challenges to the patient. There is the already mentioned fear of aggressive impulses and wishes. There is, in addition, the problem stressed by Vaillant (1974), that when alcoholic patients idealize their therapists in the transference, they experience themselves as worthless and bad.

But these are just preliminaries. The greatest difficulty is that effective work in (intensive, psychoanalytically oriented) psychotherapy, through which one can give up attachment to infantile object-representations and the infantile view of oneself, is by "effective grieving," a process analogous to mourning (Wetmore 1963). That very process spells trouble for the drug-dependent patient, who tends to dread being overwhelmed with depression, which represents to him the return to childhood trauma. Raskin and I postulate, in order to explain this phenomenon, that this type of individual has had a nearly destructive childhood trauma experience, which he fears may return, and which he experiences as a "fate worse than death" (Krystal and Raskin 1970). Elsewhere I have discussed the *technical* modifications made necessary by regression in the nature of affects and impairment of affect tolerance. If even that obstacle is overcome, and the patient is able to grieve effectively, then he faces the ultimate challenge: the conscious acceptance of his object-representations as his own mental creations. At the end of a successful analysis one is in the same position as at the end of the hypothetical completely successful mourning. The bereaved person discovers that though the lost person is dead and gone, he continues to exist in the survivor's mind. This gives him the opportunity to discover that as far as he is concerned, that is where the object had been all along — in his mind as an object-representation of his own creation. And so one has to face the "return of the repressed." All the "bad" persecutory aspects of the object could be viewed as projections, but they are really simply fantasies, impulses, wishes and feelings which were not integrated. In other words, the giving up of the repressions, the owning up to the self-sameness of one's object-representations, confronts one with the aggression which caused the alcoholic to "wall-off" his object-representation so rigidly, and subsequently to develop that tragic yearning and dread of the love object.

Earlier I said that the rigid "walling-off" of the maternal object-representation took place in the face of extreme aggressive impulses toward it. The evidence for that came from this stage of the psycho-therapeutic work with drug-dependent individuals. The intensity of the narcissistic rages, the persistence of the aggressive impulses make one wonder if all addiction is, at bottom, a "hate-addiction." The problem of aggression and its apparent threat to the safety and integrity of the self-representation and/or object-representation sets the limits to the kinds and numbers of drug-dependent patients who can be carried to completion of psychotherapy. Along the way most such patients, when confronted with their aggression, will relapse again and again into drug use and self-destructive activities. Others will be driven to prove that their childhood misfortunes were *real*, by getting the therapist angry and provoking abuse. Still others become so terrified of the dangerous, poisonous transference object that they set out on a panicked, frantic search for the *ideal mother* in some form — such as drink, love or gambling. If the therapist is otherwise equipped to bear the disappointments, provocations and failures entailed in working with these patients, and has the time and patience to permit the patient to do this work by minute steps, then it is helpful to keep in mind that the patient is confronted with problems of aggression that make him experience the transference as a life-and-death struggle. Care and caution must be exercised that the patient not be overwhelmed with his aggressive feelings or guilt. Emergencies in which the patient's life hangs in the balance will occur, for that may be the way the patient may have to test the therapist.

When Simmel reviewed his lifetime experience with alcoholics in a paper which he never completed, he was very clear about the problems of aggression in the treatment of these patients. He said:

> . . .during a state of abstinence under psychoanalysis in a hospital, substituting for the addiction to alcohol or drugs was an overt suicidal addiction or an overt addiction to homicide. During this stage the addict's only compulsion is to kill: himself or others. Usually he does not rationalize this urge; he just wants to die or, at other times he just wants to kill. [Simmel 1948, p. 24]

The aggression observable in the self-destructive lifestyle of the drug-dependent individual is, in the process of psychotherapy, traced to its ultimate sources and meanings. In this process the patient has to be able to experience with the therapist that which he has never dared to face—his hatred. Instead of seeing himself as a victim, and claiming *innocence*, now he confronts his murderous aggression. To do so, however, requires giving up the treasured view of oneself as the innocent victim, which again, has to be mourned. And so, it can be said that an unavoidable step in the treatment of a certain type of drug-dependent individual in intensive therapy is a depressive stage. During this phase of the treatment the dependence upon the therapist is extreme, and no substitutes are acceptable. While early in the treatment many patients do best in a clinic with multiple therapists, for the few who will be carried to this type of therapeutic completion, the chief therapist has to be the one who will be stationary and available to the very end.

Such are some of the difficulties resulting from the nature of object-representation in addictive personalities. They determine that successful psycho-analytic psychotherapy will continue to be the exception, mainly of research interest.

SUMMARY

The nature of the object relations of the drug-dependent patient is such that he craves to be united with ideal object, but at the same time dreads it. He thus becomes addicted to acting out the drama of fantasy introjection and separation from the drug. There is a corresponding intrapsychic defect; certain essential functions related to nurturance are reserved for the object-representation. The objective of therapy is to permit the patient to extend his conscious self-recognition to all of himself, thereby freeing him from the need for the placebo effect of the drug as a means of gaining access to his alienated parts and functions.

REFERENCES

Abraham, K. (1926). The psychological relation between sexuality and alcoholism. *Int. J. Psychoanal* 7:2.

―――― (1954). The influence of oral erotism on character formation. In *Selected Papers of Karl Abraham*. New York: Basic Books.

Chessick, R. D. (1960). The pharmacogenic orgasm. *Arch Gen Psychiatry* 3:117–128.

Clark, L. P. (1919). Psychological study of some alcoholics. *Psychoanal Rev* 6:268.

DiCara, L. (1972). Learning mechanisms. In *Biofeedback and Self-Control*. Chicago: Aldine.

Fenichel, O. (1945). *The Psychoanalytic Theory of the Neuroses*. New York: Norton.

Glover, E. The prevention and treatment of drug addiction. *Br. J of Inebriety* 29:13–18.

Hartmann, H. (1925). Cocainismus und homosexualitat. *Z Neur* 95:415.

Juliusberger, O. (1913). Psychology of alcoholism. *Zentralblatt fur psychoanal* 3:1.

Kirk, R. W. (1968). Pediatrics. In *Canine Medicine*, ed. J. Catcott, p. 809. Santa Barbara, CA: Amer. Vet. Pub.

Krystal, H. (1962). The study of withdrawal from narcotics as a state of stress. *Psychoanal Q Suppl* 36:53–65.

―――― (1966). Withdrawal from drugs. *Psychosomatics* 7:199–302.

―――― (1973a). Technical modification in affect regression and impairment of affect tolerance. Paper presented at the Annual Meeting of the American Psychoanalytic Association.

―――― (1973b). Psychic reality. Paper presented to the Michigan Psychoanalytic Society, March.

―――― (1974). The genetic development of affects and affect regression. Part 1. *The Annual of Psychoanalysis*, vol. 2.

―――― (1975). The genetic development of affects and affect regression. Part 2. Affect tolerance. *The Annual of Psychoanalysis* 3:179–219.

Krystal, H., and Raskin, H. A. (1970). *Drug Dependence Aspects of Ego Function*. Detroit: Wayne State University Press.

Margolis, M., Krystal, H., and Siegel, S. (1964). Psychotherapy with alcoholic offenders. *Q J Alcoh* 25:85–99.

Radó, S. (1926). The psychic effect of intoxicants: an attempt to evolve a psychoanalytic theory of morbid craving. *Int J. Psycho-anal* 7:396–413. (Also in: *Psychoanalysis of Behavior*. New York: Grune & Stratton, 1956.)

―――― (1933). The psychoanalysis of pharmacothymia. *Psychoanal Q* 2:1–3.

Savitt, R. A. (1963). Psychoanalytic studies on addiction: ego structure in narcotic addicts. *Psychoanal Q* 32:43–57.

Simmel, E. (1930). Morbid habits and cravings. *Psychoanal Rev* 17:48–54.

―――― (1948). Alcoholism and addiction. *Psychoanal Q* 17:6–31.

Stoyva, J. (1970). The public (scientific) study of private events. In *Biofeedback and Self-Control*, ed. T.X. Barber. Chicago: Aldine.

Szasz, T. S. (1958). The counterphobic mechanisms in addiction. *J. Am Psychoanal Assoc*, 6:309–325.

Vaillant, G. (1974). Paper on the treatment of alcoholics in the Cambridge Alcoholic Clinic. Given at a symposium on alcoholism, Boston University.

APPLYING SELF PSYCHOLOGY TO
ALCOHOLISM TREATMENT
Part VI

23: THE CYBERNETICS OF "SELF": A THEORY OF ALCOHOLISM

Gregory Bateson

The present essay is based upon ideas which are, perhaps all of them, familiar either to psychiatrists who have had dealings with alcoholics, or to philosophers who have thought about the implications of cybernetics and systems theory. The only novelty which can be claimed for the thesis here offered derives from treating these ideas seriously as premises of argument and from the bringing together of commonplace ideas from two too-separate fields of thought.

In its first conception, this essay was planned to be a systems-theoretic study of alcoholic addiction, in which I would use data from the publications of Alcoholics Anonymous, which has the only outstanding record of success in dealing with alcoholics. It soon became evident, however, that the religious views and the organizational structure of A.A. presented points of great interest to systems theory, and that the correct scope of my study should include not only the premises of alcoholism but also the premises of the A.A. system of treating it and the premises of A.A. organization.

My debt to A.A. will be evident throughout—also, I hope, my respect for that organization and especially for the extraordinary wisdom of its co-founders, Bill W. and Dr. Bob.

In addition, I have to acknowledge a debt to a small sample of alcoholic patients with whom I worked intensively for about two years in 1949–52, in the Veterans Administration Hospital, Palo Alto, California. These men, it should be mentioned, carried other diagnoses—mostly of "schizophrenia"—in addition to the pains of alcoholism. Several were members of A.A. I fear that I helped them not at all.

THE PROBLEM

It is rather generally believed that "causes" or "reasons" for alcoholism are to be looked for in the sober life of the alcoholic. Alcoholics, in their sober manifestations, are commonly dubbed "immature," "maternally fixated," "oral," "homosexual," "passive-aggressive," "fearful of success," "over-sensitive," "proud," "affable," or simply "weak." But the logical implications of this belief are usually not examined:

1. If the sober life of the alcoholic somehow drives him to drink or proposes the first step toward intoxication, it is not to be expected that any procedure which reinforces his particular style of sobriety will reduce or control his alcoholism.

2. If his style of sobriety drives him to drink, then that style must contain error or pathology; and intoxication must provide some — at least subjective — correction of this error. In other words, compared with his sobriety, which is in some way "wrong," his intoxication must be in some way "right." The old tag *"In vino veritas"* may contain a truth more profound than is usually attributed to it.

3. An alternative hypothesis would suggest that when sober, the alcoholic is somehow more sane than the people around him, and that this situation is intolerable. I have heard alcoholics argue in favor of this possibility, but I shall ignore it in this essay. I think that Bernard Smith, the non-alcoholic legal representative of A.A., came close to the mark when he said, "the [A.A.] member was never enslaved by alcohol. Alcohol simply served as an escape from *personal* enslavement to the false ideals of a materialistic society" (A.A. 1957, p. 279, italics added). It is not a matter of revolt against insane ideals around him but of escaping from his own insane premises, which are continually reinforced by the surrounding society. It is possible, however, that the alcoholic is in some way more vulnerable or sensitive than the normal to the fact that his insane (but conventional) premises lead to unsatisfying results.

4. The present theory of alcoholism, therefore, will provide a *converse matching* between the sobriety and the intoxication, such that the latter may be seen as an appropriate subjective correction for the former.

5. There are, of course, many instances in which people resort to alcohol and even to extreme intoxication as an anesthetic giving release from ordinary grief, resentment, or physical pain. It might be argued that the anesthetic action of alcohol provides a sufficient converse matching for our theoretical purposes. I shall, however, specifically exclude these cases from consideration as being not relevant to the problem of addictive or repetitive alcoholism; and this in spite of the undoubted fact that "grief," "resentment," and "frustration" are commonly used by addicted alcoholics as *excuses* for drinking.

I shall demand, therefore, a converse matching between sobriety and intoxication more specific than that provided by mere anesthesia.

SOBRIETY

The friends and relatives of the alcoholic commonly urge him to be "strong," and to "resist temptation." What they mean by this is not very clear, but it is significant that the alcoholic himself—while sober—commonly agrees with their view of his "problem." He believes that he could be, or at least, ought to be "the captain of his soul."[1] But it is a cliché of alcoholism that after "that first drink," the motivation to stop drinking is zero. Typically the whole matter is phrased overtly as a battle between "self" and "John Barleycorn." Covertly the alcoholic may be planning or even secretly laying in supplies for the next binge, but it is almost impossible (in the hospital setting) to get the sober alcoholic to plan his next binge in an overt manner. He cannot, seemingly, be the "captain" of his soul and overtly will or command his own drunkenness. The "captain" can only command sobriety—and then not be obeyed.

Bill W., the co-founder of Alcoholics Anonymous, himself an alcoholic, cut through all this mythology of conflict in the very first of the famous "Twelve Steps" of A.A. The first step demands that the alcoholic agree that he is powerless over alcohol. This step is usually regarded as a *"surrender"* and many alcoholics are either unable to achieve it or achieve it only briefly during the period of remorse following a binge. A.A. does not regard these cases as promising: they have not yet "hit bottom"; their despair is inadequate and after a more or less brief spell of sobriety they will again attempt to use "self-control" to fight the "temptation." They will not or cannot accept the premise that, drunk or sober, the total personality of an alcoholic is an alcoholic personality which cannot conceivably fight alcoholism. As an A.A. leaflet puts it, "trying to use will power is like trying to lift yourself by your bootstraps."

The first two steps of A.A. are as follows:

1. We admitted we were powerless over alcohol—that our lives had become unmanageable.
2. Came to believe that a Power greater than ourselves could restore us to sanity. [A.A. 1939]

Implicit in the combination of these two steps is an extraordinary—and I believe correct—idea: the experience of defeat not only serves to convince the alcoholic that change is necessary; it *is* the first step in that change. To be defeated by the bottle and to know it is the first "spiritual experience." The myth of self-power is thereby broken by the demonstration of a greater power.

In sum, I shall argue that the "sobriety" of the alcoholic is characterized by an unusually disastrous variant of the Cartesian dualism, the division between Mind and Matter, or, in this case, between conscious will, or "self," and the remainder of the personality. Bill W.'s stroke of genius was to break up with the first "step" the structuring of this dualism.

Philosophically viewed, this first step is *not* a surrender; it is simply a change in epistemology, a change in how to know about the personality-in-the-world. And, notably, the change is from an incorrect to a more correct epistemology.

---

[1] This phrase is used by A.A. in derision of the alcoholic who tries to use will power against the bottle. The quotation, along with the line, "my head is bloody but unbowed," comes from the poem "Invictus" by William Ernest Henley, who was a cripple but not an alcoholic. The use of the will to conquer pain and physical disability is probably not comparable to the alcoholic's use of will.

EPISTEMOLOGY AND ONTOLOGY

Philosophers have recognized and separated two sorts of problems. There are first the problems of how things are, what is a person, and what sort of a world this is. These are the problems of ontology. Second, there are the problems of how we know anything, or more specifically, how we know what sort of a world it is and what sort of creatures we are that can know something (or perhaps nothing) of this matter. These are the problems of epistemology. To these questions, both ontological and epistemological, philosophers try to find true answers.

But the naturalist, observing human behavior, will ask rather different questions. If he be a cultural relativist, he may agree with those philosophers who hold that a "true" ontology is conceivable, but he will not ask whether the ontology of the people he observes is "true." He will expect their epistemology to be culturally determined or even idiosyncratic, and he will expect the culture as a whole to make sense in terms of their particular epistemology and ontology.

If, on the other hand, it is clear that the local epistemology is *wrong*, then the naturalist should be alert to the possibility that the culture as a whole will never really make "sense," or will make sense only under restricted circumstances, which contact with other cultures and new technologies might disrupt.

In the natural history of the living human being, ontology and epistemology cannot be separated. His (commonly unconscious) beliefs about what sort of world it is will determine how he sees it and acts within it, and his ways of perceiving and acting will determine his beliefs about its nature. The living man is thus bound within a net of epistemological and ontological premises which — regardless of ultimate truth or falsity — become partially self-validating for him (Ruesch and Bateson 1951).

It is awkward to refer constantly to both epistemology and ontology and incorrect to suggest that they are separable in human natural history. There seems to be no convenient word to cover the combination of these two concepts. The nearest approximations are "cognitive structure" or "character structure," but these terms fail to suggest that what is important is a body of habitual assumptions or premises implicit in the relationship between man and environment, and that these premises may be true or false. I shall therefore use the single term "epistemology" in this essay to cover both aspects of the net of premises which govern adaptation (or maladaptation) to the human and physical environment. In George Kelly's vocabulary, these are the rules by which an individual "construes" his experience.

I am concerned especially with that group of premises upon which Occidental concepts of the "self" are built, and, conversely, with premises which are corrective to some of the more gross Occidental errors associated with that concept.

THE EPISTEMOLOGY OF CYBERNETICS

What is new and surprising is that we now have partial answers to some of these questions. In the last twenty-five years extraordinary advances have been made in our knowledge of what sort of thing the environment is, what sort of thing an organism is, and, especially, what sort of thing a *mind* is. These advances have come out of cybernetics, systems theory, information theory, and related sciences.

We now know, with considerable certainty, that the ancient problem of whether the mind is immanent or transcendent can be answered in favor of immanence, and that this answer is more economical of explanatory entities than any transcendent answer: it has at least the negative support of "Occam's Razor."

On the positive side, we can assert that *any* on-going ensemble of events and objects which has the appropriate complexity of causal circuits and the appropriate energy relations will surely show mental characteristics. It will *compare*, that is, be responsive to *difference* (in addition to being affected by the ordinary physical "causes" such as impact or force). It will "process information" and will inevitably be self-corrective either toward homeostatic optima or toward the maximization of certain variables.

A "bit" of information is definable as a difference which makes a difference. Such a difference, as it travels and undergoes successive transformation in a circuit, is an elementary idea.

But, most relevant in the present context, we know that no part of such an internally interactive system can have unilateral control over the remainder or over any other part. The mental characteristics are inherent or immanent in the ensemble as a *whole*.

Even in very simple self-corrective systems, this holistic character is evident. In the steam engine with a "governor," the very word "governor" is a misnomer if it be taken to mean that this part of the system has unilateral control. The governor is, essentially, a sense organ or transducer which receives a transform of the *difference* between the actual running speed of the engine and some ideal or preferred speed. This sense organ transforms these differences into differences in some efferent message, for example, to fuel supply or to a brake. The behavior of the governor is determined, in other words, by the behavior of the other parts of the system, and indirectly by its own behavior at a previous time.

The holistic and mental character of the system is most clearly demonstrated by this last fact, that the behavior of the governor (and, indeed, of every part of the causal circuit) is partially determined by its own previous behavior. Message material (i.e., successive transforms of difference) must pass around the total circuit, and the *time* required for the message material to return to the place from which it started is a basic characteristic of the total system. The behavior of the governor (or any other part of the circuit) is thus in some degree determined not only by its immediate past, but by what it did at a time which precedes the present by the interval necessary for the message to complete the circuit. There is thus a sort of determinative *memory* in even the simplest cybernetic circuit.

The stability of the system (i.e., whether it will act self-correctively or oscillate or go into run-away) depends upon the relation between the operational product of all the transformations of difference around the circuit and upon this characteristic time. The "governor" has no control over these factors. Even a human governor in a social system is bound by the same limitations. He is controlled by information from the system and must adapt his own actions to its time characteristics and to the effects of his own past action.

Thus: in no system which shows mental characteristics can any part have unilateral control over the whole. In other words, *the mental characteristics of the system are immanent, not in some part, but in the system as a whole.*

The significance of this conclusion appears when we ask, "Can a computer think?" or, "Is the mind in the brain?" And the answer to both questions will be negative unless the question is focused upon one of the few mental characteristics which are contained within the computer or the brain. A computer is self-corrective in regard to some of its internal variables. It may, for example, include thermometers or other sense organs which are affected by differences in its working temperature and the response of the sense organ to these differences may affect the action of a fan which in turn corrects the temperature. We may therefore say that the system shows mental characteristics in regard to its internal temperature. But it would be incorrect to say that the main business of the computer—the transformation of input differences into output differences—is "a mental process." The computer is only an arc of a larger circuit which always includes a man and an environment from which information is received and upon which efferent messages from the computer have effect. This total system, or ensemble, may legitimately be said to show mental characteristics. It operates by trial and error and has creative character.

Similarly, we may say that "mind" is immanent in those circuits of the brain which are complete within the brain. Or that mind is immanent in circuits which are complete within the system, brain *plus* body. Or, finally, that mind is immanent in the larger system—man *plus* environment.

In principle, if we desire to explain or understand the mental aspect of any biological event, we must take into account the system—that is, the network of *closed* circuits, within which that biological event is determined. But when we seek to explain the behavior of a man or any other organism, this "system" will usually *not* have the same limits as the "self"—as this term is commonly (and variously) understood.

Consider a man felling a tree with an axe. Each stroke of the axe is modified or corrected, according to the shape of the cut face of the tree left by the previous stroke. This self-corrective (i.e., mental) process is brought about by a total system, tree-eyes-brain-muscles-axe-stroke-tree; and it is this total system that has the characteristics of immanent mind.

More correctly, we should spell the matter out as: (differences in tree)-(differences in retina)-(differences in brain)-(differences in muscles)-(differences in movement of axe)-(differences in tree), and so on. What is transmitted around the circuit are transforms of differences. And, as noted above, a difference which makes a difference is an *idea* or unit of information.

But this is *not* how the average Occidental sees the event-sequence of tree-felling. He says, "*I* cut down the tree" and he even believes that there is a delimited agent, the "self," which performed a delimited "purposive" action upon a delimited object.

It is all very well to say that "billiard ball A hit billiard ball B and sent it into the pocket"; and it would perhaps be all right (if we could do it) to give a complete hard science account of the events all around the circuit containing the man and the tree. But popular parlance includes *mind* in its utterance by invoking the personal pronoun, and then achieves a mixture of mentalism and physicalism by restricting mind within the man and reifying the tree. Finally the mind itself becomes reified by the notion that, since the "self" acted upon the axe which acted upon the tree, the "self" must also be a "thing." The parallelism of syntax between "*I* hit the billiard ball" and "the ball hit another ball" is totally misleading.

If you ask anybody about the localization and boundaries of the self, these confusions are immediately displayed. Or consider a blindman with a stick. Where does the blindman's self begin? At the tip of the stick? At the handle of the stick? Or at some point halfway up the stick? These questions are nonsense, because the stick is a pathway along which differences are transmitted under transformation, so that to draw a delimiting line *across* this pathway is to cut off a part of the systemic circuit which determines the blind man's locomotion.

Similarly, his sense organs are transducers or pathways for information, as also are his axons, and so forth. From a systems-theoretic point of view, it is a misleading metaphor to say that what travels in an axon is an "impulse." It would be more correct to say that what travels is a difference, or a transform of a difference. The metaphor of "impulse" suggests a hard-science line of thought which will ramify only too easily into nonsense about "psychic energy," and those who talk this kind of nonsense will disregard the information content of *quiescence*. The quiescence of an axon *differs* as much from activity as its activity does from quiescence. Therefore quiescence and activity have equal informational relevance. The message of activity can only be accepted as valid if the message of quiescence can also be trusted.

It is even incorrect to speak of the "message of activity" and the "message of quiescence." Always the fact that information is a transform of difference should be remembered, and we might better call the one message "activity—not quiescence" and the other "quiescence—not activity."

Similar considerations apply to the repentant alcoholic. He cannot simply elect "sobriety." At best he could only elect "sobriety—not drunkenness," and his universe remains polarized, carrying always both alternatives.

The total self-corrective unit which processes information, or, as I say, "thinks" and "acts" and "decides," is a *system* whose boundaries do not at all coincide with the boundaries either of the body or of what is popularly called the "self" or "consciousness"; and it is important to notice that there are *multiple* differences between the thinking system and the "self" as popularly conceived:

1. The system is not a transcendent entity as the "self" is commonly supposed to be.

2. The ideas are immanent in a network of causal pathways along which transforms of difference are conducted. The "ideas" of the system are in all cases at least binary in structure. They are not "impulses" but "information."

3. This network of pathways is not bounded with consciousness but extends to include the pathways of all unconscious mentation—both autonomic and repressed, neural and hormonal.

4. The network is not bounded by the skin but includes all external pathways along which information can travel. It also includes those effective differences which are immanent in the "objects" of such information. It includes the pathways of sound and light along which travel transforms of differences originally immanent in things and other people—and especially *in our own actions*.

It is important to note that the basic—and I believe erroneous—tenets of popular epistemology are mutually reinforcing. If, for example, the popular premise of transcendence is discarded, the immediate substitute is a premise of immanence in the body. But this alternative will be unacceptable because large parts of the thinking network are located outside the body. The so-called "Body–Mind" problem is wrongly posed in terms which force the argument toward paradox: if mind be supposed immanent in the body, then it must be transcendent. If transcendent, it must be immanent. And so on (cf. Collingwood 1945).

Similarly, if we exclude the unconscious processes from the "self" and call them "ego-alien," then these processes take on the subjective coloring of "urges" and "forces"; and this pseudodynamic quality is then extended to the conscious "self" which attempts to "resist" the "forces" of the unconscious. The "self" thereby becomes itself an organization of seeming "forces." The popular notion which would equate "self" with consciousness thus leads into the notion that ideas are "forces"; and this fallacy is in turn supported by saying that the axon carries "impulses." To find a way out of this mess is by no means easy.

We shall proceed by first examining the structure of the alcoholic's polarization. In the epistemologically unsound resolution, "I will fight the bottle," what is supposedly lined up against what?

ALCOHOLIC "PRIDE"

Alcoholics are philosophers in that universal sense in which all human beings (and all mammals) are guided by highly abstract principles of which they are either quite unconscious, or unaware that the principle governing their perception and action is philosophic. A common misnomer for such principles is "feelings" (Bateson 1963).

This misnomer arises naturally from the Anglo-Saxon epistemological tendency to reify or attribute to the body all mental phenomena which are peripheral to consciousness. And the misnomer is, no doubt, supported by the fact that the exercise and/or frustration of these principles is often accompanied by visceral and other bodily sensations. I believe, however, that Pascal was correct when he said, "The heart has its *reasons* of which the reason knows nothing."

But the reader must not expect the alcoholic to present a consistent picture. When the underlying epistemology is full of error, derivations from it are inevitably either self-contradictory or extremely restricted in scope. A consistent corpus of theorems cannot be derived from an inconsistent body of axioms. In such cases, the attempt to be consistent leads either to the great proliferation of complexity characteristic of psychoanalytic theory and Christian theology or to the extremely narrow view characteristic of contemporary behaviorism.

I shall therefore proceed to examine the "pride" which is characteristic of alcoholics to show that this principle of their behavior is derived from the strange dualistic epistemology characteristic of Occidental civilization.

A convenient way of describing such principles as "pride," "dependency," "fatalism," and so forth, is to examine the principle as if it were a result of deutero-learning[2] (Bateson 1942) and to ask what contexts of learning might understandably inculcate this principle.

1. It is clear that the principle of alcoholic life which A.A. calls "pride" is not contextually structured around past achievement. They do not use the word to mean pride in something accomplished. The emphasis is not upon "I succeeded," but rather upon "I can . . ." It is an obsessive acceptance of a challenge, a repudiation of the proposition "I cannot."

2. After the alcoholic has begun to suffer from—or be blamed for—alcoholism, this principle of "pride" is mobilized behind the proposition "I can stay sober." But, noticeably, success in this achievement destroys the "challenge." The alcoholic becomes "cocksure," as A.A. says. He relaxes his determination, risks a drink, and finds himself on a binge. We may say that the contextual structure of sobriety changes with its achievement. Sobriety, at this point, is no longer the appropriate contextual setting for "pride." It is the risk of the drink that now is challenging and calls out the fatal "I can. . . ."

3. A.A. does its best to insist that this change in contextual structure shall never occur. They restructure the whole context by asserting over and over again that *"once an alcoholic, always an alcoholic."* They try to have the alcoholic place alcoholism within the self, much as a Jungian analyst tries to have the patient discover his "psychological type" and to learn to live with the strengths and weaknesses of that type. In contrast, the contextual structure of alcoholic "pride" places the alcoholism *outside* the self: "*I* can resist drinking."

4. The challenge component of alcoholic "pride" is linked with *risk-taking.* The principle might be put in words: "I can do something where success is improbable and failure would be disastrous." Clearly this principle will never serve to maintain continued sobriety. As success begins to appear probable, the alcoholic must challenge the risk of a drink. The element of "bad luck" or "probability" of failure places failure beyond the limits of the self. "If failure

---

[2]This use of formal contextual structure as a descriptive device does not necessarily assume that the principle discussed is wholly or in part actually *learned* in contexts having the appropriate formal structure. The principle could have been genetically determined, and it might still follow that the principle is best described by the formal delineation of the contexts in which it is exemplified. It is precisely this fitting of behavior to context that makes it difficult or impossible to determine whether a principle of behavior was genetically determined or learned in that context.

occurs, it is not *mine*." Alcoholic "pride" progressively narrows the concept of "self," placing what happens outside its scope.

5. The principle of pride-in-risk is ultimately almost suicidal. It is all very well to test once whether the universe is on your side, but to do so again and again, with increasing stringency of proof, is to set out on a project which can only prove that the universe hates you. But, still and all, the A.A. narratives show repeatedly that, at the very bottom of despair, *pride* sometimes prevents suicide. The final quietus must not be delivered by the "self" (cf. Bill's Story, A.A. 1939).

PRIDE AND SYMMETRY

The so-called pride of the alcoholic always presumes a real or fictitious "other" and its complete contextual definition therefore demands that we characterize the real or imagined relationship to this "other." A first step in this task is to classify the relationship as either "symmetrical" or "complementary" (Bateson 1936). To do this is not entirely simple when the "other" is a creation of the unconscious, but we shall see that the indications for such a classification are clear.

An explanatory digression is, however, necessary. The primary criterion is simple:

If, in a binary relationship, the behaviors of A and B are regarded (by A and B) as *similar* and are linked so that more of the given behavior by A stimulates more of it in B, and *vice versa,* then the relationship is "symmetrical" in regard to these behaviors.

If, conversely, the behaviors of A and B are *dissimilar* but mutually fit together (as, for example, spectatorship fits exhibitionism), and the behaviors are linked so that more of A's behavior stimulates more of B's fitting behavior, then the relationship is "complementary" in regard to these behaviors.

Common examples of simple symmetrical relationship are: armaments races, keeping up with the Joneses, athletic emulation, boxing matches, and the like. Common examples of complementary relationship are: dominance-submission, sadism-masochism, nurturance-dependency, spectatorship-exhibitionism, and the like.

More complex considerations arise when higher logical typing is present. For example: A and B may compete in gift-giving, thus superposing a larger symmetrical frame upon primarily complementary behaviors. Or, conversely, a therapist might engage in competition with a patient in some sort of play therapy, placing a complementary nurturant frame around the primarily symmetrical transactions of the game.

Various sorts of "double binds" are generated when A and B perceive the premises of their relationship in different terms—A may regard B's behavior as competitive when B thought he was helping A. And so on.

With these complexities we are not here concerned, because the imaginary "other" or counterpart in the "pride" of the alcoholic does not, I believe, play the complex games which are characteristic of the "voices" of schizophrenics.

Both complementary and symmetrical relationships are liable to progressive changes of the sort which I have called *schismogenesis* (Bateson 1936). Symmetrical struggles and armaments races may, in the current phrase, "escalate"; and the normal pattern of succoring-dependency between parent and child may become monstrous. These potentially pathological developments are due to undamped or uncorrected positive feedback in the system, and may — as stated — occur in either complementary or symmetrical systems. However, in *mixed* systems schismogenesis is necessarily reduced. The armaments race between two nations will be slowed down by acceptance of complementary themes such as dominance, dependency, admiration, and so forth, between them. It will be speeded up by the repudiation of these themes.

This antithetical relationship between complementary and symmetrical themes is, no doubt, due to the fact that each is the logical opposite of the other. In a merely symmetrical armaments race, nation A is motivated to greater efforts by its estimate of *the greater strength* of B. When it estimates that B is weaker, nation A will relax its efforts. But the exact opposite will happen if A's structuring of the relationship is complementary. Observing that B is *weaker* than they, A will go ahead with hopes of conquest (cf. Bateson 1946 and Richardson 1939).

This antithesis between complementary and symmetrical patterns may be more than simply logical. Notably, in psychoanalytic theory (cf. Erikson 1937), the patterns which are called "libidinal" and which are modalities of the erogenous zones are all *complementary*. Intrusion, inclusion, exclusion, reception, retention, and the like — all of these are classed as "libidinal." Whereas rivalry, competition, and the like fall under the rubric of "ego" and "defense."

It is also possible that the two antithetical codes — symmetrical and complementary — may be physiologically represented by contrasting states of the central nervous system. The progressive changes of schismogenesis may reach climactic discontinuities and sudden reversals. Symmetrical rage may suddenly turn to grief; the retreating animal with tail between his legs may suddenly "turn at bay" in a desperate battle of symmetry to the death. The bully may suddenly become the coward when he is challenged, and the wolf who is beaten in a symmetrical conflict may suddenly give "surrender" signals which prevent further attack.

The last example is of special interest. If the struggle between the wolves is symmetrical — that is, if wolf A is stimulated to more aggressive behavior by the aggressive behavior of B — then if B suddenly exhibits what we may call "negative aggression," A will not be able to continue to fight unless he can quickly switch over to that complementary state of mind in which B's weakness would be a stimulus for his aggression. Within the hypothesis of symmetrical and complementary modes, it becomes unnecessary to postulate a specifically "inhibitory" effect for the surrender signal.

Human beings who possess language can apply the label "aggression" to all attempts to damage the other, regardless of whether the attempt is prompted by the other's strength or weakness; but at the prelinguistic mammalian level these two sorts of "aggression" must appear totally different. We are told that from the lion's point of view, an "attack" on a zebra is totally different from an "attack" on another lion (Lorenz 1966).

Enough has now been said so that the question can be posed: Is alcoholic pride contextually structured in symmetrical or complementary form?

First, there is a very strong tendency toward symmetry in the normal drinking habits of Occidental culture. Quite apart from addictive alcoholism, two men drinking together are impelled by convention to match each other, drink for drink. At this stage, the "other" is still real and the symmetry, or rivalry, between the pair is friendly.

As the alcoholic becomes addicted and tries to resist drinking, he begins to find it difficult to resist the social context in which he should match his friends in their drinking. The A.A. says, "Heaven knows, we have tried hard enough and long enough to drink like other people!"

As things get worse, the alcoholic is likely to become a solitary drinker and to exhibit the whole spectrum of response to challenge. His wife and friends begin to suggest that his drinking is a *weakness*, and he may respond, with symmetry, both by resenting them and by asserting his strength to resist the bottle. But, as is characteristic of symmetrical responses, a brief period of successful struggle weakens his motivation and he falls off the wagon. Symmetrical effort requires continual opposition from the opponent.

Gradually the focus of the battle changes, and the alcoholic finds himself committed to a new and more deadly type of symmetrical conflict. He must now prove that the bottle cannot kill him. His "head is bloody but unbowed." He is still the "captain of his soul"—for what it's worth.

Meanwhile, his relationships with wife and boss and friends have been deteriorating. He never did like the complementary status of his boss as an authority; and now as he deteriorates his wife is more and more forced to take a complementary role. She may try to exert authority, or she becomes protective, or she shows forbearance, but all those provoke either rage or shame. His symmetrical "pride" can tolerate no complementary role.

In sum, the relationship between the alcoholic and his real or fictitious "other" is clearly symmetrical and clearly schismogenic. It escalates. We shall see that the religious conversion of the alcoholic when saved by A.A. can be described as a dramatic shift from this symmetrical habit, or epistemology, to an almost purely complementary view of his relationship to others and to the universe or God.

PRIDE OR INVERTED PROOF?

Alcoholics may appear to be stiffnecked, but they are not stupid. The part of the mind in which their policy is decided certainly lies too deep for the word "stupidity" to be applicable. These levels of the mind are prelinguistic and the computation which goes on there is coded in *primary process*.

Both in dream and in mammalian interaction, the only way to achieve a proposition which contains its own negation ("I will not bite you," or "I am not afraid of him") is by an elaborate imagining or acting out of the proposition to be negated, leading to a *reductio ad absurdum*. "I will not bite you" is achieved between two mammals by an experimental combat which is a "not combat," sometimes called "play." It is for this reason that "agonistic" behavior commonly evolves into friendly greeting (Bateson 1969).

In this sense, the so-called pride of the alcoholic is in some degree ironic. It is a determined effort to test something like "self-control" with an ulterior but unstateable purpose of proving that "self-control" is ineffectual and absurd. "It simply won't work." This ultimate proposition, since it contains a simple negation, is not to be expressed in primary process. Its final expression is in an action—the taking of a drink. The heroic battle with the bottle, that fictitious "other," ends up in a "kiss and make friends."

In favor of this hypothesis, there is the undoubted fact that the testing of self-control leads back into drinking. And, as I have argued above, the whole epistemology of self-control which his friends urge upon the alcoholic is monstrous. If this be so, then the alcoholic is right in rejecting it. He has achieved a *reductio ad absurdum* of the conventional epistemology.

But this description of achieving a *reductio ad absurdum* verges upon teleology. If the proposition "It won't work" cannot be entertained within the coding of primary process, how then can the computations of primary process direct the organism to try out those courses of action which will demonstrate that "It won't work"?

Problems of this general type are frequent in psychiatry and can perhaps only be resolved by a model in which, under certain circumstances, the organism's discomfort activates a positive feedback loop to *increase* the behavior which preceded the discomfort. Such positive feedback would provide a verification that it was really that particular behavior which brought about the discomfort, and might increase the discomfort to some threshold level at which change would become possible.

In psychotherapy such a positive feedback loop is commonly provided by the therapist who pushes the patient in the direction of his symptoms—a technique which has been called the "therapeutic double bind." An example of this technique is quoted later in this essay, where the A.A. member challenges the alcoholic to go and do some "controlled drinking" in order that he may discover for himself that he has no control.

It is also usual that the symptoms and hallucinations of the schizophrenic—like dreams—constitute a corrective experience, so that the whole schizophrenic episode takes on the character of a self-initiation. Barbara O'Brien's account of her own psychosis is perhaps the most striking example of this phenomenon, which has been discussed elsewhere (Bateson 1961, Introduction).

It will be noted that the possible existence of such a positive feedback loop, which will cause a runaway in the direction of increasing discomfort up to some threshold (which might be on the other side of death), is not included in conventional theories of learning. But a tendency to verify the unpleasant by seeking repeated experience of it is a common human trait. It is perhaps what Freud called the "death instinct."

THE DRUNKEN STATE

What has been said above about the treadmill of symmetrical pride is only one half of the picture. It is the picture of the state of mind of the alcoholic *battling* with the bottle. Clearly this state is very unpleasant and clearly it is also unrealistic. His "others" are either totally imaginary or are gross distortions of persons on whom he is dependent and whom he may love. He has an alternative to this uncomfortable state—he can get drunk. Or, *"at least,"* have a drink.

With this complementary surrender, which the alcoholic will often see as an act of spite—a Parthian dart in the symmetrical struggle—his entire episte-mology changes. His anxieties and resentments and panic vanish as if by magic. His self-control is lessened, but his need to compare himself with others is reduced even further. He feels the physiological warmth of alcohol in his veins and, in many cases, a corresponding psychological warmth toward others. He may be either maudlin or angry, but he has at least become again a part of the human scene.

Direct data bearing upon the thesis that the step from sobriety into intoxication is also a step from symmetrical challenge into complementarity are scarce, and always confused both by the distortions of recall and by the complex toxicity of the alcohol. But there is strong evidence from song and story to indicate that the step is of this kind. In ritual, partaking of wine has always stood for the social aggregation of persons united in religious "communion" or secular *Gemütlichkeit*. In a very literal sense, alcohol supposedly makes the individual see himself as and act as *a part of* the group. That is, it enables complementarity in the relationships which surround him.

HITTING BOTTOM

A.A. attaches great importance to this phenomenon and regards the alcoholic who has not hit bottom as a poor prospect for their help. Conversely, they are inclined to explain their failures by saying that the individual who goes back to his alcoholism has not yet "hit bottom."

Certainly many sorts of disasters may cause an alcoholic to hit bottom. Various sorts of accidents, an attack of delirium tremens, a patch of drunken time of which he has no memory, rejection by wife, loss of job, hopeless diagnosis, and so on—any of these may have the required effect. A.A. says that "bottom" is different for different men and some may be dead before they reach it.[3]

It is possible, however, that "bottom" is reached many times by any given individual; that "bottom" is a spell of panic which provides a favorable moment

---

[3]Personal communication from a member.

for change, but not a moment at which change is inevitable. Friends and relatives and even therapists may pull the alcoholic out of his panic, either with drugs or reassurance, so that he "recovers" and goes back to his "pride" and alcoholism — only to hit a more disastrous "bottom" at some later time, when he will again be ripe for a change. The attempt to change the alcoholic in a period *between* such moments of panic is unlikely to succeed.

The nature of the panic is made clear by the following description of a "test."

> We do not like to pronounce any individual as alcoholic, but you can quickly diagnose yourself. Step over to the nearest barroom and try some controlled drinking. Try to drink and stop abruptly. Try it more than once. It will not take long for you to decide, if you are honest with yourself about it. It may be worth a bad case of jitters if you get a full knowledge of your condition. [A.A. 1939, p. 43]

We might compare the test quoted above to commanding a driver to brake suddenly when travelling on a slippery road: he will discover fast that his control is limited. (The metaphor "skid row" for the alcoholic section of town is not inappropriate.)

The panic of the alcoholic who has hit bottom is the panic of the man who thought he had control over a vehicle but suddenly finds that the vehicle can run away with him. Suddenly, pressure on what he knows is the brake seems to make the vehicle go faster. It is the panic of discovering that *it* (the system, self *plus* vehicle) is bigger than he is.

In terms of the theory here presented, we may say that hitting bottom exemplifies systems theory at three levels:

1. The alcoholic works on the discomforts of sobriety to a threshold point at which he has bankrupted the epistemology of "self-control." He then gets drunk — because the "system" is bigger than he is — and he may as well surrender to it.

2. He works repeatedly at getting drunk until he proves that there is a still larger system. He then encounters the panic of "hitting bottom."

3. If friends and therapists reassure him, he may achieve a further unstable adjustment — becoming addicted to their help — until he demonstrates that this system won't work, and "hits bottom" again but at a lower level. In this, as in all cybernetic systems, the sign (plus or minus) of the effect of any intrusion upon the system depends upon timing.

4. Lastly, the phenomenon of hitting bottom is complexly related to the experience of double bind (Bateson et al. 1956). Bill W. narrates that he hit bottom when diagnosed as a hopeless alcoholic by Dr. William D. Silkworth in 1939, and this event is regarded as the beginning of A.A. history (A.A. 1957, p. vii). Dr. Silkworth also "supplied us with the tools with which to puncture the toughest alcoholic ego, those shattering phrases by which he described our illness: *the obsession of the mind* that compels us to drink and *the allergy of the body* that condemns us to go mad or die" (Bill W. in A.A. 1957, p. 13; italics in the original). This is a double bind correctly founded upon the alcoholic's dichotomous epistemology of mind *versus* body. He is forced by these words back and

back to the point at which only an involuntary change in deep unconscious epistemology — a spiritual experience — will make the lethal description irrelevant.

THE THEOLOGY OF ALCOHOLICS ANONYMOUS

Some outstanding points of the theology of A.A. are:

1. *There is a Power greater than the self.* Cybernetics would go somewhat further and recognize that the "self" as ordinarily understood is only a small part of a much larger trial-and-error system which does the thinking, acting, and deciding. This system includes all the informational pathways which are relevant at any given moment to any given decision. The "self" is a false reification of an improperly delimited part of this much larger field of interlocking processes. Cybernetics also recognizes that two or more persons — any group of persons — may together form such a thinking-and-acting system.

2. This Power is felt to be personal and to be intimately linked with each person. It is "God as *you* understand him to be."

Cybernetically speaking, "my" relation to any larger system around me and including other things and persons will be different from "your" relation to some similar system around you. The relation "part of" must necessarily and logically always be complementary but the meaning of the phrase "part of" will be different for every person.[4] This difference will be especially important in systems containing more than one person. The system or "power" must necessarily appear different from where each person sits. Moreover, it is expectable that such systems, when they encounter each other, will recognize each other as systems in this sense. The "beauty" of the woods through which I walk is my recognition both of the individual trees and of the total ecology of the woods as *systems*. A similar esthetic recognition is still more striking when I talk with another person.

3. A favorable relationship with this Power is discovered through "hitting bottom" and "surrender."

4. By resisting this Power, men and especially alcoholics bring disaster upon themselves. The materialistic philosophy which sees "man" as pitted against his environment is rapidly breaking down as technological man becomes more and more able to oppose the largest systems. Every battle that he wins brings a threat of disaster. The unit of survival — either in ethics or in evolution — is not the organism or the species but the largest system or "power" within which the creature lives. If the creature destroys its environment, it destroys itself.

5. But — and this is important — the Power does not reward and punish. It does not have "power" in that sense. In the biblical phrase, "All things work together for good to them that love God." And, conversely, to them that do not. The idea of power in the sense of unilateral control is foreign to A.A. Their

---

[4]This diversity in styles of integration could account for the fact that some persons become alcoholic while others do not.

organization is strictly "democratic" (their word), and even their deity is still bound by what we might call a systemic determinism. The same limitation applies both to the relationship between the A.A. sponsor and the drunk whom he hopes to help and to the relationship between A.A. central office and every local group.

6. The first two "steps" of Alcoholics Anonymous taken together identify the addiction as a manifestation of this Power.

7. The healthy relation between each person and this Power is complementary. It is in precise contrast to the "pride" of the alcoholic, which is predicated upon a symmetrical relationship to an imagined "other." The schismogenesis is always more powerful than the participants in it.

8. The quality and content of each person's relation to the Power is indicated or reflected in the social structure of A.A. The secular aspect of this system—its governance—is delineated in "Twelve Traditions" (A.A. 1957), which supplement the "Twelve Steps," the latter developing man's relationship to the Power. The two documents overlap in the Twelfth Step, which enjoins aid to other alcoholics as a necessary spiritual exercise without which the member is likely to relapse. The total system is a Durkheimian religion in the sense that the relationship between man and his community parallels the relationship between man and God. "A.A. is a power greater than any of us" (A.A. 1957, p. 288).

In sum, the relationship of each individual to the "Power" is best defined in the words "*is part of.*"

9. Anonymity. It must be understood that anonymity means much more in A.A. thinking and theology than the mere protection of members from exposure and shame. With increasing fame and success of the organization as a whole, it has become a temptation for members to use the fact of their membership as a positive asset in public relations, politics, education, and many other fields. Bill W., the co-founder of the organization, was himself caught by this temptation in early days and has discussed the matter in a published article (A.A. 1957, pp. 286–294). He sees first that any grabbing of the spotlight must be a personal and spiritual danger to the member, who cannot afford such self-seeking; and beyond this that it would be fatal for the organization as a whole to become involved in politics, religious controversy, and social reform. He states clearly that the errors of the alcoholic are the same as the "forces which are today ripping the world apart at its seams," but that it is not the business of A.A. to save the world. Their single purpose is "to carry the A.A. message to the sick alcoholic who wants it" (loc. cit.). He concludes that anonymity is "the greatest symbol of self-sacrifice that we know." Elsewhere the twelfth of the "Twelve Traditions" states that "anonymity is the spiritual foundation of our traditions, ever reminding us to place principles before personalities."

To this we may add that anonymity is also a profound statement of the systemic relation, part-to-whole. Some systems theorists would go even further, because a major temptation for systems theory lies in the reification of theoretical concepts. Anatol Holt says he wants a bumper sticker which would (paradoxically) say, "Stamp out nouns" (Wenner-Gren Foundation 1968).

10. Prayer. The A.A. use of prayer similarly affirms the complementarity of part–whole relationship by the very simple technique of asking for that relationship. They ask for those personal characteristics, such as humility, which are in fact exercised in the very act of prayer. If the act of prayer be sincere (which is not so easy), God cannot but grant the request. And this is peculiarly true of "God, *as you understand him.*" This self-affirming tautology, which contains its own beauty, is precisely the balm required after the anguish of the double binds which went with hitting bottom.

Somewhat more complex is the famous "Serenity Prayer": "God grant us the serenity to accept the things we cannot change, courage to change the things we can, and wisdom to know the difference."[5]

If double binds cause anguish and despair and destroy personal epistemological premises at some deep level, then it follows, conversely, that for the healing of these wounds and the growth of a new epistemology, some converse of the double bind will be appropriate. The double bind leads to the conclusion of despair, "There are no alternatives." The Serenity Prayer explicitly frees the worshipper from these maddening bonds.

In this connection it is worth mentioning that the great schizophrenic, John Perceval, observed a change in his "voices." In the beginning of his psychosis they bullied him with "contradictory commands" (or as I would say, double binds), but later he began to recover when they offered him choice of clearly defined alternatives (cf. Bateson 1961).

11. In one characteristic, A.A. differs profoundly from such natural mental systems as the family or the redwood forest. It has a *single* purpose — "to carry the A.A. message to the sick alcoholic who wants it" — and the organization is dedicated to the maximization of that purpose. In this respect, A.A. is no more sophisticated than General Motors or an Occidental nation. But biological systems, other than those premised upon Occidental ideas (and especially *money*), are multipurposed. There is no single variable in the redwood forest of which we can say that the whole system is oriented to maximizing that variable and all other variables are subsidiary to it; and, indeed, the redwood forest works toward optima, not maxima. Its needs are satiable, and too much of anything is toxic.

There is, however, this: that the single purpose of A.A. is directed outward and is aimed at a noncompetitive relationship to the larger world. The variable to be maximized is a complementarity and is of the nature of "service" rather than dominance.

THE EPISTEMOLOGICAL STATUS OF COMPLEMENTARY AND SYMMETRICAL PREMISES

It was noted above that in human interaction, symmetry and complementarity may be complexly combined. It is therefore reasonable to ask how it is possible

---

[5] This was not originally an A.A. document and its authorship is unknown. Small variations in the text occur. I have quoted the form which I personally prefer (A.A. 1957, p. 196).

to regard these themes as so fundamental that they shall be called "epistemolog-ical," even in a natural history study of cultural and interpersonal premises.

The answer seems to hang upon what is meant by "fundamental" in such a study of man's natural history; and the word seems to carry two sorts of meaning.

First, I call *more fundamental* those premises which are the more deeply embedded in the mind, which are the more "hard programmed" and the less susceptible to change. In this sense, the symmetrical pride or hubris of the alcoholic is fundamental.

Second, I shall call more fundamental those premises of mind which refer to the larger rather than the smaller systems or gestalten of the universe. The proposition "grass is green" is less fundamental than the proposition "color differences make a difference."

But, if we ask about what happens when premises are changed, it becomes clear that these two definitions of the "fundamental" overlap to a very great extent. If a man achieves or suffers change in premises which are deeply embedded in his mind, he will surely find that the results of that change will ramify throughout his whole universe. Such changes we may well call "episte-mological."

The question then remains regarding what is epistemologically "right" and what is epistemologically "wrong." Is the change from alcoholic symmetrical "pride" to the A.A. species of complementarity a correction of his epistemology? And is complementarity *always* somehow better than symmetry?

For the A.A. member, it may well be true that complementarity is always to be preferred to symmetry and that even the trivial rivalry of a game of tennis or chess may be dangerous. The superficial episode may touch off the deeply embedded symmetrical premise. But this does not mean that tennis and chess propose epistemological error for everybody.

The ethical and philosophic problem really concerns only the widest universe and the deepest psychological levels. If we deeply and even uncon-sciously believe that our relation to the largest system which concerns us—the "Power greater than self"—is symmetrical and emulative, then we are in error.

LIMITATIONS OF THE HYPOTHESIS

Finally, the above analysis is subject to the following limitations and implica-tions:

1. It is not asserted that all alcoholics operate according to the logic which is here outlined. It is very possible that other types of alcoholics exist and almost certain that alcoholic addiction in other cultures will follow other lines.

2. It is not asserted that the way of Alcoholics Anonymous is the *only* way to live correctly or that their theology is the only correct derivation from the epistemology of cybernetics and systems theory.

3. It is not asserted that all transactions between human beings ought to be complementary, though it is clear that the relation between the individual and

the larger system of which he is a part must necessarily be so. Relations between persons will (I hope) always be complex.

4. It is, however, asserted that the non-alcoholic world has many lessons which it might learn from the epistemology of systems theory and from the ways of A.A. If we continue to operate in terms of a Cartesian dualism of mind *versus* matter, we shall probably also continue to see the world in terms of God *versus* man; elite *versus* people; chosen race *versus* others; nation *versus* nation; and man *versus* environment. It is doubtful whether a species having *both* an advanced technology *and* this strange way of looking at its world can endure.

REFERENCES

Alcoholics Anonymous (1939). *Alcoholics Anonymous*. New York: Works Publishing.

———— (1957). *Alcoholics Anonymous Comes of Age*. New York: Harper.

Bateson, G. (1936). *Naven*. Cambridge, England: Cambridge University Press.

———— (1942). Social planning and the concept of "deutero-learning." In *Conference on Science, Philosophy, and Religion. Second Symposium*. New York: Harper

———— (1946). The pattern of an armaments race — part I: an anthropological approach. *Bull Atomic Scientists* 2(5):10–11.

———— (1961). *Perceval's Narrative*. Stanford, CA: Stanford University Press.

———— (1963). A social scientist views the emotions. In *Expression of the Emotions in Man*, ed. P. Knapp. New York: International Universities Press.

———— (1969) Metalogue: What is an instinct? In *Approaches to Animal Communication*, ed. T. Sebeok. The Hague: Mouton.

Bateson, G. et al. (1956). Toward a theory of schizophrenia. *Behavioral Science* 1:251–264.

Collingwood, R. G. (1945). *The Idea of Nature*. Oxford, England: Oxford University Press.

Erikson, H. (1987). Configurations in play — clinical notes. *Psychoanal. Quart.* 6:139–214.

Lorenz, K. (1966). *On Aggression*. New York: Harcourt, Brace & World.

Richardson, L. F. (1939). Generalized foreign politics. *British J. Psychology*. Monogr. Supplements.

Ruesch, J., and Bateson, G. (1951). *Communication: The Social Matrix of Psychiatry*. New York: Norton.

Wenner-Gren Foundation (1968). Conference of the effects of conscious purpose on human adaptation. New York: Knopf.

24: "THE GIANT KILLER": DRINK & THE AMERICAN WRITER

Alfred Kazin

When drunk, I make them pay and pay and pay and pay.
—F. Scott Fitzgerald

America has always been a hard-drinking country despite the many places and times in which alcohol has been forbidden by law. Even in Puritan days Americans were amazingly hard drinkers. It is history that liquor up to the Civil War was cheap as well as plentiful. In the first decades of the 19th century, spirits cost all of 25 cents a gallon domestic, and $1 imported. From 1818 to 1862 there were no taxes whatever on American whiskey, and it took the federal government's needs of revenue during the Civil War to change things. The temperance movement, the Prohibitionist movement, the anti-Saloon League were all powerful church-supported bodies, but no more powerful than the "liquor interests" and the freedom and ease that American males acquired for a 4 cents glass of beer in the saloon. America's entry into World War I and the need to conserve grain finally put Prohibition across in 1918. Whereupon the line was marked between what H. L. Mencken called the "booboisie" and the party of sophistication. In the 20's, drinking was the most accessible form of prestige for would-be sophisticates; and this continued to be the case within the professional and wealthy classes as the "tea party" of the 20's became the cocktail party of the 50's (a time when the clientele of Alcoholics Anonymous showed a more representative cross-section of middle-class society than Congress).

But even by these heavy-drinking standards, there is something special about the drinking of so many American writers. Of course there have been famous literary drunks in other countries—Burns, Swinburne, Lionel Johnson, Ernest Dowson, Paul Verlaine, and those two fat boys, Dylan Thomas and Evelyn Waugh. The Russians, famous for knocking themselves out, have produced particularly lurid, despairing, melodramatic poet-drinkers like Sergei Yesenin (the husband of Isadora Duncan) who wrote his suicide note in his own blood. But in 20th-century America the booze has been not just a lifelong, "problem" and a killer. It has come to seem a natural accompaniment of the literary life—of its loneliness, its creative aspirations and its frenzies, its "specialness," its hazards in a society where values are constantly put in money terms.

In fact, though no one ever talks about it very much, booze has played as big a role in the lives of modern American writers as talent, money, women, and the longing to be top dog. Of the six American Nobel Prize winners in literature, three—Sinclair Lewis, Eugene O'Neill, William Faulkner—were alcoholics, compulsive drinkers, for great periods of their lives. Two others, Ernest Hemingway and John Steinbeck, were hard drinkers. Hemingway was also a lover of wine, regularly had champagne with lunch when he lived in Cuba, and (at least in warm climes) drank for pleasure rather than to knock himself out.

The list of American literary drunks is very long. And despite all the fun they must have had, the post-mortem record is full of woe. F. Scott Fitzgerald (dead at forty-four) and Ring Lardner (dead at forty-eight) were celebrated, dedicated, hopeless alcoholics. Hemingway used to say that a drink was a way of ending a day. But John O'Hara swore off at forty-eight only when he was rushed to a hospital at the point of death from a bleeding ulcer. "A hell of a way for booze to treat me after I've been so kind to it. I used to watch W. C. Fields putting away the martinis at Paramount, and say to myself, 'That's what I want to be when I get big.' Well, I almost made it."

Among the famous suicides, Jack London and John Berryman were alcoholics; Hart Crane had a problem. Poe, the only hard-case alcoholic among the leading 19th-century writers, finally died of drink one election day in Baltimore, 1849, when, already far gone and in total despair, he accepted all the whiskey that was his payment for being voted around the town by the corrupt political machine. Jack London wrote a fascinating account of his alcoholism in *John Barleycorn*. At first, he wrote, liquor seemed an escape from the narrowness of women's influence into "the wide free world of men." A wanderer, making his living from the sea, could always find a home in a saloon. But "suicide, quick or slow, a sudden spill or a gradual oozing away through the years, is the price John Barleycorn exacts. No friend of his ever escapes making the just, due payment."

As a sailor, London was sometimes drunk for three months at a time. Though he could never figure out just why he drank, he hauntingly described his death wish in one extraordinary passage. He had stumbled overboard, and, drunk, was swimming for his life in the Carquinez Strait in the Bay of San Francisco.

Some wandering fancy of going out with the tide suddenly obsessed me. I had never been morbid. Thoughts of suicide had never entered my head. And now that they entered, I thought it fine, a splendid culmination, a perfect rounding off of my short but exciting career. I who had never known girl's love, nor a woman's love, nor the love of children. . . . I decided that this was all, that I had seen all, lived all, been all, that was worthwhile, and that now was the time to cease. That was the trick of John Barleycorn, laying me by the heels of my imagination and a drug-dream dragging me to death.

J. P. Marquand, Wallace Stevens, e.e. cummings, and Edna St. Vincent Millay did not write about their "problem." Edwin Arlington Robinson, Dorothy Parker, Dashiell Hammett, Theodore Roethke, Edmund Wilson did write or talk about theirs. They were all serious drinkers, some more than others, some more openly than others. There is reason to believe that W. H. Auden, a big martini man, voluntarily or involuntarily did himself in by regularly (like Marilyn Monroe) mixing drink with sleeping pills. The Englishman Malcolm Lowry, who understandably felt part of the American scene (for he did his best work in and about North America), died in an acute state of alcoholic distress.

The high point of all-out drinking came in the 20's. F. Scott Fitzgerald said that he and his generation "drank cocktails before meals like Americans, wines and brandies like Frenchmen, scotch-and-soda like the English. This preposterous melange that was like a gigantic cocktail in a nightmare." Edmund Wilson in a "Lexicon of Prohibition" (1927) solemnly listed over a hundred words for drunkenness "now in common use in the United States. They have been arranged, as far as possible, in order of the degrees of intensity of the conditions which they represent, beginning with the mildest states and progressing to the more disastrous." The list began with *lit, squiffy, oiled*, and concluded with *to have the whoops and jingles* and *to burn with a low blue flame*.

In his notebook of the 20's, Wilson described himself as "daze-minded and daze-eyed" and sobering up only when he read about Sacco and Vanzetti. An editor at *Vanity Fair*, Helen Lawrenson, remembers "hair-raising rides in cars with drivers so pissed they couldn't tell the street from the sidewalk." Robert Benchley was usually so far gone that he no longer went to the plays he reviewed for the old *Life*. A delicious confusion of the senses operated in such key books of the 20's as *The Great Gatsby*. "Everything that happened has a dim, hazy cast over it. . . . Her laughter, her gestures, her assertions became more violently affected moment by moment, and as she expanded the room grew smaller around her, until she seemed to be revolving on a noisy, creaking pivot through the smoky air. . . ." "There was blue music from my neighbor's house through the summer nights. In his blue gardens men and girls came and went like moths among the whisperings and the champagne and the stars."

Despite all this gorgeous prose, the background of *The Great Gatsby* is raw alcohol. Gatsby made his pile as a bootlegger and then bought up side-street drugstores in Chicago that sold grain alcohol over the counter. And Fitzgerald's drunkenness, which gave such malicious satisfaction to Hemingway (who, with his overdeveloped competitive sense, knew that stopping in time would give him an advantage over "rummies" like Fitzgerald), was so involved in his need to be picturesque, to ease the money and sexual strains in his life, to keep up with his crazy wife Zelda, that only a writer of such powerful and desperate imagination could have taken it. Destructiveness and charm went hand in hand, all "the good times" and the most heart-sinking depression. A friend said about them: "If you want to get your furniture antiqued up, you want to get the Fitzgeralds in— they'll antique it up in a single night—why they'll put in their own wormholes in the furniture with cigarette ends."

Fitzgerald described his feeling about himself in the weakness of Dr. Dick Diver, the charming psychiatrist in *Tender Is the Night* who sold out and comforted himself more and more by taking two fingers of gin with his coffee. Writers are not the best analysts of their own alcoholism, but psychiatry (a notorious failure in curing compulsive drinkers) is not much better about pinpointing the reason why. The many thousands of personal confessions recited in AA meetings add up to the fact that the addict to alcohol, like the addict to anything else, believes that he can will a change within himself by ingesting some material substance. Like so many of the things we do to ourselves in this pill-happy culture, drinking is a form of technology. People drink for hereditary reasons, nutritional reasons, social reasons. They drink because they are bored, or tired, or restless. People drink for as many reasons as they have for wanting to "feel better." Drinking cuts the connections that keep us anxious. Alcohol works not as a stimulant but as a depressant. But it is exactly this "unwinding," relaxing, slowing-down, this breaking down of so many induced associations and inhibitions, that creates the welcome but temporary freedom from so many restraints, tensions, obligations. Civilization is a tyrant, "hell is other people," and we all need to escape the "ordeal of civility."

But there are periods and occasions when drinking is in the air, even seems to be a moral necessity. The 20's marked the great changeover from the old rural and small-town America. It also marked the triumph in the marketplace of "advanced," wholly "modern" writers and books, ideas, and attitudes. They all entered into the big money and the big time at once. The glamorous, best-selling, restlessly excited Fitzgeralds would never be reconciled to anything less. The Fitzgeralds' drinking began as a perpetual party. Then Zelda went off her rocker, the country went bust, *Tender Is the Night* was not a best-seller, Fitzgerald was writing for Hollywood. When he was doing *Gone with the Wind*, David Selznick fired Fitzgerald for not coming up with "funny" lines for Aunt Pittypat. Gavin Lambert reports that "being taken off the script was a disastrous blow to Fitzgerald's already shaky confidence. He resumed the long on-again-off-again drinking bout that led to his unrequited love affair with the movies. And between the drinking bouts and brief assignments on B pictures, he began *The Last Tycoon*."

Fitzgerald drunk was pleasanter to be with than Sinclair Lewis, who regularly passed out. One of the most serious drinkers in American history was Eugene O'Neill, who came from a family of serious drinkers. His brother Jamie was a confirmed alcoholic at twenty. His father, the famous actor James O'Neill, regularly had a cocktail before breakfast, and became so possessive about his liquor that he locked it up in the cellar out of the reach of his equally thirsty sons.

During his one stormy year at Princeton O'Neill once finished off a bottle of absinthe in a dormitory room reeking of burning incense. He went berserk, tore up all the furnishings in his room, and tried to shoot a friend. When the friend escaped and returned with help, they "found the place a shambles and O'Neill, wide-eyed, still on a rampage. It took all four of the other students to subdue him and tie him up." Later, say Barbara and Arthur Gelb in their biography, the slightest upset would send O'Neill to the bottle—and it did not matter what the bottle contained. He once drank a mixture of varnish and water; another time, camphor-flavored alcohol. Louis Sheaffer reports that while still a very young man, worried about his clandestine marriage to Kathleen Jenkins and the imminent birth of an unwanted child, O'Neill hacked up everything in his parents' hotel room in New York. O'Neill's mother (herself a drug addict) "never knew what to expect of him, whether childlike he would turn to her and James for comfort or present the face of a dark brooding stranger impossible to reach." Shortly after this, O'Neill attempted suicide by drinking veronal.

O'Neill claimed that "I never try to write a line when I'm not strictly on the wagon." But he was never able to stay off the booze completely in the crucial twenty years 1913–33, during which he became the most significant playwright America had ever had. It was, however, in the succeeding twenty years (he died in 1953), a dry period by the direst necessity (he had Parkinson's disease), that he wrote his best five plays—*Ah, Wilderness!, A Touch of the Poet, More Stately Mansions, A Moon for the Misbegotten, Long Day's Journey into Night.*

The most boldly determined, all-out, to-hell-with-the-consequences literary soak of the 20's was Ring Lardner. He appears as Abe North in *Tender Is the Night*, a tall, morosely witty, perpetually disoriented creature getting drunk in the Ritz bar in Paris at nine in the morning. Poor Abe, witty yet lost. "Presently he was invited to lunch, but declined. It was almost Briglith, he explained, and there was something he had to do at Briglith. A little later, with the exquisite manners of the alcoholic that are like the manners of a prisoner or a family servant, he said goodbye to an acquaintance, and turning around discovered that the bar's great moment was over as precipitately as it had begun." After an involved fracas in a Paris hotel, Abe says to Dick Diver, "Could I annoy you for a drink?" "There's not a thing up here," Dick lied.

> Resignedly Abe shook hands with Rosemary; he composed his face slowly, holding her hand a long time and forming sentences that did not emerge. She laughed in a well-bred way, as though it were nothing unusual to watch a man walking in a slow dream. Often people display a curious respect for a man drunk, rather like the respect of simple races for the insane. Respect rather than fear. There is something awe-inspiring in one who has lost all inhibitions, who will do anything. Of course we make him pay for his moment of superiority, his moment of impressiveness.

The real Ring Lardner, almost ten years older than Fitzgerald, was much funnier than Abe North. "How do you look when I'm sober?" he once said to a flamboyant actor. But he was just as determined to drink himself to death. And he did. The inoperable final "Why?" haunts us particularly in his case. He came from a sturdy, cultivated Midwest family, was deeply in love with his wife, raised four remarkable sons. It was because Lardner had been "brought up right" that he became fascinated by what illiterate ball players did to the language. Ring Jr. reports his father saying — "Where do they get that stuff about my being a satirist? I just listen." Looking a little like Buster Keaton, sad-faced and quiet except when he had something to say right on target, old-looking enough in his teens to fool saloon keepers, Lardner was from his teens in Niles, Michigan, a citizen of saloon society. There (before Prohibition) a man could be quiet with himself, drink to his heart's content, and listen. Lardner's mother thought Lardner and his brothers (fellow soaks) were putting in extra hours at choir practice.

Lardner was an amazing drinker, a real hard case, even before he was transformed from a journalistic funny man to a literary figure. "I have a reputation — an unfortunate one — for infinite capacity." Living near each other in Great Neck (where Gatsby had his dream house), he and Fitzgerald, easily amused by each other's jokes and each other's alcoholism, would sometimes drink through the night. Ring would not go home on a weekday morning until his sons had left for school. Lardner had greater capacity than Fitzgerald and maintained his physical coordination when drunk for many more years than Fitzgerald did. But Ring Jr., the only living witness, thinks that "Scott may have been fascinated by Ring as the image of his own future; even though he could sleep off a drunk and get back to work with much more ease than his older friend, he must have known that he was heading in the same direction. . . .Even the pattern he came to of setting a specific beginning and ending date for going on the wagon was Ring's."

With a large family to support, Lardner pragmatically set himself a fixed period of abstinence and a fixed quota of work to accomplish in it. Despite the legends of his knocking out a story under the influence of a quart or so, he told his son: "No one, ever, wrote anything as well even after one drink as he would have done without it." But once the allotted work was finished, Lardner just as determinedly went back to the bottle. He had once thought of Prohibition as an enforced solution to his problem, but he soon saw this was an unattainable goal. He told the actress Jean Dixon that if he smelled beer he would drink it and when he drank it he would go on to something else. He went on bats for three months at a time. He knew exactly what he was doing — and could have himself written the decisive "first step" of AA's famous "twelve steps" that an alcoholic must go through in order to recover: "We admitted that we were powerless over alcohol — that out lives had become unmanageable." After Lardner's death in 1933, Fitzgerald wrote: "One is haunted not only by a sense of personal loss but by a conviction that Ring got less percentage of himself on paper than any other American author of the first flight."

Alcoholics, like other prodigies, begin young. Faulkner, always a crazy reckless drinker, came from a family of reckless drinkers. His father and grandfather were known for sprees, and would be taken off at regular intervals to the Keeley Institute, fifteen miles from Memphis, for the "cure." He himself was introduced to liquor by this same grandfather who let him taste the "heeltaps" left over in a glass from toddies. On the famous hunting trips, a necessary retreat for the men, when a drinking bout might go on for three or four days. Faulkner drank the powerful corn liquor made in illegal stills concealed in the hills and pine barrens. At eighteen, Faulkner drank in town with the town drunk. At twenty, he tried to get into World War I by joining the Royal Canadian Flying Corps, but cracked up in a training plane—in which he kept a crock of bourbon. When Prohibition descended upon the land, Faulkner showed ingenuity as well as determination. He drank white mule made by county moonshiners, clear corn liquor in the dice joints, and frequented Memphis brothels because they had a better variety of whiskey. He even did a little bootlegging and "rum-running" in order to make some money. Even when forced to work for a spell in the local post office (he quit because he was at the mercy of "every son of a bitch with a two-cent stamp"), Faulkner was able to console himself with a bottle of "white lightning." He is remembered for saying: "There is no such thing as bad whiskey, some are just better than others."

Faulkner was a social drinker, a private drinker, a convivial drinker, a morose drinker. He drank because it was a habit in the Deep South for men to drink. He drank to ease himself and to knock himself out as a result of the screaming exhaustion—"I feel as though all my nerve ends were exposed"—that came after the tension of writing *The Sound and the Fury*. After finishing this great book, he said to a friend, "Read this. It's a real son of a bitch," and went on a tear for several days without eating. His compulsive drinking regularly led to one or two serious illnesses a year for thirty years. Some of the side experiences were alcoholic exhaustion, DT's, whiskey ulcers, electroshock therapy, the many nicks and gashes in his head, broken ribs, falling down stairs, falls from horses, broken vertebrae, sweats, shakes, organic damage, fibrillation, blackouts.

He sometimes (and probably more and more) drank while writing. When he lived in Greenwich Village at one period, he wrote in small pocket notebooks he bought at Woolworth's for a nickel—occasionally sipping gin as he wrote. Faulkner did not drink in order to *start* writing. He may have been repressed as a man, but certainly not as a writer. "You just keep the words coming," he said. Like so many great novelists, he was productive because his mind kept everything he had seen, heard, lived. As a man he seems to have found existence intolerable from time to time. Who can say just why? But although he could do anything he liked with words, his "drinking habit" inflamed and spoiled his writing as much as it damaged his body.

Of course writing, for Faulkner, was already a form of intoxication. But the insensately long sentences that he went in for suggest the abandon that so often comes to a drinker as the "connections that make up anxiety" are broken off. But it is just connections that make writing—the line-by-line thinking that the writer undergoes so that the reader will see what is in the writer's mind. It was disastrous for Faulkner to lose the thread. After the period 1929–36 in which he composed all his greatest works— *The Sound and the Fury, Light in August, As I Lay Dying, Absalom! Absalom!*—Faulkner wrote windy books like *Intruder in the Dust, Requiem for a Nun, A Fable, The Town*. Donald Newlove has put it more harshly than anyone else:

Something disastrous happened when Faulkner turned forty-nine; whatever grip he had on his alcoholism faded, and so did the hot focus of his imagination. He wrote for twenty-two years, but his brain was stunned. What we get is the famous mannered diction, senatorial tone, a hallucinated rhetoric of alcohol full of ravishing if empty glory. Dead junk compared to the sunburst pages of *The Sound and the Fury*. . . . Faulkner's ruinous pose as a master of Latinate diction is the direct result of alcoholic hardening of the ego. . . .

After the 20's, later writers like John O'Hara and John Steinbeck did their best to keep up with the careless drinking style they had learned as young men in the 20's. But there was a notable lack of joy. O'Hara as a reporter had been known as a saloon fighter. When he went off the booze, totally, to save his life, he admitted that he still missed scotch and beer. He made up for it by working all through the night, night after night. He wrote so many stories that he virtually ran out of titles, and he made so much money that he boasted that no one anywhere — wanna bet? — had *ever* written short stories as well as John O'Hara. O'Hara sober was just as truculent as O'Hara drunk. Hemingway said that he could beat Tolstoy. O'Hara went after younger writers.

In Algeria during World War II André Gide heard that Steinbeck was in town as a war correspondent and tried to meet him. But Steinbeck was always drunk. Gide told Malcolm Muggeridge that he had tried in the evening, at lunch time, and finally at breakfast, but always with the same result. Dashiell Hammett, whom Lillian Hellman lovingly portrays as a Southern gentleman extraordinarily rational, resourceful, self-possessed, and informed, grimly drank himself into insensibility at regular intervals. Thomas Wolfe amazed Fitzgerald by his ability to keep things in an uproar. One night, when they were having an argument in the street, Wolfe gesticulated so vehemently that he struck a power line support, snapped the wire, and plunged the whole community into darkness. Bernard De Voto, like so many writer-drinkers of the second order, gave the impression of imitating more illustrious writers. He was a martini snob even more tiresome than the usual wine snob. Gancia was the only vermouth to mix with gin; Noilly Prat was too changeable.

Malcolm Lowry would have been shocked by all this twaddle. Lowry, one of the most stupendous drinkers in all recorded history, wrote the greatest novel I know about an alcoholic, *Under the Volcano* (1947). There is nothing like it in modern literature. It is one of the great 20th-century novels in language, form, and in its amazing visionary demonstration of the tie between the alcoholic hero's crumbling life in the 1930's and the disasters about to fall on the Western world. Geoffrey Firmin, a former British consul in Mexico, always called "the Consul," drinks anything, drinks all the time, drinks as a way of life, drinks as a way of living and dying at once. His final collapse and his murder at the hands of fascist thugs take place on a single day in 1939, "The Day of the Dead." The deadly atmosphere that has collected around the helpless Consul finally becomes a signal that the Western world is sliding into war. *Under the Volcano* could have been achieved only by an imagination that already had the qualities of drunkenness. Lowry's imagination was made more itself by drink. Then he died of it, probably feeling that it had all been worth it.

The best-known drinker of my own literary generation was the poet John Berryman (1924–72). Berryman was a natural celebrity. Poets often are, for their personality and their works seem so much of a piece. The language of a good poem is so close to fundamental emotion, to the secrets of the human heart, that the poet is traditionally honored as a prophet among men. Flamboyant poets convinced of their importance make messes in public, delight their humble students, the literary gossips, the jealous psychiatrists (who also deal in the language of emotion, but not so memorably), and get a reputation for genius based on the disorderliness of poets from François Villon to Dylan Thomas. The poet Theodore Roethke wrote a very subdued, miniature poetry about his "lost childhood." But he was an enormous hulking fellow with violent personal emotions, and a heavy drinker's gift for asserting himself loudly in public. He regularly put on such a show that it was easier to cheer big Ted Roethke on than to admit that his poems were slight, sometimes inaudible experiments in self-pity.

But of the American poets, it was Berryman who made more literary capital out of his "problem" than anyone since Lowry. Liquor made Berryman more and more special to himself—and famous. He would not have become so famous without it. Berryman was pictured by the caricaturist David Levine with an enormous bottle down his back. It is typical of his celebrity as a boozer that while he was still known mostly to a small literary audience, he was given a big story in *Life* that showed him and his enormous beard convivial in an Irish pub. After he killed himself in the winter of 1972 by jumping from a bridge off Minneapolis onto the frozen Mississippi, his unfinished novel about the "cure," *Recovery*, was published, followed by a novel, *The Maze*, by his ex-wife Eileen Simpson.

Despite his furious drinking, Berryman doggedly pursued his career. He published ten books of poetry and a brilliant critical biography of Stephen Crane. His most famous work, because it is the most personal, is the 308 "Dream Songs"—monologues "about an imaginary character (not the poet, not me) named Henry, a white American in early middle age sometimes in blackface, who has suffered an irreversible loss and talks about himself sometimes in the first person, sometimes in the third, sometimes even in the second; he has a friend, never named, who addresses him as Mr. Bones and variants thereof. . . . *Requiescat in pace*. . . ."

Of course "Henry" is "not the poet, not me"—there were too many Berrymans. What is most striking about these poems is the crossing of so many selves. Only a white man in "blackface" could suggest the layer on layer of disguise and personality that went to make John Berryman! The poems are a fantastic performance in the many voices forever buzzing in John Berryman's mind—the voices of himself as teacher and writer, of his supposed accusers, of the longing to see an end to his self-torturing confabulations with himself, of his dead father and of himself as a father who does not see his own son.

The jauntiness of tone that Berryman brought to his sorrows!

I'm scared a lonely. Never see my son,
easy be not to see anyone,

* * *

I'm scared a only one thing, which is me,
from othering I don't take nothing, see,
    for my hound dog's sake
But this is where I livin, where I rake
my leaves and cop my promise, this' where we
cry oursel's awake.

In another "Dream Song" he asks:

Why drink so, two days running?
two months, O season, years, two decades running?
I answer (smiles) my question on the cuff:
Man, I been thirsty. . . .

Berryman was "authoritative," cocky, even at his lowest. Snooty, heartbreaking, maudlin, clearly written under booze, quick to portray every side of the divided self that emerges under booze, these poems are the human heart's rushed shorthand. They are also in Berryman's most maddeningly allusive style. You have to know a lot about Berryman's friends, girls, most secret worries, and especially his relations with the best poets dead and alive to know what he is referring to more than half the time. The poems are shockingly alive in their emotional distress and in the poet's determination to keep things *looking* good. Disconnected on purpose, disconnected by necessity, abrupt, brilliant at times, and just as often throwaway, the poems are obsessive about the need to move on, to get out of difficulties, to move out of this world if finally necessary. This is what makes Berryman's stuff finally so compelling. The life and the book are one. The force of his personality (not of the poems in themselves) is overwhelming.

What explains all this excessive, delirious, and often fatal drinking? Hemingway had a theory about it. He called booze "the Giant Killer," and he could have added that the Giant is America itself, or rather the "bitch-goddess" Success which William James said was the great American deity. The history of American writers even in the 19th century was already marked by unnatural strain, physical isolation, alienation from the supposedly "sweet and smiling aspects of American life." But it is significant that the only known literary alcoholic of the period was Poe, a magazine writer and editor of genius always desperate for money, who helped to swell the marketplace psychology among American writers. And it was just when that psychology became rampant, as in the 20's the big money and the big time began to seem possible for serious and "advanced" writers, that the really big drinkers emerged.

There were no such "rebels" (in their own eyes) as those in the literary class. They were "different" from "ordinary" Americans because they lived by their wits. They had been around, they knew things. In a "Memoir of the Drinking

Life," Pete Hamill shows what an assist to your fantasies of being Hemingway, of knowing things, it can be to drink:

> For a writer, the life was particularly attractive. I learned a lot of things in saloons: about my craft, human beings, about myself. . . . We drank in all the bars of Brooklyn, and later in McSorleys, and the old Cedar Tavern (looking at Franz Kline and Jackson Pollock), and the White Horse (looking for Dylan Thomas), and a lot of other places. . . .Drink was the great loosener, the killer of shyness, the maker of dreams and courage. . . .

But in fact the literary rebels always yearned for success as much as any benighted Babbitt. Only in America have first-class novelists been driven to "prove" their acceptability by also becoming best-sellers. Even poetry has to sell, or at least make you famous. Berryman, for example, who worshipped other famous writers in America and knew all about them, was generally disappointed in himself. He wanted fame so badly that he was always hard on himself. He was far from being modest. Of course he had non-literary sorrows. His father was a suicide and probably an alcoholic. Berryman went through all the instability, hysteria, hypochondria, the broken marriages, the "bad sex," the blackouts that are indissolubly the causes and effects of excessive drinking. But fundamentally he was driven by competition with other poets and was determined to outdo them.

It was, then, the drive for success of every kind, the hunger for prestige, fame, and money, that drove all these writers to drink: the burden put upon the creative self by so many contradictory pressures was overwhelming and cried out for relief. They drank to escape the hunger; they drank to disguise it from themselves and others; they drank to be different from the unsophisticated "booboisie"; they drank to be the same as the "regular fellers"; they drank to acquire class. In one form or another the Giant exacted a final sacrifice— themselves—from the writers who tried to kill their Great Fear over and over again.

25: SELF DEFICITS AND ADDICTION

Heinz Kohut

The explanatory power of the new psychology of the self is nowhere as evident as with regard to these four types of psychological disturbance: (1) the narcissistic personality disorders, (2) the perversions, (3) the delinquencies, and (4) the addictions. Why can these seemingly disparate conditions be examined so fruitfully with the aid of the same conceptual framework? Why can all these widely differing and even contrasting symptom pictures be comprehended when seen from the viewpoint of the psychology of the self? How, in other words, are these four conditions related to each other? What do they have in common, despite the fact that they exhibit widely differing, and even contrasting, symptomatologies? The answer to these questions is simple: in all of these disorders the afflicted individual suffers from a central weakness, from a weakness in the core of his personality. He suffers from the consequences of a defect in the self. The symptoms of these disorders, whether comparatively hazy or hidden, or whether more distinct and conspicuous, arise secondarily as an outgrowth of a defect in the self. The manifestations of these disorders become intelligible if we call to mind that they are all attempts — unsuccessful attempts, it must be stressed — to remedy the central defect in the personality.

The narcissistically disturbed individual yearns for praise and approval or for a merger with an idealized supportive other because he cannot sufficiently supply himself with self-approval or with a sense of strength through his own inner resources. The pervert is driven toward sexual enactments with figures or symbols that give him the feeling of being wanted, real, alive, or powerful. The delinquent repeats over and over again certain acts through which he demonstrates to himself an escape from the realization that he feels devoid of sustaining self-confidence and of sustaining ideals. And the addict, finally, craves the drug because the drug seems to him to be capable of curing the central defect in his self. It becomes for him the substitute for a self-object which failed him traumatically at a time when he should still have had the feeling of omnipotently controlling its responses in accordance with his needs as if it were a part of himself. By ingesting the drug he symbolically compels the mirroring self-object to soothe him, to accept him. Or he symbolically compels the idealized self-object to submit to his merging into it and thus to his partaking in its magical power. In either case the ingestion of the drug provides him with the self-esteem which he does not possess. Through the incorporation of the drug he supplies for himself the feeling of being accepted and thus of being self-confident; or he creates the experience of being merged with a source of power that gives him the feeling of being strong and worthwhile. And all these effects of the drug tend to increase his feeling of being alive, tend to increase his certainty that he exists in this world.

It is the tragedy of all these attempts at self-cure that the solutions which they provide are impermanent, that in essence they cannot succeed. The praise which the narcissistically disturbed individual is able to evoke, the mergers with idealized others which he brings about, the sexualized reassurances which the pervert procures for himself, the loudly proclaimed assertion of omnipotence forever repeated through his actions by the delinquent—they all give only fleeting relief. They are repeated again and again without producing the cure of the basic psychological malady. And the calming or the stimulating effect which the addict obtains from the drug is similarly impermanent. Whatever the chemical nature of the substance that is employed, however frequently repeated its consumption, however cleverly rationalized or mythologized its ingestion with the support from others who are similarly afflicted—no psychic structure is built; the defect in the self remains. It is as if a person with a wide open gastric fistula were trying to still his hunger through eating. He may obtain pleasurable taste sensations by his frantic ingestion of food but, since the food does not enter that part of the digestive system where it is absorbed into the organism, he continues to starve.

The enriching effect of the insights supplied by the psychology of the self upon the data obtained within different psychological frames of reference can be demonstrated with special clarity with regard to the examination of the family background, of the childhood situation of the future addict. It is evidently of great importance in the present context to determine certain details concerning the behavior of the addict's parents when he was a child. We might ask, for example, whether they had been lenient or strict, or whether their identities (e.g., as male and female, or, occupationally, the mother as a housewife, the father as a truckdriver, etc.) were hazy or well defined. Yet, having obtained the answer to these and similar questions, we will look at the significance of the sociopsychological data concerning parental behavior with different eyes when we examine them against the background of our knowledge concerning the factors that contribute to the child's ability to build up a strong and cohesive self and, in the obverse, concerning the factors that stand in the way of this crucial developmental task.

Just as we know, from the point of view of the physiologist, that a child needs to be given certain foods, that he needs to be protected against extreme temperatures, and that the atmosphere he breathes has to contain sufficient oxygen, if his body is to become strong and resilient, so do we also know, from the point of view of the depth-psychologist, that he requires an empathic environment — specifically, an environment that responds (a) to his need to have his presence confirmed by the glow of parental pleasure and (b) to his need to merge into the reassuring calmness of the powerful adult — if he is to acquire a firm and resilient self. It is not enough to obtain answers to questions such as whether the mother's attitude toward toilet training is strict or lenient, for example, or whether the father's work-identity is clearly defined or not. The crucial question concerns the adequacy or inadequacy of the parents as the self-objects of the child, that is, the adequacy or inadequacy of the parents at a time when they are still performing for the child the psychological functions of self-esteem regulation which the child should later be able to perform on his own, the adequacy or inadequacy of the parents at a time, in other words, when the child still experiences them predominantly as extensions of himself or experiences himself still predominantly as part of their strength. The crucial question then is whether the parents are able to reflect with approval at least some of the child's proudly exhibited attributes and functions, whether they are able to respond with genuine enjoyment to his budding skills, whether they are able to remain in touch with him throughout his trials and errors. And, furthermore, we must determine whether they are able to provide the child with a reliable embodiment of calmness and strength into which he can merge and with a focus for his need to find a target for his admiration. Or, stated in the obverse, it will be of crucial importance to ascertain the fact that a child could find neither confirmation of his own worthwhileness nor a target for a merger with the idealized strength of the parent and that he, therefore, remained deprived of the opportunity for the gradual transformation of these external sources of narcissistic sustenance into endopsychic resources, that is, specifically into sustaining self-esteem and into a sustaining relationship to internal ideals. Thus, in asking the crucial question concerning the factors in childhood which lead to the addiction-prone personality, we will say that, in the last analysis, and within certain limits, it is less important to determine what the parents do than what they are.

26: ALCOHOLICS ANONYMOUS AND CONTEMPORARY PSYCHODYNAMIC THEORY

Edward J. Khantzian and John E. Mack

> After a successful psychoanalytic treatment a patient is definitely less neurotic (or psychotic) but perhaps not necessarily more mature. On the other hand after a successful treatment by group methods the patient is not necessarily less neurotic but inevitably more mature.
>
> —Enid and Michael Balint (1972)

INTRODUCTION

Alcoholism is a devastating illness, eroding every aspect of a person's physical, psychological, and social being. The chronic, unrelenting, yet seemingly self-elected course of alcoholism is so extreme that until recently it caused most people to consider it a hopeless moral or criminal condition. However, over the past 50 years the growing popularity and the success of a natural experiment of extraordinary proportions have proven that alcoholism is a condition that is preeminently responsive to the caring intervention of others. We are referring, of course, to Alcoholics Anonymous (AA), a self-help group that provides in special and effective ways an ongoing source of hope, support, and restoration.

Many of the strongest proponents of AA are recovering alcoholics who have benefited from "keeping it simple and pragmatic." As a consequence, there has been an unfortunate tendency to reduce and explain the basis of AA's success to its ability to instill and maintain abstinence and in providing a community of others who are understanding because they know the ravages of the illness and know the practical and necessary "steps" it takes to get better. That is, AA removes the "sufficient and necessary cause" (Vaillant 1983), the alcohol, from a person's life and replaces it with the support and comfort of AA. As simple and true as they may be, it is our contention that beyond achieving abstinence and providing support, AA is effective because it is a sophisticated psychological treatment whose members have learned to manage effectively and/or transform the psychological and behavioral vulnerabilities associated with alcoholism.

Beyond oversimplifying the basis of its success, one of the by-products of AA has been a corresponding tendency to minimize and eschew the psychological dimensions of alcoholism and to argue that alcoholism causes rather than is caused by psychopathology (Vaillant 1983). Although recent, careful diagnostic studies have produced findings to support both possibilities (Hesselbrock, et al., Schuckit 1985), the emphasis on either–or arguments about etiological links between psychopathology and alcoholism are unfortunate, counterproductive, and defy resolution at this time. In our opinion, a more fruitful line of inquiry is provided if we can explore and try to understand how alcohol, a powerful emotion-altering drug, interacts with a person's emotions and the mental structures and functions that govern and regulate a person's life to make reliance on this substance so compelling. In contrast to earlier psychodynamic formulations that laid heavy emphasis on unconscious pleasurable and destructive instincts and the symbolic meanings of alcohol, modern theorists have placed affects (i.e., feelings) and problems in self-regulation and self-governance at the core of alcoholics' vulnerabilities (Khantzian 1981, Krystal and Raskin 1970, Mack 1981, Wurmser 1974). Approached in this way, reductionistic explanations and either–or arguments about psychopathology and alcoholism can be avoided and, instead, alcoholics' suffering can be better appreciated as a complex interaction between an alcoholic's experience and expression of affect and the nature and quality of their psychological capacities to govern their affects and their lives. Accordingly, the focus and emphasis in contemporary psychodynamic approaches have been on understanding more empathically how alcoholics experience and express feelings, the quality of their self- and object relations, their capacity for self-care, and how these factors interact with the meaning and effects of alcohol.

Alcoholics Anonymous, in common with group therapy, responds to an individual's need for acceptance and sharing to overcome the sense of alienation and shame entailed in a disorder that is so disabling and in which one has lost so much control of his or her life. Like effective group therapies, AA also instills hope, contact, and a climate of mutual concern that provides a basis to regain control of one's life. The encouragement in AA of openness, self-disclosure, an insistence that one cannot get better on one's own, and the repeated emphasis on shared experiences strikes at the core issues of self-regulation and self-care involved in alcoholism as a "multiperson" psychology. In this chapter we will examine AA as a special kind of group experience that provides a context for examination, containment, and/or repair of core vulnerabilities involving affects, self-regulation, and self-governance.

SELF-GOVERNANCE AND AA

Ernst Simmel (1948) was one of the first psychoanalysts to concern himself with AA. In his work he speculated on how the group psychology of AA might therapeutically influence intrapsychic factors that contribute to the impulse to drink. He believed that the therapeutic benefits of AA were consistent with "psychoanalytic findings," namely, that AA countered through mass psychology the impulses deriving from the latent, overpowering drives with which alcoholics live. In posthumously published notes he discussed how group dynamics, the community, and religion influence ego structures, and he concluded with the hope that psychoanalysts and AA might collaborate to unravel and resolve the dangers of alcoholism.

The concept of self-governance, introduced by Mack (1981) to underscore the self–other context of self-regulation, represents one attempt to further such a psychoanalytic understanding of alcoholism, particularly the nature of the impulses involved in drinking and how the group dynamics of AA operate to effectively control and transform the impulses:

> *Self-governance* has to do with that aspect or the ego of self which is, in actuality or potentiality, in charge of the personality. Self-governance is a supraordinate function, or group of functions, in the ego system. It is concerned with choosing or deciding, with directing and controlling. The functions of self-governance are similar to what . . . [has been called] . . . ego executant functions (Henrick 1943). But "executant functioning" connotes a solitary operation of the ego, while "self-governance" is a psycho-social term, intended to leave room for the participation of others in the governance of the individual. Self-governance as a theoretical concept is intended, unlike ego executant functioning, to allow for the sharing of control or responsibility with other individuals or groups. It acknowledges the essential interdependence of the self and others. . . .
>
> There are many situations in which self-governance is impaired — manic and schizophrenic psychoses and aggressive impulse disorder are obvious examples. The disorders of substance abuse in general and alcoholism in particular offer other striking examples of such impairment. The powerlessness which the alcoholic experiences in relation to alcohol reflects an impairment of self-governance with respect to the management of this substance. It has not been ascertained whether this powerlessness is specific to the drive to drink or is experienced by alcoholics in relation to certain other strong impulses as well. In the A.A. approach acknowledgement and acceptance of this powerlessness are the first steps in the path to recovery ("We admitted we were powerless over alcohol — that our lives had become unmanageable"). [pp. 132–133]

The ability to govern oneself is a highly prized capacity. To admit that one is unable to manage one's life, especially the use of alcohol, an accepted and integral part of our culture, represents a major and often inadmissible defeat. Although admittedly there are degrees to which people lose control of their alcohol use, it is clear that those who need to struggle to maintain it are either unable to do so, or are plagued with conflict, self-doubt, and shame. Although debates continue about whether some alcoholics can resume controlled drinking, and whether some alcohol-abusing individuals on the benign end of the spectrum of alcohol excess achieve it, most of the accumulating evidence suggests that a goal of controlled drinking for most, if not all, alcoholics (i.e., those who have lost control of their lives — medically, socially, or legally — as a consequence of heavy, frequent alcohol use) is inadvisable or undoable (Helzer et al. 1985).

The "12-step" tradition (Alcoholics Anonymous 1955) provides an alcoholic with practical tools, suggestions, guiding slogans, and an expanding network of relationships (e.g., participants repeatedly hear the triad slogan, "Don't pick up, go to meetings and ask for help") that help to establish a growing capacity to control his impulse to drink. Alcoholics Anonymous is successful because of its intuitive grasp of the complexities of the biological and psychosocial nature of self-governance, not only in relation to alcohol, but far more pervasively in relation to the conduct of one's life in general. The organization appreciates and underscores that "the self never functions as a solitary entity" (Mack 1981, p. 134). In fantasy or action the self is always participating with others—other people, the family, the neighborhood, and social, religious, ethnic, or national groups—as part of one's existence and development. In this respect the self is a composite structure and an ongoing process, reflecting the interaction with the qualities, values, and norms of the individuals and groups in a person's life. Alcoholics Anonymous capitalizes on this process, recognizing that certain group activities and processes profoundly influence a person's capacity to govern himself, often far more than is possible in an individual psychotherapeutic relationship, and still more so when it occurs in a context of religious experience and values (Mack 1981). Bales (1944) was probably referring to this aspect of AA when he stated, "There is a certain type of control within the individual personality which can have its source only 'outside of the self'—for practical purposes, in the moral principles advocated by a closely knit solidarity group—and can only be internalized and made effective against self-centered, satisfaction-directed impulses by an involuntary feeling of belongingness and allegiance to such a group, i.e., a 'moral community'" (p. 276).

It is little wonder, then, that psychiatric patients outside the AA program often express both envy and a wish to belong, as Bales suggests, when they witness the hope, support, and enthusiasm that its participants derive and reflect. It also partly explains how a patient diagnosed as borderline personality and suffering from the inability to control her emotions, relationships, and behavior exaggerated her alcohol symptoms to justify pursuing the beneficial containing, comforting, and restoring aspects of AA. In this regard, the benefits that alcoholics derive from AA in controlling their alcoholism probably have implications clinically and theoretically for others who suffer from an inability to regulate their emotions and behavior as a consequence of experiencing an injured sense of self (Mack 1981).

AA, NARCISSISM, AND SELF PSYCHOLOGY

Psychoanalysis is both a method of treatment and a theory of mental life. When Sigmund Freud first discovered and described his treatment methods, he emphasized instinctual factors (i.e., pleasurable and aggressive drives) and a topographic view of the mind in which many psychic processes were seen as unconscious. Freud and his followers subsequently modified their approach by placing greater emphasis on internal, subjective processes and states (e.g., affects, attitudes, needs, etc.) and structural factors and functions responsible for controlling and regulating one's internal psychic life and adjustment to external reality. Whereas early psychodynamic formulations of mental life and its aberrations (including alcoholism) placed heavy emphasis on drives and the unconscious, more recent approaches stress the importance of affects and ego and self structures in appreciating the unique subjective and observable aspects of how individuals are organized internally and how they adapt to their environment. It is in the context of these developments in psychoanalytic theory that the contemporary psychodynamic view of alcoholism leads us to consider vulnerabilities and deficits in affect management, the sense of self, and the ego in order to understand alcoholics' suffering and decompensations.

Character Formation, "Character Defects," and AA

By the time an individual reaches late adolescence and early adulthood, he or she possesses the capacity to manage emotions, relationships, and behavior with relative success, albeit in ways that are unique to the individual, that is, there are characteristic qualities in a person that set a predictable affective tone and behavioral pattern in that individual. For example, a person may be gloomy versus cheerful, or active and outgoing versus passive and reticent, or expressive versus restrained. Traditionally, in psychodynamic theory we have spoken of this aspect of a person's unique makeup as his or her "personality style" or "personality organization." More precisely, the mental structures and functions determining personality are a reflection of our ego capacities and sense of self. Their development begins in infancy and evolves over a lifetime, incorporating attitudes and functions primarily of our parents and, subsequently, other persons and groups with whom there is significant contact, relationship, and meaning. To the extent that the growing-up environment is optimally nurturing, constant, and relatively free of major trauma and neglect, ego functions and the sense of self coalesce to give us a mature and adaptable character structure. Conversely, major flaws, defects, and distortions develop in a person's character structure as a function of environmental deprivation, inconstancy, trauma, and neglect. These are the flaws to which AA refers when it speaks of "character defects" in alcoholics.

The salient "defects" that AA targets so successfully have probably been recognized or identified over its 50-year history out of the experience and the intuitions of its founders and members, and its insistence on the simple and pragmatic, discarding what is unusable and retaining what has worked. As with psychotherapy in general, AA as a treatment modality for alcoholism has general and specific therapeutic actions. Some elements act to provide symptom reduction and containment; other elements of the AA approach are more "curative," seeking to alter the characterologic determinants of the condition. Many in AA, especially some of the older "veteran" members, argue that they benefit simply from the removal of alcohol associations, "keeping it simple," and from the provision of a supportive, social(izing) group committed to abstinence. These supportive elements are often sufficient to explain the benefits of AA.

However, we also believe that the curative aspects of AA are probably operative in these cases as well, but in more subtle and less apparent ways.

Obviously the most immediate, general benefit of AA is not at all subtle. AA succeeds in getting people to *stop* drinking. It is demonstrably effective in setting a limit on the most destructive behavior, the drinking itself. However, what it does even more successfully by addressing the psychological underpinnings of alcoholism (i.e., the "defects of character") is to prevent the resumption of drinking. This is the aspect with which we will concern ourselves primarily in this discussion.

Bean (1975, 1981) and, more recently, Brown (1985) and others (*Alcoholics Anonymous* 1978, Bales 1944, Bean 1975, 1981, Brown 1985, Leach 1973, Leach et al. 1969, Stewart 1955, Tiebout 1943–1944, 1961, Trice 1957, Zinberg 1977) extensively reviewed the history, organization, and procedures of AA and its effectiveness in establishing abstinence and recovery as a process. Bean's focus on how AA successfully challenges alcoholics' denial and Brown's emphasis on AA's successful management and pursuit of the dynamics of alcoholics' loss of control and the importance of maintaining an identity as an alcoholic, provide important and valuable insights into the group dynamics of AA and the recovery process. We also would stress the importance and centrality of abstinence and the focus on loss of control. We do not dispute the social, biological and hereditary aspects of alcoholism, and a unified theory must ultimately consider how all these aspects of alcoholism interact with psychodynamic forces. In our view important psychodynamic aspects of alcoholism have been much neglected. Recent advances in psychoanalytic theory and practice provide a better basis for understanding the psychological factors that initiate and end bouts of drinking, maintain sobriety, and predispose individuals to becoming alcoholic (Mack 1981). These are areas that deserve attention and a psychodynamic perspective can significantly add to our understanding and enable us to help alcoholics overcome their resistance to AA and other treatments that may be helpful.

Beyond the support and containment that AA provides, AA works because it has learned to recognize and respond creatively to the obvious problems alcoholics experience in self-regulation and self-governance (Khantzian 1981, Mack 1981). The problems in self-regulation and self-governance of alcoholics that AA so effectively targets relate to the alcoholic's personality (or character) structure, narcissistic vulnerability, problems in maintaining a cohesive sense of self, affect experience, and certain ego capacities concerned with self-preservation and self-care (Mack 1981). These problems are not unique to alcoholics. They are shared more or less by all human beings but it is the degree of such vulnerabilities, combined with social, biological, and other factors, that needs to be explored to further a comprehensive understanding of alcoholism. We single out these factors for heuristic purposes and because our experience and understanding suggest to us that these are fruitful and helpful avenues to pursue further.

As we have indicated, the strength and vulnerability in a person's character reflect how experiences of nurturing and caretaking have become structuralized (i.e., internalized) over the course of his or her development. The character defects referred to in AA more than any other aspect of a person's life seem to refer to the qualities and flaws in personal organization associated with narcissism and narcissistic development, that is, that aspect of life having to do with self-love.

Definition of Narcissism

Although AA does not use technical terms, it is clear that it recognizes, as do modern theorists, that problems with self-love and self-regard are central to alcoholics' problems. Heinz Kohut and his followers (Baker and Baker 1987, Goldberg et al. 1978, Kohut 1971, 1977, 1978, and Ornstein 1978), in advancing their concepts about self-psychology, have made the important observations that narcissism, or self-love, though linked to object relations, may be considered separately, that is, has its own developmental line and is manifested in mature (normal) and less mature (pathological) forms, especially in personality organization. Healthy narcissism is basic to our general emotional health and consists of a subjective sense of well-being, confidence in self-worth and potential, and a balanced valuation of our importance in relation to other people, groups, and our place in the world (Mack 1981). Satisfactory relationships and healthy involvement with work and play are fundamental to mature narcissistic development. Pathological narcissism may be expressed as an abnormal or exaggerated preoccupation with the self, its needs, and desires, and in its extreme form expressed as grandiosity. In contrast, it may also be evident in a diminished self-regard and concerns about one's needs and desires. In more extreme forms, narcissistic pathology may produce psychological fragmentation and disorganization of the self as seen in psychosis or in the regressive states associated with acute or chronic intoxication. It is for these latter reasons that alcoholics are often incorrectly diagnosed as schizophrenic or borderline and/or cause confusion in determining whether alcoholic ego disorganization is a consequence of psychophysiological deterioration or narcissistic pathology (Mack 1981).

To this extent, as we explore the manifestations of narcissistic vulnerabilities in alcoholics in what follows, we wish to emphasize that it would be incorrect and unwarranted to conclude that alcoholics' core problems are a result of narcissistic pathology. It is likely that alcoholics suffer with sectors of narcissistic vulnerability, but that much of the more severe disorganization, regression, and primitive narcissistic pathology and defenses associated with advanced alcoholism is the result of the physical deterioration and the narcissistic hurts and injury that occur with excessive and prolonged drinking.

Manifestations of Narcissism in Alcoholics

In our experience, one of the most obvious problems associated with narcissism in alcoholics is their inability to acknowledge that they cannot control their drinking. In fact, more often there is an exaggerated belief in the ability to control their impulses, especially the impulse to use alcohol. This aspect of alcoholism has recently caused Brown to consider the focus on loss of control as her most central thesis for understanding the psychology of alcoholism and recovery (Brown 1985). The alcoholics' problems of control go beyond accepting their inability to limit themselves in relation to alcohol. It is tied up more in the belief, if not insistence, that they are in charge of themselves, that they are autonomous and able to govern themselves. Although alcoholics are not alone in such exaggerated beliefs about self, we suggest that a combination of such a predisposition, interacting with long-term effects of chronic alcohol use, might especially influence alcoholics' drive to drink.

The aphorisms in AA (1978) and its literature reflect the appreciation of the healthy and unhealthy ways attitudes about self can affect alcoholics in their attempt to achieve sobriety. For Bill W., the founder of AA, "it meant destruction of self-centeredness" (p. 16). Listening to participants in AA laugh at themselves and at each other in meetings as they tell their stories, and the way they banter lightly and use the aphorisms of AA with each other, also show how play, humor and enthusiasm in the program evoke the healthier aspirations for recovery for themselves and each other. Some of the aphorisms are particularly pointed and witty in "puncturing," if not stampeding on, the egoism of alcoholics. They are instructed to "leave their egos at the door" when they attend meetings; or, in AA KISS stands for "keep it simple stupid"; woeful, egocentric laments are met with comments such as, "he suffers from terminal uniqueness" or "her majesty, the baby."And should they believe they are too smart or dumb "to get it" in AA, they might hear that "no one is too dumb to get the program; but there are a lot of people too smart."

One of the first psychiatrists to become actively involved with AA, Harry Tiebout (1943–1944, 1957) described how AA was an effective treatment for alcoholism because it focused primarily on the egoistic aspect of alcoholics' attitude and behavior. He wrote (1943–1944) that the alcoholic realized he always "put himself first" and that getting better required the realization that "he was but a small fraction of a universe peopled by many other individuals" (p. 471). The effectiveness of AA hinges on the alcoholic losing "the narcissistic element permanently" (p. 472) and trading in the "big ego" of infantile narcissism for a more humble self (Tiebout 1957, p. 5). As in the case of Phil that follows, continued study of attitudes about self should continue to unravel the issue of how much alcoholism produces the narcissistic element and how much this element might contribute to the development of alcoholism.

Phil, a very successful recovering alcoholic businessman, shared in psycho-therapy with one of us (Khantzian) how AA helped him to deal with alternating attitudes of disdain and shyness in his relationship with people, attitudes rooted in conflicts whereby he constantly over- and undervalued his capacities as a person. He was a man who suffered much neglect as a child because his mother was severely mentally ill and his father was totally absorbed with his career. Despite the neglect and being left to the care of governesses, or because of it, he developed an uncanny ability to observe and imitate others. As an adolescent he overcame his shyness and gained acceptance by entertaining family and friends as a magician. Despite his ability to tune in on what others expected (not uncommon in individuals with narcissistic vulnerabilities) and a deep fear of nonacceptance, he was also aware of his arrogance. Although he had gained 18 months of abstinence in AA, he knew from the program that he had to deal with and change the attitude of disdain he felt for people in order to maintain his sobriety. He said the "24-hour book" told him to "pray for [his] enemies." He enthusiastically emphasized that AA (1955) really helped him "let go" (i.e., derived from steps 2 and 3 in the 12 steps) of his arrogance and, once again drawing on an AA aphorism, he said that it really worked after awhile, but you had to "fake it till you make it."

From its inception AA has been aware of the pitfalls and potentials rooted in human self-centeredness, especially as it operates in alcoholics, and has been sensitive to the fact that leadership roles can artificially stimulate or inflate self-regard and archaic grandiose self-structures. Thus they have taken measure to circumvent the pitfalls of leadership roles by eliminating permanent offices or leadership positions in AA (Mack 1981). Tradition 2 of AA, for example, emphasizes that "God as He may express Himself" is the ultimate authority and the "leaders are but trusted servants; they do not govern" (Alcoholics Anonymous 1955, p. 136). Yet at the same time AA challenges the pitfalls of being in a position of authority or leadership in the program, it is clear that the successful "elder statesmen" of AA are rewarded when personal aspirations and trends are reshaped and transformed by AA. This occurs when AA respects them as inspiring transmitters of the wisdom they acquire in their recovery, one of the cardinal forms of healthy narcissism described by Kohut. In the following section we describe how AA as a special group experience challenges the less healthy forms of narcissism and evokes the healthiest parts of a person's aspirations in satisfying his or her needs.

Group Psychology, AA, and Self-Governance

Alcoholics Anonymous implicitly adopts principles of group psychology to influence and transform the psychological vulnerabilities inherent in alcoholic suffering. It also shares with group therapy the potential to provide a context for shared experiences, enabling confrontation, support, comfort, and a sense of feeling accepted (Khantzian 1985). However, beyond a description of these general, beneficial effects (Rosenberg 1984), there is, but for a few notable exceptions (Bean 1981, Brown 1985), little in the group literature that addresses how group dynamics in general or the dynamics of AA in particular influence or modify the intrapsychic dimension of the alcoholic's emotional life. Freud's (1921, 1930) writings about group psychology pertained primarily to mass organizations such as the church, the influence of the leaders, and the effect of large groups on the development of superego and ego ideal structures. The AA reference to "group conscience" is probably significant in this regard. Although other reports on group psychology consider how small and large groups may fulfill needs and be ego sustaining (Calder 1979, Kernberg 1977, Scheidlinger

1964, 1974) and, at the small group therapy level, how they influence and mobilize beneficial interpersonal factors (Brown and Yalom 1977, Vanicelli 1982), there is surprisingly little to explain how groups function to modify and transform personality organization and the vulnerabilities in ego and self structures that might predispose a person to depend on alcohol. In the following we hope to contribute to such an understanding and to begin to show how AA as a group experience is effective because it accurately targets and modifies those sectors of the self and personality organization that leave alcoholics vulnerable because they are unable to regulate their lives or to take care of themselves.

Alcoholics Anonymous teaches that the human tasks of self-regulation and self-care are not challenges best faced or mastered alone. This applies to life in general but it is a particularly crucial realization for alcoholics. When AA places powerlessness center stage as the main source of alcoholics' difficulties, it succeeds almost immediately in providing a powerful counter force (Mack 1981). Through its graduated steps, aphorisms, and structuring the process of abstinence, "keeping it simple," and doing it "one day at a time," AA helps the person to gain a growing sense of confidence in the power to manage his life. In a community that shares the same distresses and losses, accepts its members' vulnerabilities and applauds and rewards successes, AA provides a stabilizing, sustaining, and, ultimately, transforming group experience.

The focus on helping people to internalize care and controls, and to manage what has seemed so unmanageable, relates to what has been called executive functioning, or what we call self-governance because this kind of functioning is never altogether a solitary activity. Alcoholics Anonymous is effective because it appreciates that the underpinnings of self are connected with social structures and institutions. Self-governance comprises a set of functions that derive from the individual's participation in a variety of group and institutional activities and affiliations. Alcoholics Anonymous helps alcoholic individuals to achieve sobriety by providing a network of stable individual and group relationships which powerfully impact on the governance of drinking behavior (Mack 1981).

Societal norms, social institutions, attitudes, and cultural factors are powerful determinants of drinking practices and behaviors. We either take for granted or, more likely, underestimate how much of our capacity to govern and regulate our drinking patterns and amount consumed are influenced by societal and cultural norms. It is probably safe to say that such influences play a significant ongoing role, alone with internalized ego controls, in protecting some individuals who might otherwise become problem drinkers. In fact, some have proposed that "epidemics" of rampant drinking during periods of U.S. history and in other cultures have occurred when there was a breakdown of family social structures that restricted drinking to special and ceremonial events. With the absence or waning of such sanctions and rituals, men who were socially dislocated because of the industrial revolution and urbanization (Mack 1981, Zinberg and Fraser 1979) began to drink increasingly in taverns and barrooms instead of the home. Perhaps the modern counterpart occurs among high-powered, upwardly mobile "yuppies" who increasingly turn to chic, after-work singles bars in which daily consumption of significant amounts of alcohol is a part of their social and work affiliations.

Along these lines, we have speculated that the loss of the capacity to govern drinking may go beyond a breakdown of drive and ego structures within an individual but might just as likely be the result of a loss of social and community supports in an individual who is biologically or psychologically vulnerable to alcoholism (Mack 1981). Although the affective component of loss and grief as a consequence of death or separation is often invoked as a precipitant of alcoholic drinking, such explanations more often fail to take into consideration how significant persons, or related sources of social stability, often represent an important part of the self-governance system. In addition, the one who is lost may also serve as a stabilizing link to social community resources that aid a person in regulating his or her life.

Most would agree that AA succeeds because it replaces "chemical solutions" with "people solutions." It provides a group of individuals who care and who share similar life experiences. It avoids the confounding and often compounding disappointments of the individual treatment relationship (unfortunately not too uncommon an occurrence) with therapists who are inexperienced in the treatment of alcoholism and/or with patients who prematurely enter therapy before sobriety and stability are well established. It also confronts the defenses of denial and rationalization and the sense of invincibility in alcoholics. The "alcohol-controlling capacity" of the members of AA becomes part of the self-governing system and helps them to stay humble and to be realistic about their susceptibility to relapse and loss of control (Mack 1981).

Jeff, a man in his mid-30s, aptly described in group therapy how AA served as a protection and antidote against his belief that he was "strong enough" and could control his alcohol and drug use alone. He said that his most recent relapse and current hospital admission occurred after he had achieved a total state of abstinence for 8 months, but that a few "slips" over several weeks had led to his losing control of his alcohol and cocaine use. He emphasized that his 12-year history of heavy alcohol and drug use had failed to respond to several detoxifications and attempts at outpatient care until he embraced AA and began to attend daily meetings. He said that although he obtained a great deal of hope and comfort from his meetings, he stopped going regularly after several months but did not drink or take drugs. As a consequence, within a month he felt confident that he could "control things" without attending any meetings at all. He described with insight the progression of rationalizations when he then began to believe that he could take just one drink with some friends, which he did. Shortly thereafter, he said, he allowed himself two drinks and a "line" of cocaine, whereupon he quickly lost control and within a week was rehospitalized. The group therapist suggested that perhaps there is some kind of monster that operates in us, since, it would seem, we could shun or give up such a source of comfort and protection. Perhaps it might help Jeff and the other patients, who all agreed this story sounded too familiar, if we could give a name to the monster. After a short pause, it was Jeff who spoke up and said, "We'll call him

King Kong." The groups broke into spontaneous laughter and then animatedly pursued the King Kong in each member. Few or no members failed to recognize their inflated sense of self in respect to their ability to control drug or alcohol use and how illusory it was. The only reliable antidote, they felt, was the Alcoholics Anonymous/Narcotics Anonymous (AA/NA) program, which kept them more humbly connected to their vulnerability and constantly challenged their self-sufficiency and sense of being invincible by constantly admitting it in themselves or witnessing it in others.

AA and the Religious Dimension

The religious dimension of AA, especially for outsiders, is often considered an off-putting aspect of the program, deterring or discouraging participation. There is a tendency to compare this aspect of AA to formal religions or particular religious sects. This is unfortunate and misleading. Those who understand and appreciate best what is important in the religious dimension of AA place emphasis on "spirituality" and a flexible approach to defining one's "Higher Power" or God in the program. In a previous publication we have elaborated on what is essential to the religious dimension of the AA program in addressing alcoholics' vulnerabilities (Mack 1981). We will only highlight these observations here.

God as a governing influence or force within an individual may take various forms. For some, religion and religious ideas serve childish and egocentric purposes where God or religious belief and acts are felt to offer magical protection or the religious system serves as a rigid and restrictive system of beliefs and practices. For others, the power and awe engendered by the outside universe and our humble place in it instill a sense of a force or power greater than ourselves. The spiritual dimension of AA helps to move a person from a less mature, childish self-centeredness toward a more mature form of object love. The three stands of childhood narcissism described by Spruiell (1975) — namely, self-love, omnipotence, and self-esteem — are helpful and pertinent in this respect, especially the strand involving omnipotence. The sense of omnipotence begins in the second year of the toddler's life when he begins to sense his power (or the lack of it) and that he can make things happen. It is in this context that the idea of God, or a power greater than oneself, may be a step in the direction of taming and transforming infantile omnipotence and serving in early childhood to establish a capacity for object love (Mack 1981).

The spiritual and religious elements in AA act as an important counterforce to the egoistic aspects of chronic drinking by directly confronting the denial, rationalizations, and allusion of control that support the persistence of alcoholic behavior. Through its appeal to a Higher Power AA's insistence on humility acts as an anodyne to the self-serving grandiosity and the wallowing self-pity of the alcoholic. In this context God serves as a "self-object" in a transition from self-love to object love and provides much needed authority and structure within the self. Step 3 and the remaining steps in the 12-step tradition of AA help the alcoholic move from a self-centered posture to a more mature one by helping the individual give up the overly prominent, grandiose parts of the self. The self-examination involved in taking "a moral inventory" (step 4), "making amends" (step 9), and "carrying the message to others" (step 12) are steps that inspire and instill a real concern for others and an increasing capacity for mature altruism. This effect of AA is genuine and lasting (i.e., for those who embrace it) and suggests that AA may produce permanent structural change, a result that has clinical and conceptual significance for psychoanalytic theory and practice (Mack 1981).

The Self and the Implications of AA

We have emphasized that the core vulnerabilities in the self, or the nature of the "character defects," that AA counters have to do with childish and grandiose attitudes and dispositions contributing to their inability to control their lives or their drive to drink. Our emphasis has been on the total self as a concept involving a multiperson psychology which operates within individuals to govern and regulate their lives.

The growing self-psychology literature, especially the work of Heinz Kohut (1971, 1977), has provided a useful basis for understanding the vulnerabilities in self-organization that AA so effectively contains and transforms. In trying to understand how a cohesive sense of self develops, Kohut focused on early disappointments in the mother–child relationship. He attempted to explain how certain archaic narcissistic structures persist into adulthood and how these infantile structures interfere with the development of more mature adaptations. Attitudes of grandiosity, over- and underestimation of others, and persistent search for comfort from outside the self (i.e., exaggerated self-object needs), as in addictive behaviors, may be adult manifestations of these structures and vulnerabilities, and derive primarily from the disappointments in the early relationship with the mother. Alcoholics Anonymous provides an environment of caring individuals, a supportive group, which accepts the alcoholic's frustrated self-object needs. It heals and repairs those parts of the self Kohut found to be especially vulnerable in those suffering traumatic disappointments, especially a capacity for self-soothing and self-comforting and the enjoyment of ordinary exhibitionistic display.

In contrast to heavily and multiply addicted drug abusers, alcoholics, in our experience, do not suffer from global narcissistic personality disturbances. The program is sufficiently ingenious (especially in its expanded NA version), however, in providing sustenance, comfort, and repair that it can be effective in the more extreme cases where there is pervasive character pathology. Our emphasis here has been on poorly developed functions that are precursors of self-governance as opposed to pervasive structural defects in the development of self (Mack 1981).

AFFECTS AND ALCOHOLISM

Alcoholism is a complex disorder in which problems with self-governance malignantly interact with other vulnerabilities such as disabilities in regulating feelings (i.e., affects) and self-care to cause biologically susceptible individuals and others to become hopelessly dependent on alcohol. In this section we will consider how alcoholics and others with related conditions experience their feelings in unusual or atypical ways, so that the feeling-altering effects of alcohol become welcome.

Early psychoanalytic theory placed drives at the root of most emotional and behavioral disturbances. In the case of alcoholism, for example, excessive "orality" or oral drives were invoked as the main motivation for alcoholic drinking, an explanation most psychodynamic clinicians would now find embarrassingly unuseful (Khantzian 1987). Yet the drive or instincts, as Schur (1966) suggested, are important sources of psychic energy and motivation. They originate in the body and put pressure on ego-executant functions. An adequate account of mental life, including the lives of alcoholics, is needed to take them into account. However, as indicated in an earlier review (Mack 1981), and as Tomkins (1962) suggested, drives are rigid and unmodifiable in nature, whereas affects or feelings, which are more flexible and derive from drives, are the important and prime motivators in human emotions and behavior.

It would appear from our own observations and those of others (Gottheil et al. 1973, Ludwig 1961, Mathew et al. 1979, Pattison et al. 1977) that the powerlessness that alcoholics experience in relation to the impulse to drink is not simply a function of irresistible "craving" but occurs in a context of psychological distress. We have tried to focus on the nature and quality of affects (or feelings) associated with psychological distress and how a person's feeling life interacts with the effects of alcohol.

A fruitful area for further investigation would be how the unusual and atypical ways alcoholics experience their affects or emotions influence craving and related behavior. We suggest that the "flexibility" of affects, to which Tomkins referred, is lacking in alcoholics and this lack of flexibility derives from the atypical ways in which alcoholics experience and express feelings. The expressive aspects of AA may help to increase the flexibility of the feeling life of alcoholics.

Over the past 25 years, important clinical and theoretical exploration involving disturbances, deficits, and dysfunction in affect experience has produced findings that are relevant and useful in understanding how the feeling problems of alcoholics may contribute to their reliance on alcohol. Although much of this work has been with addicts and alcoholics, some of the observations have occurred with populations with psychosomatic and characterologic pathology. These observations have made note of and underscored the following:

1. Affects have a normal developmental line and are subject to developmental arrest and traumatic regression (Krystal and Raskin 1970, Lane and Schwartz 1987, Schmale 1964).

2. Addicts, psychosomatic, and acting-out character-disordered patients display extreme patterns of experiencing affects, some feeling too much and others feeling too little or being devoid of feelings (Khantzian 1979, 1981, Krystal and Raskin 1970, McDougall 1984).

3. Affects may be somatized, undifferentiated (i.e., patients cannot distinguish anxiety from depression), or not verbalized (Krystal 1982, Krystal and Raskin 1970).

4. Affective dysfunction for some is primarily characterized by denial or absence of feelings (e.g., "disaffected," "nonfeeling responses," or "hypophoria") (Martin et al. 1978, McDougall 1984, Sashin 1985).

5. Affective dysfunction may be manifest primarily in an inability to put into words ("alexithymia") feelings that are only vaguely experienced or are felt to be diffusely unpleasant ("dysphoria," "affect deficit") (Khantzian 1987, Krystal 1982, Nemiah 1970, Sifneos 1967).

6. Specific affective states may be overwhelming (e.g., rage, extreme anxiety or dread, mania) as a consequence of early environmental trauma or neglect and/or as a consequence of defects and deficits in ego structure (Khantzian 1985, Krystal 1982, Wurmser 1974).

7. The various classes of drugs (i.e., stimulants, analgesic narcotics, hallucinogens, and sedative-hypnotics including alcohol) have specific and different actions and interact with painful or overwhelming affective states and structural deficits to make them appealing (Khantzian 1985, Wurmser 1974).

It is clear from this partial list that affect deficits may be on a continuum and have differing qualities with regard to the problems of recognition, modulation, tolerance, and articulation of feelings. For some, affect deficits or dysfunction may be within the experiential realm of being unable to identify feelings; for others it is within the expressive realm where alcoholics and addicts, for example, are unable to display or put feelings into words, and for yet others the main problem or challenge has been to bear feelings.

Michael, a distinguished, middle-aged scholar with a 15-year history of alcoholism, was not as impaired as some in recognizing and expressing feelings. Instead, he aptly described in group therapy how he used alcohol to modulate both pleasant and unpleasant feelings. He described painful conflicts at a family reunion in which he debated taking over the piano playing from his older brother-in-law who was playing insipid and boring tunes. He described how painfully self-conscious he felt about performing and linked it to his puritanical and ambitious mother who instilled in him at an early age antithetical admonitions: he must achieve great stature when he grew up, yet she often warned him that he must not "show off." Finally, overcoming his painful inhibitions, which he realized prior to achieving and maintaining abstinence would have been easily relieved and overcome with alcohol, he took over the piano playing and quickly stirred the family into a rousing and enthusiastic sing-along with his spirited, rhythmic, and powerful style of playing. As he told his story in the group he realized, in retrospect, that although he had enjoyed himself, he had also worked himself into a "frenzy"; he then also realized that if he had taken a drink it would have calmed his frenzy or, better still, he would not have noticed it at all. He realized further, after this episode, how much he depended on alcohol to dissolve his painful self-consciousness. Michael ruminated for several days after the party that he had "overdone it," until he spoke with a supportive and reassuring older sister who dispelled his anxieties. He also realized that if he had been drinking he might not have experienced, or even been aware of, his anxiety and embarrassment after the party, but he would have also been deprived of his sister's reassurance and the salutory aspect of bearing and working out his worry.

Clinical examples such as this suggest that further exploration of the complexities of alcoholics' experience and expression of feelings, comparing them, for example, with nonalcoholic special populations such as psychosomatic patients, trauma victims, and patients with personality disorders, would add greatly to our understanding of the disorder itself. Such studies should continue to shed further light on the ways alcoholics are different from or similar to these groups in their attempt to use alcohol to relieve the way they experience distress, and the degree to which dependence on alcohol causes regression in ego functions and further perpetuates their distress.

SELF-CARE AND ALCOHOLISM

It is perhaps not surprising that early psychoanalytic formulations invoking drive psychology and, more particularly, "death instincts" or unconscious death wishes or trends are still often adopted to explain the motivations for heavy alcohol use, given its extreme and devastating consequences (Menninger 1938, Tabachnick 1976). What these explanations often fail to appreciate is that the degree of suffering alcoholics endure, which is often of unusual intensity, and their search for short-term relief through alcohol often override all other considerations. However, beyond this adaptive use of alcohol to relieve suffering, we (Khantzian 1981, Khantzian and Mack 1983, Mack 1981) have been interested in deficiencies and vulnerabilities in a capacity referred to as "self-care." Lack of self-care plays an important part in many impulsive disorders, seems to contribute significantly to the susceptibility of alcoholics and addicts to become involved with substances, and also contributes to relapse when abstinence is achieved. There is little evidence that alcoholism is determined by "death wishes" or even by unconscious destructive motives.

Freud, almost until the end of his life, considered the self-protective, survival functions in terms of libido theory and the "ego instincts," emphasizing the investment of narcissistic libido in the protection and preservation of the individual, as opposed to object libido which assured the survival of the species (Freud 1913, 1915, 1916–1917, 1925). Although toward the end of his life he explicitly indicated that the task of self-preservation was more within the domain of ego functions (Freud 1949), there have been surprisingly few attempts to explain this most important aspect of human existence, especially since such functions are so flagrantly or dangerously absent in certain conditions such as alcoholism, obesity, anorexia/bulimia, accident proneness, and other acting out/impulse problems.

The capacity for self-care involves a set of ego-executant functions and serves particular aspects of self-preservation. Self-care includes signal anxiety, reality testing, judgment, control, and the ability to make cause–consequence connections (Khantzian 1981, Khantzian and Mack 1983, Mack 1981). It is a capacity that we acquire in early childhood, and involves the ability to value ourselves enough to comfort and take care of ourselves and an ability to plan our actions and to anticipate harm or danger. Self-care functions evolve and develop out of an internalization of the caring and protective functions of the parents. It is established most stably and beneficially when extremes of over or underprotection (i.e., as manifested by either too much or too little concern for the child's safety) are avoided by the parents in the child's caretaking environment. In adult life, healthy self-care concerns are manifested by appropriate levels of anticipatory affects such as embarassment, shame, fear, worry, and the like when facing potentially compromising, harmful, or dangerous situations where to act or not act could do injury to oneself or others (Khantzian 1981, Khantzian and Mack 1983, Mack 1981).

We have been struck by the absence of such anticipatory responses, or the absence of delay with regard to the behaviors and impulses leading up to and associated with the use of substances. Impairments in self-care capacities are even more evident in cases of relapse after prolonged periods of abstinence where one has already had the "benefit" of the disastrous consequences of alcohol use as a guide to knowing about one's vulnerability.

One patient told how an unpleasant encounter with his self-centered father would have precipitated another bout of drinking except for the help of AA. His father visited him and his wife and children. But during the visit the older man constantly seized the conversation from the children at the dinner table, after which the patient found himself becoming increasingly agitated and then unable to sleep. He found himself invoking the AA slogan to "get help," called some friends in AA and spoke about his problems the next day at an AA meeting. In his pre-AA days, despite the availability of his therapist to whom he had easy and frequent access, he said he would have ruminated and remained upset for days, whereas in this instance he found himself remaining safe at first ("I was very anxious — and obsessing — but I didn't drink"). By the next day he felt free of the distress his father's visit engendered. He stressed how the phone calls, the meeting, and "talking himself down" with the aphorisms from AA enabled him to avoid a possible relapse to alcohol and drug use.

Examples such as this suggest that the development and establishment of self-care functions such as self-soothing and delaying pain-avoiding impulsive action are not achieved as a solitary psychological process. Perhaps self-care, more than any other aspect of self-governance, can be seen as a "multiperson" psychology (see Balint below). Working with alcohol and drug-dependent patients in psychotherapy has provided reconstructive and observational evidence of the characteristic ways such patients do or do not take care of themselves, how much difficulty they have in availing themselves of other people's help, and how their self-care problems pre- and postdate their alcoholism in the form of preventable accidents, legal, financial, medical, and related difficulties. Continued psychodynamic and clinical investigation of self-care disabilities will help to clarify the degree to which addictive processes and illness compound and heighten self-care problems.

EGO DEFENSE AND ADAPTATION

Alcoholics suffer because they have been vulnerable in sectors of their personality organization involving self-governance and the capacity to regulate feelings and self-care. Wherever there are gaps or deficits of functioning in psychological life, individuals develop and display compensatory defenses and characteristic traits and styles of coping, or "defects of character" (step 6 in the 12-step tradition), such as those that AA (1955) asks to be removed.

Many of the defenses that alcoholics use are in the service of compensating for or ameliorating the "defect of affect defense" (Wurmser 1974). In some instances these defenses take the form of exaggerated character traits or personality styles that avoid dependency needs and feelings (Khantzian 1981). In other instances, the use of alcohol itself may be seen as a defense. Its effects may relieve unpleasant or overwhelming affects such as intolerable tension and anxiety (Krystal and Raskin 1970), or alcohol may be used to produce feelings of warmth, closeness, and affection by its softening of rigid, counterdependent defenses and character styles that prevent the expression of such needs and emotions (Khantzian 1979, Krystal and Raskin 1970).

Less well-organized patterns of defense against painful affect are evident in impulsive acts of activity, including aggressive and violent behaviors, which ward off feelings of fear, loneliness, and helplessness. The effects of alcohol may augment such defensive behaviors, or may help to alleviate feelings of anxiety or fear that are generated by the behaviors themselves. Thus, self-medication with alcohol becomes a part of the defensive system or adaptation. It may be employed to relieve or eliminate feelings that are experienced as intolerable, or to produce or allow feelings that are otherwise difficult to bear or express (e.g., warmth and affection).

Rationalization and related defenses of denial and justification are prominent defenses associated with alcoholism and the alcoholic's adaptation (Bean 1981). In particular, they serve to protect alcoholics from facing their hopeless attachment to alcohol itself and the degree to which their lives have become consumed with alcohol-related associations and activities. Alcoholics employ rationalizations to explain to others and themselves a psychophysiological process of which they are incompletely aware and which they do not understand, a process that constantly erodes and destroys their composure and self-respect (Mack 1981). Furthermore, rationalization may be a characteristic defense in some alcoholic families in which the minimization or denial of heavy alcohol is transmitted intergenerationally. One recovering 38-year-old alcoholic of a wealthy alcoholic Midwestern family spoke in group therapy about how neither his alcoholic father nor his heavily drinking mother ever mentioned a word about his or their alcoholism or his recovery either prior to his hospitalization for detoxification or in the 15 months of sobriety after hospitalization. During many subsequent visits with his parents in this time they continued to drink heavily while he was abstinent. The contrast was sharply evident.

Alcoholics demonstrate a range of characterologic defenses and traits related to vulnerabilities in self-governance and self-regulation. The 12 steps of AA, especially admitting loss of control and asking a Higher Power "to remove all the defects of character," challenge these individuals to yield their investment in the primitive defenses they employ. Thus, counterphobic mechanisms, the justification and projection that accompany and compensate for self-care deficiencies,[6] and the attitudes of disdain, counterdependency, and disavowal of needs (Khantzian 1981) that are used to shield the alcoholic from old hurts and injury can give way to the beneficial humbling and softening acceptance of support, care, and comfort provided by AA.

The benefit from psychoanalytic treatment hinges less on the removal or reduction of symptoms than on a modification or restructuring of an individual's personality organization. Our own observations and the work of Brown (1985), Bean (1981), and Bateson (1972) suggest that beyond establishing abstinence and providing support, AA's therapeutic efectiveness may also include the production of structural change. Further clinical evidence will be needed to substantiate this possibility.

For Phil, the patient described earlier, the experience with AA helped him to bring about a significant personality change. In his psychotherapy he described an episode in which he was shocked and hurt after a phone call to one of his sponsors. Without warning this man rejected him brutally with a rage-filled obscene verbal assault. In contrast to a previous pattern in which Phil would have most likely reacted with counterrage and counterattack, he sat and cried, aware of feeling hurt and sad. Guided by his AA program, he called several people for comfort and reassurance. Still feeling rejected and lonely, he then went to his bedroom, literally dropped to his knees (as learned from AA), and "prayed intensely." He was surprised and pleased that by the next day his distress had left him. In his therapy hour Phil reflected and contrasted his recent hurt, which he sustained and tolerated, and his subdued response to his sponsor's attack, to his "old self" where, as an example, in his business he had a reputation for being tyrannical, aggressive, and retaliatory. Not insignificantly, during the same hour Phil also recalled that he had suffered from a "mild case of agorophobia." He recounted examples of social anxiety and shyness, growing up and in college, which he had learned to overcome by medicating himself with alcohol. When he first joined AA and went to meetings without the protection of alcohol's antianxiety effect, he "felt incredibly uncomfortable, and at first stayed in back and didn't talk." But more recently this anxiety was abating and he was confident that he would "get it" even better in the AA program, a striking shift in attitude, given his previous avoidant reactions and behavior.

COMMENT AND CONCLUSION

Whenever human psychological frailties occur, there is a corresponding tendency to disguise and deny that they exist. A contemporary psychodynamic understanding of alcoholism suggests there are degrees of vulnerability in self-regulation involving self-governance, feeling life (affect), and self-care that are involved in the predisposition to become and remain dependent on alcohol. AA succeeds in reversing this dependency by effectively challenging alcoholics to see that they disguise and deny their self-regulation vulnerabilities. Implicitly, if not explicitly, AA employs group processes to highlight and then modify the vulnerabilities that plague the lives of alcoholics. The focus of AA on the loss of control over alcohol and the insistence on maintaining identity of the suffering individual as an alcoholic (i.e., it is always that one is "recovering," never "recovered") is a useful if not essential treatment device. It permits alcoholics to acknowledge and transform vulnerabilities in self-regulation.

When AA underscores alcoholism as a "disease of denial," they are challenging the alcoholic's attempts to defend against that aspect of the self that is vulnerable, injured, or in a state of disrepair. These defenses are often evident in alcoholics in attitudes of self-centeredness, self-sufficiency, and disavowal of distress, which may alternate with or present as attitudes of abject self-rebuke and pity that defy and reject attempts at comfort and understanding. The organization confronts alcoholics' convictions that they can solve life problems alone or, worse still, that they are not solvable at all. It helps them to see that the challenge of self-governance is not a solitary process, and that yielding to and benefiting from the regulating influence of others in the program, with their care, concern, and even admonishments, is extraordinarily beneficial. By placing the alcoholics' inability to control their alcohol as the central focus, AA creates a basis to address a fundamentally important reality, namely, that as human beings we do not and cannot survive and grow on our own and that governance of our lives as well as our behaviors is intimately linked and involved with other people.

Once alcoholics "surrender" to the human reality of interdependence through AA and accept their "powerlessness" to control their alcohol alone, other beneficial aspects of AA begin to provide a basis to address, repair, and/or strengthen other vulnerabilities involving deficits and dysfunction around one's feeling life and behaviors.

Alcoholics Anonymous is uniquely suited to provide support, to proscribe detrimental behavior, and to ameliorate real guilt. It provides needed, practical coping tools, advice, and admiration, all beneficial elements that are necessary, especially early in recovery, for overcoming the psychological and physical debilitation associated with alcoholism. AA provides human contact in a structured group setting that encourages story telling and the recognition and sharing of feelings, the imparting of wisdom, the containing of emotions and behavior, and the teaching of interdependence and self-care (Khantzian 1987). These elements of the AA treatment approach respond appropriately to alcoholics' narcissistic hurts and defenses and to their incapacity to tolerate intense feelings and to take care of themselves.

The AA program is a special human invention that provides people who have been out of control, uncomfortable, and unable to communicate their distress a forum in which to practice, learn, and internalize growing capacities for containment, self-comfort, and self-expression. Although the treatment strategies are for the most part "indirect techniques" such as story telling and bearing witness to another's vulnerabilities, AA, as McGarty (1985) recently suggested, offers universalizing experiences that provide invaluable human association and an opportunity to try out alternative solutions for those who feel too anxious or traumatized to associate or to speak. It is on this basis that Enid Balint (1972) extolled the advantage of group experiences over individual ones for certain problems. She suggests that in individual therapy patients do not tolerate or are not always helped by becoming aware of the analyst's emotions nor are they helped if the analyst is incapable of them. In contrast, certain emotions and experiences can be best tolerated and enjoyed in a "multiperson" or group context. When offering these ideas Balint was not referring to the group experiences of AA but she could have been.

REFERENCES

Alcoholics Anonymous (1955). *Twelve Steps and Twelve Traditions.* New York: Alcoholics Anonymous World Services, 1977.

Alcoholics Anonymous. (1978). 4th ed. (1st ed. — 1939, 3rd ed. — 1976). New York: Alcoholic Anonymous World Services.

Baker, H. S., and Baker, M. N. (1987). Heinz Kohut's self psychology: an overview. *Am J of Psychiatry* 144:1–9.

Bales, R. F. (1944). The therapeutic role of Alcoholics Anonymous as seen by a sociologist. *Q J Stud Alcohol* 5:267–278.

Balint, E. (1972). Fair shares and mutual concerns. *Int J Psycho-Anal* 53:61–65.

Bateson, G. (1972). The cybernetics of "self": a theory of alcoholism. In *Steps to an Ecology of Mind,* pp. 309–337. New York: Ballantine.

Bean, M. H. (1981). Denial and the psychological complications of alcoholism. In *Dynamic Approaches to the Understanding and Treatment of Alcoholism,* ed. M. H. Bean and N. E. Zinberg, pp. 55–96. New York: The Free Press.

—— (1975). Alcoholics Anonymous: A.A. *Psychiatr Ann* 5:3–64.

Brown, S. (1985). *Treating the Alcoholic: A Developmental Model of Recovery.* New York: Wiley.

Brown, S., and Yalom, I. D. (1977). Interactional group therapy with alcoholics. *J Stud Alcohol* 38(3): 426–456.

Calder, K. (1979). Psychoanalytic knowledge of group processes. Panel report. *J Am Psychoanal Assoc* 27:145–156.

Freud, S. (1913). The claims of psychoanalysis to scientific interest. *Standard Edition* 13.

—— (1915). Instincts and their vicissitudes. *Standard Edition* 14.

—— (1916–1917). An autobiographical study. *Standard Edition* 20.

———— (1921). Group psychology and the analysis of the ego. *Standard Edition* 18.

———— (1930). Civilization and its discontents. *Standard Edition* 21.

———— (1949). An outline of psychoanalysis. *Standard Edition* 23.

Goldberg, A. et al. (1978). *The Psychology of the Self.* New York: International Universities Press.

Gottheil, E., Alterman, A. I., Skoloda, T. E., and Murphy, B. F. (1973). Alcoholics' patterns of controlled drinking. *Am J Psychiatry* 130:418–422.

Helzer, J. E., Robins, L. N., Taylor, J. R. et al. (1985). The extent of long-term moderate drinking among alcoholics discharged from medical and psychiatric treatment facilities. *N Eng J Med* 312:1678–1682.

Henrick, I. (1943). Work and the pleasure principle. *Psychoanal Q* 12:311–329.

Hesselbrock, M. N., Meyer, R. E., and Keener, J. J. (1985). Psychopathology in hospitalized alcoholics. *Arch Gen Psychiatry* 42:1050–1055.

Kernberg, O. F. (1977). Large group processes: psychoanalytic understanding and applications. Paper presented at the panel on Psychoanalytic Knowledge of Group Processes. American Psychoanalytic Association, December 18.

Khantzian, E. J. (1979). Impulse problems in addiction: cause and effect relationships. In *Working with the Impulsive Person*, ed. H. Wishnie, pp. 97–112. New York: Plenum.

———— (1981). Some treatment implications of the ego and self-disturbances in alcoholism. In *Dynamic Approaches to the Understanding and Treatment of Alcoholism*, ed. M. H. Bean and N. E. Zinberg, pp. 163–188. New York: The Free Press.

———— (1985a). The self-medication hypothesis of addictive disorders. *Am J Psychiatry* 142(11):1259–1264.

———— (1985b). Psychotherapeutic interventions with substance abusers—the clinical context. *J Subst Abuse Treat* 2:83–88.

———— (1987). A clinical perspective of the cause-consequence controversy on alcoholic and addictive suffering. *J Am Acad Psychoanal* 15(4):521–537.

Khantzian, E. J., and Mack, J. E. (1983). Self-preservation and the care of the self-ego instincts reconsidered. *Psychoanal Study Child* 38:209–232. New Haven, CT: Yale University Press.

Kohut, H. (1971). *The Analysis of the Self.* New York: International Universities Press.

———— (1977). *The Restoration of the Self.* New York: International Universities Press.

Kohut, H., and Wolf, E. S. (1978). The disorders of the self and their treatment: an outline. *Int J Psycho-Anal* 59:413–426.

Krystal, H. (1982). Alexithymia and the effectiveness of psychoanalytic treatment. *Int J Psychoanal Psychother* 9:353–378.

Krystal, H., and Raskin, H. A. (1970). *Drug Dependence: Aspects of Ego Functions.* Detroit: Wayne State University Press.

Lane, R. D., and Schwartz, G. E. (1987). levels of emotional awareness: a cognitive-developmental theory and its application to psychopathology. *Am J Psychiatry* 144(2):133–143.

Leach, B. (1973). Does Alcoholics Anonymous really work? In *Alcoholism:Prognosis in Research and Treatment*, ed. P. Bourne and R. Fox. New York: Academic.

Leach, B., Norris, J. L., Dancey, T., and Bissell, L. (1969). Dimensions of Alcoholics Anonymous. *Int J Addictions* 4:507–541.

Ludwig, A. M. (1961). On and off the wagon: reasons for drinking and abstaining by alcoholics. *Q J Stud Alcohol* 22:124–134.

Mack, J. E. (1981). Alcoholism, A.A. and the governance of the self. In *Dynamic Approaches to the Understanding and Treatment of Alcoholism*, ed. M. H. Bean and N. E. Zinberg, pp. 128–162. New York: The Free Press.

Simmel, E. (1948). Alcoholism and addiction. *Psychoanal Q* 17:6–31.

Martin, W. R., Haertzen, C. A., and Hewett, B. B. (1978). Psychopathology and pathophysiology of narcotic addicts, alcoholics, and drug abusers. In *Psychopharmacology: A Generation of Progress*, ed. M. A. Lipton, A. DiMascio, and K. F. Killam. New York: Raven.

Mathew, J. R., Claghorn, J. K., and Largen, J. (1979). Craving for alcohol in sober alcoholics. *Am J Psychiatry* 136:603–606.

McDougall, J. (1984). The "dis-affected" patient: reflections on affect pathology. *Psychoanal Q* 53:386–409.

McGarty, R. (1985). Relevance of Ericksonian psychotherapy to the treatment of chemical dependence. *J Subst Abuse Treat* 2:147–151.

Menninger, K. A. (1938). *Man Against Himself.* New York: Harcourt, Brace.

Nemiah, J. C. (1970). Denial revisited: reflections on pscyhosomatic theory. *Psychother Psychosom* 26:140–147.

Pattison, S. M., Sobell, M. B., and Sobell, L. C. (1977). *Emergency Concepts of Alcohol Dependence.* New York: Springer.

Rosenberg, P. (1984). Support groups: a special therapeutic entity. *Small Group Behav* 15:173–186.

Sashin, J. I. (1985). Affect tolerance: a model of affect-response using catastrophe theory. *J Soc Biol Struct* 8:175–202.

Scheidlinger, S. (1964). Identification: the sense of belong and of identity in small groups. *Int J of Group Psychotherapy* 14: 291–306.

———— (1974). On the concept of the "mother-group." *Int J Group Psychother* 24:417–428.

Schmale, A. H. (1964). A genetic view of affects. *Psychoanal Study Child* 19:287–310. New York: International Universities Press.

Schuckit, M. (1985). The clinical implications of primary diagnostic among alcoholics. *Arch Gen Psychiatry* 42:1043–1049.

Schur, M. (1966). *The Id and the Regulatory Principles of Mental Functioning.* New York: International Universities Press.

Sifneos, P. E. (1967). Clinical observation on some patients suffering from a variety of psychosomatic diseases. In the Proceedings of the Seventh European Conference on Psychosomatic Research. Basil: Kariger.

Spruiell, V. (1975). Three strands of narcissism. *Psychoanalytic Q* 44:577–595.

Stewart, D. A. (1955). The dynamics of fellowship as illustrated in Alcoholis Anonymous. *Q J Stud Alcohol* 16:251–262.

Tabachnick, N. (1976). Death trend and adaptation. *J Am Acad Psychoanal* 41:49–62.

Tiebout, H. M. (1943–1944). Therapeutic mechanisms of Alcoholics Anonymous. *Am J Psychiatry* 100: 468–473.

———— (1961). Alcoholics Anonymous: an experiment of nature. *Q J Stud Alcohol* 22:52–68.

Tompkins, S. (1962). *Affects, Imagery, and Consciousness.* Vol. 1. New York: Springer.

Trice, H. M. (1957). A study of the process of affiliation with Alcoholics Anonymous. *Q J Stud Alcohol* 18:39–54.

Vaillant, G. E. (1983). *The Natural History of Alcoholism.* Cambridge, MA: Harvard University Press.

Vanicelli, M. (1982). Group psychotherapy with alcoholics. *J Stud Alcohol* 43(1):17–37.

Wurmser, L. (1974). Psychoanalytic considerations of the etiology of compulsive drug use. *J Am Psychoanal Assoc* 22:820–843.

Zinberg, N. E. (1977). Alcoholics Anonymous and the treatment and prevention of alcoholism. *Alcohol Clin Exp Res* 1:91–101.

Zinberg, N. E., and Fraser, K. M. (1979). The role of the social setting in the prevention and treatment of alcoholism. In *The Diagnosis and Treatment of Alcoholism*, ed. J. H. Mendelson and N. K. Mello. New York: McGraw-Hill.

27: ALCOHOLISM AND REGRESSION/FIXATION TO PATHOLOGICAL NARCISSISM

Jerome D. Levin

Although alcoholics are not narcissistic personality disorders in either Kernberg's (1975) or the *DSM-III-R*'s (1987) sense, in my experience they do have more than humanly average difficulty with narcissistic issues. The notion that regression/fixation to Kohut's stage of the archaic nuclear self, a stage of pathological narcissism in adults, is the psychodynamic correlative of alcohol addiction, accounts for the empirical psychological findings on the clinical alcoholic personality, as well as reconciling and making sense of competing psychodynamic theories.

Thus Heinz Kohut's (1971, 1977) insights into the psychodynamics of addiction are directly relevant to our understanding and treatment of the alcoholic. Kohut sees narcissistic disturbance as central to the psychopathology of the addict. The core difficulty of these narcissistic personalities is the absence of internal structure; explicitly, there are deficits in the self's capacities for tension regulation, self-soothing, and self-esteem regulation. The alcoholic's pathological drinking is an attempt to make up for this "missing structure," that is, the drinking serves to reduce tension and regulate self-esteem in the absence of adequate intrapsychic resources to achieve such regulation. Thus, in early sobriety these deficits in the structure of the self, with their concomitant psychological dysfunctions, will continue to disable the alcoholic until psychic structure can be built.

Elevation in the Psychopathic deviate (Pd) scale of the Minnesota Multiphasic Personality Inventory (MMPI) in both active and recovering alcoholics, probably the most consistent finding in the literature on the alcoholic personality, can be understood as a manifestation of the overtly grandiose self, with its arrogance, isolation, and lack of realistic goals. The elevation of the Depression (D) scale on the MMPI, which is also a consistent finding in advanced active alcoholism and early recovery, reflects both the psychopharmacological consequences of active alcoholism (depletion of available catecholamines) and the impoverishment of the self, riddled with structural deficits and impaired in its capacity for self-esteem regulation, found in pathological narcissism.

Developmentally, the depression reflects the disappointment which results from inadequate phase-appropriate mirroring of the child's grandiose self by selfobjects. Additionally, active alcoholism gives one much to be realistically depressed about. Empirical findings, using adjective checklists and self-reports, of impoverishment of the self can be understood in the same way. The structurally deficient self of pathological narcissism is experienced as an empty depression, and it is reported as lack of interest in people, activities, and goals. Even the self is uninteresting to itself. The regression to pathological narcissism concomitant with the alcoholic process progressively strips the already enfeebled ego of its investments in objects and activities, leaving an empty self, an empty world, and an empty bottle.

Another consistent finding in alcoholics is field dependence. Field dependence entails a relative inability to utilize internal resources, as well as impairments in the differentiations of body image, of figure and ground, and of self and world. By definition, the field-dependent person experiences the environment as a self*object*—which is precisely the way in which the person fixated/regressed to pathological narcissism experiences the world. Thus, our hypothesis well accounts for this datum.

Confused gender identity is a frequent finding in alcoholic populations. It also can be understood in terms of pathological narcissism. (Conflict over sex roles, a related finding, has both sociological and psychological determinants.) Developmentally, the archaic self arises before the establishment of firm gender identity. Hence, regression/fixation to the stage of the archaic self entails a blurring of gender identity. The failure to adequately internalize (identify with) the ideal selfobject of the same sex, which is postulated as etiological in a vulnerability to pathological narcissism, would render difficult the establishment of a firm gender identity. The early psychoanalytic findings of latent homosexuality in male alcoholics may also reflect failure to internalize ideal selfobjects, although they are expressed in terms of libido theory and the psychosexual stages.

Ego weakness is a construct which integrates several empirically confirmed characteristics of active and early-sobriety alcoholics: impulsivity, lack of frustration tolerance, lack of affect tolerance, and lack of differentiation of the self-concept. It overlaps many of the findings just discussed: confused gender identity, conflict over sex roles, psychopathic deviancy, and impoverishment of the self. In terms of pathological narcissism, ego weakness in the alcoholic is understood in terms of the structural deficits in the self. In other words, the failure to internalize by a process of selective and depersonified identification (designated "transmuting internalization" by Kohut) the functions of affect regulation once performed from the outside by mother and other caretakers results in ego weakness. In the case of weak or incomplete internalization, the self is subject to regression to pathological narcissism, with its accompanying ego weakness.

Stimulus augmentation, which has been found to be characteristic of alcoholics and which contributes to their ego weakness, can also be understood in terms of pathological narcissism, as a failure to internalize the mother's function as an auxiliary to the innate stimulus barrier. Although constitutional factors certainly play a role in the alcoholic's stimulus augmentation, failures in internalization and structuralization just as certainly play their role.

Kohut's view of narcissism differs from both Freud's and Kernberg's. In contradistinction to Freud's view of narcissistic libido as the precursor of object libido, Kohut believes that narcissistic and object-libidinal strivings develop along independent lines. That is, narcissism is seen not as a stage in the development of object love, but rather as an aspect of human life that has its own developmental history in which the self and its libidinal investments evolve from a fragmentary stage into a cohesive, archaic form (the nuclear self) and finally into a mature form. The development of mature object and idealized selfobject love are parallel, but independent, processes.

Kohut differs from Kernberg in believing that the grandiose self (a term he coined) is a normal, albeit archaic, rather than pathological, structure. Kohut is particularly interested in early self structures: the grandiose self and the idealized selfobject (or idealized parent imago). These structures constitute the nuclear self, which Kohut views as bipolar.

SELF PSYCHOLOGICAL ISSUES

Let us attempt to elucidate these concepts. Kohut defines the self as a unit cohesive in space and enduring in time, which is a center of initiative and a recipient of impressions. It can be regarded either as a mental structure superordinate to the agencies of the mind (id, ego, and superego) or as a content of those agencies. Although Kohut believed that these conceptualizations were complementary rather than mutually exclusive, he emphasized the self as a central or superordinate principle in his later theories. It is, so to speak, the organized and organizing center of human experience, which is itself experienced as cohesive and enduring. How does this sense of an I (self), which coheres in space and endures in time, develop? According to Kohut, the infant develops a primitive (fragmented) sense of self very early. That is, each body part, each sensation, each mental content is experienced as belonging to a self, to a me, as mine; however, there is no synthesis of these experiences as yet. There are selves, but no unitary self. Nor are there clear boundaries between self and world. Kohut designates this stage as the stage of the *fragmented self;* it is the developmental stage at which psychotic persons are fixated or to which they regress. Although there are important differences, Kohut's stage of the fragmented self corresponds to Freud's stage of autoeroticism; it is another way of understanding the stage of human development that precedes the integration of the infant's experienced world.

At the next stage of development, an *archaic, nuclear self* arises from the infant's experience of being related to as a self, rather than as a collection of parts and sensations, by empathic caretakers. This self is cohesive and enduring, but it is not yet securely established. Hence, it is prone to regressive fragmentation. It is nuclear in the sense of having a center, or nucleus, and it is archaic in the sense of being a primitive (that is, grandiose and undifferentiated) precursor of the mature self. The archaic nuclear self is bipolar in that it comprises two structures: the grandiose self and the idealized selfobject. That is, in this stage there is a differentiated self, which is experienced as omnipotent, but there are no truly differentiated objects. Objects are still experienced as extensions of the self, as selfobjects. At this stage, the child's grandiose self attempts to exercise omnipotent control over his selfobjects. In healthy maturity, all loved objects have a selfobject aspect. However, here the experience of the object as a selfobject is a reversible "regression in the service of the ego," which lacks the rigidity that characterizes the experience of objects as selfobjects in pathological narcissism.

The internalization of psychic structure (albeit in rudimentary form) is co-determinous with the formation of the nuclear self. As Kohut (1977) puts it, "The rudiments of the nuclear self are laid down by simultaneously or consecutively occurring processes of selective inclusion and exclusion of psychological structure" (p. 183). Failure to adequately internalize functions originally performed for the child by selfobjects results in deficits in the self. Addiction is a futile attempt to compensate for this failure in internalization.

To paraphrase Kohut: it is the inner emptiness, the missing parts of the self experienced as a void, that addicts try to fill with food, with alcohol, with drugs, or with compulsive sexuality. It cannot be done. Whatever is compulsively taken in goes right through and no psychic structure is built; that can only be done by transmuting internalization of self–selfobject relationships. It is abysmally low self-esteem, doubts about being real or of existing at all, and terror of fragmentation that addicts, including alcohol addicts, try to remediate by their addictions. They always fail.

Of crucial importance are the internalization of tension regulation, self-soothing, and self-esteem regulation, as well as the selfobject's function as stimulus barrier. Kohut's stage of the archaic self corresponds, in some ways, to Freud's stage of (primary) narcissism. It does not develop into object love, however, but into mature narcissism, which is characterized by realistic ambitions, enduring ideals, and secure self-esteem.

Pathological narcissism is the regression/fixation to the stage of the archaic self. It is characterized by the presence of a cohesive, but insecure, self that is threatened by regressive fragmentation; grandiosity of less than psychotic proportions, which manifests itself in the form of arrogance, isolation, and unrealistic goals; feelings of entitlement; the need for omnipotent control; poor differentiation of self and object; and deficits in the self-regulating capacities of the ego (self). Further, affect tolerance is poor. The tenuousness of the cohesion of the self makes the narcissistically regressed individual subject to massive anxiety, which is, in reality, fear of annihilation (that is, fear of fragmentation of the self). Narcissistic personality disorders are also subject to "empty" depression, reflecting the relative emptiness of the self, or the paucity of psychic structure and good internal objects. In the condition of pathological narcissism, these manifestations of the grandiose self and/or the idealized selfobject may be either blatantly apparent or deeply repressed and/or denied, with a resulting façade of pseudo-selfsufficiency, but they are never smoothly integrated into a mature self, as in the case of healthy narcissism.

In Kohut's formulation, the overtly grandiose self is the result of merger with (or lack of differentiation from) a mother who used the child to gratify her own narcissistic needs. It is a "false self" in the terminology of Winnicott (1960). Kohut envisions this false self as insulated from the modifying influence of the reality ego by a vertical split in the personality. The reality ego is in turn impoverished by the repression of the unfulfilled archaic narcissistic demands by a horizontal split (repression barrier) in the personality. For our purposes, the salient point to be derived from Kohut's and Winnicott's theories is an understanding of the overt grandiosity of the alcoholic as a manifestation of a "false self," which is isolated, both affectively and cognitively, from the more mature reality ego, which is itself enfeebled by its inability to integrate the archaic self. Hence, some sense can be made of the coexistence of haughty arrogance and near-zero self-esteem so frequently seen in alcoholics.

The therapist's first task with the recovering alcoholic (and all other patients) is *building a relationship*. Because the treatment will end unless the therapist succeeds in establishing a meaningful relationship with the alcoholic, the building and preserving of bonds between therapist and alcoholic *always* take precedence in the therapeutic interview. Bonds are built by empathic listening, supplemented by the clearing of resistances.

It is the *attitude* of the therapist that is crucial, especially with patients who are as sensitive as alcoholics are in early sobriety. What is required is active listening, the projection of interest and concern, and nonjudgmental positive regard for the patient. However, the situation with the newly sober alcoholic requires some modifications of Freud's excellent advice on conducting the early stages of treatment. The modification essentially consists of greater overt activity on the part of the therapist. Although empathic listening and clearing of treatment-threatening resistances remain paramount, the therapist must also serve as an expert on the disease of alcoholism; he or she has an educative function to perform.

The therapist is also dealing with an impulse disorder that may be acted out at any time, possibly ending the treatment. Insofar as possible, this acting out must be anticipated and circumvented. It is intolerable affects that lead to the drink. Unconscious and/or disavowed affects are particularly dangerous. Any intense feelings, "positive" or "negative," conscious or unconscious, that remain unverbalized are a threat to sobriety. The therapist must therefore actively encourage the expression of feelings and must appropriately interpret some of the emotional discomfort as a symptom of recovery. In other words, the acting out of the resistance by drinking must be anticipated and dealt with before it occurs. Of course, this is not always possible; it is a goal, not a demand on the therapist. Therapy at this stage of recovery is so very difficult because the therapist has little time in which to deal with the patient's conflicts since those conflicts may be acted out by drinking and terminating the treatment. We do not have the luxury of waiting the patient out, however desirable this may be. Thus, what is required is a sort of bob and weave on the part of the therapist. Empathic listening, imparting of information, and the elicitation of feelings must be integrated into a coherent style. It requires a great deal of "therapeutic tact" for the therapist to sense when to do what in order to maintain the relationship. However, the growing attachment of the patient to the therapist provides the cement which holds both the patient and the therapeutic relationship together. Thus, Freud's recommendations for establishing the therapeutic alliance remain pure gold that we must, however, necessarily alloy in order to successfully treat early-sobriety alcoholics (Freud 1913).

INTERNALIZATION OF SOBRIETY

Virtually no chronic alcoholic wants to get sober. The pain is too great. The regressive pull is too great. That is why either actual external events — such as the loss or threat of loss of a job, or the loss or threat of loss of a mate — or events experienced as external — such as the loss or threat of loss of health — are so often the precipitants of the emotional crisis that results in the alcoholic's becoming sober. These external events furnish the apparent motives for sobriety. At this point the alcoholic is "doing it for them." Such motivation is often not sufficient, and external controls such as those provided by hospitalization are necessary to achieve sobriety of any duration. After leaving the hospital, the alcoholic may remain sober out of fear of losing something valued. It is still being done for "them." This is the stage of "I can't drink" (Zimberg 1978). The hope is that a gradual process is initiated at this point by which remaining sober comes to be something that the alcoholic wants to do rather than something that must be done.

If this process is successful, the stage of "I won't drink" is reached. The controls that were originally external or experienced as external are now internal. Now, no asylum walls or chemical barriers are necessary. Internalized controls maintain sobriety, and the stage of "I don't have to drink" has been reached.

It is not known exactly how this control becomes internalized. Identification helps; in fact it may be the key. This is one reason that AA and peer counseling can be so effective in establishing stable sobriety. The alcoholic is provided with figures with whom to identify. They too are alcoholic, but they are no longer active; they are recovering. It is not with Bob or Jane or John or Sally that the alcoholic must identify, but with Bob's or Jane's or John's or Sally's sobriety. The alcoholic may also identify with his nonalcoholic therapist's sobriety, although here the identification is less direct. At first the identification is with the sobriety of the other, but slowly that sobriety is drawn within. It is as if the sobriety of the other is mentally ingested, digested, metabolized, and assimilated until it becomes part of the mental world of the newly recovering alcoholic. Although this is only a simile, it comes as close as we can get to an understanding of the process of internalization. Through this process the controls that allow others to remain sober become the controls of the newly sober one.

With time, sobriety becomes more rewarding. The pain of early sobriety recedes, the residual pain is endurable, and the alcoholic wants to remain sober. Sobriety becomes part of the recovering alcoholic's ego-ideal — of the ideal self. Living up to one's ego-ideal increases self-esteem and that feels good; hence, it is a behavior one tries to maintain. This is the case with the recovering alcoholic's sobriety. Remaining sober is no longer a struggle; it is an increasingly comfortable decision.

Sally

Sally came to me for the treatment of a post-traumatic stress reaction. She had been in an automobile accident and was badly shaken. Her face had been scarred and she was deeply depressed. Plastic surgery later restored her face, leaving little evidence of the accident, but she didn't know that was going to happen when she first came to my office. Sally was young and very appealing. She had been referred by her attorney, who had not mentioned alcohol, so I was surprised when she told me that she was an alcoholic. She said that she had been alcoholic since the age of 12 and had "hit bottom" four years ago. I asked her how old she was. She said, "Twenty -five." My next question was, "How did you get sober?" She replied, "The part about getting sober wouldn't make sense unless I told you about my drinking too: should I do that?" I said, "Sure." This is her testimony:

"Well, I don't know where to start. I come from an alcoholic family. Both my parents died of alcoholism. Well, I think my father died of alcoholism; he deserted us when I was 4. I remember the last time I saw him. We were eating in a diner and I was spilling my food. He screamed at me and said I was disgusting. I always felt that he left because I was so disgusting. I feel like a pig; I'm a compulsive overeater, too. I know in my head that he didn't leave because of the way I eat, but I don't know it in my heart. I think I still believe it. Things got worse then. My mother drank more and more and we had very little money. Sometimes there was no toilet paper in the house, but there was always beer. Later we moved to my grandfather's. He was rich, but he grabbed my pussy sometimes and I didn't know what to do. I think he was senile, but he drank too so maybe that was it. After I grew up, my mother told me she knew what he did to me, but she was afraid to do anything about it because he might have thrown us out. She was drunk when she told me that. Why did she have to tell me? I hate her for letting it happen, and I hate her for telling me that she let it happen. How could a mother do that? I have a daughter. I'd cut off his balls, if a man did that to my daughter. How could she? My grandfather got more senile and I don't know exactly what happened after that. My mother was like two people. When she was sober she was wonderful—beautiful and interested in me. But very snobby and uptight. Then I didn't think she was a snob, I thought that she was a great lady—perfectly dressed and so elegant. I loved her so much. Then there was mother when she was drunk. Sloppy and falling down, she'd sit with her legs spread with no panties and you could see everything. She'd curse and then try to play the great lady again, 'Oh, my dear' and all that shit. I hated her then.

"I was around 10 when I started having sex play with my cousins and some of the neighborhood kids. Mostly with the boys, but sometimes with the girls too. Do you think I'm a lesbian? I loved sex—it felt so good and it made me feel good about myself. Somebody wanted me. Maybe I felt guilty underneath. Later I hated myself and maybe all that sex play had something to do with it. I was raised a strict Catholic—sort of—once I was naked—I had just gotten out of the tub and I did an imitation of the Virgin Mary—I was about 6—and my mother really whaled my ass with a ruler. When I was about 10 my mother met my stepfather. Eddy was a complete asshole. He drank all the time, too. Can you imagine marrying a fucking drunk like him? Then mother really dropped me. She was more interested in drinking with Eddy. I started getting in trouble in school—at 11 I got fucked for the first time. And I mean got fucked, not made love to, by some 20-year-old pervert. Can you imagine an 11-year-old getting fucked? I loved it or thought that I did. I hung out with all the older boys. They had cars and liquor. I can't tell you how many cocks I had in me. Big ones, small ones, white ones, black ones. And you know I was never sober once. Every one of those guys had something to get high on—beer, pot, hard stuff. I loved booze from the first time I tasted it. It was even better than sex. I drank a lot. Any boy or man who gave me something to drink could have me. Sometimes I really liked it, but I liked fooling around with other girls even more. I think I was really turned on by myself—when I played with the other girls. My mother and stepfather raised hell when they weren't too drunk to care and finally my mother had me put away. Can you imagine that? What kind of fucking mother would put a kid in the places she put me? For God's sake, one place had bars and I was locked in. I hate her for doing that. Mental hospitals, homes for delinquent girls, the House of the Good Shepherd, the whole ball of wax. Finally I got out—I wasn't actually in any of those places for very long, it's just the idea—how could you do that to a kid—and I met Calvin.

"What a bastard he was. Oh, I forgot to tell you that when I was 15 I was team banged—raped—by a gang who pulled me into an alley and fucked me until my thing was raw and bloody. They beat me real hard too, but not so hard as Calvin did later. Oh yeah, Calvin beat me all the time. I must have been crazy but I loved him. He took me away from my hometown and my mother didn't bother me anymore. He sort of made a prisoner out of me—if I even went to the grocery store without his permission he beat me. He had a big one, the biggest I ever saw and I had seen plenty, so I thought he was a great lover. He always had beer and weed and other stuff and I stayed high most of the time. He's the father of my child. When I went into labor he was stoned. He slapped me and called me a rotten whore. He wouldn't go to the hospital with me. Do you know what it's like for a 16-year-old kid to have a baby alone? Forget it.

"I never cheated on Calvin but he never stopped accusing me of being with other men and hitting me. Sometimes he hit me with a wooden plank. I think I thought I deserved it—that I needed to be punished for all the things I had done. I needed Calvin to beat me. As long as he supplied drugs and alcohol and beat me I would have stayed. It was the way he acted around the baby that made me leave. One day when he wasn't home and the baby was about 2 I ran away. I couldn't stand his insane jealousy anymore; he was even jealous of the baby. A guy crazy enough to be jealous of his own kid, that's sick. He was real sick; sick in his head. I couldn't stand any more so I ran away and went to a town in the mountains where my older sisters and brother lived. Something in me said *enough*, you've been punished enough. Of course I kept on drinking. There wasn't any more sex, not then, just falling down drunk every day. I went on welfare and sometimes I worked off the books. I was sort of dead, no, not *sort of*, just plain *dead*. That went on for a few years and I hated myself more and more. I tried to be a good mother through it all and I don't think I did too badly, but God, was I depressed!

"My stepfather was dead by then and my mother was far gone. I think I saw it in her before I saw it in me. My brother was in the program—A.A. that is. I thought he was a jerk, a real ass, an uptight loser. Who else would join those holy rollers? What I couldn't figure out was how such a raving asshole could be happy, and the damn jerk *was* happy. Even I could see that. He did something really smart; he didn't lecture me. In fact, he never even mentioned my drinking. Damn good thing he didn't, because the way I rebelled against everything and everybody I would never have listened. What he did do was tell me what had happened to him—ran his story as they say in A.A. I didn't want to hear that shit and I told him so, but I did hear it in spite of myself. I was getting worse; I was more and more terrified that Calvin would come back and kill me—I guess I thought that he should because of the way I was living, but I didn't know that then, I was just scared. I was getting sicker and sicker from all the drinking and I never had any money; it got to the point where I couldn't stand anymore. If it wasn't for my daughter I would have killed myself, but I couldn't get out of it that way. I don't know why, but one day I asked my brother to take me to a meeting. An A.A. meeting that is. I think it was the guilt—once I didn't have Calvin to beat me I couldn't stand the guilt—I *knew*—I mean I really knew what it's like to have alcoholic parents. I loved my daughter—she has such a sick fuck for a father, so I wanted her to have at least one parent with her head screwed on straight. So I went to that fucking meeting. I loved it—

I mean I *loved* it—like I never loved anything. For Christ's sake, I even identified with the coffee cups. When I do something I *do* it—I went all the way—the whole nine yards. I was sick—sick, sick, sick from my crotch to my toes, not to mention my head. I was so scared; I hadn't had a sober day in years, but I've made it a day at a time. I haven't made it any too swiftly. I still can't stand the guilt and the rage; you wouldn't believe how angry I get, and the crying. I cry all the fucking time, but I don't drink, I don't drug, and I don't care if my ass falls off, I'm not going to. At least not today.

"I didn't want to be like my mother. I *won't* be like her. She's dead now. I couldn't stand it when she died—she died from her drinking—she had an accident while drunk, it was kind of a suicide. I knew she was dead, but I didn't know it. I couldn't let her go—not the awful way it was—if she was sober and I was sober I could have let her die, but she wasn't, so I knew but I didn't know she was dead. I never accepted it; she couldn't forgive me dead, not I her. Then one day I went to the cemetery. I looked at her grave for a long time. I couldn't believe she was dead; I started screaming, 'Move the fucking grass, move the fucking grass, Mother.' I screamed and screamed but she didn't move the fucking grass and I finally knew she was gone. I went to my home group meeting hysterical. All I said was she couldn't move the fucking grass and I cried the rest of the meeting. Nobody said a word, they just let me be me; they didn't try to take away my pain and I didn't want or need anybody to take it away. What I needed was somebody to be with me in that pain, and they were.

"I love the fucking program and all the crazy screwed-up people there. They're like me; I'm crazy too, but I'm sober. For God's sake, can you imagine what it would have been like if I was drinking when she died? Thank God I wasn't. I hate her—I love her—I still can't let go of her although I know she's dead. I hate alcohol. I hate drinking; look what it did to her, to my father, to me. How did I get sober—I don't really know—I sort of had two bottoms—a beaten bottom and an alcohol bottom. In that first bottom I sort of saw myself and saw I couldn't go on exposing my daughter to that stuff; the second was luck or something. No, not exactly luck or not only luck. It had something to do with willingness—I became willing to go to that meeting. Maybe I had just had enough; I didn't want any more pain for me or for the baby; she's not a baby anymore. They say, 'Why me?' in the program. When you're drinking you have the 'poor mees,' so you're always asking, 'Why me?' If you recover, you say it differently. I don't know why me. The way I lived, I should be dead but I'm not. I don't know if I deserve it or not, but I'll take it."

MAJOR TASKS IN WORKING WITH ALCOHOL ABUSE

Sally is a very clear example of an attempted self-cure of narcissistic deficit and narcissistic injury by substance abuse. All such attempts at self-cure are futile, eventually leading to further narcissistic injury. This was so for Sally. Although alcohol and drugs turned out to be the wrong medicine, Sally had found another way to heal herself or start to heal herself before she came for therapy, and the therapist largely stayed out of her way and was nonimpinging as she continued to heal herself. His relative "inactivity" allowed identification and transmuting internalization to take place. This led to structure building, firmer self-cohesion, and greater ego strength. Most alcoholics and substance abusers do not have Sally's powerful drive for health and they require more active interventions on the part of the therapist. Self psychology has a number of powerful interventions to suggest for use in working with these patients. In their respective ways they address what theory understands as narcissistic deficit and narcissistic injury and their attempted self-cure through the substance abuse; the attempt to fill inner emptiness due to failures in transmuting internalization; the acting out of and turning against the self of narcissistic rage; idealizing, mirror, and twinship transferences to alcohol and other drugs; attempts at omnipotent control through substance use and abuse; attempts to boost abysmally low self-esteem through the use of alcohol; and shame experiences both antecedent to and consequent upon alcohol and drug abuse. The following eleven suggested ways to translate theory into concrete interventions need to be modified so a particular patient can hear them, but they are models of great utility in working with alcoholics and substance abusers.

1. This intervention addresses the narcissistic wound inflicted by not being able to drink "like other people." The admission that one is powerless over alcohol, as A.A. puts it, or that one can't drink without the possibility of losing control, as I would put it, is extremely painful. It is experienced as a defect in the self, which is intolerable for those who are as perfectionistic as alcoholics usually are. The self must not be so damaged and deficient. Additionally, to be able to "drink like a man" or "like a lady" may be a central component of the alcoholic's self-image—his or her identity. This is particularly so for "macho" men, but is by no means restricted to them. The therapist must recognize and articulate the conflict between the patient's wish to stop drinking and the patient's feeling that to do so entails admitting that he or she is flawed in a fundamental way. The therapist does this by saying, "You don't so much want to drink as not want not to be able to drink." This makes the patient conscious of the conflict in an empathic way and allows him or her to struggle with this issue. This often opens the way for the patient to achieve stable sobriety.

2. All addictions, including alcoholism, are one long experience of narcissistic injury. Failure usually stalks the alcoholic like a shadow. As one of my patients put it, "When I drink, everything turns to shit." It sure does when an alcoholic drinks. Career setbacks, job losses, rejection by loved ones, humiliations of various sorts, ill health, economic decline, accidental injury, and enduring "bad luck" are all too frequent concomitants of alcoholism. Each is a narcissistic insult. Cumulatively they constitute a massive narcissistic wound. Even if outward blows have not yet come, the inner blows—self-hatred and low self-regard—are always there. The alcoholic has all too frequently heard "it's all

your fault" in one guise or another. The therapist must empathize with the alcoholic's suffering. "Your disease has cost you so much," "You have lost so much," and "Your self-respect is gone" are some ways the therapist can make contact with the alcoholic's pain and facilitate the alcoholic's experiencing this pain instead of denying, acting out, and/or anesthetizing it.

3. Alcoholics feel empty. Either they have never had much good stuff inside or they have long since flushed the good stuff out with alcohol. "You drink so much because you feel empty" makes the connection as well as brings into awareness the horrible experience of an inner void. After sobriety has been achieved, the genetic determinants of the paucity of psychic structure experienced as emptiness can also be interpreted.

4. Alcoholics frequently lack a firm sense of identity. How can you know who you are if your experience of self is tenuous, and its inner representation lacks consistent cohesion? The therapist can comment on this and point out that being an alcoholic is at least something definite—having an identity of sorts. When an A.A. member says, "My name is _____ and I am an alcoholic," he or she is affirming that he or she exists and has at least one attribute. With sobriety many more attributes will accrue—the self will enrich and cohere. Saying, "You are confused and not quite sure who you are. That is partly because of your drinking. Acknowledging your alcoholism will lessen your confusion as to who you are and give you a base on which to build a firm and positive identity" is a way of conveying this to the patient.

5. Many people drink because they cannot stand to be alone. They drink to enjoy someone's companionship. They have not developed what Winnicott (1958) calls the "capacity to be alone." Winnicott thinks that this comes from the experience of being alone in the presence of another—from having been a small child in the presence of an empathic, nonimpinging other who has become internalized so that one is not really alone when one is by oneself. Being alone in this sense is very different from defensive isolation driven by fear. Presumably, those who drink for companionship have never acquired the capacity to be alone. This, too, should be interpreted, "You drink so much because you can't bear to be alone and alcohol gives you the illusion of having company, of being with a friend. After you stop drinking it will be important for us to discover why it is so painful for you to be alone."

6. Alcoholics form selfobject (narcissistic) transferences to alcohol, as do other drug abusers to their drug of choice. Relating to alcohol as a friend can be regarded as forming a twinship transference to alcohol. Alcoholics also form idealizing and mirror transferences to alcohol. The imago of the archaic idealized parent is projected onto alcohol and it is regarded as an all-powerful, all-good object with which alcoholic drinkers merge in order to participate in this omnipotence. "Alcohol will deliver the goods and give me love, power, and whatever else I desire" is the drinker's unconscious fantasy. The therapist should interpret this thus: "Alcohol has felt like a good, wise, and powerful parent who protected you and made you feel wonderful, and that is why you have loved it so much. In reality it is a depressant drug, not all the things you thought it was."

The therapist can go on to say, "Now that drinking isn't working for you anymore, you are disillusioned, furious, and afraid. Let's talk about those feelings."

7. One of the reasons that alcoholics are so devoted to the consumption of alcohol is that it confirms their grandiosity. Another way to say this is alcoholics form a mirror transference to alcohol. I once had an alcoholic patient who told me that he felt thrilled when he read that a sixth Nobel prize was to be added to the original five. He read this while drinking in a bar at 8 A.M. His not-so-unconscious fantasy was winning all six.

The therapist should make the mirror transference conscious by interpreting it. "When you drink you feel that you can do anything, be anything, achieve anything and that feels wonderful. No wonder you don't want to give it up."

8. Alcoholics, without exception, like others with narcissistic behavior disorders, have abysmally low self-esteem no matter how well covered over by bluster and bravo it may be. Self psychology understands this as an impoverishment of the reality ego consequent upon failure to integrate archaic grandiosity, which is instead split off by what Kohut calls the "vertical split" and which manifests itself as unrealistic reactive grandiosity. At some point the therapist needs to say, "You feel like shit and that you are shit and all your claims to greatness are ways to avoid knowing that you feel that way. You don't know it, but way down somewhere inside you feel genuinely special. We need to put you in touch with the real stuff so you don't need alcohol to help you believe that the phony stuff is real." The particular reasons, antecedent to and consequent upon the alcoholism, that the patient values himself/herself so little need to be elucidated and worked through.

9. Sometimes the patient's crazy grandiosity is simultaneously a defense against and an acting out of the narcissistic cathexis of the patient by a parent. That is, the patient is attempting to fulfill the parent's dreams in fantasy while making sure not to fulfill them in reality. This is especially likely to be the case if the patient is an adult child of an alcoholic. Heavy drinking makes such a defense/acting out easy. If the alcoholic patient's grandiosity does seem to be a response to being treated as an extension of himself or herself by either parent, the therapist can say, "One reason you feel so rotten about yourself is that you're always doing it for Mom or Dad and not for yourself. You resent this and spite them by undermining yourself by drinking."

10. Many alcoholics have a pathological need for omnipotent control. Alcohol is simultaneously experienced as an object they believe they can totally control and coerce into doing their will, and an object which they believe gives them total control of their subjective states and of the environment. This can be seen as a manifestation of their mirror/idealizing transferences to alcohol. Alcoholics frequently treat people, including the therapist, as extensions of themselves. The A.A. slogans, "Get out of the driver's seat" and "Let God and let go," are cognitive behavioral ways of loosening the need to control. Therapists interpret this need to control in the patient's relationship with alcohol, in the patient's relationship with other people, and in the patient's relationship with the

therapist. For example, "You think that when you drink you can feel any way you wish," "You go into a rage and drink whenever your wife doesn't do as you wish," or "You thought of drinking because you were upset with me when I didn't respond as you thought I would."

11. Alcoholics and their children suffer greatly from shame experiences. Alcoholic patients are ashamed of having been shamed and often drink to obliterate feelings of shame. Therapists need to help alcoholic patients experience rather than anesthetize their feelings of shame. One way to do this is to identify such feelings of shame that are not recognized as such. For example, "You felt so much shame when you realized that you were alcoholic that you kept on drinking so you wouldn't feel your shame."

Sally amply exemplifies the relationship between narcissistic deficit, narcissistic injury, and the futile attempt to remediate the former and heal the latter through the addictive use of substances—alcohol and food—and compulsive actions—sex and excitement. Sally suffered massive failures of internalization, leaving her with gaping structural deficits. She also felt dead, doubting both her aliveness and her existence, and sought out stimulation of any kind, even beatings, to feel alive. Lacking idealizable parents she found Calvin; having had little phase appropriate mirroring of her archaic grandiosity, she found alcohol. In addition to mirroring her, alcohol gave her the illusion of cohesiveness. The amazing strength she did display may have been possible because her mother very early on was "good enough." Sally's capacity for splitting also helped her preserve a good mother from whom she could draw some sustenance in face of all the "badness" of her later, and by then overtly alcoholic, mother. Sally never integrated the two mothers, which in her case worked for her, at least in some ways. Her "bad" mother became Sally's split-off grandiosity and denial. So split off from any kind of reality testing was this side of Sally's vertical split that her unassimilated grandiosity came very close to killing her. The mother's grandiosity did kill her. On the other side of the vertical split, Sally's reality ego was impoverished, depressed, empty, fragile, and never far from fragmentation. The phase-appropriate grandiosity of the stage of the archaic nuclear self had never been integrated into her reality ego—it couldn't be because it had never been adequately mirrored. In Winnicott's terms, her true self was buried for safekeeping in a dangerous, treacherous environment. Whether we understand this in Kohutian or in Winnicottian terms, it is clear that this defensive system made survival possible *and* that a major aim of treatment must be its modification.

The child of an alcoholic carries a special kind of narcissistic injury. Humiliation and shame are recurrent and the wounds go deep. Sally's narcissistic injuries were denied, repressed, and/or acted out as was the narcissistic rage as a natural reaction to these injuries. Sally's delinquency was an attempt at self-cure. As Winnicott says, when there is an antisocial tendency there is hope. Sally found some kind of solace, responsiveness, and, in however distorted a form, mirroring in her acting out. It also allowed her to externalize her rage.

However, what saved Sally was her ability to love and to seek love. She never gave up her search for good objects that she could idealize and internalize. Alcohol was one such object—one that traumatically failed her, but she didn't give up. Abandonment depression and abandonment rage were central to Sally's psychopathology, but they could be worked through in the transference because she transferred, because she was still searching for relationship. Her love for her baby, probably an identification with the early good mother, got her away from Calvin, and her ability to enter into a twinship with her brother allowed her to identify with him and join A.A. The A.A. Program then became an idealized object. She formed the same kind of transference with me, and the working through of her predominately idealizing transference, which also had aspects of mirror and twinship in it, enabled her to build psychic structure. Of course, she was sober by then or this would not have been possible.

The scene in the cemetery was crucial to Sally's recovery. As long as she couldn't let go of the bad mother or of just plain *mother*, there was no way that she could internalize a good object. Bad mother was a pathological introject, the content of the vertical split. Only by letting her die and then mourning her could Sally recover the energy to cathect a new object and by transmuting internalization acquire the psychic structure she lacked. Mourning is not possible during active addiction to alcohol or to other substances. I have found in case after case that facilitating mourning must take priority in the therapy of stable sober alcoholics. Only then can the work proceed as one hopes it will.

CONCLUSION

Self psychological psychoanalysis is not the treatment of choice for most recovering alcoholics. Rather, what is indicated is once-or twice-weekly intensive, insight-oriented psychodynamic psychotherapy that is informed by Kohut's insights into the viscissitudes of narcissism. These patients have an intense need for mirroring, or approving confirmation, as well as a need to idealize the therapist. They are also particularly narcissistically vulnerable. The treatment should therefore focus on blows to the alcoholic's low self-esteem (alcoholism inflicts such terrible narcissistic wounds), failures of the childhood environment to supply sufficient phase-appropriate mirroring and opportunities for idealization, and the alcoholic's experience of much of the world as an extension of self. Anxiety is usually understood and interpreted as panic fear of psychic death, rather than as a manifestation of intrapsychic conflict, and rage is usually understood and interpreted as narcissistic rage, fury at the failure of the selfobject to perfectly mirror or protect, rather than as a manifestation of mature aggression.

Much seemingly irrational behavior can be understood in terms of both the alcoholic's need for omnipotent control and the rage that follows failure to so control. The grandiosity and primitive idealization of the archaic, nuclear self also explains the perfectionism of alcoholics and the unrealistic standards that they set for themselves. Most alcoholics have not developed realistic ambitions or livable ideals—these are characteristics of the mature self. The alcoholic's depression can be understood in terms of the paucity of psychic structure, which was never built up through the normal process of transmuting internalization. This empty depression also reflects the repression, rather than the integration, of the archaic, nuclear self and the failure to integrate the split-off grandiosity of the vertical split. The emptiness does not abate with sobriety. Further, the narcissistic rage to which the alcoholic is so prone can be turned against the self, resulting in intensely angry depression, sometimes of suicidal proportions. Failure to internalize the stimulus barrier and poor resources for self-soothing render the alcoholic especially vulnerable to psychic injury. Therefore, events in daily life threaten the alcoholic's already tenuous self-esteem.

The insights of self psychology into the dynamics of pathological narcissism are relevant and helpful in working with stably sober alcoholics. Further, Kohut's technique can be used in a modified form in which the narcissistic transferences (attenuated in psychotherapy) are allowed to unfold, the patient's need to control and to participate in greatness is accepted, and a slow working through is used to help integrate components of the archaic, nuclear self into the reality ego.

REFERENCES

American Psychiatric Association (1987). *Diagnostic and Statistical Manual of Mental Disorders,* 3rd ed. – rev. Washington, DC: American Psychiatric Association.

Freud, S. (1913). On beginning the treatment. *Standard Edition* 12:124–144.

Kernberg, O. (1975). *Borderline Conditions and Pathological Narcissism.* New York: Jason Aronson.

Kohut, H. (1971). *The Analysis of the Self.* New York: International Universities Press.

———— (1977). *The Restoration of the Self.* New York: International Universities Press.

Winnicott, D. W. (1958). The capacity to be alone. In *The Maturational Processes and the Facilitating Environment,* pp. 29–36. New York: International Universities Press, 1965.

———— (1960). Ego distortion in terms of true and false self. In *The Maturational Processes and the Facilitating Environment,* pp. 29–36. New York: International Universities Press, 1965.

Zinberg, S. (1978). Principles of alcoholism psychotherapy. In *Practical Approaches to Alcoholism Psychotherapy,* ed. S. Zinberg, J. Wallace, and S. B. Blume, pp. 1–18. New York: Plenum.

ISSUES AND TECHNIQUES
IN TREATMENT
Part VII

28: "CRAVING" AND RELAPSE TO DRINK

Arnold M. Ludwig and Abraham Wikler

Many clinical tenets in the field of alcoholism have not been adequately conceptualized, experimentally validated or tested critically under controlled laboratory conditions. Among the most important of these is the concept of craving for alcohol (alternately termed "irresistible desire," "overpowering urge," "need," "appetite" or "psychological dependence"). An expert committee of the World Health Organization noted that the concept has been invoked to describe many different clinical phenomena, such as (a) the onset of the excessive use of alcohol, (b) the drinking behavior displayed within a drinking bout, (c) relapse into a new drinking bout after days or weeks of abstinence, (d) continuous daily excessive drinking, and (e) loss of control. Aside from the descriptive aspects of this concept, it has also acquired a number of etiological implications. " 'Craving' and its alternative terms have been used to explain drinking arising from (a) a psychological need, (b) the physical need to relieve withdrawal symptoms, or (c) a physical need which originates in physiopathological conditions involving the metabolism, endocrine functions, etc., and existing in the drinker before he starts on his drinking career or developing in the course of it" (Jellinek et al. 1955, p. 63).

In order to focus discussion, some definitions are needed. According to Isbell (1955), there are essentially two types of craving. "Nonsymbolic" craving occurs in alcoholics who have drunk excessive amounts of alcohol over a protracted period of time. It is manifested by the appearance of symptoms upon withdrawal of alcohol and is believed to be due to physiological alterations, the mechanisms of which are not completely understood. Though physiologically determined, these symptoms may be colored or altered by psychological factors. In contrast, "symbolic" craving is presumably psychological in origin, accounting for the initial misuse of alcohol and for relapse after abstinence. While clinicians and scientists generally agree regarding the conditions necessary to elicit nonsymbolic craving and the role it plays in perpetuating a drinking bout, they are not in accord concerning the role or even existence of symbolic craving.

Because of the profound implications which symbolic craving (should it prove to be an authentic phenomenon) holds for the prevention and treatment of alcoholism, we are obliged to clarify both its nature and function.

Allied with the concept of symbolic craving is the presumed phenomenon of loss of control. This is commonly understood as meaning that a drink or two of an alcoholic beverage, taken either wittingly or unwittingly by an alcoholic, will trigger an inordinate desire, a sort of chain reaction, for alcohol, leading to increased consumption and eventually to the end-point of drunkenness or stupor—a process over which the alcoholic has little control. Glatt (1967) has offered some qualifications of this rather extreme but generally accepted view of loss of control. There may be an individual threshold, a critical blood alcohol level, "above which 'loss of control' begins to set in, a level range varying from person to person, and in the same individual from time to time, depending on a variety of factors, which might be predominantly psychological and/or physiological, psychosomatic or psychosocial in nature." These factors might include (a) state of mind of the alcoholic, (b) motivation for taking the drink, (c) place of drinking and one's company, (d) certain brakes, such as responsibility, work, lack of money, and (e) occupation and environment.

In Jellinek's view (1960), craving and loss of control are intimately related. He believed that the obsessive drinking bout related to loss of control becomes partially established through a true physical demand for alcohol (adaptation of cell metabolism to that substance) in the given situation, and that the demand for alcohol gives rise to the idea of "craving." The craving, however, may be only an apparent one since it will pertain specifically not to the ingestion of alcohol, which may be viewed by the alcoholic with disgust, but rather to the expected relief from the painful withdrawal symptoms. "The demand for alcohol seems to be of a two-fold nature. One part reflects the necessity to allay the distressing withdrawal symptoms, i.e., a physical demand; the other part reflects the obsessive belief that ultimately a sufficient amount of alcohol will bring about tension reduction which, before loss of control, was achieved quite easily."

In an attempt to account for loss of control, clinicians have advanced a variety of explanations, ranging from operant and classical conditioning mechanisms, to the activation of specific hypothalamic centers eliciting craving, to alcohol-induced dissociation of control centers in the brain, to alterations in cellular metabolism which become conditioned by the first drink. For the present, it is sufficient to note that none of these possibilities have been systematically studied or documented.

As with craving, the phenomenon of loss of control, if validated, has important implications for the etiology, prevention and treatment of alcoholism. To a great extent, these concepts have been adopted as implicit or explicit axioms in most psychiatric treatment settings and are reflected in the Alcoholics Anonymous injunction to "avoid the first drink." The problem, however, is that there is no substantial experimental evidence to support this extreme position. Moreover, a body of data is accumulating which tends to contradict these clinical axioms.

CONTRA CRAVING

According to Mello (1972), the constructs of "symbolic" craving and loss of control have little clinical or even scientific utility. On the assumption that clinicians define craving by subsequent drinking behavior, she argues that the concept of craving is really a logical tautology and, as such, becomes superfluous from the vantage point of science. In further support of her contentions, she offers most of the following arguments, representing the findings of various studies.

1. No alcoholic subjects allowed freely to program their ethanol consumption showed loss of control or "drank to oblivion" (Mello 1968, Mello and Mendelson 1965, Mello et al. 1968).
2. No alcoholic subjects allowed to drink up to 32 oz of alcohol per day drank all that was available even without having to work for it (Mello and Mendelson 1971).
3. Alcoholic subjects allowed to drink 30 to 60 days continuously often started and stopped drinking bouts throughout this period (Mello et al. 1968, Mello and Mendelson 1971).
4. The amount of alcohol consumed by alcoholics consistently proved to be a function of the amount of work necessary to obtain it (Mello 1972, Mello and Mendelson 1965).
5. For a sufficient payment of money, alcoholics were willing to abstain from drinking. Moreover, a priming dose of alcohol disrupted abstinence less than a delay in payment for abstinence (Cohen et al. 1971).
6. Because alcoholics demonstrated the ability to taper their drinking to avoid the severe consequences of abrupt withdrawal from alcohol, this presumably indicated that they did have control over their drinking behavior (Mello 1972, Mello and Mendelson 1971).
7. Alcoholics could display social drinking for long periods of time (Bailey and Stewart 1967, Davies 1962).
8. Priming doses of alcohol, with taste (presumably) disguised, did not lead to increase in reported craving (Merry 1966).

Other recent studies (Cutter et al. 1970, Marlatt et al. 1973) have also failed to demonstrate loss of control in alcoholics after administration of single doses of alcohol. Also, in an extensive follow-up study by Ludwig (1972), only 1 percent of alcoholics offered reasons akin to craving as the excuse for "falling off the wagon"; most of the others cited some type of emotional dysphoria or unpleasant situation as the major cause.

There is no need to criticize the above studies, for most are of excellent caliber and add considerably to our knowledge of the behavior of alcoholics. We shall later, however, take issue with the interpretation that they constitute "evidence" against the concept of craving and loss of control.

Several misconceptions in the interpretation of the above studies need to be pointed out. First, although alcoholics may not have "demonstrated" craving or loss of control in several of these studies, they certainly drank inordinately large amounts of ethanol (i.e., sustaining blood alcohol levels between 150 and 250 mg per 100 ml) either in free-drink or work situations, either continuously or sporadically. Since these subjects were not forced to imbibe alcohol, we "naively" assume that they were somehow "driven" to drink quantities of alcohol far greater than those likely to be consumed by normal or social drinkers. Moreover, because alcoholics do not necessarily drink themselves to stupor does not mean that loss of control is absent. Drinking to the point of sustained intoxication may likewise indicate an inability to control alcohol intake. Rather than view loss of control in absolute terms, it seems much more fruitful to adopt a relativistic framework, as with any form of human psychopathology. (This viewpoint will be developed later at length.)

Second, we strongly protest the notion that subjective states, such as craving, need be reflected in behavior, or that regulation of drinking behavior (determined by either external contingencies or inner motivation) argues against a need, drive or compulsion for alcohol consumption. We may note that inordinate sexual urges, ravenous appetites, monumental angers, and so on (constructs we regard as comparable to craving) need not necessarily be expressed in rape, eating or overt aggression. Not only is it possible to curb these behaviors (i.e., sexual abstinence, fasting, forced politeness), but the expressed behavior may actually be incongruous with the inner motivational state. In other words, the presence of a subjective need or drive does not necessarily mean that cognitive control cannot be exerted over its overt expression or that it cannot be modified by external contingencies.

Third, it should be noted that except for several small studies conducted under highly artificial conditions, none have been specifically designed to investigate craving or loss of control in a systematic manner. The reflections concerning these phenomena are essentially byproducts of other investigations. Moreover, since the study by Merry (1966) has been widely cited as disproving the concept of craving, it is important to realize that the actual results prove otherwise. His nine alcoholic subjects did not report craving any more frequently following ingestion of a disguised mixture containing the equivalent of 1 oz of "65.5% proof" vodka than after a placebo in an experiment represented to them as designed "to help them remain abstinent" (we should note the very negative demand characteristics of the instructions). But all of the same subjects reported craving on the one day that an additional ounce of vodka was added to the disguised mixture. The average craving score (by our calculation) was 1.44, indicating slight to moderate craving. Although Merry interprets his data in a rather peculiar manner, he concludes his report as follows: "There is no doubt that 2 fl oz of vodka taken under experimental conditions described would have a strong disinhibiting effect and would allow a good opportunity for the emergence of psychological tendencies to relapse."

Fourth, the follow-up study by Ludwig (1972) relied primarily on spontaneous reports of alcoholics and was not specifically designed to probe into actual details concerning the cognitive aspects of drinking behavior. To remedy this, a comprehensive Craving Questionnaire was constructed and administered to sixty alcoholic patients. In contrast to prior findings, (a) 78 percent of them experienced craving for alcohol; (b) 62 percent claimed that craving was increased after one or two drinks; (c) 43 percent defined craving in terms of relief from dysphoria or discomfort while 55 percent defined it as a need, desire or want; (d) 57 percent reported an inability to stop drinking after taking one or two drinks; and (e) 55 percent and 47 percent, respectively, claimed that their craving increased when they were around people who were drinking or in places where alcohol was likely to be found. If these findings are accepted at face value, they seem to support the view that craving and loss of control represent crucial determinants of relapse and excessive drinking behavior—at least, from the perspective of alcoholics.

For an issue characterized by polarized and divergent viewpoints, it is unlikely that resolution will come solely through further polemics or even experimentation. What seems first indicated is a clearer conceptualization of the nature of the phenomenon in question and then the development of appropriate experimental paradigms to test the validity of hypotheses based on this conceptualization. It is to this end that subsequent discussion will be directed.

A RECONCEPTUALIZATION

In the past, the phenomenon of craving has been viewed either as an experiential subjective state or as an invariant psychological correlate of alcohol-acquisition behavior. With the former view, it becomes possible to reify the experience itself as having phenomenological validity without the necessity for expression in behavior. With the latter view, it becomes possible to discard this phenomenon as tautological with behavior and, therefore, unnecessary from a logical standpoint.

As a further conceptual problem, there has been the tendency to adopt an elitist orientation toward the interpretation of craving for alcohol by not incorporating insights gleaned from research and clinical observations on comparable phenomena, such as narcotic drug-seeking behavior, obesity and heavy cigarette smoking. For some inexplicable reason, theoretical formulations of alcoholism have regarded the phenomena comprising this disorder as unique and idiosyncratic and, therefore, have not benefited by cross-fertilization from findings on analogous forms of psychopathology.

In our view, much of the ambiguity and controversy surrounding the phenomenon of symbolic craving can be resolved if it can be viewed as similar to "narcotic hunger," which likewise contributes to relapse. Within this theoretical framework, we would consider craving for alcohol, comparable to craving for narcotics, as representing the psychological or cognitive correlate of a "subclinical" conditioned withdrawal syndrome. According to Wikler (1948, 1952, 1955, 1961, 1968, 1971, 1973, Wikler and Pescor 1967, Wikler et al. 1971), concomitantly with the development of physical dependence on opiates, opiate-withdrawal phenomena can become classically conditioned to stimuli (physical environment, drug-using or drug-dispensing associates, certain emotional states) through repeated temporal contiguity between such stimuli and "unconditional" opiate-withdrawal phenomena; and opiate-seeking behavior is repeatedly reinforced (instrumental conditioning) by the efficacy of self-administration of opiates in suppressing withdrawal phenomena.

After conventional detoxication and discharge of the patient to his home environment, exposure to the same or similar stimuli can now evoke conditioned withdrawal phenomena and opiate-seeking behavior (relapse). The theory is supported by experimental evidence that in the rat a selected opiate-withdrawal sign (increased frequency of "wet-dog" shakes) can be conditioned experimentally to a physical environment and that such "conditioned abstinence" can persist for many months after withdrawal of the opiate; and, likewise, that a secondary (conditioned) reinforcer generated by repeated temporal contiguity with suppression of "unconditional" opiate-withdrawal phenomena can retain its potency for months after the withdrawal (Wikler and Pescor 1967, Wikler et al. 1971). Also, the theory is consistent with statements frequently made by addicts to the effect that they relapsed to use of opiates because of "sickness" appearing suddenly on return to their home environment after a "cure," or later on encountering their former associates (active addicts or "pushers"). Usually, this sickness is called "the flu," but the symptoms specified—"aching all over," "runny nose," "watery eyes," "sweatiness," and so on—are strongly suggestive of early opiate-withdrawal phenomena (presumably conditioned).

Despite such presumed "cognitive mislabeling," the addict himself also reports that under such circumstances he experiences a "yen" (craving) for "God's Own Medicine" (opiates) and, much to his "disgust," resorts to "just one fix" (and many more "fixes" thereafter). In one sense, the use of opiates under such circumstances can be regarded as a consequence of negative rather than positive reinforcement since, from past experience, the addict associates such use with relief from discomfort. In a more important sense, however, the instrumental conditioning generated by the opiate-withdrawal–withdrawal-suppression cycle is "appetitive" in that through such conditioning the opiate-adapted individual is able to get opiate reinforcement more frequently—up to twelve times per day in one study (Wikler 1952)—in contrast to aversive reinforcement which results in less frequent delivery of the original reinforcer, for example, electric shocks (Wikler 1971).

Wikler (1971) also maintains that the anxiety due to withdrawal and its subsequent relief by morphine is of great importance in establishing a habit pattern of relieving anxiety due to other factors (e.g., neurotic anxiety) by the use of morphine and other drugs. The subjective concomitants of this drug-seeking behavior may or may not be at a conscious level. The degree of cognitive specificity is related to the addict's capacity for symbolism. In addition, it should be noted that the production of withdrawal symptoms is not only susceptible to conditioning but to suggestion as well. Through posthypnotic suggestion, Ludwig and Lyle (1964) were able to produce a variety of withdrawal symptoms, including elevated pulse rate, elevated blood pressure, mydriasis, gagging and vomiting, muscular aches and pains, and runny nose in postnarcotic drug addicts who had a prior history of numerous "cold turkey" withdrawal experiences.

If we may apply a similar thesis to alcoholism, we should expect that craving and other withdrawal phenomena would become conditioned through prior alcohol withdrawal experiences. The more frequent and severe the prior withdrawal experiences, the greater the predisposition to conditioned withdrawal symptoms with consequent desire for relief (i.e., "craving") through drink. Moreover, just as there are gradations of severity of alcohol withdrawal symptoms, ranging from hangover and tremulousness to full-blown seizures and delirium tremens, craving could also be expected to vary in degree. While the experience of craving provides an alcoholic with the necessary cognitive symbolism for goal-directed, appetitive behavior (i.e., the negative reinforcement provided by alcohol), there is no cogent reason (as with anger, hunger or sexual urge) why this subjective desire for alcohol should be directly acted upon or expressed in overt behavior, especially if there are competing drives or motivations. We would regard craving, then, as a necessary but not sufficient condition for relapse or loss of control. It is necessary since without it the alcoholic would not look to alcohol for relief or pleasure; it is not sufficient since there are other powerful factors which influence whether it will be consciously perceived, expressed directly in alcohol consumption, or manifested in some other fashion.

Granted the validity of these assumptions, we should expect that craving for alcohol, as with craving for opiates, could be conditioned either interoceptively or exteroceptively. Interoceptive conditioning would arise after ingestion of a sufficient amount of alcohol (or drugs having similar effects) with stimulation or sensitization of appropriate visceral and cerebral neuronal receptors, which, in a recovered alcoholic, act as conditioned stimuli that evoke conditioned withdrawal responses. It could also be induced by the provocation of any physiological arousal state resembling the alcohol withdrawal syndrome. For example, Ludwig, Levine, and Stark (1970) observed that many alcoholics given lysergide compared their experience to "D.T.s" or "coming off a drunk"; and in a recent pilot study, several alcoholics given Δ-9-tetrahydrocannabinol not only likened their experience to a "hangover" or "D.T.s" but also professed heightened craving for alcohol.

As for exteroceptive conditioning, this would pertain to a variety of situations associated with prior heavy drinking or with the uncomfortable psychological and physical effects of prior withdrawal experiences. A conditioned withdrawal syndrome, generally subclinical in nature, with associated craving might result, therefore, whenever the alcoholic passed a bar or was in the presence of other people drinking or encountered cues relevant to previous drinking practices. Moreover, since apprehension, anxiety, mild depression, other types of emotional dysphoria or physical discomfort (e.g., increased heart rate, tremulousness, increased respiration, autonomic lability, insomnia) represent major features of the alcohol withdrawal syndrome, we should anticipate that any combination of these factors, either interoceptively or exteroceptively induced, might likewise evoke the experience of craving.

Modifiers of Craving

While the presence of a subclinical conditioned withdrawal syndrome or a state of neurophysiological arousal seems to represent a necessary precondition for the appearance of craving, other conditions determine whether an alcoholic will consciously interpret his feelings as craving and translate these feelings into alcohol-acquisition behavior. First, situational variables, either implicitly or explicitly defined, seem to play a major role in the experience of craving. In the presence of drinking companions, in a bar or at a social gathering, or in the solitary confines of a hotel room, an alcoholic may experience an overwhelming desire for alcohol; in a psychiatric treatment unit, at an Alcoholics Anonymous meeting, or in an experimental setting, the same alcoholic will report no craving.

By not appreciating the importance of mental set and setting, many clinicians and researchers have come to erroneous, inaccurate or biased conclusions concerning the determinants of alcoholic behavior. In state hospitals and psychiatric institutions, dedicated clinicians find themselves betrayed by seemingly sincere alcoholics who, while hospitalized, profess resolutions of abstinence but who, after discharge, immediately "fall off the wagon." What must be recognized, however, is that these patients actually believe their resolutions while hospitalized, largely because they experience no craving and, therefore, have just cause to feel self-confident in their vows of abstinence. Once released from an institutional setting with its implicit and explicit prohibitions against drinking and inebriation, and then exposed to real-life settings reinforcing drinking, the same alcoholics are likely to forget their resolutions of sobriety and "the good life."

In experimental settings, the situation is similar. In certain studies of loss of control (Marlatt et al. 1973, Merry 1966) an attempt was made to disguise the taste of alcohol. The alcoholic was then required to perform certain tasks or make certain judgments; and based on the results, inferences about craving or loss of control were made. In other studies of drinking behavior, alcoholics, who might be paid for participating, were required to perform operant tasks at different reinforcement schedules for alcohol, to drink small amounts of alcohol at artificially scheduled times, or to drink unspecified amounts of alcohol in highly artificial experimental settings. If mental set and setting are crucial variables for the assessment of drug effects, as indeed most psychopharmacologists consider them to be, then it is little wonder that behaviorally oriented investigators have failed to elicit craving or loss of control. The experimental "demand characteristics" of these situations have little in common with those real-life situations, many of which are idiosyncratic for given alcoholics, in which craving and alcohol-acquisition behavior are likely to appear.

The powerful inhibitory effect and invisible constraints of an institutional setting on alcoholic behavior and craving have been noted by other investigators. Paredes,[1] in a preliminary research report, observed that nineteen alcoholics with blood alcohol levels of 150 mg per 100 ml or higher, who normally were aggressive, hostile and provocative under the influence of alcohol, exhibited none of these characteristics in the hospital. The findings suggested that if craving and the provocative behavior are to be manifested, the drinking must occur in a setting where such behavior is expected. According to Paredes, "If the social expectations are suspended—if the drinker does not have the job to worry about, if there is no nagging wife waiting for him at home, if the people around him are not expecting him to act or react in a certain way—then the alcohol does not trigger the 'uncontrollable' actions . . . seen outside."

From our viewpoint, these conclusions are not surprising. A public lavatory is not the best setting in which to stimulate hunger and eating with gusto; it is less likely that sexual fantasies and overt copulation will occur in a church during a sermon than in a bedroom; and smoking a cigar at home after supper may be far more enjoyable and relaxing than smoking it in a laboratory filled with oxygen tanks. Likewise, it seems reasonable to assume that clinical and experimental settings, especially those which impose artificial schedules on drinking and devise artificial tasks to perform in order to drink, are likely to yield artificial or biased results with regard to the phenomena of craving and loss of control. In the above situations, the exteroceptive cues would provide stimulus configurations different from those associated with ordinary drinking situations and thereby diminish the possibility of eliciting conditioned withdrawal. Moreover, even if sufficient alcohol is administered, it is possible that these powerful external influences might foster the misinterpretation of interoceptive cues. We should presume, therefore, that if craving is to be elicited in any systematic manner in experimental settings, it is first necessary to alter these external influences so that they provide optimal stimulus configurations for ordinary drinking behavior; and, second, to train the alcoholics to recognize, as such, feelings akin to those experienced during prior withdrawal states (when they sought alcohol for relief) and to label such feelings as "craving."

This latter injunction brings up another crucial determinant for the expression of craving. Most simply, we would anticipate that eliciting craving under appropriate stimulus conditions would be directly affected both by an alcoholic's capacity for symbolization and for accurate symbolization. Alcoholics, for example, may express the same feeling state in a variety of ways. Some will translate their experiences into socially desirable terms (e.g., "I want a drink to be sociable"), some will "psychologize" (e.g., "I want a drink to be sociable"), some will "psychologize" (e.g., "I want a drink to relieve my tension or depression"), some will translate their desire into a compulsion (i.e., "I just need

---

[1]Cited by Manber (1972).

a drink"), some will deny their feelings (i.e., "I don't want a drink"), some will distort their feelings (e.g., "I took a drink because it was available"), and others may be unable to find any appropriate reason for their behavior (e.g., "I don't know why I drank—I just drank").

In other words, it appears that alcoholics may employ a variety of cognitive labels to interpret similar visceral states. These labels or "excuses," however, are highly modifiable by external situational factors or internal cognitive factors. That this should be the case seems predictable, especially when the research findings from other related areas are taken into account. The work of Schacter (1971) and Schacter and Singer (1972) and Lazarus (1968) emphasizes the "plasticity" of physiological states (e.g., sympathetic arousal, fear, joy, hunger, pain), or even of "standard" drug effects, all of which can be manipulated through experimental factors. Orne's work (1962) on the power of situational demand characteristics demonstrates how attitudes or cognitions can be shaped through external instructions or implicit mental sets.

Cognitive labeling has also been demonstrated to alter classically conditioned physiological and subjective responses. Thus, Wikler (1973) reports that in subjects physically dependent on morphine or heroin, unauthorized "decoding" of the experimental design by the subjects resulted in prompt disappearance of signs and symptoms of conditioned abstinence evoked by subcutaneous injections of normal saline, which had been interpolated irregularly among subcutaneous injections of nalorphine, even though this narcotic antagonist continued to evoke typical withdrawal symptoms.

The construct of cognitive labeling has direct relevance for explaining the inconsistent results and observations made on the drinking behavior of alcoholics. Because alcoholics do not spontaneously report craving or because they offer some other reason for drinking does not necessarily mean that they are not experiencing craving or that craving is not an important determinant in the initiation and perpetuation of drinking. It may well be that the cognitive labels provided by alcoholics are either inappropriate or inaccurate. On further probing, experimenters and clinicians will likely find an intense desire, compulsion or drive for alcohol consumption beyond the veil of the glib labels or reasons supplied by alcoholics for their drinking. This was demonstrated most dramatically in a recent study in which 78 percent of the alcoholics interviewed claimed to have experienced craving; when this concept was more precisely defined for them, the incidence of reported craving increased to 95 percent.

The implications of cognitive label theory for research on craving are apparent. First, any investigator studying craving must probe beyond the initial, superficial reasons offered by alcoholics for their drinking. Not only may the symbolic processes of many alcoholics be deficient, especially those with varying degrees of organic mental impairment, but they are also highly malleable by mental set and physical setting. Second, just as behavioral raters have to be trained to increase interrater reliability, alcoholics have to be trained to discriminate among internal cues and to label such cues accurately both as to nature and degree. We suspect that almost any cognitive construct an alcoholic offers to justify initial relapse, provided he finds this construct a compelling reason to consume alcohol, is probably a reflection of underlying craving which, in turn, is an automatic concomitant of a subclinical conditioned withdrawal state or related state of physiological arousal. Third, since no one (even alcoholics) likes to admit that he is a slave to some unknown internal force, such as craving, an alcoholic must first be educated about the nature of drives and feel that he will not be looked down upon by those in authority (i.e., clinicians, experimenters) before he feels relatively free to provide an honest appraisal of his feelings.

Functions

We regard craving as a cornerstone concept for interpreting the appetitive behavior of alcoholics, especially those predisposed to relapse and numerous drinking bouts. In our view, like the hypothetical constructs of anger, fear, hunger or sex urge, the cognitive experience of craving represents an effective way of protecting the organism against sensed danger, threat or psychophysiological distress by alerting it to a potential source of relief—namely, alcohol. Without such an automatic cognitive labeling process for amorphous and ambiguous internal cues (conditioned or unconditioned), the appetitive behavior of alcoholics would be far less efficient or goal-directed and far more disorganized, fragmented and haphazard since there would be no specific consummatory response for immediate relief. Unfortunately, the consequences of this response pattern tend to become maladaptive largely because of its tendency to generalize to related dysphoric experiences and its predisposition toward unmodulated drinking.

LOSS OF CONTROL[2]

As mentioned previously, the phenomenon of loss of control is intimately associated with the concept of craving. There is considerable confusion, however, concerning the actual relationship between these phenomena. Some clinicians employ the terms craving and loss of control interchangeably; others employ the latter to refer to inordinate and overwhelming craving which increases with increased drinking; and others regard these concepts as complementary but distinctive. Regardless of definitional bias, the general construct of loss of control is crucial, for without the presumed predisposition of an alcoholic toward unmodulated drinking after the ingestion of one or several drinks, craving would be only of hypothetical rather than practical clinical interest. We might say that craving can lead an alcoholic to ethanol but it cannot make him drunk.

If loss of control is to be studied and better understood, it is essential to

---

[2]Since the completion of this paper, we have been introduced to a relatively recent article by Keller (1972) on the loss-of-control phenomenon. This represents a penetrating analysis of definitional and semantic aspects of loss of control, with important implications for the understanding of alcoholism.

resolve some of the conceptual chaos surrounding this construct. When opinions of loss of control range from regarding it as an outright myth to the "fundamentalistic" belief that, if it exists, it must act as a psychological juggernaut, increasing the momentum of drinking until the point of stupor occurs, then erroneous interpretation of the research data gathered on this phenomenon is inevitable. For example, a number of investigators have made the latter opinion a straw man for their studies and, after finding no evidence to support it, have arrived at conclusions consistent with the former opinion — namely, that loss of control does not exist. But neither of the extreme opinions is in accord with clinical reality.

From our viewpoint, based on extensive clinical experience with alcoholics, all that loss of control connotes is the relative inability to regulate ethanol consumption. Craving is the cognitive state designating ethanol consumption as a source of relief or pleasure; it need not inevitably lead to drinking. Loss of control is the behavioral state initiated by craving and characterized by activities indicative of a relative inability to modulate ethanol consumption; it need not eventuate in gross intoxication or stupor. It may even take the form of total abstinence, when an alcoholic has incorporated the belief that he must remain abstinent because he cannot handle alcohol. By no means, however, does the construct of loss of control imply (as some investigators apparently assume) that alcoholics have no volitional power at all to control the amount and frequency of drinking or that they turn into servomechanisms guided solely by the desire to attain mental oblivion through alcohol.

As we shall demonstrate, this operational definition of loss of control holds many heuristic advantages from both a clinical and research standpoint, for it permits a reconceptualization of many of the discrepant findings in the literature and suggests certain underlying mechanisms of action contributing to this behavior.

Concerning the reconceptualization of prior findings, we wish to make certain points. First, as alluded to previously, we believe that the large number of studies in which alcoholics obtain ethanol either through operant-task behavior or through free-drinking schedules, contrary to the conclusions of the investigators, is more indicative of loss of control than not. Regardless of the reasons offered by alcoholics for their excessive drinking or the demonstrated relationship of their drinking behavior to certain environmental contingencies, we assume that any alcoholics who drink sufficiently to achieve and then sustain blood alcohol levels of the magnitude of 150 to 200 mg per 100 ml over a period of days or even weeks (even though not becoming stuporous) are manifestly demonstrating a relative inability to control, regulate or modulate their ethanol intake; otherwise, why should they not be content with two or three socially acceptable drinks of an evening? The very fact that they choose to drink so much, even though they do not have to, argues in favor of some sort of internal regulatory dysfunction or excessive, nonenvironmentally derived, need.

Second, it is fallacious to assume that, because the drinking behavior of alcoholics can be modified by experimental manipulations of environmental reinforcement contingencies (e.g., the amount of alcohol consumed is inversely related to the amount of work necessary to earn it, or abstinence behavior can be "bought" for a suitable price), the behavior is not primarily influenced by neurophysiological mechanisms or internal drives. Internal drive states and external environmental factors are not mutually exclusive: they are complementary and in constant interaction. Because one of these dimensions can be manipulated does not invalidate the operation of the other. To illustrate this point, we may cite a common clinical situation: Acutely psychotic patients, such as schizophrenics or manicdepressives, can "voluntarily" modify their symptomatology or respond to environmental contingencies (Ludwig 1971) even though most of their psychopathology is likely to be metabolically or neurophysiologically induced. Why should not a similar situation pertain in the drinking behavior of alcoholics? While behavioral studies can elucidate the external reinforcers controlling drinking in experimental situations, they do not necessarily provide answers to the mechanisms of action underlying such behavior.

Third, once we view loss of control within a relativistic rather than an absolutistic framework, there is no necessary reason why it should become manifest immediately after one or several drinks rather than over a more extended time. During the initial phase of relapse, many alcoholics are able to exert considerable volitional control over the amount of ethanol consumed, often convincing themselves that they are now capable of "social drinking." In time, however, their volitional control progressively declines and their drinking behavior comes more and more under the control of internal factors. In other words, it appears that time and repeated exposure to alcohol may be important variables for the expression of loss of control.

Abstinence and Drinking

We have suggested that total abstinence may reflect loss of control. Under our operational definition of loss of control, the relative inability to regulate ethanol intake also implies behavior which indicates that an alcoholic cannot drink ordinary amounts of ethanol appropriate to certain social occasions. Total abstinence then represents the other side of the coin of excessive drinking. It belies an alcoholic's ability to handle alcohol other than in an unmodulated and extreme way. The behaviors based on abstinence and excessive drinking are certainly radically different but their common denominator is the inability to handle alcohol in moderation.

While support for this viewpoint is primarily anecdotal, it is nevertheless substantial. The countless alcoholics who profess that total abstinence represents for them the only effective way of dealing with alcohol, and A.A's wise insistence that alcoholics admit their inability to drink wisely, seem to reflect some portion of clinical reality. This does not mean that all alcoholics at all times display loss of control, for the findings of Stein, Niles, and Ludwig (1968) prove otherwise, or that they can only cope with alcohol through total abstinence. Nor does this mean that a certain portion of alcoholics cannot be taught to drink socially. It only means that under ordinary circumstances, without the use of special treatment procedures, many alcoholics can keep from "falling off the wagon" only by "staying on the wagon."

In a sense, then, we are stating that the same "defect" or "vulnerability" or "sensitivity" resides in both the abstinent and drinking alcoholic. In the former the defect is latent, in the latter manifest. Because these two behaviors are diametrically opposed does not mean that they are determined by different causes. In our view, they are simply different but consistent expressions of the same underlying problem.

Our thesis regarding abstinence represents something more than mere semantics. As we later hope to demonstrate, this broadened concept of loss of control permits precise study and elucidation.

Interoceptive and Exteroceptive Cues

In general, a social drinker tends to rely primarily on two sources of information to regulate his drinking. These sources pertain to both exteroceptive and interoceptive cues. Exteroceptive cues, for example, relate to counting the number of drinks, setting limits on the total amount, drinking at socially specified times (i.e., cocktail hour, nightcap), drinking only in appropriate social contexts, and drinking amounts appropriate for those contexts. Interoceptive cues pertain to the relative state of perceived intoxication, the degree of speech and motor impairment, the amount of "glow," and so on. These exteroceptive and interoceptive cues, then, may be regarded as a source for information feedback relevant to limiting or regulating the drinking rate and quantity. To the extent that drinkers attend to this feedback, they can be regarded as controlled drinkers; to the extent that they do not or cannot, they demonstrate loss of control. It is our hypothesis, therefore, that the presumed regulatory dysfunction in alcoholics is related to a relative deficit in ability to respond to such feedback.

In some respects, the behavior of many alcoholics in regard to ethanol intake does not seem too different from that of obese persons who likewise seem to possess a relative inability to limit the rate and quantity of food intake and whose eating behavior is often characterized by binge eating interspersed with periods of starvation diets. Moreover, obese persons, compared with the non-obese, show little correlation between the experience of hunger and stomach contractions, tend to rely more on external cues, such as the ready availability or attractiveness of food, as an inducement for eating behavior, and tend to have difficulty in appreciating visceral feedback regarding satiation or satisfaction of hunger (Schacter 1971, Stunkard 1961, Stunkard and Koch 1964). All these behaviors can be interpreted within the framework of a feedback dysfunction.

Hypothetical Model

If we assume the plausibility of a feedback dysfunction, it becomes possible to construct a hypothetical model of loss of control, capable of experimental validation, as a means of classifying alcoholics and problem drinkers according to their ability to utilize exteroceptive or interoceptive cues, or both, in order to regulate ethanol intake. Such a classification has implications for both etiology and treatment.

The model could be tested in a study of the drinking responses of subjects during two separate experimental sessions after a prior training session in which their blood alcohol level (BAL) is stabilized within a designated range (e.g., 50–70 mg per 100 ml). Over the course of the training session, subjects are provided with accurate feedback about their BAL. In the experimental sessions, they are required to remember how they felt during the prior training session and to drink enough to maintain a BAL within the designated range, regardless of exteroceptive feedback. In actuality, false feedback is given in both experimental sessions by a "rigged" blood alcohol meter. In one session, prior to being offered disguised amounts of ethanol which they may or may not choose to drink throughout the sessions, they receive feedback that their BAL are much more (e.g., 25 percent greater) and in the other session that they are much less (e.g., 25 percent less) than the actual values. By these means, it should become possible to classify subjects according to the extent to which they rely on interoceptive (i.e., blood alcohol level) or exteroceptive (i.e., experimental feedback) cues to regulate their drinking.

If we assume that subjects can metabolize approximately 1.25 to 1.75 oz of vodka (containing 50 percent alcohol) per hour, then ingestion of greater or lesser amounts (regardless of exteroceptive feedback) during the experimental sessions (lasting several hours) would indicate a relative deficit in interoceptive feedback for maintaining the specified BAL. Likewise, if subjects consumed quantities of vodka contrary to the external "feedback" provided by the blood alcohol meter (i.e., drank more in the exaggerated and less in the underestimated BAL session), this would indicate a relative deficit in responding to exteroceptive cues. Since subjects can drink amounts of ethanol which are either greater, lower or equivalent to what they can metabolize (after giving them a priming dose to bring them in the appropriate BAL range) and since they can either attend to or ignore the information provided by the blood alcohol meter, there would be three possible patterns for each of these two sessions. Each would portray the relative balance of attention which subjects pay to interoceptive and exteroceptive cues. These patterns are represented schematically in Table 29–1. The plus sign indicates relative presence and the minus sign relative absence of reliance on the particular cues.

According to this chart, we interpret the behavior of subjects displaying patterns A or F or both as indicative of maximal loss of control. Regardless of interoceptive or exteroceptive cues, these subjects are unable to regulate their alcohol intake by keeping it within the specified training-session range. Pattern A represents the propensity to drink excessively and pattern F not to drink at all under conditions which require more controlled drinking. Patterns B and E, demonstrating relative reliance on exteroceptive cues, represent moderate loss of control, since unmodulated drinking should result whenever external constraints are ignored. Patterns C and D, demonstrating a primary reliance on interocep-

TABLE 28-1.

EVALUATION MODEL FOR LOSS OF CONTROL IN DRINKING

Oz of 50% Alcohol per Hour	Feedback, Session I (meter rigged 25% more)	Feedback, Session II (meter rigged 25% less)
	A	B
>1.75	− Interoceptive	− Interoceptive
	− Exteroceptive	+ Exteroceptive
	C	D
1.25–1.75	+ Interoceptive	+ Interoceptive
	− Exteroceptive	− Exteroceptive
	E	F
<1.25	− Interoceptive	− Interoceptive
	+ Exteroceptive	− Exteroceptive

tive cues, represent minimal loss of control. We presume, then, that persons characterized by any of the latter four patterns, in contrast to the former two patterns, should be capable of demonstrating considerable regulation of their drinking behavior should they choose or be motivated to do so. In addition, there are, of course, normal or social drinkers who attend to both interoceptive and exteroceptive cues.

It must be stressed that this pattern classification is purely hypothetical. Much research (some of which is ongoing) will have to be conducted to determine its merits and usefulness. Moreover, these speculations concerning different feedback dysfunctions do not argue against other mechanisms contributing to loss of control. Since we postulate craving to be associated with a conditioned withdrawal syndrome, the conditioning could also be applied to loss of control. In this regard, it is possible to explain the psychological and physiological effects of the first drink or two as "chain conditioned" to an entire sequence of excessive ethanol intake, often terminating in intoxication, just as had occurred in many prior drinking bouts. This first drink, then, would act like an "appetizer," stimulating hunger (craving, as a conditioned withdrawal response) even further because it has become sequentially conditioned to the later consumption of an "entrée" (intoxication). It is not contradictory to assume that these hypothetical feedback dysfunctions should facilitate such conditioning.

At a practical level, if there is any scientific merit to our concept of a feedback dysfunction in alcoholics, a classification system delineating the specific types of deficits should hold not only potential diagnostic and prognostic value but should also provide important information for establishing treatment goals, such as social drinking or total abstinence for any given alcoholic. Obviously, those persons who demonstrate a relative inability to recognize or respond to both interoceptive and exteroceptive cues for the purpose of regulating their drinking would not be ideal candidates for a social-drinking treatment program unless it is specifically designed to remedy these deficits.

Without such a program, total abstinence would seem to be a far more realistic treatment goal.

In conclusion, we believe that our theories concerning craving and loss of control warrant extensive investigation. In the past, researchers and clinicians alike have not paid sufficient attention to the important role these phenomena play as potential determinants of relapse. Until the mechanisms of action underlying these very basic constructs are thoroughly understood and techniques developed to modify their manifestations, the treatment of alcoholism will always be relatively ineffective. It is unlikely that effective and efficient treatment programs for alcoholism can derive from theoretical superstructures built on inadequate knowledge.

REFERENCES

Bailey, M. B., and Stewart, J. (1967). Normal drinking by persons reporting previous problem drinking. *Quart. J. Stud. Alc.* 28:305-315.

Cohen, M., Liebson, I. A., and Faillace, L. A. (1971). The modification of drinking of chronic alcoholics. In *Recent Advances in Studies of Alcoholism: An Interdisciplinary Symposium*, ed. M. K. Mello and J. H. Mendelson, pp. 745-766. Rockville, MD: U.S. National Institute on Alcohol Abuse and Alcoholism.

Cutter, H. S. G., Schwaab, E. L., Jr., and Nathan, P. E. (1970). Effects of alcohol on its utility for alcoholics and nonalcoholics. *Quart. J. Stud. Alc.* 31:369-378.

Davies, D. L. (1962). Normal drinking in recovered alcohol addicts. *Quart. J. Stud. Alc.* 23:94-104.

Glatt, M. M. (1967). The question of moderate drinking despite "loss of control." *Brit. J. Addict.* 62:267-274.

Isbell, H. (1955). Craving for alcohol. *Quart. J. Stud. Alc.* 16:38-42.

Jellinek, E. M. (1960). *The Disease Concept of Alcoholism*. Highland Park, NJ: Hillhouse Press.

Jellinek, E. M., Isbell, J., Lundquist, G., et al. (1955). The "craving" for alcohol; a symposium by members of the WHO Expert Committee on Mental Health and Alcohol. *Quart. J. Stud. Alc.* 16:38-42.

Keller, (1972). On the loss-of-control phenomenon in alcoholism. *Brit. J. Addict.* 67:153-156.

Lazarus, R. S. (1968). Emotions and adaptation; conceptual and empirical relations. In *Nebraska Symposium on Motivation*, vol. 16, ed. W. J. Arnold. Lincoln, NE: University of Nebraska Press.

Ludwig, A. M. (1971). *Treating the Treatment Failures: The Challenge of Chronic Schizophrenia*. New York: Grune & Stratton.

——— (1972). On and off the wagon; reasons for drinking and abstaining by alcoholics. *Quart. J. Stud. Alc.* 33:91-96.

Ludwig, A. M., Levine, J., and Stark, L. H. (1970). *LSD and Alcoholism: A Clinical Study of Treatment Efficacy*. Springfield, IL: Charles C Thomas.

Ludwig, A. M., and Lyle, W. H. (1964). The experimental production of narcotic drug effects and withdrawal symptoms through hypnosis. *Int. J. Clin. Exp. Hypnosis* 12:1-17.

Manber, M. M. (1972). Social setting held decisive in alcoholic's craving behavior. *Psychiat. News*, February 16, p. 22.

Marlatt, G. A., Demming, B. M., and Reid, J. B. (1973). Loss of control drinking in alcoholics; an experimental analogue. *J. Abnorm. Psychol.* 81:233-241.

Mello, N. K. (1968). Some aspects of the behavioral pharmacology of alcohol. *Amer. Coll. Neuropsychopharmacol.*, Proc. 6th Annual Mtg, pp. 787-809.

——— (1972). Behavioral studies of alcoholism. In *Biology of Alcoholism*, vol. 2, ed. B. Kissin and H. Begleiter, pp. 219-291. New York: Plenum.

Mello, N. K., McNamee, H. B., and Mendelson, J. H. (1968). Drinking patterns of chronic alcoholics; gambling and motivation for alcohol. *Psychiat. Res. Rep.* 24:83-118.

Mello, N. K., and Mendelson, J.H. (1965). Operant analysis of drinking patterns of chronic alcoholics. *Nature* (Lond.) 206:43–46.

———— (1971). Drinking patterns during work contingent and non-contingent alcohol acquisition. In *Recent Advances in Studies of Alcoholism: An Interdisciplinary Symposium.* Rockville, MD: U.S. National Institute on Alcohol Abuse and Alcoholism.

Merry, J. (1966). The "loss of control" myth. *Lancet* 1:1257–1258.

Orne, M. T. (1962). On the social psychology of the psychological experiment; with particular reference to demand characteristics. *Amer. Psychologist* 17:776–783.

Schacter, S. (1971). *Emotion, Obesity and Crime.* New York: Academic.

Schacter, S., and Singer, J. E. (1972). Cognitive, social and physiological determinants of emotional state. *Psychol. Rev.* 69:379–399.

Stein, L. I., Niles, D., and Ludwig, A. M. (1968). The loss of control phenomenon in alcoholics. *Quart. J. Stud. Alc.* 29:598–602.

Stunkard, A. J. (1961). Hunger and satiety. *Amer. J. Psychiat.* 118:212–217.

Stunkard, A. J., and Koch, C. (1964). The interpretation of gastric motility; apparent bias in reports of hunger by obese persons. *Arch. Gen. Psychiat.* 11:74–82.

Wikler, A. (1948). Recent progress in research on the neurophysiological basis of morphine addiction. *Amer. J. Psychiat.* 105:329–338.

———— (1952). A psychodynamic study of a patient during experimental self-regulated re-addiction to morphine. *Psychiat. Quart.* 26:270–293.

———— (1955). Rationale of the diagnosis and treatment of addictions. *Conn. St. Med. J.* 19:560–569.

———— (1961). On the nature of addiction and habituation. *Brit. J. Addict.* 57:73–79.

———— (1965). Conditioning factors in opiate addiction and relapse. In *Narcotics*, ed. D. I. Wilner and G. G. Kassenbaum, pp. 85–100. New York: McGraw-Hill.

———— (1968). Interaction of physical dependence and classical and operant conditioning in the genesis of relapse. *Res. Publ. Ass. Nerv. Ment. Dis.* 46:280–287.

———— (1971). Some implications of conditioning theory for problems of drug abuse. *Behav. Sci.* 16:92–97.

———— (1973a). Dynamics of drug dependence; implications of a conditioning theory for research and treatment. *Arch. Gen. Psychiat.* 28:611–616.

———— (1973b). Sources of reinforcement for drug using behavior; a theoretical formulation. *Proc. 5th Int. Cong. Pharmacol.* 1:18–30.

Wikler, A., and Pescor, F. T. (1967). Classical conditioning of morphine-addicted rats. *Psychopharmacologia* (Berl.) 10:255–284.

Wikler, A., Pescor, F. T., Miller, D., and Norrell, H. (1971). Persistent potency of a secondary (conditioned) reinforcer following withdrawal of morphine from physically dependent rats. *Psychopharmacologia* (Berl.) 20:103–117.

29: COUNTERTRANSFERENCE ISSUES IN TREATING THE ALCOHOLIC PATIENT: INSTITUTIONAL AND CLINICIAN REACTIONS*

Ronna H. Weiss

Several years ago, I was asked to speak with the staff of a large urban college on alcohol and drug abuse in students. A number of the faculty questioned the relevance of the topic, assuring me that a drug problem did not exist at their campus. After some time, a janitor standing at the back of the room asked, "Then why am I sweeping up so many liquor bottles and crack vials from the stairwells?" Prior to his comment, I had begun to doubt my instinct that a problem was likely in this setting. I think this must be how a child of an alcoholic family feels when faced with denial in a system.

Reactions to alcoholism occur in institutions and health care systems as well as in the relationship between the clinician and the alcoholic patient. These are varying forms of countertransference that are related to the powerful unconscious feelings aroused by the phenomena of addiction to alcohol. Furthermore, countertransference is evoked in the psychotherapy relationship due to intense transference related to psychological difficulty in the alcoholic patient.

Overlooking the "elephant in the room" is a common reaction to alcoholism in a variety of systems. This has resulted in a small number of services for alcoholic patients despite the magnitude of the problem. This paradox is acutely felt by hospital emergency rooms, which find few appropriate placements in the community for the large number of alcoholics revolving through their doors.

This gap in services is aggravated by a tendency of medical and psychiatric departments to inadvertently disown the alcoholic patient. Resistance toward treating the alcoholic is bolstered by the confusion as to the domain in which the

*The author acknowledges Robert Steinmuller, M.D., and Judith Cobb, Ph.D., Emilio Morante, Margaret Hill and Stuart Rosenblatt, Ph.D., Ellen Carni, Ph.D., Michael McGuire, M.D. and Melissa Kresch, Ph.D.; Matthew Petti, Psy.D., Hermina Shaw, Janice Davis and the Recovery Team at North Central Bronx Hospital. Special gratitude is expressed to Bernard Weiss.

alcoholic belongs. Based on the Cartesian tradition, our disciplines are divided; psychiatry treats the mind, and medicine heals the body. Yet where does the alcoholic fit? Intoxication alters mental status, causing agitation, depression, suicidal ideation, and behavioral changes. With progressed or advanced disease, the alcoholic has cognitive and personality changes, yet these, too, are organically based. The chronic alcoholic's medical sequelae call for medical treatment. Yet figuring out why the alcoholic continues to jeopardize his or her health through drinking seems to be the query of psychiatry. Historically, the alcoholic patient has been a "hot potato," with psychiatry claiming the alcoholic's problems are essentially organic and medicine claiming they are primarily psychiatric.

While both medical and psychiatry departments have been slow to embrace the treatment of alcoholics, their rationales have been puzzling. Physicians routinely face patients whose chronic hypertension, diabetes, and cardiovascular and respiratory problems defy treatment due to lack of adherence to the prescribed medical regimen. Patients who continue to overeat or smoke, or fail to exercise or take medication, are accepted as the course, albeit with some frustration. However, alcoholics are often considered impossible to treat due to their continuing use of alcohol.

A psychiatrist who practiced liaison psychiatry to inpatient medical units in the 1970s shared his bewilderment surrounding a similar tendency in that service. Patients resisting medical treatment for conditions such as cardiac disease became the subjects of fascinating rounds, with psychoanalytic interpretations of the meaning of the patients' resistance. Yet the same department did not consider alcoholics as appropriate referrals, claiming lack of sobriety was an untreatable form of resistance. The psychiatrist considers psychiatry the guilty party for failing to respond to medicine's desperate requests for help with patients suffering from bleeding esophageal varices and ulcers and cirrhosis.

Viewing alcoholism treatment as outside the domain of psychiatry is serious, given the high comorbidity of alcoholism with mood, anxiety, and personality disorders (Kofoed et al. 1986, Roy et al. 1991, Weisman and Meyers 1980). Jellinek's (1962) reconceptualization of alcoholism as a disease had the impact of deemphasizing the psychological aspects of alcoholism. The residue of this problem is felt by alcoholics requiring hospitalization, as well as psychiatric treatment, for alcoholism. Alcohol detoxification units, often oriented by the disease model, are minimally equipped to treat psychiatric problems. The psychiatric facilities often view themselves as unequipped to deal with problems of alcoholism. The number of dual diagnosis units is disproportionately low compared with the number of patients seeking their services.

In outpatient psychiatry clinics, alcohol use is often one of the exclusionary criteria for admission. Despite the large number of alcoholic patients seeking services, these clinics refer patients elsewhere rather than expand their services to treat the alcohol problems that present with such regularity.

In one sense, the increasing awareness of alcoholism as a problem needing special attention is an appropriate advance in psychiatry. I have interviewed alcoholic patients as recently as the mid-1980s, who have described inpatient and outpatient treatment for depression at fine psychiatric facilities where the use of alcohol was not explored, despite its obvious importance. However, this increased awareness of the role of alcohol has resulted in viewing the alcoholic patient as someone outside the domain of psychiatric treatment. In a recent commentary, "Is use always abuse?" Peter Tilton (1993) argues that the pendulum has swung so far that reported anxiety and depression are usually not treated if use of substances is reported.

Given that the alcoholic patient is not considered a bona fide medical or psychiatry patient, she or he is often devalued or considered a second-class patient. Moreover, this lack of status is inadvertently transferred to the alcoholism providers. Alcohol or substance abuse departments and their staffs are often accorded with less prestige than other psychiatry or medical departments. This lack of status is serious, given that resources such as funding and space are allotted based on what is felt to be the value of the service. It is interesting that alcohol and drug services are more likely than other services to be relegated to off-site locations.

It is misleading to portray health care institutions as being opposed to alcoholism treatment. This is contrary to my own experience with a psychiatry department and hospital that have looked for ways to expand substance abuse services. In addition, I have seen increased numbers of alcoholism facilities with greater involvement of psychiatry nationwide. However, it appears that institutions are vulnerable to unconscious reactions toward alcohol addiction. This may inadvertently result in forms of denial, disowning, and devaluation of the alcoholic and alcoholism treatment. These largely paradoxical and illogical responses occur in institutions that are usually quite logical and responsive to the needs of clients. This discrepancy points to ways that countertransference toward the alcoholic patient can reverberate throughout an institution. This notion is supported by the intensity of reactions toward the alcoholic patients that resounds in the health care systems that treat them.

A chain of emotional reactions to the alcoholic can be seen in the hospital emergency room system. Denial of alcoholism has resulted in a shortage of facilities that treat acute alcohol-related problems. As a result, alcoholic patients often seek treatment in an emergency room. When they enter, medical staff become anxious because a bed that could go to a "real" or more pressing medical patient is being used. Patients who were previously treated for alcoholism in the emergency room are a particular frustration. If the alcoholic demonstrates agitation or other dangerous behavioral disturbances, a hospital police officer may be asked to provide protective observation. The hospital police department then becomes alarmed because coverage elsewhere has been depleted.

Pressure may be put on the psychiatric emergency room to accept the alcoholic patient. Psychiatry nurses become upset at the prospect of being handed the management of an alcoholic with behavioral manifestations. The psychiatrists become worried that they may be asked to take a patient who has not had sufficient medical attention or may not even exhibit psychiatric disturbance after the intoxication dissipates. Administrators become involved in facilitating coordination of services, which, in my experience, results in competent, appropriate treatment. The issue is not quality of care but rather the considerable emotional energy expended by a large number of hospital personnel — ambulance drivers, clerks, nurses, hospital police, physicians, psychologists, social workers, and administrators. This demonstrates how lack of specialized services for alcoholics, confusion as to the domain of alcoholism, and the intensity of reactions evoked reverberates in a health care system.

I view these emotionally charged responses as forms of countertransference. *Countertransference* is a term originally used to describe thoughts and feelings on the part of the psychotherapist, coming from the psychotherapist's personal history and dynamics. In more contemporary views, this term has come to include thoughts and feelings of the psychotherapist evoked by the patient's dynamics. Yet countertransferential feelings emerge in varying forms in the broader context of relationships between patients and providers other than psychotherapists.

In treating alcoholics, what feelings are evoked in the provider that stem primarily from the provider's own background, rather than the patient's dynamics? Clinicians of most disciplines may be uneasy treating alcoholics because the former lack the knowledge base and framework from which to work. Medical education may include as little as several weeks on alcoholism, and psychiatry residency training usually does not require an alcoholism rotation. Psychologists and social work clinicians can be licensed without having any coursework or clinical experience with patients with alcohol disorders. Moreover, the lack of alcoholism education within the respective training programs implicitly conveys a message that work with this population is not a priority.

The alcoholic may arouse uncomfortable feelings in the provider concerning his or her own use of alcohol or drugs or use by significant persons in the provider's life. Also, providers come to the treatment situation with various attitudes based on their social, cultural, and religious backgrounds (Chappel and Lewis 1992). Frequently, the provider has had more exposure to negative stereotypes of the alcoholic as bowery bum than with the positive images of the multitude of alcoholics who successfully recover and contribute to society through participation in Alcoholics Anonymous and clinical treatment.

How do the alcoholic's behaviors and unconscious dynamics contribute to the countertransferential feelings in the provider? The patient's erratic use of clinical services (e.g., not attending scheduled appointments, yet appearing at the emergency room) may arouse a sense of chaos among clinicians. Providers become discouraged and angered by lack of follow-through on treatment plans that they may regard as lack of motivation. The alcoholic's disruptive pattern is partly a function of the disease of alcoholism with its intermittent periods of intoxication and withdrawal. Yet the alcoholic's relationship with providers also reflects his or her own maladaptive and unstable object relations. Also, the alcoholic may unconsciously provoke the provider due to the patient's feelings of guilt and badness (Chappel and Lewis 1992, Wurmser 1977). The provider may be overwhelmed by the patient's repeated use of the health care system in an attempt to manage overwhelming affective states and a deteriorated medical condition.

The above distinction, however, is somewhat artificial in that the underlying emotions, fantasies, and impulses regarding alcohol use are common to both provider and patient. Extremely powerful feelings are evoked in the provider as the phenomena of alcohol addiction tap less mature, less conscious aspects of his or her own unresolved development. The telos of development is generally viewed as the attainment of more mature forms of functioning; alcoholic behavior is disturbing as it appears to run counter to this course.

Drinking itself may represent regression to the early oral stages of psychosexual development, evoking fantasies of the infant sucking breast or bottle. Intoxication may represent regression to stages of merger, loss of reality testing, and loss of consciousness, evoking images of the fetal state. In the life-style of the alcoholic, one can see dependency overriding stage-appropriate industriousness, intimacy, and generativity (Erikson 1950). The downward spiral of chronic alcoholism may tap unconscious self-destructive impulses and fears. Alcoholics may arouse in the provider anxieties over failure to gain control of the urges. According to Szasz (1958), it is this very fear that motivates the alcoholic's counterphobic use of alcohol. Providers may avoid alcoholics because of these threatening feelings.

Moreover, providers are angry and resentful over the alcoholic's apparent gratification of the very infantile urges the provider must forego (Moore 1965). Providers' punitive reactions collude with the alcoholic's own self-punitive tendencies stemming from guilt and low self-esteem. Overpermissiveness toward the alcoholic may reflect a reaction formation to the basic anger toward the alcoholic (Moore 1961).

This discussion does not focus directly on the social, economic, cultural, and political aspects of addiction and its treatment, topics addressed by Lowinger (1992), Berger (1991), and others. While this chapter examines the intrapsychic dynamics of patient and health care provider, it should be noted that these intrapsychic structural components, particularly the superego, embody larger social dynamics.

Chappel (1992) summarizes how drug abusing patients expect a "moralistic lack of understanding accompanied by rejection and even mistreatment" (p. 984). He attributes this to the patient's superego "where internalized parental and cultural values and standards" react to the misuse of drugs (p. 984). Countertransference responses from physicians often parallel the negative transference reactions of the patient. Chappel explains that the "parental and cultural messages experienced in early life by the physician were similar to those experienced by the patient" (p. 984). Among these are disapproval of intoxication, antisocial behavior, and drug abuse. Therefore, the dynamics of countertransference reflect larger social mores and dynamics.

COUNTERTRANSFERENCE IN THE CLINICAL RELATIONSHIP

Countertransference reactions emerge with great intensity in the dyadic relationship between clinician and patient in a variety of contexts, such as the medical ward, psychiatric emergency room, and in outpatient alcoholism treatment.

A resident covering the medical ward and awakened at 3:00 A.M. to respond to requests by the alcoholic for sleep medication may have difficulty understanding that restlessness and insomnia are normative symptoms of alcohol withdrawal and legitimate requests for treatment. The tendency is to be angered and see the patients as a nuisance or worse.

The psychiatric emergency service is one area where countertransference toward the alcoholic patient could have potentially lethal results. The psychiatrist is required to decide, in a relatively short period, which patients need to remain in a hospitalized setting to prevent harm to self and others. Regarding the alcoholic as unworthy of psychiatric treatment could result in an inappropriate discharge with serious consequences. In settings I have worked at, clinical policy and a hierarchical system safeguards against reactive decision making. However, I have found that the psychiatrists' ability to make mature judgments was largely due to sensitivity acquired through the psychoanalytically oriented aspect of their education.

There is a tendency among trainees to feel that patients are either alcoholics or legitimate psychiatric patients. They hold these attitudes despite their knowledge of the high incidence of psychiatric disorders and suicide in heavy alcohol users (Hyman 1988). Helping psychiatry residents develop an awareness of these countertransference reactions is particularly important because they may later have the critical responsibility of attending psychiatrists in an emergency room setting.

OUTPATIENT COUNSELING WITH ALCOHOLICS

In outpatient substance abuse treatment, unlike the psychiatric emergency room, clinicians have the advantage of an ongoing clinical relationship to work with countertransferential feelings and benefit from the input of staff and supervisors. Using these feelings to better understand the patient's experience can enrich the work. However, unprocessed countertransference reactions can result in treatment errors through overpermissiveness or extreme rigidity, loss of effective boundaries or distancing, prolonging treatment, or prematurely referring the patient elsewhere (Wurmser).

Some reasons psychotherapists give for not working with the alcoholic patient share the illogical qualities of rationales given in health care systems. Recently, I was asked to meet with psychology trainees to discuss countertransference with substance abuse patients. Because most members of the group did not plan to work with this population, I began to explore their reasons. One trainee emphasized that progress is too slow with this population. Yet, when I asked if treatment with high functioning, normal patients progressed more quickly, the trainee looked perplexed, admitting that these preferable patients had slow-to-change maladaptive patterns. Another trainee pointed to high relapse rate in alcoholics. Yet this same trainee admitted she was not deterred by the high relapse rate in schizophrenic patients. May (1991) suggests countertransference accounts for the inconsistency among psychoanalysts who require patients to give up alcohol or drugs of abuse prior to starting psychoanalysis, but do not expect patients to give up other symptoms, such as problematic relationships.

Reluctance to enter a psychotherapeutic relationship with an alcoholic, then, is likely based on the type of unconscious anxieties and resentments previously discussed rather than on the conscious reasons offered. Moreover, therapists may avoid working with alcoholics due to the intense transference/countertransference phenomena that emerge in psychotherapy. These difficulties in treatment are related to disturbances in self, ego, and object relationships prominent in the alcoholic patient. Because these disturbances are described throughout this book, we turn to a discussion of common countertransferential reactions in the psychotherapy context.

The following table (Table 30-1) outlines the most common reactions I have observed in recovery focused psychotherapy with alcoholics. These include feeling *stood up* (rejected, bewildered, abandoned), *conned* (confused, deceived, exploited), *punitive* (being pushed in the role of policeman, angry, punitive, sadistic, or the reverse, overly permissive), *bored* (losing interest, feeling shut out, sleepy), *hopeless* (helpless, impotent, devalued), *overwhelmed* (demanded upon, depleted, drained, rejecting), *charmed* (drawn to patient, physically attracted, warm, loss of boundaries), *panic* (worried or anxious over danger to patient), *sympathetic* (overconcerned, overresponsible, "rescuer" fantasy), and *genuine regard/liking* (enjoyment, interested, optimistic, comfortable, interest valued). The table also outlines types of behaviors of the alcoholic that might induce countertransference feelings. In turn, these therapist reactions and patient behaviors are related to symptoms of the disease of alcoholism and possible forms of psychopathology in the alcoholic patient. In all categories except the last, *anger* is usually also experienced by the therapist consciously or unconsciously, often leading to rejection of the patient. This is largely related to the patient's rage, which unfolds in the transference and is expressed in multiple forms, such as projective identification.

In reviewing the varied countertransference reactions, a differentiation elaborated by Racker (1968) is useful. Racker referred to *concordant identifications* as the therapist's empathic responses to the patient's thoughts and feelings through identification with the patient's ego or id. *Complementary identifications* refer to the therapist's identification with some projected (unwanted) part of the patient's self or superego (Epstein and Feiner 1983). Sympathy and concern toward a recovering patient suffering from the effects of alcoholism might reflect concordant identification. Punitive feelings toward a passive-aggressive noncompliant patient might reflect complementary identifications.

During the course of writing this chapter, I saw a therapist in the substance abuse program leaning against the wall, looking dejected. He explained, "My patient just didn't show; I feel bewildered. He seemed so motivated; I was sure he would be here." He continued, "I feel confused, like I can't read him and . . . maybe a bit annoyed . . . maybe a bit angry."

Frequently, I have observed therapists whose patients did not show hanging

TABLE 29–1.

COMMON COUNTERTRANSFERENCE REACTIONS IN ALCOHOL-FOCUSED PSYCHOTHERAPY
AND RELATED PATIENT DYNAMICS

Clinician Responses	Patient Behavior/ Examples	Alcohol Symptoms	Psychodynamics
Stood up Hurt Rejected Bewildered Fear of abandonment	Erratic attendance	Unreliability due to physical problems of intoxication, withdrawal	Inconsistency in object relations Guilt over drinking Ambivalence over giving up drinking
Conned Confused Deceived Exploited Angry	Concealing of alcohol Misrepresenting use of other doctors, clinics Using treatment only to acquire financial or economic entitlements	Alibis required to maintain drinking Needs to manage anxiety and irritability Drinking interferes with ability to work	Replays traumatic patterns Needs to split treatment Relates with part objects
Policeman Angry Punitive Sadistic Guilty	Repeated disregard for standards, pushing clinician to enforce rigid policies	Continues alcohol use due to physical dependence Disregards consequences of actions	Provokes punishment due to guilt Lacks ego control/ structure (can't manage instincts)
Bored Loss of interest Feeling shut out Sleepy	Grandiosity Repetitive speech Lack of affect Soliloquies	Lack of experience in relationships while sober	Relates to therapist as selfobject Grandiosity masks fragile self
Hopeless Helpless Impotent as helper Devalued	Denial of illness Continued drinking Sabotaging treatment	Physical dependence Repeated intoxication Advanced medical problems	Denial Faulty thinking: sees permanent flaws in self Depressive: lack of optimism Uses hopelessness to rationalize drinking

(continued)

TABLE 29–1. (continued)

Clinician Responses	Patient Behavior/ Examples	Alcohol Symptoms	Psychodynamics
Overwhelmed Depleted Drained	Frequent calls Suicide attempts Requests for Rx Requests for additional services	Chronic use Physical dependency Feels overwhelmed by decreased alcohol	Ego deficits: can't manage internal affects Dependency
Charmed Intense warmth Desires closeness Physical attraction Loss of boundaries	Seductive behavior (glances, dress, comments) Flattering therapist Idealizing treatment	Intoxication: diminishes inhibitions/ boundaries Sobriety: overwhelms patient with new states	Seeks merger to overcome aloneness Regression from differentiated state
Panic Guilty, anxious Fears own reputation will be destroyed Fears patient will be destroyed	Failure to get medical care High risk behavior (casual sex, physical or sexual abuse)	Serious medical sequelae Lack of judgment Blackouts Impaired cognition Nutritional deficiencies	Denial and grandiosity Guilt, self-destructiveness Ego deficits in self-care
Sympathy Overconcern Over-responsible Rescuer fantasies	Emphasizing their pain Conveying helplessness	Depression (organic) Patient isolation due to alcoholic behavior Problems with work, finances, and family	Rescue fantasies Dependency Wish for maternal caretaking
Positive regard Likes patient Appropriate concern Genuine interest Feels hopeful	Participation in AA Regular attendance in treatment program Conveys genuine involvement with therapist and others	Sobriety Adequate medical care and nutrition Improved thinking Recovery with work and family	Internalize group function of AA Character growth through 12 steps Internalize structure of therapy/ therapist

around, looking as if they had been stood up by a date. While clinic policies help minimize this problem, this experience is part of the work with alcoholics. This is due to fluctuating physical condition related to alcohol abuse, unacknowledged ambivalence over giving up alcohol, and disturbed object relations. Patients may replay versions of their own traumatic experiences or establish distance with the therapist because of difficulties with intimacy.

Clinic directors asked to assign an alcoholic patient to a trainee are often encouraged to select a patient who attends regularly. While this is desirable, experiencing the alcoholic's absences *is* part of the education. This lack of constancy conveys the patient's experience of his or her own object world and helps us understand the experience of family members of the alcoholic. Certainly, absences should be discouraged because they impede the patient's progress in the clinical work. Moreover, absences can leave the therapist vulnerable to countertransference feelings of abandonment. Fearing abandonment by the patient can influence a clinician's therapeutic stand (Masterson 1983). For example, a therapist may avoid confronting the patient due to fears that the patient will leave treatment.

Clinicians frequently complain of feeling pushed into the role of policeman. For example, one patient, upon periodic alcohol binges, entered inpatient detoxification units. However, repeatedly, he would leave early, against medical advice (AMA), expecting the therapist to continue seeing him in the outpatient program. The clinic therefore had to develop policies about leaving detox's AMA. The patient continued to confront the therapist with loopholes in the policy, forcing the clinic to make the policy increasingly rigid. The therapist felt punitive, almost sadistic, and felt angry about being placed in this role.

Another common reaction surrounds feeling conned or manipulated. Clinicians are repeatedly stunned to find they've been deceived. The therapist may learn information concealed by the patient. For example, the patient may have been seeing other doctors or clinicians, who may have prescribed medication. The patient may have been driven to get medication from multiple sources because of uncomfortable states related to continued drinking. Furthermore, the patient may have needed to split treatment due to difficulties in object relations. When patients do get caught, the therapist is usually angered and distanced, which may be the patient's unconscious objective. In addition, the patient may be replaying a traumatic manipulative pattern she or he experienced. Some patients attend outpatient treatment due to external motivators such as meeting requirements to receive public assistance. While the patient may eventually internalize a desire for sobriety, the clinician may feel exploited in the process.

The types of countertransference reactions compiled here from clinical experiences with alcoholism and substance abuse patients coincide with those written on countertransference with narcissistic (Wolf 1983) and borderline (Pine 1979) patients. This is not surprising given the prevalence of these disorders in the alcoholic population (Hartocollis and Hartocollis 1980). Furthermore, these countertransference reactions of alcohol treatment providers resemble those of clinicians working with suicidal patients (Maltsberger 1974).

This is understandable given the self-destructive quality of alcoholism and the high incidence of suicidality among alcoholics (Hyman 1988).

A frequent therapist complaint is feeling bored or shut out. Patients may present with a grandiose or false self that makes genuine relating difficult. Furthermore, boredom can be an unconscious response to withdrawal or affective abandonment by the patient, conveyed through intellectualization or monotonous speech. Boredom is a result of the therapist feeling excluded (Racker 1968). A patient's nonaffective quality may reflect an attempt to avoid the negative transference. According to Wolf (1983), feelings of boredom or sleepiness are often characteristic of transference/countertransference dynamics in patients with self-disturbances. Within the mirror transference the therapist is not acknowledged as a separate person; she or he is totally merged to the patient's experience. It is difficult for the therapist to listen to the patient's soliloquy, and the therapist can become irritable as empathy is lost.

Therapists may worry excessively about their patient. This may be the clinician's felt need to compensate for the patient's ego deficits in areas such as self-care (Khantzian 1981). However, excessive worry could also reflect the therapist's unconscious depreciation of the patient's potential for independent functioning. The therapist may duplicate the family's response to the patient's striving toward independence at the time of separation/individuation struggle (Colson 1982).

Alcoholic patients may pull for feelings of merger in the clinician; this may be related to the patient's panic over aloneness. From a Mahlerian perspective (Mahler, Pine, and Bergmen 1972), with the aftermath of differentiation, the individual may experience aloneness rather than differentiation of self/other. This may lead to substitute object gratification through such means as alcohol use. When the patient gives up the alcohol, the panic over aloneness may return (Pine 1979). Therefore, the patient may induce closeness with the therapist and engulfing propensities of patients may reflect this desire for merger (Wolf 1983).

Therapists who feel hopeless about their patients may also feel impotent or devalued in their capacity to help the patient. Because the therapist is the basis of the therapeutic work (Maltsberger 1974), failures in treatment leave the therapist susceptible to narcissistic injury. Therapists are vulnerable with narcissistic patients because of the devaluation that often follows idealization (Wolf 1983). Furthermore, alcoholic patients who relapse may trigger feelings of failure in the therapist.

Because the countertransference reactions described are largely negative, there is a component of anger or countertransference hate. For example, boredom in the therapist may in addition reflect the therapist's attempts to repress his or her feelings. However, the aversion is conveyed nonverbally through actions such as glancing at the clock (Maltsberger 1974).

Hopelessness in the therapist can reflect hatred toward the patient turned against the self. If the patient's transference is hurtful and the therapist cannot ward off the hostility, a sense of hopelessness may ensue. Decisions to give up a case can be the expression of underlying aversion. A reaction formation to the anger may result in the therapist being overly sympathetic with fantasies of rescuing the patient (Maltsberger 1974). Furthermore, panic or fear about what will happen to the patient may be a projection of the therapist's hatred. Thoughts that the patient will die, leave, or pose a threat to the therapist's reputation can stem from the therapist's homicidal impulses and result in rejection of the patient.

Maltsberger (1974) further points out that the therapist may use distortion and denial of reality to validate hateful countertransferential feelings, thereby using defenses similar to those of the patient. The therapist may rationalize referring out a patient, thereby repudiating the relationship. Just as the patient was in danger of a rejecting mother, the therapist becomes the rejecting object. Much of the negative countertransference induced by the patient results in distancing the therapist and reflects the primary relational difficulties of the patient.

Although the majority of the countertransference reactions reviewed were negative, not all work with alcoholic patients is unsatisfying. Although alcoholic patients are ambivalent about sobriety, a part of them is often very motivated due to social/economic difficulties, medical debilitation, and psychic pain. After giving up alcohol, patients seek new attachments; relationships with AA and therapists are often central. Consistent involvement replaces sporadic attendance. Given that the patient was alcoholic during major developmental periods, he or she is now open to many aspects of life never experienced. Through AA the patient often develops a notion of personal development and character change that becomes central to his or her life. This seriousness extends to the patient's work in psychotherapy treatment. The patient demonstrates a capacity for intrapsychic change through internalizing structures of the ego system, such as self-governance and self-care (Khantzian 1981), through forms of group and individual treatment.

WORKING WITH COUNTERTRANSFERENCE

What are ways to deal with the countertransference? For patients with severe alcoholism and psychopathology, multimodal treatment is essential and can include psychiatric consultation, individual and group treatment, and therapy with family or significant others. Regular team meetings are crucial because multiple perspectives may be needed to adequately understand the patient. The clinician should be in regular contact with other providers, such as physicians, to further prevent splitting of treatment. Clinicians need to withstand tremendous ambivalence, rage, and distancing on the part of the patient. Group meetings are helpful in providing support, and clinicians must feel safe to express their countertransferential feelings.

The patient's lack of self-care in a variety of situations should be a focus of treatment. Clinicians should help model for the patient "first things first," with physical health and safety given priority. This curbs tendencies of clinicians to take over for the patient rather than develop the patient's autonomous functioning.

The clinician can examine his or her own "addictions" in an attempt to empathize with the patient's experience. Cognitive-behavioral techniques (Marlatt and Gordon 1985) are helpful in showing the patient (and clinician) that relapses are responses to discrete situations rather than permanent personality flaws.

It is helpful for clinicians to familiarize themselves with Alcoholics Anonymous through attendance at open meetings. This helps them understand their patients' recovery process. Moreover, exposure to patients who *are* recovering engenders a sense of optimism in the clinician.

As alcoholism has been conceptualized as a disease, its treatment has largely been developed outside the domain of professional mental health. This is a concern because of the serious psychopathology and intense dynamics involved. This problem has been addressed by Wurmser (1977).

> The current debunking of thorough training in psychiatry and especially in intensive psychotherapy and with that the nearly total lack of understanding for the psychodynamics of these patients and their families has been devastating for psychiatry in general, but it has left the field of treatment of these patients almost entirely to paraprofessionals and to specialists from other fields who are naive as to the gravity and nature of the psychopathology in the majority of these cases and as to a measure for devising rational treatment strategies for each individual case. [pp. 36–72]

It is imperative that qualified mental health professionals be trained in substance abuse treatment because their clinical skills are crucial in this specialty.

Alcoholism education is one of the most powerful tools for helping clinicians deal with their negative feelings toward working with the alcoholic. Understanding the physical course of alcoholism and dependency allows the clinician to better understand the patient's experience. The psychodynamic literature is extremely valuable in further helping the therapist understand the myriad of intense emotions that emerge in the psychotherapeutic relationship.

REFERENCES

Berger, L. (1991). *Substance Abuse as a Symptom.* Hillsdale, NJ: Analytic Press.

Chappel, J., and Lewis, D. (1992) Attitudes toward the treatment of substance abuse. In *Substance Abuse: A Comprehensive Textbook,* ed. J. H. Lowinson, P. Ruiz, R. Millman, and J. Langard, pp. 983–997. Philadelphia: Williams & Wilkins.

Colson, D. (1982). Protectiveness in borderline states. *Bulletin of the Menninger Clinic* 46:305–320.

Epstein, L., and Feiner, A. (1983). Introduction. In *Countertransference: The Therapist's Contribution to the Therapeutic Situation,* ed. L. Epstein and A. Feiner, pp. 1–23. Northvale, NJ: Jason Aronson.

Erikson, E. H. (1950). *Childhood and Society.* New York: Norton.

Hartocollis, P., and Hartocollis, P. C. (1980). Alcoholism, borderline and narcissistic disorders. In *Phenomenology and Treatment of Alcoholism,* ed. W. Fann, I. Kanacan, A. Pokorny, and R. Williams. New York: Spectrum.

Hyman, J. (1988). *Manual of Psychiatric Emergencies.* Boston: Little, Brown and Company.

Imhof, J. (1991). Countertransference issues in alcoholism and drug addiction. *Psychiatric Annals* 21:292–306.

Jellinek, E. (1962). Phases of alcohol addiction. In *Society, Culture, and Drinking Patterns,* ed. D. J. Pittman and C. R. Snyder, pp. 673–683. New York: Wiley.

Khantzian, E. J. (1981). Some treatment implications of the ego and self disturbances in alcoholism. In *Dynamic Approaches to the Understanding and Treatment of Alcoholism,* ed. M. H. Bean and N. E. Zinberg, pp. 163–189. New York: The Free Press.

Kofoed, L., Kania, J., Walsh, T., and Atkinson, R. (1986). Outpatient treatment of patients with substance abuse and coexisting disorders. *American Journal of Psychiatry* 143:867–872.

Lowinger, P. (1992). Drug abuse: economic and political basis. In *Substance Abuse: A Comprehensive Textbook,* ed. J. Lowinson, P. Ruiz, R. Milman, and J. Languard, pp. 138–144. Philadelphia: Williams & Wilkins.

Mahler, M. S., Pine, F., and Bergman, A. (1975). *The Psychological Birth of the Human Infant.* New York: Basic Books.

Maltsberger, J. (1974). Countertransference hate in the treatment of suicidal patients. *Archives of General Psychiatry* 30:625–633.

Marlatt, G. A., and Gordon, J. eds. (1985). *Relapse Prevention: A Self Control Strategy for the Maintenance of Behavior Change.* New York: Guilford.

Masterson, J. (1983). Countertransference and psychotherapeutic technique. In *Teaching Seminars on Psychotherapy of the Borderline Adult,* pp. 9–12. New York: Brunner/Mazel.

May, M. (1991). Observations on countertransference, addiction, and treatability. In *Psychoanalytic Approaches to Addiction. Current Issues in Psychoanalytic Practice* (Monographs of the Society for Psychoanalytic Training), Number 3, ed. A. Smaldino, pp. 1–13. New York: Brunner/Mazel.

Moore, R. (1961). Reaction formation as a countertransference phenomenon in the treatment of alcoholism. *Quarterly Journal of Studies on Alcohol* 22:41–46.

———— (1965). Some countertransference reactions in the treatment of alcoholism. *Psychiatry Digest* 26:35–43.

Pine, F. (1979). On the pathology of the separation individuation process as manifested in later clinical work: an attempt at delineation. *International Journal of Psycho-Analysis* 60:225–242.

Racker, H. (1968). The meanings and uses of countertransference. In *Transference and Countertransference,* pp. 127–173. New York: International Universities Press.

Roy, A., DeJong, J., Lamparski, D., et al. (1991). Mental disorders among alcoholics. *Archives of General Psychiatry* 48:423–427.

Szasz, T. (1958). The role of the counterphobic mechanism in addiction. *Journal of the American Psychoanalytic Association* 6:309–325.

Tilton, P. (1993). Is use always abuse? *Clinical Psychiatry News* 21:16–17.

Weisman, M. M., and Myers, J. K. (1980). Clinical depression in alcoholism. *American Journal of Psychiatry* 137:372–373.

Wolf, E. (1983). Countertransference in disorders of the self. In *Countertransference: The Therapist's Contribution to the Therapeutic Situation,* ed. A. Feiner and L. Epstein, pp. 445–465. Northvale, NJ: Jason Aronson.

Wurmser, L. (1977). Mr. Pecksniff's horse? In *Psychodynamics in Drug Dependence* (U.S. Department of Health, Education and Welfare, National Institute of Drug Abuse [NIDA]), pp. 36–72. Washington DC: Government Printing Office.

30: DENIAL, AMBIVALENCE, AND COUNTERTRANSFERENTIAL HATE

Howard J. Shaffer

INTRODUCTION

For some clinicians, this chapter will be painful, like a cold shower—something that is necessary, but uncomfortable and perhaps even unwelcome nonetheless. This discussion is essential, however, if therapists who treat addictive behavior are going to advance their capacity to influence positive treatment outcomes. The analysis that follows shifts the focus away from the traditional view that addiction treatment failures or stalemates derive primarily from client traits. Instead, I think treatment failures come from provider countertransference and poor treatment client matches. In addition, traditional clinicians have opted for an overly simple addiction treatment rationale that rests primarily on patient denial and resistance. In the following discussion, I describe (1) how ambivalence emerges naturally during the development of addictive behavior patterns, (2) how denial relieves painful ambivalence for those who are struggling with addiction, and, ultimately, (3) how the struggle with ambivalence and addiction stimulates countertransferential hate and rage in clinicians who treat addiction. The issues of ambivalence and countertransference are relevant to clinicians of every theoretical persuasion.

A NEW APPROACH TO UNDERSTANDING AND TREATING ADDICTIVE BEHAVIORS

Clinicians now have a new treatment map. They had been asking Which therapy with which patient with which therapist produces the most favorable outcomes. Now they ask Which therapy with which patient with which therapist *at which point in the natural history of addiction* produces the most positive treatment outcomes?

Until recently, there has been a lack of meaningful integration of theory, research, and practice (Niaura et al. 1988, Tims and Leukefeld 1986). Marlatt and other observers (e.g., Maisto and Connors 1988, Shaffer and Jones 1989) describe the emergence of a significant theoretical movement: the evolution of the concept of *stages of change*[1] to understand and explain the entire addiction process. Vaillant's (e.g., 1983) natural history approach to addictive disorders provided the supportive conditions for this perspective to emerge. Prochaska and DiClemente (1985) stimulated and nourished the movement by giving theoretical substance and empirical sustenance to the idea of discrete developmental stages of addiction. The stages of change concept has had a powerful heuristic effect in the development of models of addiction (Marlatt 1988, Marlatt et al. 1988), the evaluation and understanding of treatment (Maisto and Connors 1988), and understanding natural recovery (Shaffer and Jones 1989). Some theorists have gone so far as to conclude that "A zeitgeist has emerged in which therapists from different systems are searching for common processes of change" (Goldfried 1980, Prochaska et al. 1988, p. 520).

Any discussion of contemporary approaches to the emergence and treatment of addiction is incomplete without an illustration of a current developmental stage change model of addiction. More specifically, in this section, I examine the development of addiction and the transition to recovery, with emphasis on the psychodynamics of ambivalence and how it emerges during substance abuse to provide the infrastructure of resistance to abstinence, life-style change, and recovery.

Shaffer (1992) offers a model that extends the theory of stages of change to an account of the natural recovery process reported by cocaine quitters (Shaffer and Jones 1989) and intoxicant abuse in general (Shaffer and Gambino 1990). In the following section, I outline this model very briefly to describe a common set of processes that may explain recovery from any addiction, whether it occurs within the framework of formal treatment or not. While the model has much in common with earlier models—for example, it describes several stages similar to those of precontemplation, contemplation, and action (Prochaska and DiClemente 1985, Prochaska, DiClemente, and Norcross 1992)—it provides more detail about the role of events that occur during the transition from addiction to recovery.[2] Because a full discussion of this model is beyond the scope of this chapter, in this discussion, I emphasize the specific psychodynamic aspects of this transition. I focus on how ambivalence stimulates denial and, in turn, how this ambivalent state stimulates countertransference hate and rage in clinicians. The end result is often less than optimal treatment.

---

[1]Prochaska and DiClemente (1985), Marlatt and Gordon (1985), Marlatt, Baer, Donovan, and Kivlahan (1988), and Vaillant (1983) provided the intellectual framework that stimulated much of the developmental stage change thinking that led to a modern reformation of addiction explanations. These workers are true pioneers, and I am indebted to them for providing the conceptual and intellectual platform upon which many of the stage change ideas in this chapter rest.

[2]Readers interested in this transition should see Shaffer and Jones (1989) for a more thorough discussion of this stage change.

ADDICTION AND PSYCHOLOGICAL STAGE CHANGE:
THE CONTEXT FOR AMBIVALENCE[3]

Shaffer and Jones (1989) were the first to report that natural cocaine quitters recover their independence through a sequence of phases comprised of identifiable activities. The major events associated with quitting are observable and thus provide the arena for a psychodynamic analysis of recovery.

It appears that successful quitters pass through these phases, though at differing rates. It does not follow, however, that going through these phases ensures breaking the habit. Systematic research is necessary to confirm success or to determine the circumstances under which the sequence of quitting phases proves to be insufficient for recovery. At present, I suggest that identification of these phases, and recognition that they are an integral part of the quitting process, holds great promise for those who desire more effective behavior change skills. For recovery from addiction to be possible however, a sequence of well-defined events must occur. The intensity and duration of each milestone in the sequence will vary from person to person, but the basic sequence is common to all.

Stage One: The Emergence of Addiction

Phase 1. Initiation: Beginning Drug Use.   It is obvious that in order to become an addict, and then a successful quitter, of any activity, one must participate in it at some point. Everyone who uses a drug, however, does not become a drug abuser or addict. In fact, the vast majority of those who have tried a drug do not become addicted to it (Shaffer 1987, Shaffer and Jones 1989).

Phase 2. The Substance Use Produces Positive Consequences.   If the substance use is not associated with some positive consequences, it will not be continued. Positive effects can be a direct result of the pharmacological properties of the drug or the psychological reinforcement obtained by its use (e.g., relief of depression or reduced sexual inhibition). The consequences also can be positive in a more indirect manner. For example, some drug users experience more social rewards, are held in higher esteem, and have more to do when they are using the substance. Without some positive consequences, any activity or drug use would not be continued to the point that addiction could emerge. This experience of positive consequences is essential to understanding ambivalence and the often repetitive cycle of addictive behaviors.

Phase 3. Adverse Consequences Develop but Remain Out of Awareness.   For drug use or any other activity to be considered an addiction, it must, by definition, be associated with adverse consequences. The essence of addiction is that it continues to provide some of the previous positive consequences while simultaneously producing adverse consequences that begin to weigh more heavily than before. Addictive behaviors serve while they destroy. The reason that they can

---

[3]This section is adapted from previously published work (Shaffer 1992, Shaffer and Jones 1989).

be so very destructive rests on the notion that the addict is not fully aware that the adverse effects of his or her substance abuse (or other addictive behavior) is, in fact, the result of the addictive behavior.

An epicycle of this nature can escalate without regulation because the cybernetic, or feedback, channels are impaired.[4] The addict perceives others as the source of his or her problems. During this phase, addicts believe their behavior has little to do with their suffering. The urging of friends and family to reduce or stop the addictive behavior is of little consequence; in fact, their pleading can become fuel that energizes the addictive behavior so that the pattern intensifies further. Bean-Bayog (1988) has called this type of denial a focused delusional system. At this level, addicts are capable of making sense of their world, with one exception: they cannot make any causal association between their addictive behavior and the life problems they have had to endure. In order to minimize the discomfort associated with these problems, addicts persist in engaging in those behaviors that previously produced positive consequences; that is, the addictive behavior and the cycle continue. Prevailing beliefs have suggested that there is no escape from this epicycle unless it is interrupted from the outside. The natural recovery from addictive behavior, however, stands as a scintillating contradiction (e.g., Shaffer and Jones 1989).

For addicts who successfully recover, adverse consequences of substance abuse enter awareness, and life takes a turn. This turning point into awareness, or insight, has often been considered the end of denial. More accurately, it is a reclaiming of the projections that characterize phase three. No longer are the addict's problems the result of external events; no longer can he or she continue to claim victimization. The adverse consequences associated with addictive behavior are now experienced as the addict's own. This is the beginning of an epistemological shift. The addict is confronted by his or her own recognition of the causal connection between drug-using behaviors and problems such as poor health, financial difficulty, and/or family disintegration. The addict now realizes that his or her behaviors are not anomalous and not without adverse effect. The addict often experiences this realization as a life crisis and recognizes that his or her life-style must now change if he or she is to regain control. The addict begins to recognize that he or she must give up the positive consequences of the behavior that continue while gaining access to the negative outcomes that are connected with the addictive behavior pattern. The event or events associated with turning point experiences mark the beginning of stage two, the evolution of quitting.

Stage Two: The Evolution of Quitting

Phase 4. Turning Points. A turning point represents the shift from unencumbered substance abuse to the realization that this abuse is directly responsible for the presence of profoundly negative life circumstances. The thought of quitting or controlling drug abuse first appears prior to the actual turning point.

---

[4]This circumstance is similar, in effect, to a furnace that continues to heat an excessively warm house because the thermostat is malfunctioning and cannot send a message back to the furnace indicating it should stop.

Addiction is a well-known destructive behavior. Like all patterns of human behavior, addictive behavior patterns perform some service. Usually, people have difficulty understanding the adaptive or useful value of these patterns. The result is that efforts to change these behaviors often fail. Whether recovery is self- or other-initiated, it is very important to understand that addictive behaviors serve while they destroy.

This double-edged sword we call addiction produces ambivalence for the addict who is thinking about change. Ambivalence is a feeling of conflict; it is a sense that we simultaneously want and don't want to change or both like and don't like what we have, want, or experience. Despite the obvious destructive power of addiction, addicts cling to the part of addiction that they like, the part that was adaptive originally and produced positive consequences. As drug abusers become aware of their ambivalence, they begin to express a wish that they want to quit. Increasing levels of self-observation develop, and the substance abuser now begins to realize that the costs of addictive behavior exceed the benefits. Substance abuse is explicitly identified as the major[5] destructive agent in their life. It is at this point that a quitter often asks friends and significant others to help them stop. Before a turning point, the burden of self-control had been delegated more to others than to the addict; the acceptance of personal responsibility represents the actual turning point.

A turning point is not simply a transition. It is actually the end of a complex dynamic process about drugs (or other addictive behavior). We consider it an endpoint even though abstinence and recovery might be months or years away. Needless to say, the experience of a turning point does not produce instantaneous results. Commonly experienced turning points have been described as periods of dissonance associated with feelings of self-loathing or a deterioration of personal values (Shaffer and Jones 1989). Other turning point perceptions include the recognition that substance abuse is beginning to exacerbate rather than diminish intra- and interpersonal conflict. An extremely important, yet commonly reported, turning point centers around the addict's recognition that his or her deteriorating physical condition is related to drug abuse. This is experienced as a do-or-die situation: if drugs are used, the user believes that he or she may die as a result. Other turning points, less extreme but no less important, involve the addict's recognition that he or she may lose what is important to him- or herself—for example, a job or a special relationship—because of drug involvement.

Phase 5. Active Quitting Begins.   Once a turning point is experienced, the process and task associated with active quitting can begin. Two basic approaches to active quitting have been identified: *tapered quitting* and *cold turkey quitting*. It is possible that a successful quitter will mix these approaches in order to find a method that works. The majority of quitters, however, fall predominately or entirely into one style or the other. Few successful quitters mix their stopping strategies.

---

[5]Other substances or activities may be being used addictively.

The notion of active quitting is important. Successful quitters make observable changes during this second phase of the stopping of addiction. The methods for quitting drugs include energetic attempts to avoid the drug, gaining social support for personal change, and engaging in some form of self-development. Thus, this phase is characterized by neither thoughtfulness nor ambivalence. It is identified by important and marked behavioral change and life-style reorganization. New activities are elevated to a position of prominence, and gain intra- and interpersonal value. Old behaviors become devalued and less meaningful.

Phase 6. Relapse Prevention. Very few individuals who stop their drug use remain totally abstinent from that moment. Marlatt and Gordon (1985) examined how slips, that is, single episodes of drug use, can lead to full-blown relapse. Biological, psychological, and sociological factors interact to influence the risk of relapse for any individual. The final phase of quitting involves the maintenance of new skills and life-style patterns that promote positive, independent patterns of behavior. The integration of these behaviors into regular day-to-day activities is the essence of relapse prevention (e.g., Brownell et al. 1986).

The experience of natural quitters suggests that having a number of strategies and tactics to draw upon is essential to maintaining abstinence. Successful quitters substitute a variety of behavior patterns for their old drug-using life-style. For example, they become regularly involved in physical exercise. At times, these substitute patterns also can become excessive. This risk is most probable when (a) excessive behavior patterns serve as anodynes to uncomfortable affective states, and/or (b) self-observation skills are weak and poorly developed. Flights into spiritual or religious conversions also help many individuals sustain their abstinence. For others, formal treatment was necessary. Others occasionally substitute other drugs that they consider less troublesome than their drug of abuse. The use of pharmacological substitution is extremely risky and often backfires. The results of drug substitution can be as devastating and destructive as the original drug abuse.

In sum, there are six phases that describe the cycle of addiction. The first three phases comprise the natural history stage of addiction, stage one, while the last three phases, in stage 2, are associated with quitting or the treatment history of the addictive disorder. The first stage serves as groundwork for the second stage and, thus, must not be lost sight of during the therapeutic process.

TOWARD CLINICAL INTEGRATION: UNDERSTANDING AMBIVALENCE AND COUNTERTRANSFERENCE HATE

Clinical Applications of a Stage Change Model[6]

According to a stage change model, clinicians should base treatment choices on a determination of which method of care for which patient should be applied at

---

[6]Much clinical evidence and experience support the clinical application of a stage change model as described in this section. However, systematic research is necessary to clarify the complex causal influences that affect treatment outcome.

which specific time during the process of recovery. Prescriptive treatment requires the integration and modification of clinical approaches. Wachtel (1977) was one of the first to describe the integration of clinical approaches when he considered the movement toward an integration of psychoanalysis and behavior therapy. Khantzian, Halliday, and McAuliffe (1990) recently modified traditional psychodynamic group psychotherapy techniques for substance abusers.

Integrating clinical methods is not as complicated as it first appears. Consider the third phase of our stage change model. When adverse consequences develop but remain out of awareness, most people do not seek treatment for addiction. Others (e.g., family, friends, doctor, lawyer) often entreat or coerce phase three addicts into a clinical setting. When treatment is available, confrontation and clarification are the most useful clinical interventions. These tactics help patients gain access to the ambivalence, fantasy, and wish that they want to stop their addictive behavior.

The Psychodynamics of Ambivalence. In 1911, Bleuler (1950) was the first clinician to describe ambivalence: "the tendency to endow the most diverse psychisms with both a positive and negative indicator at one and the same time" (p. 53). Although there are relatively few references about ambivalence[7] in the general psychological literature and even fewer in the addictions literature (Miller and Rollnick [1991] and Orford [1985] are important contemporary exceptions), contemporary observers have noted that ambivalence is more common an experience now than ever before:

> Nowadays, there are two sides to every answer. We don't face facts and, hell, simply decide. No. That would be too instinctual, too easy, too blithe, too unlike us. Instead, we consider every alternative and feel complete enthusiasm for none of them. We postpone. We fret. We second-guess. Whether it's a matter of deciding what to have for lunch . . . or how to spend the rest of our lives . . . neither a wholehearted yes nor an unequivocal no comes naturally. We say maybe. We try to act on both impulses . . . to have it all, foreclosing no option . . . Ours is a generation comfortably adrift, bobbing on a sea of ambivalence. . . . Ambivalence as a defining sensibility, widespread and full-blown, is something new. There is virtually nothing today about which thoughtful people — especially thoughtful younger people — do not feel mixed emotions. [Anderson 1989, p. 58]

The psychodynamic rationale for focusing on ambivalence rests on the assumption that substance users have had positive consequences from their phase 2 experience with the object of addiction. These positive consequences weigh heavily on the mind of anyone struggling with addiction. Moreover, there is a human tendency to experience identities in the past. For example, when men in their late thirties and forties disproportionately show up in emergency rooms at the start of spring with orthopedic and other sports injuries, they still think of themselves as having the bodies and capacities of men in their late teens and twenties. Similarly, science moves very slowly in how it develops a view and

---

[7]Will Rogers once quipped that "Mississippi will drink wet and vote dry so long as any citizen can stagger to the polls." This statement is an excellent example of ambivalence and how mixed feelings can energize apparently inconsistent behavior patterns.

understanding of the universe. Scientific views that lag behind technology and discovery are one way that we come to know and experience the world as stable, teachable, and learnable. If world views changed too rapidly, the smooth transition of intergenerational knowledge would be disrupted. The subjective sense of self experienced by people struggling with excessive behaviors is similar to how science maintains stability. For science and individuals struggling with addiction, conventional evidence and understanding have higher priority than newer anomalous experiences. The result is that drug abusers and others with addictive disorders both want and despise the object of their addiction. They want it for the positive experiences it has produced (in the past) and despise it for the pain it seems to cause now. The painful aspect of addiction is not always experienced, however, because denial extinguishes this conflict by splitting the ambivalence and erasing one side of the equation.

Clinicians understand this ambivalent conflict as the twin pillars of recovery from addiction: the fear of using again and the fear of never using again. Denial helps people feel better by splitting an ambivalent conflict and removing one of the components from awareness. Denial also diminishes the substance abuser's cognitive dissonance generated by behaving in ways that the larger culture frowns upon. In the next section, after introducing the notion of countertransference hate, I return to the issue of denial and examine its relationship to ambivalence and countertransference.

Countertransference Hate

"When a therapist feels or acts toward a patient in ways that are neither part of the real relationship, rationally justified by the circumstances, nor part of the working alliance, appropriate to the terms of the treatment contract, he is manifesting countertransference" (Weiner 1975, p. 244). Think about your instinctive response to those revealing they are getting married or divorced, pregnant, or detoxifying. In each case, we feel that we should be either congratulatory or sympathetic. However, this is countertransferential. A more effective clinical posture would be to ask, "When did you decide?" or "How did you decide?" or "What's that going to be like for you?" Congratulations leaves relapsing patients in a difficult position: if they share their difficulties, they might disappoint you.

Countertransference was originally though to be an obstacle that clinicians needed to overcome. Actually, observers of psychotherapy now recognize that clinicians need to identify their real feelings — which may offer little to the conduct of psychotherapy — and distinguish these from countertransference, which can be extremely helpful.

Maltsberger and Buie (1974) described countertransference hate in their very important and now classic work on the treatment of suicidal patients. Suicidal patients are not unlike those struggling with addiction. Karl Menninger once noted that addiction was like suicide on the installment plan. Maltsberger and Buie suggest that clinical hate and rage are comprised of three important elements: malice, aversion, and a mixture of these two emotions.

Malice. Malicious impulses stimulate a disgust that can make patients seem loathsome (e.g., disgust about patients who are self-indulgent). Under these circumstances, patients can become the object of punishing, torturing impulses. Maltsberger and Buie are quick to note that malicious impulses are less dangerous than aversive tendencies because malice requires clinicians to maintain a clinical relationship with a patient, whether he or she is abominated or loathed. Aversive impulses tempt the therapist to abandon the patient.

Aversion. Aversive impulses stimulate clinicians to "abandon" patients. These are the most dangerous circumstances for the patient. For the therapist, these feelings are often mistaken or confused with the impulse to behave maliciously (Maltsberger and Buie 1974).

Mixing Malice and Aversion. Unbearable malicious impulses often stimulate aversive actions. Malicious impulses are more painful to clinicians than the tendency to avoid (Maltsberger and Buie 1974). Therefore, when patients stimulate malevolent impulses, clinicians avoid confronting or continuing to work with them.

Addiction, Denial, Intractable Patients, and Countertransference

Clinicians are often disappointed with treatment progress of patients who are struggling with addictive disorders because patients are not ready to begin the tasks of recovery (e.g., Prochaska et al. 1992, Shaffer 1992) — because of either their ambivalence or their inability to think about the need to change their situation. To help move patients along the recovery path, clinicians have the difficult task of encouraging patients to experience both the positive and negative aspects of their addictive behavior. However, many clinicians, particularly those who have been recovering from addictive behavior, are unable to tolerate the patient's positive feelings about the addictive activity. These thoughts can generate too much anxiety for both the therapist and the patient to bear. The result is a superficial therapeutic exploration of the critical issues and little treatment progress. Therapists blame their patients for this stalemate by developing elaborate rationalizations — sometimes called *theories* — to explain the lack of treatment progress. Blaming patients for failing to thrive in treatment is a sophisticated form of displaying clinical hate, one expression of countertransference hate.

Recently, I presented some of these ideas at the annual Norman E. Zinberg Memorial Conference on Addictive Behaviors.[8] Shortly after this lecture, I received many letters expressing and explaining countertransferential thoughts similar to those aired by the director of an alcohol treatment program:

---

[8]Shaffer, H. J. (1993). *Ambivalence, countertransference and hate: The client/therapist interaction.* Paper presented at Harvard Medical School and the Norman E. Zinberg Center for Addiction Studies for the meeting Treating the Addictions: Stages of Change. Boston, MA, March.

We were discussing the need to explore the "positive effects" of drinking and the fact that drinking, at some point, may have been "wonderful" for the patients. The point made was that the staff members who were from alcoholic families, and to a lesser extent, those who are in recovery from alcoholism, rarely thought to explore or validate a patient's positive thoughts of drinking. Instead, they would get intent on breaking through denial and making the patient see the light. Upon examination, a number realized they were acting out of their own fears or unresolved issues. Acknowledging that drinking once was great or that it might hold magical values for them even at this point in their recovery was disconcerting. Discussing the topics of ambivalence and countertransference is already paying dividends. [Curtin 1993]

Ambivalence and Denial: The Stimuli for Countertransference Hate

Traditionally, addiction specialists and the recovery movement in general have referred to alcoholism as a disease of denial. It is common to hear clinicians and patients alike refer to someone as in denial. This language is confusing at best; at worst, thinking of someone as in denial is a countertransferential condescension. This a way of putting down someone caught in the struggle with addiction. Invoking denial is a clinician's way of rationalizing the need to apply therapeutic interventions that might be painful or oppressive. Denial is not a place where one can go to find oneself. Indeed, denial is an active process that protects each of us naturally from overwhelming and not so overwhelming fears and anxieties. As a process, denial is dynamic and constantly in flux. At one extreme, denial is expressed as psychotic behavior. At the other end of this dimension, denial might reveal itself more simply as forgetfulness.

Denial increases when patients feel pressed by clinicians to experience more than they can tolerate (Miller and Rollnick 1991). In addition, as I discussed above, among people struggling with addictive behavior patterns, denial resolves painful ambivalence—the feelings that derive from having experienced the positive aspects of phase two (i.e., positive consequences produced by the object of addiction) in the natural history of addictive behaviors (Shaffer 1992). Denial helps people avoid ambivalence that has become painful. As such, denial is not the *sine qua non* of addiction; it is simply a natural defense mechanism stimulated by shifting information that challenges personal identity.

When patients actively deny the clinical offerings (e.g., observations, clarifications, and interpretations) of those who are working so very hard to help them make the transition from addiction to recovery, and their self-destructive behavior patterns continue, therapists often become frustrated and angry. For many clinicians, this is the beginning of an emerging pattern of countertransference hate and rage. Therapists have been taught by conventional clinical wisdom to experience patient denial as a sign of resistance that must be destroyed if any modicum of treatment progress is to emerge. Faced with patients who actively deny important aspects of experience, therapists begin to assert themselves with more bold and often oppressive interventions. Clinicians who fail to address ambivalence as the major origin of therapeutic resistance will find themselves in a struggle for power that they cannot win. In addition, patients who simply flee into health are not as healthy as those who struggle with their shifting identities (e.g., Shaffer and LaSalvia 1992). As I explain later, by stimulating and exercising ambivalent feelings and thoughts, denial diminishes because it is no longer necessary, and recovery can proceed apace.

Patient Transference as Provocation for Hate and Rage

Therapist countertransference does not stand alone. Patient transference can stimulate and sustain countertransference hate via provocation and projection (Maltsberger and Buie 1974). "Transference hate operates against the therapist consciously, preconsciously, and unconsciously, and to support and justify it [clinical hate] as well as to bear it, the patient employs a reciprocating system of provoking and projecting" (Maltsberger and Buie 1974, p. 626). Norman Zinberg often quipped that clinicians should consider provocative and challenging barbs and many other utterances "as projection until proven otherwise."

Illustrations of Clinical Hate and Rage

Some common examples of clinical hate and rage are in evidence when therapists blame (i.e., malicious impulse) patients for failing to thrive in treatment. Even worse, it is common among addictions treatment programs for therapists to discharge patients (i.e., aversive behavior) from programmatic services for the very disorder that qualified them for treatment in the first place. In this example, a patient who continues to use intoxicants after qualifying for substance abuse treatment services is discharged, allegedly for not being motivated or failing to respond. In other areas of health care (cardiology, dentistry, orthopedics, internal medicine, etc.) it is malpractice to discharge patients for the very problem that originally qualifies them for services. In the addictions, this has been a common practice often rationalized by therapists as essential to help patients "hit bottom." Similarly, psychotherapists occasionally fail to advance patients from one level of addiction services to the next when the patient is displaying disinterest or resistance to psychotherapy, even though the patient makes the requisite behavioral changes that the program determined were necessary to advancement.

One very common example of malicious clinical behavior exists in publicly funded methadone programs. Many of these programs claim that urine surveillance is necessary for responsible treatment to exist. The argument is that patients are not always honest about their extracurricular substance-using patterns and that this information is essential for accountable clinical care. Yet some of these programs fail to test for the most common drugs of abuse. Alcohol problems, for example, account for about 25 percent of all methadone patient discharges (Bickel et al. 1987). Discharging patients from treatment is typically a countertransferential act that protects clinicians from both their impulses to behave maliciously and the anxiety generated by their inability to control patient behavior patterns.

Finally, throughout the United States, policymakers have been debating the propriety of needle exchange programs. Most of these discussions assume that, if allowed, the exchange program must include mandatory counseling. However, this requirement will attract fewer intravenous drug users to the program (the result of both aversive and malicious impulses among the providers and policymakers). An exchange program with the fewest strings attached meets these reluctant-to-change needle users where they are at and eventually will attract the most users into treatment. This process will put a stop to the drug user's cycle of social isolation and withdrawal. This result is precisely contrary to the impulses of malice and aversion experienced by many policymakers and clinicians toward intravenous drug users. Clinicians must begin to ask themselves, Do we really always have to have it our way?

Treating Ambivalence and Minimizing Countertransference Hate

Psychodynamic treatment for ambivalence begins with an exploration of this conflict followed by an explanation of the treatment rationale. Superego pressure begins to diminish simply by examining forbidden wishes in a safe and secure atmosphere (e.g., Havens 1989). During this uncovering work, clinicians consider the role of wishes and fantasies. Psychodynamic psychotherapists permit an examination of how these desires translate to the awareness of wanting substances as a means to resolve inner conflict or deficiency.

As underlying belief systems are uncovered, clinicians must also be willing to explore behaviors that reflect the patient's ambivalence about both wanting to stop and wanting to continue drug use. By only confronting attitudes that clinicians think will discourage drug or alcohol use, therapists unwittingly stimulate and affirm beliefs that value the use of intoxicants. In addition, failing to explore a patient's drug wishes, interest, and fantasies diminishes the credibility of treatment. Similarly, therapists must permit an exploration of the shortcomings and personal losses that come with a drug-free life-style. Clinicians also must permit open discussion of what happens to the patient when he or she acts out wants. During this dialogue, patients are encouraged to articulate their wishes for wants: what do they wish they could want? As these associative exercises strengthen the patient's capacity to recognize desires, algetic ambivalence is piqued, emotional tolerance begins to emerge, and denial starts to diminish. This aroused emotional state provides the hypersensitive environment within which drug abusers first recognize and then gradually accept responsibility for their addiction. Interest in stopping addiction becomes stronger as the drug abuser recognizes his or her capacity for producing, as well as stifling, substance abuse. With this realization, patients naturally enter the turning point crisis.

Throughout the course of treatment, substance abusers need to be held responsible for the adverse consequences of their drug abuse (as previously mentioned, the positive results also require exploration). During the development of adverse reactions, enablers unwittingly help the addict keep these negative effects out of awareness. Consequently, family and systems treatments offer great utility. Group therapy also is very helpful if the patient is willing to participate. One patient's denial is another's irritation. Both of these treatments also are useful in exploring ambivalence: the patient's ambivalence about change and the family's ambivalence about simultaneously loving and hating the patient for the current family crisis. Behavioral treatments are of little assistance during this phase of addiction.

During a turning point, when an addict begins to realize that he or she wants to want to stop, psychodynamic treatments can be very useful. These techniques assist the patient in understanding his or her life and making sense out of chaotic emotions. In addition, dynamic therapies help manage the growing awareness of adverse consequences and mobilize the executive functions of the personality to regain control. During this phase of change, behavioral treatment remains premature because it is still too difficult for patients to give up or change behaviors that some part of them actively desires. Research on natural recovery shows that people usually know exactly how to change their behavior (e.g., Shaffer and Jones 1989). What keeps drug abusers from doing what they already know is their sense of ambivalence. Addiction treatment, whether self-imposed or provided professionally, should help people work through their ambivalence. Psychodynamically oriented psychotherapy is arguably the best strategy for helping patients determine what substance abuse does for them and what it means to them.

However, once the patient resolves the ambivalence that is so very paralyzing and responsible for energizing denial, he or she usually becomes sufficiently organized to consider actively changing, and more directive behavior therapy becomes the most appropriate treatment of choice. During the fifth, or active, change phase, patients need to learn new behavior patterns and get support for testing their ability to carry these out; in particular, they have the option of failing and resolving associated negative affect. Consequently, behavior, psychodynamic, family, or systems and group therapies can all be applied judiciously and effectively. Passive, nondirective therapies have little value at this point unless they serve to help the patient integrate the emotional experience of actively changing.

During the relapse prevention phase, both behavioral and psychodynamic treatments are essential. Behavioral approaches help the patient learn how to avoid or cope with risky situations, determine the cues that begin a sequence of events that threaten sobriety, and successfully manage negative thoughts. The majority of incidents involves negative emotional states, however, and can benefit from psychodynamic techniques. New research also emphasizes the importance of behavior change (Svanum and McAdoo 1989). This work reveals that for nonpsychiatric patients who are substance abusers, those who sustain a regimen of physical exercise are less likely to relapse. Psychodynamic and pharmacologic treatments are most helpful for psychiatric patients during this phase of addiction treatment. These methods assist patients in managing the emotional turmoil that often predicts substance abuse relapse (e.g., Marlatt and Gordon 1985, Svanum and McAdoo 1989).

Shaffer and Gambino (1990) consider whether therapists must (a) cultivate a sufficiently broad base of clinical skills to provide continuous care or (b) direct the patient to other clinicians during the course of treatment. Both possibilities are acceptable. Throughout the field of medical practice, the idea of a primary care provider as case manager is common. For the therapist whose range of clinical skills is narrow, the clinical task is to coordinate treatment interventions prescriptively. Such therapists need not deliver every treatment personally. They should, however, remain sensitive to the shifting needs of the patient throughout the course of recovery and then try to provide or access specialty treatments when appropriate.

In every example mentioned, it is crucial for addiction treatment specialists to determine how patients envision their place in the sequence of addiction phases. This process helps patients engage and remain in the therapeutic process. In addition, it aids both therapist and patient in accessing a useful rationale for the treatment program that follows. If the treatment rationale is in conflict with the patient's perception of the problem, the patient often drops out of treatment. When therapy follows a formulation that is consistent with the patient's view, treatment compliance is common. In short, the patient's perception of the change process is essential to determining which clinical method should be applied.

Assessing the Patient's Perception.[9]   Earlier, I said that psychodynamically oriented psychotherapy is arguably the best strategy for helping patients determine what substance abuse does for them and what it means to them. This task is essentially a problem in self-and social perception. The most important view of addictive behavior for the drug treatment specialist is the patient's. The patient's perception of his or her disorder determines when, how, and to what treatment provider, if any, he or she goes. Understanding every patient's unique perception of his or her substance abuse and what treatment approach he or she thinks will prove useful permits clinicians to negotiate and navigate treatment interventions.

In order to develop an integrated model of substance abuse treatment, clinicians need to begin to learn how to access and then to assess their patient's view of addiction. While it may be possible to impose a clinical model on some patients, most bring their own view of addiction with them when they enter treatment. When the provider and patient see things similarly, treatment can go well. However, most clinicians recognize that the majority of substance abusers find it difficult to engage in treatment. Historically, this has been a patient problem: many treatment specialists blame the patient and his or her "disease of denial." More likely, however, this situation results when the patient's view does not match the therapist's opinion.

Kleinman (1988) and Pfifferling (1980) discussed the importance of examining a patient's perspectives for the treatment of psychiatric disorders in

---

[9]This section derives from Shaffer (1992).

general. Their work is particularly relevant for the addictions because excessive behaviors can be understood from a multiplicity of views. Aside from cross-cultural differences, addictive behavior can be understood from at least thirteen different perspectives. For example, in addition to the conventional view that addiction represents a disease process, patients often consider their excessive behavior as the result of an excessive habit, a psychodynamic deficiency or a biological dilemma. Some patients view their excessive behavior patterns as average and expectable for their social reference group.

There are more complex views. For example, there are patients who see their problems as a punishment. Some consider the problems a well-deserved penalty, whereas others view them as unreasonable and unfortunate. Clinicians often view addiction as a challenge — something to overcome. Patients may see it as an enemy and deny their capacity to resist; alternatively, these patients may resist with pronounced hostility. Other patients view their addiction as direct evidence of personal weakness, a moral loss of control. For some, addiction is a strategy by which they manage their environment and identity. Addiction can also provide relief from obligations and responsibilities. Quite often, addiction is understood as an irrevocable personal loss, a view that often leads to depression. Finally, patients can view addiction as an opportunity, a time for personal growth and reflection. This perspective can lead to personal growth and significant changes in life-style.

SUMMARY

This chapter considers the natural history of addictive disorders and the common mechanisms of change that characterize this process as a context for understanding the emergence of ambivalence and countertransference. A stage change model is offered as a template to describe the emergence of addiction and the three phases of recovery. Further, this discussion focuses on the psychological events associated with stage change and the transitions between them. Of special interest, I consider the role that addiction ambivalence plays in energizing the denial that sustains the status quo. The dynamic interaction between (1) the emergence and maintenance of addictive ambivalence and denial and (2) countertransference hate serves as the centerpiece of this chapter. Just as this model is only one of many possible perspectives that explains ambivalence, the chapter concludes by considering the variety of patient views that exist to explain addiction in general. This approach to understanding the social and psychodynamic perception of addiction yields a functional approach to this disorder: emphasis on patient and provider perceptions alike encourages clinicians to thoroughly assess the shifting meaning of addiction throughout the patient's life. This strategy also reveals how addiction can work adaptively for a patient and, therefore, stimulate ambivalence, which in turn can energize clinician countertransference hate. Awareness of this often ignored treatment dynamic yields more economical treatment tactics to help work through the painful ambivalence that often sustains addictive behaviors.

REFERENCES

Anderson, K. (1989). These are not the best of times; these are not the worst of times. At the end of the decade, we are turning ambivalent. Maybe. *Rolling Stone*, May 18, pp. 58-60.

Bean-Bayog, M. (1988). Psychotherapy and alcoholism. Presented at the symposium, Treating the Addictions. Harvard Medical School, Cambridge, MA, March.

Bickel, W. K., Marion, I., and Lowinson, J. H. (1987). The treatment of alcoholic methadone patients: a review. *Journal of Substance Abuse Treatment* 4:15-19.

Bleuler, E. (1950). The fundamental symptoms. In *Dementia Praecox: or the Group of Schizophrenias*, ed. E. Bleuler, trans. J. Ziskin. New York: International Universities Press.

Brownell, K. D., Marlatt, G. A., Lichtenstein, E., and Wilson, G. T. (1986). Understanding and preventing relapse. *American Psychologist* 41:765-782.

Curtin, P. (1993). Personal communication, March 11.

Goldfried, M. R. (1980). Toward the delineation of therapeutic change principles. *American Psychologist* 35:991-999.

Havens, L. (1989). *A Safe Place*. Cambridge, MA: Harvard University Press.

Khantzian, E. J., Halliday, K. S., and McAuliffe, W. E. (1990). *Addiction and the Vulnerable Self: Modified Dynamic Group Therapy for Substance Abusers*. New York: Guilford.

Kleinman, A. (1988). *The Illness Narratives: Suffering, Healing and the Human Condition*. New York: Basic Books.

Maisto, S. A., and Connors, G. J. (1988). Assessment of treatment outcome. In *Assessment of Addictive Behaviors*, ed. D. M. Donovan and G. A. Marlatt, pp. 421-453. New York: Guilford.

Maltsberger, J. T., and Buie, D. H. (1974). Countertransference hate in the treatment of suicidal patients. *Archives of General Psychiatry* 30:625-633.

Marlatt, G. A. (1988). Matching clients to treatment: treatment models and stages of change. In *Assessment of Addictive Behaviors*, ed. D. M. Donovan and G. A. Marlatt, pp. 474-484. New York: Guilford.

Marlatt, G. A., Baer, J. S., Donovan, D. M., and Kivlahan, D. R. (1988). Addictive behaviors: etiology and treatment. *Annual Review of Psychology* 39:223-252.

Marlatt, G. A., and Gordon, J. R., eds. (1985). *Relapse Prevention: Maintenance Strategies in the Treatment of Addictive Behaviors*. New York: Guilford.

Miller, W. R., and Rollnick, S. (1991). *Motivational Interviewing*. New York: Guilford.

Niaura, R. S., Rohsenow, D. J., Binkoff, J. A., et al. (1988). Relevance of cue reactivity to understanding alcohol and smoking relapse. *Journal of Abnormal Psychology* 97:133-152.

Orford, J. (1985). *Excessive Appetites: A Psychological View of Addiction*. New York: Wiley.

Pfifferling, J. H. (1980). A cultural prescription for medicocentrism. In *The Relevance of Social Science for Medicine*, ed. L. Eisenberg and A. Kleinman, pp. 197-222. Boston: D. Reidel.

Prochaska, J. O., and DiClemente, C. C. (1985). Common processes of self change in smoking, weight control, and psychological distress. In *Coping and Substance Abuse*, ed. S. Shiffman and T. A. Wills. New York: Academic.

Prochaska, J. O., DiClemente, C. C., and Norcross, J. C. (1992). In search of how people change: applications to addictive behaviors. *American Psychologist* 47:1102-1114.

Prochaska, J. O., Velicer, W. F., DiClemente, C. C., and Fava, J. (1988). Measuring processes of change: applications to the cessation of smoking. *Journal of Consulting and Clinical Psychology* 56:520-528.

Shaffer, H. J. (1987). The epistemology of "addictive disease": The Lincoln-Douglas debate. *Journal of Substance Abuse Treatment* 4:103-113.

———— (1992). The psychology of stage change: the transition from addiction to recovery. In *Comprehensive Textbook of Substance Abuse*, ed. J. H. Lowinson, P. Ruiz, and R. B. Millman. 2nd edition, pp. 100-105. Baltimore: Williams & Wilkins.

Shaffer, H. J., and Gambino, B. (1990). Epilogue: integrating treatment choices. In *Treatment Choices for Alcoholism and Substance Abuse*, ed. H. B. Milkman and L. I. Sederer, pp. 351-375. Lexington, MA: Lexington Books.

Shaffer, H. J., and Jones, S. B. (1989). *Quitting Cocaine: The Struggle Against Impulse.* Lexington, MA: Lexington Books.

Shaffer, H. J., and LaSalvia, T. (1992). Patterns of substance use among methadone maintenance patients: indicators of outcome. *Journal of Substance Abuse Treatment* 9(2): 143–147.

Svanum, S., and McAdoo, W. G. (1989). Predicting rapid relapse following treatment for chemical dependency: a matched-subjects design. *Journal of Clinical and Consulting Psychology* 57:222–226.

Tims, F. M., and Leukefeld, C. G. (1986). Relapse and recovery in drug abuse: an introduction. In *Relapse and Recovery in Drug Abuse,* ed. F. M. Tims and C. G. Leukefeld, (National Institute of Drug Abuse Research Monograph 72, pp. 1–4.) Washington, DC: U.S. Government Printing Office.

Vaillant, G. (1983). *The Natural History of Alcoholism.* Cambridge MA: Harvard University Press.

Wachtel, P. L. (1977). *Psychoanalysis and Behavior Therapy: Toward an Integration.* New York: Basic Books.

Weiner, I. B. (1975). *Principles of Psychotherapy.* New York: Wiley.

ACKNOWLEDGMENTS

The editors gratefully acknowledge permission to quote from the following
sources:

Chapter 1: "An Inquiry into the Effects of Ardent Spirits upon the Human Body
and Mind," by Benjamin Rush. Reprinted with permission from *Journal of Studies
on Alcohol* (formerly *Quarterly Journal of Studies on Alcohol*), vol. 4, pp. 321–341,
1943. Copyright © 1943 by Journal of Studies on Alcohol, Inc., Rutgers Center
of Alcohol Studies, New Brunswick, NJ 08903 [originally published 1785].

Chapter 2: "Heredity and Pre-mature Weaning: A Discussion of the Work of
Thomas Trotter, British Naval Physician," by Emil Jellinek. Reprinted with
permission from *Journal of Studies on Alcohol* (formerly *Quarterly Journal of Studies on
Alcohol*), vol. 2, pp. 584–591, 1941. Copyright © 1941 by Journal of Studies on
Alcohol, Inc., Rutgers Center of Alcohol Studies, New Brunswick, NJ 08903
[originally published 1804].

Chapter 3: "Alcoholism as a Progressive Disease," by Emil Jellinek. Originally
published as "Phases of Alcohol Addition," in *Society, Culture and Drinking Patterns*,
ed. D. J. Pittman and C. R. Snyder, 1962, pp. 673–683. Copyright © 1962.
Reprinted by permission of *Journal of Studies on Alcohol*.

Chapter 4: "Masturbation as the Original Addiction," by Sigmund Freud,
originally entitled "Letter #79," from *The Origins of Psychoanalysis: Letters to William
Fliess*, eds. M. Bonaparte, A. Freud, and E. Kris, pp. 238–240. Authorized
translation by E. Mosbacher and J. Strachey. Copyright © 1954, by Basic Books,
Inc. Reprinted by permission of BasicBooks, a division of HarperCollins
Publishers Inc.

Chapter 5: "The Psychological Relations between Sexuality and Alcoholism," by
Karl Abraham. Originally published in *Selected Papers of Karl Abraham*, published
by The Hogarth Press. Copyright © 1954. Courtesy of the estate of the author
and The Hogarth Press.

Chapter 6: "Dostoevsky and Parricide: Addiction and Guilt," by Sigmund Freud from *Standard Edition,* vol. 21, pp. 177–196, 1928, trans. and ed. by James Strachey. Copyright © 1928 by Sigmund Freud Copyrights, The Institute of Psycho-Analysis, and The Hogarth Press. Also from *The Collected Papers of Sigmund Freud,* vol. 5, edited by James Strachey. Published by Basic Books, Inc. by arrangement by the Hogarth Press, Ltd. and The Institute of Psycho-Analysis, London. Reprinted by permission of BasicBooks, a division of HarperCollins Publishers.

Chapter 7: "The Aetiology of Alcoholism," by Edward G. Glover. Originally published in *Proceedings of the Royal Society of Medicine,* vol. 21, pp. 1351–1355. Copyright © 1928 by *Journal of the Royal Society of Medicine* and reprinted with permission.

Chapter 8: "Alcoholism as Chronic Suicide," by Karl Menninger. Originally published as "Alcohol Addiction" in *Man Against Himself* by Karl Menninger. Copyright © 1938 and renewed 1965 by Karl A. Menninger. Reprinted by permission of Harcourt Brace & Company.

Chapter 9: "Dynamics of Addiction," by Otto Fenichel. Originally published in *The Psychoanalytic Theory of Neurosis,* by Otto Fenichel, pp. 375–380. Copyright © 1945 by W. W. Norton & Company, Inc. Reprinted by permission.

Chapter 10: "The Role of the Counterphobic Mechanism in Addiction," by Thomas S. Szasz. Originally published in *Journal of the American Psychoanalytic Association,* vol. 6, pp. 309–325, 1958. Copyright © 1958 by International Universities Press and reprinted by permission of International Universities Press and the author.

Chapter 11: "The Psychoanalysis of Pharmacothymia (Drug Addiction)" by Sándor Radó from *Psychoanalytic Quarterly,* 1933, vol. 2, pp. 1–23. Copyright © 1933. Reprinted by permission of *Psychoanalytic Quarterly* and the estate of the author.

Chapter 12: "The Psychogenesis of Alcoholism," by Paul Schilder. Reprinted with permission from *Journal of Studies on Alcohol* (formerly *Quarterly Journal of Studies on Alcohol*), vol. 2, pp. 277–292, 1941. Copyright © 1941 by Journal of Studies on Alcohol, Inc., Rutgers Center of Alcohol Studies, New Brunswick, NJ 08903.

Chapter 13: "The Ego Factors in Surrender in Alcoholism," by Harry M. Tiebout (formerly entitled "The Art of Surrender in the Therapeutic Process"). Reprinted with permission from *Journal of Studies on Alcohol* (formerly *Quarterly Journal of Studies on Alcohol*), vol. 10, pp. 48–58, 1949. Copyright © 1949 by Journal of Studies on Alcohol, Inc., Rutgers Center of Alcohol Studies, New Brunswick, NJ 08903.

Chapter 14: "Affect Tolerance," by Henry Krystal and Herbert Raskin, from *Drug Dependence,* pp. 15–44. Copyright © 1970. Reprinted by permission.

Chapter 15: "Psychodynamics in Compulsive Drug Use," by Leon Wurmser. Originally published as "Mr. Pecksniff's Horse? (Psychodynamics in Compulsive Drug Use)" in *Psychodynamics of Drug Dependence,* Research Monograph 12, 1977, pp. 36–72, National Institute on Drug Abuse. Copyright © 1977 Jason Aronson Inc. Reprinted by permission.

Chapter 16: "Alcoholism, Borderline and Narcissistic Disorders," by Peter Hartocollis and Pitsa Hartocollis. Copyright © 1980. Reprinted by permission of the authors.

Chapter 17: "Working with the Preferred Defense Structure of the Recovering Alcoholic," by John Wallace. Originally published in *Practical Approaches to Alcoholism Psychotherapy,* eds. S. Zimberg, J. Wallace, and S. Blume, 1975, pp. 19–29. Copyright © 1975 by Plenum Publishing Corp. and reprinted by permission of the publisher and the author.

Chapter 18: "Some Treatment Implications of the Ego and Self Disturbances in Alcoholism," by Edward J. Khantzian. Reprinted with permission of the author and The Free Press, a division of Macmillan, Inc. from *Dynamic Approaches to the Understanding and Treatment of Alcoholism,* by Margaret H. Bean, Norman E. Zinberg, John E. Mack, Edward J. Khantzian, and George E. Vaillant. Copyright © 1981 by The Free Press.

Chapter 19: "The Dynamics and Treatment of Chronic Alcohol Addiction," by Robert P. Knight. Originally published in the *Bulletin of the Menninger Clinic,* September 1937, copyright © 1937. Reprinted by permission of the Menninger Clinic.

Chapter 20: "Alcoholism and Addiction," by Ernst Simmel. Reprinted from *Psychoanalytic Quarterly,* 1948, vol. 17, pp. 6–31. Copyright © 1948. Reprinted by permission of *Psychoanalytic Quarterly* and the estate of the author.

Chapter 21: "The Addictive Drinker," by Giorgio Lolli. Reprinted with permission from *Journal of Studies on Alcohol* (formerly *Quarterly Journal of Studies on Alcohol*), vol. 10, pp. 404–414, 1949. Copyright © 1949 by Journal of Studies on Alcohol, Inc., Rutgers Center of Alcohol Studies, New Brunswick, NJ 08903.

Chapter 22: "Self- and Object-Representation in Alcoholism and Other Drug Dependence: Implications for Therapy," by Henry Krystal. Originally published in *Psychodynamics of Drug Dependence,* Research Monograph 12, 1977, pp. 88–100, National Institute on Drug Abuse.

Chapter 23: "The Cybernetics of 'Self': A Theory of Alcoholism," by Gregory Bateson. Reprinted from *Psychiatry,* vol. 24, pp. 1–18, 1971. Copyright © 1971 by Guilford Press and reprinted by permission.

Chapter 24: "'The Giant Killer': Drink and the American Writer," by Alfred Kazin. Reprinted from *Commentary,* March 1976, copyright © 1976, by permission; all rights reserved, and by permission of the author.

Chapter 25: "Self Deficits and Addiction," by Heinz Kohut. Originally published as the Preface to *Psychodynamics of Drug Dependence,* Research Monograph 12, 1977, pp. vii–ix, National Institute on Drug Abuse. Reprinted with permission.

Chapter 26: "Alcoholics Anonymous and Contemporary Psychodynamic Theory," by Edward J. Khantzian and John E. Mack. Originally published in *Recent Advances in Alcoholism,* ed. M. Galanter, pp. 67–89. Copyright © 1989 by Plenum Publishing Corp. Reprinted by permission of the publisher, the editor, and the authors.

Chapter 27: "Alcoholism and Regression/Fixation to Pathological Narcissism," by Jerome D. Levin. Reprinted with modifications from "When the Patient Abuses Alcohol," in *Using Self Psychology in Psychotherapy,* ed. Helene Jackson. Copyright © 1991 Jason Aronson Inc. Used by permission.

Chapter 28: "'Craving' and Relapse to Drink" by Arnold M. Ludwig and Abraham Wikler. Reprinted with permission from *Journal of Studies on Alcohol* (formerly *Quarterly Journal of Studies on Alcohol*), vol. 33, pp. 108–130, 1974. Copyright © 1974 by Journal of Studies on Alcohol, Inc., Rutgers Center of Alcohol Studies, New Brunswick, NJ 08903.